Essential Oracle8*i*™
Data Warehousing

Designing, Building, and Managing
Oracle® Data Warehouses

Gary Dodge

Tim Gorman

Wiley Computer Publishing

John Wiley & Sons, Inc.
New York ◆ Chichester ◆ Weinheim ◆ Brisbane ◆ Singapore ◆ Toronto

Publisher: Robert Ipsen
Editor: Robert M. Elliott
Managing Editor: John Atkins
Text Design & Composition: D&G Limited, LLC

This book is printed on acid-free paper.

Published by John Wiley & Sons, Inc.

Published simultaneously in Canada.

This publication is designed to provide accurate and authoritative information in regard to the subject matter covered. It is sold with the understanding that the publisher is not engaged in professional services. If professional advice or other expert assistance is required, the services of a competent professional person should be sought.

Library of Congress Cataloging-in-Publication Data:

ISBN 0-471-37678-7

Printed in the United States of America.

10 9 8 7 6 5 4 3 2 1

Advance Praise for
Essential Oracle8i Data Warehousing

Data warehousing is now an imperative in order to understand business drivers of our organizations and industries. For all companies using Oracle to power their data warehouses or e-commerce operational data stores, Dodge and Gorman provide an outstanding, complete "how-to" guide to implementation. *Essential Oracle8i Data Warehousing* is a must-read book that very deftly explains how to utilize Oracle8*i* parallel processing options to keep abreast of the increasing demands being placed on hardware architectures by growing data warehouses. The authors use humor in developing best practices for using new Oracle8*i* features in conjunction with the most important features of earlier Oracle releases, making it compelling reading for anyone tasked with implementing, updating, or improving their Oracle data warehouse. *Essential Oracle8i Data Warehousing* is a resource you won't want to miss!

Susan Osterfelt
Columnist and editorial advisor for DMReview *magazine*
Senior Vice President, Bank of America

Gary and Tim's book provides a detailed roadmap to planning, designing, and implementing data warehouses. With their real world experience, they are able to traverse the diverse world of data warehousing and provide insight to all involved in building and managing Oracle data warehouses. From concepts to code, this book provides a wealth of information.

Bob Hammer
Director, Datawarehousing
NetZero, Inc.

Essential Oracle8i Data Warehousing is a must-read for all data warehouse architects and developers. It has something for everyone—novice to expert. The opening chapters provide an excellent introduction and overview for beginners while the remainder of the book delivers enough in-depth technical details that even veteran warehouse developers are sure to learn something. Unless you have developed dozens of successful, multi-terabyte data warehouses, you will definitely learn something from this book.

Kent Graziano
Senior Technical Architect
ARIS Corporation, Denver

The convergence of data warehousing and the Internet was inevitable. Gary and Tim are ahead of the pack. This book is the definitive guide for serious Oracle8*i* professionals and is required reading for all Oracle data warehousing practitioners.

Shannon Platz
Senior Director, Business Intelligence and Warehouse Global Service Line
Oracle Corporation

Dedication

My contributions to this book are dedicated to *grace* and to some of the people who have helped introduce me to it:

Dale Flanders, whose weekly messages inspire my heart;
Philip Yancey, whose written words stir my soul;
Jackie Robinson, whose life showed grace surpassing even his athletic ability;
and, most importantly, to my family and friends who have been so forgiving in the many times that I have lacked the grace to be forgiving of them.

GD

To Jarmila, my best friend who is also my wife,
To Peter and Marika, my kids and heart and soul,
And to Gary, my friend and mentor.

TG

Contents

Foreword

The other day I looked at an industry survey that identified which database management software (DBMS) platforms held data warehouses. Leading the pack was Oracle. That Oracle serves as the nerve center for more data warehouses than any other dbms is not a surprise—it has long been the leader in versatility (among other things) in database solutions. What did come as somewhat of a surprise was how this book transcends the technology covered.

While *Essential Oracle8i Data Warehousing* is indeed about Oracle, it also contains important principles and lessons about what you need to know to succeed in data warehousing. People well outside of the Oracle environment who are building or embarking on the data warehouse experience should read this book.

One of the real joys of the book is that the authors are well aware of data warehouse theory, but they couch it in very readable, very comprehensible terms. They introduce you to theory one step at a time, so that you can absorb one set of issues before tackling the next. You end up understanding the more profound and complex issues of data warehousing in a very natural, down-to-earth manner. As a writer (take my word for it), that is not easy to do. The book is also well organized and is written at both a detailed and a summary level. The net result is a really excellent book—in fact, I can sincerely say that this is one of the best books on the subject that I have ever encountered.

Bill Inmon
Pine Cone Systems

Acknowledgments

We are grateful to those who have helped us through the production of this second edition. One would expect the second time around to be easier, but in many ways it was much more complex and difficult. Sherra Basham-Ziegler and Richard Armstrong provided substantive suggestions and helpful critique, especially in the chapter on performance tuning. Emilie Herman, at John Wiley & Sons, gently but firmly prodded us across the finish line—without her, the manuscript would probably still be in the starting blocks.

We owe thanks to all of our colleagues, clients, and especially to our families. Both of these editions were written at night, on weekends, on vacations, and during holidays. It has been wisely said that a person can *work their job, live their life,* and *write a book,* but only two at a time. We took this time from our lives and our families, and words cannot express our gratitude for their love and support.

Acknowledgments from the Previous Edition

A number of people provided assistance in the development of this book. Our thanks go to Bill Pass for his timely help with the hardware architectures of Chapter 2. Our gratitude is owed to Kim Wilson for his contributions to material on building the data warehouse in Chapter 6. Karl Johnson's guidance and insight into the workings of Oracle Express for Chapter 13 are appreciated. We are also grateful to Ulla-Carin Johnson, who helped in the production of many of the drawings. Armand Perry read the manuscript with a nontechnical eye and helped identify several opportunities to clarify technical material.

Finally, we must express our heartfelt thanks to Valerie Borthwick and Doug McArthur, our regional management within Oracle Consulting Services, for their encouragement and support in both initiating and completing this project.

Introduction

Forget the former things;
 do not dwell on the past.
See, I am doing a new thing!
 Now it springs up; do you not perceive it?
I am making a way in the desert
 and streams in the wasteland.

Isaiah 43:18-19

The first edition of this book arose, as all books should, from a need. Many books, articles, and seminars that discuss data warehousing have been available for the last decade. These sources all seem to describe what a data warehouse is, why an organization should build one, the process of organizing a data warehouse implementation team, the general design concerns of a warehouse, and the process of identifying, extracting, and cleansing data from source systems.

What seemed to be missing was a nuts-and-bolts "how to" manual for the technical team chartered with actually creating and maintaining the data warehouse. Of course, there are many products that can be used to design, build, and manage a data warehouse, but no general-audience book could attempt to deal with the specifics of each.

The Oracle relational database management system has become the most popular and effective tool for managing the large amounts of data required in a data warehouse. During the past decade we have worked with clients to develop data warehouses using Oracle version 6, Oracle7, Oracle8, and now Oracle8*i*. Along the way we've acquired or developed a lot of very practical knowledge of how the Oracle RDBMS product can be used to address the many problems faced in data warehousing. These problems come in many colors and flavors. Some are related to performance of queries, large data loads, and related activities. Other common problems are related to the administration of very large databases. Still other difficulties arise in the form of just selecting from the many technology options provided in each new release of Oracle.

The first edition of this book (*Oracle8 Data Warehousing*, 1998, John Wiley & Sons) was written as Oracle8 was first released. Only two short years later, we have had to make many additions to accommodate new features of Oracle8*i* and Oracle8*i*, release 2. It is our intent in writing this book to share as much of this practical knowledge as we can. This revision has gotten longer as we continue to identify other topics, tips, and "gotchas." To make room for this new material, we have had to scale back on the amount of information that was specific to Oracle7. This seemed reasonable since all of the data warehouses we've worked on recently have been based on Oracle8 and Oracle8*i*. If, however, you find yourself in need of Oracle7 data warehousing techniques, please refer to the first edition. It is our sincere hope that the subject matter that eventually made it into this edition will be the most practical and useful subset of the universe of current Oracle data warehousing knowledge.

Audience

This book is directed to two groups of readers. First, we anticipate that experienced data warehouse developers who have worked with a different RDBMS product, and are about to use Oracle for the first time will find this book very useful. While it will not replace the shelf full of manuals (or their digital equivalent) shipped with each copy of Oracle, we know firsthand how daunting the prospect of absorbing Oracle documentation can be. This was true when we started with Oracle version 5 in the 1980s, and the number of features and the corresponding documentation has mushroomed in the interim.

This book is designed to serve as a technical roadmap to the specific Oracle8 or Oracle8*i* features that are relevant to designing, building, tuning, and administering an Oracle data warehouse. Once the function and usage of a particular feature or option are understood, the reader can locate the more detailed information in the relevant Oracle reference manuals. Where appropriate, we have attempted to provide "pointers" to official documentation throughout this book.

The second intended audience is the individual who has been working with Oracle, perhaps for years, as a developer or DBA but who is new to data warehousing. It is not intended that this book be the only reference for learning about data warehousing—the many books and seminars mentioned above do a much more thorough job of covering the basic concepts—but it will provide a guide to thinking about how to use Oracle technology in a different way. Experienced users of Oracle may find special value in the description of how to use new Oracle8 and Oracle8*i* features, such as partitioning, the updated star query optimization, and materialized views. Knowing that data warehouses will continue to be built using both various Oracle releases for several years, we have attempted to identify feature differences of the current releases.

To achieve this goal, we have been specific in our use of terminology. We have used *Oracle8*i to reference features or techniques that are new to this release. Features specific to Oracle8 are noted with a reference to *Oracle8*. We have used the term *Oracle7* to identify those features that were specific to that release, but which have been superseded by subsequent Oracle8 enhancements. There are many occasions, however, where we have discussed topics that span across all of these releases. In these situations we have chosen to use the more generic *Oracle* terminology.

Organization

This book retains the thirteen-chapter structure of earlier editions. Chapter 1, "Data Warehousing," is a quick overview or review of the basic concepts of data warehousing. We address current developments in the data warehousing world such as data marts and OLAP.

Chapter 2, "Hardware Architectures for Oracle Data Warehousing," describes various hardware platforms that can be used to support the Oracle data warehouse. Common architectures such as symmetric multi-processor (SMP) computers are described along with more exotic configurations such as clusters and massively parallel processor (MPP) hardware. Hardware and software technology, such as RAID, for handling data file storage are covered as well. This chapter may be safely skimmed by readers who are not responsible for selecting hardware for the warehouse. You may find it sufficient to just review the description of the particular hardware architecture that your organization has already chosen.

Chapter 3, "Oracle Server Software Architecture and Features," is an overview of the architecture of Oracle7 and Oracle8 and a description of various standard and optional features that may be used to enhance the workings of a large data warehouse. Experienced Oracle DBAs may wish to just review this chapter for an introduction to the many Oracle8 and Oracle8*i* enhancements specific to data warehousing.

Chapter 4, "Designing the Oracle Data Warehouse," discusses design considerations, including the need for warehouse metadata and how to deliver it to users. This chapter also introduces a case study situation of a warehouse, which will be used throughout subsequent chapters to demonstrate specific features or techniques.

Actually constructing the data warehouse using Oracle7 and Oracle8 database technology is addressed in Chapter 5, "Building the Oracle Data Warehouse." Several very useful techniques using SQL*Plus, the Oracle interactive SQL environment, are demonstrated. Then we cover the specifics of creating Oracle databases and database objects.

Chapter 6, "Populating the Oracle Data Warehouse," describes techniques for loading data into the Oracle data warehouse.

Chapter 7, "Post-Load Processing in the Data Warehouse," builds upon this foundation by providing information on the processes used for summarizing and aggregating data within the warehouse. This second edition places primary emphasis on the use of Oracle8*i* materialized views. Less automated techniques for use in Oracle7 and Oracle8 were addressed in the first edition.

Chapter 8, "Administering and Monitoring the Oracle Data Warehouse," and Chapter 9, "Data Warehouse Performance Tuning," address administration and performance tuning requirements and techniques using a variety of tools available to the developer and database administrator. In these chapters our emphasis is on understanding the underlying technology. There are many excellent tools (such as Oracle Enterprise Manager or its optional Tuning Pack) that make the administrator's life simpler. We are strong believers, however, that in order to fully utilize such a tool it is imperative to understand the actual effects produced by each action within that tool. If the reader understands how to do tuning at the "bare metal" layer, then interpreting the findings and recommendations of a tuning tool will be effective. Without this basic grounding, the user is held hostage to the tool.

Chapter 10, "Parallel Execution in the Oracle Data Warehouse," describes the "divide and conquer" capabilities of Oracle8 and Oracle8*i* for performing parallel operations in order to accomplish massive tasks more quickly. These features are virtually indispensable in developing and maintaining large Oracle data warehouses.

Chapter 11, "Warehousing with Oracle Parallel Server," deals with an optional feature, Oracle Parallel Server, which enables simultaneous access to a single Oracle database from multiple computers in either a clustered or MPP configuration.

Chapter 12, "Distributing the Oracle Data Warehouse," presents various reasons for choosing a distributed architecture and describes specific features and techniques for implementing such a design.

Finally, Chapter 13, "Analytical Processing in the Oracle Data Warehouse," provides an overview of several Oracle facilities that provide online analytical processing (OLAP) capabilities for the data warehouse. Oracle8*i* has added several new analytical functions inside the database kernel. Oracle Express can operate independently as a multidimensional database or provide "reach through" access to a relational warehouse built with an Oracle RDBMS. Additionally, tools such as Oracle Discoverer can easily enable the user to perform analysis of warehouse data.

In essence, this book is not a work of reference. The standard Oracle Server documentation set should fill that function. Given the pace at which Oracle is adding new features, attempting to duplicate the Oracle8i Server reference manuals would be an effort worthy of Sisyphus. Rather, allow this book to get the ball rolling through a series of recommendations already proven in the field and readily adaptable to different warehousing situations.

Additionally, whenever possible we have identified techniques for verifying the internal workings of Oracle features, particularly the various parallel operations. Use these techniques to verify that Oracle is, or is not, doing what you expect in the way you expect it. Use the knowledge imparted in these chapters to verify whether the approach you are considering is reasonable or not. There is almost never a single "right" answer to questions regarding data warehouse design and usage, but we will try to provide you with the information needed to steer you away from the wrong answers.

What's on the Companion Web Site

One of the many things we learned from the first edition was that things change quickly. There inevitably will be things in this edition that we didn't explain fully enough, and answers to the questions from one reader may help other readers. We know that some of the scripts from the first edition have had to be retyped by many readers. There are many, many other scripts and tools that couldn't be provided in text. We absolutely know that there will be additional material that needs to be added—we have already generated additional information on several topics (such as data mining with Oracle's Darwin product) that could not be included within this single volume.

To provide this additional information to our readers, we invite you to visit the companion Web site. Answers, clarifications, extensions, scripts, and new material will all be made available at:

```
www.wiley.com/compbooks/dodge
```

We welcome your feedback. If you have comments, suggestions, or questions, you may send us e-mail via the links at this Web site. Please don't misinterpret this offer as an alternative to Oracle Worldwide Support, and please don't expect fast turnaround; with work and travel schedules we cannot always respond immediately to e-mails (even if they're marked "Urgent"). Also, be sure to allow for additional delays during the winter months . . . after all, there are certain priorities during ski season in Colorado!

An Invitation

Do not dwell on the past. There is much that may initially seem counterintuitive to OLTP developers and administrators about Oracle's new features to support data warehousing. Read on and learn. Then, go forth and *do the new thing*!

Enjoy!

CHAPTER 1

Data Warehousing

Gentlemen . . . we are history!

Rufus
Bill and Ted's Excellent Adventure (1989)

So, you've been given the assignment of building a data warehouse. Congratulations! The CIO read an article in *Computerworld* that said a data warehouse is a fundamental component of a modern information technology (IT) department. The CEO has also read articles in *Business Week* and *Forbes* that suggest a data warehouse is *the* vehicle for competitive advantage as we enter the twenty-first century. Everybody seems to agree that we need a data warehouse because everyone else seems to be building them.

Without any scientific studies to back it up, our observation is that many of the data warehouse projects begun in the past decade have failed to achieve the lofty rewards promised for them. This doesn't mean that most have been complete failures resulting in project cancellations (although that has certainly happened in some cases), but many so-called data warehouses have produced very modest returns on their implementation investments.

Some organizations' data warehouse failures have been due to technical implementation issues. But most failures (or modest successes) have missed the mark on more basic levels. Failing to understand the underlying concepts, philosophy, objectives, and success factors of data warehousing presents far greater risks than technical issues such as the choice of hardware or relational database management system (RDBMS). Within the correct conceptual and managerial context one successfully can deliver a useful warehouse using virtually any vendor's hardware or software offerings.

The material in this chapter is intended as a review and summary of information that should already be familiar to the reader of this book. If these topics are new, then we strongly recommend that you also study the less technical and more conceptual books and articles on data warehousing written by Bill Inmon, Ralph Kimball, and others. To offer an analogy, you might consider this book to be like the shop manual for your new sports car. It is designed for a specific, technical audience, but it presupposes all the knowledge contained within the car's owner manual as well as a fundamental understanding of engine, suspension, electrical, braking, and other automotive systems. Many drivers (data warehouse users) will need only the owner's manual and not the shop manual. The technicians who need the shop manual will find that it doesn't attempt to cover all the conceptual basics that would be included in the owner's manual and a driver's education course.

Before tackling the specifics of implementing a data warehouse using Oracle8*i*, we'll use this one chapter to summarize many of the nontechnical concepts and critical success factors of data warehousing and a few related topics.

What Is a Data Warehouse?

Data warehousing has been presented as the panacea for all the ills confronting the business and its IT organization; one might think that data warehousing would be the final hurdle. Needless to say, however, data warehousing joins all the other failed panaceas: structured programming, relational databases, CASE tools, 4GLs, client/server and object-oriented development. To be sure, each of these technologies has provided great improvements in the way organizations manage information and is not, in and of itself, a failure. The failure has been in our expectation that we've finally reached the last hill of our journey and, if we can just climb it, we'll soon gaze upon the Promised Land of information management.

As one example, during the 1980s hundreds of organizations bought computer-aided software engineering (CASE) tools with the expectation that they'd receive tenfold increases in productivity. But when the dust settled and the organization's first CASE project was not completed any sooner than a non-CASE project, the company put the CASE tool on the shelf and went back to doing things the way it always had. What failed in almost every case (pardon the pun) was not the tool or the technology. What failed was the organization—it did not adopt and internalize the philosophical change of perspective required by a new way of doing things. CASE development is primarily a change in thinking; the tools are just supporting aids to help mechanize the new way of thinking. Without transforming the organization to the new discipline of CASE development, the tools just got in the way.

Data warehousing presents the same potential situation. As we'll see later in this chapter, data warehousing requires a fundamental change in the way an organization thinks about its data. If an organization embarks on a first attempt at a data warehouse with overly optimistic expectations then it is possible that a very useful and educational experience may be labeled a failure. It is important for an organization to be realistic about the benefits to be gained from a data warehouse and to realize that these benefits will grow over time as the warehouse is used and enhanced.

A similar explanation lies behind every one of the other "panacea" technologies just mentioned. They were demonstrably successful in those organizations that had realistic expectations, introduced the new philosophy and technology in a controlled manner, and ensured that all the participants adopted the philosophy first and then used the tool to support it. For the other organizations, those that did not change their way of thinking and developing systems, the new tools were frequently labeled as failures.

To be successful with data warehousing, it is thus essential to view it first as a new philosophy, a new way of thinking. Only then should the various technologies be introduced. If you have just purchased a new UNIX server, a data extraction and transformation tool, the Oracle8i RDBMS, and a couple of query and analysis tools and now expect to simply plug them together to build a data warehouse, you are virtually doomed to disappointment. Data warehousing is not fundamentally about technology.

The following sections discuss some other misconceptions about what a data warehouse is.

A Data Warehouse Is Not a Project . . .

Projects have defined starts and schedules; projects have defined results and specified constraints. Projects have budgets and assigned resources. Most importantly, projects have definite ends. (Of course, we've all been on projects that never seemed to end, but this is how it is *supposed* to work!)

A successful data warehouse does not have an end. The data warehouse is implemented in a series of miniprojects, each of which should have all the project characteristics just described. There are two risks associated with the misconception that a data warehouse is a project.

The first risk is that when the project ends everybody assumes the warehouse is done. Most of the benefits of the data warehouse will not be realized in the first delivery. Both users and developers of the first warehouse release will learn at least as much about what additional warehousing needs were not addressed as they will about the business entities represented within the warehouse. The sponsor, the implementation team, and the first set of warehouse users should all have the attitude that they're going to deliver something during the first project, but it will not be perfect. It will be a foundation for the next, improved version that will, in turn, form the foundation of the next, further improved version. This process should continue for as long as the organization has a data warehouse, although the changes and enhancements should be expected to become less radical over time.

The second risk of confusing a data warehouse with a project is that the project team is dangerously tempted to try to do everything and meet every need right out of the starting gate. There is absolutely no problem with deciding to severely limit the initial scope of the warehouse. Successfully providing integrated data about a small handful of business subject areas in a few months is far healthier than spending years attempting to get it all right in one giant release. It is, truthfully, impossible to do the latter. You cannot anticipate all the uses to which the warehouse may be put. It cannot be done. It has never been done. You will not be the first to have tried and failed.

Plan, therefore, to initially disappoint some or most prospective users. The very fact that they begin using the data that you have provided and then start asking for additional, related data is your first sign of success! What they learn from the first release will lead them to new questions that will lead you to new data structures, new data sources, and better integration processes.

. . . Rather, Data Warehousing Is a Process

Although a data warehouse is not a project, it is implemented in a series of projects. Through successive iterations we gradually build our data warehouse. In the first release, we might implement only three or four entities that are closely tied to each other and are of interest to one specific department or group of users. Each successive release adds some additional information based on what was learned from using the prior release. The additional information may be about the existing subject areas, perhaps adding more columns or new summaries. We will also choose to add entirely new subject areas and support new departments and user communities.

In an ideal implementation, the first release is made available to a particular user group within six months or less. As they begin to use the data warehouse two things happen. First, they find useful information that leads them to ask new questions. Some of these questions cannot be answered by the limited scope of data provided in the first release, which then leads to enhancements that are rolled out in future releases. Second, however, is a byproduct of our early success with the initial release: Word spreads from our initially targeted group of users to other potential users within other departments. The initial success with the finance department produces interest and access requests from marketing and production and sales and so on.

As this word-of-mouth reputation spreads throughout the organization, the data warehouse team is presented with new opportunities, challenges, and risks. The opportunities and challenges, of course, are related to supplying the additional data subject areas that are of interest to all those other departments now clamoring at the door. The risks, too, are in letting the first-round success trap us into trying to satisfy every newly identified opportunity in our second release. It is critical that we maintain the same discipline that allowed the first release to be successful. The warehouse team should prioritize specific subject areas and user groups for inclusion in each release. Each version of the warehouse should incrementally add new data to allow for three- to six-month intervals between releases.

Each release should follow closely enough on the heels of the prior release so that we maintain momentum and build a string of small success stories rather than attempt to do too much at once. Just as in baseball, grand-slam home runs make the headlines, but they don't happen often. Nine out of 10 long fly balls are caught for an out rather than clear the fence. To extend the analogy, the teams that win games consistently are those that can regularly get runners on base and then systematically advance them into scoring position and then bring them home. Baseball games are generally won by a series of singles and doubles (and sacrifices) rather than home runs. Data warehousing is the same. By the time a three-year grand-slam warehouse project is completed (if it ever is) the interest of the sponsor and users will have waned, and funding will have been diverted to some more urgent project.

In the movie *Annie Hall*, Woody Allen's character comments, "A relationship, I think, is like a shark. You know, it has to constantly move forward or it dies." A data warehouse, too, must continue to move forward or it loses value. Begin thinking early of the warehouse as an ongoing process rather than a single project or event.

A Data Warehouse Is Not a Product . . .

In most cases, the data warehouse will store its data within the control of an RDBMS, but this is not a requirement. The data warehouse is not the database. Some historical or foreign data for the warehouse may be realistically stored on tapes, microfiche, or even paper. It may not even be in the possession of the organization that builds and maintains the data warehouse. The data warehouse is a means of discovery. Sometimes the discovery is conveniently fast because the data needed for a particular question is nicely organized within the online files of a single relational database. It is just as valuable, although not as convenient, for the database to be able to answer the first of three questions, for example, and perhaps only provide direction for the user to find the answers to several subsequent questions.

One response to the current data warehousing fervor is to offer a "data warehouse in a box" or a data mart solution. In addition to product vendors, many consultants and authors offer predefined enterprise data models for manufacturing, retail, or other industries. All of these pre-packaged solutions or designs are attempts to appeal to the desire for an easy solution to a tough problem. Sometimes the data mart pitch can sound like the late-night television infomercials that offer a "miraculous new device that can give you rock-hard abdominal muscles or the thighs of a supermodel with absolutely no exercise in only 10 minutes a day while you watch your favorite TV show!" In reality, these shortcuts to fitness can't really work without some investment of time and exercise on your part. The primary risk of this approach to data warehousing is that by buying and implementing a series of quick and easy independent data mart packages you may end up missing out on the primary advantage of a data warehouse—an integrated view of the entire organization's data. (The subject of independent data marts, whether purchased or developed internally, is examined later in this chapter.)

Building an effective data warehouse requires making very tough decisions about the data model, the naming of attributes, the agreement on definitions (and other *metadata*) of each attribute, the source of each data element, the transformations that will be applied to the source data . . . the list goes on and on. A pre-packaged warehouse or data mart design may be a very useful fast start on your organization's total data warehouse needs, but only if you're realistic in understanding that you must still make an investment in validating and integrating the package into your total warehouse.

TIP Metadata is special data that describes the contents and operations of the data warehouse. Metadata is discussed in Chapter 4, "Designing the Oracle Data Warehouse."

In particular, if one of your key source systems is a packaged suite of Enterprise Resource Planning (ERP) applications, you may find that the vendor of that suite may have the best knowledge of how to extract data from its complex data structures. That vendor may also have a very good warehouse design for the subject area(s) associated with their applications. Just remember that not every ERP vendor is also expert in decision support processing!

When evaluating any ready-made solution, however, you need to evaluate a product's data model carefully—how well does it fit with your source systems and warehousing needs? Additionally, you will need to assess critically how easy it will be to integrate the packaged data model with the other data sources and subject areas that are critical to your organization. If you like the extraction and transformation processes, will you be able to modify the target warehouse design without breaking the other parts? If you like the warehouse data model but need to retrieve data from a different source than specified by the package, will you be able to alter the extraction routines? Any "solution" that can't be extended, modified, and integrated will not solve your problems; instead, it will become an albatross around the neck of the warehouse team until it is eventually replaced.

OBJECTS AND DATA WAREHOUSING

Much effort is underway within the RDBMS vendor community to better integrate the storage of complex data other than the traditional numeric and character data currently stored in the data warehouse. Oracle8, for example, introduced greatly enhanced capability for storing images, sounds, video clips, and even more complex objects. What is still missing is an appropriately engineered set of end-user query tools that are able to manipulate and retrieve these complex data types. These will come, however, and we predict they will be available within the lifecycle of Oracle8. Unfortunately, the data warehouses being built and used today cannot exploit these capabilities yet.

As an example, consider a data warehouse that supports the marketing functions of a multinational corporation. The warehouse could be realistically expected to contain a lot of information about the corporation's past sales results and the success of several marketing campaigns in various geographic territories. The warehouse might also have industry statistics obtained from trade organizations or the U.S. Department of Commerce. Some information on the corporation's competitors would certainly be valuable. It might, however, be impractical to physically store images of each of the competitors' various advertisements. Would you want 150 copies of the actual ad or would it be better to store information about the 150 placements and perhaps a pointer to a single copy of the ad layout? It might be useful to be able to find every article ever written that mentions our products or those of our competitors. If our company has a traditional library in which trade publications and other reference materials are held, it is a reasonable accommodation for the warehouse to store only references to the physical magazines. If potentially useful journal articles (or, for instance, Ph.D. theses) are already stored electronically by their copyright owners and made available over the Internet, it isn't critical that a copy be maintained within the warehouse's database. It would be very handy, however, if our warehouse were able to store the means for locating the information later.

As much as we might like to digitize and store a copy of everything anyone might ever want within our warehouse, realistically, there are costs associated with storage and with management. Those costs have to be traded off against (1) the probability of access, (2) the likely value of that access, and (3) the probability that the currently available copy will remain available until we might want to reference it. Storing the table of contents for each issue of our industry publications and journals and providing a text search against them may be nearly as useful as trying to electronically store every word ever published in them. It will certainly be a lot cheaper and probably more prudent legally.

As one final example, it is very common for the most detailed operational data used to build the data warehouse to be made available for inquiry for a period of time, frequently several months or even a year, as part of the warehouse. At some point, however, the sheer volume of detailed data produced by any large organization forces it to do something other than continue storing the detailed data online for immediate access. One alternative is to purge the data without keeping a copy. Purging is appropriate for some data, but most data warehouse developers tend to have a defensive "pack-rat" mentality about such things. "What if somebody finds a need for that data in a form other than the historical summaries we've built?" Anything is possible, so in many cases the developers will archive the data rather than purge it. By archiving, they move a copy of the data to some lower-cost medium, such as magnetic tape or CD-ROM, before removing it from the online database. If, by chance, someone in the distant future needs to access the data, they'll retrieve it and make it temporarily available again.

Archived data may not be in the database, but it can still be considered part of the data warehouse. Accessing archival data is obviously slower, but the cost of storage is substantially less. Remember that the speed with which data can be accessed is only one of several factors to be considered when designing the data warehouse. Other factors include the cost of storage, the cost of retrieval, the probability of retrieval, and the value of the data when retrieved. We can't keep everything. And what we can keep can't necessarily be retrieved immediately forever.

Likewise, prepackaged data mart products may seem to be an easy way to bypass all the tough issues surrounding the design and integration of a data warehouse. The primary value of the data warehouse, however, comes directly from the integration of data. A standalone data mart in each department or regional office may independently meet some organizational information needs, but it will not begin to resolve problems that result from creating proprietary "islands of information."

. . . Rather, Data Warehousing Is a New Way of Thinking about Data

Programmers and users of traditional transaction processing systems have unconsciously adopted a very short-term perspective on data. What is the current value of QTY_ON_HAND in the INVMSTR file for PROD_ID = 'BD112786'? How many employees are enrolled today in the 401(k) plan? Why didn't order number 19374730 from our biggest customer ship today as promised? How much money needs to be transferred tonight to cover the accounts payable check run?

All these questions are important to the operation of the business. They cannot be ignored or avoided. As new transactions are processed within our operational systems, the specific values associated with each of these questions constantly changes. New orders as well as new inventory receipts will constantly change the quantity on hand of many products. Newly hired employees and those leaving the company will change the retirement plan enrollments daily. Today's critical order will be forgotten tomorrow as we focus on the next critical order. Treasury management will have to assess balances and requirements again tomorrow and every day.

When (and only when) all of those operational questions are handled by stable, predictable data processing systems is it possible for an organization to start asking questions from a different perspective. The operational manager is like an airline pilot who has a specific destination to reach and a specific route to fly. He or she certainly has decisions to make (in conjunction with air traffic control) about finding the most economical and comfortable altitude or about detouring around a large thunderstorm, but they are all decisions regarding this flight, on this one day. Someone other than the pilot, however, needs to take a different perspective and consider such questions as whether that particular route is profitable or if the departure and scheduled arrival times are optimal for passenger loading, gate operations, equipment and crew utilization, and so on. Such questions don't affect the pilot flying today's flight. They do, however, involve information about many flights, routes, and even competitors' schedules.

Similarly, the effective user of a data warehouse has to be able to pull away from the details of today's operations and take a broader view of the business. The data warehouse can facilitate questions asked from the new perspective, but it cannot generate the new perspective. "Build it and they will come" is not a healthy way to approach data warehousing. In fact, they may or may not come; and if they do, they may not be ready to think in ways that a data warehouse can enhance.

One of our health care clients recently began building its first data warehouse. The sponsoring group of initial users was the actuarial department. I initially thought that actuaries would probably be interested in big-picture trends and would be perfect consumers of the summarized, long-term data normally found in a data warehouse. Wrong! In reality, the actuaries insisted on having access to the lowest level of detailed data; nothing would budge them from this position. What we eventually learned was that there was an immense backlog demand for detailed, operational reporting within this department. The actuaries required specific case data on morbidity and mortality for last month, and the currently available operational reports did not meet their needs. They needed consolidation of current data across geographic boundaries, and the current systems were capable only of reporting independently for each state in which the provider did business. They were not attempting (at that moment) to identify which procedures or doctors provided a long-term reduction in follow-up medical costs. They were just trying to find out how many patients, in total, died from cancer last month. They first needed an *operational data store* to meet some current operational system deficiencies.

We frequently work with consulting clients who claim to be implementing a data warehouse, but upon closer inspection we find that their driving business requirements are to be able to do faster or more flexible reporting on their operational data. There is nothing wrong with recognizing this business need. Frequently, organizations do have unfulfilled operational reporting needs. Organizations have a hierarchy of information needs that is similar to A. H. Maslow's famous hierarchy of individual needs.

The Hierarchy of Information Needs

Just as a person requires the satisfaction of basic physical needs for food, shelter, and the like, an organization must first be able to manufacture its product or deliver its service. If it can't, then more sophisticated information needs are irrelevant. A small startup business, such as a "single-shingle" consultant, may well survive based only on the owner's ability to remember the who, what, where, and when of his promised deliveries. The first information needs can be met simply by keeping a logbook and handwritten invoices. If the consultant is at all successful, a more complete information system will eventually be needed to meet tax reporting requirements (which obviously correspond to Maslow's safety needs!).

As the business grows and additional consultants are added there will be additional information needs. The different people in the organization will require information to support assignment schedules, payment of commissions, and the like. Like Maslow's love and esteem need categories, the organization's information needs at this point are functionally ones of communication, cooperation, and coordination. The organization will need to have a new awareness of cash flow and the day's outstanding accounts receivable. Eventually, the

MASLOW'S HIERARCHY OF NEEDS

For any reader who may have somehow escaped attending virtually any management or organizational motivation seminar or college course in the past thirty years, sociologist Maslow theorized in 1943 that every person has a hierarchy of needs. Basic physiological needs such as food and water must be met before the individual will be motivated by needs of safety. Only when physiological and safety needs are met can the person begin to seek love and interpersonal interaction. At that point, the individual begins to seek esteem and position within a social organization. Finally, on the foundation of satisfied physiological, safety, love, and esteem needs, the individual can begin to "self-actualize" and become concerned about engaging in self-fulfilling activities.

mature organization will have developed various information systems to handle these operational requirements.

Only when the organization has met these operational requirements will it be ready, like Maslow's self-actualizing individual, to address data warehousing needs. If the operational reporting needs of an organization have not been met, what might be called a data warehouse will end up becoming what Inmon has termed an *operational data store*. There is absolutely nothing wrong with building an operational data store that will hold a copy of operational data in order to support various otherwise unmet reporting requirements. This is a common phenomenon in a large mainframe shop whose assembler and COBOL programs date back to the 1960s and 1970s and whose file structures don't lend themselves to easy ad hoc reporting. The need to see additional operational reports from these ancient systems cannot be met through the labor-intensive process of writing more COBOL programs.

Figure 1.1 shows one way of considering the hierarchy of information needs within an organization. Fundamentally the basis of all information is in the foundation of data. At the first level of sophistication, operational reporting answers routine questions such as "What happened yesterday?" When these needs are met, members of the organization are able to consider questions at the next level of sophistication. These questions are generally of the form, "Why did that happen yesterday?" Users, armed with their standard operational reports, begin to investigate anomalies through ad hoc queries. At the third level of this hierarchy, selected users (analysts) begin to do more complex investigation of the data, asking questions such as "What is likely to happen tomorrow?"

Another way of describing these first three levels is that users are applying their knowledge of the data and the business to ask pertinent questions which will help them (1) run the business, (2) manage the business, and (3) direct the

Figure 1.1   The hierarchy of information needs.

business. The first level uses operational data with little need for historical perspective; it uses data within the operational systems or, optionally, from an operational data store. The second level typically uses operational data (for example, for drill-down inquiries) but some queries may also benefit from the integrated and historical character provided by a data warehouse. The third level generally requires access to a data warehouse for investigation of trends and statistical correlation.

Note that Figure 1.1 also depicts a fourth level of sophistication that might correspond to Maslow's self-actualization of the individual. At this level of the information needs hierarchy, the organization transcends its own knowledge of itself and its data and begins to discover relationships and patterns that were hidden in the large volumes of organizational data. This type of investigation is provided through the use of *data mining* software that does not require that a user be able to formulate a query about some known (or suspected) relationship in the data. The objective of data mining is to discover relationships that are not readily seen. One common use of data mining is to examine the past behavior of a company's customer base to discover opportunities to cross-sell and up-sell customers who fit certain patterns.

Without a good understanding of data warehousing (and a perspective on where the organization is in this information needs hierarchy) it is very tempting to start copying data to a relational database environment and letting the users build their own reports—and then just call it a data warehouse. The operational data store meets the level of need being felt by the organization in its current state of information maturity. These reporting needs must be met *before* the organization will be capable of gaining benefit from data warehousing.

Data warehousing is *not* equivalent to ad hoc queries and reporting. Just because users are doing ad hoc querying of the database does not mean they are interacting with a data warehouse. It is very common to perform ad hoc processing of operational data. The risk of confusing the data warehouse and the operational data store is that an organization that claims to have developed a data warehouse when it has really built an operational data store doesn't recognize that there is still a giant opportunity before it. Its managers begin to wonder why they are not receiving the wonderful competitive benefits that *Computerworld* and *Business Week* told them to expect.

Operational Data

The transaction processing systems used to run the business generally have a very current focus: What is the current stock level for product number 7582 at warehouse 3? How many hours did Luann work last week for which she needs to be paid? Which orders are currently waiting to be filled because of stock outages? How many blue casings are we supposed to produce before retooling the injection-molding machine? These are critical questions that must be answerable. If the operational systems don't somehow provide screens or reports to handle these and similar questions then an operational data store may be the appropriate next step.

The warehouse will, by contrast, allow us to ask a different set of questions: During which months do we sell the most of product number 7582? Are we spending more money on temporary, hourly workers this year than last? Which of our vendors' late deliveries to us have caused us to delay production and shipment of the greatest dollar volume of orders to our customers? What is the average number of days between identical machine setups to produce the same part? These are new questions that deal less with running today's business and allow us to begin to manage the business at a higher level of understanding. This ability to view historical data and to analyze current data within a historical context is the key benefit of a data warehouse.

Just keep in mind that users who can't take or fill orders or cut a paycheck are probably not yet ready to start analyzing business performance on these levels. Satisfy the more basic needs before embarking on a data warehouse.

A Data Warehouse Is Not a Place . . .

It may be obvious to some, but a data warehouse is not a specific location to which information consumers come to get data. Data warehousing has grown out of a tradition of decision support processing that, two decades or so ago, included just such an actual physical place. Today's data warehouse is not the same as a 1980s-vintage information center, which typically provided a special room equipped with terminals, PCs (remember, this was before every desk came equipped with a computer), printers, plotters, and trained support staff.

A data warehouse need not be housed in a single place. And even those warehouses whose databases are implemented on a single server are still not likely to be in a place ever physically visited by a user. Information is distributed to users at their normal place of work—their desk—in response to their requests. This model fits the image of a warehouse as a distribution center: Orders for specific warehouse contents are located, picked, packaged, and shipped to the original requester.

The difference, of course, is that data within the warehouse is not depleted in the same way as a physical warehouse. Multiple users may request the same data, or the user may "browse" through the warehouse requesting various things until he or she finds something interesting. Data, though, does have to be

EXTENDING THE METAPHOR

The term *data warehouse* presents a useful metaphor for characterizing the mass storage and distribution of information. Various authors (and vendors) have attempted to extend the metaphor . . . sometimes even usefully. We have seen the advent of the term *data mart,* which has been used variously to describe a small standalone data warehouse or a distributed secondary level of storage and distribution in conjunction with a data warehouse. We've also acquired the terms *data mining* and *data publishing* as other industrial metaphors. Recently, vendors have announced new products that they have dubbed the "data mall" and the "data factory." One recent reference to a "data toxic waste dump" was particularly descriptive. Eventually, we will probably all be subjected to "data service stations," "data condos," "data retirement homes," and "data amusement parks" as vendors and consultants climb over each other to find new (and annoying) variations on the industrial building metaphor.

replenished in the data warehouse—not, however, because of depletion, but for the sake of renewal. To have ongoing value the data of the data warehouse has to be both current and historic. We constantly add new data to the warehouse that can be compared to and combined with the historical record of data. It is within this context that the warehouse provides value in a way that the organization's operational systems cannot.

. . . Rather, Data Warehousing Is a Supplement to Traditional Data Processing

Traditional transactional systems are oriented toward holding a data value until that value is changed, at which point the systems must hold the new value until it is changed again. Each of those transactions, however, sees many interesting data relationships as it executes but does not traditionally record them. For example, we record the fact that our particular order was for 20 lawn mowers and we incidentally record the fact that on that same day we needed to replenish our inventory of lawn mowers. All sorts of other potentially interesting connections between these two "independent" transactions, however, are lost within our traditional systems.

These operational systems don't record coincidental circumstances that might occur at the time of a transaction. One transaction might note that John Smith ordered a set of four tires; a separate transaction orders a new supply of tires to be delivered to the shop. No record, however, is likely to be kept that it was specifically John Smith's order that caused our local inventory to drop below the reorder level. That may or may not be something of interest to an analyst. It might, however, be more interesting to know that right before Mr. Smith's order, we processed an order from a rental car fleet for 400 of the same tires. The actual reorder was "caused" by a small order, but we may want to investigate the impact of large orders. How often do these large orders occur? What is their impact on stock outages and reorders? How many small orders are affected when we receive a large order like this? What is the cost of maintaining sufficiently high inventory levels to handle these occasional large orders versus the additional cost of shipping large orders from a centralized warehouse while maintaining smaller inventory at each of our regional warehouses?

Similarly, our operational systems don't generally track weather events around the country. Why should they? But an analyst might be very interested to know which products show an increase or decrease in sales when a geographic region experiences an early frost.

What products show a change in purchasing trends when a market has a professional sports team in the playoffs? Again, our operational systems are generally not expected to record such information.

The systems that we build or buy to help us run our daily business are designed and tuned for efficient operation. They don't keep track of what data values might have been last month or last year. They aren't supposed to. But there is great value in observing the trends in how values have changed over time and in being able to see what other data has also changed—and possibly discovering connections. This is where a data warehouse can supplement the operational systems. By keeping regular snapshots of the operational data, the warehouse accumulates years of data that we can analyze. By incorporating data from external sources (like the data about weather or sports playoffs), the warehouse can become the place where we discover things about our data that were never visible in the day-to-day operational files and databases.

Inmon's Four Characteristics of a Data Warehouse

Bill Inmon, who is widely credited with founding the data warehousing movement, has written and lectured extensively on data warehousing and the ways to design and build a data warehouse. His books and articles on these topics should be read by anyone embarking on a warehouse implementation effort. He has repeatedly and consistently defined a data warehouse in terms of four characteristics. According to him, a data warehouse is a "subject-oriented, integrated, nonvolatile, and time variant collection of data in support of management's decisions" (from Inmon's *Building the Data Warehouse*, Second Edition, Wiley, 1996). It is, of course, possible to quibble with minor details or provide an exceptional case in which this definition doesn't precisely apply. As a general statement, however, this is the widely accepted definition of data warehousing. Let's examine each of the four points in greater depth.

Subject-Oriented

We have traditionally built systems with an applications or functional focus. When we build or buy the operational systems for a cable TV provider we deal with the billing function, the program-scheduling function, the maintenance of the physical plant, and the installation of equipment. We build other systems to handle order entry for monthly services and pay-per-view events. We will need to be able to schedule installation and repair visits. Frequently, each of these systems may be purchased from a different vendor or internally built or replaced at different times. Each application is supported by its own set of databases or files. We would commonly interface between these applications through extract files that pull a copy of information from, for instance, order entries to populate needed data in our installation, service, and billing systems. Our cable company would also use this order data to identify specific set-top devices and their authorized services and features for the network control and transmission systems.

Each of these systems (except for program scheduling) has some awareness of the CUSTOMER entity. The billing function and the network control function, as an example, have totally different views of what a customer is. Billing cares about a name and address and what service packages have been ordered by the customer. The network control function is aware of, say, two set-top devices with cryptic network addresses and that these devices are connected to a specific headend controller. The process of enabling a particular set-top device to receive this evening's heavyweight championship fight does not require any knowledge of the customer's name or mailing address or whether the customer disconnected the Disney Channel last week. Conversely, billing doesn't care what encryption algorithm will be used by the headend controller to transmit the fight.

In the data warehouse, however, we want to look across these multiple applications to distill the essential gestalt of CUSTOMER. Some of the data about a customer is likely to be found in the operational billing system. Other customer data may be extracted from the service calls database, which needs to be included with customer data taken from our pay-per-view system. Likewise, we might also need to retrieve data from billing, customer service, repair, and physical plant maintenance systems to capture and present all the necessary information about a service outage.

Within the OUTAGE subject area in the warehouse we will want to see the cause of each incident, the number of customers affected, the duration of the outage, the cost of repair, the refund costs committed to customers who complained, and the like.

In the warehouse, the subject orientation around CUSTOMER or OUTAGE is primary. Everything we store will be brought together around one of these subjects. If we stumble across some interesting bit of data from an operational system that does not apply to one of the subject areas of our data warehouse, we will set it aside until some future release in which its subject is implemented.

Data warehouse design is data-driven design. There have been several pushes for data-driven design of application systems, but the reality of application projects is that we first define the functional scope of the project and then design the data needed for the included functions. Within the data warehouse there are no functional barriers, and we, as designers, are free to be more pure in our data focus. We identify the subject areas, we construct our design, and then we go seek the data from its various operational sources. In some cases, the data we would like to include about one of our subjects cannot be obtained because of limitations imposed by the operational source systems or by the availability of external data. We mark that particular part of our subject area as unavailable and continue on. When possible, we'll request modifications to the existing legacy systems to better capture or retain the data we're interested in or we'll investigate other sources.

What we don't do in constructing our data warehouse is to build it "bottom up" by finding what data can be obtained and then loading it into an unstructured shell.

Integrated

Very closely related to the topic of subject orientation is that of integration. Once we have a cohesive, data-driven design we have the foundation for an integrated data warehouse. As we pull together the disparate data to form each subject effort we must make a conscious effort to effectively integrate it. As designers of the data warehouse, we can and must take the time to force consistency and discipline onto data that, in the operational sources, is anything but consistent and integrated.

We find that each system frequently uses a different name for a piece of data and that each system has stored the item with different encoding or different units of measure.

- What the payroll system calls SEX_CD and stores as either M or F corresponds to the benefits system's GENDER field that contains either 1 or 0.

- The benefits department registers 401(k) contributions by percentage of income, but payroll tracks contributions in dollars and cents while treasury reports fund balances as percentages of total contribution.

- One system has lots of fields suffixed with _IND (for indicator) that contain T and F values. Another system was built using _FLAG names for fields that store 1 or 0, while a third has no standard naming but seems to have lots of fields containing either Y or N.

- The purchasing department orders liquid lubricants by volume measured in barrels or by weight measured in tons. Our warehouse system, however, tracks inventory of all fluids in gallons and our installation and service departments dispense oil by the liter.

As we bring all this discovered data into the data warehouse, we are responsible for modifying the names, standardizing the encoding, and imposing consistency in our units of measure. Of course, each of the departments is used to naming, encoding, measuring, and even thinking in the way that its supporting systems have been written. As designers we have to resolve such conflicts in some manner, such as the following:

- By what seems logical to us
- By the common usage of the first sponsoring department
- By the common usage of the department with the biggest budget
- By flipping a coin
- By inviting all departments to a "last-man-standing" wrestling match

Seriously, there is no clear-cut way of deciding such issues. As we'll discuss later, one of the critical success factors in developing a data warehouse is to form a project team with active representation from each department likely to use the warehouse. Even if the initial release of the warehouse is going to include only the subject areas of interest to the finance department, other departments will someday use some of that data as well, especially after we include some additional subjects and data in releases two and three. Certain subject areas such as CUSTOMER and PRODUCT tend to cross many organizational boundaries. It is essential to resolve questions about the naming, sourcing, transformation, and storage of this data through discussion and compromise with all the groups that will eventually want to access the warehouse.

When old departmental conflicts prevent cooperation and compromise, it becomes necessary for the core warehouse development team to make decisions. Sponsoring executives need to be told before the start of the effort that their departments' representatives must be oriented toward the corporate benefit rather than parochial, departmental tradition. They (sponsors and design participants) need to understand that *any* standard is far better than the chaos created by decades of unintegrated applications.

When all else fails, it is possible (though not advisable!) to incorporate aliases into the warehouse design and to store and present specific data in more than one way. We can carry a field measured in inches and another in centimeters, or we can write conversion functions into the database and incorporate them into views that will allow each warring faction to see the data in its customary way. Rarely is this the right approach, for it misses one of the side benefits of a data warehouse—fostering improved communication across functional and organizational boundaries to discuss business subjects.

Nonvolatile

Data once entered into the data warehouse is almost never changed. Data records an event or state as it existed at some point in time. If some other event occurs that changes that state, it should be included in the warehouse as a separate, distinct event with a later time stamp. The data should reside as it was loaded for as long as the data is retained. Thus, there are only a few operations performed on warehouse data: It is loaded, it is accessed (for building summaries or by user queries), or it is eventually purged or archived. Data in the warehouse is not generally updated.

Any pressure to violate this simplified processing model should be viewed with extreme suspicion. If someone is asking to have adjusting entries or returns applied against the original transaction's data, either he is confused about the nature of the data warehouse or really attempting to extend his operational systems into an operational data store. If that person needs additional operational reporting, this is a need that should be met outside of (and prior to) the data warehouse.

One exception that may legitimately be made to this rule occurs when the integration of data from multiple sources is delayed because of the different availability of the source data. Remember that we did a pure, data-driven design of our warehouse. Data to satisfy the design is commonly pulled from multiple sources, not all of which are made available at the same time. As one example, if the design for our CUSTOMER entity includes data fields for SIC code, annual sales, and the like that do not originate within our internal systems, we may legitimately decide to load our internal data and later include the missing data when it becomes available. When we obtain the external data (from their quarterly 10Q filings, for instance) we can add it to the warehouse record of the customer.

Another exception sometimes is made to allow for data summaries of the "year-to-date" type. If your design is made simpler by this denormalization and you consciously choose to include this current data focus to an entity, you risk having operational questions ("What are the current year-to-date sales to Acme Corporation?") directed to your warehouse. This may lead to improper interpretations of answers because we may update that field only monthly while the user may think they are getting truly *current* values. Also, it adds complexity (and, potentially, locking issues) to our data warehouse if we begin doing single row updates. If you anticipate many questions of this type, you may wish to make life simpler for the user by supplying "to-date" summaries, but be very careful not to mix them with more appropriate nonvolatile summaries.

It might be preferable to create a view that meets the users' convenience needs without requiring frequent updating of data. The following example is built on detailed data in the ORDERS table, but a better performing view could be built on top of a MONTHLY_ORDERS table if such a summary were already available:

```
CREATE VIEW YEAR_TO_DATE_SALES
    AS
SELECT CUSTOMER_ID, CUSTOMER_NAME, SUM(SALES)
  FROM ORDERS
 WHERE SALES_DATE BETWEEN ROUND(SYSDATE, 'YEAR') AND SYSDATE
 GROUP BY CUSTOMER_ID, CUSTOMER_NAME;
```

Time Variant

Most data stored for operational use has an implied time dimension: now. Each new transaction modifies the current state of data, such as an inventory level, to form a new current state. Even data that is created by the transaction (such as a new order) is typically modified to show changes in current state, such as the order status changing from "taken" to "credit checked" to "picked" to "shipped." Order data that isn't modified tends to have a rather short life span within the order processing system. Operational data is generally kept only until its innate workflow cycle is completed. This might mean until the order is shipped or until the end of the next billing cycle or perhaps, somewhat arbitrarily, for six months.

For performance reasons the designers of operational systems try to keep databases and files as small as possible. Most details about last year's orders are of relatively little use in running today's business.

Contrasted with this operational focus on currency of data and minimizing storage space and access speeds, the data warehouse has very a different perspective on time. First, data in the warehouse is expected to be retained for much longer periods, commonly 5 or 10 years. One of the most frequent types of analysis performed in the warehouse involves identifying trends and correlations over time.

Data, whether in the originating application system or the data warehouse, can be classified as being related to an event or a state. Events are the triggers that initiate a transaction. Event data includes the order that was taken at a particular time and shipped on a particular day. Events are easily positioned in time, although not all of a company's operational systems do so explicitly.

State data is changed by a transaction. Examples of state data include inventory levels, customer credit limits, and cash flow. State data can be sampled at any time and can generally change at any time. State data does not have a predefined time element, but only an implicit one—the current time when it is sampled. We can take a nightly snapshot of our inventory levels or make a monthly calculation of cash on hand. Alternatively, we can sample the current value of state data on an irregular schedule, perhaps tied to some event.

Finding a correspondence between events and state data is one of the most difficult aspects of decision support processing. Problems arise because of this dichotomy between event and state data. First, the order of events has profound effects on the changes in state. Several events may commonly occur between captures of state data, and it is frequently difficult to rebuild the successive state changes that occurred between the samples. Second, events are not necessarily discrete, and there is potentially more than one way to determine the time of an event.

A common part of taking an order is to check the state of inventory and the customer's credit limit. Another part is adjusting both the inventory level and the credit limit. If the customer makes several purchases, returns some items, and makes a payment all on the same day, it is possible for one of the purchase requests to be refused because of a credit limit violation, but the nightly report of customers who are over their credit limits may not include the customer. Why? Several events have occurred between our snapshots of state. Depending on when the payment and return transactions are processed in relation to the attempts to purchase, this customer may or may not have had a purchase refused. Similarly, a bank that does its nightly posting of checks and other debits before it posts deposits would likely have some very irate customers who were bouncing checks even though they had deposited adequate funds to cover those checks.

Another example, familiar to most businesspeople who travel a lot, is the credit card postings for airline travel. Charges seem to be posted by the airlines to your credit card immediately. Return an unused ticket to the airline or travel agency, however, and it will probably not get credited to your account for at least one extra billing cycle. The reason, of course, is that the airline is playing cash flow games using your money. But when the monthly billing statement is produced (state data) your account will not reconcile to your personal calculation of your outstanding balance. The statement is accurately reflecting the posted activity (events) that have completed, but your own balance is also accurately reflecting the events that have been initiated. This is because you've measured the start of an event (returning the ticket), and the credit card company has not yet recorded the completion of the same event (posting the credit). In between these two parts of the same event a variable amount of time may occur.

Resolving these issues and correlating event data and state data is one of the great opportunities and great challenges for the data warehouse designer. Virtually all data that enters into the data warehouse must be assigned a time dimension value. This means that events are time-stamped, and samplings of state data are also given a time-stamp. Ideally, we would like to have these perfectly correlated, but this is rarely possible. Commonly, we have an available transaction time-stamp for events, but it may vary widely in its precision. Orders are recorded with date and time, perhaps provided by a database trigger that reads the system clock. Shipping events may be recorded only by the day processed. Once a package is addressed, weighed, and placed in the outbound bin, it is considered shipped even though the shipping carrier may not come to the dock for several hours.

Similarly, it would be possible to record the current state data as part of every transaction, but the additional workload and storage requirements would be prohibitive for most operational systems. So we compromise by taking snapshots at regular intervals. In some cases, this might be hourly, in others it might be nightly, and in still others it might be only monthly. To illustrate this point, it would be possible as part of order taking to record the standard price of each

---

AN ANALOGY TO INMON'S FOUR CHARACTERISTICS

Though not commonly considered a data warehouse, the collection of data by the Securities and Exchange commission demonstrate these characteristics well. Public companies in the U.S. must produce audited financial reports every quarter.

A quarterly report deals with a single *subject* area—financial performance of the organization. The results are consolidated (*integrated*) from many subsidiary companies and operational divisions using standardized accounting practices. It is considered a major negative for a company when the financial reports, once released, must be restated (they are generally *nonvolatile*). Finally, these reports are *time variant* as they are prepared specifically for a particular operating period (fiscal month, quarter, or year).

Interestingly, both transactional activity, reported on the income statement, and state data, shown as a snapshot on the balance sheet, are included.

Deciphering these reports by industry analysts and brokerage firms has many similarities to the analysis performed by data warehouse users. Trends and comparisons are widely used to make decisions and recommendations about future directions of a particular company or an entire industry.

---

item along with the negotiated or volume discounted price. Our order processing system may have been designed, for storage economy, to ignore standard pricing whenever a negotiated price for this customer is available. Order processing is streamlined by this design, but our decision support users may later legitimately wish to analyze discounting and its correlation with order volume. If we can't convince the maintenance team for order entry to add some additional logic and data fields (and we probably can't) we may have to do the additional work as part of building the data warehouse.

We may choose to record (and time-stamp) the events of all changes to standard and negotiated prices. Alternatively, we may choose to snapshot the pricing data nightly. Either way, we have a means of adding standard price and discount percentage to each order record when we add it to the warehouse. The first approach may be harder to accomplish but provides greater accuracy. The second approach is simpler programmatically but loses precision if multiple pricing changes happened during one day or if some orders were processed before and others after the price change.

Choosing an appropriate sampling frequency is a compromise between costs and accuracy. Even though the detailed data initially loaded into the data warehouse is time-stamped with different levels of precision we are not hopelessly out of synch. In many cases, the detailed data loaded into the warehouse will be used primarily for building various summaries. Summaries, like all other data in the warehouse, should have a time dimension as part of their key structure. Sales are summarized by region and month. Hiring is summarized by department by month. In summarizing along the time dimension, we typically compress the data by giving up precision. We may summarize activity by day, week, month, quarter, and/or year. If we have captured our state data to at least the first level of summarization of our events, then most of the warehouse processing can correlate the two with adequate precision.

All data in the data warehouse should be identifiable by its position in time, in addition to its other identifying attributes.

REFRESHING THE DATA WAREHOUSE

One side note on the impact of time on the warehouse: In addition to forcing a time dimension on all data as it is entered or built through aggregation, there is an issue of timing our warehouse processing. Data should be entered into the warehouse on a regular schedule. Summarizations, too, should be processed according to a regular schedule. For the past 25 years, the emphasis of data processing has been to move as much processing as possible from batch mode to online mode. (Newcomers to the industry without an IBM mainframe background don't even use the term *batch*.) We have been brainwashed into thinking that everything must happen immediately and that delays in processing data are inherently bad. For several reasons this thinking must be reversed when working with the data warehouse.

First, performance of batch operations on large amounts of data is almost always more efficient than single-record processing. Loading 10 million rows to an Oracle database via direct path SQL*Loader is orders of magnitude faster than loading the rows individually. Likewise, building a summary table in Oracle using the parallel, unrecoverable CREATE TABLE AS SELECT command is many times faster than processing each detail row in a SQL cursor and applying changes to an existing summary. Performance requirements for a warehouse are generally relaxed over those of an OLTP system, but throughput concerns are often more stringent.

Second is the (somewhat underhanded) value of introducing an intentional delay in making data available in the data warehouse. Even if your data volumes are such that you can load daily transactional data overnight, in many cases it may be preferable to load data only weekly or even monthly. "How can that be?" the OLTP-trained masses cry. The answer is that if yesterday's data is made available today, there is an immediate temptation to start using that data for operational purposes. To keep warehouse users focused on the bigger picture of analysis and discovery we should not encourage them to get mired in details. (An operational data store [ODS] provides a means of satisfying the need for operational reporting while also supporting the loading of the warehouse.)

What Is an Operational Data Store?

One of the common difficulties during the design phase for a data warehouse is that users insist that they must have all data retained at the lowest level of detail. This is a problem for the technical architects who must design the methods for storing, indexing, and processing very large volumes of data. One of the reasons for this request is that users don't know what data will be useful to them in the future, so they request everything. That is an understandable reaction to the iterative nature of warehouse evolution.

Another reason for requesting detail data, however, was described earlier in this chapter while exploring the hierarchy of information needs. This phenomenon generally is also manifested in the stated need for the data to be published in the warehouse within one day or even a few hours of its creation. These two requests are symptomatic of users whose basic reporting needs have not been met within the operational systems that they use daily. These are valid needs and must be addressed. Many early data warehouses were unfortunately overwhelmed by the attempt to store many millions of rows of transactional data. This was made even worse by the more limited capabilities of the RDBMS and hardware available at the time.

Recognizing the gap between the operational systems' reporting deficiencies and the intended usage of the data warehouse, Bill Inmon suggested an intermediate storage location for detailed data called the Operational Data Store (ODS). The ODS shares the ease of use associated with the relational database while still maintaining an arm's-length relationship to the decision support functions of the data warehouse.

While data in the data warehouse is generally intended to be kept for multiple years (or forever), attempting to store millions of transactional details is generally unnecessary. Detailed data has a half-life like a radioactive isotope. Over time, the value of the specific transactional data loses value. As an example, it is likely that we will need the details of an order for many purposes in the time between its origination and the customer's next monthly billing statement. During the second and third month there is still some potential for doing research for complaints or returns. What is the probability of anyone needing to look at the details of that order two years from now? Much lower.

There is still value inherent in the order data, but it is because we need to see summary results around one or more dimensions of the data:

- How many red dresses were sold in winter months versus spring months?
- Which of our customers have placed an average of at least three orders per month?
- Which models have demonstrated a lower-than-average number of returns?

An ODS provides the ability to do detailed operational reporting when it is important to the operation of the business. It also becomes a primary feed for data into the warehouse on a regular refresh schedule. This minimizes the number of extracts that impact performance on the transaction processing systems.

The data warehouse provides a longer-term perspective that allows the users to answer questions about aggregates of data. Setting appropriate retention periods and archival processing in these two environments will allow both to operate efficiently in meeting their respective goals.

It should be noted that building the operational data store is a very helpful step to have completed when one does start to build a true data warehouse. It is often much simpler to obtain operational data for the warehouse from a relational operational data store. If someone has already done some of the hard work of identifying, extracting, and cleansing data from the various legacy system files then the remaining work of integrating and time-dimensioning the data during warehouse design may be simplified.

What Is a Data Mart?

Some people use the term *data mart* to mean a small data warehouse. They create several data marts to meet the needs of several departments, and everyone is happy. Well, maybe. The risk of using data marts in this way is that you may easily sidestep the tough issues of integration that must be addressed in a data warehouse. By avoiding these issues we can certainly get several independent data marts operational more quickly. Each department works in isolation and thinks it is receiving valuable information from its private decision support system (DSS) environment. What naturally follows is that the independent data marts foster the same "islands of information" typified by the old application systems, which are functionally delineated. Using this independent data mart model we still find the marketing department and the manufacturing department getting two very different answers to what appears to be the same question.

To be useful to the entire organization, a data mart needs to be an extension of the data warehouse. Data is integrated as it enters the data warehouse. Data marts, then, derive their data from the central source, the data warehouse. Each department (or whatever organizational unit gets its own data mart) determines which of the data warehouse contents are of primary interest. These subject areas are then replicated onto the smaller, local data mart so that users can get to the data they are interested in with less interference.

Of course, if we were truly just replicating the data we would probably be able to save a lot of money by just increasing the query processing capacity of the data warehouse and retaining just one copy of the data. In fact, the distribution of data from the data warehouse to a data mart provides an opportunity to build new summaries to fit a particular department's needs. A common approach to data marts is to load detailed data into the data warehouse and perform the first level of summarizations (what Inmon refers to as "lightly summarized data"). The data marts, by contrast, keep only higher levels of summarization, which are derived from the warehouse's lightly summarized data. No detail data is copied to the data mart, and the central data warehouse does not attempt to keep every possible summary. This approach keeps the size of each local data mart relatively small. It also allows the complete data mart to be quickly refreshed. Because the data mart can be reconstructed quickly, backup and recovery concerns are virtually eliminated.

In this hierarchical model, whenever users of the data mart need to drill down from their local level of summarization, their queries are routed to the primary data warehouse. This can be done automatically and transparently through the distributed capabilities of Oracle, although it may be preferable to make users aware of the change of venue. As they ask more detailed questions they should understand that the warehouse, with its larger volume of data to process and potentially greater number of users contending for system resources, will generally provide slower response times.

A good analogy for effective data mart design is that of a public library system. The central, downtown library attempts to obtain a large number of books, periodicals, and other more obscure publications. The local branch library maintains a much smaller inventory of materials. For average users, their local branch provides nearly all their needs. Children doing school papers and adults looking for an interesting mystery novel find what they need most of the time. But in the occasional situation in which the local resources are not sufficient, the local branch can obtain any of the main library's resources on an overnight basis. The electronic card catalog available in each branch shows the total set of resources, their location, and their availability status.

The user of the data mart should have the same capability to view the entire catalog of available data and decide whether the immediately available local summary data will meet his or her needs or whether to wait for delivery of a more detailed set of data from the central data warehouse.

More complete discussion of data mart implementation is provided in Chapter 12, "Distributing the Oracle Data Warehouse."

What Is OLAP?

OLAP, online analytical processing, is complementary to data warehousing. There are two variations of OLAP.

MOLAP (multidimensional OLAP) provides analysis capability on data stored within a specialized multidimensional database system (MDBS). This specialized MDBS can be on an individual analyst's personal computer, or it may be considered a departmental data mart. MOLAP databases are optimized for rapid analysis across different dimensions of generally numeric data. MDBSs are not designed to support the same operations as transaction processing databases (relational, network, or hierarchical), such as transaction management and high concurrency of access. Generally, the structure of the multidimensional "cube" is fairly rigid. Modifying the structure and reloading the cube is often a very time-consuming task.

ROLAP (relational OLAP) applies analysis tools to data stored within a relational database. ROLAP processing may be applied to the data warehouse or to a data mart. Relational databases are best known for their flexibility. Until recently they were weak in their ability to perform the same kind of multidimensional analysis for which the MDBS is specifically optimized. The introduction of hybrid relational systems with enhanced abilities to manipulate star schemas, such as the Red Brick product, brought much of the OLAP capability to the relational world. Oracle7, release 7.3, introduced star schema processing to the Oracle RDBMS product. This star schema processing was greatly enhanced in Oracle8.

These improvements still do not enable ROLAP to meet all of the "slice and dice" analysis speeds offered by a dedicated MDBS. But coupled with the traditional flexibility of the relational database and ROLAP's ability to gracefully incorporate more complex data types and structures, ROLAP is an attractive option.

Both forms of OLAP processing, using Oracle's Express line of products, are covered in Chapter 13, "Analytical Processing in the Oracle Data Warehouse."

What Is Data Mining?

Data mining software is a recently invented class of tools that apply artificial intelligence (AI) techniques to the analysis of data. The promise of data mining tools is that, given access to the raw data, the tool can dig through the data looking for patterns and discovering relationships that the user might never have suspected. These tools are still maturing and can be expected to improve over the next several years. Whether they will eventually deliver on their promise or, like the AI products and techniques so widely touted a decade ago, end up living only in academic laboratories is still to be determined.

OLAP tools and most query tools used with data warehouses require the user to identify specific queries for investigating data that is expected to be of interest. The user must formulate his or her own hypothesis and then investigate the data to see if the hypothesized data relationships exist. Data mining tools can work against the data stored in operational systems or in a data warehouse.

Because of the processing-intensive nature of data mining, it is likely that these tools, if they are ever widely adopted, will be commonly used in a data warehouse or operational data store environment.

Several different data mining software products have established a toehold in this market. By far, the largest installed base is the large set of products from SAS Institute. SAS came into the data mining space from a strong background of delivering statistical analysis software. This was a natural evolution, but SAS products still have the reputation of being difficult for nonstatisticians to use. IBM is another significant player in the data mining space with its Data Miner tool set. Another player of interest, Thinking Machines Corporation, was founded in 1983 and produced a line of massively parallel computers. Their natural evolution came through applying massively parallel processing capabilities to the problems of searching large data sets for hidden patterns and relationships. When the massively parallel computing market failed to grow solid roots in commercial applications, Thinking Machines sold off its hardware business to concentrate on just the data mining software market with its Darwin product. Darwin developed the reputation for being powerful software that exploits the parallel processing paradigm, but it never gained enough market share to be a threat to SAS dominance because of the very small size of Thinking Machines.

That situation changed dramatically in June of 1999 when Oracle Corporation acquired Thinking Machines Corporation, its 30 or so employees, and the Darwin product. At the time of this writing, integration of Darwin technology and Oracle8*i* is only in the initial stages, but this should prove to be a very synergistic acquisition, for several reasons.

- Oracle Corporation has not had a product offering in the data mining space that is closely tied with Oracle's emphasis on data warehousing.

- Thinking Machines's primary emphasis for Darwin has been in customer behavior analysis, which fits well with Oracle Corporation's move into Customer Relationship Management (CRM) applications. Additional industry strengths of Oracle Corporation, such as Internet commerce companies, have similar needs for mining large databases.

- Darwin has not had the marketing and development support of an industry-leading corporation.

- Darwin's design emphasis on parallel execution with very large data sets fits nicely with Oracle8*i*'s strengths.

In its first year under Oracle ownership, Darwin has acquired new capability of writing its scoring data back into the Oracle8*i* database. Over the next several years, we will continue to see an increasing integration of Darwin and the Oracle8*i* RDBMS. An additional chapter on Darwin data mining would not fit within the space limitations of this book. Readers interested in data mining may obtain that supplemental chapter from the Web sites listed in the Introduction.

Critical Success Factors in Data Warehousing

Certain characteristics are common to data warehouses that have been implemented successfully. Success of a data warehouse can be best defined by user acceptance and usage. It is common to justify the development of a data warehouse by forecasting a return on investment that assumes a dollar value for business decisions made more accurately or quickly because of information gleaned from the warehouse. In a small percentage of cases, the warehouse team has solicited the users' valuation of the warehouse after deployment as well. In some publicized cases, users have been able to point to specific decisions made using warehouse data that have earned their companies millions of dollars in new business opportunities or saved costs.

Such cases are no doubt real, but they are isolated. Most data warehouses provide their value through hundreds of small, incremental decisions whose individual value is difficult to quantify. Even if users cannot point to a million-dollar cost savings, a data warehouse is successful if its users are finding it subjectively valuable and if they are continuing to ask for enhancements and extensions.

Some of the common factors seen in data warehouses that are successful and growing include the following:

An identified, involved user community. Successful data warehouses are not built in a vacuum. The only reason to keep data in a warehouse is for the users who will request it. The library analogy applies here as well. A successful library listens to the needs of its users and adds books, periodicals, and technology that will enhance its patrons' usage. Trying to determine their needs without involving them can at best only be partially successful.

Executive sponsorship. An organization makes a large commitment when it decides to begin data warehousing. This commitment involves potentially large sums of money for funding hardware, software, and human resources. The opportunity cost of what those people might otherwise be doing should not have to be constantly reviewed. Only with an executive sponsor who can champion the effort through its gestational period can the warehouse team keep its focus and move toward success.

A balanced project team. Warehouse teams don't have to be large. The most successful ones aren't. They do, however, need a variety of skills and knowledge, both technical and business-related. It is easy to fall into the trap of thinking that the primary team players will have technical backgrounds. In reality, the representatives of the business units that will be the warehouse users will have the greatest impact on the eventual warehouse results. The IT analysts and DBAs are best considered as the facilitators who bring the others' business knowledge together into a design.

Quick, small, incremental successes. As stated at the beginning of the chapter, it is not advisable to attempt to build the corporate data warehouse in a single, massive project. Given a very high-level outline of the subject areas that will eventually be represented in the warehouse, the first implementation effort should attempt only to satisfy a small manageable portion. By completing that portion quickly, the team can demonstrate benefits, cement management support, and begin learning how to improve the design for future releases.

An architected environment. Simply throwing transactional data into a relational database and calling it a data warehouse is a recipe for failure. Unless the warehouse implementation team commits to making the difficult design decisions required to integrate the data into a subject-oriented plan, users will not find relevance in the warehouse. (Very likely they won't be able to find *anything* in the warehouse!) Of all possible characteristics, irrelevance is the one that will doom the warehouse fastest.

Summary

Data warehousing is not a project but an ongoing process. A data warehouse is not a product or set of products but a new way of thinking about the data of an organization. A data warehouse is also not the same as an operational data store, although they frequently are used to complement each other. If an organization has unmet reporting needs about the current operational data these needs should be addressed separately and before building a data warehouse. Finally, a data warehouse is not a specific place. It does not replace current application systems but is a supplemental outgrowth of traditional data processing.

As noted earlier, according to Bill Inmon a data warehouse is a "subject-oriented, integrated, nonvolatile, and time-variant collection of data in support of management's decisions." This means that a lot of work goes into the data-driven design of a data warehouse in order to allow users to visualize data across application and organizational boundaries and across time. Gary Larson's *Far Side* comic strip once displayed a big pile of horses and cowboys heaped in the street in front of the sheriff's office. The sheriff is seen saying to his deputy, "And so you just threw everything together? Matthews, a posse is something you have to organize!" So, too, is the data warehouse.

This chapter has briefly summarized *what* data warehousing and some related topics are all about. The rest of this book is oriented to showing you *how* to use Oracle8*i* technology to deliver a successful data warehouse that will grow in value for many years to come.

CHAPTER
2

Hardware Architectures for Oracle Data Warehousing

Hardware Wars! A thrilling space saga of romance, rebellion, and household appliances! . . . You'll laugh! You'll cry! You'll kiss three bucks goodbye!

Hardware Wars (1977)

An Oracle data warehouse may be implemented on a wide variety of systems with a number of options for data storage, fault tolerance, backup, and recovery. Each of these systems can be categorized in terms of broader hardware architectures (i.e., SMP, MPP, clusters, etc.). This chapter describes each of these architectures and discusses their suitability to the Oracle data warehousing environment. The ability of each architecture to support the Oracle Parallel Query and Oracle Parallel Server options is discussed. Oracle Parallel Query is discussed because it is considered essential for most Oracle data warehouses. Oracle Parallel Server *may* be required if the workload exceeds the capacity of a single server.

Data storage hardware and software continue to evolve side by side with the core computer systems architectures. In the later sections of this chapter, data storage technologies are discussed as they relate to the data warehouse.

Throughout this chapter the terms *node* and *system* are used to identify components of a hardware architecture. A node is the smallest hardware component of an architecture that is capable of independently running its own operating system and database instance. A system is composed of one or more nodes that together provide the hardware infrastructure for implementing the Oracle data warehouse.

> **THE AUDIENCE FOR THIS CHAPTER**
>
> This chapter describes and compares the different hardware environments in which the Oracle8*i* RDBMS can operate. The nontechnical reader who is not involved with making hardware selection decisions may safely choose to skim this material quickly. The information on clustered and MPP architectures, however, is important background for the understanding of Chapter 11, "Warehousing with Oracle Parallel Server."

Computer Architectures

A key factor in determining the likely success of a data warehouse is, in part, the organization's ability to select the architecture that best meets most of the requirements. It will probably be cost-prohibitive or technically unfeasible to meet all of an organization's requirements. Some compromises will inevitably have to be made. In this chapter we identify why it is important to develop a set of requirements in conjunction with the end users of the system, what these requirements should contain, and how to evaluate an architecture based on these requirements. We then discuss the computer architectures currently available and describe their strengths and weaknesses.

> **ONGOING ARCHITECTURAL ASSESSMENT AND IMPROVEMENT**
>
> Regardless of the architecture selected, software and hardware failures will always occur. There is a natural tendency for the operations staff to blame the hardware or software vendor for these failures. Although this may be warranted in some cases, it does not address the needs of the users. To address these needs, an assessment and improvement process should be adopted to investigate the causes for each failure. This should lead the organization to identify new procedures or architectural changes to prevent the failure from reoccurring in the future or to mitigate the impact of such a failure.

Requirements Definition

When evaluating an architecture it's necessary to assess how well the architecture satisfies your organization's requirements. These requirements need to be developed with the cooperation of the end users of the data warehouse and should take into account their expectations. They should be documented on paper so that all parties are in agreement about what the data warehouse should provide. These requirements form the basis for evaluating the various architectures and for selecting the one that best fits an organization's needs.

The requirements that impact the warehouse architecture are distinctly different from the requirements that define the contents of the data warehouse. Architectural requirements define in a quantitative manner the reliability, availability, performance, scalability, and manageability of the data warehouse. There are also other considerations (e.g., cost) that should be taken into account once these basic requirements are satisfied but that are not part of the architectural requirements.

It is common for the initial pass through the users' requirements to generate a trial solution that is more expensive than the allowable budget.

The requirements document can also be used (with some additions) as the basis for a service-level agreement. This agreement serves as the contract between the users and the operations staff. It establishes an ongoing method for measuring the effectiveness of the chosen architecture as well as the performance of the operations staff. The service-level agreement serves to pinpoint weaknesses in the architecture or deficiencies of the operations staff and to point the direction for improvement.

Evaluation Criteria

The Objective criteria need to be in place by which alternative architectures may be evaluated. Five classifications are described in the sections that follow and then are used to evaluate the available architectures. These criteria can be remembered via the acronym "PARMS":

- Performance
- Availability
- Reliability
- Manageability
- Scalability

Performance

OLTP environments typically have a large number of concurrent users who execute a small number of simple, predefined transactions that operate against small amounts of data in the database. In contrast, data warehouse environments typically have fewer users executing complex ad hoc queries that require vast amounts of data and processing resources. In addition to the online user queries, the data warehouse will need to be periodically refreshed. As a result, the typical measure of performance for OLTP environments (i.e., response time) cannot be applied to data warehouse environments. For data warehouses, a method for measuring performance that covers both the online users as well as the refresh requirements must be defined.

Performance metrics for online data warehouse users should define the workload in terms of how many concurrent users can query the database and still provide reasonable response time. To define what reasonable response time is, it's necessary to establish a series of benchmark queries that can be run under various load conditions. The emphasis should not be on the absolute response time of any single query but on the throughput of total user workload.

Another method for establishing performance requirements for the batch refresh jobs is also needed. One method is to define the total amount of time available to complete the various load, summarization, and indexing jobs. Because the load may vary for weekly, monthly, quarterly, or yearly refreshes it will be necessary to define the time window for each of these jobs. Of course, it will also be necessary to define the conditions under which these jobs will run:

- Will backups be running?
- Which jobs can or should be run simultaneously?
- What degree of parallelism will be used for these jobs?
- How many users, if any, will be permitted access during these refresh periods?

Additionally, the amount of time to perform many of these tasks (especially indexing and backups) can be expected to increase over time as data volumes in the warehouse grow. Allowance for this increased processing load must be made during the initial design of the system.

Numerous technical areas of an architecture must be examined when evaluating performance. The now obsolete TPC-D benchmark provided one data

---

ORACLE PARALLEL SERVER AND ORACLE PARALLEL QUERY WILL NOT INCREASE PERFORMANCE ON A SYSTEM WITH LIMITED RESOURCES

Oracle Parallel Server and Oracle Parallel Query provide the ability to parallelize certain operations (see Chapter 10, "Parallel Execution in the Oracle Data Warehouse," for a list) in the Oracle8*i* data warehouse. They, however, cannot shorten the run-time of an existing job if the supporting system is already limited in resources. You will be disappointed if you expect Oracle Parallel Query to significantly shorten the run-time of a job on a system that has only 10 percent CPU idle time or that is already I/O bound. In this situation, using Oracle Parallel Query in conjunction with adding CPUs or striping the data files may dramatically increase performance.

point for comparing architectures under a hypothetical data warehouse load. This particular benchmark provided a more complex query mix than previous TPC benchmarks. The TPC-D has been replaced by two new benchmarks, the TPC-H and TPC-R. These are designed to model ad hoc query performance and standardized reporting environments, respectively.

Benchmarks present only a hypothetical load, however, and are not necessarily indicative of how any specific warehouse will perform. Also, hardware and DBMS vendors tend to try every possible trick in the book to achieve performance that may not be realistic in a real-world environment. By way of example, the published benchmark results may depend on specific data partitioning that would be administratively burdensome in a real warehouse. A good approach for evaluating how an architecture will perform with an Oracle8*i* data warehouse is to analyze how quickly certain database operations can be performed. From an architectural standpoint, the chief factors that influence this are as follows:

Disk transfers. How long does it take to transfer data between the SGA and disk (msecs [milliseconds])? The primary concern here is sequential read access times. Write times also become a factor during refresh operations and any intensive recoverable data manipulation language (DML) operations. Placement of data files and the number of concurrent database operations can lead to disk contention (also called "hot spots"). Another factor is over how many spindles the load is spread. In general, the more disk spindles, the better the performance. Differing RAID levels also impact I/O performance (this will be discussed in more detail later). System bus throughput may become an issue (especially on nodes that have multiple CPUs). Oracle Parallel Server presents some additional demands for disk transfers. It requires that all database files be accessible from every node. Some of the platforms on which Oracle runs provide this accessibility through software instead of through shared direct access to the disks. These platforms impose an additional overhead in terms of software and the intranode communications required for all disk operations that cannot be satisfied locally. Also, each node increases the contention on the disks.

Lock conversions (Oracle Parallel Server only). How long does it take to convert a lock with the Oracle Parallel Server option (µsecs [microseconds] to msecs [milliseconds])? This is a factor involving the latency of the communications path between the requesting node and the node (if any) that has the lock in a conflicting mode. Additionally, if a node has the lock in exclusive mode, you must consider the amount of time to flush any dirty buffers covered by the lock down to disk as well as the rollback associated with the transaction that requested the lock. Lock conversion is an issue only during insert, update, and delete processing during warehouse refreshes, not during periods of exclusive query activity.

SGA access. What is the latency for access to the SGA (msecs to μsecs)? Each CPU on a node will require quick access to the shared Oracle SGA. Because CPU caches are less efficient in deferring memory requests for the large SGA (especially in multi-CPU environments), latency (not to be confused with throughput) is critical. Also, as the number of CPUs on a single node increases, competition for access to the SGA can cause contention on the system bus. Therefore, system bus throughput also has an impact on SGA access.

Execution speed. How many CPUs are there and how fast are they (MHz/SPECint)? More CPUs provide the ability to increase the number of users doing work concurrently as well as the ability to increase the degree of parallelism with Oracle Parallel Query. The former is really a scalability attribute, while the latter decreases execution time for some database operations. More CPUs also permit the Oracle background process to run concurrently with user requests. Of course, the faster the CPU, the faster nonblocking operations can be performed. If there are too many CPUs contending for access to common resources (memory, disks, communications channels), however, then more or faster CPUs will not substantially improve performance.

Availability

Availability is the amount of time the system is able to provide service to the end users. The system may be unavailable due to either planned or unplanned events. A service-level agreement should define the expected hours of operation. Reliability is one factor that affects system availability, but it is not the only one. Each failure may make the system unavailable for users to do their work. A related factor is the amount of time it takes to return the system to a usable state after a failure. This is typically expressed as the mean time to repair (MTTR). A final factor relates to the amount of time needed to perform planned maintenance tasks that require that the system (or database) be taken away from the users.

Another characteristic that affects availability is degraded performance or brownouts. If performance degrades to the point that the performance criteria for user queries cannot be satisfied, then the system is not available at the required performance level. Also, Oracle Parallel Server may experience temporary brownouts when a node fails. When this happens all queries are temporarily suspended. Assuming that no portion of the queries was running on the failed node, they will resume where they left off after the automatic recovery of the failed node.

It is important to set realistic availability requirements. Beware of simplistic availability models that state something like "The data warehouse must be available 98 percent of the time." This approach is unrealistic because it doesn't allow for differences between planned and unplanned downtime. There may very well be requirements for loading, indexing, summarizing, and possibly backing up data that will exceed the allowed 2 percent downtime. If users expect they'll have query access 98 percent of the time, they are likely to be disappointed. An additional reason that this simplistic availability requirement statement is unworkable is that mere percentages don't reflect the duration and impact of an incident of unavailability. A system could make the 98 percent availability target either by being down for one 15-hour period a month or by being down 1.2 seconds of every minute! The former situation will allow completion of a lot more work during the month than the latter.

The cost of achieving higher availability levels is not linear. A user or manager who requires that a warehouse be unavailable no more than once a month for no more than one hour needs to be shown the cost of such a solution. If he is willing to accept a more relaxed availability requirement of, say, one event per week of up to two hours then the cost may be only half that of the more stringent solution. Frequently the "desire" is greater than the "requirement." The trade-offs between the business requirements, the availability requirements, and the ultimate cost of providing the solution need to be carefully considered.

When evaluating an architecture's availability characteristics consider the following:

- Redundancy
- Auto failover capabilities
- Failover speed
- Recovery speed

The availability of a system can be increased by providing redundant hardware and software components that can continue to provide service when the primary component fails. Just as we can add up the probability of failure of independent components, we can multiply the reliability factors of redundant components. As a very simplified example, if the probability of failure of a particular disk device can be estimated as 1/100,000, then a database stored on two of these disks should have a failure probability of 1/50,000 because the loss of either disk would make the database unavailable. If the data is stored redundantly on both disks, though, then the probability of both disks failing simultaneously is only one in 10,000,000,000 (1/100,000 * 1/100,000).

Consider providing redundancy for those hardware components with the lowest mean time between failures (MTBF) in order to reduce downtime. Selecting components with reduced MTBFs over more reliable components is not a wise investment unless the savings are used to provide redundancy. Always begin consideration of redundancy with the component that has the highest failure rate (e.g., disks). It is not always necessary to provide a one-for-one mirror for each of these components. Some logical volume management (LVM) software and high availability (HA) software technologies provide the ability to implement redundancy with fewer hardware components. These technologies are discussed later in this chapter.

In addition to hardware failures, the warehouse's ability to survive operating system and database failures should be considered. Assuming there is sufficient hardware, the use of HA software or Oracle Parallel Server can provide a means for reducing downtime. Using HA software without Oracle Parallel Server requires that the database instance that failed be restarted on a surviving node after the failure occurs. With Oracle Parallel Server, a database instance is already running on the other nodes, and another instance simply has to perform recovery on behalf of the failed instance. This approach provides slightly higher availability.

In conjunction with redundancy, an automatic method of detecting failures and initiating failover or recovery operations is needed to reduce downtime. Some hardware vendors build in the ability to detect hardware failures (power supplies, disks, CPUs, memory, system buses) and automatically reconfigure the system around the failed component. These automatic facilities are preferable to manual intervention. They may, however, require that a node be rebooted in order to reconfigure around the failed components. When this occurs, the system will be temporarily unavailable. HA and/or Oracle Parallel Server software can be employed to detect software failure and initiate failover operations automatically. These software technologies may also be used in conjunction with automatic hardware failure detection and recovery to reduce or even eliminate the temporary loss of service caused by the reconfiguration reboot.

The method and performance of the automatic failover facility will impact system availability. Each of the potential hardware and software failures that can occur should be evaluated for the potential loss of service they may cause for each proposed architecture. When evaluating architectures, preference should be given to those that accommodate these failures with a minimal loss of service. Be sure to include any database recovery time for HA or Oracle Parallel Server enhanced solutions.

In the event of a failure that requires the initiation of database recovery, the performance of the recovery mechanism should be considered in reducing downtime. Each recovery scenario (database file[s], tablespace, entire database, import) should be tested and benchmarked to determine the best approach for each type of recovery that may be required. These procedures should be scripted to reduce confusion and ensure timely recovery when they are needed. Many of these tasks can be automated with Oracle's Recovery Manager utility, provided with each Oracle8 and Oracle8*i* license.

In some cases it may be faster to rebuild or refresh some or all of the database rather than perform recovery on it. Most newer tape technologies can sustain higher I/O rates than most disks. Most recovery/backup software, though, will support only one stream of data between a single disk file and tape device.

(Oracle8's Recovery Manager, working in conjunction with tape management software and hardware, can support a multiplexed backup of multiple files to maximize the streaming capacity of the tape device.) In virtually all cases, however, utilizing multiple tape devices to back up or recover a large number of disk files in parallel can significantly decrease both backup and recovery times. This is an opportunity for using component redundancy that is commonly (and improperly) overlooked in the interest of economy.

Reliability

Users view reliability as the frequency of unexpected system outages. The systems staff may alternatively view reliability as the amount of time between failures. Vendors typically express this as the mean time between failures (MTBF). Based on their testing, they will estimate the MTBF for each individual component in a system. Considered in total, the reliability of these components will determine the total reliability of the system.

Another aspect of reliability is the impact of a specific outage. It is important to remember that a single query on a data warehouse may require several days to complete. An outage in the middle of such a query would typically require that the query be restarted from the beginning. Oracle Parallel Server extends this concept through a new application failover capability that will allow queries to failover and reconnect to another node even if the node that a query started on should fail.

The KISS principle (Keep It Simple, Stupid) generally applies to reliability concerns. Complexity is the enemy of reliability. The more independent components there are in a system, the more likely the system is to fail. Reliability is tightly coupled with the previous criterion—availability. Insufficient or inadequate components can lead to poor availability. For example, if redundant disks are not available, then a single disk failure (a reliability issue) could result in a lengthy outage (an availability issue) while the database is restored to a consistent state.

When evaluating an architecture's reliability characteristics consider the following:

- Maturity of the product(s)
- Simplicity of design
- System load
- Usage in similar environments
- MTBF

Unless a new, unproved component, product, or configuration provides considerable cost savings or is backed by significant support resources, it is not advisable to select it as the basis for any critical project including a data warehouse. On the other hand, if a product is so mature as to be approaching obsolescence, then it may not be a good idea to depend on it either. As products approach their intended life expectancy, they are not supported as well as the newer products. Also, in our industry new products typically provide superior cost-performance to previous generations. Be wary of products that depart from a vendor's existing product line. This does not necessarily mean that you should avoid the product that has a higher clock rate or faster system bus, but is basically the same as a previous version. These, too, can have risks associated with them, but it is a lower level of risk than that typically associated with a completely new architectural approach.

Examine each proposed architectural design for its simplicity. After eliminating all the redundant components in the design, how many nodes are there and how are they connected? As the number of nodes goes up, the potential for hardware and software problems also increases. This is due to the necessarily complex hardware and software needed to coordinate the activities of all these nodes to make them function as a single system. In general, if you can meet your performance and scalability requirements with fewer nodes, that will probably be a more reliable path than a design with many more nodes.

Operating a system at or near capacity can expose hardware and software problems that would not be exposed at lower workload levels. Architectures that will allow your data warehouse application to operate at a fraction of capacity while still delivering the required performance are preferable to those that would require running it at maximum capacity.

The suitability of an architecture for the data warehouse role can be determined, in part, by talking with reference accounts that have implemented data warehouses on the proposed architecture. The vendor should be able to provide such accounts. If they can't, then the architecture is probably too new or may be inappropriate for the data warehouse role. When discussing the architecture with the reference account representative(s), be sure to inquire about the size of the total system and workload. It should be similar in size to the system you are expecting to build. A 4-node cluster may be very reliable, but a 16-node cluster of the same hardware components may prove far less reliable. A related issue, scalability, will be discussed later.

The final step in considering a system's reliability is to examine and compare the MTBF numbers of the components for the various architectures. By multiplying the MTBF by the number of components of each type you should arrive at an expected failure frequency. By example, if a disk drive component is rated as 150,000 hours MTBF but you intend to deploy 200 of these disks, you should expect a failure about every 750 hours (once a month!). This estimate can be used to guide your decisions about where redundancy is needed to meet your availability requirements. If you choose not to build in redundancy for certain components or if it is not feasible to do so, then the calculated system reliability number must not exceed the MTBF requirements of the users.

THE "A DATA WAREHOUSE IS NOT AN OPERATIONAL SYSTEM" SYNDROME

There is a tendency to design data warehouse environments that do not provide adequate availability. The rationale for this may be explained as "a data warehouse is not an operational system." While this may be true, the number of people who come to work every day and expect to ask questions of the warehouse may not see it quite that way. This situation can be avoided by working with the user community to develop realistic availability requirements and then investing in technology capable of meeting those requirements. Designing within both budget tolerance and availability requirements is essential to the success of a data warehouse.

Manageability

Although the users of the warehouse are not concerned with the manageability of the system, they are directly affected by a lack of manageability in terms of system availability. The operations staff should be keenly concerned with how manageable the system will be, especially because they are on the hook for living up to service-level requirements. This is another area where the KISS principle applies. A more complex architecture means more to monitor and manage. Even the use of sophisticated monitoring and management tools may not be sufficient to overcome the complexity of the architecture. You may have to enlarge your operations staff.

Several aspects of a system need to be monitored and managed proactively. Effective tools that work together and provide the ability to manage by exception are key to the success of a complex data warehouse environment. A lot of tools provide too much information but not necessarily the right information to the people who must manage the system. It is essential to properly select and configure monitoring and administration tools. Also consider the required experience and training level of the staff that will be using these tools. If the operations staff is not adequately trained you cannot expect them to use the tools effectively. A partial list of areas that require monitoring and managing follows:

Hardware. You need tools that provide online and offline diagnostics and alerts that inform the operations staff when a component (disk, memory, CPU, I/O controller, node) has failed or is experiencing recoverable errors that may foreshadow a failure in the near future.

Operating system. Operations staff must have the ability to monitor operating system metrics including disk I/O rates, memory utilization, CPU utilization, file system utilization, paging/swapping, active jobs, and rogue jobs. Also, job scheduling and/or tape management packages may be required.

Network. Tools to monitor the network for hardware failures, link failures, excessive errors or collisions, and utilization are necessary in today's client/server and Internet environments.

Database. Tools are required that provide the ability to back up and recover the database, perform administrative activities, and monitor space usage, latch contention, locks, parallel operations, and user sessions.

The primary architectural issue that affects manageability is the complexity of the architecture at initial implementation and as it scales up. The more components there are in the architecture, the harder it will be to manage. This complexity may be manageable with more sophisticated tools, but expect to add personnel to the operations staff as the system becomes more complex.

Scalability

Scalability is the ability of an architecture to meet current demands and to grow easily to meet greater needs in the future. To determine if the architecture will meet these demands it will be necessary to look into the crystal ball and project data and processing growth over some period of time. In addition to the amount of data that will be stored, the number of new applications and users that are projected to start using the data warehouse during that same period needs to be defined. The users' expectations in terms of performance in light of this additional load should also be defined.

Note that we can address the scalability of an architecture in which specific components or nodes may not necessarily scale. Adopting a distributed data warehouse architecture or one based on clustering may allow the warehouse to scale even though individual computers are not modified.

There are two primary means for scaling up a data warehouse to support additional users and/or applications with Oracle8*i*:

- Increasing the number of CPUs within existing nodes
- Increasing nodes/instances within a system

Most vendors boast about how well their hardware architecture scales. When running a database, however, the ability to scale a hardware architecture is highly dependent on system bus and/or high-speed interconnect bandwidth. When scaling up a system by adding CPUs or replacing existing CPUs with faster ones the common system bus typically becomes the limiting factor. Likewise, when scaling up by adding additional nodes/instances the high-speed interconnect is typically the limiting factor. Attempting to scale beyond a point at which these buses or interconnects become saturated results in diminishing returns or even degradation.

Oracle Parallel Server adds another layer of software to coordinate activities between nodes/instances. Although adding Oracle Parallel Server can help you achieve higher availability goals or scale beyond the capabilities of a single node, it does not scale as efficiently as a pure hardware scale-up. When you consider the expected growth of the system over the new few years, determine if it is possible to achieve this growth within the confines of a single node/instance. If it is, then consider Oracle Parallel Server for high availability only.

On the other hand, if you see that additional nodes will be required, then installing multiple reduced capability nodes initially will alleviate some of the migration difficulties later. Starting with two clustered nodes, each containing two processors, and later upgrading each node to four processors will generally be easier than starting with a single four-CPU node and then later adding a second node and migrating to Oracle Parallel Server. Oracle Parallel Server requires certain database design considerations and prohibits the use of file systems for multiple-instance access.

Whichever approach you take, you need to ensure that it will accommodate the increasing disk storage demands of the growing data warehouse. Also, as the number of users and jobs increases, so does the demand for memory. A growth path that will not unnecessarily limit the ability to accommodate these increased demands is essential.

Uniprocessor Systems

The uniprocessor architecture is the simplest computer configuration on which you can implement an Oracle database. The ability to run Oracle, however, does not mean that a data warehouse application, other than a small data mart, is feasible on this architecture. The following description of a uniprocessor system provides a comprehensive background for the other architectures available today and introduces the simplest of architectures in order to set the stage for the more complex architectures presented later.

A uniprocessor system is characterized by a single node containing a single CPU, which is directly attached to all the other components in the systems via a common bus. This node must do all the processing for the entire system. This includes the operating system, database queries, and any applications that may be resident. Figure 2.1 depicts the major components of the uniprocessor system architecture.

Oracle utilizes a latching mechanism to ensure protected access to memory structures stored in the SGA. These latches are usually implemented by a test-and-set operation on a shared memory address. If the latch is not immediately available Oracle will spin a number of times on the test-and-set operation. If the latch is still not available, then the Oracle process may sleep for a period of time

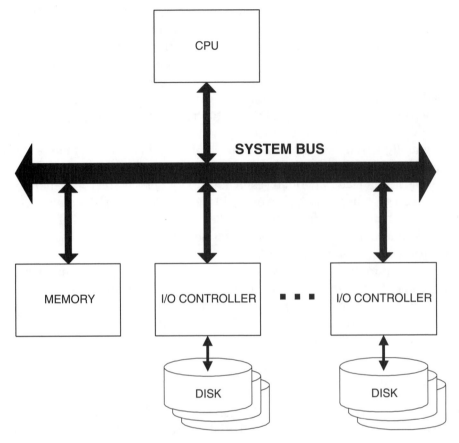

Figure 2.1   Components of the uniprocessor architecture.

before attempting to gain access to the latch again. As multiple Oracle processes attempt to obtain these latches a great deal of system bus traffic is generated to maintain cache coherence. CPU execution will pause momentarily when obtaining the latch from another CPU's cache or from main memory. This is another justification for high system bus throughput and low latencies.

Performance

Because uniprocessor architectures are not normally meant for large database applications they will typically support a small number of disk devices. More care must be taken in placing data on the limited number of disks to avoid hot spots that could adversely affect disk access times. Oracle Parallel Server is not a consideration for uniprocessor architectures (unless it is a uniprocessor node in an MPP architecture, discussed later); therefore lock conversion times are not a concern. With only the single CPU and the limited number of disk devices, system bus contention and throughput as well as memory access times are not typically a problem with uniprocessor architectures.

Because the single processor must perform all the work on the system, user queries will contend with Oracle background processes and other operating system functions for time on the CPU.

CPU CACHES AND CACHE COHERENCE

Each CPU (regardless of architecture) has a small amount of memory to cache instructions and data, which are referenced frequently (this is similar in function to the Oracle SGA). This memory is called cache and is significantly (orders of magnitude) faster to access than main memory. A CPU that can fetch instructions and data found in the cache will operate much more efficiently. Fetching from the cache instead of main memory is called a cache hit. When the fetch cannot be satisfied by the cache, it is called a cache miss. Most cache implementations are also used to defer store operations (i.e., data is immediately stored in cache and written back to main memory in the background). This prevents the CPU from pausing when storing to main memory. For these reasons, bigger caches tend to benefit CPU performance.

Another issue that is of particular concern in multi-CPU environments is cache coherence. Cache coherence is the mechanism employed to synchronize identical memory locations when cached by multiple CPUs. Hardware vendors use a variety of techniques to ensure that any single memory location contains only a single value regardless of where it is currently cached. Most approaches involve watching or "snooping" the system bus for memory requests. When an address is seen that corresponds to an address that's in the local cache, the local copy may be sent in response to the request (instead of the copy in main memory), or the local copy may be invalidated when a remote copy is modified.

Caches are more effective at caching instruction execution streams and local data. The CPU cache is less effective in caching the large amounts of data stored in the Oracle SGA. This is due to the limited size of the cache and the higher probability of repeatedly accessing the same instructions and local data memory. Because database execution is tightly coupled to how quickly structures in the SGA can be accessed, the resulting cache misses will dramatically influence performance. Therefore, it is critical to performance that the system bus provide short latencies and high throughput.

Availability

The simplicity of the uniprocessor's architecture provides for excellent reliability, which benefits availability. A few vendors provide the ability to implement redundancy for disks. Redundancy at the CPU, memory, and system bus level, though, is typically not available for this architecture. As a result, hardware failures that result in a system outage will be significantly longer than for designs that do implement more robust redundancy features.

> **SYSTEM REDUNDANCY THROUGH SOFTWARE**
>
> Software redundancy capabilities are not inherent with this architecture, although it may be possible to add this capability (see the section on high availability later in this chapter) to compensate for a lack of hardware redundancy. At some point, the addition of software and hardware to improve availability adds expense and complexity corresponding to other architectures, such as MPP or clustered.

Reliability

Uniprocessor architectures are very mature and simple. They have been around since the dawn of the computer age and because of the single processor design, do not require sophisticated bus interface logic to implement cache coherence. Likewise, the bandwidth of these buses may be kept low in comparison to other architectures. This further simplifies the design. Architecturally, this is the most reliable design. One potential area of investigation is the MTBF of the components used. A quick review of the components used should be done to ensure that they are of high quality and have MTBF numbers similar to those of components of other architectures being considered.

From a software perspective the probability of failure is also low. The software does not have to be as sophisticated as that required for multiple-CPU architectures, and timing issues present less of a challenge. On the other hand, there is no hardware or software redundancy so any outages are likely to result in a complete loss of service.

Manageability

With only one copy of the operating system, applications, and database instance, the uniprocessor architecture is by far the easiest architecture to manage. Because of its simplicity this architecture does not require a lot of monitoring and management tools. You can probably get by with simple scripts developed in house. Most of the tools that make more complex architectures manageable, however, are also available on the uniprocessor architecture.

Scalability

Scalability is severely limited on a uniprocessor architecture. There are practical as well as physical limits on the amount of disk storage and memory that can be added to these systems. The only CPU upgrade path is to replace the single CPU with a faster one. As the clock rate of the CPU increases it may be necessary to replace the system bus and/or memory on these systems. If your data warehouse is expected to grow then this is probably not the path for you.

If you are considering the uniprocessor architecture to support multiple, distributed data marts as extracts from a central data warehouse then the uniprocessor architecture may well serve the lighter needs of a departmental data mart.

Symmetric Multiprocessing (SMP) Systems

As shown in Figure 2.2, on the surface the symmetric multiprocessing (SMP) system appears identical to the uniprocessor architecture but with the addition of multiple CPUs. Each of the major components attached to the system bus requires complex logic to arbitrate between the multiple CPUs and to ensure cache coherence between them.

Performance

Implementing cache coherence in SMP architectures places an enormous load on the common system bus. As the number of CPUs increases, so does contention on the system bus. Compounding this is the number of cache misses that occur when accessing the Oracle SGA or when obtaining a latch. As a result, it may not be feasible to effectively utilize all the CPUs that may be theoretically configured for a given SMP architecture. When evaluating SMP architectures, the following prioritized factors should be compared for maximum configured systems:

- System bus latency
- System bus throughput
- CPU cache size
- CPU speed
- Number of CPUs

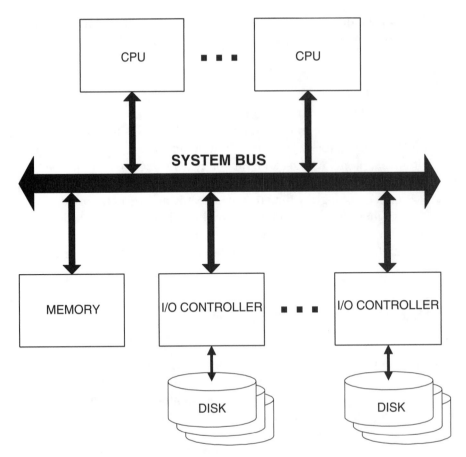

Figure 2.2   Components of the SMP architecture.

Even with the common system bus contention issues, SMP architectures provide excellent performance within their scalability range when compared to other
architectures. The two best performers according to recent TPC-D benchmarks
are SMP-based architectures. Of course, as vendors upgrade their products and
perform additional benchmarks, TPC results will change frequently.

Because the SMP architecture uses hardware to apply multiple CPUs to a
problem, it is more efficient than architectures that use software (i.e., MPP and
cluster) to apply multiple CPUs to the same problem. As such, SMP architectures require less hardware to provide equal levels of performance. Another
way of saying this is that the SMP architecture is more efficient because it

needs to spend less of its available CPU time coordinating the activities of multiple nodes.

Availability

Availability in SMP architectures varies greatly and is dependent on the amount of hardware redundancy built into the system and the method of reconfiguring around these failures. Consider all single points of failure and the system's ability to reconfigure and continue running in the event of a component failure. Single points of failure should be carefully considered as they can lead to lengthy outages while you wait for a replacement part to be shipped and replaced. Most SMP vendors support a method of reconfiguring around a failed disk (assuming redundant disks are available). Some capability for redundancy at this level should be considered mandatory for large data warehouse applications. Also consider whether the disk storage technology supports hot swapping for increased availability. Fewer vendors support the ability to reconfigure around CPU, memory, system bus, or power supply failures. Those that do may require an outage for the system to automatically reconfigure or, even worse, may require a manual reconfiguration in order to return the system to a degraded mode of operation. All these factors must be taken into consideration when evaluating vendors' alternative solutions.

Software impacts on availability will be primarily affected by the maturity of the software release and the load placed on it. Because there is only one operating system and database instance running, the system will be unavailable in the event of a failure. The amount of time needed to restart the system can dramatically affect availability. Restart times vary between architectures and vendors. SMP architectures generally will have faster restart times than an MPP or cluster architecture. Because the MPP and cluster architectures may have built-in failover capabilities, the probability of needing to restart the entire system may be lower than with SMP systems.

Reliability

SMP architectures have been around for a number of years and have established themselves as fairly reliable systems. They are quite a bit more complex than uniprocessor architectures and are always pushing technology to improve performance. Each new generation of SMP uses newer technology and tricks (e.g., shortening system buses) to overcome the limitations of physics to achieve the next level of performance and scalability. As this occurs the systems become more delicate and sensitive to timing issues that can cause failures. These may be manifested as hardware failures or as operating system or even database bugs. Hardware failures can be overcome by increasing the redundancy and automatic failover capabilities of the systems. Software bugs, on the other hand, can be overcome only by subsequent software releases or patches. For this reason, it may not be prudent to be the vendor's guinea pig for these new systems until they have proven themselves.

As the size of these systems increases, simple extrapolation of the MTBF will lead to higher failure rates. Small variances in the MTBF of specific components between systems can have a dramatic effect when multiplied by the number of components needed to reach the proposed configuration. These numbers are an excellent indication of the long-term stability of the system.

As with uniprocessor architectures, the SMP architecture also depends on a single operating system and database instance. Failures of any one of these components will likely result in a compete outage.

Manageability

The SMP architecture is inherently as simple as the uniprocessor architecture to manage because it has only one operating system and database instance to monitor and control. SMP architectures, though, can support a lot more users and storage than the uniprocessor architecture can. As a result, more sophisticated tools for monitoring system performance are required. Also, with the increased storage capacity, more sophisticated tools may be needed for managing database backup and recovery. Note that this additional administration overhead is due to the larger configuration capacity, not to limitations in the SMP architecture itself.

Scalability

Implementing cache coherence in SMP architectures places an enormous load on the common system bus and limits how many CPUs can effectively be added to the system. In the previous section, we discussed how to evaluate SMP architectures for maximum performance. These same evaluation criteria can also be used to determine the scalability of an SMP architecture. In addition to the practical limit on how many CPUs may be effectively utilized in an SMP node, a physical limitation also exists. For this reason, SMP architectures have limited scalability when compared to MPP and cluster architectures. Scalability improvements are frequently seen even between releases of the vendor's operating system on identical hardware. As CPU contention issues are identified they are researched and fixed as bugs.

If a single SMP node can satisfy the growth requirements of your organization then that is an acceptable option. If the growth requirements are beyond the capabilities of a single SMP node then the MPP or cluster architectures should be examined.

Nonuniform Memory Access (NUMA) Systems

Nonuniform memory access (NUMA) architectures share characteristics of both the SMP and cluster architectures. They run a single operating system and database instance and generally provide a single memory address space, like SMP architectures. The NUMA architecture connects one or more CPUs to local memory and local I/O devices via a local shared bus to form a local processor group. This local processor group is, in turn, connected to other processor group(s) via a high-speed interconnect. Each local processor group provides a portion of the total memory space that is available to the node. Operations that can be satisfied within the memory of the local processor group do not generate traffic on the high-speed interconnect. Accesses to local memory are faster than accesses to the memory in remote processor groups, thus the term *nonuniform memory access*. Figure 2.3 depicts the components of the NUMA architecture.

Performance

Early experience with NUMA systems has shown them to have excellent performance characteristics. Certainly, if the high-speed interconnect of the NUMA architecture can deliver performance similar to that of the SMP system buses, then it should provide better performance. The NUMA vendors, though, are not currently implementing high-speed interconnects that operate at the same throughput and latencies as the high-end SMP configurations. Therefore, it is essential to reduce the number of accesses that must cross the high-speed interconnect. The caches in NUMA architectures should be as effective as SMP architectures at reducing requests for instructions and local data over the high-speed interconnect. The same issues that were of concern with the SMP architecture are also of concern in the NUMA architecture. Oracle SGA accesses and Oracle latch accesses will frequently have to be resolved over the interconnect.

The Oracle SGA is a large, shared memory area that all Oracle foreground and background processes must access. Assuming no special changes are made to the Oracle server code, the location of the SGA is up to the operating system. Likewise, the contents of the SGA are not partitioned to localize accesses by processor group. As such, the probability that an Oracle process running in a local process group will be able to find a portion of the SGA it requires locally will be a factor of the percentage of the SGA that is local. It is probable that the total number of accesses to the SGA that result in traffic on the high-speed interconnect will be lower than accesses over the system bus in SMP architectures. It is not clear that the reduced number of remote accesses will be sufficient to overcome the higher latency paid for these accesses when compared to

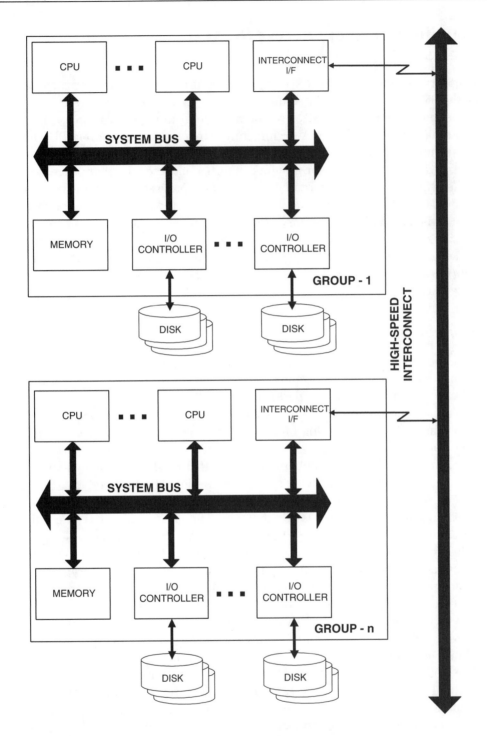

Figure 2.3 Components of the NUMA architecture.

high-end SMP architectures. Of course, if in some future release Oracle were able to partition the shared pool and buffer cache (which are structures in the SGA) evenly across all the local processor groups' memories and provide local processor group affinity, then the number of remote accesses might be dramatically reduced. This presumes that the NUMA system's operating system can provide process group affinity for individual processes.

The same issues that resulted in remote SGA accesses also affect latch requests by the Oracle foreground and background processes. Without any changes to the Oracle server code the result may be a lot of remote accesses that cause slower CPU execution because the CPU has to wait for a consistent copy of the latch to be retrieved from a remote processor group's memory. This is another situation in which it is not clear that NUMA architectures will necessarily outperform a similarly configured SMP system. Oracle8*i* has the potential to further optimize NUMA performance by partitioning these latches along with the SGA to reduce remote requests and to speed execution.

Based on these issues, it is not clear that NUMA will always deliver higher performance than comparably configured SMP systems without making significant changes to the Oracle server. In situations in which an SMP architecture is overloaded and is experiencing a lot of contention on the system bus, a NUMA architecture should provide better performance. If an SMP architecture is not experiencing system bus contention, however, then the SMP architecture should be able to perform better because it may have lower bus latencies than the interconnect of the NUMA architecture.

When evaluating NUMA architectures the following prioritized factors should be compared for maximally configured systems:

- High-speed interconnect latency
- High-speed interconnect throughput
- Local processor group bus latency
- Local processor bus throughput
- CPU cache size
- CPU speed
- Number of CPUs per processor group
- Number of processor groups

Availability

Availability of the NUMA architecture is influenced by the exact same factors as those of the SMP architecture and should be comparable for similar levels of redundancy. These systems may initially experience decreased availability owing to some of the reliability concerns addressed in the next section. Once the reliability stabilizes, availability should be very similar to that of SMP architectures.

Reliability

The NUMA architecture is the newest of the architectures described here and therefore is not as mature as the others. Also, only a few vendors offer systems based on the NUMA architecture. Like MPP systems, this means that there are fewer organizations that have actually implemented data warehouses based on these systems compared to the more prevalent SMP architecture. As more organizations adopt this architecture for their data warehouse applications more information will be available on its reliability.

NUMA SYSTEM VENDORS

Sequent Computer Systems, Inc. was the first open systems hardware vendor to make an active commitment to converting its product line to a cache coherent NUMA architecture they called NUMA-Q. The Sequent design groups four processors together with memory and several I/O slots on a local bus. This unit is called a "quad" and becomes the building block for putting together large systems via an interconnect. Multiple NUMA-Q nodes, each of one or more quads, may be clustered together.

Since the release of the first edition of this book IBM acquired Sequent, adding NUMA-Q to its existing SMP and MPP product lines. No announcements have been made regarding plans for assimilating Sequent's DYNIX/ptx operating system into IBM's AIX.

From a hardware perspective, the NUMA architectures are based on the same technology as the other architectures. The difference is in the manner in which the components are assembled and connected. From a hardware perspective, reliability is expected to be similar to that of SMP solutions (assuming similar MTBF numbers for the components). From a database and applications software perspective, there are no changes required in order to run on this architecture. There may, however, eventually be some performance benefits to optimizing the database software to run on it.

The operating system, obviously, must be modified to support this new architecture, just as uniprocessor operating systems had to be modified to support SMP configurations. These changes may introduce unanticipated bugs as vendors port their SMP-based operating systems to NUMA systems. These problems should be resolved as these systems become more prevalent in the marketplace.

The complexity of the NUMA architecture is similar to that of the SMP architecture and should have similar reliability as it develops a well-established installed base.

Manageability

The manageability of NUMA systems is similar to that of SMP architectures. Enhancements are required to the monitoring and administration tools (from the hardware vendor or third-party software vendors) to provide visibility to the additional structures and connections within the NUMA configuration. As an example, an important new statistic to monitor through your enterprise management software is the ratio of memory accesses that are satisfied in the local memory versus those that require interconnect access from a different processor complex.

Scalability

During the discussion of cache coherence for SMP architectures it was explained how cache coherence and system bus throughput/latency affect CPU performance and scalability. The NUMA architecture is a direct response to these issues. The concept is this: If the majority of accesses can be satisfied within a local processor group, less contention will be generated on the high-speed interconnect. This should allow a single-node NUMA-based system to scale better than single SMP nodes.

Although performance is affected by the increased latency for the Oracle SGA and latches with NUMA architectures, scalability is not impacted because the high-speed interconnect has high throughput and very little contention. This, combined with the fact that more processors can be added to the NUMA architecture than to the SMP architecture, should provide for better scalability within a single-node system.

As with SMP architectures, if more scalability is required than can be addressed within a single node, then clustered or MPP options must be considered.

Clustered Systems

Clustered architectures combine multiple nodes of the uniprocessor, SMP, or NUMA systems to increase availability, scalability, and/or performance. The nodes may be connected by a system interconnect that is based on either a standard network or a specialized high-speed interface. This interconnect is used to support the lock management communications required by the Oracle Parallel Server option or the heartbeats required for non-Oracle Parallel Server high availability (HA) software. Cluster systems also share a common pool of disks that can be directly accessed from all systems in the cluster. When using

Oracle Parallel Server, disk accesses from Oracle are coordinated by using a lock management protocol. If HA software is used in lieu of Oracle Parallel Server, then only one node at a time has exclusive access to the shared disks. This is enforced by the HA software. The advantage of Oracle Parallel Server is that in addition to providing higher availability, higher performance and scalability may be achieved. Figure 2.4 depicts the components of the cluster architecture.

Performance

For the cluster to provide better performance than SMP or NUMA architectures, Oracle Parallel Server (and usually Oracle Parallel Query) must be used to implement a parallel database.

Given an equal number of CPUs in a single node versus the same number of CPUs spread across multiple nodes, the single-node approach provides better performance (up to the point at which contention issues limit scalability). This is due to the overhead of the lock manager software that is used to coordinate access to the shared disks from multiple nodes. If more CPUs are needed than can be configured in a single node, however, the cluster architecture is an excellent second choice for data warehousing.

Clusters are more efficient than MPP architectures because they require fewer nodes to implement a parallel database using Oracle Parallel Server for a comparable level of performance. This is due to smaller operating system overhead as well as the method for implementing shared disks. MPP architectures also depend on software and high-speed interconnects to provide access to all disks by all nodes. Compare this to the more simplified coordination effort required for direct shared disk access within a cluster.

Availability

One of the primary objectives of cluster architectures is to increase system availability by eliminating the node as a single point of failure. When a node fails, another node is available to take up the load of the failed node. Depending on which approach is taken (Oracle Parallel Server or HA), the amount of time the system is unavailable will vary. When using Oracle Parallel Server, the database is already up and running on the other node(s). When a node failure occurs, a surviving node recognizes the failure and initiates recovery for the failed instance. During this recovery all user requests at all surviving nodes temporarily pause. The amount of time this recovery takes depends on the amount of time that has passed since the last checkpoint and the number of PCM locks. Processing of these requests resumes once recovery is complete. With Oracle7, users that had queries running on the failed node need to reconnect/resubmit their jobs. Oracle8 can be configured so that the reconnection and resubmis-

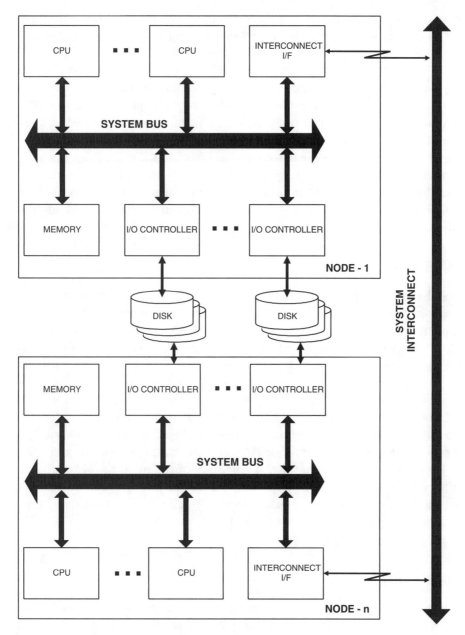

Figure 2.4 Components of the cluster architecture.

sion of queries is invisible to the end user. Data modification (INSERT, UPDATE, DELETE) activities, however, must be resubmitted. If there are a large number of PCM locks, then the recovery time can cause the temporary pause in service to be longer than the time required to shut down and restart the database. (Shutting down and restarting, though, would result in the termination of all currently executing queries, requiring them all to be resubmitted.)

The HA approach continuously polls all the nodes in the cluster for a node failure. Upon detecting that a node has failed, the HA software starts up the Oracle instance of the failed node on another node and optionally reassigns its network address so that users do not realize the instance has moved. The amount of time required to return the instance to an operational state is dependent on the amount of time it takes to obtain access to the shared disk and to start up the replacement for the failed database instance. The database instance startup time may be lengthy if it has been a long time since the last checkpoint of the failed instance. The HA approach may sometimes be faster than Oracle Parallel Server in restoring access to an instance, but it does not provide the performance and scalability advantages of Oracle Parallel Server.

Reliability

Clusters have been around for quite a while, and Oracle has a long history of running on these architectures. This architecture was introduced by Digital Equipment Corporation over a decade ago with VAX clusters, and Oracle version 5 provided a multi-instance mode that was the predecessor to Oracle Parallel Server. Thus, the basic cluster architecture is a mature and proven technology, although vendors of UNIX systems have begun providing clustered solutions only much more recently. Reliability of the cluster architecture will actually be lower than that of the constituent nodes that constitute it. This is due to the multiplication effect on the MTBF for the additional hardware. The addition of Oracle Parallel Server or HA software can also result in more frequent interruptions. This is due to the criticality of timing to the HA software and the complexity of the Oracle Parallel Server software. If high availability (not scalability) is the goal when using Oracle Parallel Server, then using only one system to support online users at any time may reduce the potential for outages.

Manageability

Managing a cluster is more difficult than managing a single-node SMP or NUMA architecture, but it is not as difficult to manage as an MPP architecture, which typically has many more nodes. More sophisticated tools are required to monitor the parallel database when using the Oracle Parallel Server option in conjunction with the cluster architecture. The multiple operating system copies and Oracle instances required for a multinode cluster require coordination. Care must be taken to ensure that configuration changes on one node are propagated to the other nodes.

Scalability

When combined with Oracle Parallel Server, clusters provide the ability to scale a data warehouse up from single-node NUMA or SMP machines to multiple-node systems composed of these same systems. The ability to scale in this manner is limited by the number of nodes a disk subsystem can concurrently connect to and the bandwidth of the system interconnect. In practice, the disk subsystem is the primary concern. Most hardware vendors support only a small number of concurrent connections to their disk subsystems. Because of this physical limitation, cluster-based architectures cannot scale to the extent that MPP architectures can.

Oracle Parallel Server imposes specific database and application design requirements for OLTP systems in which users must simultaneously perform INSERT, UPDATE, and DELETE activity. There is very little impact, however, on simultaneous query performance, so nearly linear scalability within the warehouse environment is achievable—two nodes can handle almost double the workload of a single node.

Massively Parallel Processing (MPP) Systems

The MPP architecture provides for maximum scalability of an Oracle parallel database using Oracle Parallel Server and Oracle Parallel Query. This architecture overcomes the physical limitations of the cluster architecture disk subsystems to connect multiple nodes by utilizing a high-speed interconnect and software to make it appear that disks that are actually local to a single node are available at all nodes in the system. The Oracle Parallel Server option requires direct access to all disks in the database from all nodes in the system, and this approach satisfies that requirement. An MPP node is an autonomous system with its own CPU(s), I/O devices, memory, and operating system. Each node also runs an instance of an Oracle parallel database. The high-speed interconnect ties all of the nodes together. Figure 2.5 depicts the components of the MPP architecture.

Although Oracle software runs on several varieties of MPP hardware, the majority of MPP data warehouses today are implemented on the IBM RS/6000 SP (commonly still referred to as the "SP2," even though IBM dropped that designation quite a while ago).

Performance

The MPP architecture is the least efficient of all of the multi-CPU architectures. This is due to the overhead imposed on each node to run its own operating

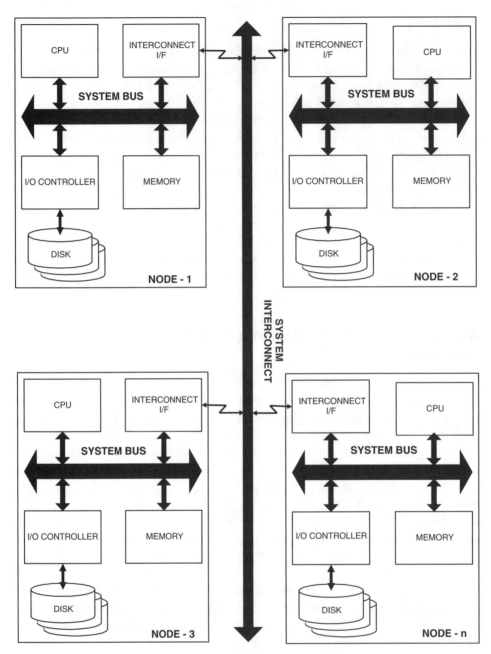

Figure 2.5 Components of the MPP architecture.

system and database instances as well as the overhead necessary to implement the virtual shared disk subsystem and lock manager for coordinating access.

The nodes of the MPP system are connected by a high-speed interconnect. Depending on the implementation of this interconnect and the number of nodes in the system, contention can become a problem. The vast majority of traffic over this interconnect is disk data being transferred in support of the virtual shared disk subsystem. This represents a massive amount of data. As the data warehouse grows, so grows the amount of data that must be transferred over the interconnect. In contrast to the buses in SMP and NUMA architectures, the main concern here is throughput rather than latency.

Some efforts have been made with Oracle Parallel Server to reduce the amount of disk data being transferred over the high-speed interconnect. In later versions of Oracle7 disk affinity was implemented for parallel operations. Disk affinity gives preference to nodes on which data physically resides in order to perform operations on that data. As a result, the disk data does not need to be transferred across the interconnect. In Oracle7 only a few operations could be parallelized. With Oracle8 and Oracle8i a larger number of operations are parallelized, resulting in reduced internode traffic. Subsequent releases of Oracle8 are expected to continue this trend toward reducing the amount of data that must be moved across the interconnect. Much of the need for data transfers over the interconnect is determined by the physical design of the database and its partitioning of data.

Availability

The MPP architecture is identical to the cluster architecture in terms of the handling of node failures with Oracle Parallel Server. Although this is not depicted in Figure 2.5, it is possible to "twin tail" disks between multiple nodes so that in the event of a single node failure, another node can provide access to the rest of the system for that node's disks. It is also possible to provide redundant disks so that a single disk failure will not make database files unavailable. Because of the large number of nodes in a typical MPP system, it can absorb many more node failures than a cluster architecture typically can.

Startup times for today's MPP systems are longer than for clusters. This is due to the large number of separate redo threads (each node has its own redo thread) that must be recovered at database startup. Because of the way in which Oracle keeps track of transactions, it is not possible to perform instance recovery on all nodes in parallel. Only one node will perform the instance recovery on behalf of all the nodes on the system at startup. Also, at system boot all the nodes in the cluster must go through their own boot process and restart the virtual shared disk software before starting the Oracle database. The amount of time required to start systems with large numbers of nodes can exceed an hour.

Reliability

The reliability of the MPP architecture is worse than that of all the other architectures. The MPP architecture requires many more components than the other architectures to provide a comparable level of performance. The autonomous nature of each node contributes to lower reliability from both a hardware and software perspective. Each node has an operating system and a database instance that can potentially fail. The software used to implement the virtual shared disk and Oracle Parallel Server capability is complex and more prone to failure as the number of nodes increases. There is also limited redundancy.

Scalability

MPP architectures have the fewest physical restrictions on the number of nodes that can be interconnected. As a result, they can scale to many more processors and nodes than can all the other architectures. The interconnect is the primary hardware limitation on how far this architecture can be scaled. As more nodes and their disks are added to the system, they place higher demands on the high-speed interconnect. The resulting contention effectively limits how far this architecture can be scaled.

Another consideration is the design of Oracle Parallel Server itself. For certain operations, there are a few global enqueues that must be obtained in exclusive mode across all instances in a parallel database. Waiting on these enqueues can cause jobs to serialize. They are highly dependent on the operations performed by users and, as such, can be subject to contention as the system scales. When this occurs, adding more nodes to the system may provide no additional capacity or may even reduce total system throughput. Again, partitioning the database and the application tasks plays a critical role in avoiding this situation.

Manageability

Managing current MPP systems is very difficult. With a large number of nodes, each running its own operating system and database instance, it is difficult to keep configuration changes in synch across all the nodes. Software upgrades must be coordinated across all nodes. Monitoring the system is also complicated by the large number of nodes. When attempting to track down a problem it is not unusual to jump from node to node looking for the cause. Although there are some good tools for managing this environment, they fall short. It is often necessary to develop custom scripts to monitor and manage these systems. Even with all these tools it takes a big staff to operate a large MPP system.

Backup and recovery also require a carefully considered plan and a sophisticated backup/recovery tool. Not only do you need to back up all the database files, but you must be able to restore the operating system and configuration for every node in the MPP system.

Summary: Computer Architectures

The Oracle Parallel Server and Oracle Parallel Query options give you the ability to parallelize operations across multiple CPUs and nodes. Table 2.1 summarizes the computer architectures discussed in this chapter and the combinations of Oracle Parallel options that are preferable, useful, or unnecessary. Using Oracle Parallel Server and Oracle Parallel Query where they are not necessary or appropriate may result in diminished performance. In the situations in which Oracle Parallel Server and Oracle Parallel Query are preferable, you can frequently improve performance by using them.

All the architectures discussed earlier in this chapter are capable of supporting a data warehouse. Table 2.2 summarizes the architectures and how they

Table 2.1 Oracle Option Recommendations by Architecture

HARDWARE ARCHITECTURE OPTIONS	ORACLE PARALLEL QUERY	ORACLE PARALLEL SERVER
Uniprocessor	Not Necessary	Not Necessary
SMP	Useful	Not Necessary
NUMA	Useful	Not Necessary
Cluster	Useful	Useful
MPP	Preferable	Preferable

Table 2.2 Architecture Evaluation Ratings

CRITERIA/ ARCHITECTURE	RELI- ABILITY	AVAIL- ABILITY	MANAGE- ABILITY	PERFOR- MANCE	SCAL- ABILITY
Uniprocessor	Excellent	Poor	Excellent	Poor	Poor
SMP	Good	OK	Good	Excellent	OK
NUMA	Good	OK	Good	Excellent	Good
Cluster	OK	Excellent	OK	Good	Very Good
MPP	Poor	Good	Poor	OK	Excellent

rate in each of the evaluation criteria. Of course, only a really small data warehouse or data mart with very few users can use the uniprocessor architecture. The SMP and NUMA architectures are similar and are simpler to manage than the cluster and MPP architectures. These should be considered first before moving on to the more complex cluster and MPP architectures. Should higher availability or performance be required than can be achieved with stand-alone SMP or NUMA architectures, the cluster architecture is the next step. Finally, should the performance requirements exceed the capabilities of a cluster, then the MPP architecture provides the ultimate in scalability, although at the cost of manageability and reliability.

Data Storage Architectures

As computing architectures have evolved to meet the computing requirements of the data warehouse, so have data storage technologies. The primary motivations for this evolution are the higher processing speeds of these new computer technologies and the rapid growth in the amount of information being stored in data warehouses. This evolution has come through advances in both software and hardware technology. This section focuses on these advances and their applicability to the data warehouse.

Software

Software advances have occurred in the areas of file systems and redundant storage technologies. New file systems have been developed that decrease the amount of time needed to recover from system outages, increase performance, and reduce the waste of valuable disk space. Methods of storing data on multiple disks have been developed that provide higher data availability through varying degrees of redundancy.

ORACLE FILE I/O REQUIREMENTS

For data integrity, Oracle requires that for each disk write the data be flushed all the way to persistent storage. If data were to be written to a file system cache and not flushed to disk and then a system crash occurred, the database would be left in a corrupted state. When the system was rebooted and the database instance restarted it might not detect that a block was not flushed. In other situations media recovery might be required to restart the instance. Any data storage technology that does not provide the ability to force synchronous or guaranteed writes is not appropriate for storing Oracle data.

Raw Files

The most direct and efficient method for accessing database files is through raw files. Raw files provide the ability to bypass the file system and access data without the overhead associated with accesses through the file system. File systems are layered on top of raw files and introduce CPU and memory overhead, which results in reduced I/O performance. On the other hand, raw files are more rigid in their configuration and typically require a system administrator as well as a DBA to move or resize a database file. For this reason they are less flexible than file system files. Without special logical volume management software, only a small number of raw files may be defined on a single disk, and a raw file cannot span multiple disks.

> **NOTE** At present, Oracle Parallel Server in UNIX requires that all database files (including control, redo, rollback, temp, and data files) be stored as raw files. This is due to the buffering of file system data and lack of a cache coherence policy for these buffer caches between multiple systems. Work is continuing to create file systems that can be shared between systems, but these are not yet available.

Because of the difficulty of managing raw files they are not recommended for development environments or production environments where it is anticipated that data files will need to be resized or moved often. Raw files and file system files may be mixed within a single Oracle database, although this is rarely recommended.

Logical Volume Managers (LVM)

Logical volume management (LVM) software provides the ability to combine multiple disk partitions or entire disks so they appear as a single raw file (called a logical volume). Several methods for combining these disks to provide increased performance and/or redundancy exist; they will be discussed in more detail in the following section on Redundant Arrays of Inexpensive Disks or RAID. Once a raw logical volume has been defined using the LVM, a file system may be on the raw file, thus providing the same performance and redundancy benefits for all files (including database files) stored in the file system.

The LVM software typically provides GUI and command-line tools for configuring and monitoring logical volumes. Because most LVMs provide a finer granularity of control over the placement of raw files than raw files by themselves, they may reduce some of the management burden of raw files alone.

Because of the usefulness of LVM software for both raw files and file systems, it should be considered mandatory for any large data warehouse environment.

Redundant Arrays of Inexpensive Disks (RAID)

Redundant arrays of inexpensive disks (RAID) is an engineering approach to organizing multiple disks that provides varying degrees of performance and redundancy. Multiple disks are used together to provide reliability or performance characteristics that could not be economically provided by a single disk. RAID may be implemented solely in software via an LVM, or it may be implemented through intelligent array hardware combined with LVM software. The currently defined levels for RAID are as follows:

RAID 0. Provides for nonredundant disk striping. Each disk is subdivided into smaller units called stripes. Stripes from multiple disks are concatenated together to provide a larger striped logical volume that then appears to be a single raw file. Performance and concurrency are increased by spreading I/O requests across multiple devices.

RAID 1. Provides for mirroring of data between multiple disks. Each disk has a mirror copy on another disk, providing 100 percent redundancy.

RAID 0+1. Combines RAID levels 0 and 1 to provide striped/mirrored logical volumes. When combined in this manner RAID 0+1 provides increased performance and redundancy.

RAID 3. Provides for storage of parity data on a single disk. Multiple disks are grouped together into a single logical volume with one disk dedicated to storage of parity. If any single disk fails the data can still be reconstructed from the remaining disks by using an XOR (exclusive or) operation, resulting in increased availability.

RAID 5. Combines RAID levels 0 and 3 to provide striped parity across multiple disks. Parity is distributed across a number of disks at the stripe level, thus providing the availability attributes of RAID 3 with increased performance benefits similar to RAID 0.

Each of the RAID levels provides varying degrees of redundancy and performance for different types of I/O operations. Table 2.3 summarizes the various RAID levels and ranks them based on performance and redundancy for normal operations. Some RAID levels (5 and 3) experience dramatic reductions in performance when a single disk fails because all disks must be accessed for I/O that is directed to the failed drive. These rankings are for software-only RAID implementations and do not take into account array hardware, which may accelerate the performance of certain RAID levels. Hardware RAID implementation will be discussed in a subsequent section.

Some vendors are coining their own RAID levels and terms for describing what is essentially one of the previously defined RAID levels combined with intelligent array hardware for overcoming some of the performance limitations associated with certain RAID levels. We will discuss hardware-embedded RAID solutions later in this chapter.

Table 2.3   RAID Level Rankings (Higher Numbers Are Better)

RAID LEVEL	REDUN-DANCY	SEQUEN-TIAL READ	SEQUEN-TIAL WRITE	RANDOM READ	RANDOM WRITE
0	1	3	3	1	3
1	3	3	2	1	2
0+1	3	3	2	1	2
3	2	1	1	3	1
5	2	2	1	2	2

One of the key factors that affect the performance of striped RAID levels (0, 0+1, and 5) is the stripe width (or stripe size). Stripe width is the amount of data that is stored across all disks in a logical volume before wrapping around to the first disk in the logical volume. When a single write request is larger than the stripe width, then the single logical I/O results in more than one physical write to one of the disks. This causes the I/O request to enqueue on itself, resulting in diminished performance.

A stripe segment (or stripe unit) is the amount of data written to one disk before starting to write to the next disk. The stripe width is equal to the size of the stripe unit multiplied by the number of disks in the striping group. Raw files are mapped in a round-robin fashion across the set of disks, which provides for an even distribution of data (and usually I/Os) in the logical volume.

Stripe size has a direct effect on how well certain access methods (sequential or random) perform under certain load conditions (high or low concurrency). Low concurrency means a small number of nearly simultaneous I/O requests; a large number of I/O requests indicates high concurrency. Table 2.4 summarizes the various types of data files that make up an Oracle data warehouse, their access patterns, and the recommended *minimum* stripe sizes.

In general, the objectives of striping are to spread the I/O load evenly across multiple disks while avoiding any single I/O request from enqueueing on itself. Rather than attempt to individually tune each type of file, selecting a uniform stripe size of 1 or 2 megabytes can provide the best balance of performance and simplicity.

File Systems

Another method of storing database files is in a file system. A file system is an extra layer of software that allows the storage of multiple files per raw file. File systems are built on top of raw files. Therefore, the previous discussion of LVM and RAID also applies to file systems (i.e., file systems may be mirrored, striped, etc.). The biggest advantage of file systems is their flexibility. Files can

Table 2.4   RAID Stripe Size Recommendations

DATA FILE TYPE	ACCESS METHOD	CONCURRENCY	RECOMMENDED MINIMUM STRIPE SIZE
Control Files	Sequential	Low	2 * DB_BLOCK_SIZE
System Tablespace	Random	High	2 * DB_BLOCK_SIZE
Redo Logs	Sequential	Low	DB_BLOCK_SIZE
Rollback Segments	Sequential	Low	2 * DB_BLOCK_SIZE
Temp Segments (Sort Space)	Sequential	High	2 * DB_FILE_MULTI_ BLOCK_READ_COUNT * DB_BLOCK_SIZE
Indexes	Random	Varies	2 * DB_BLOCK_SIZE
Tables	Mixed	Varies	2 * DB_FILE_MULTI_ BLOCK_READ_COUNT *DB_BLOCK_SIZE

be created, moved, resized, and deleted at will without the need to coordinate with a system administrator every time you wish to make a change. On the other hand, this extra layer of software does add extra CPU overhead for every I/O request. Depending on the file system implementation, this overhead can range from very small for some of the new specialized file systems to as much as 10 to 15 percent for older file systems such as the UNIX file system. Also, if the file system utilizes a buffer cache (and most do) then you will need additional memory for storing database blocks twice (once in the file system cache and once in the SGA). In this section we examine three different file systems and their associated overhead and performance characteristics.

UNIX File Systems (UFS)

The UNIX file system (UFS) is the oldest of the file systems we will consider. It has been around since the genesis of UNIX but has evolved over time, with each vendor making its own improvements and customizations. In many cases vendors have coined new names for their particular implementation of UFS.

UFS was designed to provide efficient access and storage of relatively small files. Large files, on the other hand, are not as efficiently stored. Each file in a UFS is accessed via its inode, which contains information on where each block of the file is stored. As files become large, multiple inodes are required to keep track of all the blocks. These inodes are structured in a hierarchical fashion like a B*Tree index in a database. The more inodes there are, the more I/Os are required to locate and access a single data block. The overhead of database files in UFS can be as high as 15 percent in terms of access times as well as additional CPU load. More and/or faster CPUs are required to accommodate database files in UFS compared to raw files.

As files are created in a UFS, the blocks are allocated from a free pool. This pool is not defragmented when blocks are returned to it. This can lead to individual files being scattered all across the disks underlying the file system. This can result in poor performance when doing sequential I/O operations, as is often required with data warehouses.

Untuned UFS file systems also waste a lot of space when database files are stored in them. Because they are typically meant to contain large numbers of small files, the default storage parameters are not optimized for storing a few large database files. If you intend to store database files in a UFS, be sure to tune the file system to hold back less space and to allocate fewer inodes. It is also advisable to store only database files or only program files in a given UFS. Mixing file types within a single file system is not recommended.

A UFS employs caches for more frequently accessed data blocks (similar to the database block buffers of the SGA) and inodes for files that are open. Blocks that are part of the database end up being double cached (once in the file system cache and once in the SGA block buffer). When using UFS for database files, plan on configuring additional memory for this purpose.

NOTE Because of the default way in which Oracle avoids SGA buffering of blocks retrieved as part of a full table scan, UFS buffering can occasionally improve performance when a table is scanned repeatedly.

Journal File Systems (JFS)

A journal file system (JFS) is any file system that provides the ability to record file system metadata in a log similar to the redo log in Oracle. Only metadata is written to the JFS; file data is written directly to the file system. The advantages of a JFS are that it reduces the probability of file system corruption and decreases file system recovery time. The JFS log is used to recover metadata changes that had not yet been applied prior to doing the file system integrity check. As a result, the check typically completes almost instantaneously when the system is being rebooted. One disadvantage of a JFS when used in conjunction with an Oracle database is that there will be a minimum of two synchronous writes for each database write operation. One is for the data block that must be synchronously written through the file system to the underlying disks, and one is for the metadata (for any write operation, the last modification timestamp in the file's inode must be updated), which is stored in the JFS log.

Placing the log for a JFS is critical to the performance of a JFS file system. The log itself is written sequentially in a circular fashion and is typically relatively small. It should be placed either on disks separate from the JFS it is protecting or striped across a small portion of all the disks in the file system to reduce contention with regular file data transfers. The JFS logs should also be mirrored to provide an extra level of protection against file system corruption.

If you are planning to use file systems to store your database files, a JFS is highly recommended to protect that data against potential loss and to increase availability. Even if you do not plan to use the file system for database files it is a good idea to protect the remaining system components and the archive log files with a JFS.

Some implementations of JFS use a log for both metadata and file data changes. This significantly increases the amount of data being logged. Because Oracle does synchronous writes, data logging is not needed. For this reason this implementation of JFS is not recommended for storage of Oracle database files.

Extent-Based File Systems (XFS)

Extent-based file systems (XFS) is a relatively new file system design that does not utilize an inode structure to map data blocks to files. Instead of mapping individual data blocks, XFS groups contiguous blocks into extents. Multiple extents (if required) can be grouped together to access the entire data file. This approach is far more suitable for storing large files such as those required by a database. It is not suitable for very dynamic environments containing small files. The allocation/deallocation of these files will result in fragmentation and reduce the effectiveness of XFS in handling large files. When used for database files only, however, XFS has far less overhead for finding data blocks. Also, data files are more likely to be stored contiguously. Some implementations of XFS provide tools to defragment a file system (in some cases while it is online) or to implement a strict contiguous storage policy.

Although XFS implementations typically provide a caching capability similar to UFS, this feature can often be turned off or bypassed, resulting in performance similar to that of raw file accesses. Bypassing the cache also results in less memory waste due to the double-buffering effect seen in UFS implementations.

XFS, like UFS, is implemented as a software layer on top of raw files. As such, XFS can be used with the RAID technologies previously discussed to increase its performance and/or redundancy characteristics.

XFS provides an effective compromise between the performance of raw file access and the flexibility of UFS, while overcoming each technology's shortfalls. Assuming that Oracle Parallel Server is not required, XFS should be considered before raw files due to its UFS-like manageability characteristics. In the future there are likely to be XFS implementations that support Oracle Parallel Server. Until that time, however, warehouses that require Oracle Parallel Server must continue to use raw files.

Hardware

There have been several advances in hardware storage technology to keep abreast of the increasing performance, availability, and growth demands origi- nating from data warehouse applications. These advances have manifested themselves as intelligent controllers that can handle a large number of disks, commonly referred to as disk arrays. In this section we will consider several types of arrays, which offer varying degrees of intelligence.

Caching Arrays

Caching arrays are used to increase the performance of all read/write opera- tions by utilizing a persistent cache embedded in the array controller. The size of these caches varies and has a direct effect on performance. Although this technology increases the performance of the RAID levels described earlier, it does not directly implement any of them. Software running on the host operat- ing system is completely unaware of the caching going on in the controller and must continue to implement any required RAID support.

Write operations are the main beneficiaries of this technology. Whenever Oracle requests a write operation, the block being written must be persistently stored before control is returned to Oracle. The disk block in question is trans- ferred to the array's persistent cache for storage, and control is immediately returned. The array then has a process that ensures that the dirty block gets written to disk in background. The write-to-cache operation completes in a fraction of the time required to write directly to disk. The cache must be per- sistent so that in the event of a power outage, the data is not lost. Once power is restored, the background process resumes writing the dirty blocks to disk. The cache should be sufficiently large so that the background write process in the controller can stay ahead of demand. Should the write process consistently fall behind, performance will revert to writing directly to disk.

Data blocks that are cached in the array because of a recent read or write operation may be used to satisfy read requests. The SGA and file system cache (if you are using file systems) will satisfy most read requests that might be cached in the array. Those read requests that eventually make their way to the array are more likely to request data that is not cached, resulting in a physical disk read operation. As such, the benefit of caching arrays for read operations in a data warehouse environment is limited.

Embedded RAID Arrays

The embedded RAID array, in addition to providing the caching array function- ality discussed earlier, also implements some or all of the RAID levels in hard- ware. This effectively offloads the host operating system from performing the multiple I/O operations required by software implementations of the various RAID levels. Each I/O request results in a single request from the operating system to the intelligent controller. The controller satisfies the request and returns control to the operating system.

In general, embedded RAID arrays will react in a manner similar to caching arrays. Overall performance will be better, and system load will be reduced compared to caching arrays. Write operations will continue to benefit more than read operations for the same reasons described for caching arrays. Embedded RAID arrays typically provide larger caches than caching arrays, resulting in better cache hit rates and higher performance. Some RAID arrays allow replacement of a failed disk without interrupting access to the array. This feature is commonly referred to as "hot swappable" disks. Arrays that support hot swapping of disks will hide the performance degradation for resynchronization better than software implementations.

Several embedded RAID array solutions on the market provide a variety of other capabilities. Some provide read ahead capabilities that attempt to guess which data blocks may be requested next. Others provide hot swap capabilities to increase availability. They may also support connections from multiple hosts (required for Oracle Parallel Server cluster solutions).

One drawback to the embedded RAID array is that it becomes a single point of failure that can bring your entire system down. This risk can be mitigated with arrays that provide for multiple host connections from the same host coupled with automatic sensing and failover circuitry. Some arrays may even provide redundant power supplies and intelligent controllers to further increase availability.

Remote Replication Arrays

Remote replication arrays provide the ability to replicate data over great distances. This capability provides the ultimate in availability, redundancy, and disaster recovery. Should any disaster cause a system or array to become temporarily or permanently unavailable, the remote site can be activated using an up-to-date copy of the data from the failed site. The replication capability is an option that is added to either the caching or embedded RAID arrays.

The remote site is a read-only site (from an application perspective) until it is activated. As writes occur at the online site they are synchronously transferred to the remote site to keep it up to date. In order for the remote site to be viable from an Oracle perspective, updates must occur synchronously. They cannot be propagated via a write-behind approach. Depending on the amount of write activity to the array, one or more parallel communications paths may be needed to keep up with the demand without impeding the online database performance. In addition to the throughput needed to keep up with this demand, communications delay must be considered when replicating over long distances.

Oracle software provides some similar capabilities through replication and the standby database feature (introduced in Oracle7, release 7.3). This level of protection and investment, however, is rarely considered necessary for data warehousing.

Network Storage

A traditional file server uses a general-purpose computer with attached storage to provide network access to its files. That general-purpose computer and its operating system were originally designed to perform lots of different functions, one of which was the storage and retrieval of files. Lots of the operating system and hardware capabilities are wasted when used for a single purpose. The inevitable conclusion that we draw from this is that a specialized file server could be designed to very efficiently perform a small subset of operations dedicated to just file management.

Several storage vendors have recently started promoting such dedicated file servers, which are designed to serve as independent network devices. Each device has a small operating system (usually called a micro-kernel) that provides the necessary device management. It has its own network interface and can communicate with other devices using standard network protocols, such as TCP/IP. These devices are commonly referred to as network attached storage (NAS) or storage area networks (SAN). (Every vendor of these devices, however, seems to have coined its own trade name for its particular design.)

To make the files on the NAS visible to the other servers in the network, each server maps the NAS file systems to make them *appear syntactically* to be local files; that is, users access the files using the same commands they would use if the files were actually stored on their server. In a UNIX world, this is generally done through network file system (NFS). NFS, originally developed by Sun Microsystems but now universally supported by UNIX vendors, has provided network mounting of remote file systems for many years. It was a natural basis for accessing NAS files.

The logical reasoning behind the invention of NAS is sound, but caution should be applied before jumping into this new architecture. Many uses of files lend themselves to a file server approach—many users on many hosts needing occasional access to a file, for example. The Oracle8*i* database, however, will not be sharing its access to its files with any other hosts. Oracle requires exclusive access to the database files for extended periods of time. There are two considerations here: performance and reliability. Potential purchasers should carefully evaluate both before selecting this architecture.

Oracle Worldwide Support has, for years, strongly cautioned against placing Oracle files on NFS-mounted devices. Until very recently, the performance of the local area network (commonly Ethernet) was many times slower than access to local disks. With more widespread availability of Fibre Channel connections in the network connecting servers, this performance differential should decrease in the next few years.

Reliability and data integrity are a second factor to evaluate when deciding whether to use an NAS device to house your Oracle warehouse. NFS has been around long enough to be pretty well shaken out. Unfortunately, the porting of NAS and various hardware/software components of the new NAS products are not as well tested. An I/O error (from any cause) in retrieving a user's spreadsheet is far less serious than an I/O error experienced by the database management system in accessing one of its files. Similarly, a write to disk that gets reported back to Oracle as complete cannot be allowed to get lost between the buffer and the physical disk!

After considering all of these cautions, it is appropriate to also consider potential benefits of using network storage for your database. When a database server with locally attached storage is unavailable, the database on that local storage cannot be accessed. Some shops implement various distributed architectures (see Chapter 12) to increase availability. If the database were physically stored on network storage and the database server becomes unavailable, then an alternate server in the network could start an Oracle instance to access the database. This approach will be less expensive than a standby database or replicated database that would require redundant storage on two separate servers. Of course, cost isn't the only consideration—network storage doesn't address the potential loss of the storage node, but it can provide a simple level of redundancy for inexpensive servers. Also, unlike Oracle Parallel Server, this architecture does not permit the two servers to access the database simultaneously, so there is no scalability improvement.

Be very sure of the actual behavior of any NAS device you consider. There are very few large Oracle databases running in this environment today. Even if the storage vendor can provide references regarding performance, the issues of reliability and data integrity are harder to address. Just because a site hasn't had a failure that corrupted its database doesn't mean that it won't happen, only that it hasn't happened *yet*. Since Oracle Corporation has only recently begun officially supporting databases in this configuration, there should be a very big cost savings to justify being on the bleeding edge of technology!

Summary

Five computer architectures (uniprocessor, SMP, NUMA, clusters, and MPP) have been introduced and evaluated in relation to several criteria: reliability, availability, performance, scalability, and manageability. The uniprocessor architecture is recommended only for small-scale data marts. Most Oracle data warehouses today are implemented with SMP configurations. The newer NUMA architecture extends many of the benefits of SMP. When a single SMP or NUMA computer cannot provide the performance of scalability that is required, Oracle Parallel Server in conjunction with clustered SMP or NUMA nodes may be the answer. For extremely high-end warehousing needs an MPP solution may be required, albeit at a cost of both dollars and administrative time.

Complementing the evolution of computer architectures has been a corresponding evolution in data storage technology. Raw disk files and various file system implementations were described. Logical volume managers, various levels of RAID, and four types of storage array hardware were presented.

There is clearly no one single computer or storage architecture that is ideal for every data warehouse. Each architecture offers specific advantages and disadvantages when compared to the others. From the descriptions and evaluations provided in this chapter you should be able to begin evaluating alternative configurations from various vendors.

Oracle Server Software Architecture and Features

The secret temple of the Piranha women—their architecture is surprisingly advanced!

Dr. Margo Hunt
Cannibal Women in the Avocado Jungle of Death (1988)

This chapter introduces the wide variety of architectural components and features that make up the Oracle Server. Experienced Oracle DBAs may feel comfortable skimming over this introductory material, perhaps stopping only to peruse the description of new features. More detailed information on the topics of this chapter is available in the *Server Concepts* manuals published by Oracle Corporation for each release of Oracle.

The Oracle data warehouse is created, accessed, and managed through the facilities of the Oracle Server. Most of these facilities are provided through the core Oracle Server product while others are available only through separately licensed options.

We begin our examination of Oracle's architecture from the outside and identify and describe the components that can be observed from the operating system level—what we'll call the external architecture. Then we move inside the Oracle database to see the components and substructures that Oracle uses to perform its various functions—what we'll term the internal architecture.

ORACLE SERVER RELEASES AND OPTIONS

Throughout this book we sometimes refer to features of Oracle, Oracle7, Oracle8, or Oracle8*i*. While these alternative names may appear to be confusing, we have chosen which to use in a particular context based on when the feature was introduced into the product.

We use the term *Oracle* generically to indicate the Oracle server of any currently supported release. Alternatively, we use *Oracle8* when discussing features or behavior introduced in the Oracle8 product (release 8.0, 1997).

Oracle8*i* was introduced in 1999 (with the 8.1 release of the Oracle Server). When referencing specific features that are new to Oracle8*i* we explicitly use that product name.

Although this book does not target Oracle7 features, it is sometimes necessary to differentiate between that release and the newer releases.

The packaging of features by Oracle Corporation into its base server product, its Enterprise Edition, and the various options (e.g., Oracle Parallel Server) has changed over time for both technical and marketing reasons. Some of the features described throughout this book are available only as extra-cost options to the Oracle Server. The user is responsible for compliance with current licensing restrictions.

Oracle Server: External Architecture

The external architecture includes those things that can be seen or monitored from the operating system. It includes various disk files, several processes (or threads, depending on the operating system's design), and the allocation of memory by those processes. Figure 3.1 illustrates the primary components of Oracle's external architecture.

We discuss each of the components in more depth later in this chapter. Before getting into the specifics of the Oracle architecture, it is important to clarify some terminology specific to the Oracle environment.

Oracle Database versus Oracle Instance

New Oracle users and administrators who are familiar with other DBMS products commonly get confused about Oracle's use of the terms *database* and *instance*. In Oracle's terminology, a database is a set of related physical files that exist on permanent storage, usually disk. The database continues to exist even if the computer system is shut down. The additional software processes and shared memory structures that are needed to access and use the database are referred to, in Oracle terms, as an instance.

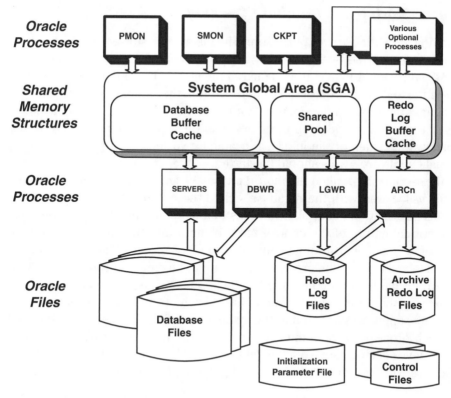

Figure 3.1 High-level external architecture.

In normal operations one database is associated with one instance; typically, they even have the same name. It is no wonder then that, in casual conversation, even an experienced Oracle administrator, consultant, or support representative may use the terms interchangeably—which, of course, helps feed the confusion. There are times, however, when it is important to understand the distinction between these terms.

An Oracle database can exist even without an instance. The instance may have been shut down, for example, to perform an offline ("cold") backup of the database. If an instance does not have the database open, no information within the database can be accessed, read, or manipulated. Only operating system functions (such as the cold backup) on entire files can be performed on the database.

Less intuitively, however, it is possible to have an Oracle instance without an Oracle database. Specifically, when creating a new database the administrator will start up an instance and then issue the CREATE DATABASE command. Even with an existing database, the process of starting up Oracle and making the database available to users has three distinct steps. Not until the third step is the database actually involved.

Instance Startup and Database Opening

In the first step, the *startup* phase, only the instance is started. That is, several processes are started by the operating system, each of which runs the Oracle RDBMS software. An allocation of shared memory is made that is accessed by each of these Oracle processes. To perform this first step, Oracle reads a file containing initialization parameters that define how to configure the instance. These parameters provide important information such as the name of the database, how much memory should be allocated for various operations, and which optional Oracle processes should be started.

In the second step, called the *mount* phase, the Oracle software opens a special file associated with the database, called the *control file*. The control file contains information about all other files that make up this database. Because of the critical nature of the control file it is important that you keep multiple copies of it. Oracle will automatically maintain these copies. The names of each copy of the control file are provided to the instance through the CONTROLFILES parameter in the initialization parameter file opened in step 1.

Finally, in the third step (the open phase) each of the files that make up the database is opened. At this point, the instance and the database are associated with each other until the administrator shuts the instance down. Oracle can now retrieve specific data from the database files for a user. Any changes made to the data will be recorded in the redo log files and the database files.

Multi-Instance Oracle

One other situation makes it critical to understand the distinction between an Oracle instance and an Oracle database. In clustered architectures and massively parallel processor (MPP) configurations (introduced in Chapter 2, "Hardware Architectures for Oracle Data Warehousing"), multiple computers, each having its own memory and processes, can all access a set of database files on disk. In these hardware configurations, a special Oracle option, the Oracle Parallel Server Option, must be used to control simultaneous access to the database from the separate computers. Using Parallel Server, an Oracle instance is started on each of the computers in *multi-instance mode*. In this mode, each instance agrees to cooperate with each of the other instances to protect the integrity of the data in the database. Only one instance, for example, will be allowed to actively work with a specific block (or, more typically, a set of contiguous blocks) at a time. Figure 3.2 illustrates Oracle's ability to start two instances on two nodes of a clustered configuration, which then share access to a single Oracle database. Each instance has its own set of redo log files, but they share access to the database files.

In Chapter 11, "Warehousing with Oracle Parallel Server," we discuss the issues involved in designing, loading, and administering a data warehouse using Oracle Parallel Server in clustered and MPP environments.

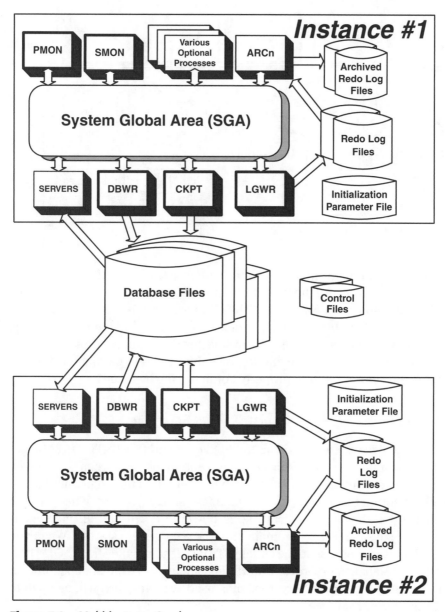

Figure 3.2 Multi-instance Oracle.

File Architecture

Because by definition a database is the organized storage of data—and generally large amounts of it—it is appropriate to begin our examination of Oracle architecture by considering the data files that provide the storage. In addition

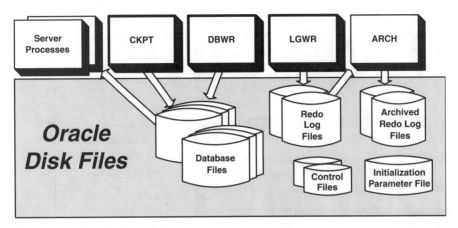

Figure 3.3   Oracle file architecture.

to the files that actually hold the data, Oracle uses other files to provide integrity controls to ensure that the data is not lost or corrupted. These various Oracle files are shown in Figure 3.3. The database data is stored in database files. Changes made to blocks in the database files are logged in redo log files, which are later permanently copied to archive log files. Control files keep track of the status of all the database and log files. Initialization parameter files are read during instance startup to properly configure the instance.

Database Files

An Oracle database is created using the SQL command CREATE DATABASE. (The Oracle Installer can issue this command automatically, if requested, when the Oracle Server software is installed.) Several files are created in this process that will constitute the actual physical database stored on disk. Whenever the computer system hosting the database is powered down and all memory is erased, these physical files will remain until the next system startup. When you need the database again, issue the Oracle STARTUP command (from SQL*DBA, Oracle Server Manager, or Oracle Enterprise Manager programs, depending on which version of the Oracle Server is being used), and the files will be open to make the database available.

When you create a database you must create at least one database file for the SYSTEM tablespace (which we discuss further in the section on Oracle internal architecture). This tablespace contains the essential components that must be part of every Oracle database, namely, the data dictionary. Your data warehouse will, of course, require you to create other database objects, such as tables and indexes, to store the information that your users want to see. Oracle uses the data dictionary to store its information about those other objects that you will create.

Each database file stores some special control information in its file header. This information is not generally seen or used by the database administrator or end user. It is used by the Oracle RDBMS software to ensure the integrity of the database and prevent a file from being substituted or overlaid in error. As an example, consider a fairly common situation in which a disk failure causes one (or more) of the database files to become unavailable. The database administrator then restores an old copy of the files from a tape backup and attempts to restart the Oracle instance and open the database. When Oracle compares the control file information to the data stored in the header of the restored data files, it immediately recognizes that the restored files are out of date and some changes may have been lost. The instance forces the administrator to complete the recovery before allowing any users to connect.

Redo Log Files

An additional set of files is automatically created as part of the Oracle database. At least two redo logs must be part of every Oracle database. Redo logs are Oracle's journal of the changes being made to database data. In case of the failure of a disk or other hardware, Oracle can use the redo logs' record of changes to perform recovery so the changes are not lost. There must be at least two redo log files because Oracle must switch between the two files repeatedly as changes are logged. The operation of redo logs is illustrated in Figure 3.4.

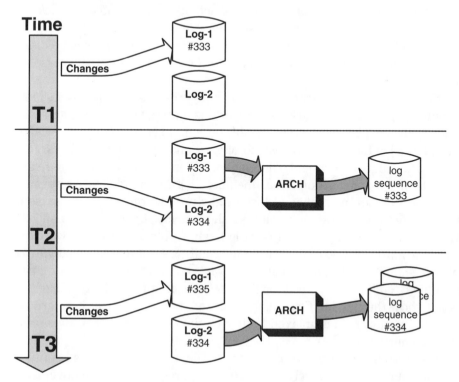

Figure 3.4 Online redo log file processing and archiving.

At time T1, we see all changes being written to log-1 until it is filled. At T1, log-1 is currently holding the 333rd log file created by this instance. When log-1 is filled (at time T2) Oracle begins writing changes out to log-2. At time T3, the second log (sequence #334) has completely filled and Oracle again performs a log switch to start writing change records into the log-1 file again—this time as log sequence #335.

Each log switch also initiates a checkpoint. During checkpoint processing Oracle writes out every database block within the buffer pool of the System Global Area (or SGA, discussed later in this chapter) that has been modified but not yet written out to disk. Remember that Oracle does not write the actual data blocks to disk as changes are made. If the instance should fail due to a hardware, operating system, or Oracle software problem, the unwritten changes stored within the SGA's memory structures would be lost—except for the record maintained within the redo log. Therefore, Oracle cannot overwrite the information in log-1 until all the modified data blocks are safely stored out on disk. When the checkpoint is completed we are assured that the change information that was written out to log-1 is no longer needed in case of an instance failure, and Oracle can begin reusing the log-1 file when log-2 is full, as shown at time T3.

A problem can arise in a database in which many changes are occurring. What happens if log-2 fills up before the checkpoint can be finished? Well, a bad thing happens: All insert, update, and delete activity in the database comes to a complete halt until the checkpoint finishes. Oracle will not allow the possibility of changes getting lost by being prematurely overwritten or not being recorded in a log file. The solution to this problem is for the administrator to increase the number of log files.

Another risk to the integrity of the database is presented by the possible loss of an online log file due to a disk failure. For this reason, Oracle provides a simple facility for keeping multiple copies of the redo logs. The copies are called members of a log file group. So, instead of log-1 and log-2 we have two log file groups, each with two members. The first, log group 1, has members log-1a and log-1b. The second, log group 2, has members log-2a and log-2b. We strongly recommend that you multiplex all logs of any production Oracle database in this way. Redo logs are generally small (usually between 30 and 300 megabytes), so keeping a second copy is likely to require at most two extra disks. With most data warehouses today requiring hundreds of gigabytes of data storage, making the additional copy of all redo logs adds only 1 or 2 percent to the overall disk expense for the warehouse. For simplicity, Figure 3.4 does not show the two log files being duplexed, but in practice these critical files should always be multiplexed (either by the Oracle facility or by storing the files on mirrored disks).

Because the change information written to the online redo logs is kept until the actual data blocks are safely written to disk, Oracle is able to recover from the various types of hardware and software failures that would cause the volatile memory that contains the SGA to be destroyed. All committed changes either are stored on disk in the database files or are available in the online redo logs so they can be "replayed" during instance recovery to ensure that no committed changes are lost.

INSTANCE RECOVERY

During instance recovery the database is returned to a consistent state. That is, all completed (committed) transactions will be fully restored. Incomplete (uncommitted) transactions will be fully undone (rolled back). Because these transactions never had the chance to complete before the instance failure, Oracle will not allow the partially completed changes to be visible after recovery. Every transaction is either fully completed or fully erased.

Yet another risk may threaten the database—loss of a database file from disk failure. When a database file is lost, the change information since the last backup of the file must be available in order for the database to be recovered. If redo log files are being reused, say, every hour or so, how do we possibly recover from a file backup made one or more days before the disk loss?

Oracle conveniently provides for this situation through an optional process called redo log archiving. When enabled, the database is said to be operated in *archivelog mode*. When in archivelog mode, the instance will make a copy of the online redo log whenever it fills and before it can be overwritten. At time T2 in Figure 3.4 the archiver process (ARCH) begins copying the contents of log-1 to a new archive log file. This copy is assigned a file name that corresponds to the log sequence in which it was created. In this example, it inherits the number 333. Later, at time T3, when log-2 is filled and Oracle switches back to writing changes to log-1, ARCH again goes to work copying the contents of the filled log file to an archived log file. Just like checkpoint processing, the archiving must be completed before Oracle will be able to reuse an online log file.

If recovery from a media failure is necessary, Oracle will automatically prompt the DBA to provide the necessary archived logs (in the proper order) to replay all the changes since the backup copy of the lost data file was created. We cover this topic in much more depth in the discussion of backup and recovery in Chapter 8, "Administering and Monitoring the Oracle Data Warehouse."

Even though archivelog mode is not the default mode of operation for the database, nearly every production Oracle database should be run in archivelog mode to protect the database from media failures. The few exceptions to this rule are also discussed in Chapter 8.

Control Files

Creating a database also creates at least one control file. The control file is where Oracle keeps a record of every other file (database and redo log) that is part of the database. Although only one control file is required for the database, because of its critical nature and small size it is highly recommended that several control files be defined on different physical disks. Oracle will then maintain each of them as identical copies so that no single disk failure will make the database unusable. Oracle uses the control file(s) during database startup processing to find every other file that must be opened and also to verify that each of those files is indeed the correct file and has not been dropped or substituted while the database was shut down.

Information identical to that stored in the header of each database file and redo log is also kept in the control file. Oracle will maintain this information automatically without any direct intervention by the administrator or user. This information includes such things as the file name and the last time Oracle checkpointed the file (when all changes made in memory were flushed out to the physical file). Also, whenever the administrator issues a command that adds a file to the database (e.g., CREATE TABLESPACE, ALTER TABLESPACE . . . ADD DATAFILE, ALTER DATABASE . . . ADD LOGFILE), drops a file, or renames a file Oracle updates the control files as well as the header of the affected file.

If during the open phase of startup Oracle finds that there is any difference in the file header information and the information maintained in the control file, it will interrupt the startup process and direct the DBA to correct the problem. This check is one of the primary integrity features of the Oracle RDBMS, which prevents accidental corruption of the database.

Initialization Parameter Files

There are literally hundreds of parameters that can affect the way Oracle behaves. Most, luckily, have default values that work well without an administrator having to set them. A few (e.g., DBNAME and DB_BLOCK_SIZE) control how the database is initially built and cannot be changed once the database is created. Some parameters (such as DB_BLOCK_BUFFERS, SHARED_POOL_SIZE) control how the allocation of shared memory will be made. Others (NLS_LANGUAGE, MTS_SERVERS, for instance) control various optional features of the Oracle RDBMS. Still others are used to configure security options, and others provide "knobs" for performance tuning. Some initialization parameters that are particularly relevant to data warehousing are shown in Table 3.1.

Descriptions of each of these parameters is provided in the *Oracle7* and *Oracle8 Server Reference* manuals. The warehouse DBA should become familiar

Table 3.1   Initialization Parameters for Data Warehouses

BITMAP_MERGE_AREA_SIZE	PARALLEL_MAX_SERVERS
BUFFER_POOL_KEEP	PARALLEL_MIN_PERCENT
BUFFER_POOL_RECYCLE	PARALLEL_MIN_SERVERS
CREATE_BITMAP_AREA_SIZE	PARTITION_VIEW_ENABLED
DB_BLOCK_BUFFERS	SORT_AREA_RETAINED_SIZE
DB_BLOCK_SIZE	SORT_AREA_SIZE
DB_FILE_DIRECT_IO_COUNT	SORT_DIRECT_WRITES
DB_FILE_MULTIBLOCK_READ_COUNT	SORT_WRITE_BUFFER_SIZE
HASH_AREA_SIZE	SORT_WRITE_BUFFERS
HASH_JOIN_ENABLED	STAR_TRANSFORMATION_ENABLED
HASH_MULTIBLOCK_IO_COUNT	

with the listed parameters. Some of these parameters (such as STAR_TRANS-FORMATION_ENABLED) control important data warehouse features but default to False. These parameters, in particular, will need to be explicitly set to True to enable these features.

Each database has its own initialization parameter file and may sometimes have several alternative files. One file might be used to configure the instance for normal daily operations, and another might be used to configure the instance differently for special weekly database load and summarization processes. When more than one parameter file is available, the administrator (or the startup scripts he has written) will have to specify the name of the parameter file to be used during startup whenever it is not the default name or if it is stored in a directory other than Oracle's default location.

NOTE Some undocumented initialization parameters whose names are prefixed with an underscore (and even some documented ones) should not be modified except under the direction of Oracle Worldwide Support.

Although this file is properly known as the *instance initialization parameter file*, many Oracle administrators find that to be more than a simple mouthful and continue to refer to it by the shorthand term *init.ora* ("init dot ora"). This more manageable name comes from the common format of the names assigned by Oracle to these files: *init_instname.ora* (where *instname* is the name of the instance to be controlled by this particular file).

Memory Architecture

Oracle uses a combination of shared and private memory structures. The System Global Area is a shared memory structure that is allocated during instance startup. It provides a means of communication and coordination for the many processes, both system and user, that need to access data within the database. Additionally, each process may need some memory usage that is irrelevant to any other process and is allocated privately by the individual process.

System Global Area (SGA)

The primary memory structure, which is accessible to all Oracle processes, is called the System Global Area, or, more commonly, the SGA. Figure 3.5 shows the primary structures within the Oracle SGA. It is common for the SGA to be the largest single consumer of memory on a computer dedicated to running an Oracle database application. The SGA may often be several hundred megabytes or even gigabytes in size. How this shared memory structure is created and attached by processes varies by operating system. In UNIX, the most common platform for Oracle data warehouses, the SGA is created during instance startup as a shared memory segment.

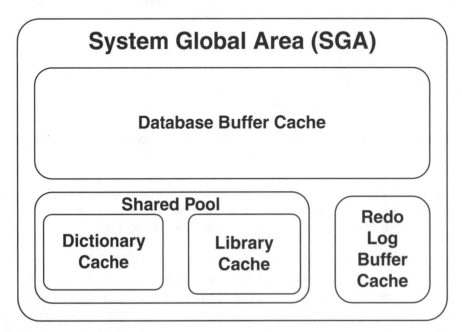

Figure 3.5   SGA structures.

Database Buffer Cache

The SGA holds three very important structures. The largest, typically, is the database buffer cache. The buffer pool for a data warehouse will commonly be defined as having several hundred or even a few thousand database buffers. A single buffer pool is used for all the database blocks needed by all users. Each buffer is capable of holding one database block of data. This database block (or *Oracle block*) size applies to every block in the entire database and is defined by the value of the DB_BLOCK_SIZE parameter when the database is created. It cannot be modified without completely recreating the database.

SETTING DB_BLOCK_SIZE

DB_BLOCK_SIZE is normally between 2,048 (2 KB) and 16,384 (16 KB) bytes, but allowable values vary by operating system and Oracle version. It is the amount of data Oracle will either read or write at a time. Generally, for data warehousing applications the larger block sizes should be chosen over the small (usually 2 KB) default. Ideally, for best performance the Oracle block size should be the same as the operating system's block size. This will have to be coordinated with the system administrator, who is otherwise likely to choose a smaller block size than this ideal.

In normal operations, the data needed by a user can be manipulated only after it is retrieved from the database files and stored in one of the buffers in this pool. In Figure 3.1, note that the server processes assigned to users' requests are able to retrieve data blocks from disk into the database buffer. When changes are made to a block in the buffer pool, the block must be written back out to disk by the database writer (DBWR) process. These changes are not written as part of the transaction that made the change, but asynchronously. At the longest, this write will be performed as part of the next checkpoint.

The various buffers in the pool are managed using a least recently used (LRU) algorithm. An LRU list keeps track of how recently each block in the pool has been accessed. Each time a block is read or modified it is moved to the tail of the LRU list—that is, the "most recently used" end. If a block is brought into the buffer pool and then not used again, it gradually moves toward the "least recently used" end of the LRU list. Buffers at this end of the list become candidates to be "stolen" to hold another user's blocks that need to be read in from disk. Each server process that performs the reads will use the LRU list to determine the buffers in which to store newly read blocks.

There is an exception to this LRU process that is used for handling full table scans. Because a single table may consume far more space than the total number of database buffers in the SGA, a full scan using the normal LRU mechanism would completely flush all other blocks from the buffer cache. This would hurt performance for other queries that would otherwise find blocks in memory but now must reread them from disk. To prevent this effect from occurring, when a server process is performing a full table scan by default it places the buffers it uses at the least recently used end of the LRU list. These buffers, then, tend to get immediately reused even by the same query. The downside of this special behavior is that, for a smaller table that various queries are likely to access repeatedly, the table must be repeatedly read from disk by each subsequent query! To balance these conflicting needs, Oracle allows the DBA to modify table scan behavior to record retrieved blocks of certain tables on the most recently used end of LRU list, just like blocks that are accessed randomly. Blocks of a table created with the CACHE keyword will be retained in the buffer cache after a table scan so they may be accessed by another query. The DBA must be careful in assigning the CACHE behavior to tables in the data warehouse. Use it for relatively small reference tables, but avoid using it for very large tables that do not fit entirely within a portion of the buffer cache or are not likely to be repeatedly queried.

MULTIPLE SUBPOOLS IN ORACLE8

Oracle8 provides the administrator with another technique to more carefully control the handling of blocks of particular tables. The large database buffer cache may be divided into subpools with independent LRU handling. Up to three subpools may be defined using the BUFFER_POOL_*name* initialization parameter. Objects may then be assigned to the subpool using the new BUFFER_POOL clause on the CREATE TABLE, ALTER TABLE, CREATE INDEX, and ALTER INDEX commands.

The first subpool, the KEEP cache, may be defined to hold blocks from small reference tables (such as dimension tables) and high-performance indexes that might otherwise be flushed by the overwhelming numbers of blocks from large (e.g., fact) tables and indexes.

The second, the RECYCLE cache, may be specified to store blocks of large tables that are accessed randomly but have a low probability of reusing any specific block before it ages from the buffer pool. Whatever remains of the total buffer pool after defining either or both of these special subpools is assigned the DEFAULT cache. The DEFAULT cache behaves identically to the Oracle7 single buffer pool and will contain blocks of all objects not specifically assigned to the KEEP or RECYCLE caches.

Some experimentation is required to determine the optimal size and contents of each subpool in order to actually improve on Oracle's default LRU handling. More information on the use of multiple buffer pools is provided in the *Oracle8* or Oracle8*i Server Tuning Reference* manual.

Conventional Oracle wisdom holds that a larger buffer cache is almost always better for performance than a smaller cache. This is not always true for OLTP applications, and it is often not true for data warehouses. If at least some tables aren't defined with the CACHE attribute, relatively few buffers may be used if lots of full table scans are performed. This may be the case in data warehouses based primarily on summary tables. (This isn't the case, however, with warehouses built around star schemas, which will frequently use indexes to identify and retrieve random blocks from tables.) To use the memory allocated to a large database buffer cache effectively, ensure that you strike a reasonable balance between random block requests, scans of small cached tables, and scans of large tables without the CACHE attribute.

SIZING THE DATABASE BUFFER CACHE

To determine whether the buffers currently being allocated are being used effectively, set the parameter DB_BLOCK_LRU_STATISTICS to true and query the X$KCBCBH table. This table has one row for each allocated buffer and will provide a count of how many times each relative position on the LRU chain was used for a subsequent access. The results are generally more easily interpreted if the large number of rows is grouped together into about 10 to 20 buckets. A query to do this grouping along with more detail about how to interpret the results can be found in the *Server Tuning* manuals for Oracle7 or Oracle8. These manuals also describe how to use DB_BLOCK_LRU_EXTENDED_STATISTICS and the X$KCBRBH virtual table to determine the potential benefit of increasing the value of DB_BLOCK_BUFFERS.

Redo Log Buffer Cache

Every time a user changes the value of data in the database, Oracle must record the specifics of the change into the current redo log. Each of these changes typically requires recording only a few bytes—an identification of the data block affected, the transaction making the change, and the specific bytes modified. Because of these small record sizes, it would be very inefficient to write these changes out as they occur. Also, because several transactions (at least in an OLTP database) are likely to be occurring simultaneously, controlling and coordinating a large number of writes would be a bottleneck to performance and a nightmare for administration.

To avoid these two problems, Oracle buffers the change information and then the Log Writer (LGWR) process issues a write request after several changes, by multiple users, are accumulated. The write is triggered by any transaction issuing a COMMIT statement or whenever this buffer pool reaches one-third full. The administrator controls the size of the redo log buffer cache using the LOG_BUFFER initialization parameter.

Shared Pool

The second structure in the SGA is the *shared pool*, which is a common area of memory used primarily for two different functions. The shared pool contains the *dictionary cache* and the *library cache*.

When a user issues a SQL statement (or invokes a block of code written in PL/SQL, Oracle's procedural programming language) that statement or block of code is loaded into the library cache. The statement (or program) is parsed to validate syntax and ensure that all the referenced objects (such as database tables or other stored procedures) exist and are accessible with this user's current security privileges. To do this parsing and security checking, Oracle must reference the data dictionary, which is the part of the database where Oracle keeps track of everything about the structure of the database. Definitions of all the users, tables, indexes, and the like are maintained in the data dictionary tables, which are stored in the system tablespace. To avoid the disk I/O expense of repeatedly having to go out to the database files associated with the SYSTEM tablespace to look up this information, Oracle keeps a copy in the dictionary cache.

When the statement has been parsed and security checks are completed, the Oracle query optimizer develops an execution plan that will determine how best to retrieve the information requested by that SQL statement. (Oracle security mechanisms and the query optimizer are discussed later in this chapter.) All the information about referenced objects and execution plans is then stored in the library cache along with the original text of the SQL statement.

Prior to the release of Oracle7, this statement parse information was stored in private memory by each user's server process instead of by a shared memory structure. Making the information shareable can provide major savings in memory and parse effort for OLTP systems. Typically, hundreds or thousands of users of a large OLTP system are running one application and issuing identical SQL statements. Instead of forcing each user's process to individually absorb the overhead of parsing and determining an optimal execution plan and storing this information privately, Oracle7 and Oracle8 require only the first process to issue a particular SQL statement to incur these costs. All other users' server processes will be able to take advantage of most of this effort. (Each user must still be individually evaluated for necessary security privileges associated with the statement.)

Of course, data warehousing and OLTP systems operate in many fundamentally different ways. One of the key differences is in the amount of shared SQL processing typically performed. In the OLTP situation, it is common for many users to issue the same SQL statements as they navigate through application screens or submit application reports for processing. Data warehouse users, on the other hand, tend to issue different SQL statements.

There are several reasons why data warehouse users are less likely to be issuing identical SQL statements. First, the data warehouse has fewer simultaneous users (although each one may be causing the database to do much more work!). Second, each user is more likely to be investigating different data relationships. One analyst may be looking at the last quarter's average cost of sales for a new product line across each sales region. Another may be examining the correlation between manufacturing rejection rates at various factories and the suppliers of various raw materials. Yet another might be trying to determine the relative effectiveness of a recent change in the marketing organization structure in the international divisions.

For these reasons, Oracle's shared SQL feature of the library cache does not provide the same memory and processing savings for the query activity in the data warehouse that it does for a database used for OLTP applications. The dictionary cache, however, provides potentially greater advantage to the data warehouse because more SQL statements are being parsed and, therefore, more references to data dictionary information must be made. Even though the many decision-support queries submitted to the data warehouse are likely to be different, they will generally reference the same set of tables and will need the same data dictionary information about tables, columns, indexes, and so on.

In addition to query processing, however, the data warehouse has other processing requirements as well. Frequently the warehouse design allows data to be loaded using direct-path SQL*Loader. In some cases, because of the complexity of the data or the additional processing needed during the load, it is necessary to use traditional INSERT statements. One of our recent Internet commerce clients has a custom load process that generates an INSERT statement for each row to be loaded. The generated SQL, however, used literal values in the VALUES clause so each INSERT appeared as a new statement that needed to be parsed before it could be executed. By rewriting the generation process to use bind variables instead of literal values, the millions of independent INSERT statements were reduced to only one per table. This simple change to their application design reduced the parsing overhead dramatically by effectively using the Oracle8 shared pool architecture.

Oracle maintains space within the shared pool dynamically using an LRU algorithm. Each time a SQL statement or dictionary element is referenced, it is, in effect, time-stamped. As additional parsing is performed, the new SQL statement or retrieved data dictionary information will reuse space within the shared pool by flushing out the information that has the oldest time-stamp. Oracle maintains statistics about how frequently items in the shared pool are flushed and then have to be reloaded. These allow the administrator to determine when additional space should be allocated by changing the value of the SHARED_POOL _SIZE initialization parameter and restarting the instance.

Large Pool

Certain operations make rather large requests for memory allocations that may cause undue stress on the shared pool. Effective with Oracle8, the database administrator can define a separate space within the SGA to handle these large requests. This specialized area is called the large pool and is defined using the LARGE_POOL_SIZE initialization parameter.

Connecting large numbers of users to OLTP systems using the multithreaded server (MTS) facility or XA-compliant teleprocessing monitors (such as Tuxedo) is the most common reason for configuring the large pool.

More relevant to data warehousing, another feature that makes use of large memory allocations from the large pool is the Oracle8 Recovery Manager (commonly referred to as RMAN). Backup and restore operations of RMAN are discussed in Chapter 8.

Program Global Area (PGA)

Each user's session will require some allocation of private memory to maintain information that is of no value to other processes connected to the database. Generally, this memory is allocated within the Program Global Area (PGA) by the server process that is working on that user's behalf. This memory is used for functions like keeping track of how far a specific query has progressed in its retrieval of data or storing values for variables that may be declared within the session. Additional memory may also be allocated by the user's server process for performing sort operations.

The introduction of the shared SQL feature in the Oracle7 release greatly reduced the amount of private storage needed by each user's server process.

Process Architecture

Several processes make up the Oracle instance. Five of these processes perform key background functions and are required. These five are shown in bold boxes in Figure 3.6. Several other background processes are optional and will be initiated during instance startup based on initialization parameters. Finally, a third set of processes are created to do server work on behalf of users who connect to the instance. One of these server processes is started for each user and is dedicated to performing work for that user until he disconnects from the database. These dedicated server processes are represented in Figure 3.6 with dashed boxes.

Required Processes

There are five required Oracle processes: DBWR, LGWR, PMON, SMON, and CKPT.

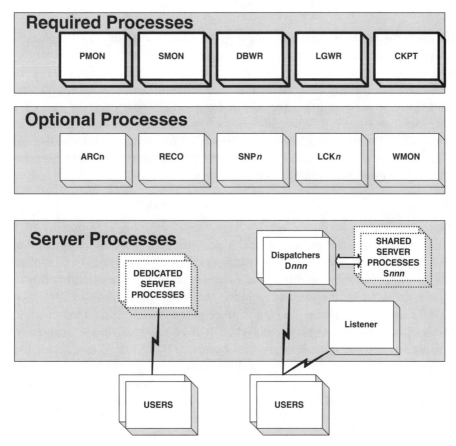

Figure 3.6 Oracle process architecture.

DBWR

The database writer process (DBWR) is responsible for writing modified data blocks from the database buffers of the SGA out to the database files.

In Oracle version 6 DBWR was the only process that ever wrote to the database files. As new features have been added in subsequent releases, some special exceptions to this rule have been made. When loading large volumes of data using SQL*Loader in direct path mode, the dedicated server process doing the load is allowed to directly write to an empty part of a database file. This feature is discussed in depth in Chapter 6, "Populating the Oracle Data Warehouse." INSERT statements in Oracle8 can also be performed in this same direct path mode. The other primary exception is the SORT_DIRECT_WRITES feature, added in release 7.3, which speeds sorting operations by allowing the dedicated server process to bypass the database buffers in the SGA when writing intermediate sort results to temporary storage. This capability is discussed as part of Sort Operations later in this chapter.

LGWR

LGWR, the redo log writer process, has responsibility for doing all writes to the online redo log files. Each time any user or program ends a transaction by issuing a COMMIT command, LGWR is awakened to write the accumulated contents of the redo log buffers out to the current redo log. Log writer is also signaled to begin writing log information out to disk whenever the redo log buffers reach one-third full. This can occur when large transactions do massive amounts of work with only infrequent COMMITs. Such batch jobs may be used in a data warehouse environment to load data into the database or to do summarization processing on that data after loading.

PMON

PMON, the Oracle process monitor, has the responsibility of cleaning up after failed user processes. Occasionally, a user process gets disconnected from its Oracle server processes due to an aborted program or a lost network connection. Any locks held by the user transaction and any data changes made prior to the failure are held by the server, awaiting a transaction-ending COMMIT or ROLLBACK statement. But because the user process is no longer connected, the transaction will never be completed. PMON recognizes these "orphaned" servers, connects to them temporarily, and issues a ROLLBACK command and then disconnects. This restores any modified data to its state prior to the start of the transaction and releases all locks and memory being held by the interrupted transaction. PMON tends to do relatively little work and spends most of its time waiting for a wake-up call to check for any failed servers.

SMON

SMON, the Oracle instance monitor, has several functions. Its primary job is to ensure the integrity of the database during instance startup. If the database had not been previously closed and the instance had not been shut down cleanly then there may have been change records placed in the redo logs whose actual data buffers were never written down to the database files. During the startup process, SMON checks the logs and the headers of the database files and then performs or coordinates the necessary recovery to ensure that any previously committed transactions are restored. Additionally, SMON has several other responsibilities, including cleanup of leftover temporary segments that are no longer needed and the coalescing of adjacent free extents.

CKPT

In Oracle8 the checkpoint process, CKPT, was optional and was initiated by the DBA through the CHECKPOINT_PROCESS initialization parameter. CKPT became one of the standard background processes in Oracle8*i*. When active, CKPT takes over some of the coordination and file header management duties that would otherwise be performed by LGWR during a checkpoint.

Optional Processes

In addition to the five required processes just discussed (DBWR, LGWR, PMON, SMON, and CKPT), there are several other processes that may be initiated as part of the startup of the Oracle instance. These optional processes are started depending on which options of the Oracle Server are in use and what the values of various initialization parameters are.

ARCn

The archiver processes, ARCn, are present only when the database is operating in archivelog mode. One (ARC1) is started automatically if the DBA has issued the ARCHIVE LOG START command. This is the normal method for invoking archiver, but the DBA may manually initiate the archiving of each redo log with other variations of the ARCHIVE LOG command. Only in very rare circumstances should a database be operated in *noarchivelog mode.*

In Oracle7 and Oracle8 there was only a single ARCH process, although the DBA could manually trick the database into starting another to keep up with a heavy archiving load. Oracle8*i* is able to automatically start multiple archiver processes whenever the workload warrants. The DBA sets the maximum number of archiver processes using the initialization parameter LOG_ARCHIVE_MAX_PROCESSES.

RECO

The recoverer process, RECO, is used only with distributed databases. RECO's function is to recover distributed transactions that might fail during the very brief span between phases of a two-phased commit process. The first phase of committing a distributed transaction ensures that every participating site is prepared to complete the commit. If all sites are prepared, then the second phase makes the transaction's changes permanent on all sites. Should one of the instances or the network fail between the prepare phase and the commit phase, the transaction at that site is left in the prepared state. After restarting the failed instance or recovering the connecting network, RECO resolves each pending transaction found in the prepared state by contacting its partner database to determine the final disposition (either committed or rolled back) of the transaction. It then commits or rolls back the local portion of the transaction to match the action taken at the transaction coordinator site. Distributed transactions are discussed in more depth in Chapter 12, "Distributing the Oracle Data Warehouse."

WMON

WMON, the wake-up monitor, is probably the most obscure of the background processes. It is seen on only a few operating system ports of Oracle. It aids in the wake-up signaling of the other Oracle background processes, which are designed to operate intermittently.

SNPn

The job queue processes, SNPn, are not intuitively named. This is for historical reasons. The Oracle8 Advanced Replication facility is a generalized capability that grew out of the Oracle7 snapshot replication feature. These processes are used by Oracle replication facilities to copy data changes from one database to another. These processes also execute any other scheduled jobs that have been submitted to the Oracle job queue maintained with the DBMS_JOB package. The Oracle8*i* materialized view feature builds on this queuing foundation.

LCKn

The Oracle Parallel Server lock processes, LCKn, coordinate the actions of multiple Oracle instances that have opened a single database using the Oracle Parallel Server option (n is an integer, from 0 to 9, used to uniquely identify each lock process that is part of an instance). The Oracle Parallel Server option is discussed briefly later in this chapter and then more completely in Chapter 11.

Dnnn

Multithreaded server dispatchers, Dnnn, are part of the Multi-Threaded Server (MTS) feature of the Oracle Server (nnn is a three-digit integer that uniquely names each dispatcher associated with the instance). This feature is discussed more fully under "Server Processes" in the next section. A user connected to an Oracle instance via MTS does not get a dedicated server to process his requests. Instead, the user commands are passed to a dispatch process to which the user remains connected. The dispatcher then passes the request to one of a pool of shared servers. The temporarily assigned server performs the requested work and then passes its response back to the same dispatcher, which then relays them back to the user. Each dispatcher handles the requests of several users.

Snnn

Shared servers, Snnn, are also a component of the MTS architecture. The next section on "Server Processes" discusses these processes in more depth.

Server Processes

The standard configuration for Oracle uses a *two-task* architecture. Each user session (or batch program) has a second task (or process) that starts automatically to perform its database work. On UNIX, the most popular operating system for large data warehouses, it is dangerous to let a user session or program connect directly to the SGA. Because the SGA is a shared resource, any program that connects to it could possibly corrupt data in the SGA that is needed by other users. To prevent this, the user session or program passes its requests (in SQL or PL/SQL) to a server process, which is running Oracle-provided code. The server process, connected to the SGA, performs the requested database operations and passes results back to the user process. This effectively insulates the critical SGA structures from any possible program bugs in user code. Normally these server processes are started for each user when the user connects to the database and remain dedicated to that user until the session is completed.

An alternative server architecture provided by Oracle is called the Multi-Threaded Server (MTS). When users connect to the database through MTS they do not receive a dedicated server. Instead, user requests are processed by a shared pool of server processes. MTS is useful for situations where a large number of users need to be connected simultaneously, but each has relatively infrequent interaction with the database. This commonly occurs with OLTP systems that might support thousands of connected users doing data entry into online screens. The user might take a few seconds to enter data into a screen field and then a very quick validation query might be programmed to occur. Only when several fields have been entered is the data submitted to the database for insertion. The database might be actively in use for only a small percentage of the total time the user is connected. MTS is designed to allow the server to be working for many other users in the interim.

MTS is rarely used with data warehouses, however, for at least three reasons. First, data warehouses usually have far fewer simultaneously connected users than the number needed for MTS to become useful. The additional process overhead of dedicated servers for 50 or even 100 users is negligible on the large computer systems typically used for data warehousing. MTS is even less useful for the dozens of users who typically might be interacting with a data mart on a smaller UNIX or NT server. Second, the server usage pattern of data warehouse users is not uniform as in the OLTP example given earlier. Typically, the warehouse analyst will spend many minutes composing a query that may then take many seconds, minutes, or sometimes hours to complete. This pattern doesn't fit well with the MTS load-balancing paradigm. Third, passing large amounts of data back from the shared server to the user takes longer than doing so from a dedicated server. Warehouse users may frequently issue queries that retrieve large result sets. The extra work performed in returning the data might nullify whatever process relief MTS provided.

SINGLE TASK

In some operating systems, such as Digital Equipment Corporation's OpenVMS, this high level of isolation can be provided within a single process. In this environment, Oracle can be run in single-task mode, and no additional server process is required. It is possible to link programs as single-task in the UNIX environment, but this exposes the shared SGA to corruption by program code, which might inadvertently address into the Oracle server code. Therefore, with the single exception of Oracle-provided utilities such as IMP, this approach is never recommended.

Oracle Server: Internal Architecture

Many structures internal to the Oracle database do not correspond directly to the physical database file structure. The organization of these structures cannot be seen except from within the database. These structures include tablespaces, segments, and extents and are shown in Figure 3.7. Each database typically has several tablespaces. Each tablespace holds one or more segments. Each segment is made up of at least one extent. Each extent is a contiguous set of database blocks.

Several types of segments exist, including tables and indexes as well as more specialized segments used for system functions. The data dictionary is a special set of tables, clusters, indexes, and views that provide the means for observing the rest of the internal structure of the database.

Tablespaces

Since the introduction of Oracle version 6, the *tablespace* has been the fundamental unit of Oracle database object storage, backup and recovery, and other administrative functions. Whenever an object that requires storage is created, it must be created within a currently available tablespace. Whenever the database administrator performs on online ("hot") backup, it is done for an entire tablespace at a time. If a database file is lost because of a disk problem, the entire tablespace is unavailable until the problem is resolved.

A tablespace is the link between the physical files observable at the operating system level and all the logical database objects (such as tables and

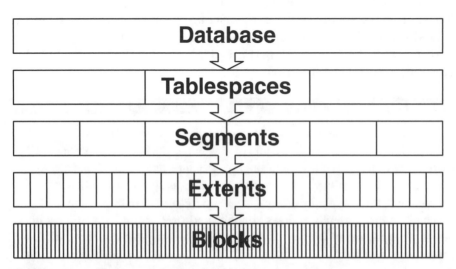

Figure 3.7 Oracle internal database architecture.

indexes) that are visible only from within the Oracle environment. Each tablespace consists of one or more operating system files that, in total, define the size of the tablespace. A tablespace is created using the CREATE TABLESPACE command. When the tablespace is created (or enlarged through the ALTER TABLESPACE . . . ADD DATAFILE command) the space from the database file on disk is immediately allocated to that tablespace and cannot be used for any other purpose.

The following example shows the SQL statement for creating a tablespace called USER_DATA in a Windows NT environment, which uses a single 100-megabyte file. Oracle takes over the 100 megabytes, which are then considered freespace in the USER_DATA tablespace. By querying the dictionary view DBA_FREE _SPACE, as shown in the following example, we see that this space is now available. When an object is created in the tablespace, the amount of freespace is reduced by the object's size.

```
SQL> CREATE TABLESPACE USER_DATA
  2    DATAFILE 'H:\ ORADATA\ DWP1\ USER_DATA_01.DBF' SIZE 100M
  3    DEFAULT STORAGE
  4      (INITIAL      1M
  5       NEXT         1M
  6       PCTINCREASE 0)
  7  /

Tablespace created.

SQL> SELECT SUM(BYTES)
  2    FROM DBA_FREE_SPACE
  3    WHERE TABLESPACE_NAME = 'USER_DATA'
  4  /

SUM(BYTES)
---------
104855552

1 row selected.

SQL> CREATE TABLE TEST_TABLE
  2    (CUST_ID         NUMBER(6,0),
  3     CUST_NAME       VARCHAR2(30),
  4     REP_ID          NUMBER(5,0))
  5     TABLESPACE      USER_DATA
  6     STORAGE
  7      (INITIAL      1M
  8       NEXT         1M
  9       PCTINCREASE 0)
 10  /

Table created.
```

```
SQL> SELECT SUM(BYTES)
  2    FROM DBA_FREE_SPACE
  3    WHERE TABLESPACE_NAME = 'USER_DATA'
  4  /

SUM(BYTES)
---------
103800832
```

WHY DOESN'T THE INITIAL FREESPACE EQUAL 100 MB?

The actual initial freespace, 103,800,832 bytes, is 2,048 bytes (the size of one Oracle block on this example database), smaller than the actual 100 megabytes allocated in USER_DATA_01.DBF. This block contains the file header and cannot be used to store user-created database objects.

Every Oracle database must have at least one tablespace, named SYSTEM. Occasionally, inexperienced Oracle administrators will not create additional tablespaces and will place all the application tables and indexes within the SYSTEM tablespace. For a small database that resides entirely on one or two disks this may not present any problems. Typically, however, the large database will occupy multiple disk drives, and the administrator must take more explicit control of where database objects get stored. This is done by creating multiple tablespaces and then creating specific objects in appropriate tablespaces. Objects are assigned to tablespaces either to group certain objects together or, more commonly, to separate specific objects and keep tablespaces to a manageable size.

Read-Only Tablespaces

Starting with Oracle8, the DBA may elect to make a particular tablespace *read-only* using the ALTER TABLESPACE command. Once a tablespace is converted to read-only status, Oracle8 will allow no changes to be made to the underlying data files. Even file headers, normally updated at every checkpoint, will be untouched.

This new feature is of particular interest in data warehousing applications. Because the datafiles of a read-only tablespace do not change, they do not need to be repeatedly backed up. A single backup of the files made immediately after the tablespace is altered to read-only status will protect those files from loss for as long as the tablespace remains read-only. The warehouse's emphasis on maintaining historical perspective of data is easily adapted to this feature, especially when combined with partitioning of large tables and indexes.

Transportable Tablespaces

In Oracle8*i*, the concept of read-only tablespaces was extended to provide the capability of easily copying data of one database to another database. In all prior releases, such a transfer would have required either unloading the data and reloading it in the new database or transferring the data using database links and SQL*Net. Neither of these options is ideally suited to very large data sets because they must process each row, one at a time. A million-row table will require 1,000 times more processing than a thousand-row table.

Transportable tablespaces, on the other hand, allow for the transfer of the actual data files that make up a tablespace. Now transferring a million-row table can be performed in only a few seconds more than a thousand row table!

To utilize this feature, the DBA must export the meta data about the tablespace's contents from the data dictionary but not the contents themselves. The export file is transferred along with copies of the actual datafiles, and the small amount of meta data is then imported into the new database. Now that database's data dictionary has all of the necessary information to access the contents of its new tablespace.

There are some restrictions, however, in the use of transportable tablespaces. Chief among these is that the datafiles may not be transferred between different operating systems. The Oracle file format is not universal, and HP-UX files are not identical to Solaris or NT files. The other restriction of note is that the contents of a transportable tablespace must be complete tables or indexes, not individual partitions of a partitioned object that also has partitions in other tablespaces.

Uses of this feature, particularly to support dependent data marts, are discussed in Chapter 12.

Locally Managed Tablespaces

Oracle8*i* also has a new method of tracking the various extents, both free and used, within a tablespace. While the default, dictionary managed, is the same as in previous releases, the DBA may specify EXTENT MANAGEMENT LOCAL when creating a tablespace. Instead of maintaining a row within the data dictionary tables for each extent, Oracle creates a bitmap as part of the header information for each file in the tablespace. As extents are allocated or freed, these bitmaps are locally manipulated to track where freespace in the tablespace can be found.

This reduces the amount of recursive SQL (SQL that is generated by Oracle to access the data dictionary in order to perform a user's request) necessary when objects are created, extended, or dropped. In most warehouses with proper storage parameters for database objects, this type of recursive SQL is rarely a burden.

If the nature of your particular warehouse is for many of the users to frequently create and drop objects of their own (perhaps for intermediate results of one query to be used in another query), then there may be value in letting them build those objects in a locally managed tablespace. In many cases, though, this type of private storage requirement may be handled using Oracle8*i*'s temporary table feature instead.

Optimal Flexible Architecture (OFA)

Several years ago, Cary Millsap, formerly head of Oracle Consulting Services' System Performance Group, published a white paper on an Optimal Flexible Architecture (OFA) for Oracle version 6 databases. The paper has been updated several times over the years to account for new releases and adapt to the issues raised by the ever larger databases being maintained in Oracle. The concepts of OFA have been included in the Oracle product documentation. Beginning with Oracle7 release 7.3, they have also been incorporated into the Oracle Installer product so that the "default" database optionally created as part of installing the Oracle RDBMS will follow the guidelines of OFA.

OFA deals with many database configuration issues beside tablespaces, but effective decisions about tablespaces and their assigned objects are one of its key principles. The goal of the OFA recommendations for tablespace assignment is to be able to characterize each tablespace with respect to segment growth patterns (and fragmentation), administrative requirements, and I/O loads. Segments with short life spans (such as temporary segments that are dynamically created and destroyed) should never be placed in the same tablespaces as permanent objects. Objects (tables, partitions, or indexes) that are to have data added or modified should not be located in tablespaces with static, read-only tables. Tables that are frequently scanned should not be placed in the same tablespace with objects that are normally accessed in a random manner. Objects expected to have high I/O demands should be separated from those that will not be accessed frequently.

The updated OFA paper and many other excellent white papers are available for public download from www.orapub.com. We highly recommend that this paper be reviewed before you install Oracle8*i* and create the warehouse database.

Segments

Each database object that requires space for its storage will be created in a specific tablespace. Tables and indexes are the most common database objects of this type, although the DBA will have to make arrangements for other specialized objects. Oracle's term for these created objects is *segments*. Using the same example as in the discussion on tablespaces, we can query the data dictionary to find out information about segments stored within our USER_DATA tablespace.

```
SQL> SELECT SEGMENT_NAME, OWNER, SEGMENT_TYPE, BYTES
  2    FROM DBA_SEGMENTS
  3    WHERE TABLESPACE_NAME = 'USER_DATA'
  4  /

SEGMENT_NAME OWNER    SEGMENT_TYPE        BYTES
------------ ------   ------------        ---------
TEST_TABLE   GDODGE   TABLE               1,054,720
```

We see that the table we created in the earlier example is the only segment in USER_DATA.

In addition to the basic tables, clusters, indexes, and specialty segments (rollback and temporary) found in Oracle7, Oracle8 added some new variations. An Oracle8 partitioned table consists of multiple segments—each partition of the table is stored as a separate segment. Also, a new hybrid structure, the index-organized table, was introduced in Oracle8 that combines the data storage of a table with the hierarchical organization of an index.

Oracle8*i* also adds the ability to create temporary tables (and temporary indexes) that are automatically cleaned up at the end of the session in which they are created. These are discussed a little later in this chapter.

WHY ISN'T THE SEGMENT EXACTLY 1 MB?

The segment is 1,054,720 bytes in size, slightly larger than the 1 megabyte we specified when we created it. To avoid small fragments of freespace, Oracle may round up the requested size of an object by as much as five blocks.

Tables

Tables are the type of segment most easily recognized by users of the data warehouse. They are where the warehouse data is actually stored. When the analyst wishes to see information about customers, he will issue a SQL SELECT statement against the CUSTOMERS table. To see information about which products have standard prices at least 50 percent higher than their cost, he would probably need to query the PRODUCTS table.

When the DBA creates a table, both the logical structure (column definitions) and physical structure (tablespace name, storage parameters) are defined. Setting these properly before loading data makes the future life of the DBA much easier; it is generally an unpleasant situation when the DBA finds that a 20-gigabyte table has to be reorganized because a storage parameter was incorrectly defined! Oracle7 v7.3 introduced the ALTER INDEX . . . REBUILD command to rebuild and reorganize indexes, while Oracle8*i* introduces the ALTER TABLE . . . MOVE command to rebuild and reorganize tables. However, the best solution to the table reorganization problem is to avoid having to do reorganizations. In Chapter 5, "Building the Oracle Data Warehouse," we discuss effective space management techniques that can eliminate the need for table reorganization.

Partitioned Tables

A new specialized type of table, introduced in Oracle8, is the partitioned table. Data warehouse tables frequently hold millions of rows and may require many gigabytes to store. Managing segments of this size can be a particular burden on the warehouse DBA. An Oracle8 table may be created with multiple partitions. Each partition is defined to contain a particular subset of the total table's rows. Values in any column (or columns) can be used to do the partitioning, but in most cases data warehouse tables are partitioned by some date field. This allows a partition to be loaded as one month (or other period) and then have its tablespace converted to read-only status. When a partition's data is sufficiently old, the entire partition can be archived or purged easily. Each partition is also defined independently with respect to its tablespace location and storage parameters. Each partition can be independently administered, which makes the total management task more manageable. Partitioning is discussed in more depth in Chapter 5.

As Oracle databases have gotten larger over the years, administration requirements for these databases have increased. Particularly in data warehousing applications we see the need for tables of millions or even billions of rows. A billion-row table that has a million rows added to it during a periodic refresh of the warehouse requires a backup of the entire tablespace in which it resides. This leads to major problems in having to back up an entire terabyte warehouse even though only a few gigabytes of data may have actually been loaded.

Oracle8 provided a means for reducing this unnecessary administrative burden. Instead of loading all billion rows into a single table in a single tablespace, the warehouse designer may now elect to create the table with multiple pieces (*partitions*) that can be individually sized and placed into separate tablespaces. Figure 3.8 illustrates this capability. In the unpartitioned table, rows from various months' orders are potentially intermingled. This makes one large object to administer and negatively affects performance for queries that include a specification of the order date. It also greatly complicates the task of removing the oldest month's orders if a rolling window of only the most recent 12 months' data is to be maintained online.

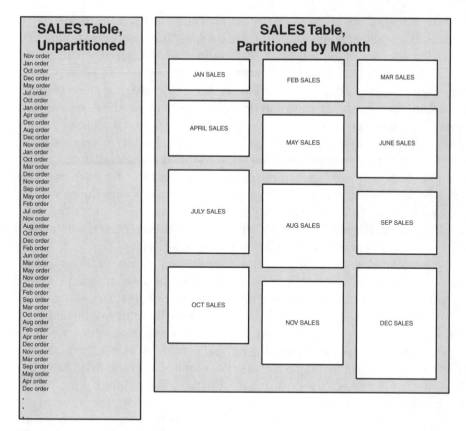

Figure 3.8 Partitioned table.

Although there are significant performance benefits to partitioning a large table, the primary advantages are for simplified administration and maintenance. Even though partitioning is an additional cost option to the Oracle8*i* Enterprise Edition Server, it is an absolute necessity for any serious data warehouse project. This is the only place throughout this book where a particular option is recommended as a mandatory addition to database licensing. Other options (discussed at the end of this chapter) may be beneficial in particular situations, but they aren't universally used to the same degree as partitioning.

More detailed information on how to use partitioning is covered in many subsequent chapters of this book.

Temporary Tables

It is common for an application to need to save the results of one query temporarily for use later in the transaction or session. These results, typically, then need to be cleaned up at the end of the user's session. Prior to Oracle8*i*, the DBA would grant each user the CREATE TABLE privilege and give the user disk quota in a permanent tablespace. Of course, special routines would also have to be created to handle cleanup of any of these tables that didn't get dropped by the creating user for some reason. Users could, if they desired, create these tables with any storage parameters. Storage management could be very complex in some of these situations. Additionally, in cases where hundreds of users might be simultaneously creating and dropping these tables, the overhead and contention of these operations can become a bottleneck to scalability.

Enter Oracle8*i* *temporary tables*. To be perfectly descriptive, these temporary tables are not actually tables in the way described in the earlier section on tables. Rather than create (and later drop) one physical table for each user, the space used for those users' temporary tables is allocated within the extents of a temporary segment similar to the way sort space is allocated when needed by a user. Even though the table name will appear in the USER_TABLES dictionary view, it will not appear when looking at USER_SEGMENTS.

Unlike normal tables, temporary tables do not allocate space at the time they are defined. The allocation of space occurs when the user transaction first inserts a row into the temporary table. From that point on, the user may do normal SQL DML processing, and, as needed, additional extents will be added to hold the data. Because the data stored by a particular session is not available for other sessions to see or change, the normal overhead of maintaining transaction integrity through locking of rows is not required for temporary tables.

When the user creates a temporary table, the table is defined as either transaction specific or session specific. *Transaction specific* means that rows in the temporary table are removed whenever the user completes a transaction with COMMIT or ROLLBACK. This is the default behavior. *Session specific* indicates that the rows will be removed when the user's session ends. Session-specific behavior is designated by adding the ON COMMIT PRESERVE ROWS clause to the CREATE GLOBAL TEMPORARY TABLE command.

These tables may be indexed, however, when retrieval requirements make this a performance aid. It is also possible to define views that reference temporary tables and even join them to permanent tables where this is useful. If desired, multiple users may use a single temporary table, but the data inserted by one user session will never be visible to another session. Each user's data will be stored in separate extents, so that if five users have each inserted one row, then looking at DBA_EXTENTS will show five extents allocated. When the user completes the transaction (or session) the extent will be automatically released.

A few restrictions, however, on the use of temporary tables should be considered as part of the decision to use this feature. Temporary tables may not be partitioned, index-organized, clustered, or replicated, and they may not have referential integrity constraints defined. Also, the data rows within a temporary table cannot be exported although the definition of a temporary table can. None of these restrictions is likely to be a problem with temporary tables when used in the intended manner. However, two other important facilities, parallel query and SQL*Loader, are not supported for use with temporary tables. These could be severe limitations if very large temporary tables are envisioned.

Indexes

Users of the data warehouse generally are not concerned about the names or location of index segments. Unless they are including optimizer hints in their queries, they never need to specify anything about indexes. The DBA, however, is responsible for determining which tables should have indexes on specific columns to help queries execute faster. An index allows Oracle to rapidly find specific rows in a table when a query includes conditions that limit the requested rows. As an example, the following query wishes to retrieve only those customers whose address is in the primary zip code assigned to downtown Denver:

```
SELECT CUST_ID, CUST_NAME
  FROM CUSTOMERS
 WHERE ZIPCODE = 80202;
```

If we have a million customers, but only 1,500 are in downtown Denver, then an index on the column called ZIPCODE would allow this query to execute very quickly. Without the index, Oracle would have to examine each of the million rows in the CUSTOMER table and test the value of ZIPCODE to see if it equals 80202. The relative performance gain from using the index is determined by several factors, including the size of the table, the percentage of the total number of rows that need to be found, and how the rows are distributed in the table. Deciding where indexes will be useful is one of the primary responsibilities of the DBA and is examined in the next chapter. In general, however, data warehouses tend to have more indexes per table than most OLTP systems because of the wide variety of selection criteria used in data warehouse queries.

B*Tree Indexes

Oracle provides two types of indexes. The first is based on a balanced B*Tree structure that is processed hierarchically to find the values of interest. Figure 3.9 represents a small B*Tree index. If a query wants to find information about product number 21694, Oracle will have to first read the top block of the hierarchy (called the "root" block) to determine which of the second-level blocks to read next. Reading the appropriate block from the second-level block determines which third-level block to read. In this small example, the third level is the last (known as the leaf nodes) and will contain the ROWIDs (addresses) of the actual data block that contains the data we want to see. Oracle will then retrieve the specific data block and present us with our answer. This allowed us to find the data for product number 21694 with a total of four logical block

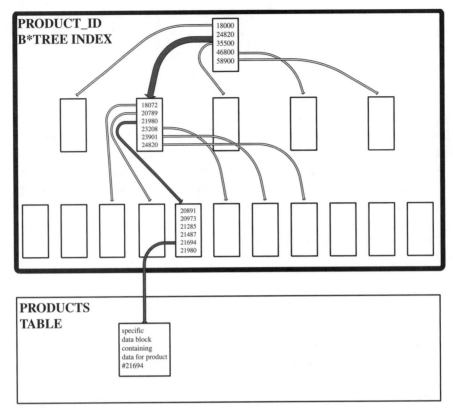

PRODUCT_ID
B*TREE INDEX

PRODUCTS
TABLE

Figure 3.9   B*Tree index.

reads—three in the index and one in the table. This access path would be particularly efficient compared to reading the hundreds of data blocks that might make up the entire PRODUCTS table.

Two varieties of B*Tree indexes are available in Oracle. A unique index allows at most one data row to contain any particular value. This is how Oracle enforces *unique* or *primary key* constraints. These constraints are useful for preventing the corruption of an OLTP database, which would occur if someone were able to enter two employees with the same employee number or two customers with the same customer identifier value. The DBA would typically define the PRODUCT_ID column of the PRODUCTS table with the primary key constraint to ensure that no duplicate customer IDs would ever be allowed in the table. The example shown in Figure 3.9 appears (from the limited data shown) to be a unique index.

The other type of B*Tree index, nonunique, is created by the CREATE INDEX command. In a nonunique B*Tree index, multiple pointers to data rows are allowed for any particular value. This type of index would be appropriate for indexing the CUST_ID column of the ORDERS table where it is reasonable (and desired!) that a given customer would place multiple orders. Retrieving all of a customer's orders quickly could be facilitated by creating this nonunique index. Generally, nonunique indexes will speed query processing whenever a small percentage of the total rows needs to be retrieved. Building a B*Tree index on a very nonselective column (such as the SEX_CODE of the EMPLOYEES table) is generally of little value because it is likely that finding all the women or all the men would involve reading every data block anyway. Simply reading the blocks sequentially (doing a full table scan) would be more efficient than using the index.

Reverse Key Index

Oracle8 introduced a new variation on the B*Tree index structure. An Oracle8 reverse key index uses the same B*Tree structure, but it reverses the order of the data bytes when building the index. This helps randomize where an entry to the index needs to be made. This can be particularly helpful when indexing a column whose new values are constantly increasing while the oldest values are being regularly purged. A normal B*Tree index will have new values always added at the right side of the index structure but will never reuse the space being emptied by the deletes occurring on the left side of the structure. In the reverse key index, inserted rows and deleted rows can be equally dispersed across the entire width of the index structure. The ability to do index range scans, however, is sacrificed in reverse key indexes because contiguous data values will not be stored adjacently in the index; value "1234" will be stored with the "4"s, and "1235" will be stored with the "5"s. As long as the search is for the specific value "1234" then this style of index works equivalently to a standard B*Tree index. Only for queries that request a range of values (such as BETWEEN "1200" and "1250") is the reverse key index unusable.

Bitmap Indexes

The second type of index structure provided by Oracle is a bitmap index. This type of index was introduced to the Oracle7 product with release 7.3. Bitmap indexes are particularly useful in situations where traditional B*Tree indexes are useless—when we have a large number of rows but only a small number of distinct values. Figure 3.10 shows a logical layout of the organization of bitmap indexes. For each distinct value in the indexed column, a bitmap contains one bit corresponding to each row in the indexed table. When we examine all the bitmaps associated with the values bitmap index we find that each row will be represented in only a single bitmap with a 1 and in all others by a 0.

Physically, the bitmap index is identical in hierarchical structure to a B*Tree index except in the layout of the leaf nodes. Where a B*Tree index stores the ROWID pointer to each data row with a particular data value, the bitmap index contains a bitmap that includes one bit corresponding to each row in a

EMPLOYEE TABLE

EMPID	EMPL NAME	SEX	STATUS	DEPT	JOB_TITLE
1234	Foley	Male	Full	Mrktng	Clerk
1397	Pass	Male	Part	Manuf	Assembler
8372	Simpson	Male	Full	Shippng	Manager
3875	Tai	Male	Part	Mrktng	Clerk
9736	Birk	Female	Full	Sales	Sales Rep
6430	Stack	Male	Full	Shippng	Clerk
8757	Livingston	Male	Part	Mrktng	Brand Mgr
8876	Fosnight	Male	Full	Shippng	Clerk
3732	Parker	Male	Full	Manuf	Assembler
3309	Melgaard	Male	Full	Sales	Manager
9393	Johnson	Male	Part	Manuf	Assembler
3984	McConahay	Female	Part	Manuf	Assembler
3857	Shouldice	Female	Full	Sales	Sales Rep
8439	Bush	Female	Part	Mrktng	Brand Mgr
9496	Wikstrom	Femail	Full	Manuf	Manager
7495	Windle	Male	Part	Sales	Clerk

BITMAP INDEX ON "DEPT" column of EMPLOYEE TABLE

EMPLID	"Manuf"	"Mrktng"	"Sales"	"Shipng"
1234	0	1	0	0
1397	1	0	0	0
8372	0	0	0	1
3875	0	1	0	0
9736	0	0	1	0
6430	0	0	0	1
8757	0	1	0	0
8876	0	0	0	1
3732	1	0	0	0
3309	0	0	1	0
9393	1	0	0	0
3984	1	0	0	0
3857	0	0	1	0
8439	0	1	0	0
9496	1	0	0	0
7495	0	0	1	0

BITMAP INDEX ON "SEX" column of EMPLOYEE TABLE

EMPID	"Male"	"Female"
1234	1	0
1397	1	0
8372	1	0
3875	1	0
9736	0	1
6430	1	0
8757	1	0
8876	1	0
3732	1	0
3309	1	0
9393	1	0
3984	0	1
3857	0	1
8439	0	1
9496	1	1
7495	1	0

BITMAP INDEX ON "STATUS" column of EMPLOYEE TABLE

EMPID	"Full"	"Part"
1234	1	0
1397	0	1
8372	1	0
3875	0	1
9736	1	0
6430	1	0
8757	0	1
8876	1	0
3732	1	0
3309	1	0
9393	0	1
3984	0	1
3857	1	0
8439	0	1
9496	1	0
7495	0	1

BITMAP INDEX ON "JOB TITLE" column of EMPLOYEE TABLE

EMPLID	"Assembler"	"Brand Mgr"	"Clerk"	"Manager"	"Sales Rep"
1234	0	0	1	0	0
1397	1	0	0	0	0
8372	0	0	0	1	0
3875	0	0	1	0	0
9736	0	0	0	0	1
6430	0	0	1	0	0
8757	0	1	0	0	0
8876	0	0	1	0	0
3732	1	0	0	0	0
3309	0	0	0	1	0
9393	1	0	0	0	0
3984	1	0	0	0	0
3857	0	0	0	0	1
8439	0	1	0	0	0
9496	0	0	0	1	0
7495	0	0	1	0	0

Figure 3.10   Bitmap index.

contiguous range of data rows in the table. (Multiple ranges of contiguous blocks, such as from multiple table extents, will each be represented by a separate bitmap entry in the index.) Each row will be represented with a 1 if that row has this particular value or by a 0 if it doesn't. Oracle performs compression on the bitmap strings so that a long series of zeros (as may frequently be expected) can be stored in less space than the actual string would require.

The SEX column of the EMPLOYEES table in Figure 3.10 is a perfect example of a candidate for bitmap indexing. There are only two values across our entire list of employees, so only two bitmap strings need to be created. If we also build bitmap indexes on other columns within the same table (such as STATUS, which includes only two values, DEPT and JOB_TITLE, each having only a small set of allowable values), then Oracle can very efficiently combine the information in these four bitmap indexes to answer questions such as "How many part-time, male clerks are employed in the marketing department?" Bitmap indexes provide an excellent component, therefore, in the complete data warehouse solution. Figure 3.11 demonstrates Oracle's use of these four bitmap indexes to quickly answer this question. Queries of this type, which

How many part-time, male clerks are employed in the marketing department?

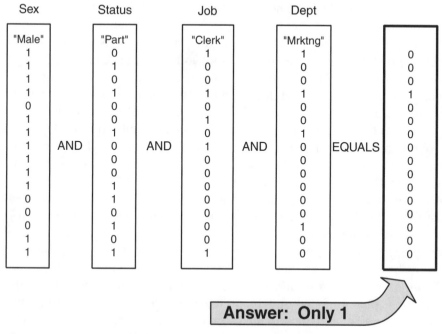

Figure 3.11 Using multiple bitmap indexes to satisfy a query.

look for the highly selective intersection of several criteria that are individually very nonselective, are commonly used in decision-support queries.

Doing this type of "AND" (as well as the similar "OR") processing between the equal-length bitmaps is extremely fast. Performing the next step, if the query requires it, of looking up the actual data rows is done using a normal ROWID lookup into the table. As we'll see in Chapter 4, "Designing the Oracle Data Warehouse," and Chapter 5, "Building the Oracle Data Warehouse," we'll exploit this feature of bitmap indexes to quickly access rows in the central fact table in an Oracle8 star query. (Oracle7 performed star queries but required a concatenated B*Tree index and cannot use the more effective and efficient bitmap indexes for this purpose.)

Function-Based Indexes

Indexes in Oracle8 and previous releases are based on the data stored in one or more columns of the indexed table. Searches that specify values in those columns can often be optimized using the index in order to identify the rows that meet the query criteria. When a query is based on a calculation or function of the stored data, such as the uppercase of a column called NAME, the index cannot be used. If this were a frequent type of query, then the database designer might be forced to create a new column that stores the UPPER(NAME). Then an index can be created on the new column to facilitate this type of query. Of course, there is a major disadvantage in that the new column requires additional storage in every row equal to the length of the existing NAME column.

Oracle8*i* provides a new type of index that solves this problem. If you need to optimize a set of queries that apply a function or calculation on one or more columns, you may now create an index on the functional value without having to store the results of the calculation in the table. The calculation can be very simple, such as the sum of two columns. It is also possible to base the index on more complex logic written into a stored PL/SQL function. These custom-written functions must be deterministic. That is, the function must be guaranteed to return the same value whenever it is called. Building a function that calculates age, for instance, by subtracting BIRTHDATE from the current system date would not be deterministic because it gives a different value if you invoke it on two different days.

Like other new features in Oracle, function-based indexes are available only to the cost-based optimizer (discussed later in this chapter). The older rule-based optimizer is unable to utilize function-based indexes when determining the best access plan for a SQL statement. It is important for the DBA to ensure that up-to-date statistics are maintained about the index by regularly running an ANALYZE of the table whenever new data is added that is likely to alter the distribution of data from the function.

Partitioned Indexes

Oracle8 allows indexes, just like tables, to be partitioned into multiple segments. This is generally done to make each segment smaller and more manageable. Partitioned indexes may be either locally partitioned or globally partitioned. A *local index* is partitioned on the same basis as the underlying partitioned table. Another way to say this is that every ROWID pointer in a partition of a local index will point to a row in the corresponding table partition. A *global index* is either not partitioned or else is partitioned on some other basis. Hence, pointers from one partition may be directed to any of the partitions of the table. The primary disadvantage to global indexes is that the entire index must be rebuilt whenever partitions are added to (or dropped from) the underlying partitioned table. Local indexes are automatically maintained by Oracle8 when partition maintenance is performed on the table.

More information on the creation and use of partitioned indexes is presented in Chapter 5.

Index-Organized Tables

Oracle8 introduced a new type of segment called an index-organized table. This structure is a hybrid between a table and a B*Tree index. An index-organized table is a table and is created by including the ORGANIZATION INDEX clause on a CREATE TABLE statement. It contains all the data columns defined for the table. The data in the table is stored inside a B*Tree index structure. By using the hierarchical search facility inherent in the hierarchical index structure and then storing all the data in that structure, Oracle can optimize retrieval of table data by primary key values. This is in contrast to a normal B*Tree index that would store the key data and also a ROWID pointer, which Oracle would use to look up the rest of the data in the separate table segment.

ROWIDS

Traditionally Oracle has used a physical *ROWID* to uniquely identify each row in an Oracle database. Physical ROWIDs combine an identification of the data file, the block within that data file, and the relative row within that block. This ROWID is used primarily as the pointer to the row in each index for the table. In Oracle8*i* the idea of a logical ROWID is introduced to allow unique identification of rows within index-organized tables.

The index-organized table does not assign a physical ROWID to each row of the data because a row is not constrained to live within a single data block, as would be the case in a normal table. A data block of a B*tree index (and therefore an index-organized table) may need to be split to accommodate new row insertions.

Not storing a physical ROWID in a separate index saves a little bit of storage for each row (6 bytes in Oracle7, either 6 or 10 bytes in Oracle8). Also, the primary key data is also just stored once in the index-organized table instead of twice (once in an index and again in the table), which saves some more storage space. The total space savings can be significant when the primary key data makes up a large percentage of the total data row length.

Additionally, if saving space is a major concern, especially when the primary key is defined over many columns, the DBA may optionally request that the key structure be compressed. In this case, values in a specified number of leading columns of the key that do not change between one row and the next will not have to be physically repeated in the second row. This feature is generally avoided in OLTP systems where there is frequent insertion and deletion of rows, but in the warehouse where row data is generally very stable over time, this is a valuable option to consider if an index-organized table with complex primary keys is to be built.

The retrieval speed and storage space advantages of index-organized tables can be significant. There are also disadvantages to index-organized tables that make them generally of more use in transaction processing applications than in data warehousing. The index-organized table is highly optimized to benefit lookups of data based on primary key (either by equality lookup or by range scan), but other secondary forms of access are more restricted.

Specifically, because no physical ROWID is assigned to each data row of an index-organized table, it is not possible in Oracle8 to build additional indexes on an index-organized table. Oracle8*i* does provide this capability through the use of new logical ROWIDs, based on the primary key of the row. This allows for the creation of additional indexes on an index-organized table in Oracle8*i*.

When initially introduced in Oracle8, index-organized tables could not be partitioned, but range-based partitioning (on one or more of the primary key columns) is allowed in Oracle8*i*. Additional restrictions in both Oracle8 and Oracle8*i* are that index-organized tables cannot be either clustered or replicated.

Clusters

Oracle provides a means, called a *cluster*, for physically organizing data from one or more tables based on the values of a particular column or set of columns. The *cluster key* is the data shared by the various rows that are to be stored together. Typically, the cluster key is the primary key of one table and the associated foreign key column(s) from other tables. The cluster key will be used to determine where each newly inserted row gets placed.

This physical organization may, on first examination, seem like a violation of a basic axiom of relational database—that row order is not important. Clusters, however, should be simply considered a physical access optimization similar to indexing. SQL access to each table remains unchanged, and users and programmers do not need to modify their code because of clustering. As an example, Figure 3.12 shows all the sales order data for a particular customer as physically stored in the same block.

ORDER_ID was defined as the cluster key, and a cluster index was built on this key. Data from both the ORDERS and ORDER_LINES tables is then sorted so that everything about order number 1234 can be found in a single data block. This can provide exceptional performance in some OLTP systems that commonly need to retrieve all this information or perform joins on ORDER_HEADERS rows and their associated ORDER_LINES entries. The DBA needs to determine how much total storage will be needed for all the data about an order. This SIZE parameter (part of the CREATE CLUSTER command) will determine how many ORDER rows (and associated ORDER_LINE data) will be stored in each block.

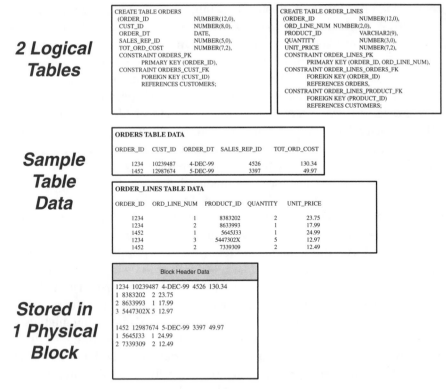

Figure 3.12   A block of an index cluster in which related data from two tables are physically stored together.

There is some benefit from reduced storage requirements as well because the cluster key data needs to be stored only once instead of in each row. For very long key values this savings can be significant.

A second type of cluster, called a hash cluster, was introduced with Oracle7. In this type of structure, rows are organized by applying a hash algorithm to the value of the cluster key and then calculating the relative block address within the total set of blocks allocated to the cluster. No index is required to determine where to insert (or later retrieve) all the rows that have a particular cluster key value. This makes lookups based on the value of the cluster key very fast, but only equality searches can be performed. This occurs because rows with "adjacent" key values may be hashed into data blocks anywhere in the cluster, so no range scans (where we wish to find all matches for a range of values rather than for one specific value) can be performed unless an index is also created on the same column(s) as the hash cluster key.

Both types of clusters are useful in very specific situations in which one type of data access needs to be optimized. Other forms of access are, unfortunately, compromised in either type of cluster. Full table scans, in particular, suffer in both cases. The nature of data warehouse processing is so varied that it is generally impossible to predict that one particular type of access to a table should be optimized to the detriment of all other forms of access. Full table scans (especially when Oracle Parallel Query is used) are common within the data warehouse environment. Clusters, however, typically spread data out over more data blocks so that a full table scan has to read more blocks to find all the rows. This is particularly true with hash clusters, which must be initially created with enough blocks to store the projected maximum number of rows. The first row inserted into a hash cluster table is equally likely to be inserted into the last physical block or the first. This means that every full table scan of a hash cluster may have to read a large number of empty blocks.

For this reason, clusters are rarely, if ever, used in the design of a data warehouse. In very specific cases, a DBA who is familiar with clusters and the many trade-offs involved with them might find a way to incorporate one into a warehouse design. Dave Ensor, formerly of Oracle's consultancy in the United Kingdom, provided the best advice on the use of clusters: "Used properly, a cluster might provide a 10 percent performance boost for one out of a hundred situations; in the other 99 cases, however, the improper use of clustering might easily cause a severalfold performance degradation!" His comments were primarily directed to OLTP configurations. The data warehousing scenario, where flexibility and overall throughput are generally of greater importance than the performance of any single query, is even less encouraging.

Rollback Segments

Rollback segments are Oracle's structure for keeping track of *undo* information—the "before" image of data prior to a transaction's modifications. Should the transaction end with a ROLLBACK statement or have to be undone because of a transaction failure, the information stored in the rollback segment is sufficient to restore all the data to its condition before the transaction started. Should a transaction end with a COMMIT statement, then the undo information is no longer required and that portion of the rollback segment is marked as available for use by another transaction.

Rollback segment information is also used by Oracle to provide *read consistency* across multiple transactions. Read consistency is needed when a transaction wishes to look at a block that has been modified but not yet committed by a second transaction. Rather than allow the transaction to see the uncommitted changes (which are not yet completely finished and which may be rolled back), Oracle uses undo information from the rollback segments to rebuild, in memory, a temporary copy of the data block as it would look if the second transaction were not occurring. Thus, each transaction or query sees the database as if no other transaction were active in the database. Because of this feature the Oracle user does not need to do anything special to ensure that he is not reading "dirty" data. In other popular DBMSs the user commonly has to specify an isolation level such as "repeatable read" and acquire locks on each data block as it is read in order to ensure that changes by other users don't cause inconsistent results to be returned.

In the pure, theoretical data warehousing model where access is always read-only, read consistency would not be a critical feature. No data warehouse, however, is ever completely read-only. Data in the warehouse has to be periodically loaded and resummarized. Ideally, no users should be executing queries against tables (or at least partitions) that are being loaded or modified. Even if read consistency isn't required during normal warehouse operations, it also incurs minimal additional cost. The only time that Oracle's read consistency model requires extra query overhead is when a block image has to be reconstructed because a query and a modifying transaction are simultaneously active in the same block.

Temporary Segments

As we might guess from the name, temporary segments are database objects that are used only during the operation of a single SQL statement and are then released so their space can be reused for another purpose. The most common use of temporary segments in the data warehouse is supporting large sort operations. Sort operations are discussed more completely later in this chapter. Note that these temporary segments are not equivalent to temporary tables that were discussed earlier in this chapter—temporary tables in Oracle8*i* use temporary segments for their storage, as do sort operations.

Each user is allowed a specific amount of memory in which to perform sorts. In the data warehouse environment, a SELECT statement may frequently retrieve large amounts of data. If the query includes an ORDER BY or GROUP BY clause that causes the data to be sorted, it may be impossible to fit all the data into the allocated memory. In this case, Oracle will sort whatever portion of the data will fit into memory and then write the intermediate sort results out to temporary storage in the database.

In Oracle7 Server releases prior to 7.3, each time a disk sort was needed by a SELECT statement it was dynamically allocated. After the query was completed, the temporary segment was recovered by SMON. In a system, such as a data warehouse, where large sorts are frequently required, the overhead of dynamically allocating temporary space could be significant. Additionally, because SMON has several functions and does not run continuously, there is sometimes a delay and additional overhead when recovering the temporary segments released by completed queries.

Since release 7.3, however, the DBA has a tool to alleviate this unnecessary overhead in dynamically allocating and deallocating temporary segments. Now when the DBA creates a tablespace to be used for storing temporary segments, he may create it with the TEMPORARY keyword. Oracle will then be able to avoid the extra space management overhead of dynamically creating temporary segments for each query by preallocating temporary extents in the tablespace. When a SELECT statement (or other SQL statement) requires sort space, these temporary extents can be quickly "checked out" for temporary use. Oracle prevents the creation of any permanent segments in a tablespace created with (or altered to) TEMPORARY status.

Once one or more tablespaces with the TEMPORARY attribute are created, the DBA must define the TEMPORARY TABLESPACE attribute of each user to ensure that sort extents will be allocated correctly.

Extents

Each segment, of any type, is made up of one or more extents. The *extent* is the unit of space allocation by which a segment is initially created and later grows. When the DBA creates a table, index, or other segment, he is able to specify several parameters in the STORAGE clause that affect the size of the segment's extents. The following CREATE TABLE command illustrates these parameters:

```
CREATE TABLE SALES_REPS
       (EMPL_ID              NUMBER(7,0) PRIMARY KEY,
        EMPL_NAME            VARCHAR2(30),
        SALES_REGION         VARCHAR2(12),
        QUOTA                NUMBER(9,0))
   TABLESPACE DIM_DATA
   STORAGE
       (INITIAL              10M
        NEXT                 20M
        PCTINCREASE          100
        MINEXTENTS           1
        MAXEXTENTS           20);
```

In this simple example, one extent of 10 megabytes will be created initially. As rows are added and that extent is filled, a second extent of 20 megabytes will be added. When the second extent is filled a third extent of 40 megabytes will be added to the segment. This third extent will be 40 megabytes because the PCTINCREASE parameter was set to 100 percent. Each additional extent will be twice the size of the previous extent. Incidentally, the value of PCTINCREASE shown in this example is rarely used. The default value for this parameter is 50 percent, which leads to odd-sized extents and various space management difficulties for the administrator. Typically, the DBA should set PCTINCREASE to 0 (zero) so that each additional extent will be the same size.

In some cases, the DBA wishes to initially allocate more than one extent rather than wait for growth to trigger the creation of additional extents. Each extent is a contiguous set of database blocks and, therefore, must be contained within a single database file. If a table of 19 gigabytes needs to be created and the operating system only allows file sizes up to 2 gigabytes, then a minimum of 10 files will be required. Therefore, a minimum of 10 extents will have to be created. The DBA can do this at table creation time by specifying MINEXTENTS equal to 10.

TIP The DBA can also take explicit control of the size and placement of extents through the ALTER TABLE . . . ALLOCATE EXTENT command, which will be discussed in Chapter 11.

Database Blocks

We introduced Oracle database blocks earlier in this chapter. Each time Oracle reads from or writes to the database files it moves data in units of database blocks; the data buffers within the SGA are each sized to fit one database block.

The database block size may be set as a multiple of the underlying block size used by the operating system. (Ideally, the Oracle block should correspond directly to one underlying operating system block.) The default database block size used by Oracle in most operating systems is 2,048 (2 KB) bytes. To override this default value, the DBA must specify a value for the DB_BLOCK_SIZE initialization parameter when creating the database. In almost every case, the large data warehouse benefits from using a larger block size of 8 KB or even 16 KB. The maximum value allowed for the DB_BLOCK_SIZE parameter is dependent on both the Oracle release and the operating system you are using.

Views

Oracle provides a means of predefining query criteria and keeping this information in the data dictionary. This may be helpful in simplifying complex access (by predefining join criteria, for instance) or to enforce security rules (users are able to see only a subset of rows in a table based on their department).

These query definitions are defined using the CREATE VIEW command. The *view* is a logical way of looking at data that is physically stored in one or more tables. No data is actually stored as part of the view. Each time a query references the view, Oracle combines the view definition with the other criteria specified in the query. This combination of criteria is the final query that is actually executed against the database.

Consider a table of sales order information that requires 200 megabytes of storage. Users in each of 12 regions might have a need to see only those orders that were taken in their region. If a view is created for each region, the data storage requirement would still be only 200 megabytes. When a user requests data from the ROCKY_MOUNTAIN_ORDERS view, the restriction of which orders belong to this region is automatically imposed on the query. The final results are the same as if the user had added "AND REGION='ROCKY MOUNTAIN'" to the WHERE clause of their SELECT.

Materialized Views

As we discussed in the last section, the primary disadvantage to using views is that they have to be resolved at execution time by going to the detailed data in the underlying base table(s). If the view summarizes a million-row table into 100 rows with a GROUP BY, a query against the view will require accessing the million-row table. The traditional data warehousing answer to this issue is to avoid the view and instead store the resultant 100 rows in a summary table. Two problems remain with this approach. First, the summary table has to be maintained or re-created every time any changes are made to the data in an underlying table. Second, the user needs to be aware of the summary table and must remember to use it when formulating all appropriate queries.

Oracle8*i*'s materialized views address both of these issues. A materialized view physically stores the data that corresponds to the view's defined query. Oracle8*i* maintains the materialized view so that data changes to a base table are automatically propagated into the materialized view. The administrator can define the type and timing of refreshes to be performed.

Simplicity and performance are both enhanced by an additional feature of materialized views. When a query is received that references the base table(s) and that could be equivalently executed against the materialized view, the Oracle8*i* cost-based optimizer is able to rewrite the query dynamically to use a more efficient access to the materialized view. In the example just described, a query against the million-row table that uses the same GROUP BY criteria as the materialized view will by redirected to use the 100 rows stored there instead.

Materialized views are used extensively in the Oracle8*i* data warehouse to streamline the creation and management of summary tables subsequent to loading of detailed data. Chapter 7, "Post-Load Processing in the Data Warehouse," explores these uses in depth.

The Oracle Data Dictionary

The SYSTEM tablespace is the home of the data dictionary where Oracle will store its information about all the other data to be put into the database. Every Oracle database must have a SYSTEM tablespace. The structure of the data dictionary consists of tables, indexes, clusters, and views (just like our data warehouse will have), but the dictionary is owned by the Oracle system (a schema, or user, named SYS). The user and even the database administrator have very little reason to directly query the actual tables that make up the data dictionary. Such direct access can be very confusing because many of the table and column names are rather cryptic and because most useful queries require data from more than one table. To avoid these problems, a large number of data dictionary views have been created that make the dictionary much friendlier. There are data dictionary views to tell us about tables, indexes, tablespaces, and many other things involving the contents and structure of the database. Most of these views are named with a prefix like USER_, ALL_, or DBA_ to identify their intended audience.

As an example, three dictionary views present information about all of the tables defined in the database. The first view, USER_TABLES, shows information only about the tables owned by the user querying the view. If I issue the query SELECT TABLE_NAME FROM USER_TABLES I will see the names of the tables in my own schema. If you issue the same query you will, most likely, get a different list of table names reflecting the contents of your schema. The second view, ALL_TABLES, shows us information about the tables we own as well as all other tables whose owners have given us the ability to access them. Even if we don't own any tables ourselves (a common configuration for a data warehouse in which all the data is contained within one or more special schemas that are not associated with actual users), when we issue SELECT OWNER, TABLE_NAME FROM ALL_TABLES, we will get a listing of all the tables we have permission to access. The final view in this set, DBA_TABLES, is accessible only to those with special database administrator privileges. This view shows all the tables in the entire database.

In addition to these views of database tables, the Oracle data dictionary contains information on all other database objects. A complete listing of all the data dictionary views is contained in the *Server Reference* manual for the release of Oracle Server you are using. The actual structure of the data dictionary views varies somewhat in each release and also depends on which server options have been installed. The basic dictionary views have remained fundamentally the same since the introduction of Oracle version 6 over a decade ago.

Metadata

Metadata is data about the structure of the "real" data stored in the data warehouse. The Oracle data dictionary contains much of the metadata needed to navigate through the data warehouse. Unfortunately, the data dictionary can be somewhat cryptic to users who don't work with it on a regular basis like DBAs. Additionally, some metadata is important to the data warehouse but is not tracked automatically by the data dictionary, such as identification of the source location and transformation algorithms used to populate the warehouse. Chapter 4 presents suggestions for structuring metadata in a way that can be used more conveniently by warehouse users.

Schemas

The concept of a *schema* will be explored more in the security section later in this chapter, but we need to introduce the topic now as part of our discussion of the data dictionary. A schema is the set of database objects (such as tables and indexes) that are created and owned by a particular user. The schema and the user are virtually synonymous in Oracle8; when a user is created, an empty schema is created at the same time. In many cases, however, the users are not allowed to create any objects in their schema because they will be working only with objects provided by the DBA. On the other hand, the DBA may provide those objects by creating user schemas just to hold them. No actual user will ever connect to the database using these user schemas.

Qualifying Object Names

Table names must be unique within a schema, but two schemas may each own a table of the same name. These are, however, completely separate tables and must be differentiated by specifying the OWNER as well as TABLE_NAME. The following is a query of the dictionary view ALL_TABLES that reports multiple tables named CUSTOMERS:

```
SELECT OWNER, TABLE_NAME
  FROM ALL_TABLES
 WHERE TABLE_NAME = 'CUSTOMERS';


OWNER                           TABLE_NAME
------------------------------- ----------
CANADA_SALES                    CUSTOMERS
EAST_SALES                      CUSTOMERS
WEST_SALES                      CUSTOMERS

3 rows selected.
```

Here the column "OWNER" identifies the owning schema.

This situation is similar to the church youth group of Gary Dodge's son, Ryan. His best friend there is also named Ryan. If the group leader needs to get the attention of one of them, calling "Ryan" is not sufficient. He needs to call either "Ryan Dodge" or "Ryan Flanders" to uniquely identify which Ryan he wants. Calling out just the last name is not sufficient either, because both have siblings involved in the same group. Even though they share the same name, they are certainly not the same boy! In Oracle terms, we refer to this unambiguous naming as "qualifying the object name." It is done by specifying the owner, then a period separator, and then the table name. So the customer table, owned by the schema WEST_SALES would be uniquely identified as WEST_SALES.CUSTOMERS (generally, this would be spoken as "westsales dot customers").

QUOTED NAMES

Ordinary Oracle SQL syntax imposes some rules on the characters that can be used in the name of a table, column, or other object. Lowercase letters within these names are automatically translated into uppercase when used within a context where Oracle can recognize the text string to be one of these object names.

It is possible, however, to enter the name within double quotes and bypass these rules. For instance, CREATE TABLE TEST_TAB . . . and CREATE TABLE test_tab . . . are equivalent statements. CREATE TABLE Test Tab . . . would not be legal syntax, however, because the space in the table name would confuse the SQL parser. With quotes, though, CREATE TABLE "Test Tab" . . . is legal syntax. It will create a table with mixed uppercase and lowercase and with a space embedded in the name!

Even though this is legal, it is not a very good idea. All future references to this table will have to use the same quoted string, complete with spaces and mixed-case characters. This is likely to create unnecessary confusion for users and administrators alike. Avoid using the quotation marks in naming objects.

Taking a quick look at the number of rows in each of the CUSTOMERS tables shows that they are, indeed, different objects. Note that the table names had to be qualified in these two queries so that Oracle could determine which specific object we wanted to see.

```
SELECT COUNT(*)
  FROM WEST_SALES.CUSTOMERS;

COUNT(*)
--------
  234984

SELECT COUNT(*)
  FROM EAST_SALES.CUSTOMERS;

COUNT(*)
--------
  763916

SELECT COUNT(*)
  FROM CANADA_SALES.CUSTOMERS;
```

```
COUNT(*)
--------
     926
```

These examples all show us selecting "*" (an asterisk, usually spoken as "star" in this context) from some table. This is SQL shorthand for requesting all columns. When you wish to specifically request one or more columns instead of all columns, you will sometimes need to further qualify your statement. If there is no ambiguity, just naming the columns in the select list is sufficient, but if the same column name occurs in two tables that are being joined in a query then Oracle needs to be told which of the two columns is being selected. For one additional example, if you wanted to see how many of our customers had actually placed orders, you would enter the following:

```
SELECT COUNT (DISTINCT CUSTOMERS.CUSTID)
  FROM CANADA_SALES.CUSTOMERS, CANADA_SALES.ORDERS
 WHERE CUSTOMERS.CUSTID=ORDERS.CUSTID;


COUNT(CUSTOMERS.CUSTID)
-----------------------
                    428
```

The Distributed Data Dictionary

If desired, the Oracle data warehouse can be distributed across multiple databases on multiple servers. This topic is discussed in much more depth in Chapter 12. From the perspective of the data dictionary, however, it is important to recognize that each of these databases in a distributed warehouse is autonomous. Each physical database will have its own data dictionary, independently tracking its database objects, users, and privileges.

If a user connected to database A wishes to access the CUSTOMERS table that is stored on database B (and assuming the user has been granted access to the table by the administrator of B) then a further level of qualification is necessary. It is possible (though potentially confusing) for a CUSTOMERS table to be owned by a schema of the same name on both databases A and B. To identify the remote CUSTOMERS, the user would have to further qualify the table name with its location as well as its owner. Here we query the remote data dictionary to find other CUSTOMERS tables on a database known as INTERNATIONAL:

```
SELECT OWNER, TABLE_NAME
  FROM ALL_TABLES@INTERNATIONAL
 WHERE TABLE_NAME = 'CUSTOMERS';
```

The location qualifier INTERNATIONAL in this query is a database link. These database links are created by the database administrator using the CRE-

ATE PUBLIC DATABASE LINK command. It is possible for individual users to create their own private database links, but most administrators will see the advantages of creating and maintaining public database links to all the other databases that their users may need to access.

Location Transparency through Synonyms and Views

In many cases the users of the distributed data warehouse don't want to know about the physical distribution of schemas and tables. Why should the user have to remember that CANADA_SALES data is kept in the same database as the East and West regions of the United States, but EUROPE and ASIA SALES information is kept in a separate INTERNATIONAL database? To remove this complexity (and to give the administrator the freedom to move objects to accommodate hardware capacity, processing schedules, or other considerations) Oracle allows the qualification or even the actual table names to be hidden through the use of *synonyms*.

A synonym is an *alias* or nickname for an object. It can be created by the administrator to give a simple, consistent name to objects that hides the physical implementation decisions from the users. The decision to create multiple CUSTOMERS tables in separate schemas and then to deploy them onto multiple servers may have been necessary for administrative reasons. Unless these administrative reasons correspond to functional or organizational structures that all the users understand, however, it may be best to disguise the physical complexity by providing a simple logical structure to the users. The following series of commands will develop a simple, consistent structure:

```
CREATE PUBLIC SYNONYM EAST_US_CUSTOMERS
    FOR EAST_SALES.CUSTOMERS;
CREATE PUBLIC SYNONYM WEST_US_CUSTOMERS
    FOR WEST_SALES.CUSTOMERS;
CREATE PUBLIC SYNONYM CANADA_CUSTOMERS
    FOR CANADA_SALES.CUSTOMERS;
CREATE PUBLIC SYNONYM EUROPE_CUSTOMERS
    FOR EUROPE_SALES.CUSTOMERS@INTERNATIONAL;
CREATE PUBLIC SYNONYM ASIA_CUSTOMERS
    FOR ASIA_SALES.CUSTOMERS@INTERNATIONAL;
```

Now we have created five synonyms that are consistent and easy to remember. There is no longer a need to know which regions are represented in the "domestic" database and which are stored in the INTERNATIONAL database.

If desired, we can even remove the fact that there are five separate sales organizations by creating a view that combines information from all five customer tables into a single CUSTOMERS view:

```
CREATE VIEW CUSTOMERS AS
    SELECT 'EAST_US' REGION, *
```

```
            FROM EAST_SALES.CUSTOMERS
UNION ALL
   SELECT 'WEST_US' REGION, *
      FROM WEST_SALES.CUSTOMERS
UNION ALL
   SELECT 'CANADA' REGION, *
      FROM CANADA_SALES.CUSTOMERS
UNION ALL
   SELECT 'EUROPE' REGION, *
      FROM EUROPE_SALES.CUSTOMERS@INTERNATIONAL
UNION ALL
   SELECT 'ASIA' REGION, *
      FROM ASIA_SALES.CUSTOMERS@INTERNATIONAL;
```

This approach presents a simple perspective on our global customers list. A user can find information about any customer by querying the CUSTOMERS view. There are, of course, many other issues besides user simplicity that must be considered. The view just described, for example, which combines data from multiple databases, may introduce unnecessary performance problems. Each query for customers in, say, Cleveland, will be resolved by searching the CITY column in five tables spread across both databases even though a more informed query could have been directly executed against just the EAST_SALES.CUSTOMERS table.

This trade-off between simplicity and performance is a common enigma that the data warehouse designer and administrator must somehow solve. One step toward reaching a solution is possibly to identify multiple audiences among the user community. Commonly some warehouse users will use the warehouse infrequently and will not take the necessary training to become sophisticated in their access. For these users, the administrator should probably provide only simplified access to summary data that, due to its smaller volume, will not present opportunities for truly painful performance problems. The tables containing more voluminous detailed data may be made available for drill-down only by warehouse "power users" who receive additional training on query tuning and warehouse navigation.

We will discuss design alternatives and metadata for warehouse users in the next chapter. Performance issues related to the use of views and distributed queries are treated in Chapter 9, "Data Warehouse Performance Tuning."

Security Features

Oracle has very strong security capabilities that provide the necessary granularity for the most demanding separation of responsibilities. These security features are used extensively in OLTP systems, but, all too often, minimal consideration of security is given in the data warehouse. Some have argued that because the warehouse allows only reporting of data, there is less opportunity for fraud or other security concerns. Further, the argument goes on, the warehouse is supposed to "open up" the organizational information for everyone.

Even though there may be less stringent security demands in the warehouse, it is generally not appropriate to simply say that all users may have SELECT privilege on all tables. Fraud or other compromises of the organization's interests can be performed through read-only access to inappropriate information. What, for instance, is the value of your full national customer list if it is sold to a competitor by an unscrupulous employee?

The designers of the data warehouse should be familiar with Oracle security facilities and make an analysis of the data needs of various user groups. Oracle makes the management of security relatively easy. Oracle8 security has been enhanced over previous releases to provide better control over users' passwords. Oracle8*i* further enhances the ability of the administrator to provide access at the row level rather than at just the table or view level.

As a universal rule, no Oracle user can perform any action in the database until a specific privilege to perform that action is granted to that user. The default set of privileges, therefore, is the null set—no privileges at all. Starting from that point of no access, let's look at several security features that will then allow users to get to the appropriate data in the warehouse.

Schemas and Users

Before Oracle7, Oracle users were each assigned a username and a password for connecting to the database. Depending on the system privileges granted by the DBA, some users could create tables or other objects and others could not. Oracle7 introduced a new term to the Oracle lexicon, *schema*, which can be considered equivalent to the older concept of *user*. The newer term more precisely includes the concept of ownership of database objects. Even though the two terms are synonymous, within the data warehouse it may be useful to consider them distinctly.

A schema may be considered a special form of user account that is used to hold a set of tables and indexes to store warehouse data. In doing warehouse design it is helpful to create a separate schema to hold all the database objects related to a subject area. Normally this will mean that a warehouse will have a handful of schemas used for storing data. Generally, no user will ever actually connect to the database using one of these accounts—they are reserved for special administrator functions.

> **NOTE** There is actually only one activity that must be done from within the table-owning schema: Initially granting access to the tables of a schema cannot be done from the administrator's schema. All other actions, including creating or dropping schema objects, loading data, truncating tables, and building indexes, can be done by the administrator without connecting to the owning schema.

The warehouse will have another, larger group of users who will need to access the data stored in the table-owning schemas but will probably never need to create permanent objects of their own.

Each user of the warehouse should have his own personal userid and password. It is often tempting to set up a single userid and then give the password out to a whole department or even to all users. This mistake, rooted only in laziness, has two ramifications. First, when the userid/password is a community resource, then the database administrator has surrendered all pretext of security. Every time a user leaves the department or the company the keys to the treasure vault go with him. Second, when every session is using the same connection information, the DBA's life is complicated when trying to trace a performance problem or kill a runaway query. Without a unique userid, it is much more difficult to identify a particular session. In short, if your company needs better cooperation and teamwork, find something other than passwords to develop these behaviors.

Profiles

Every schema (i.e., user) of the database is assigned a *profile* that can limit various resources that may be consumed by the user. Example resources that may be controlled are CPU and logical I/O for each database call. In the warehouse, where very large queries may be inadvertently submitted, this feature can be used to stop execution of runaway queries. Unless altered by the DBA, new users are assigned a profile named DEFAULT that has no limits imposed.

Password Management

Oracle8 added new automated features to allow the administrator more control over the passwords of database users. These controls are also implemented through the use of profiles. The administrator may establish simple rules about passwords, such as the frequency with which users must modify their passwords or how soon a selected password may be reused by a user. Special routines may even be written to verify a specific level of complexity in the construction of a password, such as enforcing minimum length restrictions or requiring the use of special characters or even preventing the use of specific easy-to-guess passwords such as the username or "WELCOME."

System Privileges

A large number (approaching 100) of different privileges, which give them the ability to perform some type of action, may be granted to users. These system privileges include basic capabilities such as CREATE SESSION (which allows the user to make a database connection) and more exotic ones such as ALTER

RESOURCE COST or BACKUP ANY TABLE, which would be expected to be granted only to administrators.

Normally, an entire group of users will need a consistent set of system privileges. Three or four groups would be typically identified for a data warehouse: ADMINISTRATORS, SCHEMA_OWNERS, USERS, and POWER_USERS might be four candidate groups that would each need a different set of system privileges. Rather than repeatedly grant the necessary set of privileges to each member of a group, the set of privileges can be granted to a role (discussed later), and then a single grant of the role to each new user will provide the full set of privileges.

Object Privileges

Just as system privileges allow their recipients to do some type of action, object privileges give recipients the ability to perform a particular action on a specific object. Thus, the schema owner DW_OWNER may grant SELECT privilege on the PRODUCTS table to the user account JSMITH. This then allows JSMITH to read the data stored within the DW_OWNER.PRODUCTS table.

Roles

Just as with system privileges, object privileges are more easily managed through roles. *Roles* are named collections of privileges. The administrator creates a new role and then grants privileges to the role. The administrator can then subsequently grant that role to a group of users.

A large number of tables and views may be defined in the warehouse. There may also be a large number of users who are to access those tables and views. If 500 warehouse users are going to be given access to 200 tables, individual grants of these privileges would require 10,000 grant statements. If access to the 200 tables had been granted to a DW_USER role and then that role was granted to the 500 users, then a total of only 700 grants would be required—a 93 percent savings in administrative workload. (This example assumes that all users require access to all tables—a more granular approach is generally recommended, however.)

A role should be created that includes access to the tables within each subject area. Users in the finance department might then be granted the roles corresponding to the three or four subject areas of interest to their analysis. Users within manufacturing will likely require access to a different set of subject areas, as would the users from the marketing department. Of course, there is not usually a simple, distinct mapping of users to subject areas. There will be overlaps. Some users in one department will be granted multiple roles, and roles associated with a given subject area will need to be granted to more than one group of users. The user groups don't generally align neatly along organizational boundaries, although this is a good place to start. The reality of cross-group responsibilities is facilitated by creating two levels of roles, as shown in Figure 3.13. Here, the typical users from each department are granted access to a subset of the data warehouse subject areas. The chief financial officer is, however, granted access to the roles created for both marketing and finance users.

The other advantage of using two levels of roles, as shown in Figure 3.12, is that we can very easily make a portion of the data warehouse inaccessible during maintenance by revoking a small number of the grants between the two levels of roles. After the maintenance window is over and the data has been checked and validated, the access may be quickly restored by remaking the interrole grants. This is much simpler to manage than trying to handle the large number of individual grants based on the total user base or the total number of warehouse objects.

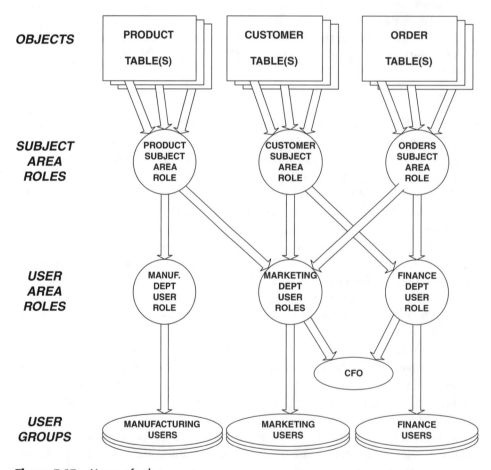

Figure 3.13 Usage of roles.

Auditing

The DBA may choose to enable auditing of specific database operations. The Oracle database will then log any activity of the specified type to an audit trail. The DBA may choose to have the audit trail as a special table inside the database or to use an external operating system audit facility. Auditing, in addition to its security-related uses, can be helpful to the administrator in tracking usage of the warehouse. For instance, it is common to audit the logon/logoff activity of users (especially failed attempts to connect to the database, which may expose a user-training issue or an attempted breach of security). Auditing of SELECT activity on specific warehouse tables will identify which parts of the warehouse are being used heavily or lightly.

Virtual Private Databases

Previously known by the less-than-inspiring names of row-level security or fine-grain security, the phrase virtual private database (VPD) accurately describes how this new feature is intended to be used. The basic idea is to allow many virtual databases to exist inside one physical database.

Prior to Oracle8*i*, mechanisms within the RDBMS provided security for entire accounts or schemas, each of which could be made up of hundreds or thousands of tables. At a finer level, mechanisms such as permissions and roles could be used to control access to individual tables. Views could be used to provide a very simplistic means of allowing subsets of data within a table, but there were no sophisticated capabilities for controlling access to individual rows within tables. Issues such as these were the responsibility of the application, not the database engine itself. In essence, program modules (whether forms, reports, batch programs, or stored procedures) become proxies to enforce row-level security through their SQL statements.

While this situation seemed satisfactory for most situations, defeating this illusory form of security meant simply finding a way around the programmed modules. Ad hoc utilities such as SQL*Plus and any form of application programming interface such as OCI, Precompilers, JDBC, or SQLJ can be used to circumvent application-enforced row-level security by simply bypassing the application. Stored procedures could protect the application code from being bypassed but did not provide a means for allowing ad hoc queries.

However, there is another need for row-level security, which is best illustrated by a real-life example involving Oracle Applications (Financials, ERP/Manufacturing, Human Resources, etc.). The full suite of Oracle applications can involve dozens of schemas and literally thousands of tables and indexes. Putting it all together, installing, and configuring, can be a tremendous task, involving weeks or months of effort. And once everything is successfully configured and installed, ongoing maintenance might mean applying several upgrades and "patches" over the course of the next few years.

This is more than enough work for one system. Since your multinational corporation has forty or fifty separate operating units, does this mean that you'll need to have forty or fifty nearly identical such installations? Ideally, you should be able to use the single installation for all forty or fifty organizations. In the world of Oracle Applications, this is called multi-org, and it keeps data for each organization segregated from each other when in fact everything resides in one database. How this is accomplished is through a relatively primitive form of row-level security.

Virtual private databases, or VPDs, take some of the mechanisms used by the multi-org functionality and improve on them. In addition to extremely simple security schemes such as differentiating between values for an "ORG_ID" column, VPDs can be used to implement extremely complex rules, if necessary. They work like this:

1. A PL/SQL package is written to encapsulate the rules of the security scheme. One or more procedures within the package are used to set a security context within an Oracle session using the SET_CONTEXT procedure in the DBMS_SESSION supplied package. One or more functions within the package are used to enforce the security scheme, based on the value of the previously saved security context string within the session. This string is retrieved from the session using the supplied function SYS_CONTEXT.

2. An overall security policy is defined in the database and the above-mentioned package is designated as the trusted enforcement package of that policy. This is done with the CREATE CONTEXT command.

3. Individual tables are assigned to the security policy using the ADD_POLICY procedure in the DBMS_RLS supplied package. Functions within the trusted package are assigned for an action (i.e., INSERT, UPDATE, DELETE, SELECT, or any combination of all four).

Once all of these components are in place, the Oracle query optimizer pulls it all together. Whenever a SQL statement references a table covered by a security policy, the optimizer detects this during the parse of the SQL statement. It executes the enforcing packaged function (set by DBMS_RLS.ADD_POLICY) and returns a string that is incorporated into the SQL statement as a predicate in the WHERE clause. This new string is thus attached to the SQL statement and becomes part of it. The VPD mechanism allows developers to execute some user-defined code while a SQL statement is being parsed, as long as that code returns either a NULL string or a string which can be incorporated into the SQL statement being parsed.

Because all enforcement is coded only within the trusted package, this mechanism cannot be "hacked." There is no way to alter the security rules without altering the trusted package itself. Also, this mechanism cannot be bypassed. Regardless of the source of the SQL statement, the VPD mechanism will be applied.

The implications on performance can certainly vary. In the best possible scenario, the enforcement function will return a very simple predicate to the executing SQL statement, minimizing the impact on performance during execution. Sometimes, the enforcement function itself may have to perform some very costly and time-consuming logic, but remember that this occurs only once, during the parse phase rather than many times, once per row, during execution. Therefore, VPDs provide a mechanism which can impose minimal or zero additional impact on SQL statement execution. It all depends on the security policy itself and how it is coded.

This can be extraordinarily useful in data warehousing. Without this feature, anybody using an ad hoc query tool or browsing utility had complete access to all rows within the tables for which they were given privileges. Thus, the only way to keep one organization from accessing data belonging to another organization was to segregate the data into different tables, or into different schemas, or even into different databases on different servers. Using VPDs, a single data warehouse or data mart system can appear to be several (or several dozen) completely isolated systems. In addition to providing finer degrees of security, VPDs can also enhance the manageability of large and complex data warehouses.

Oracle Optimizer

An RDBMS optimizer is given the task of deciding between multiple access paths to satisfy the data needs of a particular SQL statement. Oracle, for instance, provides several alternative methods for performing joins. There may well be several potential indexes that might be used, and Oracle always has the option of scanning a complete table.

Oracle actually provides two optimizers. The rule-based optimizer remains basically unchanged from Oracle version 6. Without specific action on the part of the administrator, both Oracle7 and Oracle8 will default to using the rule-based optimizer. For applications that were written and tuned specifically for the rule-based optimizer in version 6 or early releases of Oracle7, this default choice may still be appropriate. The rule-based optimizer chooses between alternative access plans by following a predefined list of rules and selects the access path that uses the highest-level rule. Thus, the rule-based optimizer will always choose to use an available index on even a small table even though it might be more efficient to scan the entire table.

The second optimizer available with Oracle7 or Oracle8 is cost-based. The initial releases of Oracle7 had several difficulties that made the cost-based optimizer a problem in many cases. Enhancements made in release 7.3 and Oracle8 make the cost-based optimizer a far better choice, especially for the unplanned queries typical of the data warehouse. Several access options of particular interest to data warehouse queries have been added in these releases. These new access path options are not available to the older rule-based optimizer.

Before the cost-based optimizer will be used to resolve a query plan, statistics must be gathered on the data in the tables and indexes of the data warehouse. These statistics are gathered using the ANALYZE TABLE command. Two options on this command allow the administrator to gather very accurate statistics based on reading every row of the table (ANALYZE TABLE . . . COMPUTE STATISTICS) or potentially less accurate statistics (ANALYZE TABLE . . . ESTIMATE STATISTICS) based on reading only a sample of the rows in the table. When a table is analyzed, statistics are also gathered for each index on the table. If needed, an index may be analyzed directly with the ANALYZE INDEX command.

One of the improvements made in successive releases of the cost-based optimizer has been in the sampling process. Each new release has allowed accurate estimates to be made based on smaller sample sizes. By release 7.3 (and Oracle8) it is possible to obtain sufficiently accurate statistics based on sample sizes of 4 or 5 percent of the total rows. The ideal sample size is a balance between the shorter execution time of a small sample and the increased accuracy of a large sample. The optimal sample size will vary by table, however. If the data in the table is very consistent and evenly distributed, a very small sample will do nicely. If the data is very irregular in its distribution then a larger sample will be needed to get a good estimate. To find the correct sample size for a given table the administrator should first issue the ALTER TABLE . . . COMPUTE STATISTICS command and save the resultant values from DBA_TABLES and DBA_INDEXES. Then the table should be analyzed several more times using various sample sizes. Each set of values should also be saved before the next ANALYZE. Comparing the resultant values will allow the administrator to determine the smallest sample size that yielded the same (or very nearly the same) statistics as the initial COMPUTE STATISTICS. Once determined, this same sample size will probably be appropriate for future statistics gathering on that table.

NOTE Column-level statistics can be gathered in the form of a height-balanced histogram when the data in one particular column deviates substantially from a uniform distribution. Histograms allow the optimizer to make a better decision about how many rows are likely to be retrieved on a particular range of values specified in a WHERE clause condition. Building a histogram on a column is done with ANALYZE TABLE . . . ESTIMATE STATISTICS FOR COLUMNS. These statistics are viewed in DBA_TAB_COLUMNS and DBA_HISTOGRAMS.

A table (and its indexes) should be reanalyzed whenever changes made to the data are likely to have altered the distribution of data enough to make the old statistics inaccurate and potentially cause the optimizer to make an improper choice. If 100,000 rows are added to a table of 10 million rows, it is likely that the statistics will not change materially. If those 100,000 rows are added to a table with only 200,000 rows it is almost guaranteed that the table needs to be reanalyzed. Even the first example with a small percentage of newly added rows may require the regathering of column-level statistics if the added data rows cause a skewing that might affect a particular column's histogram.

Most warehouse administrators tend to include statistics gathering as a regular step in their periodic data loading/summarization cycles. After each load, indexes are built (as needed) and estimated statistics are obtained. When Oracle8 partitioned tables (or partitioned indexes) are used then only the newest partition (assuming partitioning is done by date) where rows have been added will need to be analyzed. This is a great time saver and eliminates one of the disadvantages of Oracle7 cost-based optimization when analyzing a very large table could take hours to execute. New syntax for analyzing a single partition has been added in Oracle8 to handle this chore.

I/O Operations

Oracle performs I/O in different ways on different file types and for different types of access. Modified data blocks and index blocks are always written to the database files by DBWR in single Oracle blocks. Reading index blocks and individually requested data blocks from disk is done in units of single Oracle blocks. If the underlying operating system blocks are smaller than the Oracle block size, then the I/O request may turn into multiple underlying I/O requests. Given a choice, it is best to format the underlying file system so that block sizes correspond between these two levels.

One major exception to this rule of requesting single Oracle blocks occurs during performance of a full table scan. During a full table scan, the Oracle server process will request a number of sequential blocks in each I/O request as defined by the initialization parameter, DB_FILE_MULTIBLOCK_READ_COUNT, which defines the number of Oracle blocks to be requested in each request. To determine the total I/O request size this value must be multiplied by the value of DB_BLOCK_SIZE. By example, a database with 8 KB Oracle blocks and with DB_FILE_MULTIBLOCK_READ_COUNT set to 4 would request transfers of 32 KB of data in each successive read during each table scan.

Another exception to the standard I/O request size of one Oracle block occurs while performing backup, recovery, direct read, or direct write operations. These occur, for instance, during direct path SQL*Loader jobs or when

SORT_DIRECT_WRITES is enabled in the initialization parameter file. These direct read and write operations are performed using the value of DB_ FILE_DIRECT_IO_COUNT. Just like the previous example, this parameter is the number of Oracle blocks to be transferred in each request.

Sort Operations

Oracle typically has to do sorts when a user issues a query that includes an ORDER BY or GROUP BY clause. Some joins (those using the SORT_MERGE or HASH join method) also require a sort operation. Index builds also require sorting data. When possible, Oracle will perform these sorts entirely in memory. This is determined by the value of the initialization parameter SORT_AREA_ SIZE, which controls the amount of memory that can be allocated by the server process to perform a sort. If the entire sort can be completed within this memory allocation then no disk sort activity will be needed.

If the amount of data to be sorted exceeds this value then Oracle will sort as much data as it can within memory and then write it to disk in a temporary segment. Each subsequent set of data will be read, sorted, and written to the temporary segment until all the data is processed. Each of the sets of data written to the temporary segment is then merged to finish the sort process.

Where the temporary segment is created for a particular user is determined by the TEMPORARY TABLESPACE attribute, which was set using the CREATE USER or ALTER USER commands. Each database should have one (or possibly more) tablespaces set aside for just this purpose. Each user should then be altered to direct his sort activity to this location. If the user is not altered to set this attribute, then sorts will be directed to the SYSTEM tablespace, the absolutely worst possible location!

Beginning in release 7.3, the tablespace that is created for this purpose can be dedicated to this single function using the ALTER TABLESPACE . . . TEMPORARY command. This command prevents any other segments from being created in this tablespace and will preallocate the entire tablespace into temporary extents for use by queries. This reduces the overhead associated with allocating temporary space for a sort. The administrator should set the TEMPORARY attribute for each temporary tablespace.

Backup and Recovery Features

Oracle provides several options for backing up data so it can be recovered after a disk failure. Backups of data can be either logical or physical. Logical backups can be performed on a table using the export utility, EXP. This approach allows the data in a single table (or Oracle8 partition) to be restored to the point in time when the export was performed. In most cases, data warehouses are too large to use EXP as the primary backup method.

Physical (image) backups involve copying the datafiles to a safe location and later restoring them when the actual data file is lost due to media failure. Two types of image backup are available in Oracle. A cold backup, the simpler approach, requires the database instance to be shut down and a copy made of every datafile and redo log file. Recovery from a failure requires every file from the most recent backup to be restored from its backup location, usually on tape. Cold backups are time-consuming and take away time from user availability. Cold backups may be sufficient for the data warehouse as long as the time required for performing the backups fits within the scheduled window for unavailability. Too many warehouses, unfortunately, are built using this assumption, but the administrators soon find that the available backup window is shrinking even as the amount of work to be done is expanding.

The second physical backup option is to use hot backups. Hot backups require that the database be operated in archivelog mode in which the ARCH process will make permanent copies of each log file before it is reused. Hot backups do not require the database to be shut down. This may be critical for a data warehouse with high availability requirements, perhaps because of a global user base. Hot backups can be performed on individual tablespaces even while users continue to access the database.

When a database file is lost, only the lost file needs to be restored, and then tablespace recovery will allow the logged changes to be replayed in order to bring the data file back up to the point of failure. In general, every production Oracle database, used for either OLTP transactions or DSS queries, should be operated in archivelog mode and hot backups should be performed. The few disadvantages of doing hot backups on OLTP databases are nonexistent in the warehouse where heavy query activity does not conflict with hot backups. Further, the use of read-only tablespaces can greatly reduce the magnitude of backup effort in the warehouse—it is possible that only the SYSTEM and ROLLBACK tablespaces will be the only portions of the warehouse that need to receive hot backups.

Many of the backup and recovery features of Oracle7 could be automated by using the Enterprise Backup Utility, which coordinates backup activity with tape management software. Oracle8 introduced some additional backup capabilities above and beyond those of Oracle7. The Oracle8 Recovery Manager enhances the functions of Enterprise Manager and adds a new capability for doing incremental backups of only the blocks in a data file that have changed since the last backup.

Further information on backup and recovery of the Oracle warehouse are covered in Chapter 8. Additionally, an excellent reference on this topic is the

Oracle8 Backup & Recovery Handbook by Rama Velpuri and Anand Adkoli, Oracle Press, 1998.

Oracle Server Options

This book describes the use of several features that are not part of the base Oracle server product. Some of these features, such as bitmap indexes, are available with upgraded levels of the Oracle server (such as the Oracle8*i* Server, Enterprise Edition, but not the base Oracle8*i* server). Others, such as partitioning or Parallel Server, are provided as part of special options that must be separately licensed. Features are bundled into these optional product packages for a variety of technical and marketing reasons.

Over the history of Oracle version 6, Oracle7, and Oracle8 several of these features were initially introduced as part of an extra-cost option but later incorporated into the base server product. Although it may be frustrating to pay for an extra-cost option only to see it rolled into the base product in a subsequent release, it seems to be the price to pay for the newest and most innovative technology. The reader should verify, before installing or using a feature, that it has been properly licensed.

Some of the server options that have been offered as supplements to various Oracle releases include the following:

- **Transaction Processing Option (version 6).** Provided the ability to execute anonymous PL/SQL blocks within the RDBMS and enabled row-level locking.
- **Procedural Option (Oracle7).** Allowed the creation of stored procedures, functions, packages, and database triggers.
- **Parallel Query Option (Oracle7).** Allowed multiple processes to share the work of performing large queries, loads, and index builds.
- **Distributed Option (Oracle7).** Enabled the two-phased commit protocol necessary to support distributed transactions.
- **Advanced Replication Option (Oracle7).** Provided for updateable snapshots and multiple-master replication.
- **Partitioning Option (Oracle8).** Enables the ability to partition tables and indexes and to use parallel DML operations on those partitioned objects.
- **Parallel Server Option (Oracle7, Oracle8, Oracle8*i*).** Allows multiple Oracle instances to simultaneously access a shared database from the various nodes of a clustered or MPP system.

- **Objects Option (Oracle8, Oracle8*i*).** Allows the use of Oracle8's new object types, tables, and views.

- **ConText Option (Oracle7), ConText Cartridge (Oracle8), Inter-Media (Oracle8*i*).** Provide special indexing features for manipulating large-text objects.

Several other data cartridges have been offered to manage particular types of data, such as video, images, time-series data, and so on. It is likely that more changes and additions to the offered options and cartridges will continue throughout the life of Oracle8. It would therefore be inappropriate (and impossible!) to attempt to present an accurate and complete list in this book.

While not options to the Oracle8*i* database engine, Oracle Corporation has many other complementary products that may be used in a complete data warehouse solution. These products include Oracle Warehouse Builder, Oracle Data Mart Suites, Oracle Darwin, Oracle internet File System (iFS), and many others. Rather than trying to describe them all in this RDBMS architecture chapter, we have provided an introduction to each (along with links to the official Oracle site) through the Web sites listed in the Introduction.

Summary

This chapter provides an overview of the architectural components of the files, memory structures, and processes that make up the Oracle database server products. An Oracle *database* consists of data files, redo log files, and control files. Initialization parameter files are used to control the characteristics of the Oracle *instance*. The Oracle instance is made up of a series of processes that all access a shared memory structure known as the *System Global Area (SGA)*.

Within the database, objects such as tables and indexes are stored as segments that are created within tablespaces. Tablespaces are made up of one or more operating system data files. Special segments are used internally by the database for storing rollback (or undo) information and temporary sort data. A special set of tables and indexes make up the Oracle data dictionary, which keeps track of all the other structures within the database. Many features for the security and administration of the database are provided to enable the DBA to control the warehouse.

CHAPTER 4

Designing the Oracle Data Warehouse

"I'm good enough. I'm smart enough. And, doggone it, people like me."

Stuart Smalley
Saturday Night Live's *"Daily Affirmations"*

The success of a data warehouse project depends on many factors, such as the need for an executive sponsor and an effective project team organization. In the final accounting, however, the measure of success of the warehouse itself will be based on how useful it is to its users. Is useful information available? How easily can users find that information? How easily and accurately can users interpret the data they retrieve? Is performance of the warehouse acceptable to users? Can administrative tasks, such as data loads, purges, and backups and recovery be performed within the available processing windows so that users will have access when they need it?

All these questions reflect the quality of the warehouse design. Inaccurate, disjointed, or unintelligible data cannot be used to make effective business decisions. Questions that take too long to answer will, in short order, cease to be asked. A warehouse that can't be accessed can't be used. The tasks of loading and summarizing data, performing necessary administration, and providing adequate performance are all affected—for better or worse—by the quality of the underlying design.

Many shops create a dumping ground of old data, without form or organization, and call it a warehouse. Others seek to create an easier, more accessible environment for doing regular daily reporting and then call it their warehouse. With some planning and thought it is possible to structure our warehouse to maximize user value and control the various hardware and administrative costs. This chapter will discuss various design considerations that affect these two concerns.

Before discussing specific techniques of database design for the Oracle data warehouse, we will address the issue of providing information about the contents of our data warehouse through metadata.

Users Need to Understand the Warehouse Structure and Operation

Typically, departments use different operational systems to support their part of the business and therefore use different names to describe identical data and, sometimes, use the same name for very different data. The warehouse design team, however, must attempt to derive single, unambiguous data names, formats, calculations, and meanings. Ideally, representatives of the various departments are consulted during the design of warehouse entities they are likely to use. Not infrequently, these discussions of what data is to be included, where it is to be obtained, and what it is to be called become spirited or even confrontational, with each representative honestly believing that his way is the only right way. The warehouse designer must combine excellent communication, negotiation, mediation, and peacemaking skills to facilitate progress and avoid project "paralysis by analysis."

Inevitably, however, compromises have to be made that conflict with the common usage of one or more groups. Even if the representative from marketing finally agrees that manufacturing's definition of the term PRODUCT is acceptable, there are likely to be dozens of other marketing employees who will someday access the data warehouse. If they interpret PRODUCT in their department's customary way, they are likely to make erroneous conclusions or ask nonsensical questions.

The data warehouse design and delivery team must have a means for telling the users of the data warehouse all about the data they are being given. This is a similar, but significantly more difficult, task to communicating database design information throughout the programming staff of a traditional IT project. It is similar because the handful of programmers all need to share a common understanding of what data they're working with and how it is stored. It is more difficult, however, for several reasons:

- Data warehouse users are not professional programmers and may not be used to dealing with such issues.

- Data warehouse users are typically not all from the project team (or even department) and therefore are not as likely to share a common understanding of how the data is used.

- The number of users of a successful data warehouse is likely to be very large, making personal Q&A sessions much more burdensome.

- Many data warehouse users are only occasional users. Unlike members of a programming project team who work with a database every day, some warehouse users may access the data warehouse only once or twice a month. The nature of decision support activity means that, frequently, they will need to investigate data and data relationships they've not previously explored.

- Data warehouse users are, in many cases, located in different buildings, cities, or even countries from the warehouse designers. The users of the data warehouse are likely to have no more than one training session at which they will have a chance to discuss such issues with a member of the design team. Future users may receive their training only casually from another local user in their own department.

- Data warehouses are evolutionary in their design. New data is defined and added to the data warehouse regularly. Users must be able to identify, access, use, and interpret the data added in each new release as easily as the original data on which they were trained.

Because of these factors, and many others like them, the data warehouse team must find a way to communicate unambiguously to a large, possibly casually trained audience with minimal personal contact. The training for warehouse users needs to follow the model of the old proverb, "Give a man a fish and you feed him for a day, teach him to fish and you feed him for a lifetime." Rather than try to teach a new user every detail about the contents of the data warehouse, the goal should be to provide a means to let him find those details in the metadata.

Metadata

Metadata is commonly defined as "data about data." It is a description of what data is stored in the data warehouse, including where it is stored, how it is stored, where it originated, or how it was derived. It is a great deal more, as we shall see in the next several pages. As the designers of our corporate data warehouse, we will make many design decisions that will impact our users. All the decisions and compromises we make while designing the data warehouse will potentially affect how the users locate, utilize, and interpret the data we work so hard to make available.

Our warehouse users, for instance, will need to know that within our data warehouse the following things happen:

- The data in the SALES table is summarized on a daily basis by CUS-TOMER_ID (the detail of multiple SALES invoices for a given customer on a given day is not retained).

- The data in the SALES table is retained only for the past 13 complete fiscal months, then purged.

- Warehouse users can obtain weekly, monthly, quarterly, and annual summaries of that SALES data for the past four years by querying the PERIOD_SALES table.

- The CUSTOMER_NAME and CUSTOMER_ADDRESS columns in the SALES table were obtained by referencing the corporate accounts receivable system rather than the various regional sales support systems.

- Daily SALES data from all international regions has been converted from local currency to U.S. dollars based on the currency conversion factor in effect on the last day of the fiscal month.

- The column of the SALES table named SALES_DATE corresponds to the BOOKING_DATE field in the order entry system for all transactions that required credit checks and corresponds to the DATE_OF_SALE field for all others.

- Split transactions that involve sales across multiple regions reflect the actual percentage split of the transaction and do not include the 20 percent "cooperation incentive" bonus introduced in 1995 in the Sales accounting system.

These and thousands of other decisions that seem perfectly reasonable to the warehouse designers may be anything but intuitive to the regional compensation analyst in Chicago who can't understand why her warehouse reports don't balance with the monthly sales commission reports she works with daily.

Besides informing our warehouse users, metadata serves as a record of decisions and activities that are valuable to the analysts and administrators of the warehouse over time. Remember that a data warehouse is not a single project; it is not an event; and it is definitely not a product. It must be an ongoing process. By the very nature of decision support processing—a discovery process—it is impossible to know in advance what uses may be found for the data stored within the warehouse. As users become familiar with the available data they will think of new questions to ask. It will not be possible to answer many of those questions based on the current warehouse design. New data, whether from existing or new transaction processing systems—or perhaps purchased from external sources—will need to be identified and integrated into the warehouse structure. Maintaining a data warehouse is a much more active role than maintaining operational systems. As support personnel inevitably change during the never-ending "design" phase, the newcomers will need to refer to metadata about the data sources (and rejected alternative sources), transformation algorithms, and other details of the current structure.

Recording Warehouse Processing as Metadata

We need to keep event "processing logs" that record details of when extracts were performed, when and how much data was loaded (whether refreshed or appended), when summaries and indexes were rebuilt, and so on. Traditionally, system logs of this type are generated as text files by the batch processes that perform the work. These text files are generally unavailable to all but the system administrators—and are rarely examined even by them! Much useful information, however, can be gleaned from the statistics, volumes, and timings that can be obtained from these batch jobs.

Imagine a simple table added to your data warehouse in which each routine batch job does a single insert when it starts and a single update when it ends. (Note that the overhead incurred by this extra recording is negligible within the total amount of work done by any of these processes.) In a simple case, the data to be recorded might include the following:

- The name of the process (and perhaps its version/release number)
- Input file name, size, and the like (if applicable)
- The date and time of job start and end
- The job completion status
- The number of rows processed (inserted, updated, purged, etc.)
- The number of rows rejected or errored (if applicable)

Another newly defined process can be added at the end of the regular maintenance window to snapshot additional statistics about the data warehouse itself. These statistics are gathered automatically by Oracle whenever a table or index is analyzed. (See Chapter 5, "Building the Oracle Data Warehouse," and Chapter 9, "Data Warehouse Performance Tuning," for more information about using the ANALYZE command to gather statistics for use by the Oracle query optimizer.) The optimizer statistics are available in the data dictionary using simple, low-overhead queries. They need to be captured, however, into another table before they are overwritten by the next cycle of loading and analyzing. In this way you will retain a history of these statistics that can be examined to observe changes over time.

VIEWING THE STATISTICS GATHERED BY ANALYZE

The primary tables containing these useful statistics are DBA_TABLES and DBA_INDEXES. A more complete monitoring might also find interesting statistics from DBA_TAB_COLUMNS, DBA_IND_COLUMNS, DBA_HISTOGRAMS (Oracle7), DBA_TAB_HISTOGRAMS (Oracle8), DBA_TAB_COL_STATISTICS (Oracle8), and DBA_FREE_SPACE. If auditing is used to track warehouse usage, it may be helpful to regularly snapshot information from DBA_AUDIT_OBJECT, DBA_AUDIT_SESSION, or DBA_AUDIT_TRAIL. For Oracle8 partitioned objects, additional useful statistics can be obtained from DBA_TAB_PARTITIONS and DBA_IND_PARTITIONS.

Having this information in the database allows the administrator to ask a variety of interesting new questions about trends. (Why does the weekly load cycle seem to take longer than it used to? Which specific processes are taking more time than they used to? When did this start? Did it occur suddenly or gradually? Is it related to changes in the volume of data being processed or the total volume of data being stored?) Specific observations of B*Tree indexes growing out of proportion to their tables can identify the need for rebuilding them to accommodate a load/purge cycle that leaves older branches of the index sparsely populated even while newer branches are being created.

If one job should fail to complete, there may be a logical discrepancy in the implied relationships between data in different tables. Consider the case of a summary table that fails to be re-created after loading additional data into a corresponding detail table. Attempts to drill down from the summary to detail may return bizarre, confusing results.

Even warehouse users can find useful information within this "processing log" type of metadata. Just knowing that a particular load or summarization process did not complete successfully can help an analyst avoid (or explain!) a query that might return erroneous results. Also, the stored trend information about number of rows processed (or rejected) may be of more interest to the business analyst than to the administrator. Why were last week's store receipts from the central region 23 percent less than the week before? The answer might be a business issue (spring flooding in the Midwest?) or it might be because a processing problem in the Chicago office's computer prevented delivery of one of five extract files. If the analyst can see only that the dollar volume was down for the region, he may have a hard time understanding the cause; if, on the other hand, he can also investigate the record volume and processing log then the investigation may take a totally different direction.

What Metadata Does Oracle Provide?

At a bare minimum, users will need to be able to determine the name and structure of each table that contains information important to them. As we'll see shortly, this information is available via the Oracle data dictionary. Figure 4.1 shows a simplified diagram of the type of metadata that is maintained by the Oracle data dictionary. While necessary, this level of metadata may not be sufficient to allow the warehouse users to make informed decisions about which

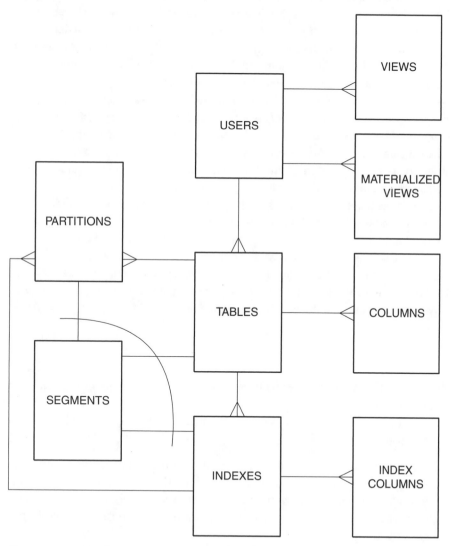

Figure 4.1   Metadata maintained by the Oracle data dictionary.

CONTROLLING USER ACCESS DURING WAREHOUSE REFRESH PROCESSING

Ideally, the administrator of the warehouse should prevent access to the warehouse, or a specific subject area, if data in one table is not properly synchronized with data in other related tables because one process out of several failed to complete. As we'll see later in this chapter, the normal OLTP system practice of using declarative foreign key constraints to ensure data integrity is not widely used in the data warehouse. Also, because of the large volumes of data typically processed in a load cycle, updates to more than one table in the warehouse are not coordinated through the normal transaction processing capabilities of Oracle. Each table is typically loaded or summarized independent of others. Either automatically or manually, the administrator should ensure that users do not view inconsistent data.

Access to warehouse data should be controlled using Oracle's role-based security feature. Roles make it very easy for the administrator (or subject area owner) to add new users to the warehouse and give them access to appropriate data. As a side benefit, this same facility makes it very easy to temporarily restrict access to one portion of the warehouse. Each subject area should be controlled by a different pair of roles. To prevent users from accessing a particular subject area during the time that data is being maintained (loaded, indexed, summarized, purged, etc.), the administrator need only issue a single REVOKE statement; after completion of all related maintenance within that subject area, only a single GRANT statement will reopen the warehouse for access. Should any portion of the maintenance cycle fail to complete, the GRANT statement should not be issued until the problem is investigated and resolved. This process can be performed manually.

warehouse data they need, how to formulate a query to retrieve it, or how to interpret the results.

Additional metadata that may be helpful to the users of our warehouse can include the following:

- Information about the source of warehouse data. This might name the operational system, file, and field from which the data was extracted, or it might identify where external data was acquired. Rarely will this be a simple 1:1 mapping of a warehouse table back to a single file or table in the legacy systems world.

- Information about how the data is transformed, filtered, and preprocessed during the extraction and loading of detailed data.

In this situation, the administrator or subject area owner will manually review the results of the most recent maintenance cycle. After verifying that all processing completed properly, the GRANT statement is executed manually. The advantage to this approach is that the verification process can be more intelligently performed; the administrator or subject area owner can examine the data for reasonableness by issuing a variety of queries rather than just verifying the completion of jobs.

The disadvantage, of course, is that someone must assume this responsibility after each maintenance cycle, whether that is monthly, weekly, or daily. As a daily responsibility, this may present problems. Vacations, illness, weather, and the like may all prevent the timely granting of access to other users. The manual approach does not require that all of the run statistics be kept in the database, although doing so is likely to facilitate the process.

Alternatively, this process can be performed automatically. To do so, run results must be made available in the database as recommended. A simple program or stored procedure needs to be written that will examine whichever results and statistics are determined to be important to reasonably ensure the integrity of the just completed data maintenance cycle. If each of these checks is successful, then the program or procedure will issue the appropriate GRANT statement (and add its own execution record to the processing log). Should any problems be detected, Oracle provides stored procedures capable of sending an e-mail message (or, with some additional programming, a telephone call to a pager) to the appropriate administrators and subject area owners. Once written, this program or procedure needs to be added to the processing schedule after all the jobs whose execution it will verify.

- A schedule and history of load, summarization, purge, and other administrative jobs including record counts and other control information.

- Definition of units of measure. As data is loaded into the warehouse, it is transformed into standardized units of measure. This allows the direct comparison of different data. Some users, however, will be more familiar with alternative units of measure (meters versus feet, for one simple example—the real world is frequently far more complex), and they need to be provided with conversion factors to help interpret results.

- Information about how summarizations were performed. This should also guide the user in how to perform drill-downs from the summary to the next lower level of summarization or to the detailed data from which the summary was constructed.

- The rules for exclusion if some data is excluded from loading or summarization because of missing or invalid values.

- Aliases information. Because all data loaded into the data warehouse is integrated (as discussed in Chapter 1, "Data Warehousing") we have determined a single standard name for each element of warehouse data. Invariably, different work groups and departments will be familiar with the data under different names than the one standard name chosen. Until users become familiar with the standard names, they will need to have help making the translations. This help can be provided with additional metadata that allows the user to look up a familiar business (or specific legacy system) term and be told the "proper" name for that data within the data warehouse.

- Versioning of data structures and definitions. Data warehouse structures are not permanently frozen. Almost by definition, data warehouses are constantly being evaluated for enhancement opportunities. Additional data elements are added to existing tables, new tables are added and, occasionally, some columns of current warehouse tables may be eliminated. New DSS analysis leads to new types of questions, which lead to new data requirements. If data from the warehouse is archived and later restored, it will also be necessary to restore the metadata that was current when the data was archived.

- Job execution status. As we discussed earlier in this chapter, the failure of one or more load or summarization jobs may invalidate the results of some queries. If the monthly regional summaries of SALES_REVENUES completed successfully but the corresponding summaries of COSTS_OF_SALES did not, then queries that seek to determine profitability by region are not going to deliver meaningful answers. In some such cases, the failure will be obvious and the queries will simply fail. In other cases, the queries may be complete but give erroneous results.

Delivering Metadata

There are several alternative means for allowing users to view metadata about the contents of the warehouse. They are discussed in the following sections.

Printed Metadata Reports

Early data warehouses typically provided metadata to their users via printed reports—often generated directly from the Oracle data dictionary. Each new user was provided with a book of simple metadata, often limited to the same type of physical database design information that DBAs would provide to a programming team for an operational system. This book typically included a layout for each table that showed column names, data types, and length. This simple approach to providing users with information about the contents of the data warehouse has several drawbacks.

- As discussed earlier, the need for additional metadata was recognized over time as the warehouse support staff found themselves having to repeatedly explain where some data element originated and how it was processed en route to the warehouse. Warehouse users have a greater need to correctly interpret the data they work with than do programmers, and they therefore need more than just physical layouts. The additional information about the warehouse data can, of course, be added to these reports using a word processor, but other problems remain.

- A printed report is of use to the user only when he takes the time to look something up in it. It is inherently passive. Modern query tools, however, are able to take advantage of metadata when it is stored in the database. As the user of one of these tools browses through the data warehouse and develops a query, the tool can become an intelligent helper by automatically displaying descriptive aliases on reports, by graphically displaying probable join criteria, or by referencing statistical information from the database to roughly predict query performance.

- Another major deficiency of printed metadata reports is that they become rapidly outdated as the warehouse evolves. New subject areas are added, each with multiple tables and relationships. Existing subject areas are frequently enhanced with new summary tables as analysts identify expensive queries that repeatedly summarize detailed data. Finally, new columns may be added to existing tables as users request additional data. Printed reports, therefore, have to be regenerated and redistributed frequently. Users who don't receive or file their updates are unable to take advantage of new warehouse features.

The Oracle Data Dictionary

The Oracle data dictionary lies at the core of each Oracle database. Oracle uses it to keep track of all database objects, freespace, users, and security. An incredible amount of detail is maintained in the data dictionary that is quite helpful to the DBA, who frequently has the need, time, and experience to delve into the gory internal workings of the database and its objects.

Many query tools also take advantage of the Oracle data dictionary to assist the user in navigating through the data warehouse. These tools can often present a graphical view of the database, including relationships and join criteria. (This capability may require defining foreign keys, which are often a problem in a data warehouse; see the discussion of database constraints later in this chapter.)

There are, however, two characteristics of the data dictionary that limit its usefulness to general data warehouse users: incompleteness and excessive detail.

Not Complete

First, the information that is maintained in the data dictionary is very heavily oriented toward physical database structures. Warehouse users certainly have some need for physical descriptions of the tables they access. They need to know the names of tables and of columns within those tables. They need to know what type of data is stored in each of those columns. They need to know about the primary keys that define how the data in a table is organized. More experienced users will be interested in knowing which indexes are available to speed the execution of a contemplated query. Unfortunately, the data dictionary does not hold other information needed by the warehouse user. The data dictionary does not, for instance, keep track of which operational system a particular data element is populated from or what calculations were performed on it. The data dictionary does not remind the user that a specific column name has several alternative names.

Further, the data dictionary provides only a current view of the database structure—it does not maintain any history. Given the evolutionary nature of the data warehouse, it is important to be able to understand the changes in structure that have occurred. This is particularly true when archival data is maintained in an older format than current data.

Too Detailed

Second, the level of physical detail that is needed by the DBA is not easily navigated by a less technically trained user. The casual or infrequent warehouse user may not recognize that the name of the "table" in his SELECT statement might actually be stored in the data dictionary as a table, a view, or even a synonym to another schema's table or view. Even experienced Oracle developers sometimes get confused about the actual location of data they're accessing when they create a private synonym, table, or view that supercedes an intended public synonym reference to another object. While necessary for administering the warehouse database, all this complexity is confusing to the business analyst trying to use the data warehouse to obtain answers to business questions. Ideally, the average warehouse user should be able to see metadata for all his available objects in one standardized set of metadata objects.

Extending the Oracle Data Dictionary

The simplest means of extending the Oracle data dictionary is to use comments. The standard data dictionary has a built-in capability for storing additional textual information about each table and each column defined in the database. It is surprising how few Oracle database administrators are aware of this capability or use it at all.

Using Comments

Comments are appended to the definition of the table or column using the COMMENT command. As an example, to add source system information for the CUSTOMERS table in the schema named DW, the administrator might issue the following SQL command:

```
COMMENT ON TABLE dw.customers
    IS 'Source is CUSTMSTR file within the ORDPROC system.';
```

Views can be commented just the same as tables. Use the COMMENT ON TABLE command just as if the view were a table. Here is a comment added to the definition of the LOCAL_CUSTOMERS view:

```
COMMENT ON TABLE dw.local_customers
    IS 'Local customers are those with HQ located in Colorado.';
```

To further note that the CUSTOMER_NAME column of this table has been edited before loading it into the warehouse, an additional column-level COMMENT command could be issued:

```
COMMENT ON COLUMN sales.customers.customer_name
    IS 'Name edited to all capital letters during load.';
```

Once the information has been added to the data dictionary with COMMENT commands for each table and column, it can be viewed by inquiring on the dictionary views ALL_TAB_COMMENTS and ALL_COL_COMMENTS using the OWNER (schema name), TABLE_NAME, and COLUMN_NAME columns as keys. This is fairly easy to do if printed reports are to be generated. To provide this data to warehouse users without forcing them to do two queries or to repeatedly join the data, the administrator may create two new views (perhaps just called TABLES and COLUMNS) that predefine the joins to effectively add the COMMENTS column to the other information. Here is an example that builds the TABLES view:

```
CREATE OR REPLACE VIEW dw.tables As
    SELECT T.TABLE_NAME, TC.TABLE_TYPE, TC.COMMENTS
      FROM ALL_TABLES T, ALL_TAB_COMMENTS TC
     WHERE T.OWNER = TC.OWNER
       AND T.TABLE_NAME = TC.TABLE_NAME(+)
```

```
        AND T.OWNER = 'DW'
   UNION ALL
   SELECT VIEW_NAME, TC.TABLE_TYPE, TC.COMMENTS
     FROM ALL_VIEWS V, ALL_TAB_COMMENTS TC
    WHERE V.OWNER = TC.OWNER
      AND V.VIEW_NAME = TC.TABLE_NAME
      AND V.OWNER = 'DW';
COMMENT ON DW.TABLES
     IS 'View displaying COMMENTS and other dictionary info';
```

During training, the users can be instructed to use these new views to obtain their metadata:

```
SELECT * FROM dw.tables;

TABLE_NAME                          TABLE_TYPE
---------------------------- ----------
COMMENTS
-------------------------------------------------------
CUSTOMERS                           TABLE
Source is CUSTMSTR file within the ORDPROC system.
LOCAL_CUSTOMERS                     VIEW
Local customers are those with HQ located in Colorado.
TABLES                              VIEW
View displaying COMMENTS and other dictionary info
3 rows selected.
```

There are, however, a few limitations on using the COMMENTS feature to extend the Oracle data dictionary:

- The textual data is unformatted by Oracle. It is treated only as a character string, so any structure to the information must be carefully defined and enforced by those who enter the COMMENTS.

- The comments for any one table or column can not exceed 2,000 characters in Oracle7 or 4,000 in Oracle8. This may not provide enough room to maintain all the additional metadata needed by an organization.

- At any given time, there can be only one comment for each table, view, or column known to the data dictionary. There is no historical record of dictionary structure or of our extended comments.

- Comments can be added only to tables, views, and columns. Other structures, such as indexes, sequences, or clusters, cannot be commented. Individual Oracle8 partitions cannot be separately commented.

- Most query tools are not likely to automatically perform the joins to ALL_TAB_COMMENTS and ALL_COL_COMMENTS in order to display comments because the comments feature is so rarely used.

■ The information stored in comments cannot be easily edited. It is replaced each time another COMMENT command is issued on the table or column. To make changes to existing comments the administrator would need to retrieve the current information to a text file, edit the text file, and then reissue the COMMENT.

TIP Extract data from the data dictionary to a text file using the SPOOL command in SQL*Plus followed by a SELECT statement for the specific data you want written to the file. To generate the extracted data in the form of the necessary SQL statements to re-create the data, use SQL to generate SQL. This technique is presented in Chapter 5.

If the limitations of using comments to extend the Oracle data dictionary impair the designer's ability to document and present metadata, it may be time to consider another alternative.

Creating Additional Tables

The entire Oracle data dictionary is composed of standard Oracle tables, indexes, clusters, views, and sequences. Application developers routinely create tables, indexes, and views to store data needed by their applications. The warehouse developer can just as easily build a mini-application to handle warehouse metadata. To employ this option, the warehouse developer will need to have a solid understanding of the Oracle data dictionary because everything built in the metadata application will need to be coordinated with it. An Oracle DBA assigned to the project should provide this necessary knowledge. An additional skill in building online screens to maintain the metadata, however, will be needed. Normally, a warehouse project does not have an assigned programmer familiar with Oracle*Forms, Visual Basic, or other screen development tools. If your project elects to provide metadata using custom tables, be sure to include this resource early in the project plan.

There is no one right set of tables and views that will satisfy the metadata needs of a warehouse. The design will be driven partly by the sophistication of the users, partly by the choice of query tool (or tools), and partly by the design of the warehouse itself. Some warehouse builders will not choose to implement a versioning strategy. Some may want to document archived data; others may not. As an example, the Oracle Discoverer query tool creates more than 40 tables to maintain its End User Layer (metadata) and support its queries.

Whichever approach is chosen to supplement the Oracle data dictionary, it will be necessary to provide a means of maintaining metadata in the repository.

Maintaining the Extended Data Dictionary

If comments are used to extend the metadata stored about tables and columns in the dictionary, then the additional metadata stored within those comments must be maintained by reissuing the COMMENT command. Each new COMMENT command will overwrite the previous comment on the object. The easiest way to maintain the data will be in an external file using a text editor. The data dictionary will be used primarily to present the data to the user, via SQL queries, but the real maintenance will be done outside of the database and then applied via a COMMENT command.

If, on the other hand, extended metadata is provided via additional tables, then maintenance can be performed using the shop's chosen application development tools. Oracle's Developer/2000 tools, Microsoft's Visual Basic, or other 4GLs designed for quickly developing SQL applications will fit the bill.

The biggest difficulty with this approach of keeping extended metadata in separate tables will be encountered when you try to keep the tables synchronized with the Oracle data dictionary. Because actual SQL statements issued by the user will interact with the tables, views, and columns as known to the data dictionary, it is essential that the helpful metadata provided to the users be consistent with the data dictionary. If we add a column to a warehouse table (via the ALTER TABLE SQL statement) the data dictionary will be immediately updated to reflect its existence. We must simultaneously add the same information to our extended metadata tables. Unless the administrator is very careful, there is a strong possibility that errors will be made while performing dual maintenance.

There are three approaches to ensuring that updates to the basic data dictionary and our extended dictionary are coordinated:

1. The first approach is after-the-fact verification. Simple SQL scripts can be run to validate that the contents of your extended metadata tables are synchronized with Oracle's data dictionary record of the actual physical structure of the warehouse.

2. The second approach is to generate skeleton updates to the extended tables from the data dictionary. Using the SQL-to-generate-SQL technique (presented in Chapter 5), a script can read the data dictionary to initially populate the extended metadata repository. Screen-based programs would then be created to allow the warehouse designer to fill in the blanks with the additional logical metadata needed by the user and future maintainers of the warehouse.

3. The final approach is to make all the changes directly to the extended metadata tables and then generate the corresponding SQL DDL to update the Oracle data dictionary. This approach could also utilize SQL to generate SQL, or it could alternatively be executed from triggers on the

extended metadata tables, using the DBMS_SQL package to immediately perform the corresponding DDL. This approach probably provides the best support for historical versioning of metadata.

Building and maintaining your own metadata repository as part of the data warehouse design process are challenging and time-consuming tasks. Unless the data warehouse project faces severe budget limitations (as during a proof-of-concept phase) it is preferable to acquire a predefined repository that can accomplish the same goals with much less effort.

Predefined Metadata Repositories

Even though the Oracle RDBMS's built-in data dictionary does not include all the information needed to support a data warehouse, other components of the complete data warehouse solution may provide the necessary capabilities.

ETT Tools

Most data warehouse projects will require the use of specialized tools for extracting, transforming, moving, validating, integrating, and loading data from various source systems into the warehouse.

WHAT'S IN A NAME?

These specialized tools are sometimes called ETT (extraction, transformation, transportation) tools. Other people refer to them as ETL (extraction, transformation, load) tools. Whichever name you use, be aware that their responsibilities are broader than these three-letter acronyms (TLAs) indicate—integration and validation are major responsibilities of these tools. Acknowledging these limitations, we'll continue to use the more traditional term, ETT, in this book.

I suppose that there might be copyright issues if they were properly termed "the nighttime extraction, transformation, transportation, validation, integration, and load, so you can rest, medicine."

Frequently data warehouse projects are initiated on a shoestring budget, and the organization decides to save money by not acquiring an ETT tool. These products can be, admittedly, rather expensive with price tags ranging well into six figures. The opportunity cost of using in-house programmers and the actual cost of engaging contractors and/or consultants to manually write and maintain the necessary extract programs, transformation logic, and file transfer scripts (and, of course, metadata), however, will eventually exceed the software licensing costs for a well-designed ETT tool.

One of the benefits provided by these tools is a metadata documentation layer. Each tool will vary in the emphasis it places on supplying user metadata as well as how and where it will store the metadata. The tool needs to store metadata for its own use. It needs to remember where to find the needed source data and how to transform it. This is also information of interest to the users. To be completely functional as a metadata repository, however, it should also be capable of storing the additional information needed by warehouse users. As discussed earlier, this should include items such as aliases, definition of standardized units of measure, conversion factors, methods of summarization, and so on. One of the many criteria for selecting an ETT tool should be the completeness of the metadata it is capable of storing as well as how easily it can be maintained by the warehouse designer or administrator and accessed by users.

The developers of an ETT tool have several alternative locations in which to store their metadata. Be sure that the one you select is capable of storing its repository inside the data warehouse so that users can access it using their standard query tools. An external repository on a dedicated ETT workstation may be most convenient for the ETT tool, but it will not meet the additional metadata needs of the warehouse users. If ETT tool metadata must be stored in a proprietary form and location, ensure that an adequate export function is provided that allows useful metadata, including versioning, to be loaded into the warehouse for user access. Synchronizing and integrating this source of metadata with other sources (such as the data dictionary, processing logs, and various query tools) is left as an exercise to the warehouse development team.

Query Tools

As an alternative to maintaining warehouse metadata manually or on the "front end" in an ETT tool, many of the current generation of end-user query tools provide a metadata layer as well. If your data warehouse project will be selecting a single, standardized query tool then this is a perfect opportunity to provide a robust navigation and interpretation tool at the same time. Using the "administrator" mode of the query tool, the analyst can document everything the user might want to know about the structure, contents, and meaning of the warehouse. The tool can then help guide the user easily through the navigation of the warehouse and automatically perform joins, drill-downs, and star and snowflake consolidations.

Of course, the end-user query tool's metadata will not directly support the needs of the extraction, transformation, transportation, and loading functions. One potential risk in piecing together an entire data warehouse solution is that the warehouse administrator will need to maintain multiple metadata repositories with some overlapping needs. If this is the case, keeping the multiple repositories in synch with each other (and the real data!) will become an additional point of concern.

THE PROMISE OF CASE TOOLS

CASE tools were widely touted in the late 1980s as the salvation of information technology. (Relational databases, GUI development tools, object-oriented development, and the Web have all taken their turn in this limelight.) Like any product, some CASE tools were (and are) better than others. Many organizations purchased and then discarded even the best CASE tools because their first in-house usage did not generate the 50 percent (or more) project time savings touted by the CASE vendors. In virtually all of those situations the problem was not in the tool but in the organization. Systems engineering, supported by CASE, is fundamentally a change in organizational discipline. Organizations without the necessary discipline (or the endemic desire to adopt it) were doomed to fail. A carpenter who fails to measure carefully will not become more successful because he replaces his handsaw with the best circular saw; he will just be able to make a mess more quickly.

CASE Tools

A third alternative for acquiring a metadata repository is the set of tools used by designers of application systems to document their table and process models. Some Computer Aided Systems Engineering (CASE) tools are very good at defining and using multiple levels of metadata. Others are little more than diagrammers for drawing pretty pictures. There are, however, a few limitations of the current crop of CASE tools that may limit their applicability to providing metadata for a data warehouse:

- Most CASE tools have not been designed to handle the special design considerations of a data warehouse. OLTP systems focus on the current value for any data element, while data warehouses provide a historical view of changes in values. Entity relationship diagramming (ERD) techniques are useful for designing a traditional detail-and-summary style of warehouse, even though relationally pure foreign keys may not apply to the new warehouse relationships. Newer techniques, however, are required to support dimensional analysis of a star schema warehouse.

- Relational OLTP systems have a strong emphasis on foreign keys based on value equality between two tables. These relationships are generally clouded in the data warehouse where time becomes part of most tables' key structures. The warehouse relationship of summary-to-detail is not the same as OLTP's parent-to-child.

- Star and snowflake schemas are unique to the data warehouse. CASE tools designed for OLTP systems design will not support this diagramming technique or generate the appropriate supporting DDL.

- Some CASE tools support versioning of applications but generally with a revolutionary mind-set. That is, version 2 is being built to replace version 1. In a data warehouse, it is frequently necessary to maintain and retrieve data in version 1 format for years, even after new data has been added in the format of versions 2, 3, and 4.

- Most OLTP systems do not require active interaction with extended metadata at run-time. Therefore, most CASE tools are generally oriented toward generating DDL or application code offline. Most users of the data warehouse will not be using code generated by a programmer but will be interacting directly with the database and metadata repository to discover new information.

As data warehouses became a major focus of the entire IT field in the 1990s, some of these capabilities have been incorporated into CASE tools. If your organization is currently using a particular CASE tool successfully, you should evaluate its capabilities for supporting the specific design requirements of a data warehouse. Perhaps you need to get an upgrade from the vendor to obtain necessary features. Beyond its usefulness as a design tool, you should also evaluate its capabilities for presenting an active metadata interface to users and their investigative tools.

Eventually these separate classes of tools (RDBMS, ETT, query, and CASE) may become better integrated into the entire data warehouse process. When that occurs, we will no longer have to maintain multiple repositories of our metadata.

A STANDARDIZED METADATA REPOSITORY

For several years, an effort has been underway within Oracle Coporation to define and provide a standardized metadata repository for data warehousing that would be used by all of Oracle's decision support tools. In 1999, Oracle (along with IBM, Unisys, NCR, and Hyperion) submitted a proposal for a Common Warehouse Metamodel (CWM) to the Object Management Group (OMG). Literally as this book is going to press, OMG has just announced the formal adoption of the CWM standard. Oracle products (Oracle Warehouse Builder, Discoverer, Express) are already being converted to begin using this new standard repository. Please visit the companion Web site for the latest news regarding CWM.

Introduction to a DW Case Study

Throughout the next several chapters it will be helpful to provide examples based on a simple case study. We will use a data warehousing effort within a fictitious consulting company, Consultants 'R' Us.

The primary business of Consultants 'R' Us is providing a variety of consulting services to many clients in a number of different industries. This organization employs thousands of consultants who provide these services. They have different skills and different levels of experience. Each consultant is assigned to a specific organization, but the consultants often work on projects managed by a different organization. Each organization focuses on a geographic territory or a specific industry. Because of our excellent staff and high-quality engagements we frequently obtain repeat business and consult on many different projects for the same customer.

Our business tracks consulting assignments using a time and expense system that was developed in-house about five years ago. Every project, client, consultant, and organization exists in the TEAM (Time Expense and Management) system. Each consultant is required to enter his or her time into the system every week and must assign every working hour to some project. We have created some nonclient projects associated with internal assignments, training, vacations, and the like so a time record will frequently have hours assigned to more than one project. Further, we have established function codes that are used to indicate the specific activities on any project. Although our transactions occur at least on a weekly basis, we will need to aggregate and report data for a given consultant, project, organization, and function on a monthly basis. Our extract and load procedures run monthly.

Our management wants to better understand the fundamental nature of our consulting business and wishes to conduct a range of analyses. Some of the expected analyses are as follows:

- Comparative analysis of budget and actual revenues among organizations over time
- Revenue associated with different types of consulting services
- Revenue and profitability associated with our work in different industries or geographies
- Profitability of specific projects, organizations, etc.
- Utilization rates of consultants in various organizations

We have been asked to develop a data warehouse to support these types of analysis.

Figure 4.2 shows the logical model for the Consultants 'R' Us TEAM operational system. The programming team that maintains the TEAM system will be extracting data for our warehouse into flat files that will be transmitted to us after the close of each monthly billing cycle.

Organizations are grouped into regions, regions are grouped into areas, and areas are rolled up into divisions. This is a classic hierarchy, and for the TEAM

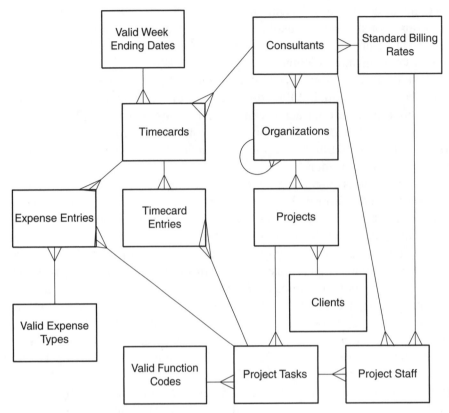

Figure 4.2 OLTP source system database design.

application our company's development team designed the hierarchy with an ORGANIZATIONS entity and a recursive relationship that would allow us to combine each element in the hierarchy with its parent organization. This type of design would provide flexibility for changing the hierarchy, and Oracle's CONNECT BY function would allow us to rebuild the hierarchy structure. Such a design is not appropriate for a data warehouse, however. The performance overhead we would incur by having to process a CONNECT BY in order to calculate summaries at different levels of the hierarchy would simply be too great. For the warehouse, we will collapse the organization structure to a single level with a time component so we can later accommodate changes in the organization structure by adding a new row with a new effective date.

Our initial analysis indicates that there will be approximately 25,000 projects, 200 organizations, 10,000 consultants, 50 functions, and 5 million transactions in the ACTIVITY table. Incidentally, this would generally be considered a relatively small data warehouse.

We will come back to this case study in a few minutes to help us visualize the differences between two alternative warehouse design approaches. First, though, we take a look at the process by which warehouses are designed and contrast that with the methodologies used to develop transaction processing systems.

Warehouse Design Process

The process of designing the data warehouse database is a variation of that used in designing traditional OLTP systems' databases. Figure 4.3 demonstrates the typical "waterfall" approach used in the design of OLTP systems. Countless systems design methodologies have been developed that follow this general approach.

The warehouse design process shares some characteristics with the OLTP "waterfall" methodology. We have the same general steps to complete, but we visit the steps in a very different pattern. Figure 4.4 demonstrates our very short phases. For each phase, we iterate through the entire set of steps.

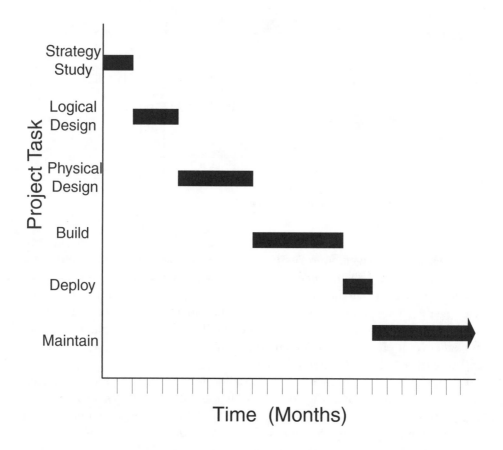

Figure 4.3 Traditional OLTP "waterfall" methodology.

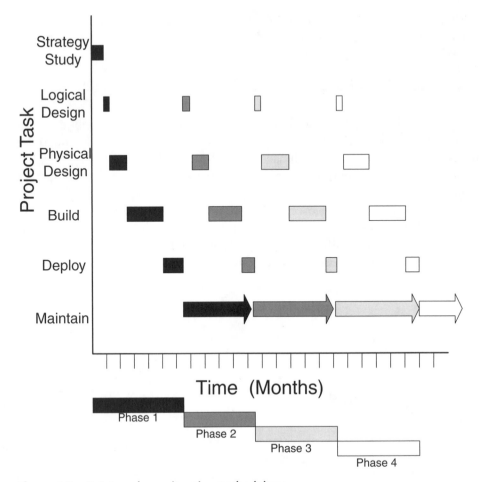

Figure 4.4   Data warehouse iterative methodology.

For the data warehouse, we typically still perform a strategy study that presents a case for management to justify building a data warehouse and defines the objectives, costs, rough implementation schedule, and resources needed. We will develop a logical design that documents the data requirements and relationships. Because the data warehouse is developed in incremental stages, we will typically start logical design by doing a very high-level subject area design that will be used to plan several phases of implementation. This corresponds to the preliminary design of the OLTP design methodology.

We can then do the detailed data modeling for Phase 1. The logical design does not take into account the specific implementation issues (such as clustering, partitioning, or indexing) of a particular database management system. When we have a complete logical model for a particular phase we translate it into a physical design that is very specific to the chosen DBMS. At this point we introduce specific features and capabilities of the DBMS that make our warehouse more manageable and provide optimal performance. We also take into account any DBMS limitations that might influence us to avoid specific design/implementation options.

After completing the physical design for Phase 1, we will begin the actual development (build) and deployment tasks. As soon as Phase 1 has been released to the users, we will immediately return to review and possibly revise the high-level subject area design and then start on the detailed logical design phase for Phase 2. That will lead to the physical design and deployment for Phase 2 and so on.

As described in Chapter 1, warehouse development is an ongoing, evolutionary process. One of the most common risks to the warehouse is the natural tendency of developers to feel the need to "get it right" before they deliver a system. For those of us who grew up in the OLTP world, we cower like a beaten dog at the thought of missing a key user requirement. In the warehouse world, this ingrained need leads to analysis paralysis and quickly consumes too much time and energy that could be better directed toward delivering *something* to which the users can then respond.

While this admonition should not be used as an excuse for sloppiness, it is important to remember that it is okay—even necessary—for a phase of the warehouse to be less than the complete solution. Just like the daily affirmation

GETTING USERS TO SPECIFY REQUIREMENTS

The potential users of a new data warehouse generally don't know what they want. If the analyst asks them for requirements, they will repeatedly respond with "Everything" or "I don't know." These responses are totally honest.

If this is frustrating to the analyst/designer, then an interesting exercise can perhaps help explain the user's plight. We all have a pretty good understanding of automobiles. If you walk into a car dealer, you will be easily able to answer questions about your needs—four doors, seating for five adults, lots of headroom, at least 20 miles per gallon, etc.

Now imagine yourself stepping, today, into the new spaceship dealer that just opened across the street from your office. Quickly, now make a list of the 10 most important requirements you have for selecting the new models of "personal intergalactic surface-negating, orthogonally unified transporters" (PIGSNOUT).

Well, are you done? Where did you start? How do you know if this device is more like *Star Trek* or the *Jetsons*? Was it inspired by Asimov or Smirnoff? (Perhaps you could get a better start on selecting a PIGSNOUT model if the salesperson were to take you out for a test-ride first.)

This is about the same sense of disorientation our potential users get when we start asking them if they need ROLAP or MOLAP. The Phase I release will give them their test ride.

of Stuart Smalley, the feel-good therapist from *Saturday Night Live* quoted at the opening of this chapter, "My warehouse is good enough. It is smart enough. And, doggone it, my users like it!"

Logical Warehouse Schema Design

To make our warehouse useful to our users we will need to go beyond loading raw data and just letting them figure it out. We will load the raw data, probably preprocessing it to resolve name and formatting inconsistencies. We will then perform various aggregations to produce summary data in a form useful for our users. Through interviews and prototyping we discover that the finance department wants to view information about consulting projects from a monthly revenue perspective. Marketing, however, wants to ask questions about the amount of business being performed in various industries. Our recruiting and internal training groups are interested in spotting trends in the hours being worked in various job functions being performed so they can keep ahead of a growing demand for certain skills. Each of these groups anticipates issuing multiple queries that will need to see data summarized in different ways.

How we approach the logical design of the database generally follows one of two styles.

Detail and Summary Schema

We have already talked in some depth about detailed and summary data. Within traditional data warehouse design (does "traditional" mean anything in a field as new as data warehousing?), we provide data in a somewhat predigested form for our users. The raw source data (from various sources) contains all of the information that can potentially be derived from the warehouse. Without any processing constraints imposed by today's hardware and RDBMS software we could just add a time-stamp, load the voluminous raw data, and call it a warehouse.

There are, however, real-world constraints that prohibit this simplistic approach. We don't want to incur the processing costs entailed in having multiple users repeat very large queries to get similar information. We also don't want to force our users to traverse a confusing network of third normal form relational tables and foreign keys to construct eight table joins with multiple-level correlated subqueries!

Detailed Data

Because of the large volume of detailed data produced by any modern corporation, organizations must seek ways to limit their need to store and repeatedly process it. In some data warehouses, detailed transaction data is never loaded. Light summarization is done during the extract process to minimize the cost and time transferring and loading the extract files. If you can accurately determine the lowest level of summarization that will be needed, then this approach has merit. It also helps avoid the operational reporting trap that can accompany detailed data into the warehouse.

In other situations, the decision is made to load detailed data. Early in the design of Phase 1 of the data warehouse a "requirement" is frequently stated that data will be retained for some extensive period of time, such as 5 years. One should at least question the need to view specific detailed transactional data from that far back. An alternative approach is to retain the detailed data for, say, 12 months and various summarizations for 5 (or more) years.

A decision will eventually have to be made about retention, archival, or purging of old detailed data. Fortunately, this is not one of the pressing decisions during the initial setup and design of the first phase of the data warehouse; unfortunately, many warehouse teams don't even consider the question. A tentative plan to purge 13-month-old detailed data each month can be reconsidered anytime during the first year of the warehouse's operation. You may later determine that archival may be a better strategy or that an 18-month retention period is more appropriate. Until you actually perform the first purge you have the freedom to reevaluate. But the tentative decision will affect elements of your physical design.

The new Oracle8*i* capability of "unplugging" transportable tablespaces is a great aid to archiving warehouse data. Archival processing will be discussed in more detail in Chapter 6, "Populating the Oracle Data Warehouse."

Summary and Aggregate Data

In most cases users will find the summarized data much easier to navigate. In building a summarization we can incorporate data from other related tables to avoid having to do joins from the summary. Of course, relational purists have to make some adjustments to their thinking—in the warehouse such denormalizations are proper.

The only difficulty arises from changes in the nonkey data. Is it possible for an organizational unit's name to change? For most companies, the answer is "of course." How will that be addressed in the warehouse? What approach will accommodate the name change in the middle of February when doing a summarization on a quarterly or annual basis? You face a Hobson's choice dilemma:

- Include one name or the other in the summary row and allow selection based only on that name.

- Include neither name in the summary but allow a query-time lookup (still of one name or the other).

- Report separate results for queries based on the two different organizational names (but merged data if a similar query were issued based on ORG_ID).

None of these three alternatives is perfect. Each will cause some confusion and the potential for erroneous results (or rather, erroneous interpretations of the results!). Generally, warehouse designers go with the third alternative. When nonkey data changes, we create a new row in whatever table (or, more likely, tables) includes that data and set appropriate values for effective and expiration date-time columns in both rows.

In our example of changing organization names, we might see the following entries in our summary data:

ORG_ID	ORG_NAME	AREA	DIV	MONTH	QTR	YEAR	INDUSTRY	HOURS	EXPENSES
123	Colo-Wyo-Utah	West	US	JAN	1	1997	Telecom	1,469	37,124
123	Colo-Wyo-Utah	West	US	FEB	1	1997	Telecom	897	19,459
123	Rocky Mountain	West	US	FEB	1	1997	Telecom	664	14,882
123	Rocky Mountain	West	US	MAR	1	1997	Telecom	1,629	42,668

Users who issue queries based on the new organizational name will receive only results starting with February 1997, and those results might be misinterpreted to suggest, for instance, that month-to-month growth between February and March (or Q1 1997 versus Q1 1998) was greater than it actually was. Users who queried based on the ORG_ID value would see a more complete picture of the telecom-related business performed within a given geographic territory. Actually, as this example illustrates, there is no single answer to this issue other than to keep data only in its most detailed form and process through it explicitly for each query. Because we cannot realistically do that with today's hardware and software this approach is the least painful alternative. (We should not hold out hope for advances in hardware and software to resolve this issue in the future either. Even as quickly as these technologies evolve, our ability to create data seems to grow even faster.)

Two other difficulties arise when providing data through multiple summarizations. The first is anticipating what summarizations are necessary. Frequently users won't know what questions they will eventually need to ask until after they've worked with the warehouse for a while. This is the normal evolutionary development pattern of a data warehouse. There is nothing to prevent adding more summary tables in later phases while also expanding the variety of subject areas and data sources. This approach does, however, require that a sufficiently low level of detail be available on which to base new summary tables. In the absence of a "final" warehouse design (which should never be expected) deciding to initially load and retain sufficiently detailed data is a reasonable insurance policy. After several design and delivery iterations the warehouse team will have a much better grasp of what data is likely to be needed in the future.

Detail and Summary Case Study

From the case study of our fictitious consulting company described earlier in the chapter we can design a data warehouse schema based on the concept of detailed data and various levels and types of summarization. Figure 4.5 shows one potential set of summary tables that might be derived from the detailed timecard data. Not shown in the diagram, but necessary to perform the denormalization discussed earlier, will be other source data about projects, consultants, organizational units, and so on. We will use these during our summarization process to include meaningful real-world descriptive information within our summary tables.

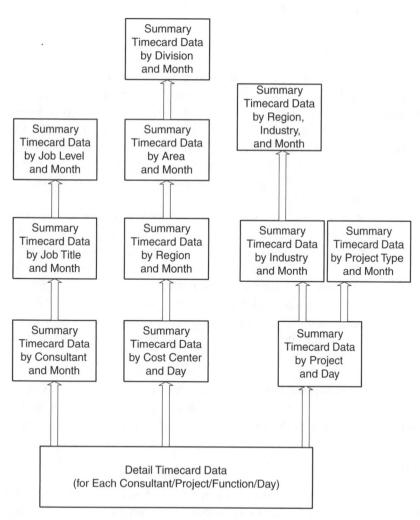

Figure 4.5 Relational "detail and summary" schema.

The logical design of this type of schema can be implemented using Oracle7 or Oracle8. We will discuss the differences later in this chapter in the section on physical database design.

Oracle8 provides efficient parallel operations for populating the summary tables from the detailed data (or from another lower level of summarization). Building a summary from detail tables can be efficiently performed with parallel CREATE TABLE AS SELECT. In Oracle8*i*, the materialized view feature simplifies the process and allows automation of the creation and maintenance of these summaries. Materialized views also provide major performance benefits through automatic query rewriting to take advantage of the summary even when the user specifies the detail table in the query. The specific techniques for building or maintaining these summary tables will be presented in Chapter 7, "Post-Load Processing in the Data Warehouse."

Star Schemas

The concept of a star schema (or its variation, the snowflake schema) was a relatively late arrival in the data warehouse design option list. Bill Inmon's initial data warehouse writings from 1992 and 1993 don't make reference to this design alternative. The primary reference works on this topic are Ralph Kimball's *The Data Warehouse Toolkit* (1996, Wiley-QED) and *The Data Warehouse Life Cycle Toolkit* (1998, Wiley Computer Publishing). Kimball's books are highly recommended for a more in-depth explanation of star schema concepts and design than is possible here.

The relational star schema is derived from multidimensional database design. Each star is designed as a central, usually large, table of facts—typically the recording of a particular type of event. Each event (fact) occurs within the context of several dimensions. Just as in Newtonian physics, where each point is conceived as existing within the dimensions of space and time, our facts must be located within the dimensions that are important to our business. When we think about a sales order (fact), we might note that it occurred on a particular day, for a distinct customer, in one of our regional offices, and was completed by a specific salesperson. Each of these ways of identifying orders is a dimension.

Of course, we are not limited to the physical dimensions of Newtonian space and time. We might find it useful to model additional dimensions such as the type of financing used on an order or the source of the original sales lead.

Fact Tables

Fact tables are commonly the largest collection of data in the data warehouse. One of our Internet commerce clients is currently recording more than 100 million rows of fact data every day! With even minimal recording of data about Web activity (page views and clicks) this quickly leads to an accumulation of 500 gigabytes of fact data each month. Telecommunications companies generate even larger volumes of call record detail.

To handle this volume of data, it is imperative to partition the fact table. Typically the warehouse fact tables are partitioned by the transaction date, possibly by month, week, day, or even hour. The proper level will be determined by the volume of data recorded, the conditions of typical queries, and the archival plan for the data.

Each row in the fact table has a column (or set of columns) corresponding to the primary key columns of each of the dimension tables in the star. In addition to these foreign key columns, the fact table consists of one or more columns that describe the volume, frequency, dollar value, or other numeric measure that can be summed, averaged, or aggregated in a query.

Fact tables, by their very nature, are highly normalized—they consist of a concatenated key (which is the intersection of the various dimension keys) and one or more measures (or attributes) that are related directly to that key. Textual attributes are generally of little value in fact tables because they cannot be arithmetically combined when a query seeks to retrieve many rows. Virtually all attributes in a fact table turn out to be measurements that can be meaningfully summed. In many cases the descriptive text attribute is more properly assigned to one of the dimensions—many fact rows with the same values for a text attribute suggest that there may be a missing dimension. Queries that are looking for specific values of an individual row's attributes are probably not ideally suited for the star schema or the data warehouse in general.

Dimension Tables

Dimension tables tend to be relatively small compared to the fact tables. Dimensions may include a few dozen or a few thousand rows. Fact tables frequently hold millions of rows. The voluminous fact tables would be very difficult to process frequently, even with index lookups. The objective of the star schema is to be able to efficiently select a subset of the total fact table by restricting the number of fact rows through limiting conditions specified about the dimensions. Consider an artificially simplified case in which a 10-million row fact table has 6 defined dimensions. Each dimension has 100 rows. A query that selects a single row from each of only 3 dimensions would, assuming a normal data distribution, retrieve only 10 rows out of the 10 million (.01*.01*.01*10,000,000). This fact lookup (assuming appropriate indexes) can be performed very efficiently!

True to traditional relational design, any descriptive attributes about the dimension will be stored in the dimension tables rather than the fact table.

Numeric values that wouldn't make sense being summed (such as a consultant's hourly billable rate) are probably dimensional attributes, not fact attributes. These dimensional attributes can be used to help select data to be reported, or they can be included in the query output.

The number of distinct values in a dimension is critical to its usefulness. A dimension with only a few values isn't particularly selective; by itself it is not very useful. As the number of possible values in the dimension approaches the number of rows in the fact table, the dimension also loses its value. At one extreme, a dimension with only one value is meaningless—it is related to every fact and doesn't help us discriminate between independent facts. At the other extreme, where a dimension is declared on a primary key (such as the sales order number) the dimension also has no value. In this case it is too discriminating—we can't use it to find a proper subset of the facts universe. In the ideal case, even though any one dimension may not be particularly selective, a combination of criteria involving multiple dimensions will identify a useful subset of the fact table for some form of analysis.

Standardizing a Continuous Dimension

When dimensional data is nearly continuous (as opposed to a series of discrete values) it will be necessary to standardize the dimension. Values along the continuous dimension should be divided into a set of ranges. The total dollar value of an order would be a useful attribute of a fact table. To be useful as a dimension, however, the total order value would have to be standardized—that is, for all values less than $100, we might assign the order a value category of 1; orders with values greater than or equal to $100 and less than $200 would go into price category 2, etc. Now a dimension based on price category would have perhaps a few dozen distinct values and would allow us to do more meaningful analysis of our sales data.

Determining the proper granularity of the dimensional values is a critical step in balancing the utility of the dimension with manageability of the warehouse. It is perfectly acceptable to carry the exact value as an attribute of the fact table while also carrying the standardized (or binned) value in another column that then relates to a standardized dimension. At the cost of some extra storage, this allows the efficiency of accessing the data via a standardized dimension while still maintaining the lower level of detail in the fact record.

The Time Dimension

Virtually every star will have a dimension related to time. Even though every transaction in the source system may be given a timestamp, this value may not be the best granularity for the warehouse. In most warehouses it isn't particularly useful to find a list of all facts for a particular second or even minute of the day.

For some business processes, determining the day for a fact may be sufficient. In this case, the time-stamp data may be trimmed during the load process to just eliminate the time portion of the Oracle DATE data type. In other cases, it may be more appropriate to be able to do analysis by hour. If the data is to be loaded using the conventional path of SQL*Loader, this can be accomplished using the TRUNC function of SQL. Even with direct path, you can easily ignore the unwanted time portion by specifying the TO_DATE format mask to read only the portion of the input record that contains the appropriate level of detail. Less significant levels of detail will be lost as Oracle defaults these portions of the DATE datatype to zero.

It may be important to do analysis based on time of day, without regard to the day. The user might be interested in analyzing the differences in Web traffic between the 9:00 a.m. hour and the 8:00 p.m. hour. If this kind of analysis were common, it might be useful to build a dimension around this view of time using 24 hourly categories (or bins) into which each Web activity record would be assigned. Using a column based on the Oracle DATE data type would not work well for this kind of analysis because it considers time to be a continuous function—9:00 a.m. tomorrow is not the same as 9:00 a.m. today. A separate dimension based on the day of the week may be useful for supporting other types of analysis.

The good news, for the designer, is that it will be easy to add dimensions of this type after the initial delivery of the warehouse as long as the full time-stamp is maintained in the fact data.

When selecting a particular level of granularity, the designer is preventing warehouse users from obtaining information at any lower level of detail. The balance must be made between the possible uses of the data and the capability for storing even greater volume. Fortunately, new features for partitioning of large fact tables, combined with improvements in the star query algorithm, allow Oracle8i to conveniently manage much larger volumes than were feasible before.

Hierarchical Dimensions

Dimension tables may be normalized around the specific dimension key. In many cases, however, where the dimension is naturally hierarchical, the hierarchy may be collapsed so that all but the lowest level of the hierarchy becomes nonkey attributes of the dimension. Figure 4.6 shows an example of taking the hierarchy from our company organization chart as it might be implemented in our OLTP systems and collapsing it into a warehouse dimension. (In Figure 4.4, the OLTP schema ERD showed this as a recursive relationship on ORGANIZATIONS.)

Any additional attributes of the higher levels of the hierarchy (such as DIVISION_NAME, REGION_NAME, and AREA_NAME) will also be made attributes

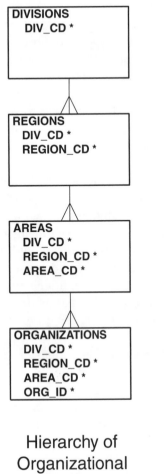

DIVISIONS
DIV_CD *

REGIONS
DIV_CD *
REGION_CD *

AREAS
DIV_CD *
REGION_CD *
AREA_CD *

ORGANIZATIONS
DIV_CD *
REGION_CD *
AREA_CD *
ORG_ID *

ORGANIZATIONS
ORG_ID *
AREA_CD
REGION_CD
DIV_CD

Hierarchy of
Organizational
Units

Collapsing the
Dimension
Hierarchy

(asterisk indicates a key)

Figure 4.6 Collapsing a hierarchical dimension.

of the resulting collapsed dimension. This is a denormalization but continues to reflect the reality in that each value of ORG_ID is associated with a single value of DIV_CD. Instead of being reflected via the one-to-many relationships of the hierarchy this is reflected in a single value of the attribute for each individual key. Within the OLTP world, such a denormalization would potentially require additional maintenance because a change of DIVISION_NAME would require updates to multiple rows.

Collapsing the hierarchy results in a single dimension within our star schema in which the user may specify any level of the hierarchy in his query. By specifying a value for any one of the attributes derived from the higher levels of the hierarchy, multiple rows of the ORGANIZATIONS dimension will be used to restrict the associated rows in the fact table to which the dimension is joined. As long as the number of rows in the resulting collapsed dimension is relatively small, this is an acceptable design.

The time dimension is frequently collapsed so that each daily record includes the week, month, quarter, and year associated with that day. Alternatively, the designer may choose (as we did in our case study) to maintain the week as the lowest level of granularity, or detail, in the fact table. This is particularly useful for viewing time in ways other than Oracle's normal understanding of the calendar. Recording the fiscal month and quarter for each daily dimension entry will allow analysts to use this criterion when specifying queries. The collapsed dimension will allow Oracle8 to efficiently translate the specification of a fiscal quarter into the equivalent 91 days.

DIMENSIONAL DATA CHANGES OVER TIME

Note that changes to the name or other attribute of any level of the collapsed hierarchy still present a problem for reflecting history in the data warehouse. This problem is unchanged by collapsing the hierarchy. It can be avoided only by adding a time element (or version number) to the key of each dimension just as in the detail-and-summary schema discussed earlier in this chapter. This is an unfortunate aspect of the real world that complicates the purity of both forms of design.

If, on the other hand, we need to store additional descriptive information about the values at each level we may choose to represent the hierarchy in a series of tables, one for each level. A foreign key at all but the top level of the hierarchy would define the relationship between adjacent levels. In this way we might represent our organization in the way shown on the left side of Figure 4.6. This would provide a convenient place to store extended descriptions, locations, etc. about each organization, area, region, and division.

Oracle8*i* Dimensions

While dimensions are a logical component of any star query, Oracle8*i* has added a new physical object type called a DIMENSION. At the risk of some confusion, we'll describe the new structure using the uppercase "DIMENSION," but remember that it is not necessary to define these hierarchical relationships in order to build or use a star schema.

DIMENSIONS are used to facilitate Oracle8*i*'s query rewrite in conjunction with materialized views. Consider the case in which a materialized view has been created to summarize activity data on a daily basis. A query that requested a summary of the detail data for April 20, 2000 would be able to take advantage of the query rewrite capability and obtain its results from the materialized view instead. Similarly, a query that requested data for dates between April 18 and April 30 would still be able to find its data in the materialized view. What if, on the other hand, the user wished to select data for the fiscal month of April 2000? Oracle has no way of inherently knowing our fiscal calendar. Assuming we use 13-week quarters of 4-4-5 week months, then fiscal April 2000 might correspond to calendar days of Saturday, April 1 through Friday, April 28. Of course, other fiscal calendar definitions are possible. Queries of this type cannot be automatically resolved by the Oracle8*i* optimizer to the corresponding days. At least not until we define the peculiar hierarchy of days, weeks, quarters, and years that make up our fiscal calendar—we do this by defining a DIMENSION.

Similar examples of hierarchies frequently occur in our dimensions (lowercase). Similar to Figure 4.6, sales offices report to areas that are part of regions that then roll up to divisions. Each of our products might be part of a product category that, in turn, is assigned to a channel. Every organization's hierarchies will be different. This is why we have to pass along some additional information to the Oracle8*i* optimizer so that it can correctly decide that the data needed for a particular query is (or isn't) already stored in a more granular form within a materialized view.

We will investigate the specific syntax to define a DIMENSION in Chapter 5. The key, during design, is to recognize that hierarchical dimensions exist within our warehouse. Each hierarchy can be collapsed, as described in the previous section, to a single table. Because of additional descriptive information that we might choose to store along with the keys at any particular level, we may decide to structure the logical hierarchy as a physical hierarchy of tables. The DIMENSION object can be defined on either of these approaches as long as there is a means to define an unambiguous relationship from each child to its single parent.

A Final Note

The process of deciding the granularity of a dimension and potentially collapsing a hierarchy is identical to the decision made in designing the detail tables of the summary-based warehouse.

In either form of design, once we have defined each hierarchical relationship we will be able to build DIMENSIONS to support our use of materialized views.

The Relationship between Facts and Dimensions

In relational terms, the fact table has a foreign key relationship to each dimension table. That is, each row inserted into the fact table will have values in various foreign key columns that correspond to primary key data in the dimension tables.

> **NOTE** Even though these *relationships* between a fact table and its dimension tables are foreign keys, Oracle8 does not require them to be defined using foreign key *constraints*. See Chapter 6 for an example of how to validate foreign key integrity during the load process, without incurring the costs of storing and maintaining constraints.

Oracle7 release 7.3 required that a concatenated index on the foreign key columns in the fact table be used to perform the joins to the dimensions. The difficulty with this approach was that, to be useful, the index must include as its leading edge the columns used in the lookup. An index on columns A, B, C, D, E, and F could be used by a query that provides values (or join conditions) to A and B or A, B, and C, for instance. It could be used for a query that specifies A, B, and D, but would only use the restrictions obtained from A and B (not D). The index would not be used at all for a query that specified B, D, and E because the leading edge (A, B . . .) is not available. This situation results in the frequent need to create multiple indexes over various combinations of the foreign key tables in order to satisfy a wide variety of queries using different dimensions. These concatenated indexes on several columns of a multimillion-row table take a lot of effort and time to build and maintain. Keeping multiple indexes compounds the problem and requires a lot of storage space.

Oracle8 introduced a great improvement on this optimization scheme. Rather than require the use of a concatenated B*Tree index on the foreign key columns being used to join to the dimension tables, Oracle8's star transformation optimization will work with a separate bitmap index on each foreign key column. This is a perfect configuration. The relationship of small dimensions to large fact tables naturally creates low cardinality (i.e., few valued) indexes (ideal for bitmaps). The specification of multiple dimensional criteria allows the use of the very efficient bitmap merge operation to precisely determine the correct rows from the fact table. These bitmap indexes are much more efficient, in both space consumption and processing overhead, than in Oracle7 release 7.3.

Further, in Oracle8, the large fact table may be partitioned on a frequently specified dimension. In many cases, an Oracle8 star schema query can be executed in comparable time to a corresponding query against a predefined summary table. The star schema design, however, is much more flexible and saves a lot of space and advance processing effort. In the two years since Oracle8's introduction, we have seen more data warehouses designed around star schemas than traditional detail and summary tables.

It is not necessary to consider these two design alternatives as exclusive options. Don't feel obligated to design a pure star schema warehouse. It is very common to design a star but additionally create summary tables based on commonly specified criteria. The reasons for initially creating summary tables to speed queries against detail tables still apply.

It is also common to have several different fact tables within a single warehouse. Each subject area of the warehouse may be implemented as its own fact table. Many of the dimensions, however, will be shared across many of the stars. If the granularity of the time dimension, for instance, is appropriate to both schemas, then only one time dimension table will be needed. In some cases it is even possible for a star to serve as a dimension to another star.

More exotic variations of the star schema, known as snowflake schemas, extend this model further. The snowflake "branches" correspond to different predefined levels of summarization in a traditional detail-and-summary warehouse schema. Kimball describes such designs extensively in his book. The implementation techniques demonstrated in this book for the simpler star design are directly extended to form a snowflake.

Star Schema Case Study

The same information included in the detail-and-summary schema of Figure 4.5 can be modeled in a star schema as in Figure 4.7. Instead of predetermining which summary levels and GROUP BY columns are appropriate, the star schema allows users to select the dimensions that interest them and display whatever aggregate values are important.

Generally, we will create our dimension tables so that for the lowest level of dimension detail we will store all the hierarchy information in the same row. This makes maintenance of the dimension hierarchies more difficult, but presumably the hierarchical organizations change infrequently. We will deal with these slowly changing dimensions by maintaining multiple rows for the low-level detail information with an effective date column so that we can identify the correct hierarchy at any point in time if we have to maintain history. In our example, when a cost center is moved to a new region, we will create a new row in the dimension table with the new region and area data with a new effective date. This strategy allows us to look at the data from various points of view. We can look at our activity data by either the current organization projected back

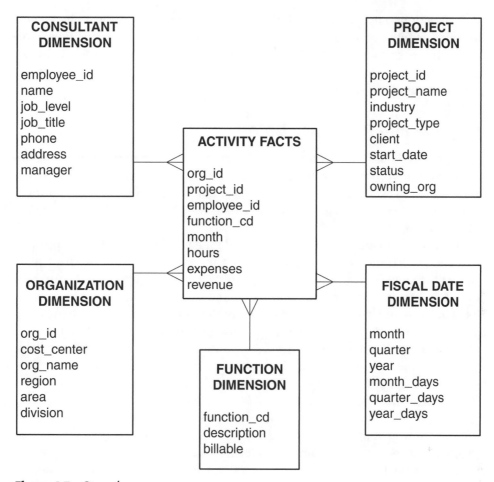

Figure 4.7   Star schema.

in time or the old organization projected forward in time, or we can apportion the activity data to the correct organization according to a point in time.

We design the FISCAL_DATE table using similar reasoning. In this case, we flatten out what is essentially a time hierarchy. Time is a dimension of interest to users in almost every data warehouse. Given Oracle's capabilities for dealing with dates it is possible to manage a time dimension without actually having to implement a separate table. Our experience suggests that it is easier over the long run to implement a time table and treat it just like any other dimension. This is particularly true if a business uses accounting periods that are different from normal calendar time periods, for example, 13-week quarters with 3 months of 4, 4, and 5 weeks, respectively. In these situations, Oracle's standard date functions such as ADD_MONTH will not understand the nonstandard accounting functions. Using a time dimension table makes such "artificial" calendar processing simpler. Users may still choose to use date functions in their queries to avoid having to join the date table when appropriate, such as when selecting data for a specific week.

External and Reference Data

So far we have discussed warehouse data as if it all originated within the application systems operated by our organization. To a great extent that may be true. There are, however, valuable sources of data that are not generated by our company but that can be integrated into our data warehouse to enhance the value of our own data.

One can, for instance, obtain an amazing range of data on industrial production and sales from the U.S. Department of Commerce. The U.S. Department of Agriculture makes available information on agricultural supply and consumption. Climate data is available, and so on and on. One of the most commonly used forms of external data in the United States is census data, which provides a wealth of demographic information that can overlay an organization's sales territories to give the analyst a totally new insight into data interpretation. Postal code and telephone country/area code reference data can also be obtained externally. Industry trade groups are another useful source of reference data for the warehouse.

The designer of the data warehouse should be constantly aware of the opportunities for obtaining data from sources outside of the company that will complement and enhance the value of internal data. In many cases, open-ended questions asked of the warehouse users will uncover the potential value of some form of external data. Then the research begins for where to obtain it, how much it will cost, how frequently it will have to be refreshed, and how to integrate it with other contents of the warehouse.

Natural Keys versus Artificial Keys

The debate over whether to use naturally occurring keys or generate artificial keys when designing tables has raged for years within the ranks of experienced DBAs and database designers. There are valid arguments to be made for each approach.

Natural keys are the identifiers of entities in the real world. People and companies have names. Automobiles have license plates. Buildings have addresses. Unfortunately, these real-world keys are not as pure and precise as our systems and databases require. Natural keys fail in three common ways:

Uniqueness. People and companies find that they do not have unique names when they are considered on a large-enough scale. Just look at the repetition of names in phone books for a couple of large cities. Even automobile owners change license plates to create a unique persona. In databases, sometimes an artificial key has already been created and has been in use long enough that it functions like a natural key. Taxpayer IDs (social security numbers) and automobile VIN numbers fill this same role. But even these, as we have learned, are not always perfectly unique.

Complexity. Timecard entries are naturally keyed by the company (or possibly division within the company!), by the identification (whatever it might be) of the employee whose time is being reported, by the date on which the employee worked, and by the specific project and task that was worked on. Very long and cumbersome natural keys like these are difficult to work with, both for people and for the RDBMS.

Absence. Some things and events in the real world just do not have identifiers. A household watching a particular television show and changing channels during a specific commercial might be of interest to a marketing analyst, but it would be difficult to find a key short of the total data available. Telephone calls fall into the same category. The latest incarnation of this phenomenon is seen in warehouses based on Web logs. Operational systems that have been designed to track, measure, bill, and report such events have been forced to generate artificial keys for them.

With all these failings, perhaps artificial keys are the one right answer. Some designers would take this position. Many Oracle OLTP systems in production use sequence-generated artificial keys for every table. Within the processing logic hidden in the database foreign keys and application programs this works very efficiently. If properly designed, the resulting systems don't put a big burden on users to have to remember or reenter these key values. This potential user burden (and source of error) is the major argument against using artificial keys.

The same questions arise when designing the data warehouse database. Frequently, however, the issue becomes moot within much of the data warehouse. Unique identifiers on each row are particularly important in an operational system when we need to get to a specific row unambiguously and efficiently. As we load detail data into the data warehouse from the operational system, we want to avoid accidentally inducing duplicates by running a load job more than once. Other than that precaution, we typically won't have much need to quickly grab specific rows. Data validation and the enforcement of integrity rules are the responsibility of the operational source systems. Our responsibility is primarily to not introduce any additional errors during our processing; only secondarily do we have a responsibility to identify problems in the source system so that we can pass that information back to the application support teams for investigation and correction.

In a detail and summary schema design, our two most common accesses to the detail data will be scripts to generate summary tables or user queries based on a variety of user-specified conditions. In the first case, we generally will be summarizing data in such a way that its unique identifiers get lost in the summary. When we examine timecard data summarized to the monthly level, the artificial key that identified each row in the TIMECARD or TIMECARD_ ENTRIES tables disappears—it is not part of our query's GROUP BY clause or calculated summarization columns.

In the second case, user-specified conditions are most easily specified in terms of the real-world keys where they exist. The second most useful conditions turn out to be those based on artificial keys introduced by the operational systems that have become "almost natural" through repeated use. Retrieving all the consultants and their total hours worked on a particular project during the third quarter of 1997 could be done by the project name or through a drill-down from the client name. If the user issuing the query were the departmental administrator who works every day with all the current project numbers, it might be simpler to enter that artificial key instead. The point is that in the data warehouse we have to provide for both accesses depending on our users' needs.

With Oracle8 star schemas we do need to have a means of joining (connecting) rows in the fact table with rows in the various dimension tables. Occasionally we encounter situations where no natural key (or source system artificial key) is available. In these cases we will have to generate an artificial key value and include it in the definition of both fact and dimension tables.

Sometimes the length or complexity of the natural key causes storage concerns. Embedding an 80-byte natural key in every row of a large fact table (and in an index) can easily consume gigabytes of storage. If space is a major concern, consider introducing an artificial key and retaining the natural key data as attributes within the dimension table.

One additional difficulty arises when assigning artificial keys in the data warehouse. Because data entering the warehouse is not processed as a transaction, we commonly load new data into multiple tables independently. It can be very difficult to assign an artificial key to a new row in a dimension table and then later be able to assign the same value during loading of rows into the fact table. Doing so will prevent direct path loading of the data. Direct path SQL*Loader, described in Chapter 6, is the fastest means of loading large amounts of data, but it doesn't allow any triggers or SQL functions to be applied during the load process.

In the context of the data warehouse, artificial versus natural keys is not much of a debate. We need not introduce new artificial keys just because a pure relational system's table must be "dependent on the key, the whole key, and nothing but the key (so help me, Codd)." Where artificial keys are part of the source data, we should carry them forward into our detail data of the warehouse whenever there is user value in having them available. As always, a strong demand for being able to report on specific detail data should raise a red flag about the users' expected use of the warehouse—they may well be planning to perform operational reporting that might be better satisfied within the source application.

Physical Design

Physical database design is the process of translating the plan for either the detail and summary schema or the star schema into actual database structures. During this process the designer will accommodate the specific idiosyncrasies of the chosen database management system to meet the requirements of availability, performance, flexibility, and manageability.

Tablespace Design

An Oracle8 database is organized into several tablespaces. Each tablespace receives an amount of disk space through one or more operating system files. Each object (e.g., table or index) that requires storage space is assigned to a tablespace and receives its necessary space allotment from the available space of the tablespace. The tablespace is the connection between the Oracle database structures and the physical world of disk files.

> **TIP** Even though we will discuss tablespace design issues first in this section, it is important to first complete the design and understand the processing needs of your tables and other database objects. Only through this process can you understand how many tablespaces will be needed, what size they will need to be, and which tablespaces should be separated from others on disk.

The first design objective of tablespaces is to separate objects that have different requirements or "lifestyles." Tables should be separated from their indexes. Small tables should be separated from large tables. Two tables that are frequently joined should generally be in different tablespaces. Dimension tables should be stored apart from fact tables. Tables that are frequently scanned should be separated from those that are usually accessed randomly. Tables and indexes that are static—once loaded, data is not added or modified—should not be placed in the same tablespace with tables that receive regular maintenance. Extremely large tables or indexes are candidates to be split—partitioned—into smaller pieces that can then be placed into separate tablespaces.

Oracle's special types of segments (rollback and temporary) need to be placed in dedicated tablespaces of their own. The Oracle data dictionary, which resides in the SYSTEM tablespace, should not be impacted by putting any other data into SYSTEM.

The only hard limit on the number of tablespaces is imposed by the number of files that can be included in a single database. In Oracle7 this was 1,022 files per database. Oracle8 effectively eliminated this restriction by increasing the number of files on most operating systems to 1,022 per tablespace and 65,533 per database.

The files associated with each tablespace should be striped across multiple disk drives whenever possible. This striping may be performed using the hardware or logical volume manager software techniques discussed in Chapter 2, "Hardware Architectures for Oracle Data Warehousing," or it may be done manually by creating multiple datafiles and then placing each onto a separate disk. The former approach will require less maintenance effort and will usually result in a better distribution of I/O.

If raw files are used (for parallel server installations, for instance) then some small set of standard partition sizes should be utilized across the entire database. If all raw files are sized at either 100 MB or 500 MB (as an example), it will be easier to redistribute I/O between busy and idle disks by exchanging files. Choosing a large variety of raw file sizes makes this sort of swap difficult or impossible.

The second design objective involved with tablespace design is administrative. Because the tablespace is the unit of backup and recovery, you should understand your load and archival requirements before planning tablespace assignments. Loading and archival needs are a primary determinant of a partitioning strategy. Any very large objects are good candidates for partitioning. Individual partitions can then be placed into separate tablespaces. Any very large objects are good candidates for partitioning.

The final consideration for creating tablespaces and assigning objects to them is that all objects in a particular tablespace should share the same storage parameters. This will allow you to use the tablespace DEFAULT STORAGE clause and never specify STORAGE for individual objects.

Predicting Space Requirements

Chapter 5 discusses methods for predicting the size of individual tables and indexes. Unfortunately, this task is very difficult to do precisely before actually creating the tables and loading a sample of data. Once some data is loaded, the DBA should run ANALYZE to compute statistics that will provide a good estimate of the average length of a row and how many rows can be stored in each individual data block. Index storage is even harder to predict. To extrapolate an index's final size from sample data, the initially loaded sample must be well distributed across the full range of data values. If data from only one department is loaded, for instance, then an index on ORG_ID will not be representative of the storage requirements for all departments.

Planning for Growth

Data warehouse tables have very different growth patterns. Some detail tables (or fact tables) grow by a predictable number of rows each week or month. Some reference or dimension tables rarely change at all. In some cases, it is impossible to predict the volume of each periodic load because of the nature of the business application that feeds the data warehouse.

In every case, it is critical for the warehouse administrator to ensure that there is sufficient space available to accommodate the data to be loaded. Because load jobs tend to be scheduled in the wee hours of the morning, it is essential that the processes are able to complete without manual intervention in order to add a data file to a tablespace. Beginning with release 7.3, the Oracle server has provided a way for a data file to grow when its tablespace does not have enough freespace for the allocation of an object extent. It is implemented using the AUTOEXTEND clause as part of the file specification in the CREATE TABLESPACE and ALTER TABLESPACE . . . ADD DATAFILE commands. Allowing data files to automatically grow provides some insurance against the midnight failure of a load or index job.

There is a downside, however, in giving up control of the use of disk space utilization. When multiple datafiles are manually striped across several disks, the DBA will typically want to provide more space by manually adding a file on a different disk. If large file systems (this feature does not apply to UNIX raw files) have been striped using either hardware or LVM software, then allowing files to automatically grow might be an appropriate strategy. The file system must have available space for growth of the data files. Using AUTOEXTEND doesn't solve the problem—it just pushes it one level lower in the technology stack. Being DBAs (generally read as being more than a little retentive) we never use the AUTOEXTEND feature.

Planning for Archival or Purging of Data

In addition to planning for the regular growth of the warehouse during periodic loads, the design team needs to consider the opportunity to remove older data when its value has passed. This seems like heresy to many first-time data warehouse designers. Most warehousing neophytes tend to think in a "first in, never out" manner. Keeping detail data forever may be appropriate for some subject areas in some data warehouses. Then again, it may be inappropriate in other situations. You should remain open to the opportunities for removing aged detail data from the warehouse. Keeping detail data from only the most recent 12 (or whatever appropriate number of) months will go a long way toward solving the warehouse growth problems. Specific techniques for performing archival and purging of data are presented in Chapter 6.

Partitioning Data

Extremely large tables and indexes should be considered as candidates for partitioning. Dividing a large object into smaller pieces can make each piece more manageable. While partitioning has some performance benefits, the primary advantage to partitioning is to ease administrative requirements.

PARTITIONING IN ORACLE7

Oracle7 and Oracle8 have very different approaches to partitioning. Oracle7 started with separate tables and applied a UNION ALL view over them to make them appear to be a single object. This prevented a single index from being created to reference data in all the tables—each table required separately created indexes. Keeping separate tables in Oracle7 required more additional administrative work than does an Oracle8 partitioned table. In Oracle8, a single table can be created that has multiple partitions. A global index may be created on the entire table, and several maintenance options are provided for managing the partitions. A very large index can also be partitioned in Oracle8. Chapter 5 provides more information on this topic and demonstrates the SQL syntax to create partitioned objects in both Oracle7 and Oracle8.

The goal is not to split the data randomly just to make smaller pieces. Oracle8*i* can do this type of distribution of data—called hash partitioning—but it serves only as a performance aid. Not that there is anything wrong with performance aids, but the primary objective should be to divide the data up in such a way that operations (like loading, backing up, and archiving) will be able to execute efficiently using an entire partition as opposed to having to locate rows spread across multiple partitions. This approach to partitioning will still provide performance benefits. For instance, partitioning on one or more columns whose values will frequently be used to specify queries will allow the query optimizer to eliminate several partitions and look for data in just a small part of the total table. Where the division of the table based on reasonable data ranges still yields partitions that are unmanageably large, then consider using Oracle8*i* composite partitioning by hashing on another column to further spread the data evenly across multiple subpartitions of each range partition.

PARTITION SIZES

Ideally, the choice of partition keys should yield partitions of roughly the same size, but this is not an absolute requirement. You can control the storage space (and subpartitioning) on each individual partition, but life is simpler if the DBA doesn't have to manually determine the size of partitions that range from 80 megabytes through 300 gigabytes. Also, parallel DDL operations (such as UPDATE and DELETE) are parallelized based on the partitioning scheme. If this type of operation is anticipated in our warehouse then we'd like to optimize the process by having each parallel task complete in roughly the same amount of time.

Like Goldilocks, we want to balance the anticipated accesses to the data so that each partition is "not too big, not too small—but just right."

Because of the normal time-related aspect of data warehouses, partitioning is typically done based on some transaction date within the fact data. Each period (whether year, month, day, hour) of detailed data is assigned to a separate partition that, in turn, can be placed into its own tablespace. Selecting the right time period for partitioning is similar to the decision about granularity of data. Several factors interact to determine the ideal partition size:

- First, consider size and quantity. Partitions should be small enough to be efficiently archived, backed up, and recovered. But choosing too small a period presents us with another manageability challenge—the DBAs don't want to have to deal with thousands of partitions for personal reasons as well as performance reasons. Overhead is associated with the Oracle dictionary tracking thousands of partitions and, more importantly, in presenting the query optimizer with many more options to evaluate. Several hundred or a thousand partitions should not present a problem to Oracle, but hundreds of thousands would be excessive.

- Second, consider the anticipated bulk operations that will need to be performed. If you are doing daily loads, then daily partitions might be appropriate even though the size of monthly partitions might still be manageable. If we load daily into a monthly partition then we will have to consider the extra burden of backing up the entire month's data every day during the month even though only one day's activity has been added. Our strategy for archiving data also plays a part, although smaller, in this decision. If, for instance, we anticipate archiving data on a monthly basis, then our partitioning scheme should support that. This doesn't mean that we should select monthly divisions of the data, but we probably shouldn't select weekly partitioning because a month doesn't neatly fit within a fixed number of weeks. Likewise, quarterly partitions would not facilitate monthly archival. Daily partitions, however, could easily support our monthly actions.

- The third set of criteria surrounds issues of query performance. For queries that include predicate conditions based on the partitioning key of the table, Oracle can quickly eliminate consideration of all of the partitions that it knows can't contain that data. For example, a query that requests a count of all orders placed on 31-DEC-1999 will have to examine only our DEC99 partition. NOV99 (and all earlier partitions) and JAN00 (and all subsequent partitions) can be safely ignored. This partition elimination feature of the Oracle8 optimizer can be a great tool in making billion-row fact tables perform as if they were only a few gigabytes in size! Another specific example came up with one of our clients. They had chosen to partition their data by month. A majority of their queries, however, were to create daily activity summaries. What they found was that reports run at the beginning of the month that ran in a few minutes took nearly an hour to run by the end of the month. This was due to having to process an extra 30 days' worth of data to retrieve the last day's activity. A simple change from monthly to daily partitioning eliminated this effect, and these reports now run consistently in the fastest timeframe.

  Also, if a large number of our queries will be selecting data for a particular day, then this becomes a natural range to choose. For those queries that select data without regard to date (e.g., all orders for a given customer) Oracle will likely have to look in multiple partitions of the CUSTOMER_ID index in order to locate all of the historical activity. (This assumes that we have equi-partitioned the index with the table; as we'll see in the next section, this LOCAL indexing strategy is almost always used for large partitioned fact [or detail] tables.) Each index partition will need to be probed to see if any of the customer's orders reside in the corresponding table partition. Doing parallel index probes with a reasonable number of partitions can actually provide a performance gain. Having to issue thousands of parallel requests, though, is likely to be a performance problem.

- Fourth and finally, consider whether DML operations will need to be performed on a regular basis. In the pure, never-changing warehouse design, there would not be any need to run large UPDATE statements against the detailed data. Many warehouse designs, however, are built with real-world considerations that vary from this pure ideal. If your design will require such a process, remember that Oracle's parallel DML can only be parallelized to the level of one process per partition. Queries, incidentally, do not share this limitation and are parallelized based on ranges of blocks. Unless the partitions are very small, Oracle will be able to efficiently divide the query workload across multiple processes by carving out multiple block ranges from each partition.

The designer does have a few partitioning tricks that can be applied when these four criteria don't all point to a consistent recommended partitioning scheme. If your analysis indicates that daily partitions are appropriate for sizing or performance reasons, but you intend to do monthly archival, remember that daily partitions will easily support monthly archival or purge processing while still preserving the advantages of the smaller size.

Also, there is no requirement that each partition be placed into its own tablespace so one option is to place all of the daily partitions for a month into the same tablespace. When it is time to archive, all of the month's partitions may be archived easily by manipulating the entire tablespace, especially with the Oracle8*i* transportable tablespace feature.

Deciding on an appropriate partitioning scheme is a key design step for large database objects. Of all the features added in Oracle8 to support warehousing, partitioning is probably the most important.

Indexing

In trying to find the data of interest to a particular query, Oracle always has the option of reading all the data in the table. For small tables, this is often the preferred access method. In many other cases, an index is needed to allow Oracle to more rapidly find a single row or a small subset of the total table. In still other cases, multiple indexes on various columns in the table can be used together to determine the rows to be returned. Indexes are created after the creation of a table and may be built based on one or more columns of the table.

Which columns need to be indexed is determined by knowing the data and anticipating the types of queries that will be issued by users. The WHERE CLAUSE (and, in some cases, the ORDER BY clause) will determine which indexes can be used by the query.

The Oracle query optimizer's job is to determine which of many available access paths through the data will provide the fastest (or least-effort) solution. The newer cost-based optimizer should always be used in data warehouses managed by Oracle8. Only the cost-based optimizer can take advantage of new access paths such as the star query optimization feature. While many applications have been written and tuned to use the older rule-based optimizer, most data warehouse queries do not allow for this sophisticated tuning. To allow the cost-based optimizer to make informed choices between alternative solutions, current statistics on each table and index need to be gathered using the ANA-LYZE command (which is covered in Chapter 5).

By monitoring use of the data warehouse and the queries submitted by users, it is be possible to identify the need for additional indexes that might not have been anticipated when the warehouse was initially delivered. Unnecessary indexes, while wasteful of space, generally do not impair query performance under the cost-based optimizer because it will choose to ignore an index that would cause additional work for the query. The older, rule-based optimizer, however, would go ahead and use an index even though doing so might be very inefficient.

B*Tree Indexes

B*Tree indexes are hierarchical structures that allow a rapid search (usually in no more than three or four logical I/Os) in order to obtain the address (ROWID) of a specific row in the data table that has a particular value. The structure of B*Tree indexes is covered in Chapter 3, "Oracle Server Software Architecture and Features," and shown in Figure 3.8.

In a unique index only one row is pointed to by each index value. A nonunique index may have pointers to several different rows from each distinct value. As the number of rows addressed per key value increases, the efficiency of using the index falls. Each value of a low-cardinality B*Tree index, such as SEX_CODE that has only two values (at least in most designs!), would generally point to rows in every block of the table. Simply scanning the entire table would be more efficient than bouncing back and forth between the index and the table.

> **TIP**   When the data distribution is heavily skewed, a B*Tree index may have greater value to some queries than to others. An index on SEX_CODE might be very efficient for finding all the female patients in a Veterans Administration hospital assuming that they make up only a few percent of the total. On the other hand, using that same index to find all male patients would be very inefficient. For the cost-based optimizer to know the distribution of data within a column it is necessary to gather column-level statistics. This can be done by specifying the FOR COLUMNS option of the ANALYZE command.

Consider adding B*Tree indexes on a column of a large table when you antic-ipate queries that will need to return a small (less than 5 percent) subset of the total table based on WHERE clause restrictions on that column. (Nested loop joins will also be able to do this type of restriction based on looking up rows that match values found in another table.) Where multiple columns will be frequently used together to restrict rows returned by a query, then create one index on that set of columns. Position the most frequently specified column to be first in the index.

Partitioning Indexes

Just like tables, large indexes in Oracle8 can be partitioned to make smaller pieces that are more manageable. In addition to the need to make smaller pieces for administrative purposes, there is another driving force behind the partitioning of indexes. As we saw in Chapter 3, partitioned indexes can be either global or local. When we build an index on a large partitioned table we may choose to make the index unpartitioned or to partition on a different basis than the underlying partitioned table. These are global indexes, and they cause some additional administrative headaches, even if their size is manageable.

Every time we choose to do partition-level maintenance (e.g., ADD, DROP, EXCHANGE) on the table, all global indexes on the table will have to be rebuilt. The amount of time required to rebuild the global indexes is time that cannot be used by queries that require the use of one of those indexes.

For large partitioned tables we should generally plan to build locally partitioned indexes. In the ideal case, the index involves the columns used to partition the table. When the same partitioning key is used for both table and index queries it will be able to use the partitioning key as if it were the first level of the index. Searches in the index will be more efficient because the search of only one partition will generally be smaller than searching through an equivalent nonpartitioned index.

We can locally partition even when the index is on columns other than those used for partitioning the table—this is a nonprefixed local index. These indexes do have disadvantages when compared to local prefixed indexes, however. Because any indexed value may exist in any partition, a query will have to look ("probe") into each index partition to look for matching rows. For a large number of partitions, this may require significant extra resources. When queries that specify a value for the partition key along with criteria for the nonprefixed local index, Oracle8 will be able to limit its search to a subset of index partitions. This greatly reduces the extra cost of using nonprefixed indexes for many queries.

Bitmap Indexes

Bitmap indexes were also introduced in Chapter 3. Their logical structure and use are shown in Figure 3.10. Bitmap indexes are appropriate in situations where only a few distinct values occur within a column (or series of columns). This is called a low-cardinality column. Bitmap indexes on low-cardinality columns are very efficient in their physical storage. A separate bitmap is constructed for each distinct value. Logically each bitmap is as long as the number of rows being indexed. Internally, though, Oracle compresses each bitmap because, on average, there are many more 0s than 1s in any given bitmap.

A query can be very efficiently executed when the conditions of a WHERE clause allow multiple bitmap indexes to be used to restrict the rows of the table. Several nonselective bitmaps can be combined to provide a very narrowly restricted list of rows. An example of using multiple bitmaps was provided earlier in this chapter in the description of Oracle8 star query execution.

Consider using bitmap indexes on a table when several columns are likely to be used in combination for many queries and each individual column has only a few distinct values and would be, on its own, very nonselective. While no syntactical limitation prevents you from creating bitmaps on high-cardinality columns, this should generally be avoided with one exception. In order to facilitate the star query transformation bitmaps are required on each foreign key related to the various dimensions. If one of these dimensions has a large number of values but is likely to be used in conjunction with other, more modest dimensions, it is appropriate to create the bitmap index on the foreign key with many values. Even though storage space and build time will be greater for this one index, it is probably a useful trade-off for the increased functionality of the star transformation.

Bitmap indexes may not be created as UNIQUE (although we cannot imagine a situation where this would be desirable). Even though a bitmap index can be constructed on a column of unique values, it is not allowed for a bitmap index to be built with the UNIQUE attribute.

Bitmap indexes may be partitioned similar to B*Tree indexes. Because one of the most common uses of bitmap indexes is to support star query transformation, they tend to be built on very large fact tables. Locally partitioned bitmap indexes support star transformation and still meet the administrative need for adding, dropping, and exchanging partitions. Globally partitioned bitmap indexes are not allowed.

Function-Based Indexes

Using indexes to find rows that contain a particular value (or range of values) within a set of columns has been a universal technique of database management systems for over 30 years. But what if the value you need to specify is not actually stored in the database? What if you need to find all consulting contracts in which expenses have exceeded 25 percent of hourly billable charges? Our PROJECTS table was built with a summarization of expenses and another column that shows the total revenues, but we never created a column to store expenses as a percentage of billings. Prior to Oracle8*i* we would have had two alternatives. First, if this were a one-time query, we could just plow through the entire table with a full table scan and find the appropriate projects. If we expected to need to do this type of query frequently, then we would probably have to add a new column to our PROJECTS table to show this computed value and then build an index on the column. This second choice is fine if this kind of new requirement comes up infrequently. If, on the other hand, we find ourselves having to rebuild and reorganize our tables frequently to add denormalized[1] computations then we will waste a great deal of time and use a lot more disk space.

Oracle8*i* provides another useful alternative to the designers. If we determine a need to look up rows based on a function of one or more columns' values but we don't want to physically store the computed value within each row, we can instead create an index based on that function or expression. Whenever a query utilizes that function or expression in its clause this function-based index can be used to retrieve rows efficiently.

The functions and expressions can be as simple as the expenses-as-percentage-of-billings example, or they can include complex PL/SQL functions (even including callouts to C programs) that have been custom developed for your organization's unique requirements. The only restriction is that the function must be *deterministic*—each invocation of the function must always return the same result given the same set of input arguments. It can't, therefore, make reference to changing values such as the time of day or the state of package variables.

Function-based indexes may be built either as B*Tree or bitmap structures. The same criteria of which index type to use, such as issues of cardinality and the need to perform bitmap merge operations, apply equally to function-based indexes. Examples of how to build this new index type are provided in Chapter 5.

Materialized Views

We have always built a variety of summary tables within our data warehouse to allow rapid and efficient access to commonly used aggregated data. If many users will want to see the sum of sales, grouped by month and region, we can facilitate their queries by performing this aggregation once and storing the results in a summary table.

This design works well, but there are two potential disadvantages. For each summary table that we build we must also create specific programs to perform the aggregation, and we must make sure that these programs are executed after

---

[1] Storing a value that can be calculated from two existing values in a table is a violation of Fifth Normal Form in relational design. As warehouse designers, though, we frequently ignore many normalization rules in favor of ease of use.

each load of data to the underlying tables. Further, to be able to benefit from this table, each user must know that it exists and remember to specify it in the query instead of the table containing the detailed data.

Oracle8*i* materialized views are able to assist us with both of these issues. With materialized views, we will still have to define the nature of the aggregation as a SQL SELECT statement, but we will not have to build the rest of the processing infrastructure—enclosing the SELECT statement in a program unit (stored procedure, C program, SQL*Plus script) and the control logic necessary to handle program scheduling and potential failures. Oracle8*i* will perform these functions on our behalf.

As an additional benefit, if one user forgets about a particular summary table and issues a query that performs (poorly) against large detail data tables, that user (and potentially all other users on the system) will pay the price of the additional I/O, sorting, and computation required to repeat an aggregation that as already been performed. Materialized views, on the other hand, support a new feature of the Oracle8*i* optimizer called *query rewrite*.

For queries that specify access to detail tables when an equivalent materialized view is available, the optimizer can automatically recast the query to use the materialized view, saving precious system resources and delivering dramatically improved performance to the user. This performance boost depends entirely on the nature of the aggregation, but improvements of two or three orders of magnitude can frequently be obtained. For the query rewrite facility to be considered by the optimizer, the specific materialized view must have been created (or altered) with the ENABLE QUERY UPDATE syntax.

Materialized views may be partitioned and indexed much the same as tables. The tables used in the defining query of the materialized view may also be partitioned but may not be index-organized. Examples of building materialized views will be provided in Chapter 5, and much of Chapter 7 is devoted to their use.

Additionally, in the distributed environment of multiple data marts being fed from a master warehouse, materialized views (also called *snapshots*) provide the perfect means for copying appropriate subsets of data to each remote site. This usage will be covered in Chapter 12, "Distributing the Oracle Data Warehouse."

Index-Organized Tables

Where you have the need to create a table that consists entirely (or mostly) of the primary key, an index-organized table may be appropriate. Ordinarily an Oracle table would store the data rows and a separate index would be created to enforce the primary key constraint as well as improve query performance in locating specific rows in the table. An index-organized table can reduce this table-and-index pair down to a single object. All of the data from the table is, in effect, stored within the index structure, saving the redundant storage of identical data in two places. Performance of data access is also improved because there is no need for the final I/O to the table once an entry is located within an index.

Index-organized tables are appropriate for relatively small tables used for validation and lookup of reference data in a detail and summary schema or as dimensions in a star configuration.

Two limitations of index-organized tables may prevent them from being used in many cases, however. In Oracle8 building additional indexes that referenced the index-organized table was not allowed because rows in this structure do not have a ROWID as in normal tables. In Oracle8*i* this restriction was lifted by allowing indexes to be built that used a primary key pointer rather than a ROWID pointer to locate specific rows in the index-organized table. We suspect that going to this level of complexity may not justify the use of the index-organized table, but the designer/builder of the warehouse is welcome to investigate the trade-offs within his own warehouse.

Additionally, Oracle8*i* materialized views may not be defined on index-organized tables; if you anticipate building materialized views that are based on your reference or dimension tables, then use traditional tables with separate indexes. There doesn't appear to be any fundamental conflict between these two object types, so it is possible that this restriction could be lifted in a future release.

Temporary Tables

Some queries are very complex, involving joins and subqueries of multiple tables. For ease of understanding (and sometimes for performance reasons as well) it is sometimes preferable to issue one simpler query and then save the intermediate results to use for another query. The intermediate results do not have any lasting value that warrants keeping them around once the second query is completed.

Temporary tables are a new Oracle8*i* structure that are accessed with the same SQL INSERT, SELECT, and DELETE statements as traditional tables, but they have a different lifestyle. Rather than create a permanent object that will store rows on disk, you may use a temporary table that will hold rows but then automatically remove them when the transaction or session is complete. More than one user can work with a single temporary table but rows from other sessions will never be visible to anyone but their creator.

By default, the rows that you insert into a temporary table are automatically removed at the end of the current transaction. This is a potential problem if you intend to use the intermediate results as input to a CREATE TABLE . . . AS

SELECT or other DDL operation because these statements all cause an implicit COMMIT and an end of the current transaction. If this is an issue for your situation, then you may choose to perform all DDL operations before inserting rows into the temporary table or you may create the temporary table with the ON COMMIT PRESERVE ROWS option. Rows inserted into this type of temporary table will not be automatically removed until the end of the session.

Of course, there are some other limitations on the use of temporary tables. They cannot be partitioned, index-organized, or clustered, and you may not define foreign key constraints on them. Additionally, you may not specify a particular TABLESPACE or any of the LOGGING/NOLOGGING or MONITORING/NOMONITORING attributes. (MONITORING is a table attribute used to instruct Oracle8i to dynamically gather performance statistics. It will be discussed in Chapter 9.)

Further, they cannot be accessed via parallel queries nor populated using SQL*Loader. These restrictions are not problematic as long as the temporary table is used as intended—to temporarily hold a reasonably small result set from one query to another. If large data sets need to be manipulated it is probably more appropriate to create a normal table to store the data. This more traditional approach also aids in the restart of a long process should the session be somehow disconnected before the whole process is completed. Remember, however, that the programmer/user will be responsible for freeing up the storage by dropping or truncating the regular table when its contents are no longer needed.

Consider including temporary tables in the design to support specific standardized reports that can take advantage of this structure. Many users will be able to run the report and safely share the single temporary table without need for manual housekeeping efforts to manage storage.

Other Structures

Oracle8 provides for other types of structures that are less relevant to data warehousing. These include index clusters and hash clusters. These were all described in Chapter 3. Chapter 5 provides an example of the syntax used to create each of these objects.

Database Constraints and Triggers

Starting with Oracle release 6.0, the Oracle database designer has had the ability to declare data constraints as part of the definition of a table. Effective with Oracle7, the Oracle kernel can enforce these rules to prevent data from being entered (or modified) that would violate the constraints. The types of constraints available to the Oracle7 or Oracle8 database developer include the following:

Check. The check constraint allows the designer of a table to establish rules about the specific values that are allowed to be stored in a particular column. The rules allow comparison to constant values ("QTY_SOLD must always be greater than zero") or to the value of another column within the same row of the table ("SALES_DISCOUNT cannot be greater than LIST_PRICE"). Comparisons can be encoded using normal SQL comparison operators (such as =, >, <, IN, BETWEEN), and multiple conditions may be specified through the use of the SQL logical operators (NOT, AND, OR).

Not null. This one constraint has been enforced in releases of Oracle prior to Oracle7. It requires that some value be provided for the specified column in each row of the table. No row is allowed to contain a null (or absent) value. It is enforced by Oracle7 and Oracle8 as a special variety of a check constraint.

Unique. The unique constraint on a column (or combination of up to 16 columns in Oracle7 or 32 columns in Oracle8) of a table prevents two rows in the table from having the same value (or set of values) at the same time. Uniqueness is actually enforced by the automatic creation of a unique index that, before Oracle7, was the way this rule would have been enforced—the DBA would have manually created a unique index.

Primary key. Declaring a primary key for a table forces the values of data inserted (or updated) in the primary key column(s) to be both unique and not null. There can be at most one primary key defined for a table. The primary key on a table is used to define the identifier that can be used to uniquely distinguish between every row in the table.

Foreign key. This constraint is the only one that provides for evaluating data in one table based on values currently stored in another table. Rules such as "the PRODUCT_ID specified in an ORDER_LINE row must be a valid PRODUCT_ID in the PRODUCTS table" are implemented using foreign key constraints.

These five types of declarative constraints can represent most simple business rules as part of a table definition. More complex business rules can also be implemented by the database designer by writing database triggers. In Oracle7 and Oracle8, database triggers are developed in PL/SQL, Oracle's procedural language for database triggers, stored procedures, and functions, and for the application logic within Oracle's application development tools such as Designer/2000.

Database Constraints in OLTP Systems

Designers of OLTP databases should always use Oracle's declarative constraints and triggers to ensure the integrity of the database. These constraints allow the database to do the important work of verifying that data being added or modified to a table follows some basic rules. When data in the database is corrupted, it frequently falls on the database administrator to develop a strategy for restoring data integrity. Even if the application programmers are to do some quick custom coding to restore order, while the database is under repair it is the DBA who frequently feels the heat from users and management. Self-preservation is reason enough for the DBA to insist on encoding basic data integrity rules into the OLTP database. There are, luckily, other more objective advantages to using database enforcement of rules.

It is preferable to have the database do this integrity checking in operational systems rather than depend on the application code to enforce rules about the data. It isn't that the application programmers are irresponsible or untrustworthy; but frequently there are multiple application programs chartered with making changes to any one database table. Often these application programs are written by different programmers, frequently in different programming languages. Even when, 20 or so years ago, development teams made a concerted effort to write exhaustive analysis and design documents before starting to code, we frequently had problems with different interpretations of business requirements finding their way into the code of different transactions. For better or worse, today's 4GL client/server development environment is less disciplined and controlled than the old mainframe teams. Rules coded into the database have to be written only once as part of a table's definition and will apply to every transaction that affects that table. We get consistent enforcement of our rules.

Additionally, these constraints (and triggers) generally have performance advantages over equivalent rules embedded in application code. Performance is enhanced for many constraints by being implemented at a lower level of the Oracle kernel than SQL. These constraints therefore don't require the overhead of being parsed and executed as would application code. Even for more complex rules that are implemented using database triggers, there is efficiency in having only a single block of code to maintain in the shared pool as well as the significant savings in network traffic over a client/server dialog requiring multiple calls to the database.

Database Constraints in the Data Warehouse

In many ways, however, the data warehouse and the OLTP database have different objectives and approaches. Rarely is it appropriate to enforce the same level of constraints in the warehouse as in an operational system's database. This is true for several reasons.

Performance

Performance considerations for the data warehouse are very different from those in the OLTP system. Transaction processing generally focuses on the performance of a single update. It is balanced against the integrity of the data touched in that single update. The overhead of a constraint or even a trigger acting on that one row is a small incremental cost when compared to the possibility of having inaccurate data entered into the database because of a data entry error or program logic bug.

Performance in the data warehouse must still be evaluated against data integrity, but the equation is different. Data integrity can be reasonably ensured once without constant monitoring. Also, because the data is initially entered into the data warehouse through large batch file loads as opposed to single row inserts, it is easier to examine the data integrity of the entire file as one batch step prior to loading.

The other side of the equation, performance, is also affected indirectly by the batch nature of data loads. Typically, the warehouse builder will want to take advantage of some of the very specialized tools provided by Oracle for dealing with bulk data loads. Chapter 6 covers the use of the direct path option of the SQL*Loader utility. Direct path SQL*Loader gains its speed by formatting and writing complete data blocks directly to disk, thus bypassing the overhead of buffer management and SQL-level processing in the Oracle kernel. Part of the overhead that is avoided is the handling of constraints and triggers.

Most constraints are automatically disabled on a table when it is loaded using the direct path. They can be reenabled after the load is completed, but this requires the complete examination of all data rows in the table. If the load added 1 million rows to a 30-million row table, reenabling constraints will have to do a lot of extra work—30 times as much! Unique and primary key constraints are enforced using indexes and are automatically reenabled (unless a parallel direct path load was performed) by building a new temporary index on the data that has been added and then merging it with the original index to form a new, bigger index. While this approach is usually faster than building the new index completely from scratch, it does require enough extra space in the tablespace to temporarily hold two copies of the index during the process. Triggers (a procedural means of enforcing more complex business rules) are also disabled during direct path loads. Data entered while the triggers are disabled will not be processed by the trigger logic, even when they are reenabled.

In short, one must choose between the potential integrity advantages of constraints or triggers and the substantial performance advantages of direct path SQL*Loader, particularly if it is run in parallel direct path mode. Later in this chapter, though, we'll see how to get the advantages of integrity constraint checking during the load of a partitioned table without the performance and storage overhead of maintaining database constraints.

Storage

Two types of database constraints require additional storage. Primary key and unique constraints both require Oracle to build and maintain a unique index on the key columns. In the case of a fact table, the primary key is generally several columns wide—at least one column per dimension. A concatenated index over these columns on a large row fact table may require over half of the amount of disk space used to store the data itself. In one sample case, a billion-row fact table required slightly over 700 gigabytes for storage of the data itself, approximately 10 gigabytes for all of the bitmap indexes, and nearly 30 gigabytes for the primary key index.

This extra overhead of the primary key's index would be affordable if it provided some value. In many cases it does not. Remember that constraints and indexes are potentially valuable in enhancing performance of queries and in ensuring uniqueness of data. A primary key constraint on a fact table may actually provide neither benefit.

First, most or all of the queries performed against our fact tables will actually be performed using bitmap indexes on each of the foreign keys that are associated with each dimension. It is rarely useful to query the fact table directly using specific values for each of the columns that make up the primary key. If any column is omitted from the predicate of the query or specified as a range of values, then the query will not be able to utilize any of the subsequent columns of the primary key index. (In Oracle7 partitioned views, this type of concatenated index was required to execute star queries. Because many queries will supply restrictions against only a few of the dimensions, DBAs frequently had to create multiple concatenated indexes with different column ordering. It was not uncommon to consume more space in indexes than in the table!) So, performance is rarely enhanced by a concatenated primary key constraint on our fact tables.

Second, because data does not change once it is loaded into our fact tables, there is little if any value in using the primary key index to enforce uniqueness. As long as the prospective primary key includes our partitioning key column, we can provide the integrity check more efficiently during our load process. This process is described at the end of this chapter and demonstrated in Chapter 5.

In most cases, maintaining a primary key constraint on a fact table is just wasted storage.

Relationships

One of the most useful types of database constraint for ensuring integrity of data in a transaction processing database is the *foreign key constraint*. With a typical operational system database, relational tables are related to each other in a variety of ways. A common value for CUST_ID provides the linkage whereby a particular order is associated with a particular customer. The combination of CUST_ID and ORD_NUM links each of the appropriate order lines to that order and to that customer. Similarly, the sales order is linked to a particular salesperson record by embedding a value from the SALES_REPS table's primary key as a foreign key in the ORDERS table. Determining who the actual sales representative is, his department and manager, and so on can be done in the operational system by joining ORDERS to SALES_REP based on the equality of SALES_REP_ID in the ORDERS and SALES_REPS tables.

Some similar equality relationships exist in the data warehouse. This is particularly true for our fact tables that must relate to each dimension table. Just as with primary keys, it is frequently easier to evaluate the integrity of foreign key relationships during the load process and not necessarily maintain them on the whole fact table. That said, foreign key constraints do not have the same costs (requiring an index) as maintaining primary keys. Even though the Oracle8 kernel does not require foreign key constraints in order to take advantage of star query transformation, many query tools will use these constraints to help users structure a query. For this reason, you should declare foreign keys on fact tables. If you've validated the data before making the new partition part of the larger table, then optional syntax instructs Oracle not to reverify that each row has corresponding dimensional entries. This syntax is shown in Chapter 6.

Another style of relationship is required for much of the data warehouse that is not based on a simple equality relationship. This is generally caused by the warehouse's different perspective on time. The operational system only has to track the current or latest state of the data. If a value is changed in the operational system, it is changed "in place" and supercedes the previous value.

In the data warehouse, by contrast, we frequently need to track each of the various iterations of the data. As we examine historical data about sales on particular days or weeks or months, we may require related information as it existed at various points in the past. If the supplier for one of our products changed on October 1, we will later have warehouse queries wanting to know the cost of components that went into our product in September. We will also have to determine a different cost when we consider products manufactured in October. Depending on our accounting rules for inventory handling (FIFO, LIFO, etc.), we may discover interesting and valuable information in the warehouse besides the cost of sales shown in the accounting reports. We may also want to examine reliability differences in the product as it is delivered by the different suppliers.

But note the interesting change in the nature of the relationship. Instead of a straightforward equality of PRODUCT_ID in our operational ORDER_LINES table and PRODUCTS table, we have a warehouse PRODUCTS table with multiple entries for the same product, but each entry has effective dates included in the key structure. For a specific batch of our product we'll have to compare the DATE_ OF_MANUFACTURE to the date ranges within our PRODUCTS table along with the equality comparison on PRODUCT_ID. This type of range comparison is just as valid a relationship as an equality test, but it cannot be implemented using a relational foreign key constraint.

Another kind of relationship is introduced into the data warehouse that does not have a counterpart in the operational world. The relationship of summary to detail data is not the same as a foreign key although it may often appear similar in that it is fundamentally one-to-many. As we build summary tables we may choose to partition or restrict data in different ways. The detail data (the "many" side of the relationship) may include specific CALL_DETAIL data for every call placed or received by one of our cellular customers. We might, however, create a summary table that includes a monthly summarization of only toll calls or roaming calls. The summary row in this table (the "one" side of the relationship) relates to multiple rows in the detail table. But not every row in the detail table (for local calls in this example) has a corresponding row in this summary table. This would violate a relational foreign key relationship that requires each "child" to have a corresponding "parent."

As another example, we may choose to form several different summary rollups on our detail data. In one we might summarize domestic sales by region (excluding international sales), and in yet another aggregation we might just maintain a count of sales over $1 million by region, excluding smaller sales. The data in each of these aggregations is related to the detailed data from which it was developed, but not in the same sense as required by a pure foreign key relationship.

Changing Business Rules

Transaction processing systems are oriented around current rules and current snapshots of data. When a business rule or database structure change is needed, the current data in the OLTP system is restructured and processing continues. A data warehouse, however, generally keeps months or years of data. The data from two years ago was oriented around a set of business rules and structures that may no longer be current.

In some cases, it may be possible to restructure historical data to fit the new rules and structures. Even when possible, this is rarely a wise thing to do unless it can be done through an alternative rollup structure while preserving the historical integrity of the data as originally recorded.

In a much larger number of cases, there is no means of translating the historical data to cleanly fit the new business rule. Consider the changing sales territories in a fast-growing software company. Two years ago there may have been only 12 sales offices. The company's application systems may have included a check constraint to ensure that no other value could be entered. Last year, growth to 20 offices required an easy change in the operational systems' constraints. Now there are 28 offices, and the rule has been changed accordingly. Which rule would you consider appropriate to add to the warehouse? The latest set of offices would have to be included to constrain current data. Data from 2 years ago would not be properly constrained, however, to the 12 offices current at that time. So what is the purpose of the constraint?

The proper approach to handling constraints would be to depend on (and verify) the correctness of the operational systems so that extracted data is correct at the time it is added to the warehouse. Any additional information about sales offices should be kept in a separate table that includes a description of when each office was opened (and possibly closed).

But how would you change historical sales data if you decided to do so? If sales office territories are purely geographic, then it might be possible to determine which current office would have made the sale if it had been open. For some trend examinations, this might be useful information, but then we would lose access to other useful information, such as average annual sales per office over time. If the sales territories changed on more than just this one dimension, perhaps by the vertical industry and the size of the customer, it may not even be possible to determine a proper mapping. No record may have been saved of the customer size at the time of the sale two years ago. The customer may no longer exist or may be much larger (or smaller) today.

In general, it is not a good idea to try to restructure historical data in the warehouse. It is a difficult task to version your data structures and metadata, but it is a manageable one. Trying to constantly keep historical data in conformance with current organizational structures and business rules is a Sisyphean quest.

Proper Uses of Constraints in the Data Warehouse

All this is not to imply that there is no place for database constraints in the data warehousing environment. Constraints have value and are sometimes required, but the warehouse designer also needs to understand their costs before employing them.

Database constraints serve two distinct purposes in an Oracle database. Oracle allows the administrator to either enable or disable any constraint. When enabled, a constraint will enforce a specific rule about the integrity of data in that table any time the data is inserted, updated, or deleted. When disabled, no enforcement is performed. The other purpose of a constraint is for documentation. The constraints are stored in and can be viewed from the data dictionary. This documentation may be of some value in meeting our metadata needs. It may also be of some value in supporting various query tools. Several query tools on the market do not install their own metadata layer, but they do attempt to use the Oracle data dictionary to support user query formation. When these tools determine that a foreign key relationship exists between two tables, they can anticipate the join criteria for any query that references both tables. In many cases, the tool is smart enough to see the relationship but (luckily) not smart enough to examine whether the relationship is enforced. Even if you don't want the overhead of enabling and enforcing constraints, sometimes it may be useful to "trick" a query tool into making life easier for your users.

NOT NULL Constraints

NOT NULL constraints are one exception to the general rule of constraints being disabled during direct path loads. NOT NULL constraints are inexpensive to process, and they are automatically enforced during all loads. If the warehouse designer determines that a particular column should always have data and that there is some documentation or integrity advantage in having the database perform this check, then he should feel free (that is, unconstrained) in using the NOT NULL constraint.

Primary Key and Unique Constraints

Primary key and unique constraints provide three functions for the data warehouse. One is to document the structure of the database and provide an identifier for locating individual rows within a table. The second is to benefit query performance through the underlying index. The final function is to help ensure data integrity; commonly, that might mean preventing a bulk data load from being executed a second time. The designer of the warehouse database should not necessarily follow the relational rule that every table must have a primary key. If there is a valid performance reason for needing the key to be indexed then, by all means, create the primary key constraint. There are cases in the data warehouse environment when tables may be created without a primary key.

The data initially loaded into a detail or fact table within the warehouse may well not have a naturally occurring key. In an operational system, the Oracle designer faced with this situation would immediately define an artificial key and create a sequence generator to provide unique values. If, as is often the case, this lowest-level transactional detail data is being loaded into a warehouse strictly to allow the creation of various aggregations and summaries, then there may be no reason for a user to want to locate a specific row of detail. If there are no performance or integrity reasons for building an index, then the index should not be built!

The designer should evaluate the potential documentation advantages. Perhaps they can be met by declaring, but not enabling, the constraint.

Further, there may be other cases when no anticipated query is going to take advantage of an index on the ORDER_ID column, which is the key generated for our ORDERS table back in its source operational system. Users may be expected to drill-down to the detailed data to see particulars about an interesting row in some summary, but this drill-down would be based on the columns used in generating that summary. Normally, users of the data warehouse should not be trying to inquire into the details of order number 1873549. (If they are, there is a good chance that the warehouse is being misused to fill some deficiency in the operational systems.) If no query performance gain is expected from the underlying index, there may be no good reason to expend the effort to store and maintain the index.

During the load process it may be appropriate to generate new sequence number values for the keys of dimension tables and then use these values within the foreign key columns of fact data. When no natural key to the dimension exists (or when it is long and awkward to work with) this is probably justified. Just be aware that this will require an extra "lookup" step while loading the fact table that may add considerable overhead to the whole process. If the fact data will be loaded to a separate table for validation before eventually being exchanged into the fact table then this extra lookup step will delay user access to the new data but not impair users' ability to access existing data.

It is, however, hard to imagine a case when it would be necessary to generate a new artificial (or "synthetic") key for the fact table. As discussed earlier in this chapter, fact rows are identified for a query via their combination of foreign key values. Never should a user be expected to look up a specific row from the fact table by specifying an unnatural artificial key value. If uniqueness is required among the fact rows (note, this is not always the case!) then it can usually be efficiently ensured during the load process, as discussed in Chapter 6.

If your situation does require generation of unique key values for either dimension or fact/detail tables, three methods for performing the key generations are discussed later in this chapter.

Foreign Key Constraints

As discussed earlier in this chapter, foreign key constraints are appropriate for defining some of the relationships within the data warehouse. Chief among these are the fact-to-dimension relationships in a star schema. There is no unavoidable overhead to maintaining foreign key constraints so they may be defined whenever the relationship is truly many-to-one. To be created, though, a foreign key in Oracle must define a relationship to a primary or unique key in the referenced table. That is, the referenced table <u>must</u> have one of these key constraints defined. For dimension tables this shouldn't be a problem—each should have a primary key to support query performance anyway. Other relationships among detail and summary tables should be evaluated to ensure that the value of the foreign key and primary key constraints exceed the cost of maintaining the primary key index.

Check Constraints

Check constraints allow the database designer to define specific rules about the data values in a particular row. Unless the data is loaded using the direct path mode of SQL*Loader, each row is evaluated during the insert process to verify that these rules are followed. Expressions involving specific columns may be compared to constants to other columns. The rules may not, however, look at other rows of data in the table or other tables in the database. Each row's data must stand alone.

PARTITION VIEWS

Partition elimination using partition views in Oracle7 release 7.3 required check constraints on each underlying table so that Oracle7 could be sure that data rows would be found in only the appropriate table. Creation of partition views is briefly described in the Chapter 5. The partition view feature was an early (and inferior) approach to partitioning. If your warehouse is built on Oracle8 or Oracle8*i*, eschew this in favor of the more robust Oracle8 partitioning feature.

There are times when the data being added to the database must be validated to ensure reasonableness of column values. When loading a small number of rows to dimension tables, the overhead of check constraints is usually not excessive.

Bulk loading of detail or fact data presents a set of problems, however. When direct path SQL*Loader is invoked on a table, it disables all constraints (except for NOT NULL conditions that are, in fact, a special case of check constraints). Because the constraints are disabled, no checking is actually performed while the data is being loaded. At the completion of the direct path load, by default Oracle will attempt to reenable the constraint. This is where two problems arise. First, reenabling a constraint requires that all data in the table be reverified because Oracle has no way of guaranteeing that existing data did not get changed while the constraint was disabled. This can be very expensive if the new 200,000 rows have been added to a table of 2 million rows! The evaluation of the existing 2 million rows may well take more time than was saved by using direct path for the load. Second, if there are data errors in the data, finding them and resolving them may be more trouble after the data is loaded. When enabling the constraint, you may specify the EXCEPTIONS INTO syntax to have Oracle create a record of each invalid row. Another process (manual or automated) will have to be performed to either delete the offending rows or correct the errors before you will be able to successfully reenable the constraint.

There is hope, however. It is possible to do this field-level editing even more economically within the extract or transformation processes. If a commercial ETT tool is not being used and all ETT functions are being locally developed, an option would be to pass the data through one or more filters on the way to being loaded. This is frequently done, for instance, to take advantage of the efficiencies of generic sort utilities to simplify and speed the creation of an Oracle index after the data is loaded. Adding another filter, such as a short awk or sed program into the data stream leading to SQL*Loader, may satisfy the requirement with a minimal effect on total processing speed. Of course, this approach requires the development and ongoing maintenance of yet another piece of hand-written code.

There is another way to manage the need for data validation without incurring the costs of maintaining constraints on the unchanged data in our large detail or fact tables.

Ensuring Uniqueness without Maintaining Constraints

If you are using partitioned tables in the manner recommended in this chapter and detailed in Chapter 6, then your data loads will be initially made into a standalone table that (after validation and indexing) will be exchanged into the partition. This standalone table contains only the newly loaded data and whatever integrity checks made against it that will not have to consider the millions or even billions of rows already loaded (and validated) to the existing table. It is perfectly appropriate to verify this newly added data by enabling whatever check and foreign key constraints are necessary to ensure that the data is fit for use. Once the data is validated, these constraints can then be dropped prior to performing the partition exchange.

If our fact table is partitioned by TRANSACTION_DATE we will want to verify that each row in our newly loaded table has only the proper value(s) in this partitioning key column before doing the exchange. SQL*Loader can do this automatically through use of the WHEN clause. If, however, the data is loaded through some other means it is appropriate to verify the partitioning key's integrity through a check constraint that, once enabled, can then be dropped.

Verifying uniqueness, if appropriate for your particular table, is only a slight variation of this approach. Declaring a primary key constraint on our standalone load table ensures that no duplicates exist within this newly loaded data. As long as the partitioning key is part of the primary key constraint definition, then we can be assured that the new data does not duplicate any existing keys.

An enhanced capability to perform this uniqueness check has been added to Oracle8*i* specifically to support data warehousing. Creating and enabling the primary key constraint ordinarily requires the creation of a unique index. Index builds have three major components. First, all of the data must be read. Second, the values for the key fields must be sorted and then checked for duplicates. Third, the structure of the physical index must be built and populated with the sorted key values and the pointers to the actual data rows. If the index we are proposing to build is being used only to initially guarantee uniqueness and will not be needed for supporting ongoing queries, there is really no value in performing step 3, actually building the index—we intend to drop the constraint immediately after it is enabled!

Oracle8*i* allows you to skip the final step by defining the primary key constraint with optional DISABLE VALIDATE syntax. DISABLE instructs Oracle8*i* not to build an index while VALIDATE indicates that the uniqueness check must still be performed. In short, the read and sort steps must be completed. Once the data is validated, it cannot be modified through any DML statements (INSERT and UPDATE, specifically, could introduce violations to the uniqueness). Because we have finished our load and validation, we will not have any further need to modify the data in the standalone table; our only remaining operation on the data is to make it a partition of the permanent partitioned table. This ALTER TABLE . . . EXCHANGE PARTITION statement is an allowed DDL operation, so our goal is met. Keep in mind, though, for this approach to ensure uniqueness throughout the extended partitioned table, the primary key must include the partition key, otherwise we would have to revalidate the values in every partition to know that none of the new rows were duplicated.

DISABLED FOREIGN KEYS

In Oracle version 6, constraints could be declared, but they were not enforced by the RDBMS. Few database designers took the time to declare them for just their documentation value. Even back in the late 1980s, users of data warehouses and some query tools discovered the trick of using disabled foreign key constraints to guide anticipated joins.

Generating Unique Key Values

In the ideal world, all incoming data to the warehouse would be nicely normalized and have primary key values already assigned and validated. Of course, the real world has some different characteristics. Earlier in this chapter we discussed the issues of using naturally occurring keys versus artificial keys. If your situation requires the introduction of artificial key values, then you have three potential means of generating them within the Oracle environment.

Table of Key Values

The first (and oldest) option is to maintain an administrative table within your warehouse that stores the current highest value being used in the particular key. Each new row being added to the table is assigned the next higher value, and the administrative table's stored maximum is updated. Before Oracle version 6, this technique was frequently used in transaction processing systems. We occasionally still run into applications that are written to be entirely database independent that use this technique. For OLTP applications, this approach is a major limitation to scalability. Locking, even at the row level, soon causes a growing queue of transactions waiting to obtain a unique key value.

In the warehouse, however, scalability in the number of transactions that can execute simultaneously is rarely an issue. There are still costs associated with this approach that make it unacceptable in some warehouse situations. When loading a very large number of rows, the overhead of having to do additional SELECT and UPDATE statements may double the time to execute the loading process. This approach also makes the direct path mode of SQL*Loader unusable. If the number of rows to be added is small, however, when adding perhaps a few hundred new rows to a dimension table, this overhead may barely be noticeable.

Oracle Sequence Generators

The second option for generating unique primary key values has been built into the Oracle RDBMS kernel since version 6. Sequence generators are particularly valuable because there is no record locking required to select a unique value from these memory-based structures. For scalable OLTP applications this is the only acceptable choice.

In the data warehouse, however, this may not always be the best choice. If the data is to be loaded using SQL*Loader direct path mode, then this option is not available because rows are not inserted to the database through the RDBMS kernel.

Generated by SQL*Loader

Finally, SQL*Loader has the ability to generate sequential values as it loads rows into a table. This technique works well and will be discussed further in Chapter 6. The SEQUENCE option of SQL*Loader allows you to specify the starting value and an incremental value. To avoid having to modify the control file before each execution to specify the new starting value, you may specify the keyword MAX instead of a starting integer value. SQL*Loader will then select the current maximum value from the table and add the incremental value to begin the load. Again assuming that the rows are being loaded into a table that already has an enabled primary key constraint (with corresponding unique index), this technique works well.

Designing for High Availability

Availability refers to the user's expectations that the data warehouse will be ready and able to provide answers to his questions when needed. Early warehouses established a schedule that allowed many hours for the batch operations of loading, validating, indexing, backing up, and archiving/purging of data and then assigned any remaining hours for user access. Two major changes have happened in the past decade of data warehousing, however. First, the amount of data that needs to be loaded has grown dramatically, and second, users have come to rely more heavily on the warehouse for supporting their decision making and planning.

The first, data volume, without adaptations to the batch versus online scheduling would result in more and more hours being consumed by administrative work and less and less being available for user work. The second, greater dependence, has simultaneously made demand for warehouse access by users grow to even broader windows. These two effects are obviously in conflict as long as we think of the day being divided between two incompatible types of processing. Fortunately, features have been added to the Oracle RDBMS that allow us to overlap these two processing modes so that user access does not need to be interrupted to allow the administrator to perform regular maintenance activities. Designing a high-availability data warehouse is no longer an oxymoron.

What Is High Availability?

High availability is a relative term. Space shuttle operations and medical life support systems have a definition that probably doesn't apply to the warehouse. On the other hand, as our user community expands outside of the corporate headquarters building to accommodate divisions (or perhaps our suppliers or customers) located in Tokyo, London, and Sao Paulo, expectations change. A new global data warehouse with a 9-to-5 user-access window actually requires nearly 24 hours per day! Unfortunately, high availability is typically measured simplistically as a percentage of uptime: 98 percent or 99.999 percent availability. This type of measure doesn't accurately reflect the nature of true availability. Consider two alternative scenarios of a system that delivers 98 percent availability: In the first case brief interruptions of less than a minute occur once every hour or so; in the second example outages are rare, but take longer to restore—perhaps one full day every couple of years. Both situations have approximately the same percentage of uptime; however, the first will make it very difficult to complete an index build or a query that typically requires an hour to execute!

To properly measure availability, the design and operations teams need to work with users to define a *service-level agreement* that measures the (1) frequency of outages, (2) the duration of outages, and (3) the impact of outages. By impact, we mean it is necessary to evaluate how much of the warehouse is unavailable or how many user queries could not be performed during the period of unavailability. For instance, if our warehouse presents data to support 20 different departments or regions, a partial outage that prevents one division from getting its reports, while admittedly a failure, is not as critical as the entire warehouse being unavailable to all 20 user groups. When we are designing very large databases, disk failures are one of our most common sources of unavailability. In the properly designed warehouse, however, the failure of a particular disk can be limited to data of importance to only a subset of our entire user base. We must design with this concept of partial unavailability in mind to minimize the magnitude of outages that, unfortunately, will occur. At the same time, we will evaluate architectures that also reduce the frequency and duration of those outages.

At the same time, our design needs to recognize that availability is not free. The discussion of hardware architectures in Chapter 2 identified several options that present higher reliability and availability, but at higher costs. Within the Oracle software layer the same effect can be seen—Oracle Parallel Server can be used to deliver a warehouse with excellent availability, but there are additional costs in acquiring both the optional software and the underlying clustering or MPP hardware and O/S. Also, the sophistication of the environment requires additional training and expertise within the systems and database administration staffs.

Figure 4.8 is a simplified demonstration of the relationship between availability and total system cost. It is not linear. Approaching the mythical 100 percent availability costs many times more than a more modest objective. Just as important as delivering sufficient availability is the goal of not wasting money buying more availability than is truly needed by the warehouse users.

Types of Interruptions

When designing for high availability it is necessary to understand that interruptions to service occur in several forms. We must consider *planned outages*

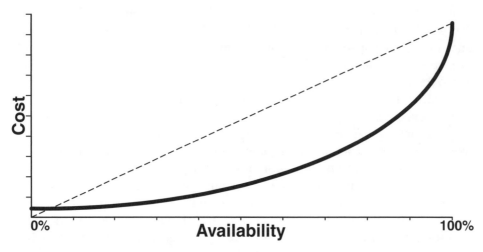

Figure 4.8   Relationship between availability and cost.

for software or hardware upgrades, load/validate/index/summarize/publish processing, and database or schema redesigns and reorganizations. Our design will directly affect the frequency, duration, and impact of these planned interruptions.

The second category of interruptions are *unplanned outages*. These include all of the things that can go wrong—we typically think of hardware, software, or network crashes. We must also consider other failures that prevent the users from obtaining reliable data from the warehouse. A load or summarization job that does not complete successfully potentially leaves data in the warehouse inconsistent and the system should, therefore, prevent users from accessing the affected (and related) data until the error is corrected.

The third categorization, *partial outages*, can be either planned or unplanned. The key point is that we should use partial interruptions as a tool to limit the impact of whatever outages do occur. With proper design, reorganizing a particular table or the failure of a single disk should not require all access to the warehouse to be denied.

Design Techniques for High Availability

While we will never be able to prevent all failures we can design with specific objectives and techniques that limit the frequency, duration, and impact of outages that occur. The following Oracle8 features and techniques have already been described, and many will be demonstrated in subsequent chapters. Each of these techniques, when properly applied, can help avoid outages, allow you to recover from the interruption more quickly, or limit the number of queries that are prevented by the problem:

- Read-only tablespaces
- Parallel Server
- Partitioning
- Hot or incremental backups
- Parallel CREATE TABLE AS SELECT . . . NOLOGGING
- Parallel CREATE INDEX . . . NOLOGGING
- Parallel SQL*Loader DIRECT
- ALTER INDEX . . . REBUILD
- Replicated, distributed, and standby databases
- Separate database objects into multiple tablespaces
- Materialized views (Oracle8*i*)
- Transportable tablespaces (Oracle8*i*)
- Sampling (Oracle8*i*)
- Online index defragmentation (Oracle8*i*)

Additionally, you should consider the supporting capabilities of the underlying hardware and operating system, such as RAID storage and clustering, as elements within your high-availability design.

Limiting Planned Outages

While many of our design decisions can help control unplanned interruptions, we have to take full responsibility for all planned outages. The choices we make will directly control how resilient our database is to the need for planned outages.

Regular Data Load Processing

The most important technique in limiting planned outages is to avoid the trap of considering our batch administrative processing to be incompatible with user access to other data in the warehouse. Earlier we described the primary regular source of unavailability as *load/validate/index/summarize/publish* processing. By using partitioned tables and indexes in the ways described in this chapter, it is possible to perform the loading, validation, indexing, and summarization steps without affecting the data that current users are viewing. Only the publishing step (the briefest step!) will affect the visible data. Given this design objective, we may spend over 23 hours doing our background work to prepare each day's data; when it is fully ready and tested, then a quick exchange of partitions on our fact tables or a change of synonyms pointing to our summary tables makes the change effective.

Backups

The next critical design choice that will eliminate planned outages is to avoid the trap of depending on cold backups of the data warehouse database. Oracle8 features such as read-only tablespaces can make the majority of our warehouse immune to the need for regular backups. Additionally, many warehouse actions such as loading, indexing, and summarization can be performed with the NOLOGGING option that limits the amount of redo being generated (and needing to be archived). In many cases, it may be faster to reload a partition or rebuild an index in case of a failure between the time of object creation and being made read-only for a single backup. For these portions of the databases that have been made read-only, it may be perfectly acceptable to avoid the extra costs of RAID Level 1 (mirroring) or RAID Level 5 (distributed parity) in favor of the higher performing and less expensive RAID Level 0 (striping) or even CD-ROM storage that is even less expensive.

Some parts of the warehouse database, however, are more susceptible to failure than others. Losing part of the SYSTEM tablespace in particular can be devastating to operations. Tablespaces containing rollback segments or recently updated data are also potential loss concerns. For these critical portions of the data warehouse, using a more expensive storage medium (e.g., RAID Level 0+1) is appropriate. Also, these volatile tablespaces that cannot operate in read-only mode, necessitate the use of ARCHIVELOG mode for the database to enable hot or incremental backups.

Reorganizations

Schema redesigns are a fact of life as the warehouse matures. Consider implementing these changes in a controlled manner that does not directly modify the current data structures. Building new tables and summaries under different names and then completely testing their usage will not prevent users from working with their former incarnations. When all is ready, a quick change of synonyms or even two RENAME operations will swap the old and new with minimal disruption of user access.

Reorganizing of tables and indexes themselves generally is rooted in fundamental design errors early in the life of these objects. Partitioned tables allow for efficient purging of older data without leaving empty space within the object that might slow performance and consume unnecessary disk. Locally partitioned indexes have this same feature.

Where index disorganization does occur, consider whether a reverse-order index will meet the performance requirements. In the remaining cases ALTER INDEX . . . REBUILD will build a new, reorganized copy of the index without interrupting queries that are currently using the original structure. Plan for this requirement by ensuring sufficient extra space in each index tablespace to allow for holding a second copy of your largest index during the rebuild.

Upgrades

It will, inevitably, be necessary to upgrade your hardware, operating system, or Oracle software from time to time. In most cases, these activities will require a scheduled outage of the entire warehouse. The best control available is to perform adequate testing of the changes prior to applying them to the live warehouse server.

While each node of the Parallel Server complex must execute the same version of Oracle and operating system code, it may be potentially useful to remove one node from the shared database environment and complete its upgrade while the other node(s) continue to execute the older release. When everything for that node is ready and tested, then shut down the instances on the other nodes and then reopen the database from the upgraded node. Upgrade each node and then add it back to the shared database. This approach can limit the absolute time that the database is completely unavailable. During the process, however, the database will be operating with less than full scalability and failover protection from some unplanned interruption on a single node. This risk may be acceptable when compared to the need to simultaneously upgrade all nodes, providing no availability.

Balancing Design Objectives

Design of the data warehouse must, of course, anticipate users' data requirements. It should also maximize the manageability of the environment. It should support the anticipated number of users and queries and provide for growth over time. Although too often an afterthought, it must also incorporate features that ensure adequate availability for users as well as administrative processes to complete their necessary work.

Summary

One of the requirements for making a data warehouse useful is the need for metadata—data about the other data in the warehouse. There are various levels of metadata possible and various ways of maintaining and presenting metadata to our users.

One primary design decision is determining the appropriate level(s) of data granularity and the length of data retention. There are two primary models for designing an Oracle data warehouse—a traditional design based on precreation of summary tables and the newer alternative of star schemas. Either style of schema can be implemented using Oracle8 features such as indexing and partitioning. Most warehouses will use both techniques, often creating summaries to handle the most common queries and allowing the underlying star to manage queries with uncommon criteria. Materialized views can simplify the administration of summary data and allow the optimizer to automatically rewrite queries that could benefit from using the already summarized data.

Database constraints and triggers, commonly used in OLTP database design, have limited use in the data warehouse. Where necessary to ensure data integrity, constraints should be applied during the load process.

The historically relaxed view of availability for the data warehouse is being replaced as more warehouses are becoming critical components in an organization's decision-making infrastructure.

Building the Oracle Data Warehouse

But this is absolute madness, Ambassador! Why should you build such a thing?

President Merkin Muffley
Dr. Strangelove or: How I Learned to Stop Worrying and Love the Bomb *(1964)*

The previous chapter examined the "what" and "why" questions regarding various components of the Oracle data warehouse. This chapter will concentrate on the "how" questions. In the real world, of course, there is no such absolute and clear-cut division between the design topics of Chapter 4, "Designing the Oracle Data Warehouse," and the build topics presented here. The two chapters should work together so that as you read here you may find the need to reference Chapter 4.

Careful planning when developing and implementing the database schema will help you ensure acceptable performance and avoid maintenance problems. This chapter refers to a number of SQL commands and provides some examples of the use of those commands. The chapter is not intended, though, to be a tutorial on Oracle database administration and does not provide exhaustive descriptions of SQL command syntax. The Oracle reference manuals and other books are available for more complete syntax. Instead, we will focus on introducing commands and usage that are of particular relevance to implementing a data warehouse using the Oracle database.

We introduce several development techniques that may seem obvious to experienced Oracle developers. In our experience, however, these may be unknown to developers new to the Oracle environment and are all too often ignored by experienced developers (yes, sometimes even painfully by the authors as well).

Finally, we demonstrate how to implement the data warehouse by creating the database, its tablespaces, and various types of tables, indexes, views, and other Oracle database objects. We show how to provide statistics about the tables and indexes to the Oracle cost-based optimizer. We conclude with a discussion of the need for testing the data warehouse with a representatively large sample of data.

ETT Tools for Building the Warehouse

ETT (or ETL, if you prefer) tools were introduced in the design chapter. Properly designed and effectively used, these tools can greatly simplify the tasks necessary to create a data warehouse. ETT products can provide the following:

- Enhanced ease of use, commonly with an advanced graphical interface for design

- Enforced consistency between iterative phases of design and build

- Change control mechanisms for implementing schema design changes

- Consistency of the user interface for extracting data, even from multiple disparate source environments

- Support for coordinated usage by multiple members of the warehouse design team

- Documentation of all warehouse metadata

- Metadata coordination with reporting, query, and analysis tools

- Generation of scripts to perform tasks such as creation of database tables, data validation, and loading

- Complete support for generating and managing enhanced Oracle8*i* data warehousing capabilities, such as partitioning, materialized views, transportable tablespaces, etc.

- Execution and control of the load and periodic refresh processing so that errors in one step are trapped and handled appropriately before invoking subsequent steps

- Support for data extraction using a variety of methods of identifying incremental changes

- Extensible support for efficiently performing both simple and sophisticated, multistep transformations of data

Unfortunately, there is no one tool that is best at all of these responsibilities. One product might be especially powerful in accessing mainframe data while another might have twice the number of built-in transformations. One might be optimal for rapid design of the warehouse but somewhat weak in defining data validation rules. Correspondingly, the needs of one warehouse development team will be different from those of another. You may have a majority of your data coming from mainframe VSAM and IDMS sources, or all of your source data may reside in Oracle on UNIX; your data transformation needs may be simple and straightforward translations or may involve complex algorithms that require customized procedural coding.

While we will discuss, somewhat briefly, the new Oracle Warehouse Builder product as an example of one tool in this very broad category, this is not to imply that it will be the only—or necessarily the best—choice for your particular data warehouse. This book does not attempt to endorse any particular tool or to objectively rate the large variety of choices available in the market. We can, however, describe some of the criteria by which we would judge the suitability of ETT tools for a particular warehouse, but how those criteria are ranked in importance is left to each warehouse team to decide. In addition to basic considerations (does the tool support extraction from all of your source environments?), some particular criteria for the Oracle8 warehouse should include the following:

Handling of warehouse metadata. This topic was addressed in the previous chapter on design, but the ETT tool's metadata should ideally be stored in an Oracle database so that it can be easily referenced by warehouse users. Metadata, in this discussion, includes the obvious design documentation but also should incorporate the control and tracking of all administrative jobs, such as loading, validating, summarizing, and archiving. Metadata defined to the ETT tool should not require reentry into the repository of the selected query and analysis tools.

Support for critical Oracle8*i* storage features, such as partitioning. As we will see in more depth in the next chapter, partitioning support goes beyond just the syntax to create partitions. It also includes the critical specialized handling of partitions during load and publish operations as well as archival and purging tasks.

Awareness of and support for high-performance Oracle8*i* facilities, such as direct path SQL*Loader, parallel query, materialized views, and function-based indexes. If the chosen tool is generic in its database handling then the administrators will have to manually modify generated code to incorporate these features. This presents an opportunity for error at every generation. Each manual intervention reduces the value of using the automated tool.

Support for Oracle8 distributed and communication facilities. If the warehouse is expected to incorporate data marts or utilize features such as Oracle8 Advanced Queuing or replication facilities, the ideal ETT tool would allow the design and administration of these capabilities to be handled in the same way as other warehouse features.

ORACLE WAREHOUSE BUILDER

In Chapter 4 we introduced Oracle Warehouse Builder as a tool to aid in the design and administration of the data warehouse. One of the features of OWB is its ability to generate and run the necessary DDL to create the tables, indexes, partitions, and materialized views of the data warehouse. (OWB was given its first production release just as this text was being submitted for printing. For current information on effective use of OWB, visit the authors' Web sites provided in the Introduction.)

Given the large set of advantages potentially provided by an ETT tool, this chapter is primarily dedicated to how to perform various steps in the building of a data warehouse using the SQL language. We strongly feel that it is appropriate for the DBA to understand the underlying technology of any tool he might use, whether for creation of warehouse tables, refreshing warehouse contents, or monitoring and tuning of warehouse performance. This is true for at least six reasons:

1. If the chosen ETT tool doesn't completely (or correctly) support a desired feature, you will have to understand how to implement it manually. The same is true even for the Oracle Enterprise Manager console. The DBA must know what it is doing (and why) to be able to use it effectively and to properly interpret its output.

2. No tool does it all. There are very powerful SQL techniques (such as the one we'll introduce in the next section) that can sometimes save the DBA hours of repeatedly clicking buttons in a GUI tool.

3. Most GUI administration and ETT tools on the market run on a Windows platform. Most warehouses are created on the more scalable UNIX platforms. Generally this client/server arrangement is fine, but there are times, especially when Oracle is being first installed and the database is being initially created, when all the pieces may not be in place. Further, there may be times throughout the project when the necessary communications links are not available. More times than we like to recall we have had to connect to our clients' networks via dialup links from home (or even vacation!) to diagnose or solve various problems.

4. Not all generated code is created equal. As much as we try to avoid doing manual maintenance on generated code, it is sometimes necessary in order to get required performance or to correct errors.

5. If you know only one tool, you are less able to help on another project where that specific tool is not available. The warehouse DBA will not be able to step easily into the DBA role for another project (or even at another company) should that opportunity arise. Not understanding the database features and the SQL to implement and control those features is a significant CLM (career-limiting move).

6. Finally, you may be about to embark on one of the many initial warehouse implementation teams that have not elected to purchase and use an ETT tool. While this is not the best plan it is a common one.

Having laid out that foundation (and exposed our biases) we will proceed to introduce the interactive SQL*Plus tool that is provided with every Oracle environment. It is primarily a simple environment for executing interactive SQL commands. Additional features for editing and spooling and formatting make SQL*Plus useful for a variety of situations.

Using SQL*Plus to Create the Data Warehouse

In many cases the initial data warehouse project may not justify the purchase of CASE or ETT tools. Oracle's SQL*Plus provides a wonderful environment for both the developer and the DBA. We can just log into SQL*Plus, type in an SQL or PL/SQL command, execute it, edit it again, and reexecute until we get it right. Great —a developer's dream!

We should, however, resist the temptation to develop our warehouse in this haphazard fashion. No one would ever admit that this is how he works, but far too many of us slip into using just this approach when building a data warehouse. The warehouse tends to be evolutionary; it is easy to tweak and adjust, and at the margin there is never a clear need to create a formal script just to execute a fairly simple SQL command. There is one certainty in this approach, however: We will regret it eventually. We should always use scripts whenever we execute any SQL command. We will never do anything once, no matter what we may think at the time. We will execute the same command or something very similar in the future, we will be rewarded for the few extra minutes it may take to create a script file when we first execute a command. Moreover, to paraphrase the famous bumper sticker, "Bad Stuff Happens"—no matter how careful and how certain we are or how easy something is, we will occasionally make mistakes. Sometimes the mistakes manifest themselves in subtle ways and are not observed until much later during data loads or even user access. It makes life much easier (and promotes career longevity!) to maintain a record of exactly what actions were taken before the appearance of the error(s). It's easy to maintain a history of our activities using Oracle.

Keeping Logs of Your Actions

The SQL*Plus SPOOL command can be used to create log files for all our activities. Ensuring that we spool the output of our script will enable us to easily track any errors that may occur while we are creating the database schema.

```
SPOOL KEEP_LOG.LST
<list of SQL and SQL*Plus commands>
SPOOL OFF
```

In this simple example of a SQL*Plus script, everything from the SPOOL command through the SPOOL OFF command will be logged to the file named KEEP_LOG.LST. A long list of commands may scroll quickly by on our screen or may even require hours to run overnight. In either case, it will be easier to review the log after the completion of the script. We will also use SPOOL later in this section to help us save generated SQL output into a new SQL script file.

SQL*Plus Formatting Commands

The SQL*Plus environment provides a number of special commands that can be used to control how SQL*Plus displays output. We refer the reader to the Oracle7 or Oracle8 *SQL*Plus User's Guide and Reference* for a complete description of the SQL*Plus commands. SQL*Plus commands are completely different from SQL commands. SQL*Plus commands are recognized only in the SQL*Plus environment, and they are unique to Oracle. SQL commands are used in many different Oracle tools, and they are frequently standard across various vendors' RDBMS environments (most vendors use ANSI standard SQL with their own extensions). It is possible to create very sophisticated reports with totals and subtotals, word wrapping, titles, footers, and other complex formats using only SQL*Plus. Most developers will choose a more graphical reporting tool than SQL*Plus to create sophisticated reports.

Because our primary interest in this chapter is in creating the data warehouse and not creating reports, we focus on the several commands that are indispensable to a data warehouse developer or manager. A number of variables that control SQL*Plus processing can be manipulated using the SQL*Plus SET command. The general syntax of the SET command is SET *variable_name value*. We simply include the necessary SET commands in our SQL*Plus script file to create the desired execution environment for our script.

For example, we may sometimes want SQL*Plus to print a page break after 62 lines when we are sending output to a laser printer. We may want to set page breaks to occur after every 22 lines when we are displaying to a monitor, and we don't want the output to scroll past too fast. We use two SQL*Plus commands to create an environment where the page will display on one terminal screen and then prompt us to scroll to the next page of output. SET PAGESIZE 22 (typically abbreviated as SET PAGES) will produce a 22-line output page. Next we need to make sure the display just doesn't scroll right past the page break all the way to the end. We accomplish this with the SET PAUSE command. SET PAUSE ON will cause SQL*Plus to display a full page of data (which we just defined to be 22 lines) and then stop until the user presses a key on the keyboard. We would like to present a prompt (so the user knows to press a key and doesn't think the command is just executing slowly). We can use SET PAUSE message to pause and print the reminder message. When we use SET PAUSE More, SQL*Plus will print a page of output, print the message "More" on the display, and pause until it receives a keystroke. Our script file will look like this:

```
SET PAGES 22
SET PAUSE ON
SET PAUSE More
SELECT TABLE_NAME FROM DICT;
SET PAGES 62
SET PAUSE OFF
```

We set our page size back to the value used for printing and turn off the pause function after we execute our SQL command.

A large number of SET commands are available. Some of the more useful ones include the following:

ECHO (ON/OFF). Controls whether the command file will display each command as it executes it. The default value is OFF.

FEEDBACK (OFF/ON/n). Controls whether SQL*Plus will display the number of rows returned from a query at the bottom of the query result set. Setting FEEDBACK OFF suppresses the display. It is possible to provide a value so that FEEDBACK is provided only if there are more rows than the value specified. Setting FEEDBACK 10 will result in FEEDBACK only if there are more than 10 rows returned. The default value is 6.

HEADING (OFF/ON). Controls whether SQL*Plus will display the column heading at the top of each output page. SET HEADING OFF suppresses column headings.

LINESIZE (n). Controls the width of the display before the line wraps. The default value is 80.

NEWPAGE (n). Controls the number of blank lines printed at the top of each new page. Setting NEWPAGE 0 will result in a page feed before the start of each new output page.

PAGESIZE (n). As demonstrated earlier, SET PAGESIZE controls the number of lines per output page. SET PAGES 0 will result in no page breaks at all. It also suppresses column headings.

TERMOUT (OFF/ON). Controls whether the output displays to the terminal. Frequently, we will set TERMOUT OFF if we are executing batch scripts and are spooling output to a file. Even if we are executing scripts in an interactive session, it may be useful to set TERMOUT OFF to speed execution. Remember to spool the output to a file and be careful not to use the SET PROMPT command when setting TERMOUT OFF (SQL*Plus will wait for a keystroke, but the user will not be able to see the prompt).

Using SPOOL to Unload Table Data

We frequently need to create a "flat" file from a table, and using SQL*Plus commands allows us to do this easily. This is useful for dumping data from a source system to be loaded into the data warehouse or for archiving data from the warehouse into a file that could be easily loaded back into the warehouse using SQL*Loader. To unload a portion of our ACTIVITY table to a flat file we could use the following command file:

```
SET FEEDBACK OFF TERMOUT OFF PAGES 0 HEAD OFF
SPOOL FLAT_FILE.LST
SELECT ORGANIZATION_ID, REVENUE
  FROM ACTIVITY
 WHERE MONTH = '1999DEC'
/
spool off
```

Note that we can place several options to a single SET COMMAND on one line.

We present a more complete example of using SQL*Plus to extract data from an Oracle source system and build a corresponding SQL*Loader control file in Chapter 6, "Populating the Oracle Data Warehouse."

Passing Values to a Script at Run-Time

Because one of our goals is to consistently use scripts for managing our data warehouse, we should strive to make them as generic as possible by using the SQL*Plus capabilities for passing variable values to a script. If we preface a variable name in the SQL*Plus command with a single ampersand (&), SQL*Plus will prompt for the substitution value by printing the variable name and waiting for input. SQL*Plus will prompt each time it encounters *&variable_name*. Suppose we want to run a simple script to check for the total number of records loaded into the data warehouse and the total revenue value for a given month. These values will be checked against totals calculated from our source systems to ensure we have accurately extracted and loaded the data. We can create a simple script using a substitution variable for the month we want to check.

```
SPOOL   CHECK_LOAD.DAT
SELECT COUNT(*), SUM(REVENUE)
  FROM ACTIVITY
 WHERE MONTH = '&MONTH';
SPOOL OFF
```

To avoid having to enter the same value repeatedly in a SQL*Plus script that references the *&variable* several times, we can use the *&&variable_name* construct. The double-ampersand variable will prompt for a value only the first time the particular variable is encountered and will automatically substitute thereafter. In the following example, we choose to use two SELECT statements that will both require specification of the MONTH variable. Because the first is referenced by &&MONTH, the value will be saved and we won't be asked for a value when the second SQL statement is executed.

```
SPOOL   CHECK_LOAD.DAT
SELECT SUM(REVENUE)
  FROM ACTIVITY
 WHERE MONTH = '&&MONTH';
SELECT COUNT(*)
  FROM ACTIVITY
 WHERE MONTH = '&MONTH'
SPOOL OFF
```

Frequently, we will want a more descriptive prompt than simply the name of the variable. We can use the SQL*Plus ACCEPT command to provide a more descriptive prompt. The ACCEPT command specifies the name of the variable and then specifies the keyword PROMPT followed by a string that defines what should be displayed on the user's screen when input is expected.

```
SPOOL CHECK_LOAD.DAT
ACCEPT   CHECK_MONTH   PROMPT 'Enter the month (YYYYMON): '
SELECT SUM(REVENUE)
  FROM ACTIVITY
 WHERE MONTH = '&&MONTH';
SELECT COUNT(*)
  FROM ACTIVITY
```

```
WHERE MONTH = '&&MONTH';
UNDEFINE MONTH
SPOOL OFF
```

We issued the SQL*Plus UNDEFINE command at the end of this script, which clears the saved value from this variable. This is particularly useful if we are using the *&&variable* construct to maintain persistence of the variable across several references as the script runs but we would also like to be prompted again for the variable value each time the script is reexecuted. (*&&variables* are automatically UNDEFINEd when exiting SQL*Plus.)

Writing Scripts for Execution in Batch

Some scripts are best run as batch procedures because they may take a long time to run or should be executed during nonbusiness hours. It is easy to set up an environment to execute batch SQL*Plus procedures using parameters. This requires a slight modification to our SQL*Plus scripts. Because we are going to pass parameters from the command line, we will need to ensure that our scripts use substitution variables that are numbers (e.g., "&&1," "&&2," etc.). The number refers to the relative position of the parameter value on the command line. We will remove the ACCEPT command from the script file because we are not going to prompt for a value interactively but will pass the parameter value from the command line when we invoke SQL*Plus.

When we enter SQL*Plus we must provide our Oracle userid and password, shown here as UID/PWD. We can also pass the name of a SQL*Plus command file using the @ symbol followed by the name of the command file to execute. We place our substitution values after the command file name, with each value separated by a space. To run our example script, we would issue the following command:

```
sqlplus UID/PWD  @CHECK_LOAD 1999DEC
```

TIP Entering the userid and password on the command line poses some security risks in the UNIX environment. Any user who issues a UNIX ps command will be able to see the full command line of executing processes. A more secure approach to providing connection information to scripts is to use Oracle's operating system authentication feature (frequently referred to as "OPS$" accounts for the default prefix given to the Oracle account name). Security checking by Oracle is simplified for Oracle accounts defined in this way. The user is automatically allowed to connect to the Oracle account that corresponds to his or her operating system account, which, presumably, has already been verified.

Because our script is going to run in the background, we will need to tell the script to exit SQL*Plus after completing our processing. The actual script that we modified now looks like this:

```
SPOOL CHECK_LOAD.DAT
SELECT SUM(REVENUE)
  FROM ACTIVITY
 WHERE MONTH = '&&1';
SELECT COUNT(*)
  FROM ACTIVITY
 WHERE MONTH = '&&1';
SPOOL OFF
EXIT
```

Now that we know how to execute a SQL*Plus script and pass parameters directly from the command line, we want to extend our ability to submit a job that will run in batch. Unfortunately, the exact syntax for that depends on the operating system on which Oracle is run. Because many data warehouse projects are implemented on a UNIX operating system, we will describe how to create a simple batch procedure for UNIX. UNIX provides the nohup command that enables you to start a UNIX process that will continue to run even if the connection between your terminal and the UNIX server is broken. By combining the nohup command with the & command to execute a UNIX process in the background it is possible to create a very simple, yet flexible, method for submitting batch procedures on UNIX. We can execute our CHECK_LOAD.SQL script in batch mode using the following UNIX syntax:

```
nohup sqlplus UID/PWD @CHECK_LOAD 1999DEC > chkld_1999DEC.log &
```

UNIX NOHUP COMMAND

The UNIX nohup command gets its name from "no hangup." When UNIX was initially developed, users frequently connected from a dial-up TTY device. When running long operations there was no guarantee that the online session could be maintained until the script completed. Thus, nohup was invented to allow the process to continue even if the user's connection was broken.

The > in the UNIX syntax redirects the output to the specified file name ("outfile") and the & command instructs UNIX to run this command in the background. For an educational exercise we can make this even easier by creating a generic UNIX shell script that will invoke "sqlplus" and pass our UID/PWD, SQL*Plus script file, and necessary parameters using the UNIX command processor. We create a simple UNIX shell script called GO_SQL as follows:

```
sqlplus "$1"  @"$2" "$3"
exit
```

The "$1," "$2," and so on are UNIX parameters that receive arguments from the UNIX command line and, where appropriate, substitute the values and pass them into the Oracle script. In our example, $1 represents the Oracle UID/PWD, $2 is the file system name of our SQL*Plus command file, and $3 is the SQL*Plus parameter that passes the date to our SQL*Plus script. Using the UNIX nohup command described earlier we now have a flexible method for executing any SQL*Plus command file in batch mode as follows:

```
nohup GO_SQL UID/PWD CHECK_LOAD 1999DEC > chkld_1999DEC.log &
```

In the process of managing a data warehouse you will accumulate many different scripts. Ideally, these will be maintained within a source code control library just like the programs of a transaction processing system. If for some reason the project is not using such a library, it is possible to remain organized with the small team size typically assigned to a warehouse project. Of course, it is also very possible to get disorganized even with a team of one! There are three goals in organizing our scripts:

1. **Identification.** Name scripts in a meaningful, standardized way. All scripts used for creating database objects might be prefixed with "cr_". All SQL scripts use a default extension of ".sql", but you may find value in naming particularly dangerous scripts (that drop or truncate tables, for instance) with a different suffix that forces you to explicitly type an override when executing. (In UNIX, the uppercase ".SQL" would work for this.) You might decide to name all data validation scripts with a "val_" prefix. SQL*Loader control files will all be suffixed with ".ctl" extensions while ".bad" might be the standard for files of rejected load records. Where appropriate, the table name (or a standardized short name for it) should be included. The goal is to be able to find the appropriate script later when it is needed. Commonly that will be during a crisis.

2. **Management.** At the start of a project it is tempting to simply create all of our scripts in a single directory. As the project continues, hundreds or even thousands of scripts (and logs) will be created. Plan early for a directory structure that allows for manageability. Above all else, make certain that the production version of a script is housed where it can never be unintentionally confused with a development version of the same script. If you need to use the same script against multiple databases you can keep

one central copy and then create symbolic links from each instance's directory. Establish standard environment variables and aliases for navigation around these directory trees. For good ideas on maintaining your directory structure see the discussion of Optimal Flexible Architecture in Chapter 3, "Oracle Server Software Architecture and Features," and in the Oracle installation documentation.

3. **Documentation.** It seems so obvious when out of the heat of battle, but every script needs to be documented before leaving it for later use. It is easy to try to avoid documentation by declaring that this is a "one-time-use" script. Fine, then delete it. Otherwise, use a standard form of recording what the script does, its parameters, who wrote it, what other scripts it calls or is called by, and known limitations. Use a template to copy an identically formatted header into every script you write and save. Don't plan on going back and documenting what each script does after the warehouse is up and running. Because a warehouse is an evolutionary creation, there is rarely a point at which we will feel we can "spare" the time to create the documentation. We just keep adding more and more routines (just a few at a time, so it doesn't seem that bad) until we have an unmanageable mess. Document the scripts as you create them. You will be glad you did!

The preceding thoughts are the foundation of a source code control system, whether part of the operating system, a purchased product, or something built from scratch by the project team. If you must create your own, it is very convenient to store the names and functions of the scripts in the database. Simply create a table that includes a column for file name, a column for description, and a longer column for any appropriate documentation. This is a rudimentary start to your process-side metadata!

```
CREATE TABLE SCRIPTS
       (SCRIPT_NAME          VARCHAR2(30),
        SCRIPT_PATH          VARCHAR2(200),
        SCRIPT_TYPE          VARCHAR2(8),
            CONSTRAINT SCRIPT_TYPE_CK
                     CHECK (SCRIPT_TYPE IN ('SQL','SHELL')),
        SCRIPT_DESCRIPTION   VARCHAR2(200),
        AUTHOR               VARCHAR(30),
        LAST_MODIFIED        DATE,
        DOCUMENTATION        VARCHAR2(2000),
            CONSTRAINT SCRIPTS_PK
                     PRIMARY KEY (SCRIPT_NAME, SCRIPT_TYPE) )
     TABLESPACE USER_DATA
     STORAGE (INITIAL 10M NEXT 10M PCTINCREASE 0);
```

You can use the techniques described earlier in this chapter to create a script that prompts for the necessary information and inserts it into the database. All of this effort makes it much easier to find a script that performs a particular function that you may have written months ago.

Note that Oracle8 allows data in a VARCHAR2 column to be up to 4,000 bytes (2,000 in Oracle7). It would be possible to store larger amounts of documentation using either the Oracle8 CLOB data type (storing up to 4 gigabytes) or the LONG data type (in Oracle7, which can store up to 2 gigabytes). Before using the LONG data type, be sure that its many restrictions will not present a problem. LONGs cannot be replicated or used in the SELECT list of a CREATE TABLE AS SELECT statement. They cannot be used in a WHERE clause or in SQL character functions (such as SUBSTR), which makes LONGs difficult to search. In general, Oracle8 databases should be created using the CLOB data type rather than LONG.

Of course, it is possible to be much more sophisticated in building a script library. This idea may be extended to include one-to-many relationships to document an execution tree for scripts that call other scripts and may even store the text of the script in the database. Source code text for Oracle stored procedures and triggers is maintained (in two different ways, unfortunately) in the database. Whatever level of sophistication you decide to adopt, just be sure that the text and documentation you need is available when you need it—don't keep database recovery scripts inside the same database they are used to recover!

Now let's examine another use for the SQL*Plus environment that can save us many hours (and many errors!) when we have to perform repetitive tasks against data that is in our database.

Using SQL to Generate SQL

One additional technique that we need to explore in detail is a method for using SQL itself to create other SQL statements. This technique is very powerful, and we will use it frequently in managing our data warehouse. Let's suppose that we just happened to create some test tables in our data warehouse and, because we knew they were just test tables, didn't bother to create a script to execute the CREATE TABLE command. Those tables turned out to be so useful that we really want to move them into our production environment. We want to reverse-engineer our CREATE TABLE scripts from information in the data dictionary. (This is a good exercise even though this action would be easy using the Oracle EXP/IMP utilities or if we were using an automated design tool.) This is a perfect opportunity to explore how to use SQL to generate other SQL statements.

TIP Even if you use a graphical ETT tool, you will find this techniques helpful for doing many repetitive actions as a DBA.

Generating Text Output

First, it's obvious that if we were to issue the following SQL statement and spool it to a file, we would end up with a command file that could be used to create a very simple table.

```
SELECT 'CREATE TABLE TEST '||
'(TEST_COLUMN VARCHAR2(10), '||
'TEST_COLUMN2 NUMBER(5,2));'
FROM DUAL;
```

This SQL statement gives the following output:

```
CREATE TABLE TEST (TEST_COLUMN VARCHAR2(10), TEST_COLUMN2 NUMBER(5,2));
```

This works because we are simply selecting a constant string. We simply need to extend this to select information from the data dictionary. The data dictionary table DBA_TAB_COLUMNS contains the column names and data types for every column in every database table. We can issue a SQL SELECT statement to produce a list of the columns, data types, and data length for every column in our PROJECT_REV table:

```
SELECT COLUMN_NAME, DATA_TYPE, DATA_PRECISION, DATA_SCALE,DATA_LENGTH
  FROM USER_TAB_COLUMNS
 WHERE TABLE_NAME =  'PROJECT_REV'
   AND OWNER = 'DW';


COLUMN_NAME            DATA_TYPE  DATA_PRECISION  DATA_SCALE DATA_LENGTH
-----------            ---------  --------------  ---------- -----------
PROJECT_ID             NUMBER                 13           0          22
COST_CENTER            VARCHAR2                                       30
LEDGER_DATE            DATE                                            7
TOTAL_REVENUE          NUMBER                 15           2          22
```

Generating Output from Multiple Queries

There are still a couple of problems we have to solve. First, our output has several sections that have different numbers of lines. The first section will be a single line of output that contains the phrase "CREATE TABLE *tablename* (". This repeats only once for the table we are working with. Then we will need a second section with several lines of output corresponding to each of our column names and data types. This portion of the output will repeat as many times as we have columns in the table. Finally, we will need to end our output with a third section (including our closing parenthesis!) that will again occur only once for each table.

We can solve this problem—multiple parts of our desired output requiring different SELECT statements—using the UNION operator. UNION allows us to combine the results from several SELECT statements into a single result set. We can UNION any SQL statements together as long as the number and data types of columns in each SELECT statement are identical:

```
SPOOL CR_TAB_PROJECT_REV.SQL
SET PAGESIZE 0 FEEDBACK OFF
SELECT 'CREATE TABLE PROJECT_REV ('
  FROM DUAL
UNION
SELECT column_name||' '||data_type||'('||data_length||'), '
  FROM USER_TAB_COLUMNS
 WHERE TABLE_NAME = 'PROJECT_REV'
UNION
SELECT ')TABLESPACE PROJECT_TS;'
  FROM DUAL;
SPOOL OFF
```

Executing this SQL statement produces the following output:

```
COST_CENTER VARCHAR2(30),
CREATE TABLE PROJECT_REV (
LEDGER_DATE DATE(7),
PROJECT_ID NUMBER(22),
TOTAL_REVENUE NUMBER(22),
)TABLESPACE PROJECT_TS;
```

Sorting the Output

This is getting close, but we need to change the order so that the output of the first SELECT statement sorts at the top and output from the second SELECT sorts next (and in the proper column order), followed by the output of the third SELECT. We can control this by introducing a dummy column that is used for nothing more than controlling the sorting order. We use the SQL*Plus NOPRINT command to suppress output of the sorting column.

We still have another problem in substituting the correct values for each column's size specification. We can use the DATA_LENGTH column for our VAR-CHAR2 columns, but we need to specify a precision and scale for our NUMBER columns. For DATE columns, we don't need to specify a length at all. We can address the problem of providing precision and scale for NUMBER columns, length for VARCHAR2 columns, and no size arguments for DATE columns by using several different SELECT statements combined with the UNION operator. (There is a more elegant method for accomplishing the same thing that uses the DECODE function. We will discuss various uses of DECODE later in this chapter).

```
COL DUMMY NOPRINT
SELECT 1 DUMMY, 'CREATE TABLE PROJECT_REV ('
  FROM DUAL
UNION
SELECT 2, COLUMN_NAME||' '||
       DATA_TYPE||'('||DATA_LENGTH||'),'
  FROM USER_TAB_COLUMNS
 WHERE TABLE_NAME = 'PROJECT_REV'
   AND DATA_TYPE = 'VARCHAR2'
UNION
SELECT 3, COLUMN_NAME||' '||
       DATA_TYPE||'('||DATA_LENGTH||'),'
  FROM USER_TAB_COLUMNS
 WHERE TABLE_NAME = 'PROJECT_REV'
   AND DATA_TYPE = 'NUMBER'
   AND DATA_PRECISION IS NULL
UNION
SELECT 4, COLUMN_NAME||' '||
       DATA_TYPE||'('||DATA_PRECISION||','||DATA_SCALE||'),'
  FROM USER_TAB_COLUMNS
 WHERE TABLE_NAME = 'PROJECT_REV'
   AND DATA_TYPE = 'NUMBER'
   AND DATA_PRECISION IS NOT NULL
UNION
SELECT 5, COLUMN_NAME||' '||DATA_TYPE||','
  FROM USER_TAB_COLUMNS
 WHERE TABLE_NAME = 'PROJECT_REV'
   AND DATA_TYPE = 'DATE'
UNION
SELECT 6, ')TABLESPACE PROJECT_TS;'
  FROM DUAL;
 ORDER BY 1;
```

This yields the following:

```
CREATE TABLE PROJECT_REV (
COST_CENTER VARCHAR2(30),
PROJECT_ID NUMBER(10,0),
TOTAL_REVENUE NUMBER(13,2),
LEDGER_DATE DATE,
)TABLESPACE PROJECT_TS;
```

Our sorting still isn't quite correct. So far, we've used a brute-force method of handling each different data type appropriately, but we need to sort the columns based on their order in the original table. Fortunately, the USER_TAB_COLUMNS table includes a column, COLUMN_ID, that defines this order. We will add another sort column to do this sorting within our second section. Because the number and type of data columns in each SELECT of a UNION query must match, we'll also have to add another dummy column within our first section. We'll use the first DUMMY column strictly to control in which section an output line will appear. The new DUMMY2 column will control the order within the section. This leads us to our next iteration:

```
COL DUMMY1 NOPRINT
COL DUMMY2 NOPRINT
SELECT 1 DUMMY1, 1 DUMMY2, 'CREATE TABLE PROJECT_REV ('
  FROM DUAL
UNION
SELECT 2, COLUMN_ID, COLUMN_NAME||' '||
       DATA_TYPE||'('||DATA_LENGTH||'),'
  FROM USER_TAB_COLUMNS
 WHERE TABLE_NAME = 'PROJECT_REV'
   AND DATA_TYPE = 'VARCHAR2'
UNION
SELECT 2, COLUMN_ID, COLUMN_NAME||' '||
       DATA_TYPE||'('||DATA_LENGTH||'),'
  FROM USER_TAB_COLUMNS
 WHERE TABLE_NAME = 'PROJECT_REV'
   AND DATA_TYPE = 'NUMBER'
   AND DATA_PRECISION IS NULL
UNION
SELECT 2, COLUMN_ID, COLUMN_NAME||' '||
       DATA_TYPE||'('||DATA_PRECISION||','||DATA_SCALE||'),'
  FROM USER_TAB_COLUMNS
 WHERE TABLE_NAME = 'PROJECT_REV'
   AND DATA_TYPE = 'NUMBER'
   AND DATA_PRECISION IS NOT NULL
UNION
SELECT 2, COLUMN_ID, COLUMN_NAME||' '||DATA_TYPE||','
  FROM USER_TAB_COLUMNS
 WHERE TABLE_NAME = 'PROJECT_REV'
   AND DATA_TYPE = 'DATE'
UNION
SELECT 3, 1, ') TABLESPACE PROJECT_TS;'
 ORDER BY 1, 2;
```

This yields the following:

```
CREATE TABLE PROJECT_REV (
PROJECT_ID NUMBER(10,0),
COST_CENTER VARCHAR2(30),
LEDGER_DATE DATE,
TOTAL_REVENUE NUMBER(13,2),
) TABLESPACE PROJECT_TS;
```

Final Formatting

To make our script more generic, we'll remove the hard-coded table name from each of the SELECT statements' WHERE clauses and use a substitution variable.

We still have the problem of the extra comma on what should be the final line of our column definitions. Solving this problem will involve a quick usage of the DECODE function, which will be more fully described later in the chapter. On the surface it appears that our problem involves deciding which is the final line of output and then suppressing the comma. This approach is a bit complex because we don't know, in advance, how many columns any given table will contain. We can use a subquery to determine the maximum value of COLUMN_ID and print a comma for all lines that don't match this maximum value.

Another (simpler) solution is possible if we restate the problem. The goal is to separate each column's definition from other columns with a comma. Rather than thinking of putting a comma after every line but the last, we can choose to put a comma before every line except the first. It is very easy to find the first column (COLUMN_ID = 1) for every table. Putting the comma at the start of the next line will make our output look a little odd, but it will function identically.

The DECODE function serves as a test. It takes, in this simple case, four parameters. Whenever the first two parameters are equal, the DECODE will return the value of the third parameter. If the first two are not equal, then the value of the fourth parameter will be returned. We will test the value of COLUMN_ID to see if it is equal to 1. If so, we will print a space, but if not we will print a comma. Here, then, is our final script to regenerate the basic CREATE TABLE statement for any table in our schema:

```
ACCEPT table_name PROMPT 'Generate CREATE TABLE for which table? '
COL DUMMY1 NOPRINT
COL DUMMY2 NOPRINT
SELECT 1 DUMMY1, 1 DUMMY2, 'CREATE TABLE &table_name ('
  FROM DUAL
UNION
SELECT 2, COLUMN_ID, DECODE(COLUMN_ID, 1, ' ', ',')||COLUMN_NAME||' '||
       DATA_TYPE||'('||DATA_LENGTH||'),'
  FROM USER_TAB_COLUMNS
 WHERE TABLE_NAME = '&table_name'
   AND DATA_TYPE = 'VARCHAR2'
UNION
SELECT 2, COLUMN_ID, DECODE(COLUMN_ID, 1, ' ', ',')||COLUMN_NAME||' '||
       DATA_TYPE||'('||DATA_LENGTH||'),'
  FROM USER_TAB_COLUMNS
 WHERE TABLE_NAME = '&table_name'
   AND DATA_TYPE = 'NUMBER'
   AND DATA_PRECISION IS NULL
UNION
SELECT 2, COLUMN_ID, DECODE(COLUMN_ID, 1, ' ', ',')||COLUMN_NAME||' '||
       DATA_TYPE||'('||DATA_PRECISION||','||DATA_SCALE||'),'
  FROM USER_TAB_COLUMNS
 WHERE TABLE_NAME = '&table_name'
   AND DATA_TYPE = 'NUMBER'
   AND DATA_PRECISION IS NOT NULL
```

```
UNION
SELECT 2, COLUMN_ID, DECODE(COLUMN_ID, 1, ' ', ',')||COLUMN_NAME||' '||
       DATA_TYPE||','
  FROM USER_TAB_COLUMNS
 WHERE TABLE_NAME = '&table_name'
   AND DATA_TYPE = 'DATE'
UNION
SELECT 3, 1, ') TABLESPACE PROJECT_TS;'  FROM DUAL
 ORDER BY 1, 2;
UNDEFINE table_name
```

Our final formatted result is as follows:

```
CREATE TABLE TEST (
 PROJECT_ID NUMBER(10,0)
,COST_CENTER VARCHAR2(30)
,LEDGER_DATE DATE
,TOTAL_REVENUE NUMBER(13,2)
) TABLESPACE PROJECT_TS;
```

This same technique can be used for any number of repetitive tasks the DBA may have to perform. As another example, if the DBA needs to drop and re-create a table it will be necessary to reissue GRANT statements to all the schemas or roles that have access to the original table. We can use SQL to generate all the GRANT statements before dropping the table:

```
SET PAGES 0 FEEDBACK OFF ECHO OFF HEAD OFF
ACCEPT table_name PROMPT 'ENTER TABLE NAME FOR GRANTS: '
SPOOL GRANT_&table_name.SQL
SELECT 'GRANT '||PRIVILEGE||' ON '||TABLE_NAME||' TO '||GRANTEE||'; '
  FROM USER_TAB_PRIVS
 WHERE TABLE_NAME = UPPER('&table_name');
SPOOL OFF
UNDEFINE table_name
```

Using SQL to generate other SQL statements is a very useful technique for the data warehouse developer and DBA. With practice, you'll see more and more opportunities to use it. This is one of the most flexible tricks to put into your toolkit. We will use this technique again later in this chapter and the next.

Creating an Oracle Database for the Data Warehouse

During the installation of Oracle a default database can be created for you. In most cases, however, the warehouse administrator will need to create a new database after completion of the install. A number of parameters that can be manipulated will have a direct effect on performance. These parameters should be tuned so they provide the best performance for your specific applications that use the database. The defaults supplied by Oracle are very unlikely to be appropriate for a large data warehouse. Many of the parameters can be changed by shutting down the database instance, changing the desired parameters, and then restarting the instance. Some can even be changed "on the fly," but there are some critical parameters that can be set only at the time of database creation. We will have to use the CREATE DATABASE command to get our data warehouse started.

Unpleasant as it may be, we will have to do some analysis and planning before we create our database. We need to have a rough estimate of the size of our tables and indexes. We will need to understand the plan for using Oracle Parallel Query so that we may ensure that data is adequately spread across the available disk drives. We will need an estimate of the number of expected concurrent connections to the database.

Estimating the Size of the Database

It is useful to have an estimate of the size of objects in the data warehouse so we can ensure that our hardware architecture is adequate to support it. Estimating the size of the tables and indexes will allow us to allocate sufficient space to those objects when we create them. Although Oracle can dynamically allocate additional space (extents) to a table or index as it is required, this may result in fragmentation that could lead to administrative complexity and, in extreme cases, to performance degradation. This is particularly true during data loading if Oracle has to frequently manage space. Contrary to much Oracle folk wisdom, fragmentation of a table is rarely a performance problem. Nevertheless, the safest approach is to allocate a sufficient amount of contiguous space to a table or index in only a few, properly sized extents.

Appendix A of the *Server Administrator's Guide* manual presents several algorithms that can be used to estimate the storage requirements for a table and an index. These algorithms are perhaps too precise and too complex to obtain a ballpark estimate for our needs. (Moreover, there's a Catch-22: These formulas refer to some system data values that can be seen only by examining the data dictionary, which therefore requires the database be loaded and available; we want to do some rough estimates before creating our database.)

Our basic position is that the best way to accurately estimate space requirements is to use an empirical approach. Once a development database is up and running, create the tables (as currently designed), load a subset of data into it, and execute a SQL query that shows how much storage space is being used for the known number of rows. These sizes can then be extrapolated (within a margin of error of one Oracle block) to project the final table size.

We can use the following methods (derived from Oracle's recommended algorithms) to give us the rough estimates that will be useful for some up-front planning even before we have any database available.

First, we need to determine how much space we will have in our Oracle data blocks for our data. The critical factor is the size of our Oracle data block. The database block size has a substantial effect on database performance (particularly in index lookups) and storage efficiency. For now, let's assume a data block size of 8 KB. Oracle requires a small portion of each data block for some internal information, referred to as the block header. For our ballpark estimate, we can assume the block header requires 200 bytes. Second, we need to know how much space will be reserved for future updates of data and how much will be available for our initial inserts. This parameter is referred to as PCTFREE (percent free). PCTFREE also has an effect on data warehouse performance and storage efficiency. For now, let's assume PCTFREE is the default value of 10 (not an optimal value for a data warehouse, as we will see). So the amount of space in each data block available for our data is equal to DATA BLOCK SIZE − BLOCK HEADER − (PCTFREE/100 * DATA BLOCK SIZE). In our example, 8,192 − 200 − 820 = 7,172 bytes.

Now we need to determine how much space an average row in our table will require. We have to estimate the average column length for each column in our table. Most Oracle data types are stored in a variable length format so the average will be determined by the actual data loaded, not the length specified in the CREATE TABLE command. VARCHAR2 character data will require the actual length of the data entered. Dates will require 7 bytes to store. Numbers will require 1 byte more than one half the number of digits to be stored, rounded up. Estimating these variable lengths is, at best, difficult. To get a more precise estimate of the average length of a particular column's data, load a sample of the data and then query the AVG(VSIZE(column_name)) for each column.

We have to add 1 byte for column overhead if the length of the column is under 255 bytes and 3 bytes if the column length is over 255 bytes. We will add 4 bytes for row overhead. The length of a row is the sum of the column lengths and column overhead plus the row overhead. This calculation is not precise because Oracle stores different types of data differently, but it provides a generally conservative estimate.

You must repeat this estimation for each table in our database. Using a spreadsheet to calculate and track these estimates and then to sum them by assigned tablespace will prove very helpful. We see that, as expected with a star design, the vast majority of our space requirements are devoted to supporting the central fact table. The dimension tables usually require relatively little space. We need to ensure that our hardware environment is adequate for supporting this size of database.

Planning cannot stop at this point. It is also necessary to estimate the amount of space required for indexes and summary tables. A data warehouse will often have more space allocated to indexing and summaries than to the actual data.

Again, there are some relatively complex algorithms presented in Appendix A of the *Server Administrator's Guide* (and in the Reference section of the same manual for Oracle7) that can help you estimate the space requirements for indexes. Initially estimating the amount of space needed for summary tables and materialized views is done using the same approach as our detailed data tables, except that we'll need to estimate the number of rows to be stored in each summary based on knowledge of the GROUP BY clause used for building the summary.

We also need to have space for our temporary tablespace, our rollback segments, and the system tablespace. A very rough rule of thumb is to plan for a total warehouse database of three to four times as much required storage for the actual detailed data to support the indexing, summarization, and other requirements. As always, your mileage may vary.

One final note on space calculations. Our experience suggests that (1) people will underestimate the space requirements of a data warehouse and (2) it is far more difficult to manage a large data warehouse that has tight disk space constraints. We also have found that management does not like to deal with repeated requests for additional disk space (it makes us look as if we don't really know what we're doing) and, unfortunately, management is unusually suspicious about requests for very large amounts of disk storage for a data warehouse project. Nevertheless, request sufficient disk storage for your planned growth for the first two years; unless your warehouse is quite unusual you will doubtless use it all in the first year. Be generous, you will have enough to worry about without concerning yourself with disk availability.

Creating Tablespaces

Oracle stores tables, indexes, materialized views, partitions, etc. in *tablespaces*. A tablespace consists of one or more data files on disk. Before we can create any tables, we must have a tablespace for the table. Each user/schema may have a default tablespace defined in which objects will be created if a specific tablespace is not named. It is best to always explicitly name the tablespace in CREATE TABLE and CREATE INDEX statements rather than allow for default placement. Even if all the tables and indexes for a schema are to go into the same tablespace (not recommended) explicitly declaring the tablespace provides additional documentation value.

There are several considerations to be kept in mind as we prepare our data warehouse by creating tablespaces. We should, at a minimum, place index data and table data in separate tablespaces. Because tablespaces consist of one or more data files, it is possible to distribute the data files for a tablespace across several disk drives or file systems. This is generally useful when we have not taken advantage of either hardware or software striping or when we are partitioning our data for access via Oracle Parallel Server.

Each tablespace should be defined with a DEFAULT STORAGE clause that will become the default for all objects created in that tablespace, unless it is overridden in the CREATE TABLE statement.

There are four basic parts of the CREATE TABLESPACE command. The first provides a name for the tablespace. The second defines one or more physical files. The third establishes characteristics for the tablespace, and the fourth defines default characteristics for objects subsequently created in the tablespace. The following command illustrates these four parts (formatted here to fit on four lines) and will create a tablespace for a set of dimension tables.

```
CREATE TABLESPACE DIMENSION_TS
    DATAFILE '/u002/oradata/dwp1/dim_data_01.dbs' SIZE 500M
    MINIMUM EXTENT 5M
    DEFAULT STORAGE (INITIAL 5M NEXT 5M PCTINCREASE 0);
```

This creates a tablespace called DIMENSION_TS with a single data file that is 500 MB in size.

The next parameter, MINIMUM EXTENT, was new syntax in Oracle8 and forces all objects' extents in this tablespace to be a multiple of 5 MB. If a user creates a table with a value for INITIAL of 13 MB, then Oracle8 will round the value up to 15 MB. This will further aid the administrator in maintaining regular extent sizes that can be easily reused if an object is dropped. Other syntax to define the characteristics of the tablespace would include TEMPORARY or PERMANENT (the default). In Oracle8*i*, we may also define whether storage extent management within the tablespace should be done through data dictionary tables or through a local bitmap stored within the tablespace.

On the final line, the DEFAULT STORAGE clause specifies that whenever a table or index is created in this tablespace it will, by default, initially be given 5 MB of storage. Whenever additional storage is required for a table or index, it will be assigned another 5 MB increment. PCTINCREASE is set to the recommended (but not default!) value of 0, which means that subsequent extents will also be allocated additional storage in 5 MB extents. If PCTINCREASE is nonzero, then each additional extent would grow by the percentage specified in PCTINCREASE. (PCTINCREASE defaults to 50, which eventually leads to very odd-sized extents that make it difficult to manage space within the tablespace.) It is strongly advised to use the DEFAULT STORAGE parameter when creating tablespaces and then allowing each object in the tablespace to use these same storage characteristics. This simplifies the DBA's work and helps keep incompatible objects from inhabiting the same tablespace. As an additional parameter to control the tablespace's objects, we may also specify NOLOGGING or LOGGING (default) in Oracle8.

The trend toward less manual tweaking of storage management is essential when dealing with the very large databases encountered in data warehousing. Reorganizations of billion-row tables are not something to be casually undertaken! A bit later in this chapter we see how this trend continues into Oracle8*i* with the introduction of locally managed tablespaces.

Defining Datafiles with AUTOEXTEND

It is also possible to specify AUTOEXTEND in the CREATE TABLESPACE command. AUTOEXTEND can tell Oracle that if we exhaust the 500 MB allocated in our data file, it should increase the data file size by a predetermined amount. Oracle will continue to automatically increase the size of data file until it reaches MAXSIZE. The use of AUTOEXTEND in the UNIX environment requires the use of filesystem files instead of raw files so this feature cannot be used with Oracle Parallel Server.

AUTOEXTEND can help us avoid loading errors that may occur during our batch load window, but it does introduce the possibility of losing some control over your disk and data files. It should be used very cautiously, and we must institute monitoring procedures to maintain control over our data files. Most administrators of very large Oracle databases find that they want to take more explicit control over their disk utilization and add more data files to a tablespace when necessary.

In some situations, however, when many tablespaces will be created in the same file system and then each will be loaded with a variable amount of data, it becomes difficult to effectively estimate and monitor the space requirements for each tablespace independently. This occurs more frequently with Oracle8 than with earlier Oracle releases, primarily due to the use of partitioning that leads us to create more tablespaces. Using AUTOEXTEND on the files associated with each tablespace will allow the tablespace to use as much space as it needs without requiring multiple files for large partitions or wasting storage for small ones. The file system is able to use its available space effectively where it is needed while retaining the DBA's ability to add and drop tablespaces on a regular basis.

Read-Only Tablespaces

It is possible to declare a tablespace to be a *read-only* tablespace. Once a tablespace has been declared read-only, you may no longer perform any DML operations on the tables and indexes in that tablespace. The primary advantage of a read-only tablespace is that you do not have to back it up once a first backup is made. For very large databases, the backup processes can become very complex, and reducing the amount of backup volume is very beneficial. A read-only tablespace may be used to reduce the cost of data warehouse storage because it can be stored on less expensive media than a disk drive such as a CD-ROM or WORM device. For very large data warehouses, storing some read-only data on CD-ROM can result in sizable cost savings. Of course, there may be a substantial performance decrement if these devices do not support rapid access. Using read-only tablespaces as part of an archival strategy for older data that is infrequently accessed but needs to remain available can be an effective strategy.

The procedure for creating a read-only tablespace is as follows:

1. Create a tablespace and create the appropriate tables, indexes, or partitions within it.

2. Load all the table data (or build all the indexes) in the tablespace. You must include only objects that, once loaded, will not need any updates or future inserts. In our example, if we were storing each month's data from the ACTIVITY table into its own monthly ACTIVITY table partition (Oracle8), we would plan to store a month's data in each read-only tablespace. (If, at some later time, it is necessary to make changes to the objects within the read-only tablespace, it can be converted back to read-write status.)

3. Execute a query on each table in the tablespace, which will induce a full table (or partition) scan. For performance reasons, Oracle does not always complete the cleanout of lock information in the headers of newly loaded or modified blocks when the modifying transaction is committed. The next time the block is touched by another transaction or query, delayed block cleanout is performed. Performing a full table scan on each table will ensure that each block has been touched. (When block cleanout is performed it can be controlled by the DELAYED_LOGGING_BLOCK_CLEANOUTS initialization parameter.)

4. Ensure that there are no active transactions anywhere in the database. This can most easily be accomplished by shutting down the database instance and starting it in RESTRICTED MODE. The key is to ensure that no transactions are active in any of the blocks in the tablespace, but Oracle does not provide any simple means of verifying the absence of transactions at a tablespace level.

5. Ensure that the only objects in the tablespace are tables, partitions, and indexes. Rollback segments and temporary segments need to be written (or dropped), which requires that they be in a read-write tablespace. The SYSTEM tablespace cannot be made read-only.

6. Issue the command ALTER TABLESPACE *tablespace_name* READ ONLY.

Transportable Tablespaces

Transportable tablespaces were introduced as a new feature of Oracle8*i* to facilitate the movement of data from one Oracle database to another. Chapter 6 provides examples of how to use transportable tablespaces. Within the current context of building the warehouse, there is no special action that the DBA must take while creating the database in order to create a transportable tablespace.

The only consideration required at database build time is to ensure that objects are placed in appropriate tablespaces so that the correct set of objects can later be managed as a unit. For instance, a partitioned table must be completely contained within the set of tablespaces being made transportable—you cannot take only some of the partitions. An index cannot be part of the transportable tablespace set unless the table it references is also included within the set. Foreign key references may be optionally enforced as part of the process. A PL/SQL packaged procedure, DBMS_TTS.TRANSPORT_SET_CHECK, is provided to verify that no violations of the rules are caused by a particular set of tablespaces.

A tablespace or set of tablespaces become transportable by declaring TRANSPORT_TABLESPACE=Y when invoking *exp*, the export utility. Rather than dumping the actual data to a flat file, this form of export dumps the metadata associated with all of the objects in the tablespace. The exported metadata along with the data files making up the tablespaces can then be copied to another database and imported. Just like this special use of export, import of this metadata-only dump file will not require physically loading the data—the metadata only is loaded to the receiving database's data dictionary so that the new database can begin accessing the objects contained within the copied data files.

Locally Managed Tablespaces

For years one of the primary duties of Oracle DBAs has been to manage the space consumed by their databases. As those databases have grown from megabytes to gigabytes to terabytes, this responsibility has grown—both in terms of time commitment and the consequences of error. The first lesson we learned was to avoid using the default value of PCTINCREASE. Eventually we learned that using uniform extent sizes for all objects in a tablespace could greatly simplify the issues of fragmentation and wasted space.

All of these lessons of how to do space management more effectively were just setting the stage for the real solution. As of Oracle8*i*, many of the complexities of space management have been eliminated. Now the system can assume responsibility for ensuring efficient use of the space within a tablespace. By defining a tablespace as locally managed, the DBA has to make fewer decisions while getting better results in the end.

Prior to Oracle8*i*, the only means of managing tablespace extents was through the data dictionary. For compatibility this is still the default behavior. Create an Oracle8*i* locally managed tablespace by adding the EXTENT MANAGEMENT LOCAL clause to the CREATE TABLESPACE command.

When the tablespace is created, Oracle8*i* reserves the first "extent" as a bitmap that will be used to track the usage of all the other extents, whether free or in use for storage of user objects. The size of this extent map area is determined by Oracle8*i* based on the size of the tablespace and the total number of extents that it expects to need to track. If the expected extents won't evenly fill the data file, the extra space is added to the extent map. The system can determine the size of these extents or the DBA may specify a value.

To allow the system to determine the size of each extent, you may specify AUTOALLOCATE (or accept it as the default) as part of the EXTENT MANAGEMENT LOCAL clause. To take explicit control of the extent size, the DBA may instead specify UNIFORM along with a SIZE parameter. In both cases, the traditional meaning of the STORAGE clause of objects created in the tablespace changes. Traditionally, INITIAL and NEXT parameters defined the actual size of extents to be allocated. In locally managed tablespaces, these still control the amount of storage to be allocated but frequently the initial allocation will be made up of several extents.

> **NOTE** Any permanent or temporary tablespace can be created as locally managed. An existing tablespace, however, cannot be converted to local management from dictionary management. Note that the SYSTEM tablespace cannot be locally managed as of Oracle8*i*, Release 2. This restriction may change in some future release.
>
> Locally managed tablespaces may not have the MINIMUM EXTENT or DEFAULT STORAGE clauses specified. To use local extent management on a temporary tablespace, you must use the new CREATE TEMPORARY TABLESPACE command instead of the TEMPORARY clause of CREATE TABLESPACE.

This example creates a tablespace with local extent management to be entirely controlled by Oracle8*i*:

```
CREATE TABLESPACE local1
    EXTENT MANAGEMENT LOCAL AUTOALLOCATE
    DATAFILE '/u004/oradata/dwp1/local1_01.dbs' SIZE 500M;
```

Depending on the size of the tablespace and the size of the object being created, the database will determine an appropriate extent size and then allocate as many of those extents as needed to satisfy the object's INITIAL storage request. When secondary allocations are needed as the object grows, the database will again use as many extents as required to meet the NEXT allocation request. Different objects in this tablespace may be created with different extent sizes as determined from the requested values of INITIAL and NEXT.

The following example does not allow Oracle8*i* to take complete control of extent management. Rather than use the AUTOALLOCATE parameter, this shows the use of the UNIFORM parameter that lets the DBA determine a single extent size that will be uniform throughout the tablespace:

```
CREATE TABLESPACE local2
    EXTENT MANAGEMENT LOCAL UNIFORM SIZE 10M
    DATAFILE '/u004/oradata/dwp1/local2_01.dbs' SIZE 500M;
```

For tablespaces in which the DBA will place only a single object there are no clear-cut advantages to one approach over the other. Both will work equally well. Taking explicit control over extent size using UNIFORM may allow the DBA to use fewer total extents, but there is no real advantage to this. Alternatively, however, when creating a tablespace that will be used to hold many objects of varying sizes, it is almost always preferable to use the AUTOALLOCATE alternative and allow Oracle8*i* to manage all the details. In general, using AUTOALLOCATE (the default) is the appropriate solution. Take explicit control only when an actual problem is identified with the AUTOALLOCATE algorithm.

Temporary Tablespaces

Another special type of tablespace required in a data warehouse is the TEMPORARY tablespace. When Oracle performs sorts, it attempts to sort in memory and then writes intermediate results to disk if the sort is too large. If a TEMPORARY tablespace is provided, Oracle will use that as the disk area for sorting. This can result in substantial performance gains because Oracle is able to handle space allocation and deallocation more efficiently in a TEMPORARY tablespace.

Again there are a few steps to creating and using temporary tablespaces:

1. Create a tablespace to be used exclusively for storing the temporary, intermediate results of sort operations using the TEMPORARY keyword.

2. If you are converting an existing tablespace, issue the command ALTER TABLESPACE *tablespace_name* TEMPORARY.

3. Alter each database user to assign his use of the new temporary tablespace.

As users begin executing queries that require disk sorts, you will observe a single temporary segment, owned by SYS, get created and extended to accommodate the temporary storage requirements of those users. This single segment will not be deallocated, nor will it shrink in size, as long as the instance is active. Space within that segment will, however, be reused by subsequent queries.

Another common question that arises is how to determine the correct size of the temporary tablespace(s) for a warehouse. Unfortunately, there is no straightforward formula, such as allow 5 percent of the total database. The answer depends on the number of users, the type of queries, and the degree of parallelism used by those users. It is not closely correlated to the size of the warehouse itself. A 3 TB warehouse with queries that exploit partition elimination, indexes, star queries, materialized views, or hash joins may need much less temporary storage than a 200 GB warehouse that instead uses highly parallelized full table scans and sort-merge joins. In general, however, the amount of disk space set aside for temporary storage is a relatively small piece of the total warehouse database.

During the initial creation and loading of the warehouse, parallel index builds and the creation of summary tables and materialized views will be the biggest consumers of temporary storage. Monitor the temporary tablespace by observing the size of the temporary segment as it grows to handle peak demand. Make sure that there is always, at a minimum, enough free space to allow adding several more extents to the temporary segment. Add a data file to the temporary tablespace if needed to ensure that jobs do not fail because of insufficient sort space. At this point in the warehouse life, only the administrators will be inconvenienced if the storage estimate was too low.

To add more space to the tablespace, use ALTER TABLESPACE *tablespace_name* ADD DATAFILE or, optionally, use the AUTOEXTEND feature, discussed in the previous section.

Once the warehouse is opened to users, you should perform the same regular storage monitoring. Remember that the size of the single temporary segment will reflect the maximum demand for sort work space since the instance was last started. Unless the instance is shut down regularly, this provides a simple way to monitor peak demand.

TIP Monitoring of a TEMPORARY tablespace is much easier than attempting to determine peak loads if you haven't altered the tablespace to TEMPORARY status. While PERMANENT tablespaces can be used as users' sort areas (and had to be prior to Oracle8) they allocate and deallocate temporary segments separately for each query. After the queries have ended, no temporary segments remain, so you must monitor demand as it occurs. On the other hand, it is more difficult to monitor current demand for sort space in a TEMPORARY tablespace because the allocated segments are not dropped when no longer needed. Looking at allocation will show you the result of historical peak demand for sorting.

Your monitoring may indicate that you have over-allocated temporary storage space and you may decide to reclaim that wasted space for other usage. While it is sometimes possible to free unused space in a tablespace through various ALTER DATABASE commands, it is often simpler to just re-create the tablespace. During a maintenance window when no queries are active, drop the tablespace, edit the script that you used to create the tablespace to reduce the number or size of files allocated, and reexecute it. (You are keeping scripts of all your DBA actions, right?)

Locally Managed Temporary Tablespaces

With the inclusion of locally managed tablespaces in Oracle8*i*, a means was added for using this more-efficient extent management capability with temporary tablespaces. As mentioned before, you may not use both the TEMPORARY and EXTENT MANAGEMENT LOCAL parameters in the same CREATE TABLESPACE command. A new SQL DDL command, CREATE TEMPORARY TABLESPACE CREATE TEMPORARY TABLESPACE, was added in Oracle8*i* to handle this situation:

```
CREATE TEMPORARY TABLESPACE local_temp
    TEMPFILE '/u012/oradata/dwp1/local_temp_01.dbs' SIZE 1024M
    EXTENT MANAGEMENT LOCAL UNIFORM SIZE 32M;
```

This example defines a locally managed tablespace in which the size of each temporary extent will be 32 MB. The appropriate value for the extent size should be set based on the number and expected size of disk sorts and coordinated with the value of the SORT_AREA_SIZE initialization parameter.

This command uses *tempfiles* as opposed to the data files specified for other tablespaces. Tempfiles have a few specific characteristics that allow for more efficient processing because they are used in only the restricted fashion of sort work areas. Tempfiles are always set to NOLOGGING and are ignored by Oracle8*i* media recovery routines. Because the intermediate work of sort operations is not reused after a failure of the instance or loss of the tablespace's media, this doesn't introduce any real limitations. Additionally, tempfiles cannot be renamed or added to a tablespace using the ALTER DATABASE command. In the rare circumstance in which sorting activity must be moved from one disk to another, you should just drop the temporary tablespace and re-create it using tempfiles in the preferred locations. Adding a tempfile to an existing temporary tablespace is performed using the ALTER TABLESPACE ADD TEMPFILE command.

The normal data dictionary views for monitoring data files do not show information about tempfiles. A new dictionary view (DBA_TEMP_FILES) and a new dynamic performance view (V$TEMPFILE) have been added to provide information regarding these files.

Planning for Full Table Scans

Until several years ago there was a mantra among Oracle database tuners: "Index—Good, Full Table Scan—Bad." This may still be generally good advice for tuning OLTP applications. It definitely does not always apply to data warehouses, though. Oracle has spent much time developing efficient algorithms to optimize the performance of full table scans. The introduction of Oracle Parallel Query and its ability to use multiple query servers greatly improve the efficiency of full table scans. Oracle8 partitioning and the ability to eliminate partitions based on their content provide another high performance alternative to index access.

Full table (or partition) scans are frequently the most efficient way to process large tables. The cost-based optimizer will frequently choose a full table scan for a wide range of different queries, especially when it has Parallel Query available. For these reasons, the data warehouse designer should spend at least as much attention implementing strategies to maximize the efficiency of full table scans as he used to spend trying to devise strategies to avoid them.

One obvious and effective strategy for improving the efficiency of a full table scan is to minimize the size of the table that must be processed. More specifically, we should reduce the number of data blocks that are read during a scan. There are several ways of doing this. First, minimize the amount of wasted space in each block by setting PCTFREE to 0 on tables that will not have rows updated (most tables in the warehouse). Second, minimize the number of empty blocks that must be read during the scan. This becomes an issue only when data rows have been deleted from a table. For warehouse tables that are regularly emptied and then reloaded, use the TRUNCATE command rather than DELETE. TRUNCATE is much more efficient and resets the table's high-water mark, unlike DELETE. A third approach to limiting the number of blocks to be scanned is to use Oracle8 partitioned tables. When a query's WHERE clause restricts the needed rows to a single partition then the optimizer will eliminate the scanning of any other partitions. Finally, when reference, dimension, and even summary tables are expected to be scanned frequently and their size is not overwhelming, we can change the way Oracle handles them by defining the tables with the CACHE attribute and possibly assigning them to the KEEP buffer pool so that they will remain cached in memory. We'll investigate this feature more when we discuss creating tables later in this chapter.

The strategy we use to lay out our tables on the disk drives may also have a direct effect on the performance of full table scans. The goal is to ensure that we maximize the operating system's capability to efficiently process I/O requests simultaneously. This is particularly important if we are planning to use Oracle Parallel Query. To process I/O simultaneously, we typically need to have the I/O requests directed toward different disks or different disk controllers. This means we want our large fact table to be spread across several disk drives (in many cases, a fact table is large enough that it wouldn't fit on a single drive even if we wanted it to). We need to plan which drives we want to use for large fact tables. An important consideration of our physical design should be to maximize the capability to make simultaneous reads of multiple disks.

If we must stripe our ACTIVITY_TS tablespace manually, we can create it with the following command:

```
CREATE TABLESPACE ACTIVITY_TS
    DATAFILE 'datafile_on_disk1' SIZE 536879004,
    DATAFILE 'datafile_on_disk2' SIZE 536879004,
    DATAFILE 'datafile_on_disk3' SIZE 536879004,
    DATAFILE 'datafile_on_disk4' SIZE 536879004
  MINIMUM EXTENT 512M
  DEFAULT STORAGE (INITIAL 512M NEXT 512M PCTINCREASE 0)
  NOLOGGING
  PCTFREE 0;
```

This provides just over 2 gigabytes of storage space for the ACTIVITY_TS tablespace, spread across four disk devices. Making each file slightly larger than the size of the object extents provides room for the file header block—each file requires additional space equal to one database block (8 KB in this example). The MINIMUM EXTENT and NOLOGGING parameters are new with Oracle8. MINIMUM EXTENT forces all extents for segments created in this tablespace to be multiples of 512 MB. No odd-sized extents will be allowed.

NOLOGGING is a segment (table, partition, or index) attribute that will be inherited by all the objects created in this tablespace unless specifically overridden when an object is created. It directs Oracle to perform minimal redo logging when creating an object or performing certain actions (for instance, direct path loads). This speeds these operations but also means we will not be able to recover the object from a media failure after one of these operations. It is critical to immediately back up the tablespace after creating or loading data!

The strategies for maximizing full table scan performance are best applied to the large fact table(s) in a star schema design or the detailed data if we've elected to use a more traditional summary design. In most data warehouse implementations, the relative size difference between the fact table and the dimension table is so large that few meaningful benefits occur from attempting to minimize the size of dimension tables.

Planning for Parallel Query

There are several ways that we can tell Oracle how many parallel query processes to use when performing a query against a particular table. We can provide a hint as part of the query that directs the optimizer to use multiple processes (or not to use multiple processes); we can specify the number of query processes to be used when querying or indexing a specific table by including the PARALLEL clause in the CREATE TABLE command; finally, parallel operations may be defined for the entire instance through initialization parameters. The scalability benefits of parallelizing queries will be limited by the I/O capacity of the disks used to store the large table. Ensure that large tables that you expect to scan with Oracle Parallel Query are spread over several disks.

Spreading Tablespaces across Disk Drives

Once we have some idea of our storage requirements, we can ensure that we have a sufficient number of disk drives available to support our warehouse. Unfortunately, it is not quite that simple. We need to have a plan for how we will deploy our disks. There are some standard architectures that we should use when installing an Oracle database to ensure maximum performance. It is commonly understood that rollback segments, data segments, index segments, and temporary segments should be located in separate tablespaces so they can be placed on separate disk drives. If we plan on using Oracle's Parallel Query extensively within our data warehouse, we need to develop a further plan to spread our data across disk drives.

The Oracle Parallel Query facility provides the capability to break a query into smaller tasks and then utilize multiple processes to complete the tasks. In Oracle8 the capabilities of Parallel Query were extended to include parallel DML (update and delete) on partitioned tables. If multiple CPUs are available, then these separate processes will execute in parallel, and the results from each component process will be merged into the final result set. The benefits of Oracle Parallel Query can be substantial; it is particularly effective in the data warehouse environment where large index builds and full table or partition scans may be common. If we can distribute the data for a table across several disk drives, we will reduce the probability that the parallel processes will contend for I/O resources. As a rough rule of thumb, we would like to ensure that large tables are distributed across at least as many disk drives as the Parallel Query processes we plan on using (as we will see in Chapter 10, "Parallel Execution in the Oracle Data Warehouse," there are several methods for telling Oracle how many parallel processes to use when processing a particular table). Ideally, we would also like to distribute the data across disk controllers in addition to just disk drives.

Spreading Data with RAID Technology

One of the implications of the need to distribute even an individual table across many disk drives is that we are far better off (for performance) with a large number of smaller disk drives than fewer, larger drives. Most sites use some

RAID technology, implemented either in hardware or software, to manage striping across disk drives. RAID level 0 (striping), RAID level 0+1 (striping with mirroring), and RAID level 5 (striping with distributed parity) are the most frequently utilized RAID configurations for the Oracle environment. These RAID levels were discussed in depth in Chapter 2, "Hardware Architectures for Oracle Data Warehousing."

RAID level 5 is less costly than RAID level 0+1. Rather than maintain a complete mirrored copy of all data (storage = 2 * data), RAID level 5 uses a group of disks to share the redundancy duty for all disks in the group. For instance, a RAID level 5 group of five disks could store the same amount of data as four disks without any level of RAID redundancy. Thus, this RAID level 5 approach would cost 25 percent more than raw disks while using RAID level 0+1 would cost 100 percent more. Using 100 disks in the group, RAID level 5 would cost only 1 percent more than raw disk while RAID level 0+1 would still require 100 percent additional. From just a cost standpoint, RAID level 5 with a large parity group seems to be a good choice.

Too many DW implementers take the easy route and simply define all available disks as RAID level 5 volumes. There is nothing inherently wrong with this approach—it is simple and gives reasonable performance and availability at a reasonable price. Before blindly adopting this approach, however, it is important to understand the trade-offs associated with RAID level 5 storage. There are serious performance impacts for certain types of access to files stored in RAID level 5, and there is some compromise in data availability as well.

The performance impact of RAID level 5 occurs when writing data to disk. Because the parity is distributed across all of the drives in the parity group, each time Oracle writes to disk, the RAID software or hardware has to do more work. As part of writing a block to disk it is necessary to retrieve the corresponding parity block from another disk in the group, check its values, and update them for each bit changed in the original data block. Because the parity is distributed, each parity bit corresponds to the sum of all of the corresponding bits from each disk in the parity group. The file system can't write a block without modifying the corresponding parity block, and it can't modify that parity block until its current values are read in from the disk (because they may have changed due to changes made to some other disk in the same parity group). This means that one write actually requires one read and two physical writes! Hardware RAID systems can handle this more efficiently than those implemented in software, but in every case there is additional overhead to writing to a RAID level 5 file.

Another performance aspect is worth considering as well. We saw that using a parity group of five disks costs us 25 percent overhead while a parity group of 100 disks costs us only 1 percent. This cost savings comes with another price, however. As the number of disks in our parity group grows, the possibility of contention for the parity block increases because 99 possible block writes would have need of this particular parity block instead of just four. This contention can become an additional penalty if we are doing very heavy load activity to multiple files in a large RAID level 5 parity group.

The large parity group can cause other problems besides performance. The distributed parity approach gives us protection from the failure of any disk in the group. Because we know the value of every bit in every block of the remaining disks in the group (including the special parity bit) it is possible to rebuild the lost disk. Two points need to be considered, however. First, reading the values from 4 surviving disks will not take as long as rebuilding from 99 remaining disks. Therefore, recovery time is directly proportional to the number of disks in the parity group. If time to recover is an important consideration, then don't try to save money by using extremely large parity groups.

The second point regarding availability is that RAID level 5 provides protection against the loss of only a single disk in the group. If 2 disks are lost, then it will be impossible to reconstruct the missing data bits. This is a consideration for RAID level 5 in general, but it is compounded by large parity groups. The probability of losing any 2 out of a group of 5 is significantly less than the probability of losing any 2 out of 100. On the other hand, complete disk mirroring with RAID level 1 can survive any loss except the loss of both copies of the same mirrored disk, but at significantly higher cost. (Thus, RAID level 0+1 can be viewed as a special case of RAID level 5 using a 2-disk parity group with even parity.) Using RAID (of any level) is NEVER a substitute for having alternative means of restoring data—through backups or reload/rebuild. RAID technology does not prevent data loss; it just postpones data loss.

The final point in this discussion is that there is nothing wrong with RAID level 5. Your warehouse (or even portions of your warehouse) may be well suited to these trade-offs of cost versus performance and availability. Portions of the warehouse (e.g., historical data maintained in read-only tablespaces) may be better served via lower-cost RAID level 0 (striping only) at the risk of lower availability during file recovery. On the other hand, other portions of the warehouse (e.g., the SYSTEM tablespace) may justify the higher safety and cost of RAID level 0+1 mirroring.

The design of the physical disk subsystem does not necessarily have to be one size fits all! Only you, the warehouse designer, can effectively determine the appropriate mix for your environment. Your system administrator should be consulted and will have to implement the chosen strategy, but only you will have the availability requirements and knowledge of the load demands to effectively make the best decision.

Spreading Data without RAID

If we do not have the capability for striping out data through RAID hardware or software, we can accomplish somewhat similar results by creating tablespaces that have multiple data files, with each file located on a different drive. The series of concatenated files that make up the tablespace give us a very coarse means of distributing data across multiple disks. Then we create a table with multiple extents, with each extent having a size that allows it to fit precisely into one of the data files. If more than one table is to be created in the manually striped tablespace, then the DBA will need to manually force each extent of each table into a separate data file. This can be done by manually allocating extents before loading data, with the following command:

```
ALTER TABLE table_name ALLOCATE EXTENT DATAFILE 'file specification';
```

The result of this command will be a table that has extents located on different disk drives, and when data is loaded it will naturally end up distributed across disk drives. This "poor man's approach" to striping creates much more administrative work and is less effective than RAID striping at the filesystem level.

Once our tablespaces have been created, using appropriate striping techniques, we are ready to create tables and other database objects in those tablespaces.

Creating the Schema

Some database objects, such as rollback segments and tablespaces, are not owned by any particular user. Other objects, however, are clearly owned by a particular user or *schema*. Prior to Oracle8*i* Release 2, these two terms are used synonymously—each user has a schema to hold objects, even if they are not granted the permission to actually create any objects. In this newest release it is possible to create a user that is not associated with its own schema. This makes a great deal of sense for both OLTP and data warehouse databases. In both cases, there are usually one or two schemas that will contain all of the objects that make up the application or warehouse. The majority of users connect to the database to run an application or execute queries against one of these centralized schemas. Recognizing this separation of storage (schema) and access (user), Oracle8*i* Release 2 allows the DBA to create many users who attach to a single schema containing the warehouse tables of interest.

Creating Tables

In a previous section we created a tablespace, ACTIVITY_TS, that is manually striped across four disk drives. We want to create our large fact table, ACTIV-ITY, in this tablespace so we can take advantage of Oracle Parallel Query when doing full table scans. We also want to ensure that we have as few data blocks as possible. Because our fact table is never updated, we don't have to reserve space for updates to avoid chaining. We will use all the available space in each data block.

```
CREATE TABLE ACTIVITY
    (MONTH              VARCHAR2(7),
     ORG_ID             NUMBER,
     FUNCTION_CODE      VARCHAR2(2),
     PROJECT_ID         NUMBER,
     REVENUE            NUMBER,
     HOURS              NUMBER,
     EXPENSES           NUMBER)
TABLESPACE ACTIVITY_TS
STORAGE (INITIAL 512M  NEXT 512M MINEXTENTS 4 PCTINCREASE 0)
NOLOGGING
PCTFREE 0;
```

This command results in the ACTIVITY table receiving four extents at the time of table creation. The PCTINCREASE 0 clause tells Oracle that every data extent allocated to the ACTIVITY table should be 512 MB. The NOLOGGING attribute informs Oracle8 to minimize the amount of redo information that is logged for this table. Finally, we use PCTFREE 0 to make the best possible use of all the space available and minimize the number of data blocks required. Note that most of these parameters are redundant because they were specified as part of the tablespace definition. We show them here as a reminder of their function, but in general it is best to specify these parameters only at the table-space level. Every object in the tablespace should inherit STORAGE (other than MINEXTENTS), LOGGING/NOLOGGING, and PCTFREE characteristics from the tablespace. If two objects require different values of these fundamental characteristics, it is likely that they should probably be in different table-spaces.

Several other optional clauses that can be used in CREATE TABLE may have limited use in a data warehouse project. Oracle reserves 23 bytes in a data block for each transaction that is simultaneously updating that data block. The parameters INITRANS and MAXTRANS control the number of transactions that can simultaneously modify a data block. These parameters can be quite important for OLTP but are less important for data warehouses. Generally, we will not have concurrent processes updating data blocks in our warehouse tables. This is a critical point to verify, however, because we have specified PCTFREE as a value of 0—once a data block is filled during load there will be no room for dynamically creating another transaction entry in the block. INITRANS defaults to 1, which is usually appropriate for the warehouse. (If you anticipate that multiple DML commands will be used for simultaneously updating some particular table, you might set PCTFREE to 1 percent or INITTRANS equal to 2.) MAX-TRANS should always be allowed to default—the specific value varies by operating system but is always much higher than we'll ever need, and no space is wasted by allowing a high maximum.

Oracle manages space allocation for a table by using a list that contains the addresses for blocks that are available for insertion in a structure called a *freelist*. If there are simultaneous processes attempting to insert into the same table, there can be contention in accessing the freelist. Oracle permits you to create a table with more than one freelist. Set FREELISTS to the number of simultaneous processes that will be loading data into the same table with INSERT statements. Direct path SQL*Loader does not require you to set FREELISTS because it avoids the use of SQL INSERTs and writes directly to new, empty blocks.

As we mentioned earlier in this chapter, we can explicitly tell the Oracle query optimizer the ideal level of parallelism for a table. This is done with the PARALLEL clause.

We will enhance our CREATE TABLE command to include these additional clauses. Because we have four available processors on our data warehouse machine, we will create the ACTIVITY table to use four parallel query processes and to provide support for four simultaneous insert processes:

```
CREATE TABLE ACTIVITY
    (MONTH                 VARCHAR2(7),
    ORG_ID                 NUMBER,
    FUNCTION_CODE          VARCHAR2(2),
    PROJECT_ID             NUMBER,
    REVENUE                NUMBER,
    HOURS                  NUMBER,
    EXPENSES               NUMBER)
    TABLESPACE ACTIVITY_TS
    STORAGE (INITIAL 512M  NEXT 512M MINEXTENTS 4 PCTINCREASE 0 FREELISTS
4)
    NOLOGGING
    PCTFREE 0
    PARALLEL (DEGREE 8);
```

Two other changes would be appropriate if our warehouse is being created on a clustered or MPP system for use with Oracle Parallel Server. The PARALLEL clause may be enhanced with the specification of the number of instances across which the parallel query processes should be spread:

```
PARALLEL (DEGREE 8 INSTANCES 2)
```

Also, our means of dealing with INSERT contention by defining additional freelists may not be sufficient in the Oracle Parallel Server environment. An additional parameter, FREELIST GROUPS, should be set to the number of instances that may simultaneously try to insert data into the table. Usually, our warehouse tables are inserted through a single instance, but this parameter provides this way to spread heavy INSERT activity if necessary.

Partitioned Tables

Although we frequently focus on the challenges a large data warehouse poses to query operations, the greatest difficulties are commonly associated with loading, indexing, and general management of the data warehouse. If we have a limited "load window," it is imperative that we be able to complete data loading, transformations, summarization, and indexing as quickly as possible. There are usually things that can be done to improve query performance (i.e., creating summary and aggregation tables), but if the data cannot be made available in a timely fashion the warehouse will fail.

One of the primary challenges with data warehouses arises from the presence of the very large detail or fact tables. A fact table may contain millions or even billions of rows and be several hundreds of gigabytes in size. Several classes of problems must be addressed when we are confronted with the presence of a multimillion-row table. Simply being able to load the actual data into the table in an acceptable period of time can be problematic. Even if we can get the data loaded, there are daunting problems associated with creating or maintaining even a single simple index on a table this size. It is typically necessary to maintain several indexes, possibly including concatenated indexes, for a very large table, which makes the problems even more challenging.

Once we have the data loaded and the indexes created for the table, our challenges continue. Eventually we will want to remove old data from the table, and so we must have a purge or archive scheme that will enable us to delete rows from the fact table and possibly store them in some fashion outside of our main fact table. Finally, it is necessary to have a recovery strategy that can restore or rebuild every table in a reasonable period of time.

Breaking up a very large table into smaller pieces that can be managed independently is the key to successfully meeting the challenges presented by multimillion-row tables. Breaking up a single table into component parts is referred to as partitioning. Oracle7, release 7.3, somewhat crudely supported partitions using partition views, and Oracle8 supports true table partitioning. Oracle8 provides a simple method to migrate from the older partition views to true partitioned tables.

Partitioning Concepts

There are two conceptual ways to partition a table—*vertical partitioning* and *horizontal partitioning*. Vertical partitioning is useful when the very large table has many columns and when certain sets of columns are almost always referenced together. It is possible to create several separate tables that break the columns into their common sets and maintain a common key across tables. This approach reduces the overall size of a single table but does not reduce the number of rows in a table. Consequently, vertical partitioning does nothing to help solve the indexing problems associated with a very large table. In fact, vertical partitioning exacerbates our problems because now we have several multimillion-row tables for which we must maintain indexes. Vertical partitioning rarely finds a use in a data warehouse architecture. Except in very specific situations involving the physical storage of large object (BLOB or CLOB) data types, Oracle8 does not support vertical partitioning.

The other method of partitioning a table is to use horizontal partitioning. In a horizontal partitioning scheme, subsets of rows are stored together in separate segments. Oracle8 partitioned tables allow a single table to be divided into smaller units (partitions) for administrative functions while allowing the single table to be referenced by user queries. With Oracle7 partitioned views, each subset of rows was stored in its own table, and a UNION ALL view allowed user SQL to treat them all as a whole. Both techniques reduce the number of rows to be managed in a single database segment.

Partitioning is not just a random assignment of rows to the partitions of a table. You must define a means for Oracle to know where to store, and later to retrieve, specific rows. That is, all the rows in a given partition need to share some common data value (or set of values) in one or more of their columns. We refer to this column as the *partition key*. This assignment of rows to partitions can be based directly on a range of specified values (range partitioning) or it can be based on a hash function that determines the appropriate partition.

In either case, it is important to select the partition key carefully. It should not be updated (which, assuming the table is defined with row movement enabled, would require a physical delete from one partition and an insert into another partition and a change of its ROWID). This is generally not a problem in a data warehouse. The partition key should produce partitions that are of manageable and roughly equal size. Ideally, the partition key should work so that each data load will load into only one relatively small partition. If each periodic refresh needs to load and index every partition we still may have a problem completing the loading process for all partitions in an acceptable amount of time and a further complication in having to backup all partitions after each load.

In the warehouse, we usually select a time column (typically a transaction date) to meet the requirements for a good partition key. In our example, we would select MONTH as the partition key for our ACTIVITY table. Once we have loaded and indexed a month's worth of data into a range partition, we will never have to load or index that data again. The tablespace containing the data can be made read-only and further backups avoided. Partitioning by date also addresses the issues of archival. When the oldest data no longer needs to be kept online, that partition can be backed up and then dropped. Because archiving is frequently based on the passage of time, date-based partition keys make the archiving and recovery scheme very easy to implement.

There is no absolute requirement, however, for partitioning by date. An organization might choose to partition by a regional or departmental code if a majority of the expected queries will be constrained by that column, but this will limit the ability to take advantage of read-only tablespaces.

Reasons to Partition

There are two reasons for partitioning large objects in the database. The first, and most important, reason is for administrative simplicity. Second, there are potential performance advantages to accessing partitioned tables.

The ability to add, drop, and exchange range-based partitions provides a very easy method for us to manage the periodic addition of new data to our warehouse as well as to facilitate the archival or purging of old data. Specific techniques to perform these operations will be discussed in depth in the following chapter.

This method of adding data to the warehouse also dramatically reduces the work necessary to perform backups of our warehouse. The data partitions holding older data can exploit the simplified backup and recovery capabilities of read-only tablespaces. Only the current partition of a large table (or local index) is affected during a load and is the only partition that must be backed up. By contrast, if the current data were loaded into an unpartitioned table then the entire table would have to be fully backed up on a regular basis.

Performance is enhanced when the optimizer is able to limit its search to a single partition (or small subset of partitions) rather than having to search an entire unpartitioned table—called partition pruning. The selection of appropriate partitioning keys is crucial to this facility.

Update and delete statements against a partitioned table can be executed in parallel—one process per partition. DML statements against an unpartitioned table can be performed only by a single process. It is not a common requirement to updates to large tables in the warehouse, but there are occasions when we elect to recast historical data into a different form. Also, purging data from a hash partitioned table might take advantage of this capability to execute a delete of the oldest data more quickly in parallel.

An additional performance benefit can sometimes be obtained when two or more tables are identically partitioned and then joined using the columns of the partitioning keys. In this particular situation Oracle8*i* is able to do a *partition-wise join*. Oracle knows that rows from any particular partition will need to be joined only with the rows of the same partition of the other table, so it can (in effect) do many small joins of corresponding partitions rather than having to process huge tables as a whole.

Two additional partitioning options—hash and composite—are provided in Oracle8*i*. These can provide performance benefits, but they do not help with simplifying our administration burdens.

New Partitioning Options in Oracle8*i*

Hash and composite partitioning, introduced in Oracle8*i*, use a hash function against one (or more) columns of the table to determine the partition where each row should be stored. This approach spreads the data across multiple partitions, but not randomly. A table with 16 hash partitions might store data with hundreds or thousands of different partition key values. The hash function takes, as input, the value of the partitioning key and outputs a value between 1 and 16 that will determine the correct partition for storage or retrieval.

This hash algorithm implies a couple of things. All rows that share a particular value of the partition key will be stored in the same partition, but rows with a dramatically different value of the key might also be stored in the same partition. Similarly, rows with just a slightly different value might be stored several partitions away. So a query that requests a specific value of the partitioning key would be able to find all of its candidate rows in exactly one partition, but a query that requests a range of values would potentially need to search in every partition to find its result set. Thus, for some queries, hash partitioning can provide the same performance benefits as range partitioning; however, hash partitioning generally does not provide the same administrative advantages.

Composite partitioning, as might be guessed from the name, uses features of both range and hash partitioning. The data of a range partition is further divided across multiple subpartitions using a hash function based on a different set of partitioning key columns. The range partitioning aspect provides the same ability to separate new data from old while the hash subpartitioning further spreads data to provide smaller partitions and increase the opportunity for using parallel DML. Composite partitioning can be particularly useful when you expect a large number of queries that are based on the time component (range partitioning key) as well as another common column, such as a geographic region code (the hash subpartitioning key). It is sometimes possible to use these two criteria, as satisfied through the partitioning information in the data dictionary, to entirely avoid having to build indexes on the columns of the two partitioning keys. Performance may actually be faster than index access, and you also save the storage costs and maintenance effort of the indexes!

CREATING A PARTITION VIEW

Partition views were introduced in Oracle7, release 7.3, and remain available in Oracle8 only for backward compatibility. The README files distributed with all production Oracle8 releases indicate that the feature will be completely desupported in some future release. There is no valid technical reason to create new partitioned views in Oracle8.

Creating an Oracle8 Range Partitioned Table

Rather than have to create and manage individual tables and then use a view to make them appear to be a single object, Oracle8 allows a single table to be stored in multiple partitions. The syntax to create our ACTIVITY table as a partitioned table with one partition for each month of 1999 would be as follows:

```
CREATE TABLE ACTIVITY
    (MONTH               NUMBER(6),
     ORG_ID              NUMBER,
     FUNCTION_CODE       VARCHAR2(2),
     PROJECT_ID          NUMBER,
     REVENUE             NUMBER,
     HOURS               NUMBER,
     EXPENSES            NUMBER)
    STORAGE (INITIAL 50M NEXT 10M PCTINCREASE 0)
    PCTFREE 0
    NOLOGGING
    PARALLEL (DEGREE 8)
    PARTITION BY RANGE (MONTH)
            (PARTITION ACT_1999JAN VALUES LESS THAN ('199902')
                    TABLESPACE ACT_1999JAN,
             PARTITION ACT_1999FEB VALUES LESS THAN ('199903')
                    TABLESPACE ACT_1999FEB,
             PARTITION ACT_1999MAR VALUES LESS THAN ('199904')
                    TABLESPACE ACT_1999MAR,
             PARTITION ACT_1999APR VALUES LESS THAN ('199905')
                    TABLESPACE ACT_1999APR,
             PARTITION ACT_1999MAY VALUES LESS THAN ('199906')
                    TABLESPACE ACT_1999MAY,
             PARTITION ACT_1999JUN VALUES LESS THAN ('199907')
                    TABLESPACE ACT_1999JUN,
             PARTITION ACT_1999JUL VALUES LESS THAN ('199908')
                    TABLESPACE ACT_1999JUL,
             PARTITION ACT_1999AUG VALUES LESS THAN ('199909')
                    TABLESPACE ACT_1999AUG,
             PARTITION ACT_1999SEP VALUES LESS THAN ('199910')
                    TABLESPACE ACT_1999SEP,
             PARTITION ACT_1999OCT VALUES LESS THAN ('199911')
                    TABLESPACE ACT_1999OCT,
             PARTITION ACT_1999NOV VALUES LESS THAN ('199912')
                    TABLESPACE ACT_1999NOV,
             PARTITION ACT_1999DEC VALUES LESS THAN ('200001')
                    TABLESPACE ACT_1999DEC);
```

There are a couple of things to note in this example. First, in order to tell Oracle8 which rows will be stored in each partition, we use the VALUES LESS THAN clause. The order in which partitions are created is important. Partitions with lower values for the partition key must be declared before those for higher values. Therefore, we must define the ACT_1999JAN partition before ACT_1999FEB. Also, to make the sorting work based on the MONTH column it was necessary to change the way we planned to store the actual data. Earlier, our table design included MONTH as a seven-character VARCHAR2 column. If we were to partition based on that data, Oracle would be sorting by the alphabetic value of the month abbreviation (APR, AUG, DEC, FEB, etc.), which would be very confusing! Changing the data to be stored as a six-digit number with year followed by month will work much better. Of course, if the original definition of MONTH as character data were important for users' access, an additional column could have been added to the table (e.g., MONTH_NUM) and used for the partition key.

The next thing to note about the partitioned table in this example is that we defined STORAGE, PCTFREE, NOLOGGING, and PARALLEL attributes at the table level. In this style, each partition will inherit those characteristics from the table. It is also possible to specify any of these parameters as part of the definition of an individual partition, in which case it will override the table-level value. This can be used, for instance, to adjust monthly storage requirements when the natural business cycle causes a large number of ORDERS to be taken in November and December and a much smaller number in January. Partitions do not have to be the same size or have the same degree of default parallelism.

If the data volume on the ACTIVITY table were smaller, we could very easily choose to partition by quarter instead of month. The change in syntax to accomplish this partitioning scheme would be as follows:

```
PARTITION BY RANGE (MONTH)
        (PARTITION ACT_1999Q1 VALUES LESS THAN ('199904')
                TABLESPACE ACT_1999Q1,
        PARTITION ACT_1999Q2 VALUES LESS THAN ('199907')
                TABLESPACE ACT_1999Q2,
        PARTITION ACT_1999Q3 VALUES LESS THAN ('199910')
                TABLESPACE ACT_1999Q3,
        PARTITION ACT_1999Q4 VALUES LESS THAN ('200001')
                TABLESPACE ACT_1999Q4)
```

Of course, if the volume of activity were higher (such as when capturing telephone call detail data or web log activity, then daily or even hourly partitioning might make more sense. These cases can be handled in the same way of partitioning based on a numeric string or, more economically, using an Oracle date column. (Using the native date data type becomes especially helpful when defining dimensions and hierarchies to support materialized views in Oracle8*i*.)

To make things easier to understand and track, this example names each partition and tablespace identically, but this is not a requirement. Partitions do not have to be placed in separate tablespaces, and the names for partitions must follow only the standard Oracle naming of any object and must be unique within the schema. Using meaningful names will make the administrator's life easier in the long run. Partitions are defined based on a balance between the manageability and performance requirements of the data volume to be stored. Tablespaces are defined based on the need for backup and archival processing.

Consider a warehouse in which millions of facts per day need to be recorded. A large percentage of the query load is expected to be retrieved of a single day's activity. The vast majority of queries will be interested in data from the current month, although there are some queries that are expected to summarize longer periods (usually by month or quarter). These characteristics suggest daily partitioning. We have an additional requirement to archive data, as an entire month, after 36 months. It is possible, of course, to archive the 30 or so daily partitions for a month, but this approach requires us (and Oracle) to constantly juggle nearly 1,100 tablespaces and files.

Another alternative worth considering is to create a tablespace for each month's data and then build daily partitions within that tablespace. Queries for a single day's data still benefit from the smaller partitions, but maintaining only 36 monthly tablespaces simplifies the administrative burden and facilitates archival of the entire month. Additionally, there is an advantage in situations where daily activity volume is very volatile even though the monthly total volume is more predictable. By allocating tablespace storage on a monthly basis, predicting daily storage requirements is less critical. The disadvantage to this approach is that we cannot make the monthly tablespace read-only until the final day of the month has been loaded. This approach will generally necessitate taking larger backups each day throughout the month. So the trade-off is fewer files to manage versus daily backups of larger size. Which resource is more critical to your operation?

It is possible to also reduce the dictionary's load of tracking the 1,100 daily partitions by merging the many daily partitions in a monthly tablespace once the early daily queries have given way to the monthly queries. The merge operation, however, is expensive in that data must be physically rewritten and will require double storage during the merge. Also, the syntax of merging partitions allows only for the merging of two adjacent partitions so merging an entire month would require up to 30 successively large rewrites of the data. Only in rare conditions would the overhead of keeping a very large number of partitions justify this additional workload.

Finally, we need to understand what happens if any data rows are inserted to this partitioned table with MONTH values prior to January 1999 or after December 1999. The first partition (ACT_1999JAN) is defined as having all rows with MONTH less than 199902. So, a row with a MONTH value from 1998 or even 1997 would be placed into the ACT_1999JAN partition. This is probably not desired behavior, so a CHECK constraint can be placed on the table to prevent any values less than 199901 from being inserted. A row with a value greater than

199912 would be rejected during the INSERT process by this table. This is commonly the proper behavior for date-ranged partitions. Optional syntax is available, however, to deal with other situations. Rather than supply a value in the VALUES LESS THAN clause of the final partition, it is valid to use the keyword MAXVALUE. This would allow the final partition to take on any values greater than or equal to the range defined in the next-to-last partition. Using MAXVALUE would, therefore, allow any 2000 activity to be placed into the ACT_1999DEC partition. This is generally not the desired behavior, however, within the data warehouse. We should reject any incoming records that don't fall within the expected range of dates. If the nature of the data requires us to handle "advanced notice" (such as data from a reservations system), then we could, as an alternative, precreate our future partitions to provide a proper home for these early arrivals.

As we will see in the next section (and in more detail in the next chapter) in many cases we will not actually load data to the partitions of a partitioned table. Instead we will frequently choose to load into a standalone table that, once the data is verified, will be exchanged with an empty partition of our main table. This strategy will give us more flexibility and time for performing validation and indexing of the loaded data before it is seen by users. Using this approach will require us to ensure that only data for the correct period is loaded.

Maintaining an Oracle8 Range Partitioned Table

The partitioned tables created in the last example provided for only the storage of 1999 activity data. Of course, there will be a need to add data after each month of 2000 and beyond. Adding a partition to store the new data is very easy—much easier than re-creating views and synonyms as required with a partitioned view. There are two options for adding a new partition's set of data to the partitioned table. The first, and most obvious, way is to simply add a partition, such as

```
ALTER TABLE ACTIVITY
   ADD PARTITION ACT_2000JAN VALUES LESS THAN('200002')
      TABLESPACE ACT_2000JAN;
```

Once again it is possible, if necessary, to override the STORAGE or other parameters defined at the table level. Also, the tablespace must have been created before the partition can be created. Once the partition has been added, data can be loaded and validated and indexes created (or re-created).

A second alternative, which has many benefits, allows for taking a standalone table with data already loaded and adding it to the partitioned table. This approach allows the data to be loaded and completely validated (including enabling constraints that might be too expensive to enable on the very large partitioned table) before making it visible to the users. This is absolutely the best way to provide the verification and publishing function on newly added data as described in the next chapter. While working with the standalone table, the administrator can take as much time as necessary to validate the data and resolve any problems. When each period's new data has been checked and "blessed" as correct, a single script can be run to include the new partitions in each partitioned table. Adding partitions in this manner is a nine-step process:

1. Add a new partition to the partitioned table. This partition will never be actually used. It is only a placeholder that will be swapped for the loaded standalone table and then dropped. Therefore, it can be made very small and placed in any convenient tablespace (such as USER_DATA).

```
ALTER TABLE ACTIVITY
      ADD PARTITION ACT_2000JAN VALUES LESS THAN('200002')
      TABLESPACE USER_DATA;
```

2. Create the new standalone table in the appropriate tablespace using the same column definitions as the partitioned table. Use appropriate STORAGE, PARALLEL, and other clauses. Using a subquery to obtain the table definition will save some typing and potential errors. (Generating it from a CASE tool would certainly work as well.)

```
CREATE TABLE ACTIVITY_LOAD
      TABLESPACE ACT_3000JAN
      STORAGE (INITIAL 50M NEXT 10M PCTINCREASE 0)
   AS SELECT * FROM ACTIVITY
      WHERE 1=2;
```

3. Load the new data to the standalone table.

4. Modify the table to create and enable whatever constraints are needed to verify data accuracy. Execute whatever PL/SQL procedures or SQL statements to further ensure the data is correct.

5. Drop or alter constraints to match those maintained on the partitioned table.

6. Build indexes on the standalone table corresponding to all local indexes on the partitioned table.

7. Analyze the standalone table to obtain optimizer statistics.

8. Exchange the standalone table with the placeholder partition created in step 1. This is the only step that requires syntax not already familiar to the DBA. If any indexes were created on the standalone table that correspond to local indexes desired on the final partition, then INCLUDING INDEXES will convert them in the same operation. WITHOUT VALIDA-

TION should be used if the data validation process on the standalone table has ensured that only rows with the proper range of the partitioning key are included. The default action is to verify each row's data during the exchange.

```
ALTER TABLE ACTIVITY
        EXCHANGE PARTITION ACT_2000JAN WITH TABLE ACTIVITY_LOAD
            INCLUDING INDEXES
            WITHOUT VALIDATION;
```

9. Drop the new empty table that was originally the placeholder partition.

```
DROP TABLE ACTIVITY_LOAD;
```

Other forms of administering range partitioned tables are available. Partitions can be moved, renamed, split, merged, and truncated. The Oracle8 *SQL Language Reference* manual describes each of these actions. Individual partitions may also be exported. This is described in the Oracle8 *Utilities Reference* manual.

Purging from an Oracle8 Range Partitioned Table

When older data eventually needs to be removed from the partitioned table, the administrator may drop the partition using the following:

```
ALTER TABLE ACTIVITY
    DROP PARTITION ACT_1999JAN;
```

You must use the export utility or other means of backing up the data before dropping the partition if later retrieval of the data is required.

As an alternative (and better) strategy for archiving data from an Oracle8 range partitioned table, the oldest partition may be exchanged with a placeholder table (the reverse of the process by which a new partition is added). This makes the oldest partition into a standalone table still residing in its original tablespace. The tablespace then can be made READ-ONLY, copied to CD-ROM, and taken offline. This allows the data to remain part of the database but not kept on expensive disk storage. If the data is ever needed again, the tablespace may be brought back online. Oracle8's expanded limits on the number of files in a database make this form of archival a viable possibility.

In Oracle8*i* the archival process is made even simpler. Transportable tablespaces allow a tablespace containing the standalone table to be disconnected from the database and, if ever needed in the future, reattached to this or even a different database. Archiving data with transportable tablespaces is discussed in more depth in Chapter 6.

Building Oracle8*i* Hash and Composite Partitioned Tables

The syntax necessary to create a hash partitioned table is not substantially different from the syntax for building a range partitioned table. Rather than specifying the upper range boundary for each partition, you must, at a minimum, define how many hash partitions should be created. You may define up to 65,535 hash partitions, although for the most effective distribution of data, Oracle Corporation recommends setting the number of partitions to a power of 2. You may name each partition explicitly or allow Oracle8*i* to automatically name each using the form SYS_P*nnnn* where *nnnn* is a sequential number. Just like automatic naming of constraints, it is easy to let the system assign default partition names. These names are not very meaningful, however, but, unlike range partitions, you rarely need to reference individual hash partitions by name.

Additionally, it is common to assign partitions to tablespaces. This can be done individually for each explicitly named partition, or you may specify a series of tablespaces. Oracle8*i* will assign partitions to tablespaces in the order listed—when more partitions are defined than the number of tablespaces listed, Oracle cycles through the list repeatedly until all partitions are assigned.

This example defines our ACTIVITY table with 16 hash partitions, spread across 4 tablespaces and automatically named by the database:

```
CREATE TABLE activity_hash
   (MONTH                NUMBER(6),
    ORG_ID               NUMBER,
    FUNCTION_CODE        VARCHAR2(2),
    PROJECT_ID           NUMBER,
    REVENUE              NUMBER,
    HOURS                NUMBER,
    EXPENSES             NUMBER)
PARTITION BY hash (ORG_ID)
PARTITIONS 16
STORE IN (ts1, ts2, ts3, ts4);
```

Tablespace ts1, for instance, will be used to store partitions 1, 5, 9, and 13. From a query performance standpoint, there is no advantage to spreading the data over 16 partitions rather than just 4 since the data would occupy the same number of disk devices. If we expect to perform UPDATE or DELETE statements, however, this arrangement would allow 16 parallel DML processes to work simultaneously to complete the task. In addition to parallel DML operations, there may be performance benefits for queries that search for specific values of ORG_ID because of partition pruning. Rarely is this benefit large enough in the warehouse to justify the use of hash partitioning.

More useful in the warehouse than hash partitioning is composite partitioning. In this situation, we get all of the administrative benefits of range partitioning, but with additional subdivision of data across subpartitions. This can be useful for parallel DML, additional I/O distribution, and occasionally enhanced partition pruning. Using our ACTIVITY table again, we partition the table initially by MONTH, but within each partition we will create 8 subpartitions using system-assigned partition names. Each MONTH's data will be spread identically across the same 8 tablespaces.

```
CREATE TABLE ACTIVITY_COMP1
        (MONTH              NUMBER(6),
        ORG_ID              NUMBER,
        FUNCTION_CODE       VARCHAR2(2),
        PROJECT_ID          NUMBER,
        REVENUE             NUMBER,
        HOURS               NUMBER,
        EXPENSES            NUMBER)
    PARTITION BY RANGE (MONTH)
    SUBPARTITION BY HASH(PROJECT_ID)
    SUBPARTITIONS 8
    STORE IN (ts1, ts2, ts3, ts4, ts5, ts6, ts7, ts8)
            (PARTITION ACT_2000JAN VALUES LESS THAN ('200002'),
             PARTITION ACT_2000FEB VALUES LESS THAN ('200003'),
             PARTITION ACT_2000MAR VALUES LESS THAN ('200004'));
```

This example defines the subpartitioning scheme at the table level. Each partition will inherit the characteristics of eight subpartitions spread across eight tablespaces. Also, no explicit storage parameters have been specified, so each subpartition will use the default storage attributes of its assigned tablespace. Had storage been specified for the table or partition level, the subpartitions would have inherited those specifications instead.

Here is a second example of creating a table with composite partitioning. In this case, we have elected to explicitly name the subpartitions and place them into specific tablespaces.

```
CREATE TABLE ACTIVITY_COMP2
        (MONTH              NUMBER(6),
        ORG_ID              NUMBER,
        FUNCTION_CODE       VARCHAR2(2),
        PROJECT_ID          NUMBER,
        REVENUE             NUMBER,
        HOURS               NUMBER,
        EXPENSES            NUMBER)
    PARTITION BY RANGE (MONTH)
    SUBPARTITION BY HASH(PROJECT_ID)
            (PARTITION ACT_2000JAN VALUES LESS THAN ('200002')
                (SUBPARTITION ACT_2000JAN_s1 TABLESPACE ts1,
                 SUBPARTITION ACT_2000JAN_s2 TABLESPACE ts2,
                 SUBPARTITION ACT_2000JAN_s3 TABLESPACE ts3,
```

```
                 SUBPARTITION ACT_2000JAN_s4 TABLESPACE ts4),
        PARTITION ACT_2000FEB VALUES LESS THAN ('200003')
            (SUBPARTITION ACT_2000FEB_s1 TABLESPACE ts2,
             SUBPARTITION ACT_2000FEB_s2 TABLESPACE ts3,
             SUBPARTITION ACT_2000FEB_s3 TABLESPACE ts4,
             SUBPARTITION ACT_2000FEB_s4 TABLESPACE ts1),
        PARTITION ACT_2000MAR VALUES LESS THAN ('200004')
            (SUBPARTITION ACT_2000MAR_s1 TABLESPACE ts3,
             SUBPARTITION ACT_2000MAR_s2 TABLESPACE ts4,
             SUBPARTITION ACT_2000MAR_s3 TABLESPACE ts1,
             SUBPARTITION ACT_2000MAR_s4 TABLESPACE ts2));
```

These two examples of composite partitioning show two pure alternatives for naming and placement of subpartitions. There are many possible variations, however. You may elect to use a mixture of the two styles. It is allowable to define the subpartitioning scheme at the table level (as in the ACTIVITY_ COMP1 example) and then override the subpartitioning for a particular partition using the explicit syntax of the ACTIVITY_COMP2 example. Consider using such a hybrid approach when you have a large variation in the number of rows to be loaded for different periods. You might define table-level syntax to normally store data in 16 subpartitions but specify a larger or smaller number for a specific month when the ACTIVITY level is much larger or smaller than normal.

Again, we avoided specification of explicit storage parameters in this second example, choosing instead to use the default storage declaration of the tablespaces. This is preferable to having to individually code each subpartition. You have that option, however, when there is a wide variation in the number of rows to be stored.

Retaining Table Data in Memory

Unlike some high-performance OLTP databases, it is never reasonable to expect that an entire warehouse database can be resident in memory. We can, however, determine those parts of the warehouse that are likely to be referenced frequently and "encourage" Oracle8 to keep those objects in memory where they can be accessed without slowing down to wait for physical reads from disk. Also, for the large tables or partitions that we expect to require scans, we are able to tell Oracle8 to use a separate memory pool so that they will not unnecessarily displace other popular data blocks (such as indexes) from the in-memory buffers.

Ordinarily during a scan of a table or partition, Oracle alters its normal buffer handling to avoid having hundreds or thousands of blocks from a large table force other randomly-accessed blocks out of memory. When a block is accessed individually (as in an index read) it is placed at the most recently-used end of the LRU (least-recently-used) chain of buffers. Blocks that are accessed frequently tend to remain in the buffer pool as they keep getting bumped to the front of the line. Blocks that haven't been used recently, however, tend to get shoved back in the line until they reach the least-recently-used end of the list. These are the buffers that are "stolen" when a reading process needs to bring a new block into memory. That system works well for OLTP systems where almost every block access is individual.

Table scans, however, don't access single blocks, but (for disk transfer efficiency) issue multiblock I/O requests that bring in many consecutive blocks in a single I/O. Because the number of blocks in a large table might greatly exceed the number of database block buffers in the SGA, a full table scan could completely flush out blocks that are being frequently accessed if the scanned blocks were also placed at the head of the LRU chain. So, to protect the residency of randomly (but frequently) accessed blocks, Oracle changes the way it handles scanned blocks. When it reads in a set of blocks during a scan Oracle places those block addresses at the LRU end of the chain. Therefore, they tend to be the first candidate buffers to be replaced by the next free buffer request.

So far, so good. Oracle tries to keep randomly accessed blocks in memory and doesn't let massive scans overwhelm the available buffer pool. But what about scans of smaller tables or of tables that we expect to scan again very soon? Well, unfortunately, Oracle is quite smart enough to be able to predict what future queries might do. But, as DBAs, we have been given the ability to tell Oracle to alter its scan behavior for specific tables that we know will be accessed frequently. When we add the CACHE attribute to the table's definition we instruct Oracle to always place blocks of this table at the MRU end of the LRU chain, even if they are read as part of a scan operation. We should be careful in determining which tables to cache, however, because applying this attribute inappropriately will lead to greater buffer handling overhead and displacement of more critically needed blocks from memory.

Beyond just defining the CACHE attribute, Oracle8 introduced a further enhancement. As discussed in Chapter 3, the database buffer pool in the SGA can be divided into two or three subpools. You may define a subpool called KEEP that should be used specifically to hold these smaller reference and dimension tables in memory. The number of buffers assigned to this special subpool is defined by the BUFFER_POOL_KEEP initialization parameter. (Note that the KEEP buffers are taken from the total number of buffers allocated by the DB_BLOCK_BUFFERS parameter.) The number of buffers assigned to the KEEP pool should be calculated to hold all of the commonly referenced tables and indexes that you intend to retain in memory. Each of these objects should then be ALTERED to include the CACHE attribute and to assign the object to the KEEP buffer pool. The following example will direct blocks from the TIME_DIM table into the KEEP pool:

```
ALTER TABLE TIME_DIM
    CACHE
    STORAGE (BUFFER_POOL KEEP);
```

The CACHE and BUFFER_POOL attributes, of course, can also be defined as part of a CREATE TABLE or CREATE INDEX similarly to this ALTER TABLE. Individual partitions of a partitioned object can be independently assigned to different buffer pools. By also specifying the CACHE attribute, we will be able to preload the cache with this data by performing a full scan of the table.

For objects that we don't want to retain in memory after a full scan we may choose to assign the table to another available pool called RECYCLE. This size of this pool is defined with the BUFFER_POOL_RECYCLE parameter. The RECYCLE pool is useful when only occasional full scans are expected to be executed against a large table or partition. Doing multiblock reads during a scan of one of these objects will not adversely affect the retention of blocks of other tables and indexes assigned to the DEFAULT pool.

If the KEEP and RECYCLE pools are not defined, then the entire DB_BLOCK_ BUFFER allocation is assigned to the DEFAULT pool. Once the KEEP and/or RECYCLE pools are defined, the remaining DB_BLOCK_BUFFERS are assigned to the DEFAULT pool. This pool exhibits the traditional Oracle LRU buffer handling described earlier in this section.

Database Constraints in a Data Warehouse

One of the greatest challenges in implementing a data warehouse is to ensure that only "clean" data is present in the warehouse. All data must be "fit for use." By "fit for use" we mean that only valid ranges are present, that all integrity constraints are met, and so on. Every warehouse development team finds that a substantial amount of time is spent defining just exactly what "fit for use" or "clean" data means and then implementing procedures to ensure that the data meets these requirements. Nothing can kill a data warehouse project as fast as having the end users decide they cannot trust the data in the warehouse. Inevitably, each end user ends up performing his own acceptance tests. The users will identify some set of reports they can produce out of the operational systems and devise some query in the data warehouse that they believe should yield identical results. They will test it out. It is important that the data warehouse be able to pass this "sniff" test. It is possible that the warehouse will fail this test because the data in the warehouse is better, or more "fit for use," than the data in the operational systems. It is not at all unusual for a data warehouse to reveal flaws in business practices or operational systems. The critical thing is that the data warehouse not be incorrect. It is hard to recover credibility, hence the need for very close attention to issues of data quality.

Oracle offers a method for using the database itself to perform various validation checks (referred to as constraints) on the data when it is loaded into the database. One common type of constraint is referential integrity. The database itself can ensure that all foreign key columns refer to a valid primary key value in the referenced table. In our example, we could use referential integrity constraints to ensure that every ORG_ID in the temporary ACTIVITY_LOAD table corresponds to a valid ORG_ID in the ORGANIZATION table. To create a referential integrity constraint on our ACTIVITY_LOAD table to guarantee that no invalid ORG_ID gets inserted into the database would require the following SQL commands:

```
ALTER TABLE ORGANIZATION ADD PRIMARY KEY (ORG_ID);
ALTER TABLE ACTIVITY_LOAD
  ADD CONSTRAINT ORG_FK
      REFERENCES ORGANIZATION(ORG_ID)
      EXCEPTIONS INTO BAD_ORGS;
```

Before creating a foreign key constraint it is necessary to ensure that the corresponding column(s) in the parent (or referenced) table have been defined as a PRIMARY KEY (or UNIQUE) constraint. This is done by the first statement just given. The EXCEPTIONS INTO clause specifies a table in which Oracle will store the ROWID, EXCEPTION_NAME, and TABLE_NAME of any rows that fail to meet the ORG_FK data integrity constraint. This makes it easier to identify any offending data and make the necessary corrections.

In addition to primary key and referential constraints, Oracle provides CHECK constraints that enable the database to check for valid data values or perform other validation processes on the data as it is inserted into the database. To also ensure that all HOURS values are between the range of 0 and 80 (we have a firm policy that no one can work more than 80 hours in a week and, despite some managers' suspicions, we have also determined it to be impossible to work a negative number of hours) we can create a CHECK constraint on the ACTIVITY table:

```
ALTER TABLE ACTIVITY
  ADD CONSTRAINT CHECK_HOURS
      CHECK (HOURS BETWEEN 0 and 80)
```

A check constraint is able to use any columns' values from the data row as well as literals (constants) to perform its validation. Using Oracle's data integrity capabilities provides an easy method for ensuring consistent data and also provides a centralized location for metadata rules.

Many data query tools (as well as materialized views and query rewrite in Oracle8*i*) use the referential integrity rules present in the data dictionary to control their operations. These sophisticated data query tools are able to generate SQL statements that join tables automatically when required, based on referential integrity definitions. Such tools greatly ease the load on developers by reducing the need to create views or train users in joining tables. These tools can also provide a substantial performance benefit over predefined views because they generate table joins only when necessary, based on which columns a user wants to include in the query.

The relative merits and drawbacks of using database constraints were discussed in Chapter 4. If the amount of data to be loaded is small and the additional overhead for loading is acceptable, by all means employ constraints to help ensure valid data. On the other hand, if a large number of rows must be processed with a relatively short time window available, full use of database constraints may be too expensive. In these situations, data validation can be performed during the extract process, or cleansing should be performed before the database loading process. As a third alternative, data can be direct path loaded into a relatively small, temporary table with constraints and be validated before moving it into the larger table on which constraints may not be appropriate.

In order to have the constraints present in the data dictionary (for metadata reference and to provide information to our query tools), it is possible to create the desired constraints without suffering the overhead of enforcing them. In the simplest case, you may define a constraint without enabling it. A disabled constraint still exists in the data dictionary, but Oracle does not attempt to enforce it during data loads. To disable a constraint on the ACTIVITY table we can issue one of the following commands:

```
ALTER TABLE ACTIVITY DISABLE CONSTRAINT ORG_FK;
```

Simple disabling of constraints is available starting in Oracle7, but this technique has some limitations. First, whenever a constraint is disabled and then reenabled, Oracle7 will revalidate every row in the table. Keep this in mind before disabling a constraint on a large table. This may, in some cases, be used to advantage. In some situations it may be a valid compromise to load data that has been validated during the extract process (and presumed to be fit for use) every day, with the constraints disabled, and validate the data every weekend, when more time is available, by enabling the appropriate constraints. Second, even though the disabled constraint may help guide a query tool, the Oracle7 optimizer knows that the disabled constraint is not being enforced and therefore will not depend on it for determining an execution plan. This becomes critical for using certain advanced query execution facilities, such as Oracle8*i* hierarchies and dimensions in conjunction with materialized views.

Oracle8, however, allows you to enable a constraint without revalidating all of the existing data. This is done by enabling the constraint with the NOVALIDATE keyword. When enabled in this state, the existing data is not verified, but any subsequent changes will be tested. This saves some overhead, obviously, but it still doesn't quite meet the requirements of data warehousing. Oracle8*i* extends the options a few further steps.

Oracle8*i* Enhancements to Database Constraints

Fortunately, the Oracle8*i* developers have provided other means of obtaining the query benefits of constraints without incurring the costs of evaluating and enforcing them. This enhancement is a direct result of increased attention to data warehousing needs. Constraints, as originally incorporated into Oracle version 6 and Oracle7, were designed to support transaction processing databases. The idea was to move the logic for enforcing data integrity inside the database where it could be performed more efficiently and consistently than in program logic. Those releases of Oracle were not, however, fully attuned to the needs of data warehouse developers. This isn't to say that those products were inferior to other RDBMS competitors of their time for doing data warehousing—quite the contrary—but we warehouse developers were pretty much left to our own devices for data integrity assurance of our billion-row tables.

As new, improved query execution mechanisms were added to support warehousing, it became critical for the database to know certain rules about the data if it were to be able to "shortcut" the access accurately. Constraints were needed, but practical experience indicated that the *use* of the rule had to be separated from its *enforcement*. In short, the warehouse developer needed a "trust me" clause that could tell the optimizer that the data could be trusted even though the RDBMS kernel hadn't actually done the validation. This has been added in Oracle8*i*.

Perhaps a short history review would be helpful here. This evolution is also summarized in Table 5.1. In Oracle version 5 the only constraint that could be declared was the NOT NULL constraint. Uniqueness was enforced by creating a unique index. All other constraints had to be enforced through application code. Oracle version 6 added the syntax to declare other constraint types for documentation purposes, but they were not actually enforced. In Oracle7 enforcement of all constraints was included, and the DBA could choose to either enable or disable a constraint. When a disabled constraint was reenabled, all existing data in the table had to be revalidated.

Oracle8 added the capability to enable a constraint without revalidating all of the existing data. Oracle8 also added the capability to define when the validation of constraints occurs. By default, validation is performed as part of the DML statement that affects the data; by declaring the constraint as DEFERRABLE validation can be postponed until the end of the transaction. This is useful, for instance, when the first of several DML statements would violate a rule, but a subsequent DML statement would make other changes that set things right again. Modifying the values of a primary key and its corresponding foreign keys (a task we would like to think should not be needed very often!) would take advantage of this capability.

Table 5.1   History of Oracle Constraint Capabilities

CONSTRAINT CONDITION	VERSION 5	VERSION 6	ORACLE7	ORACLE8	ORACLE8*i*
NOT NULL only	X				
Declaration/ documentation		X			
ENABLE/ DISABLE			X	X	X
ENABLE NOVALIDATE				X	X
DEFERRABLE validation				X	X
DISABLE VALIDATE					X
RELY state					X

Oracle8*i* completes the separation of enforcement (of new changes) and validation (of existing rows). The Oracle8-provided ENABLE NOVALIDATE state turns on future enforcement without validating current data. On the other hand, the newer Oracle8*i* DISABLE VALIDATE state checks the current data but does not attempt to check new data. Because the DISABLE VALIDATE state does not do any enforcement, it must also disable the use of any DML that could possibly violate the validated data. It does, however, still allow data modifications performed through DDL. This is fortunate in that it still allows us to add data to a partitioned table using the ALTER TABLE . . . EXCHANGE PARTITION feature.

The final piece of the puzzle completed by Oracle8*i* is the "trust me" clause mentioned earlier in this section. It is now possible to declare a constraint with DISABLE NOVALIDATE (telling Oracle8*i* not to bother validating existing data or enforcing the constraint for new data) coupled with the RELY keyword that further instructs the query optimizer that it can trust the data to have been validated through some other process. This is the final step that allows the optimizer to perform query rewrite to use materialized views without enduring any enforcement or validation overhead.

Alternatives to Enforcing Database Constraints

Earlier in this section we mentioned some alternatives to enforcing constraints on large warehouse tables, such as validating the data during extract or after loading into a small temporary table and before exchanging it into its permanent home as a partition of a huge fact table. Further discussion of this topic is in order. There are times when even enabling a constraint on our temporary load table takes too long. In other cases, the enabling process detects errors that then have to be corrected. We discussed the EXCEPTIONS INTO clause that allows the DBA to populate a table with all rows that violate a constraint, but this overhead further slows the enabling process. It also presents a problem if the cleansing is not to be performed immediately. Because the exceptions table lists the ROWID of offending rows, it is necessary to correct errors before the data rows get procedurally moved into another table (which may be necessary for additional transformation or summarization).

In some cases, Oracle's very efficient parallel CREATE TABLE AS SELECT (pCTAS) technique can be utilized to great advantage in validating data integrity. For instance, to evaluate a foreign key relationship and create a record of violating rows using primary key values, you might perform the following:

```
CREATE TABLE BAD_PROJECT_IDS_&LOADDATE
        TABLESPACE EXCEPTION_TS
        NOLOGGING
    AS SELECT '&LOADDATE' LOAD_DATE, AL.PROJECT_ID, AL.ROWID BAD_ROWID
          FROM ACTIVITY_LOAD AL, PROJECTS P
        WHERE AL.PROJECT_ID = P.PROJECT_ID(+)
          AND P.PROJECT_ID IS NULL;
```

By using the outer join (+) to "create" dummy project_ids that don't actually exist in the projects table (and then testing whether the actual value is null) this SQL statement can, in many cases, perform faster than the corresponding ALTER TABLE . . . ADD CONSTRAINT while providing the DBA with a table of the rows that require further investigation.

By capturing both the physical ROWID and the logical primary key value we also enhance our investigative process. If desired, the complete contents of the row can be captured into this table and the original rows in the load table deleted in a second step (use the ROWID, not the logical primary key—especially if no primary key index is in place on our load table!).

Another advantage of this approach is that you may evaluate something less than a full table's data—constraints are an attribute of a table and cannot be evaluated on a partition basis or other subset of an entire table. By specifying a partition name in the FROM clause or adding an additional filter in the WHERE clause you may control the number of rows to be evaluated. This is particularly useful if your situation, for whatever reason, prevents you from loading into a standalone load table.

Further, should you wish to abort the validation process based on reaching a threshold level of errors, you may do so by adding

```
AND ROWNUM < (&MAX_ERRORS +1)
```

to the WHERE clause of the subquery. Once that number of rows have been identified and added to your new table, Oracle will quit looking for additional errors.

A subsequent query in this job stream can also be used to permanently record the count of the rows in the BAD_PROJECT_IDS table into our metadata tables so that we can maintain a historical record of integrity problems. Having this metadata recorded also lets us define a threshold of errors that a later job step can use to determine whether to complete the "publishing" of our load or, alternatively, interrupt processing and possibly page the warehouse administrator.

This same technique can be used to evaluate other types of constraint conditions as well. With a little creativity in defining and linking WHERE clause conditions, multiple rules can be evaluated with a single pass of the data. Whether the performance of creating a new table based on a subquery will be better or worse than the equivalent ALTER TABLE ENABLE CONSTRAINT will need to be determined on a case-by-case basis.

It may be perfectly acceptable for a given warehouse to allow a data load with a small number of errors to be published and "trust me" constraints to be applied, using the RELY keyword in Oracle8*i*.

The data in error may be allowed to remain in the warehouse. Alternatively it may be automatically deleted and later investigated. On the other hand, it may be more appropriate to stop further processing of this periodic load until the necessary corrections can be made. The choice is to be made by the warehouse development team, in consultation with the warehouse users. Clearly the rules may need to be more strictly enforced in some parts of the warehouse than in others. There are no absolute rules. There are flexible options, however, if we choose to use them.

The central point, again, of this whole section on constraints is that we, the warehouse designers and administrators, are responsible for ensuring an acceptable level of accuracy within our warehouse. How and when we perform the validation and (if necessary) correction is up to the warehouse team. Using constraints in the RELY state in Oracle8*i* allows us to find and use whatever means of validation we find to be most efficient or convenient while still taking advantage of the awareness of data rules at query execution time.

Creating Index-Organized Tables

As described in Chapter 3, Oracle8 provides a new segment type, the index-organized table. This segment uses the hierarchical structure of a B*Tree index but stores the complete data row in the index structure. This allows data to be accessed quickly based on the columns used to build the index structure. However, data rows in an index-organized table have no associated ROWID. This means that, prior to Oracle8*i*, no additional indexes may be created to allow alternative access paths. This makes the index-organized table of relatively little value in the data warehouse. A large table would typically be expected to need multiple access paths, and a small table would not gain much benefit from avoiding the extra storage and I/O required for normal B*Tree lookup.

One possible use for an index-organized table in the detail-and-summary warehouse is to provide a code-translation table that might consist of only a short CODE_VALUE and longer CODE_DESCRIPTION. Provided that no user would ever want to query on CODE_DESCRIPTION (a dangerous assumption!), this table could be easily joined to another table when the description is needed. Most warehouse designers will choose to denormalize to include the CODE_DESCRIPTION in the base tables unless the space savings were extreme. (As another alternative, consider using a hash cluster to store the code-translation table; this would meet the same lookup requirement with even less I/O overhead, as long as no range-based searches are needed.)

Another use for an index-organized table is for the storage of very simple dimensional data without any additional attributes. The time dimension sometimes fits this pattern when only the valid dates are used as the dimension with no embedded hierarchies (such as fiscal calendar) to be superimposed.

To create an index-organized table, a few additions are needed to the normal CREATE TABLE syntax:

```
CREATE TABLE CODE_VALUES
   (CODE_VALUE               NUMBER(3),
    CODE_DESCRIPTION         VARCHAR2(500),
    CONSTRAINT CODE_VALUES_PK PRIMARY KEY (CODE_VALUE))
   ORGANIZATION INDEX
   TABLESPACE LOOKUP_DATA
   PCTTHRESHOLD 10;
```

Index-organized tables are very sensitive to the length of the data rows being stored. PCTTHRESHOLD defines how much of each block should be reserved for each data row. Rows that do not fit within this amount of storage are, by default, rejected during INSERT processing. Optional syntax (not shown) allows an overflow area to be specified for data columns that don't fit in the primary storage block.

Creating Temporary Tables

Oracle8*i* introduces a new variety of table, used to store data of a temporary nature. This is useful when you need to retain intermediate results from one query to be used in a subsequent query. This feature is specifically designed to serve as a "scratch pad" for OLTP transactions that need to retain, for instance, a running total of the number of items ordered. This can be more convenient than inserting the data in a regular table that would have to be explicitly deleted before transaction or session end. In the warehouse environment, there may be other situations where the user needs to issue several independent queries and later combine the results from all of them. A temporary table can serve as the holding area for the results until all of the queries are completed.

Temporary tables are defined using the new GLOBAL TEMPORARY clause of the CREATE TABLE command. Once created by the DBA, the temporary table may be used to store multiple users' data. It is not necessary to create a separate temporary table for each user. Even though rows created by several users are stored within the same physical table, only the user who inserts a row is able to see or modify it.

The structure of the temporary table is retained until it is dropped, but data inserted into the table lasts only until the end of the current transaction or session. By default, Oracle8i will delete the rows from the temporary table when the transaction ends. Optional syntax during the creation of the temporary table, ON COMMIT PRESERVE ROWS, causes the data to be retained beyond the transaction boundary until the end of the user's session. Alternatively, ON COMMIT DELETE ROWS, specifies the default behavior of data being automatically removed at the end of the user's transaction. The following statement is used to create a temporary table in which users can store results from several independent queries.

```
CREATE GLOBAL TEMPORARY TABLE temp_results
       (rpt_name              VARCHAR2(30),
        rpt_date              DATE,
        rpt_count             NUMBER)
    ON COMMIT PRESERVE ROWS;
```

There are some restrictions on temporary tables that also make it different from general tables. Temporary tables may not be partitioned, index-organized, or clustered. Foreign key constraints may not be declared on them. They may not include object constructs such as nested tables or varrays. Finally, parallel queries against temporary tables are not supported. You may not specify the TABLESPACE or STORAGE clauses. The ANALYZE TABLE COMPUTE STATISTICS command may be issued against a temporary table, but no statistics are actually stored.

Use ALTER TABLE to add columns or constraints to a temporary table or to make other allowable changes. To drop a temporary table when it is no longer needed, use the normal DROP TABLE command. A temporary table may be dropped only when no users are using the table to store data.

Building Indexes for the Data Warehouse

Indexes have two purposes in an Oracle database. They are used to enforce uniqueness of data values within one or more columns of a table, such as a primary key. They are also used to reduce the number of rows in a table that need to be examined to satisfy a query. The older, rule-based optimizer puts a high value on being able to use an index. It will blindly use an index even though it might be much more efficient to do a full table (or partition) scan. The newer, cost-based optimizer is much more intelligent—assuming it has accurate statistics available—in determining when using an index is appropriate.

B*Tree Indexes

The original, and most common, form of index in Oracle is a B*Tree index. The structure and use of B*Tree indexes were covered in Chapter 3. B*Tree indexes may be created on a single column of a table or a series of up to 32 columns in Oracle8 (16 columns in Oracle7). B*Tree indexes may be optionally created as UNIQUE (no duplicate values allowed). A unique index is automatically created when a PRIMARY KEY or UNIQUE constraint is enabled on a table. Star queries in Oracle7, release 7.3, required a concatenated B*Tree index on the columns of the central fact table, which correspond to the primary keys of each dimension table.

Creating a B*Tree Index

Creating and dropping indexes is quite straightforward. The CREATE INDEX has many of the same clauses found in the CREATE TABLE command. We can specify a tablespace to hold the index, the amount of freespace to be reserved in the index blocks for future growth (PCTFREE), the maximum degree of parallelism to use when creating the index, or the way we want to allocate additional space to the index segment as it grows (using the standard STORAGE clause with INITIAL, NEXT, and PCTINCREASE parameters).

One very handy additional clause available when creating an index is NOLOGGING (UNRECOVERABLE in Oracle7). Creating an index with NOLOGGING tells Oracle not to log the creation of the index. This avoids a lot of overhead and speeds the index build but means that if media failure occurs before a backup is made, the index will not be present after we recover the tablespace. This is typically a reasonable risk for the data warehouse where index build times are often critical and where backups are generally made immediately after each load cycle.

We also can specify a degree of parallelism to use when building the INDEX. Performing a parallel index build combined with the NOLOGGING option will greatly enhance index creation. For our example, we can create a simple (unpartitioned) index using the following command:

```
CREATE INDEX ACTIVITY_MO_PROJ_IDX on ACTIVITY (MONTH, PROJECT_NUMBER)
    NOLOGGING
    TABLESPACE ACT_IDX
    STORAGE (INITIAL 20M NEXT 20M PCTINCREASE 0)
    PARALLEL (DEGREE 8);
```

There are a couple of issues to note when creating an index.

Using the parallel option during the creation of an index gives each parallel process a full extent allocation for disk space, determined by the supplied STORAGE clause parameters. In the example just given, the index segment will be initially allocated 160 MB in eight 20-MB extents. Take this into account when defining the storage parameters: Divide the calculated space requirement by the number of parallel processes to derive the correct storage parameter values.

Similarly, each of the parallel processes will receive the full allocation of sort memory as defined by the SORT_AREA_SIZE initialization parameter. This, too, must be considered when defining the initialization parameter or may be overridden for the session performing the index build.

Index segments should always be separated from the tables to which they point. Do this by placing the index segments and data segments in separate tablespaces. If necessary, index extents can be manually striped across multiple drives using the same procedures described earlier for table extents. Striping of indexes, however, is not quite as critical as striping of tables because indexes are generally smaller and accessed more randomly.

Finally, because B*Tree indexes guarantee equal search path length regardless of the path through the tree, the index must be occasionally rebalanced when new data is inserted. Rebalancing a large B*Tree can take some time. When loading a large number of rows the index will be rebalanced frequently, resulting in diminished load performance. In many cases, when loading a large number of rows it may be faster to drop the index, load the table, then re-create the index using the UNRECOVERABLE/NOLOGGING and PARALLEL options. Partitioning the index (discussed later in this section) can also avoid many issues of rebalancing. The recommended approach of loading to a standalone table (with only local indexes), building indexes, validating the data, and then exchanging the table into a partitioned table avoids this problem entirely.

NOSORT Option

On a newly loaded table it is sometimes possible to save much of the time required to create one index on the table by using the NOSORT option. This option allows Oracle to avoid sorting the data by simply reading the table and directly building the index structure. To use this feature, however, the data must have been presorted and then loaded in the sorted order. This would prevent the use of parallel direct path SQL*Loader to initially load the data into the table, however, because parallel loads would not preserve the presorted order.

Oracle8 Reverse Order Indexes

It is possible in Oracle8 to build a B*Tree index in which the byte order of the indexed data is reversed. This avoids a common problem with B*Tree indexes that are defined on a column whose values constantly increase—new values are always added to the "right" edge of the indexed range. This commonly occurs in date columns with artificial primary keys that receive their values from Oracle sequence generators. The problem occurs when older data is also being regularly deleted from the "left" edge of the indexed range. Under these conditions, the index structure constantly grows to accommodate higher values while still maintaining the original (now empty) structure for the lower values.

By reversing the order in which the bytes of the indexed value are stored, new entries (and deleted old data) tend to randomize more evenly over the entire reverse-order index structure. These indexes cannot, however, be used to perform index range scans in which the user's query uses the BETWEEN, > (greater than), or < (less than) operators.

To build a reverse-order index, merely add the keyword REVERSE anywhere after the list of columns to be indexed. Bitmap indexes cannot be built in reverse order.

Only consider using a reverse-order index in the warehouse when (1) values in the indexed columns constantly increase while old data is regularly purged, (2) the index is too large to occasionally reorganize by rebuilding, (3) the table is not partitioned based on the indexed column, and (4) it is known that user queries will not need to perform inequality or range comparisons against the indexed columns. In short, there are few opportunities in data warehousing in which to effectively use a reverse-order index.

Bitmap Indexes

Bitmap indexes were also introduced in Chapter 3. Bitmap indexes are used when there are a small number of distinct values in a particular column. They are much more compact than an equivalent B*Tree index in that only a single bit is required to represent a row as opposed to a full ROWID pointer.

Bitmap indexes can also be used just like B*Tree indexes to retrieve actual row data for computing summary information or retrieving individual row data. If a query actually has to retrieve row information and refers to only one bitmap-indexed column in the WHERE clause, it will usually be more efficient to perform a full table scan than to look up a large number of rows pointed to by the bitmap index. But if several bitmap-indexed columns are referenced in the query's WHERE clause then combining the restrictions made by the indexes can be very efficient. The bitmaps are combined using simple bit arithmetic corresponding to the AND and OR conditions of the WHERE clause. The number of rows that meet all the specified conditions is likely to be a very small subset of the table that can be efficiently retrieved.

Bitmap Indexes in Oracle8

In addition to the uses for bitmap indexes described earlier, Oracle8 employs bitmap indexes to implement its star transformation algorithm. You may create a bitmap index on each foreign key column in the fact table to take advantage of Oracle8's way to perform star join transformations. In our example, bitmap indexes would be created on the PROJECT_ID, CONSULTANT_ID, ORG_ID, FUNCTION_ID, and MONTH columns in the ACTIVITY table. When we issue a query that joins the ACTIVITY table with the dimension tables, Oracle will first use provided WHERE clause criteria to limit the rows from each dimension table. The primary key values of these remaining dimension table rows are then compared to the bitmap indexes to identify the fact table rows needed using the efficient bit merge operations to resolve these sets into a single result set of qualifying rows. The final step in executing the star join is to join that result set back to each dimension table, using the most appropriate join technique (e.g., hash join, sort merge, nested loop). The Oracle8 star transformation algorithm is extremely efficient, and we should ensure that it is enabled by creating the necessary bitmap indexes.

TIP To allow Oracle8 to use bitmap indexes to perform star query transformation, you must set the initialization parameter STAR_TRANSFORMATION_ENABLED to TRUE (or override the default with an ALTER SESSION command).

Creating a Bitmap Index

The only change to the CREATE INDEX command described for creating a B*Tree index is to add the keyword BITMAP. To create a bitmap index on our PROJECT table for the SERVICE_LINE column we use the following command:

```
CREATE BITMAP INDEX PROJ_SL_IDX on PROJECT(SERVICE_LINE)
    UNRECOVERABLE
    TABLESPACE PROJ_IDX
    STORAGE (INITIAL 2M NEXT 2M PCTINCREASE 0)
    PARALLEL (DEGREE 8);
```

The storage requirements for the bitmap index will be less than those needed for an equivalent B*Tree index. The actual amount of savings will depend on the actual data distribution of the column(s) being indexed. Bitmap indexes on columns of lower cardinality will save more space than those with many values. Also, the storage efficiency increases with the number of rows being indexed. Creating bitmap indexes is also much faster than creating B*Tree indexes. The maintenance of a bitmap index, however, is much slower than equivalent changes in a B*Tree index because Oracle has to uncompress and recompress the bitmaps as data rows are modified. In some cases, it may be much faster to drop a bitmap index before performing loads (or purges) and then rebuild the index. Once again, partitioning large indexes frequently avoids this issue.

Function-Based Indexes

The new function-based index feature in Oracle8*i* allows you to define a new access path to a table based on a function rather than actual stored column data. For example, the standard SCOTT.EMP example contains a column for each employee's salary and another for his commissions. We might desire to query based on total compensation, the sum of these two columns. Of course, the user can do so directly in the WHERE clause, e.g., WHERE (SAL + COMM > 2000. This query will find the right rows, but it will not be able to use any index on either the SAL or COMM. If the EMP table contained several thousand rows, the resultant full table scan would be expensive to perform. Prior to Oracle8*i*, if we expected many queries of this type we might have decided to include a new column, TOT_COMP, in our table and then create an index on TOT_COMP. Now, we can save the unnecessary storage of another column by simply creating an index on the sum of the two existing columns. Very simply,

```
CREATE INDEX SCOTT.TEST ON SCOTT.EMP(SAL+COMM);
```

would build this index.

Partitioned Indexes

Just as large tables may be broken up into multiple pieces, Oracle8 allows indexes to be partitioned. Both B*Tree and bitmap indexes may be partitioned. A partitioned index may be built on either a nonpartitioned or a partitioned table. In the latter case, the index may be partitioned on the same partition key as the table or on some other column or columns. An index that is partitioned identically with its partitioned table is called a *local* index. Oracle will automatically maintain any local indexes if the base table is repartitioned. Local indexes are identified using the LOCAL keyword in the CREATE INDEX command.

Prefixed Local Indexes

Local partitioned indexes may be either *prefixed* or *nonprefixed*. Prefixed local indexes are partitioned by the same column(s) that form the leading (first defined) edge of the index. Any index on our partitioned ACTIVITY table that is partitioned on MONTH is *local*. An index that is built and partitioned on the MONTH column is *prefixed local*. In order to take advantage of this index a query must have specified a value (or range) for MONTH, so the Oracle8 optimizer can determine the subset of index partitions that must be examined. This partition-pruning feature generally makes prefixed local indexes the most efficient type of index for query performance. The ability to do partition manipulation of the partitioned table with automatic management of the corresponding index partitions makes local indexes the most convenient to administer.

Nonprefixed Local Indexes

Of course, some of our queries need to specify conditions that do not include our partitioning key. We will probably need to index several of these columns as well. Another local (i.e., partitioned by MONTH) index, defined on just the ORG_ID column, would be considered nonprefixed. Because each monthly index partition is likely to have timecard records from every organization, a lookup based on ORG_ID will not be able to eliminate any index partitions. This means that a range scan against a local nonprefixed partitioned index will require a search in each index partition. This may have performance impacts, of course, on queries using the index, especially if there are many partitions that must be probed. These searches in multiple index partitions can, luckily, be performed in parallel. Partition pruning, however, can still be performed for queries using this nonprefixed index if they also specify month criteria.

A common question, then, is whether to include the partition key to make a prefixed local index when indexing a nonkey column. Prefixed local multicolumn indexes obviously require an increase in storage costs over a nonprefixed index. For queries that specify criteria for both columns, partition pruning frequently makes performance comparable for both approaches. This is particularly true if the range partitioning scheme assigns only a single value of the partitioning key to each partition. With a different partitioning approach, however, there may be variations. If we store daily data in a monthly partition, a local prefixed index will generally provide a performance benefit for queries that request rows for a single day. Partition pruning will narrow the request to a single month's partition, but the nonprefixed index will probably not be used by the optimizer to further target the retrieval. The example index on ORG_ID, locally partitioned on a monthly range of daily rows, will point to roughly 30 times the number of rows needed by this query; a full scan of the partition will probably be more efficient at this point. A prefixed index (on the ACTIVITY_DAY and ORG_ID columns) would be able to take advantage of both partition pruning and subsequent use of the index to locate specific rows.

Consider one further case before deciding to prefix all of your local indexes. For queries that specify values only for the ORG_ID column the prefixed index couldn't be used because the leading-edge column of the index isn't being used in the query. So, as always in database design, there is a trade-off to consider. The final solution will depend on the nature and frequency of queries to be executed. Given an equal need to support both of these query types using the nonprefixed index is likely to give the better overall performance compromise (short of creating both types of index). One other aspect of nonprefixed indexes should be considered. Nonprefixed local indexes cannot be created as unique. A unique index must either be global or include the partitioning key so that Oracle8 may verify that duplicate values do not occur across partitions. This might be an issue when building a primary key that doesn't include your chosen partitioning key. Adding the extra column to the physical primary key might be one solution, but this approach could allow nonunique entries to the original logical key. (Of course, this would have the same net effect as using a nonunique index on the original key!) As discussed earlier in this chapter, it is possible in Oracle8 to declare a constraint in the DISABLED VALIDATE state (or RELY state in Oracle8*i*) and thereby use a nonprefixed, nonunique index. The extra effort required to revalidate this constraint after each load may, on the other hand, recommend a different partitioning scheme.

Global Indexes

A partitioned index that is partitioned differently than its base table is known as a *global* index. Each partition of a global index may have entries that point to any of the table partitions. There are several restrictions on the use of global indexes in Oracle8:

- Only prefixed global partitioned indexes are supported. This means that a global index must be partitioned by the leading-edge column(s) of the index. This is not a practical limitation since there is no potential advantage to building a non-prefixed global index.

- Global indexes on partitioned tables must be B*Tree indexes. Global bitmap indexes are not supported.

- Partitioned bitmap indexes may not be created on nonpartitioned tables.

Global indexes require additional maintenance when built on partitioned tables so they should be avoided whenever possible in the data warehouse. Each time you add or drop a partition of the table, all global indexes have to be completely rebuilt. This generally eliminates the primary advantages of partitioning, so normally only locally partitioned indexes are used in the data warehouse.

Only if your partitioning scheme were based on something other than date, if you are, therefore, going to do purging/archiving through SQL DELETEs, and if you expect to do many queries that will not include the partitioning key, then a global index might be useful.

A local nonprefixed index will generally provide acceptable performance with less administrative overhead. Unless the number of partitions is very large, the searches of multiple local partitions can be performed in parallel, which will mitigate the adverse effects. (Incidentally, all nonpartitioned indexes are considered global.) Of course, as always, testing for your particular situation will give you the correct answer. Luckily, this is a decision that can be reviewed and reversed after the warehouse is built and delivered to users. Rebuilding an index in a different format may take some time but it need not disrupt the warehouse operations and accesses.

Building Partitioned Indexes

The following SQL statement will create a local partitioned bitmap index on ACTIVITY to allow for quick lookup using both MONTH and ORG_ID columns. Because it is declared to be a LOCAL index, it is unnecessary (and actually forbidden) to specify the PARTITION BY RANGE or VALUES LESS THAN clauses. These index partitioning values are taken by Oracle8 from the table partitioning values.

```
CREATE BITMAP INDEX ACT_MONTH_ORD_IDX ON ACTIVITY (MONTH, ORG_ID)
   STORAGE (INITIAL 5M NEXT 5M PCTINCREASE 0)
   PCTFREE 0
   NOLOGGING
   PARALLEL (DEGREE 8)
   LOCAL
            (PARTITION ACT_1999JAN_ORG_IDX
                    TABLESPACE ACT_1999JAN_ORG_IDX,
             PARTITION ACT_1999FEB_ORG_IDX
                    TABLESPACE ACT_1999FEB_ORG_IDX,
             PARTITION ACT_1999MAR_ORG_IDX
                    TABLESPACE ACT_1999MAR_ORG_IDX,
             PARTITION ACT_1999APR_ORG_IDX
                    TABLESPACE ACT_1999APR_ORG_IDX,
             PARTITION ACT_1999MAY_ORG_IDX
                    TABLESPACE ACT_1999MAY_ORG_IDX,
             PARTITION ACT_1999JUN_ORG_IDX
                    TABLESPACE ACT_1999JUN_ORG_IDX,
             PARTITION ACT_1999JUL_ORG_IDX
                    TABLESPACE ACT_1999JUL_ORG_IDX,
             PARTITION ACT_1999AUG_ORG_IDX
                    TABLESPACE ACT_1999AUG_ORG_IDX,
             PARTITION ACT_1999SEP_ORG_IDX
                    TABLESPACE ACT_1999SEP_ORG_IDX,
             PARTITION ACT_1999OCT_ORG_IDX
                    TABLESPACE ACT_1999OCT_ORG_IDX,
             PARTITION ACT_1999NOV_ORG_IDX
                    TABLESPACE ACT_1999NOV_ORG_IDX,
             PARTITION ACT_1999DEC_ORG_IDX
                    TABLESPACE ACT_1999DEC_ORG_IDX);
```

Obviously, each organization may have activity data in multiple partitions of the ACTIVITY table that was partitioned by month. To create a global index with five partitions (to allow lookup in any table partition) by just the ORG_ID, use the following:

```
CREATE INDEX ACT_ORD_IDX ON ACTIVITY (ORG_ID)
   STORAGE (INITIAL 5M NEXT 1M PCTINCREASE 0)
   PCTFREE 0
   NOLOGGING
   PARALLEL (DEGREE 8)
```

```
GLOBAL PARTITION BY RANGE (ORG_ID)
        (PARTITION ACT_ORG1_IDX VALUES LESS THAN ('200')
                TABLESPACE ACT_ORG1_IDX,
         PARTITION ACT_ORG2_IDX VALUES LESS THAN ('400')
                TABLESPACE ACT_ORG2_IDX,
         PARTITION ACT_ORG3_IDX VALUES LESS THAN ('600')
                TABLESPACE ACT_ORG3_IDX,
         PARTITION ACT_ORG4_IDX VALUES LESS THAN ('800')
                TABLESPACE ACT_ORG4_IDX,
         PARTITION ACT_ORG5_IDX VALUES LESS THAN MAXVALUE
                TABLESPACE ACT_ORG5_IDX);
```

Note that this syntax to create a global partitioned index applies only to B*Tree indexes. Bitmap indexes must be local or else nonpartitioned.

Local partitioned indexes are administratively simpler than global indexes because of the automatic handling provided by Oracle8 when repartitioning the table. A local index is generally smaller than a global index and needs to be maintained only when data in the corresponding table partition is modified. Other local index partitions, for instance, are unaffected when we load data into the most recent table partition.

Because we frequently need to index columns that don't include the table's partition key, it will sometimes be necessary to create global indexes. Additional processing by Oracle8 is needed to deal with global indexes because they are affected whenever data in any table partition is added, modified, or deleted. The administrator must also perform additional work to deal with global indexes. Anytime a partition of the partitioned table is added, dropped, split, moved, truncated, and so on, all global indexes are marked as unusable and must be re-created by the DBA. This activity needs to be planned and pre-scripted to accommodate the required global index maintenance whenever table repartitioning is performed.

Global index partitions may be repartitioned (using ALTER INDEX SPLIT PARTITION command) in a manner similar to that of partitioned tables, as described earlier in this chapter. Local indexes are automatically maintained when their base table is repartitioned. Individual index partitions, local or global, may be rebuilt independently when necessary.

TIP   It is critical that the DBA specify a tablespace whenever a partition is added to an index partition. Without an explicit tablespace declaration, Oracle8 places the new partition into the same tablespace as the base table.

For a local index on an Oracle8*i* hash or composite table, the index partition will be created, by default, in the same tablespace as its corresponding table partition. Other than an explicit name, TABLESPACE is the only attribute that may be specified—all other physical attributes of the hash partition are inherited from the table definition. Subpartitions inherit attributes other than TABLESPACE and name from the partition definition.

Oracle Database Clusters

Oracle provides several methods for allowing rows that share common data values to be stored together in the same data blocks. The result of storing rows together is that they can be retrieved more quickly when they are used together such as in a join. Clusters are not frequently used in data warehousing, but in some specific situations, they can improve retrieval performance.

Index Clusters

Index clusters were introduced in Chapter 3. There are some OLTP situations in which clustering a hierarchy of tables can provide optimized access for join processing. Rarely can the warehouse designer predict join requirements as precisely as the developer of an OLTP database.

There is one potential use for index clusters in a data warehouse. That is to cluster a single table. A table with many rows that have a common data value in a column (or series of columns) may be a candidate for a single table cluster. The advantage of a single table cluster is to reduce the number of data blocks required to store the table. This is possible because the cluster key is stored only one time, and all the rows for that cluster key simply reference that cluster key. If the cluster key columns are large, the space savings of a single table cluster can be substantial. Additionally, any queries that need to retrieve these common-valued rows as a set will require less physical I/O to locate them.

Prior to the Oracle8 introduction of star transformations, we could use index clusters to provide some of the faster access benefits. A logical star-like design was sometimes denormalized by including information that would now be stored in dimension tables into the actual fact table, essentially prejoining the fact table and several of the dimension tables. By using data from several dimension tables, we could create a single-table cluster that would be impossible with a multitable cluster. For example, we could store our organization hierarchy information in the fact table by including the cost center, region, area, and division names in the fact table. We could also store some of the information from the PROJECT table, such as service line, industry, and project type, in the fact table. This would eliminate the need to join the ACTIVITY, ORGANIZATION, and PROJECT tables for a large percentage of our queries.

Without the use of a cluster, we would avoid doing this because of the huge price we would pay in extra storage requirements. If we had one million rows in the ACTIVITY table and we attempted this kind of denormalization with a normal table (adding approximately 300 bytes of denormalized columns from dimension tables), we would require approximately 50,000 data blocks (assuming an 8-KB block size). By creating a single table cluster using these denormalized columns as the cluster key, we would require a much smaller amount of incremental storage because the values would have to be stored once per block instead of once per row.

This alternative has major drawbacks (as off-the-wall alternatives frequently do) in that we would have to create additional indexes on a million-row table to efficiently answer all the possible queries that might be posed using criteria from dimension data. Additionally, it was necessary to predict the total amount of space needed to store the entire set of rows that share any given cluster key value. Unless the data distribution across dimension keys is fairly uniform, storage efficiency in the cluster will be lost. In most cases, the possible performance and storage gains were not sufficient to warrant making this denormalizaton. Fortunately, the introduction of star transformation optimization in Oracle8 made this kind of unnatural act unnecessary.

As an example, the following SQL commands would be used to create a prejoined ACTIVITY table as an indexed cluster:

```
CREATE CLUSTER PREJOIN_ACTIVITY
   (CCNUM          VARCHAR2(4),
    MONTH          VARCHAR2(7),
    SERVICE_LINE   VARCHAR2(40),
    INDUSTRY       VARCHAR2(40),
    REGION_NAME    VARCHAR2(40),
    AREA_NAME      VARCHAR2(40))
  TABLESPACE ACT_CLUSTER
  STORAGE (INITIAL 100M NEXT 100M PCTINCREASE 0)
  PARALLEL (DEGREE 8);

CREATE INDEX PREJOIN_IND1 ON CLUSTER PREJOIN_ACTIVITY;

CREATE TABLE ACTIVITY
   (MONTH         VARCHAR2(7),
    CCNUM         VARCHAR2(4),
    INDUSTRY      VARCHAR2(40),
    SERVICE_LINE  VARCHAR2(40),
    REGION_NAME   VARCHAR2(40),
    AREA_NAME     VARCHAR2(40),
    CONSULTANT_ID NUMBER,
    FUNCTION_CODE VARCHAR2(2),
    HOURS         NUMBER(11,2),
    EXPENSES      NUMBER(11,2),
    REVENUE       NUMBER(11,2))
  CLUSTER PREJOIN_ACTIVITY
     (CCNUM, MONTH, SERVICE_LINE, INDUSTRY, REGION_NAME, AREA_NAME)
  PARALLEL (DEGREE 8);
```

The order in which the statements are executed is important. The cluster must be created first, then the cluster index, then the table. The storage parameter in the CREATE CLUSTER works as the default storage parameters for tables created in the cluster, and the PARALLEL parameter sets up the number of parallel processes that can operate on the cluster and tables in the cluster. (There are a number of other parameters that relate to creating a cluster; these are described in detail in the Oracle7 and Oracle8 Server SQL reference manuals.) We can create regular B*Tree indexes on any column in the clustered table. Applications are not aware of whether a table exists in an index cluster, so we can move tables into and out of a cluster with no effect on any application SQL code.

The best performance with a single table cluster will result when the leading (i.e., first defined) columns in the cluster key are referenced in the WHERE clause. Just as with a regular B*Tree concatenated index, when the leading edge of the cluster key is referenced in the WHERE clause, the cluster index may be used for the query. Careful analysis of user access patterns and selectivity is required when choosing the order of the columns cluster key. The prime considerations in choosing a cluster key are that (1) it can be used in as many queries as possible and (2) it is selective enough that chaining will be minimized. If (as is usually the case) the queries cannot be predicted, then multiple indexes might have to be created. Ideally, data columns in the cluster key should not be updated.

Using a single table cluster will typically slow performance on INSERT operations because Oracle must first locate the appropriate data block for the specific cluster key for each row rather than just select an available block from the table's freelist. A single table cluster would not be effective for tables with millions of rows for which we cannot create a cluster key that is sufficiently selective to avoid chaining.

Tricks such as these are rarely of value in a warehouse where consistent performance over a large range of queries is more important than optimization of any specific queries. Although we would not generally recommend the use of single table indexed clusters for data warehouses, the technique might be effective in certain situations and is worth knowing. The improvements made to star query optimization in Oracle8 make this technique far less appealing.

Hash Clusters

Oracle offers a second type of clustering, *hash clusters*. Hash clusters differ from indexed clusters primarily by the way Oracle determines where the data block is located. A hash cluster creates a hash key based on either an internal algorithm or an algorithm supplied by the developer as part of the table data. The hashing algorithm processes the cluster key columns and computes the hash key. The hash key points Oracle directly to the data block containing that set of cluster key columns. Hash clusters operate faster than indexed clusters for lookups based on specific key values because there is no need to traverse a

B*Tree index to locate the address of the cluster columns. This can result in a substantial improvement in performance for a specific subset of possible queries. Unlike an indexed cluster, a hash cluster stores the cluster key values for each row in the cluster. Consequently, we cannot use the single table clustering technique discussed in the previous section as a way to prejoin our tables. Index range scans and full table scans generally suffer when the table is placed in a hash cluster. Adding data to a hash cluster also presents difficulties—the entire table's space must be allocated at initial creation and cannot later allocate additional extents. Hash clusters are also very sensitive to chaining. For these reasons, there is rarely an opportunity to take advantage of hash clusters in a data warehouse.

The syntax to create a hash cluster is very similar to that shown earlier to create an index cluster. An additional clause, HASHKEYS (and optionally HASH IS), must be provided to tell Oracle how to organize the data within the allocated data blocks.

Analyzing Schema Objects

Once tables and indexes have been created, we need to ensure that the cost-based optimizer has sufficient information to make an intelligent choice among various alternative query execution strategies. Oracle uses the ANALYZE table command to gather information about the number of rows, the distribution of index values, and the like. To analyze a table we issue the following command:

```
ANALYZE TABLE ACTIVITY COMPUTE STATISTICS;
```

When we analyze a table we analyze both the table and its partitions along with all of the indexes on that table. In order to analyze a table, Oracle must perform a full table scan and sort the table data. This requires a substantial amount of CPU and memory resources. For very large tables (multimillions of rows) analyzing the table is quite an expensive operation. It is possible to analyze a table and sample only a subset of rows. The command is as follows:

```
ANALYZE TABLE ACTIVITY
   ESTIMATE STATISTICS SAMPLE 10 PERCENT;
```

It is possible to sample any percentage of the rows in a table or to specify a number of rows to sample. Since the introduction of the cost-based optimizer in Oracle7, each release has shown improvements in the sampling algorithm that allow good statistics to be gathered with smaller sample sizes. Sampling about 5 to 10 percent of the rows yields acceptable results in most cases. Large detail or fact tables should be analyzed whenever about 10 percent of the data in the table changes. A smaller load, however, that significantly alters the distribution of data in one or more columns may justify obtaining a new set of statistics. Most warehouse administrators try to schedule an ANALYZE step after each periodic load whenever possible. The dimension tables and individual partitions of partitioned tables are usually sufficiently small that the ANALYZE command is relatively inexpensive and can be executed after each load.

Most Oracle8 data warehouses, however, use partitioning to avoid adding rows into existing large tables. By loading new data into a separate partition, only that partition will require new statistics to be gathered. Older data partitions, commonly retained in read-only tablespaces, will not need to be analyzed again. This feature alone can eliminate the concern over including an analyze step in the regular load process. To gather statistics on a single partition of an Oracle8 partitioned table, the modified syntax is as follows:

```
ANALYZE TABLE ACTIVITY PARTITION ACT_2000JAN
    ESTIMATE STATISTICS SAMPLE 10 PERCENT;
```

An optional clause can be added to the ANALYZE TABLE command in order to build a histogram of the data values in various columns:

```
FOR ALL INDEXED COLUMNS SIZE 20
```

This example shows one of several variations of the optional syntax for gathering column-level statistics. Statistics for each indexed column will be stored in 20 histogram "buckets." It is also possible to name specific columns or to request statistics for all columns in the table. (This final option provides no real value to the optimizer because retrieval based on data from nonindexed columns will require a full table scan.)

The syntax to gather (COMPUTE, in this example) statistics on an individual index is as follows:

```
ANALYZE INDEX ACT_PK
    COMPUTE STATISTICS;
```

The cost-based optimizer will not work correctly if the tables have not been analyzed. Users will receive no error messages, but the optimizer will simply make assumptions (that are probably not valid) about the data distribution and proceed. This generally results in suboptimal query performance. There is a PL/SQL package that can be used to analyze all the objects in a schema. DBMS_UTILITY.ANALYZE_SCHEMA takes two arguments, the name of a schema and the analysis method (COMPUTE or ESTIMATE). This package, however, does not allow you to specify the percentage of rows on which to base the estimate. Further discussion of the cost-based optimizer and its use of statistics is provided in Chapter 9, "Data Warehouse Performance Tuning."

Using Views in the Data Warehouse

A view is a virtual table that gives a data warehouse developer the ability to control exactly how the underlying data structures in the database appear to the user. Views can be used to hide complicated underlying physical database designs from the user. Even though one of the strengths of a star design is that the relationships between the tables are simple and intuitive, we would still like to avoid having to teach our users about joining tables. This becomes even more important if we can avoid having to introduce the concepts of outer-joins and antijoins (an antijoin is a query used to select rows belonging to one table that do *not* have a corresponding row in another table) to the users. We used an antijoin technique earlier in this chapter to demonstrate an alternative to validating foreign key relationships.

Using views enables the user to "prejoin" tables, ensuring that the join is correctly defined and efficient. Some simple but useful views that we will use in our project accounting data warehouse might include PROJECT_REVENUES and ORGANIZATION_REVENUES to present summary information. Another candidate view might be BAD_CONSULTANT_IDS, which is an antijoin used to identify any CONSULTANT_IDS that are in the ACTIVITY table but are not in the ORGANIZATION table.

```
CREATE OR REPLACE VIEW PROJECT_REVENUES AS
    SELECT PROJECTS.PROJECT_ID, PROJECT_NAME, SUM(REVENUE)
      FROM PROJECTS, ACTIVITY
     WHERE PROJECT.ID = ACTIVITY.PROJECT_ID
     GROUP BY PROJECTS.PROJECT_ID;

CREATE OR REPLACE VIEW ORGANIZATION_REVENUES AS
    SELECT ORGANIZATIONS.ORG_ID, ORGANIZATION_NAME, SUM(REVENUE)
      FROM ORGANIZATIONS, ACTIVITY
     WHERE ORGANIZATIONS.ORG_ID = ACTIVITY.ORG_ID
     GROUP BY ORGANIZATIONS.ORG_ID;

CREATE OR REPLACE VIEW BAD_CONSULTANT_ID AS
    SELECT CONSULTANT_ID
      FROM ACTIVITY
     WHERE CONSULTANT_ID NOT IN (SELECT /*+ HASH_AJ */ CONSULTANT_ID
                                   FROM CONSULTANT);
```

This last view could also be written using the MINUS operator or as an outer-join. In any event, it is an antijoin view. The Oracle optimizer will frequently recast antijoin SELECT statements into a form that can be processed in the most efficient manner. It is possible to direct the optimizer's approach to completing an antijoin using an initialization parameter (ALWAYS_ANTI_JOIN) or as shown using a hint (HASH_AJ, MERGE_AJ) in the subquery.

Using Views and DECODE for Complex Analyses

Users frequently want to display information that is stored in separate rows in our database as columnar data. This capability allows them to produce cross-tab or matrix reports. Consider an example from the project accounting data warehouse. Each of the external projects has been assigned to a specific service line. Warehouse users would like to analyze the total revenue associated with each service line for each organizational unit. We will create a view that presents the data as a matrix between ORG_ID and SERVICE_LINE.

In order to create columns out of rows, we will need to use the DECODE function. DECODE works much like an IF statement. The basic DECODE function takes four arguments: two data values, expressions, or columns and two possible output values. If the two data parameters are equal then the DECODE returns the first output value. If the two values are not equal, it will return the second answer. The syntax is as follows:

```
DECODE(first_test_value, second_test_value, result_if_equal,
other_result)

CREATE OR REPLACE VIEW SERVICE_REVENUE AS
   SELECT CCNUM, MONTH,
          SUM(DECODE(SERVICE_LINE,'INTERNET',REVENUE,0))      INTERNET,
          SUM(DECODE(SERVICE_LINE,'APPLICATIONS',REVENUE,0))
APPLICATIONS,
          SUM(DECODE(SERVICE_LINE,'DATABASE',REVENUE,0))      DATABASE,
          SUM(DECODE(SERVICE_LINE,'BPR',REVENUE,0))           BPR,
          SUM(DECODE(SERVICE_LINE,'EDUCATION',REVENUE,0))     EDUCATION,
          SUM(DECODE(SERVICE_LINE,'OTHER',REVENUE,0))         OTHER
     FROM ACTIVITY A, PROJECT P
    WHERE A.PROJECT_ID = P.PROJECT_ID
    GROUP BY CCNUM, MONTH;
```

Each column will be the sum of the value of REVENUE for each row in which SERVICE_LINE equals the constant provided in the second parameter. All other rows will contribute 0 to the sum. Executing the query

```
SELECT *
  FROM SERVICE_REVENUE
```

```
WHERE CCNUM IN ('477', '488')
  AND MONTH IN ('1999NOV', '1999DEC');
```

results in Table 5.2.

A common criticism of an RDBMS being used in data warehousing is that it is difficult, if not impossible, to perform time-based analyses. Even relatively simple time-based analyses like comparing last year's data with the current year's can be challenging with a relational database. This is functionality that multidimensional databases such as Oracle Express (covered in Chapter 13, "Analytical Processing in the Oracle Data Warehouse") typically manage better than relational databases. This technique of creating views with the DECODE function will allow us to easily manage time-based analyses. To create a view for the project accounting data warehouse that allows analysis of each month's revenue by organization use the following:

```
CREATE OR REPLACE VIEW MONTHLY_REVENUE AS
   SELECT CCNUM,
          SUM(DECODE(MONTH,'1999JAN',REVENUE,0)  JAN1999,
          SUM(DECODE(MONTH,'1999FEB',REVENUE,0)  FEB1999,
          SUM(DECODE(MONTH,'1999MAR',REVENUE,0)  MAR1999,
          SUM(DECODE(MONTH,'1999APR',REVENUE,0)  APR1999,
          SUM(DECODE(MONTH,'1999MAY',REVENUE,0)  MAY1999,
          SUM(DECODE(MONTH,'1999JUN',REVENUE,0)  JUN1999,
          SUM(DECODE(MONTH,'1999JUL',REVENUE,0)  JUL1999,
          SUM(DECODE(MONTH,'1999AUG',REVENUE,0)  AUG1999,
          SUM(DECODE(MONTH,'1999SEP',REVENUE,0)  SEP1999,
          SUM(DECODE(MONTH,'1999OCT',REVENUE,0)  OCT1999,
          SUM(DECODE(MONTH,'1999NOV',REVENUE,0)  NOV1999,
          SUM(DECODE(MONTH,'1999DEC',REVENUE,0)  DEC1999
       FROM ACTIVITY
     GROUP BY CCNUM;
```

Obviously, this could be extended to include as many years' worth of data as desired. Once the view is created the user simply can refer to any desired months in the select list of his query and combine months to show quarterly

Table 5.2 Cross-Tabular Report of Revenue by Cost Center and Service Line

CCNUM	MONTH	INTERNET	FINAN-CIALS	DB	BPR	ED	OTHER
477	1999NOV	55,120	47,620	25,050	11,270	12,450	53,200
477	1999DEC	43,830	52,500	22,110	12,335	12,500	52,400
488	1999NOV	37,442	41,207	13,400	9,500	7,000	27,000
488	1999DEC	34,300	40,270	12,530	10,110	8,430	25,600

results, compare differences between time periods, and the like. Grouping months into quarters could be done with a query such as the following:

```
SELECT CCNUM,
       NVL(JAN1999,0)+NVL(FEB1999,0)+NVL(MAR1999,0) Q1,
       NVL(APR1999,0)+NVL(MAY1999,0)+NVL(JUN1999,0) Q2,
       NVL(JUL1999,0)+NVL(AUG1999,0)+NVL(SEP1999,0) Q3,
       NVL(OCT1999,0)+NVL(NOV1999,0)+NVL(DEC1999,0) Q4
  FROM MONTHLY_REVENUE
 GROUP BY CCNUM;
```

We can use this technique along with our SQL to generate SQL technique and information in the database to create these views dynamically. That way, after we load new data we can run the script to create a new view based on the new data in the database. The view will always be up to date. To maintain the MONTHLY_REVENUE to always have a running 24-month history in the view we can use the following SQL statement to create the necessary SQL script:

```
COL DUMMY NOPRINT
COL DUMMY2 NOPRINT
SET FEEDBACK OFF PAGES 0 HEAD OFF
SPOOL CREATE_MONTHLY_REVENUE.SQL
SELECT 1 DUMMY, SYSDATE,
       'CREATE OR REPLACE VIEW MONTHLY_REVENUE AS SELECT CCNUM '
  FROM DUAL
UNION
SELECT 2, TO_DATE(MONTH,'YYYYMON'),
       'SUM(DECODE(MONTH,'''||MONTH||''''||',REVENUE,0)'||'  '||
       SUBSTR(MONTH,5)||SUBSTR(MONTH,1,4)
  FROM FISCAL_DATE
 WHERE MONTHS_BETWEEN(SYSDATE,TO_DATE(MONTHS,'YYYYMON') < 25
UNION
SELECT 3, SYSDATE,  'GROUP BY CCNUM'
  FROM DUAL
ORDER BY 1, 2;
SPOOL OFF
```

We want to ensure that the columns are created in ascending order, so that the first column is the oldest month, the second column is the second oldest, and so on. We include a second "dummy" column in the query that will be used to sort the rows returned by the second SELECT statement. Because each query in a UNION must have the same number of columns and each column must have the same data type, we must include a dummy value (SYSDATE) in the first and third SELECT statements. These dummy columns are not used other than as placeholders. In the middle query we return the date value; when we sort by the second column, this results in the rows being sorted in the desired order. The subsequent CREATE VIEW statement will have the columns created in the proper order.

NOTE The DECODE statement provides powerful capabilities that will be used frequently in a data warehouse project. A common use for DECODE is to test and transform data values during load processing. Because DECODE is a SQL function and is used in SELECT statements, we can take advantage of parallel processing for our test and transformations. This is contrasted to the common alternative of using a series of IF tests in a PL/SQL procedure. While the PL/SQL procedure is more intuitive to a programmer, PL/SQL does not take advantage of parallel processing capabilities. Using DECODE can provide substantial performance benefits over using PL/SQL and processing each row one at a time.

There is one caution to keep in mind when using views to hide the complexity of joins from end users. Typically, we create a view that has all the useful columns from each table that we join. The end user is presented with a list of available columns that all appear to come from the same table. One column seems as good as another column in the view. If the end user should happen to select a set of columns that are all in a single base table, the query will still have to suffer the performance overhead of performing the joins. The use of views from ad hoc query tools means that every query will have to join all of the tables.

A better approach would be to use a query tool that allows the administrator to provide the end user with a single list of available columns but have the tool maintain its own metadata, so that each query accesses only those tables absolutely necessary to resolve the query. Oracle Discoverer, for example, has this capability. Another alternative is to save the results displayed through such a view in summary tables that can be refreshed after each load into the underlying base tables. This summary table approach has been a fundamental part of data warehousing since its inception. Oracle8*i* helps us automate the maintenance of summary tables (and automatically rewrite queries to use these summaries) by implementing materialized views.

Creating Materialized Views in the Data Warehouse

There are tremendous performance benefits available by using Oracle8*i* materialized views and query rewrite in the warehouse. Rather than attempt to cover all of the material here, we have devoted an entire chapter to the topic of building summaries and aggregations using materialized views. We will, instead, provide one single example here and then go into much more depth on this very important topic in Chapter 7, "Post-Load Processing in the Data Warehouse."

```
CREATE MATERIALIZED VIEW ACTIVITIES_PROJECTS_MV
    STORAGE (INITIAL 128K NEXT 128K PCTINCREASE 0)
    TABLESPACE FOOBAR_DATA01
```

```
          NOLOGGING
          PARALLEL
          BUILD DEFERRED
          REFRESH FAST ON DEMAND
          ENABLE QUERY REWRITE
  AS
  SELECT PROJECTS.ID,
          PROJECTS.NAME,
          COUNT(*) CNT,
          SUM(ACTIVITIES.HOURS) HOURS,
          SUM(ACTIVITIES.EXPENSES) EXPENSES,
          SUM(ACTIVITIES.REVENUE) REVENUE
    FROM ACTIVITIES,
          PROJECTS
   WHERE ACTIVITIES.PROJECT_ID = PROJECTS.ID
   GROUP BY PROJECTS.ID
             PROJECTS.NAME;
```

For the most part, the syntax of this example looks similar to the creation of a view with the addition of STORAGE, TABLESPACE, NOLOGGING, and PARALLEL clauses from the CREATE TABLE. A few new attributes that are peculiar to materialized views, shown in bold type, allow us to define when the view's base query will be executed to populate the view, specify how and when refreshes will be performed, and enable the query rewrite facility.

Views, Materialized Views, or Summary Tables?

In our project accounting data warehouse, we have created some views that are used to present summary information. An alternative approach would be to create actual summary tables (using materialized views Oracle8*i*) for the same purpose. Summary tables will provide more rapid response to queries. Does this mean that summary tables are always to be preferred over views? Not necessarily. Summary tables can be expensive to create and to store. It is not unusual for a substantial portion of the periodic loading time to be spent creating summary tables. This price may be small if it saves dozens or hundreds of queries through the summary view.

Because summary tables collapse the detail data across one or more dimensions, many summary tables are typically required. A "traditional" data warehouse can consume more disk space for storing summaries than is devoted to the detail data. As the number of summary tables grows, the task of the DBA becomes more complex. The user also can be overwhelmed by a large number of summary tables and his inability to figure out which table he should access to answer a particular question (this latter concern applies equally to the presence of a large number of views).

Some sophisticated query tools can help us deal with the proliferation of summary tables and views. Oracle Discoverer allows us to specify the relationship between a summary table and the detail tables on which the summary is based. Discoverer then determines which table will provide the correct answer to a query and the fastest response time to the query. It directs its generated query to the summary table when possible or to the detail table when necessary. The user, therefore, does not have to be aware of the relationship of summary and detail tables. Oracle8*i* materialized views extend this same capability to queries from any tool.

If we decide to create summary tables we can use Oracle's parallel CREATE TABLE table_name AS SELECT (pCTAS) command to quickly calculate the summary data:

```
CREATE TABLE ORG_REVENUE_SUMMARY
    UNRECOVERABLE
    PARALLEL (DEGREE 8)
    STORAGE (INITIAL 5M  NEXT 5M PCTINCREASE 0)
    PCTFREE 0
    AS SELECT CCNUM, MONTH, SUM(REVENUE)  MONTHLY_REV
        FROM ACTIVITY A, ORGANIZATIONS O
        WHERE A.ORG_ID = O.ORG_ID
        GROUP BY CCNUM, MONTH;
```

This command will typically execute very quickly if sufficient hardware resources are available. Creating summary tables using pCTAS and with materialized views is covered in depth in Chapter 7.

The primary reason for creating summary tables is to improve query performance. We expect that, as more data warehouses are implemented using Oracle8, the need to build and maintain summary tables will be reduced because adequate performance will be available with star joins against the detail (fact) table and through materialized view.

Traditional database views have the advantage of not requiring additional storage or refreshing when underlying data is updated. New views can be created and existing ones redefined with only trivial resource consumption. The disadvantage, of course, is that the view has to be processed each time it is referenced. As long as a view provides adequate runtime performance and users are able to identify the correct view to use, then this approach is perfectly acceptable.

When a large, painful performance difference exists between a view and a corresponding summary table, then it is probably appropriate to spend the storage dollars to retain the summarized data. Given a choice between manually maintaining summary tables and using materialized views, there is really no decision to make. Unless you are somehow stuck using a release prior to Oracle8*i*, you should absolutely invest the time to learn the materialized view facility. If you have just recently made the upgrade to Oracle8*i*, now is the time to begin registering your prebuilt summaries as materialized views.

Testing the Data Warehouse

Like all large projects, a data warehouse needs extensive testing. Typically, insufficient time is set aside for testing (or, more commonly, the planned testing time is consumed with resolving data extract problems). All data extraction, data cleansing, transportation, and load, summarization, and aggregation processes must be tested. Additionally, expected data access methods need to be verified and tuned.

These types of tests can be referred to broadly as data quality testing. Does our data warehouse provide data of sufficiently high quality to be useful? Although the data quality testing should start early, it is not possible to complete it until all the various components are finished and the equivalent of integration testing can begin. The amount of time required for this wide range of testing will be considerable. The data warehouse implementation plans must provide enough time for testing and making changes based on the results of the testing.

In addition to the data quality testing that must be conducted, you should also conduct architecture feasibility tests using sufficiently large volumes of data. There is a bit of a Catch-22 in volume testing. Because the testing is of fundamental architecture features, like the physical database design, hardware and network design, and so on, this testing must occur sufficiently early in the project to allow time to make changes. Waiting until the week before the warehouse opens to test the architecture's ability to support the planned data volumes may leave the project in serious trouble! It is very difficult to make fundamental architectural changes late in the project. The Catch-22 is that there generally isn't enough data early in the project that can be used for volume testing. Without data extraction and loading procedures completed, how can we have a sufficient amount of data to perform any useful tests?

The primary concern in generating test data is to maintain the necessary referential integrity between the fact table and the dimension tables. Because the dimension tables tend to be relatively small, it is feasible to use simple manual methods to populate them with meaningful data. The fact table will need to have hundreds of thousands or millions of rows, and each row will need to properly reference each of the dimension tables. Unfortunately, you can't just populate the fact table with random data and be able to adequately test your warehouse. It is possible, though, to generate a "quick and dirty" set of test data for your data warehouse using PL/SQL. If you haven't done so already, create referential key constraints for the fact table and the dimension tables. Then, if you supply the name of a fact table, it is possible to determine from the data dictionary all the referenced dimension tables and the name of their primary key columns. The following SQL statement demonstrates this for a fact table named ACTIVITY:

```
SELECT COLUMN_NAME, UCC.TABLE_NAME
  FROM USER_CONS_COLUMNS UCC, USER_CONSTRAINTS UC
 WHERE UCC.CONSTRAINT_NAME = UC.R_CONSTRAINT_NAME
   AND UC.TABLE_NAME = 'ACTIVITY'
```

The output of this SQL statement will be the name of each table and the associated primary key column(s) for every table that is referenced by the fact table. This information can be used to generate SQL statements that insert records into the fact table that will support the necessary referential integrity. Use the SQL-to-generate-SQL (or in this case PL/SQL) methods discussed at the start of this chapter to create a PL/SQL routine that will load the fact table. The first step in the PL/SQL routine will be to create CURSOR FOR LOOPS that reference each dimension table and column. There will be one CURSOR FOR LOOP for each dimension table. Loop through each table, selecting the primary key values into a PL/SQL table. (A PL/SQL table works as an in-memory, single-dimension array.) At this point you will have several PL/SQL tables, one for each dimension table. You are now ready to create an insert statement for the fact table. The insert statement can reference some random data for the nonkey data fields and reference one of the values in each PL/SQL table for the foreign key values. The PL/SQL table values are referenced as variables in the INSERT statement. Control the number of rows inserted by using nested loop logic, with the inner loop processing each row in the PL/SQL table and the outer loop processing N times (where N is a parameter passed to the procedure).

This technique will generate evenly distributed data for a test fact table. Depending on the pattern used to select rows from the PL/SQL tables the rows will not be randomized and will be evenly distributed. Each key will have an equal number of fact rows. Still, this method can allow you to quickly generate sufficient data volumes to begin early load testing of the warehouse.

Regardless of the method used to load the data warehouse with test data, the effort to load and test the data warehouse with large volumes of data early in the project will be richly rewarded. It is impossible to overemphasize the need to validate the warehouse design with large volumes of data. Don't limit testing to query response times, but test the time it takes to perform the incremental loads, indexing, archival, and planned backup/recovery processes. It is very likely that procedures that work well with smaller data volumes simply will not be acceptable with large volumes. The only way to ensure that volume-related problems are identified and addressed is by thorough testing. To be useful, this testing must begin even earlier in the development life cycle than in a custom application development project.

Summary

This chapter introduced several features of the SQL*Plus environment that can be exploited by the administrator of an Oracle data warehouse to make life simpler. These included spooling and formatting of output, the use of substitution variables, and the use of SQL to generate SQL.

We then described the process for creating an Oracle database, tablespaces within the database, and then various database objects in these tablespaces. The primary object types that make up the warehouse are tables (including partitioned tables) and indexes (both B*Tree and bitmap).

The use of ANALYZE to gather statistics for the cost-based optimizer was covered along with the use of views and Oracle8i materialized views to simplify the way data appears to the warehouse users. The chapter concluded with an exhortation to plan for (and execute!) early testing of the warehouse using realistic volumes of data.

CHAPTER

6

Populating the Oracle Data Warehouse

We need more input. We gotta fill this thing up with data. We gotta make her as real as possible, Wyatt. I want her to live. I want her to breathe. I want her to aerobicize!

Gary
Weird Science (1985)

Of all the work done before the data warehouse is ready to open, the average warehouse development team will spend less than 20 percent of its time designing the warehouse, configuring hardware, installing software products, and the like. Easily 80 percent of the work involved in setting up a data warehouse is devoted to locating, extracting, filtering, scrubbing, and finally loading data. Of these tasks, loading is by far the easiest—both to perform and to describe. Resolving the various (and nefarious!) problems that arise when we bring together data from multiple source systems is invariably more difficult than we anticipate.

We haven't devoted a lot of space in this book to planning an overall data warehouse project, but we do provide one guideline here. Take whatever amount of time you believe will be necessary for creating data extracts, performing data validation and transformation, and loading and indexing data; then double that total amount and add it into the schedule just for resolving data problems. And then make sure there is some additional slack in the schedule to allow for the data that still isn't quite right!

It is always hard for the first-time warehouse analyst to accept, in advance, the absolute fact that most of our operational systems (with which we are successfully running our businesses) are not internally consistent—that somehow they continue to function even with dirty data! After the first warehouse load experience, however, a healthy dose of skepticism is inevitably introduced. Among many other valid reasons for starting on a small scale, this is sufficient justification for basing phase 1 of the warehouse on only a very small number of subject areas and source systems.

The complexity of the integration process grows rapidly as the number of subject areas and source systems is increased. For a very simplified example, Figure 6.1 demonstrates that the probability of a data conflict is proportional to the number of system integration points to be resolved. If we are integrating data from 2 sources, there is only 1 integration point to be resolved. With a triangle of 3 sources, there are 3 "edges" to be integrated. As we move to 4 sources, we have to deal with 6 potential conflicts. Five sources yields 10 opportunities for integration problems, while with 6 sources we have to resolve discrepancies arising from 15 different integration points.

It is easy to see how the complexity of integrating data from many sources rapidly becomes unmanageable. By starting the data warehouse with, say, 3

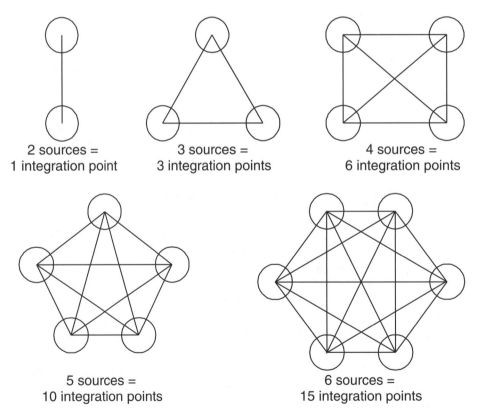

Figure 6.1 Complexity effect of multiple data sources.

subject areas or sources, we can gain experience while dealing with a relatively small number of data integration points. A second phase can then add 3 more data sources to the existing warehouse with only an additional 6 areas of potential conflict (because the existing integrated warehouse now acts as a single source). This phased approach actually presents less total work (3 + 6 = 9 integrations) than attempting to do a "big bang" implementation (15 integrations!) and is more manageable.

Dealing with Dirty Data

Integrating data from multiple sources is difficult under the best of circumstances. Unfortunately, we have never seen the best of circumstances! One should expect differences between the names, formats, and encoding of data being extracted from multiple sources. An organization's many operational systems should naturally be expected to have been designed by different teams at different times and probably built using different file or database management systems. The old payroll system tracks employees by social security number in VSAM files while the newly purchased project accounting system tracks consulting employees by name. Sometimes project accounting's employee name doesn't exactly match the name carried in the payroll system. Payroll also keeps track of all employees, some of whom aren't in project accounting because they don't work on billable projects. To make things worse, the project accounting system tracks some independent contractors who aren't even company employees.

On top of these expected differences that have to be resolved, it is virtually guaranteed that we will find other surprises in the data we extract. Our newly designed data warehouse has a carefully architected environment in which we document and incorporate specific data rules. We find that many of our existing operational systems were built without rigorous enforcement of various business rules. In other cases, we find that the application code has been enforcing some rules that aren't documented—we "discover" these rules as we try to make sense of the extracted data.

It may seem surprising, but it is not uncommon, to encounter dirty data: duplicate records, missing "parents" from what should be parent/child relationships, denormalized data that can't be renormalized. Imagine a system developed in COBOL and VSAM files in which the record layout is designed to hold everything necessary about an employee's weekly timesheet. (This design allowed the original COBOL programmer to avoid complex multiple input logic.) The record contains repeating groups to track the multiple projects, hours, and days on which an employee might work during the week. The record also carries information about the employee, his pay grade and organization code. Such a structure makes the payroll processing fairly simple. What happens, however, if the organization code or other employee information changes from one week to the next? The next week's payroll record simply carries the new values, and payroll churns along happily. What happens, however, if the pay grade changes on the first day of a month that falls on a Wednesday? Well, the original programmers found an easy solution; they just created two timesheet records for that employee for that week, one with sixteen hours and the other with twenty-four hours at the higher rate of pay. Payroll processing still works fine, but when we extract for the data warehouse we expect to load data into a normalized structure with primary keys. We have to resolve the two records into one parent row with multiple child rows for each day and project code.

We also expect that every project code we encounter in a payroll record will already be part of our PROJECTS dimension table. Because the payroll system is concerned only with how many hours the employee worked and how much money to pay per hour, it never cared about specific project codes. During our warehouse integration effort we have to reconcile discrepancies.

Dealing with Missing Data

One special case of dealing with dirty data is the situation in which not all data needed for an extract has been entered as of the time of the extract. In our case study of data taken from a company's project accounting system, we expect each employee to file a timecard each week. But what if they are late? The vacationing consultant who didn't enter his or her time report before leaving for two weeks in Hawaii will not be represented in our extract. On returning, he will probably be chastised and will enter the missing weeks' data, and the operational systems will be able to pay the employee and issue client invoices. But what about the data warehouse?

Similar situations can occur in lots of operational systems besides project accounting. There is no straightforward technical solution to this problem. We have several possible ways of dealing with it:

- Ignore the missing data. In some cases, the amount of missing data may be insignificant in relation to the whole. When combined with the next option, this solution works well in many cases.

- Wait to do our extracts until we can be sure that all (or virtually all) of the necessary data is entered. Of course, this approach will require more or less waiting depending on the source system. This approach is generally the best answer. Those critics who argue that they absolutely need the data warehouse to be updated within 24 hours of a transaction are probably trying to do some form of operational reporting instead of pure data warehouse analysis. Enhancing (or fixing) the operational system might be the correct solution.

- Mark rows/records as they are extracted so that unextracted data can be identified at the time of the next extract. One disadvantage to this approach is that it requires more work to do an UPDATE in addition to a SELECT during extract processing. Another major disadvantage is that any summaries performed on a time basis (as most warehouse rollups are) will have to be reexecuted after the missing data is later obtained. This approach, unlike the first two, requires updates to warehouse data. Updating warehouses should be avoided so that users do not receive different answers to the same question asked at different times.

- Extract data based on time of data entry as opposed to the business period to which it applies. This is tempting when the source system timestamps records, but it is generally not a very satisfactory solution. It shares the disadvantage of requiring that summaries be reexecuted to include late-arriving data. Additionally, it may cause a corollary problem by getting small amounts of data from the next period. Doing a summarization based on less than a statistically significant sample of the data may lead to erroneous decisions based on incomplete data. We will further address the concept of "publishing" data later in this chapter.

UPDATING WAREHOUSE DATA

Although not absolutely forbidden, updating data in the warehouse after it has been "published" to users leads to problems when the same query issued on different days yields different results. This has the same negative effect as creating multiple departmental "data marts" with different data sources—it causes confusion and doubts about the accuracy of all warehouse information. We should seek to avoid making changes to data in the warehouse once it has been published. If updates are required (for instance, when we define our summary as "monthly, with the current month showing totals through yesterday") then we must explicitly define this to our users through metadata. We must also be careful to define our summary calculations in a way that won't confuse the user when comparing different past months to the current. AVERAGE_DAILY SALES might be a better measure in this situation than TOTAL_MONTHLY_SALES.

Our next decisions are how and where to do the required data resolution and reconciliation. We have three general choices: We can use a tool that automates the extraction, transformation, integration, and transfer of the data from sources to warehouse; we can perform the complex transformation and reformatting as part of custom-written extraction programs and scripts; or we can extract the necessary data in "raw" form and then perform the necessary transformations and integration on the warehouse side during (or after) the load process.

Reconciling with ETT Tools

We've already discussed the use of data extraction, transformation, and transfer tools in the context of defining and building the data warehouse. In addition to these functions, your ETT tool will also aid in the loading of data into the warehouse.

Figure 6.2 demonstrates the option of performing data scrubbing and integration using an ETT tool to define the extract processing, to perform necessary data reengineering, and then to control the load process.

The primary advantage of using an ETT tool is that it can provide a single "control panel" to handle several steps in the data warehouse's design, development, and implementation. The ETT tool can serve as the repository of all warehouse design metadata. It can generate the needed extract programs to process the source data. It can control the transfer of extract data files from their source system to the computer hosting the warehouse. Finally, the ETT tool can control the loading of data into the Oracle warehouse.

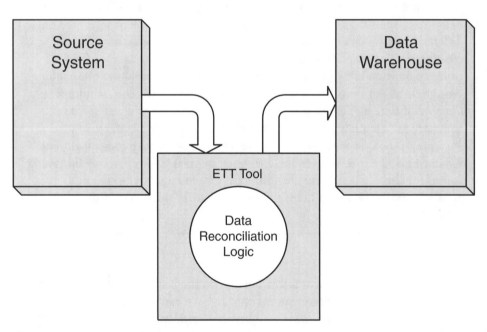

Figure 6.2   Data reconciliation using an ETT Tool.

The primary disadvantage of ETT tools is their cost. It is not uncommon to spend as much or more on the ETT tool as on the Oracle RDBMS that will host the data warehouse. The tool may be worth the price if it is used to its full advantage. There is a risk of an organization acquiring such a tool but not investing enough commitment into training and navigating the subsequent learning curve. Management that funds the purchase must also understand the total costs and insist that the tool be used rigorously.

Several criteria should be considered when selecting an ETT tool. The warehouse team should evaluate the user interface of the repository. Will the analysts and programmers assigned to the warehouse use the ETT tool for all their work, or will they be tempted to hand-modify the generated code? How fully does the tool understand the Oracle database's features? What about newer features such as table and index partitioning, bitmap indexes, parallel operations, direct path SQL*Loader, and star schemas? How easily can the analyst define the structure of both the source systems and the warehouse? Especially important is the ease with which the tool allows modification of the design. If you change the structure of a table in the warehouse, can the tool generate the necessary DDL to make the change? If the change cannot be performed without rebuilding the table (e.g., in dropping a column prior to Oracle8i), does the tool generate all the necessary code to perform the operation? Does it do so with PARALLEL CREATE TABLE AS SELECT (pCTAS) or by unloading and reloading?

Because of the high initial licensing cost of ETT tools or because of the discipline they require, many shops elect to build their data warehouse "manually." In the long run this approach will cost far more in script and program maintenance, but it certainly does allow for more customization.

Reconciling during Extract

Extracting data from application files in specific formats just requires another set of application programs. We develop specifications, write and test programs, and deliver the output to the data warehouse for loading. When the warehouse analysts have a good conception of exactly what data will need to be extracted from an application's files or databases, we can provide the applications team with the necessary program specifications. Figure 6.3 demonstrates the approach of performing the complex data cleansing logic as part of the extract process.

The advantage of this approach is that the complexities of the legacy application files are removed from the warehouse and will be addressed by the programming team, which already knows and maintains the application. The disadvantage is that the complexities must still be addressed, and the application team may not see the warehouse as its highest priority. Also, only a certain

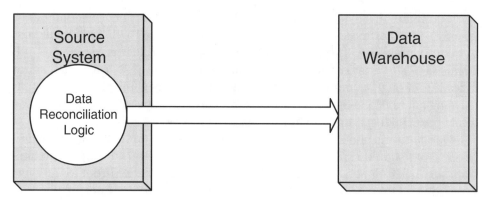

Figure 6.3   Data reconciliation during extract processing.

level of reconciliation can be performed during an extract. While single-source validation and record formatting can be done during the extract process, we probably won't be able to handle multiple source integration issues at this stage.

Many Oracle data warehouses are populated, at least partly, with data extracted from IBM mainframe applications. Many of those applications are written in COBOL, and the programmers who will be doing the extraction are frequently going to write those extracts using COBOL. The assigned programmers will typically already have the file definitions for the source application files or database. They will have to write the necessary procedure division code. In most cases, it will take some complex logic to properly reconcile, extract, and format normalized data out of the chaos of legacy systems whose quirks have frequently taken decades to develop!

The data that is extracted from the source system will need to be loaded into the data warehouse, usually with the SQL*Loader utility. We discuss SQL*Loader in more depth later in this chapter. SQL*Loader has the capability to load logical records from multiple physical input records. If possible, this feature should be avoided because it adds complexity to the loader setup and slows the load process. Try to get the extract programmers to provide the data in simple physical records that map neatly to the tables into which the data must be loaded. Fixed record formats are easiest to define to SQL*Loader, but using field delimiters will work just as well and will waste much less space if the data consists largely of variable-length text strings.

You can help the application programmers provide all the necessary data in a convenient format by specifying the layout of the extract files. It is possible to write a simple SQL*Plus script that will read the warehouse data dictionary to generate an appropriate COBOL DATA DIVISION layout in a format that will be very easy to process using SQL*Loader. Each extract file will correspond to a single table to be loaded.

A sample of such a script (SCRIPT6-1.sql) is available from the publisher's and authors' Web sites (see "Introduction" for URLs). A few notes about this script are in order. To generate a meaningful and legal name for this copybook member, the example script will use the first eight characters of the table's comments, if available. Otherwise, the file will be named the same as the table. These default names may have to be edited before transferring the file to the mainframe programmers.

The example script handles the Oracle data types most commonly used in data warehouses, but it does not know how to specify a COBOL PICTURE clause corresponding to other Oracle data types. For LONG, RAW, LONG RAW, CLOB, BLOB, or any object data types, the output will print the string UNDE-FINED? instead. Because Oracle allows for numbers of up to 38 digits of precision, the COBOL PICTURE clause may also not be legal for very large precision numbers (or columns defined as NUMBER without specification of precision). If you expect to use this technique to aid in the extract process, be sure to use only these basic data types in your warehouse tables that will be populated from COBOL programs. Otherwise, you will have to determine how you wish to map other data types back to the COBOL file layouts and modify the script accordingly.

If your extract programmers will be working with a language other than COBOL, similar scripting can be used to generate the appropriate file descriptions for FORTRAN, C, or any other language. Later in this chapter we use a similar technique to generate a SQL*Loader control file and a SQL*Plus file for unloading data from an Oracle table.

Once you've developed the extract specifications and provided a file layout, you can then write the rather simple SQL*Loader control files to process the files in the Oracle warehouse. Then you can just wait for the files to appear!

PARTNERING WITH THE APPLICATIONS TEAM

An "us versus them" division between the owners of the application and the owners of the data warehouse develops all too easily and much too frequently. An ideal warehouse project team involves a partnership between the application and the warehouse. As we discussed in Chapter 1, "Data Warehousing," a data warehouse should be considered as an extension of the operational systems. In forming a warehouse team, whenever possible, get the owners of the applications that will feed the warehouse involved. Otherwise, the warehouse team is likely to be viewed as just an extra, unnecessary burden. Let the applications teams share in some of the glory of delivering additional benefits to the users who are the real owners of the data. Their active assistance and cooperation will be well worth the investment!

Reconciling during Load

Most data warehousing project teams are given responsibility for the data warehouse but not for the extract process. The source application owners are generally very protective of their files and databases. They are hesitant (when they aren't downright obstructive!) to allow "outsiders" direct access to these precious resources. Instead, the applications team typically volunteers (read: "grudgingly submits") to do the extract processing for the warehouse. The warehouse team typically accepts the offer as an easy way to offload some work while the application team thinks they're volunteering for a one-time effort that will get those warehouse pests off their back.

Although it's unfortunate, it is also common to find that there are major unexpected project delays introduced each time we ask the applications team to create or modify an extract file. Because of the iterative, heuristic nature of data warehouse development, the warehouse team frequently needs to ask for additional files or fields that it hadn't requested earlier. As each extract request is received (and then prioritized) by the applications team, the warehouse team ends up waiting for days or weeks to get the new extract. Meanwhile, progress on the warehouse is stalled.

One way to avoid these frequent requests for extract changes is shown in Figure 6.4. In this model, we take a generic extract (or complete file copies) from the application systems. We then pick and choose which specific data fields to use and how to manipulate them during the load process. If we later determine that some additional source data is needed, we just change the load process to include the new data. The extract process is unaffected, and the applications team isn't interrupted. The trade-off for this simplicity may be much larger extract files to transfer and process.

The warehouse team can now absorb all the responsibility and work of getting the data right. Of course, they must also take on the additional responsibil-

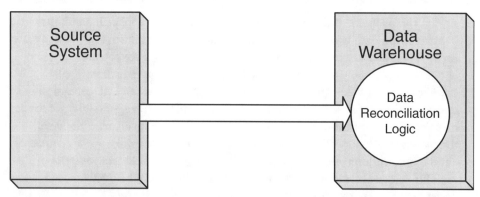

Figure 6.4 Data reconciliation during load processing.

ity of accommodating any changes in file structures introduced by application changes. So the need for close communication between applications and warehouse teams is not eliminated, but rather reversed. In most cases, this approach works as long as the warehouse team has a full-time commitment from an experienced programmer transferred or on rotation from the applications team. The data complexities and exceptions embedded within the applications files will still have to be unraveled!

An additional benefit of performing our data scrubbing and integration on the warehouse side is that we have access to the data from multiple source systems. This is, of course, the crux of the integration problem. Most of the integration work will have to be performed here even if the choice is made to do complex extract processing at each application source.

SQL combined with PL/SQL provides an easy means of manipulating raw data once it has been loaded into the warehouse. In some cases, however, it may not be terribly efficient. When the raw data can be processed using SQL's set processing features, joins, and Oracle's parallel capabilities, the work can usually be done very efficiently. If the processing must be performed in a row-at-a-time manner using PL/SQL cursors, then special care must be taken to design the post-processing tasks. One of the final sections of this chapter will explore some aspects of this topic of additional processing of data after initial bulk loading. Chapter 7, "Post-Load Processing in the Data Warehouse," will address other aspects, in particular the creation and maintenance of summary tables and Oracle8*i* materialized views.

Loading Data

For those shops that invest in an ETT tool, it will usually become the primary means of extracting data from their source systems, moving it to the data warehouse, transforming it to the warehouse's standard format and encoding schemes, and then loading it into the data warehouse. Many of these tools will provide an interface to Oracle's SQL*Loader utility. Others may attempt to perform "generic" database loads using SQL INSERT statements (we would not recommend such a product for moving large volumes of data!).

DIRECT PATH LOAD APIS

One of the new features of Oracle8*i* is a published interface to the direct path load routines used by SQL*Loader. Vendors of ETT tools may now begin to use the routines to obtain the same load speeds without having to write intermediate files and invoke SQL*Loader.

For the majority of shops that are just starting their first data warehouse project, a less automated approach is frequently adopted. In this section we examine Oracle's SQL*Loader utility in depth. SQL*Loader is the most common and best-suited means of adding large volumes of data to the Oracle data warehouse. We then explore some other means for getting smaller amounts of data into your Oracle data warehouse including Oracle's gateway technologies and some special facilities for transferring data that is already maintained in an Oracle database.

We close the chapter with a discussion of several topics closely related to loading data. We explore the need to further process bulk-loaded data to integrate it with existing data. We discuss the issues related to index maintenance whenever large amounts of data are being added to a table. Then we tackle the topic of verifying and publishing data. Finally, we look at how to get data back out of the data warehouse—either to purge or to archive detailed data once its useful lifetime has passed.

Timing of Loads

How often should the warehouse be refreshed? There is no single answer to this question, but we can share some observations made over the past decade of assisting clients in building data warehouses. When warehousing was new (circa 1990) it was commonly assumed that we would do loads on a monthly basis. Only Fortune 500 companies were attempting data warehousing, and this schedule fit well with the nature of the mainframe accounting systems that frequently were the primary data source of these early warehouses. Scheduling batch extracts on these systems was a serious constraint. And, because many of these early warehouses were built on the same mainframe systems, load scheduling was nearly as big an issue. Similar to many OLTP systems of the time, warehouse refreshes were scheduled in a batch window, query access was allowed in an online window, and the two never overlapped.

Over several years, as warehouses expanded beyond initial Finance and Marketing departments into other parts of the organization, we witnessed two phenomena that moved us to doing weekly loads. First, the increased amount of data being extracted, transformed, and loaded became too much to handle in a single monthly load. Second, we found that the second round of warehouse user departments (Manufacturing or Sales, for instance) had data that wasn't naturally oriented around an accounting month. Typically, users tended to think of this data on a daily basis. During this second wave, we still retained the batch mentality that there was a window of time during which users would not have access to the warehouse to allow dedicated refresh processing. For IT scheduling reasons, we tended to schedule refreshes on a weekend, with user access provided during the weekdays. Conveniently, during this phase, more warehouses were being implemented on dedicated UNIX servers, minimizing mainframe scheduling conflicts.

Over time, user demand for seeing their daily data on a daily basis led to today's more common scheduling of refreshes every night. This is the current, third wave of warehousing. Once again, however, in many warehouses we are reaching the point where the amount of data to be processed in the "batch window" is causing conflicts with our "online window" for access. Additionally, there is a simultaneous pressure to expand the availability of online access to accommodate users (internal users around the world as well as suppliers and customers) at any and all hours of the day.

The next wave, we predict, will involve a more substantial change in thinking. Rather than just shorten the interval between loads, we must rethink the assumption that there are two distinct windows—batch and online—that are mutually exclusive divisions of the month, week, or day. We are now seeing the first warehouses being delivered that successfully overlap the concurrent addition of new data and the querying of existing data.

Note that this overlapping of functions does not necessarily imply an uncontrolled "trickle" of data arriving and becoming visible throughout the day. It is still important for users to be able to do consistent queries—that is, being able to do two queries against the same data and get the same results. There are many situations in which this is important, but a simple example is drilling from a summary down to the supporting detail. One naturally expects that the two should match!

Later in this chapter we'll explore ways of publishing data—adding new data to the warehouse without disrupting the simultaneous activities of users.

Using SQL*Loader

Oracle provides a general-purpose utility, SQL*Loader, for loading large amounts of data into an Oracle database. SQL*Loader is a very easy product to use, but it has dozens of options that can present a formidable puzzle to the first-time user. The best approach is not to attempt to memorize all the specifics of the utility—few users will ever use even half of the optional syntax—but to learn the basic concepts and functions and then tackle one data-loading task at a time. With a basic idea of what the product can do, it is fairly easy to use the examples provided in the *Server Utilities* manual to solve a specific problem (although it is necessary to do quite a bit of jumping back and forth within the six chapters devoted to SQL*Loader).

In this section, we discuss SQL*Loader's capabilities, its major options, and its few limitations. We provide several examples of using SQL*Loader in a data warehousing environment. We do not attempt to explore every option and keyword.

SQL*Loader Concepts

Whenever you find yourself with a file of data that needs to be entered into the Oracle data warehouse, your first thought should generally be to use SQL*Loader. With only a few exceptions (which we'll discuss at the end of this section), SQL*Loader is the proper tool for processing any file of data that needs to be loaded into the Oracle data warehouse.

SQL*Loader takes an input file of raw data and loads the data into one or more Oracle tables. A control file is used to tell SQL*Loader the format of the input data file and to map these fields to the proper Oracle columns. The control file also allows the user to define WHEN clause criteria that instruct SQL*Loader to bypass the loading of certain input records.

In addition to the data loaded into the database, SQL*Loader can create up to three output files. The *log file* records a summary of the activity performed by each invocation of SQL*Loader. The *bad file* is written whenever records are rejected by SQL*Loader because of errors in the input file or by the Oracle database because of errors that prevent the data from being inserted. This may include violations of the database's data type definitions or constraints defined on the table being loaded. Finally, the *discard file* is created only when requested via the control file. It then receives a copy of each record that SQL*Loader did not attempt to load because of WHEN conditions specified in the control file.

SQL*Loader has two modes of operation, conventional path and direct path, which we discuss more fully later in this chapter. In its conventional path, SQL*Loader issues SQL INSERT statements for loading the data. These INSERT statements can use the efficient array insert facility of Oracle. There is still significant overhead associated with performing SQL processing—Oracle processes each row through the SGA's buffer cache and performs all the constraint checking and index maintenance that would be performed on any INSERT. As we'll see, the faster direct path avoids most of this overhead but imposes some other limitations.

Invoking SQL*Loader

SQL*Loader is intended to be used as a noninteractive "batch" program, so it normally cannot be called from graphical user interface (GUI) front-end presentations. The Personal Oracle product line, intended for single-user operating systems such as Windows 9x, provides an icon for SQL*Loader and a simple graphical front end, but Oracle7, Oracle8, and Oracle8*i* server product lines do not. For the most part, these products are expected to be invoked through the operating system command-line prompt, thus ensuring that SQL*Loader can be readily used in the native batch scripting language.

Once you are at the operating system command-line prompt, finding out how to invoke SQL*Loader is easy. Simply entering

```
$ sqlldr
```

at the UNIX shell command-line prompt or

```
C:\ > sqlldr
```

at the Windows NT command prompt will cause basic help text to display, as follows:

```
SQL*Loader: Release 8.1.5.0.0 - Production on Mon Nov 22 13:25:07 1999

(c) Copyright 1999 Oracle Corporation.  All rights reserved.


Usage: SQLLOAD keyword=value [,keyword=value,...]

Valid Keywords:

    userid — ORACLE username/password
   control — Control file name
       log — Log file name
       bad — Bad file name
      data — Data file name
   discard — Discard file name
discardmax — Number of discards to allow          (Default all)
      skip — Number of logical records to skip    (Default 0)
      load — Number of logical records to load    (Default all)
    errors — Number of errors to allow            (Default 50)
      rows — Number of rows in conventional path bind array or between
direct path data saves
               (Default: Conventional path 64, Direct path all)
  bindsize — Size of conventional path bind array in bytes  (Default
65536)
    silent — Suppress messages during run
(header,feedback,errors,discards,partitions)
    direct — use direct path                      (Default FALSE)
   parfile — parameter file: name of file that contains parameter
specifications
  parallel — do parallel load                     (Default FALSE)
      file — File to allocate extents from
skip_unusable_indexes — disallow/allow unusable indexes or index
partitions  (Default FALSE)
skip_index_maintenance — do not maintain indexes, mark affected indexes
as unusable  (Default FALSE)
commit_discontinued — commit loaded rows when load is discontinued
(Default FALSE)
```

```
      readsize — Size of Read buffer                      (Default 65535)
```

```
PLEASE NOTE: Command-line parameters may be specified either by
position or by keywords.  An example of the former case is 'sqlload
scott/tiger foo'; an example of the latter is 'sqlload control=foo
userid=scott/tiger'.  One may specify parameters by position before
but not after parameters specified by keywords.  For example,
'sqlload scott/tiger control=foo logfile=log' is allowed, but
'sqlload scott/tiger control=foo log' is not, even though the
position of the parameter 'log' is correct.
```

The last paragraph of this display, starting with PLEASE NOTE, is helpful. In addition, it should be noted that all but the first two parameters, USERID and CONTROL, have default values and are therefore optional. The parameter PARFILE has no default, but if it is not specified it is simply not used.

And, of course, the entire topic of SQL*Loader is explained in very fine detail in the Oracle7 or Oracle8 *Server Utilities* guide, which is part of the standard Oracle documentation set. Starting with basic concepts, SQL*Loader is explained with numerous examples across five or six chapters.

Parameters to control SQL*Loader can be specified in three different ways. In the most basic form they are specified on the operating system command-line prompt, as follows:

```
$ sqlldr userid=scott/tiger control=test.ctl
```

One of the required parameters, shown in this example, is to name a control file. We discuss the control file in more depth in a few pages, but its purpose is to provide specifics about the layout of the input data and map the data to the database tables to be loaded. Other parameters, as a second option, are supplied within the control file, using the OPTIONS keyword.

Or, in the third case, they can be stored inside an optional SQL*Loader parameter file, which is then specified at the command-line prompt:

```
$ sqlldr parfile=test.par
```

Parameters specified in a parameter file are listed one per line:

```
userid=scott/tiger
control=/usr/local/dw/scripts/load/test.ctl
log=/usr/local/dw/logs/load/test.log
data=/stage1/test.dat
```

. . . and so on. Of course, it is possible to mix the use of parameters specified on the command line, the control file, and a parameter file. As an example:

```
$ sqlldr userid=scott/tiger parfile=/usr/local/dw/scripts/load/test.par
```

The salient question, however, must be "Why would you specify parameters one way or another?" For the most part, it is a matter of style, but there are some situations in which one method is clearly superior to the other. One clear case involves password security, which is compromised in UNIX systems when a password is specified at the command-line prompt. In this case, the command-line invocation shown just before this paragraph allows the userid and password to be seen by any other user on the system, thereby rendering the password of the Oracle account SCOTT public to the world. By embedding the userid parameter and its values in a parameter file and then setting the permissions for reading that file appropriately, the Oracle account password can be safeguarded. Many people tend to ignore basic security like this, but security risks are not defined simply as malicious teenagers with Internet access and too much time on their hands. Rather, security risks include all situations in which an unauthorized individual can see, change, or remove data, even accidentally. Allowing a critical DW administrative account password to be plucked off the UNIX command line is a very preventable example of this.

Having three ways of specifying input sounds as if it might be confusing, but there is method in this madness. The best approach is to use the multiple sources to maximize flexibility while minimizing duplication of effort. Use the parameter file to supply those things (like userid and password) that will apply to many different loads but that you'd like to be able to change in only one place when necessary. Use the control file to specify items that are tied to one particular type of load (e.g., the daily incremental load of the ACTIVITY table) and use the command line only for those parameters that change with each execution of the specific load type (for instance, the input data file name). Develop a standard for your warehouse and follow it for all loads. Always place the same parameter in the same location. You may always use the command line to override a parameter when necessary for a special case. This approach will prevent inevitable errors caused by editing files (and possibly forgetting to reedit after the one special execution).

Whether they are specified directly on the operating system command line or embedded in the control file or a parameter file, the various parameters may be briefly explained, as shown in Table 6.1.

Table 6.1 SQL*Loader Parameters

PARAMETER NAME	DEFAULT VALUE	DESCRIPTION	COMMENTS
USERID	Oracle account username, password, and optional SQL*Net connect string.		Required parameter
CONTROL	Name of the SQL*Loader control file.		Required parameter
PARFILE	Name of the SQL*Loader parameter file.		Not used if not specified
DATA	Name of the input file replaced with a file to be loaded into Oracle. Can be specified in the INFILE clause in the SQL*Loader control file. Specification here overrides specification in the control file.	If not specified in the control file, then the name of the control file is stripped of its file extension and replaced with a file extension of ".dat."	
LOG	Name of the output file to hold a log of all activities performed by SQL*Loader.	If not specified in the control file, then the name of the control file is stripped of its file extension and replaced with a file extension of ".dat."	
BAD	Name of the output file to hold all the input data records that were rejected because they violated either the SQL*Loader control file specification or some kind of database constraint.	If not specified in the control file, then the name of the control file is stripped of its file extension and replaced with a file extension of ".dat."	

PARAMETER NAME	DEFAULT VALUE	DESCRIPTION	COMMENTS
DISCARD	Name of the output file to hold all the input data records that were discarded because they did not satisfy the WHEN clause in the SQL*Loader control file.	If not specified in the control file, then the name of the control file is stripped of its file extension and replaced with a file extension of ".dat."	
DISCARDMAX	Number of discarded records to allow in the discard file.	All	
SKIP	Number of logical records from the input data file to skip over.	0	
LOAD	Number of logical records from the input data file to load.	All	
ERRORS	Number of logical records to allow to fail due to violations of either the SQL*Loader control file specification or a database constraint, before forcing the SQL*Loader to quit.	50	
DIRECT	Use "direct path" load mechanism, which bypasses Oracle's normal INSERT mechanism (a.k.a. "conventional path") in favor of performance but with possible reduced flexibility and functionality.	FALSE	
ROWS	Number of logical records in bind array, to be included in a single INSERT operation. A COMMIT is performed after each array INSERT.	64	Conventional path only

continues

Table 6.1 Continued

PARAMETER NAME	DESCRIPTION	DEFAULT VALUE	COMMENTS
ROWS	Number of rows between direct path data saves. Setting this to a finite integer value allows periodic saves, which can decrease the impact of failure during loading, at the cost of some performance overhead and restart complexity in the event of failure.	All	Direct path only
SILENT	Suppress messages during run (header, feedback, errors, discards, partitions). Header is the banner produced by SQL*Loader that shows versions. Feedback is the output shown after each commit or data save (see the ROWS parameter). Errors is the logging of all error messages in the log file (see the ERRORS, LOG, and BAD parameters). Discards is the logging of messages in the log file each time a record is discarded (see the DISCARD and DISCARDMAX parameters). Partitions is the logging of summary statistics for each partition to the log file. All covers all of the above keywords.	None (all forms of feedback are produced unless suppressed)	Partitions for Oracle8 only
BINDSIZE	Size of the bind array in bytes. If the ROWS parameter multiplied by the width (in bytes) of each logical record exceeds BINDSIZE, then the ROWS parameter will be reduced to fit.	65536	Conventional path only

PARAMETER NAME	DESCRIPTION	DEFAULT VALUE	COMMENTS
READSIZE	Size of the read buffer in bytes. Both BINDSIZE and READSIZE default to the same size. If BINDSIZE is specified smaller than READSIZE (or vice-versa), the smaller parameter value will be increased to match the larger.	65536	Conventional path only
PARALLEL	Setting to TRUE allows multiple direct path loads on the same table to be performed in parallel; normally only one direct path load can be performed on a table at a time. Please note that this parameter is not necessary when using conventional path because Oracle allows multiple concurrent INSERT statements as part of its base functionality.	FALSE	Direct path only
FILE	Internal Oracle data file in which to allocate extents. The data file must belong to the tablespace in which the table being loaded resides. The data file must be specified by its full name, as shown in the FILE_NAME column in the view DBA_DATA_FILES.	Oracle chooses where to allocate extents in the tablespace by default.	Direct path only
SKIP_UNUSABLE_INDEXES	If TRUE, allows SQL*Loader to load into tables that indexes in UNUSABLE state prior to the start of the load, without causing the SQL*Loader session to fail.	FALSE	Direct path only
SKIP_INDEX_MAINTENANCE	If TRUE, does not maintain indexes during the load, leaving them in UNUSABLE state when the load completes successfully.	FALSE	Direct path only

Altogether, SQL*Loader has two input files: the input data file and the SQL*Loader control file. The input data file contains the data to be loaded and can be a regular operating system file, a tape device, or a UNIX named pipe. The latter two choices are useful in the event the input data file is simply too large to reside in an operating system file; many operating systems have a limit of 2 gigabytes on file size. Also, being able to use either a tape drive or a named pipe saves time during loads, removing the need to "stage" the input data file onto disk before loading it into Oracle.

An example, in a UNIX environment, demonstrates the power of this technique:

```
mkfifo /pv19990901.dat
nohup zcat /pv19990901.Z | sed -f sep.sed >/pv19990901.dat &
```

This small shell script first creates a named pipe (also known as a fifo), then begins a background process to read a compressed file from disk and pass the uncompressed output through a preediting program (using the UNIX stream editor, sed) and then direct the output into the named pipe. Note that the named pipe doesn't exist as a separate file that would consume a large amount of disk space. As the SQL*Loader program consumes data from the named pipe, this background process will "replenish" the buffered data in the named pipe. As we will see in Chapter 9, "Data Warehouse Performance Tuning," this technique is much faster and consumes far less disk space than sequentially uncompressing the data into a file, editing that file, and then starting a load job.

It is even possible for this combination of reading, uncompressing, editing, and loading to run in less total time than just loading from a preprocessed, uncompressed file! This can occur on a machine that is I/O bound, and the data is highly compressed because of the smaller number of blocks to be read, coupled with the parallelism of using separate processes for reading and for loading.

The SQL*Loader Control File

The control file contains a description of what the input data file looks like, using SQL*Loader's own data definition language. This language is very similar to Oracle's internal data definition language, used for creating tables and specifying columns. The important thing to remember is that these are two separate data definition languages, despite their similarities. One very common mistake when using SQL*Loader is to specify a data type for a field in the SQL*Loader control file using a data type from the Oracle RDBMS, and vice versa.

The Oracle RDBMS has relatively few native data types: CHAR, VARCHAR2, NUMBER, RAW, DATE, etc. In Oracle7, there were LONGs and LONG RAWs, but in Oracle8 these were supplemented by character CLOBs and binary

BLOBs. Additional predefined data types that are valid in the RDBMS, such as INTEGER, are just variations on these basic data types.

SQL*Loader, however, has to be able to recognize far greater numbers of input data types, so its set of defined data types is larger and richer. Rather than provide you with a list of all these data types here, it is very much worth your while to consult the chapters on SQL*Loader in the Oracle8 *Server Utilities* guide when you confront an unfamiliar data format.

One important thing to remember that will help avoid confusion: Names of objects in the SQL*Loader control file refer to tables and columns in the database, while everything else in the control file refers to items in the input data file. The control file provides a mapping between the input data file and the database tables into which data is being loaded, nothing more. It provides a guide for SQL*Loader, enabling it to read appropriate data items from the input data file, interpret them correctly in order to translate them from the external format to Oracle's internal format, and then insert them into the correct table and column.

The basic format of a SQL*Loader control file is simple:

```
LOAD DATA
INTO TABLE table-name
(
    column-name          external-datatype,
    column-name          external-datatype,
    ...
)
```

Of course, a world of options are excluded from this basic description. In fact, optional keywords and phrases enable a multitude of functionality that can be inserted just about everywhere in this oversimplified example. But the important point is that even this basic example shows all the basic components for loading data into a database. The input data file has been specified either as a SQL*Loader command-line parameter or here in the control using the INFILE clause (not shown in the example). At least one database table to be loaded from the input data file has been identified with the INTO TABLE clause. In that table, one or more database columns have been identified, which have been mapped to input data file *fields*. Because SQL*Loader can access the Oracle data dictionary, it already knows what the internal Oracle data type of each database column is. The control file syntax that specifies the external data type provides most of the information needed to perform a translation, if one is necessary. If the input data file is in a character set or language different from that of the database, this too can be specified as an option.

Two important points that are missing from this brief example are record format and field format. SQL*Loader supports three basic record formats: stream, fixed-length, and variable-length. The default record format is stream, which is also the default text file format for UNIX systems. The stream record format implies a "stream" of characters separated by a record-separator, which is usually a line-feed character on UNIX systems. Thus, SQL*Loader is designed to load free-format text files from UNIX systems by default. Be aware, though, that the stream record format is best used only with text data. If you are loading any nontext (i.e., binary) information such as binary integers or packed-decimal data, it is not good to use this record format. The character chosen as a record-separator may randomly appear in the binary data field and thus cause SQL*Loader to confuse the binary information for the end of the current record of data.

For large-scale data loads from mainframe systems, the most common record format is fixed, where each record comprises a fixed number of bytes. This is, in fact, the most efficient record format to use for loading with SQL*Loader because the SQL*Loader process is freed from the chore of reading ahead for the next record-separator character. SQL*Loader can simply allocate a buffer large enough to hold one or more records and then read the data straight into that buffer for additional processing. If you are trying to optimize performance in SQL*Loader, use a fixed-length record format.

The last record format, variable-length, is the least often used. Variable-length record format implies that each record is preceded by a record-length field. The format of the record-length field can vary from operating system to operating system, consisting of anything from a two- or four-byte binary integer to a five-digit character text field. Consult the *Server Utilities* reference manuals for more detail.

Once the record format has been specified, you should now be aware of the field format. Luckily, for each record format a particular field format is commonly used. For stream record formats, it is common for fields to be delimited by a field-separator character, much as records are delimited by record-separator characters. Common field-separator characters include the comma (,) or pipe characters (|). Another common alternative is for fields to be enclosed by single quote (') or double-quote (") characters and optionally separated by commas. SQL*Loader has syntax to cover all these possibilities and more.

With a fixed-length record format, it would be quite odd to use anything other than fixed-length field formats. The most common way to specify fixed-field formats is to use the POSITION(p, n) syntax, where p is the byte offset within the record where the field starts, and n is the length of the field. Of course, delimited or variable-length fields are possible in fixed-length records, but this is not common.

With variable-length records, either variable-length fields or fixed-length fields are common. Generally, the reason the record is variable length has to do with one or more fields that are variable length, usually located toward the end of the record.

At any rate, these are only the simplest of many situations that can be handled by SQL*Loader. Once again, please be sure to at least browse the relevant chapters in the *Server Utilities* guide to decide whether SQL*Loader can effectively solve the issue of loading data into your data warehouse database.

One important note: When Oracle8 was initially released SQL*Loader didn't quite get all of the necessary capabilities for loading data into the new object-oriented constructs such as nested tables or user-defined columns. Luckily, these limitations are removed in Oracle8*i*. In SQL*Loader, you can now *nest* column specifications using the COLUMN OBJECT clause to reflect a complex object column such as a *varray* or *nested table*. For example:

```
LOAD DATA
INFILE 'dept.dat'
INTO TABLE dept
       (dno           POSITION(01:03) CHAR,
        dname         POSITION(05:15) CHAR,
        mgr           COLUMN OBJECT
           (name            POSITION(17:33) CHAR,
            age             POSITION(35:37) INTEGER EXTERNAL,
            empno           POSITION(40:46) INTEGER EXTERNAL)
           )
      )
```

The data might look something like this:

```
789 Business     Doris Mingione  32 1234
876 Physics      Milan Stolka    39 5678
```

If you must load into tables that include object-oriented features using Oracle8 release 8.0, you may want to use SQL*Loader to load into non-OO temporary tables. You may then finish the load using PL/SQL or possibly custom OCI programs (using a third-generation programming language such as C) to move the data from the non-OO temporary tables into the permanent OO tables.

Conventional Path SQL*Loader

As mentioned earlier, the two methods used by SQL*Loader for inserting data into the Oracle database are *conventional path* and *direct path*.

Conventional path means that SQL*Loader uses normal SQL INSERT statements. Based on the information provided in the control file, the SQL*Loader program uses OCI to construct INSERT statements dynamically. This mechanism has been in place since SQL*Loader was known as ODL (Oracle Data Loader), before version 6 of Oracle. Figure 6.5 illustrates the operation of SQL*Loader's conventional path.

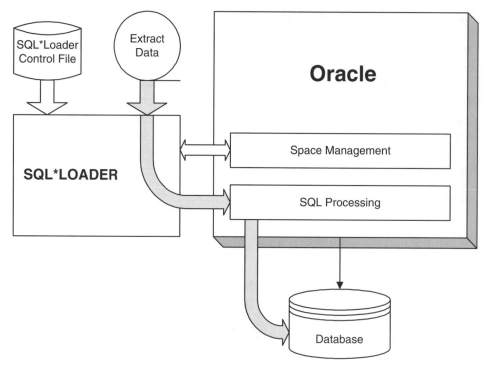

Figure 6.5 SQL*Loader conventional path.

The use of conventional path is the default in SQL*Loader. Because it uses SQL statements, conventional path provides the most flexibility and functionality. With SQL INSERT statements, indexes are maintained automatically, database triggers are fired appropriately, database constraints are enforced at the time of insert, and normal COMMIT/ROLLBACK mechanisms are used.

FAST LOADER IN ORACLE FOR MVS, VERSION 6

Actually, the predecessor to SQL*Loader direct path was introduced with Oracle for MVS during the version 6 product life cycle. Designed to provide competitive parity with the loading capabilities of IBM's DB2 database, the feature was originally dubbed "fast loader." The technology to perform direct disk writes was made part of the general SQL*Loader product on all ports, effective with the release of Oracle7.

Direct Path SQL*Loader

Starting with Oracle7, the *direct path* mechanism was introduced. This option, enabled by setting the parameter DIRECT to TRUE (from its default of FALSE), permits better performance by bypassing the entire SQL layer in Oracle. Instead of dynamically constructing and issuing SQL INSERT statements, the direct path mechanism formats database blocks entirely in the SQL*Loader process' private memory space, then writes these preformatted database blocks directly down to the datafiles within the Oracle tablespaces. Normal SQL INSERT statements merely access database blocks cached in the buffer cache in the System Global Area (SGA), and the writes of the blocks are performed by the database writer (DBWR) process. Figure 6.6 shows the ability of SQL*Loader direct path to bypass the Oracle kernel's SQL layer and write directly to the database files.

Obviously, it is much faster for SQL*Loader to perform all this work itself rather than possibly contend with other Oracle processes for access to the SGA while waiting for the DBWR process to wake up and do its job. The problem is, how does this "antisocial" behavior on the part of the direct path mechanism fit in with the highly social structure of normal SQL operations in Oracle?

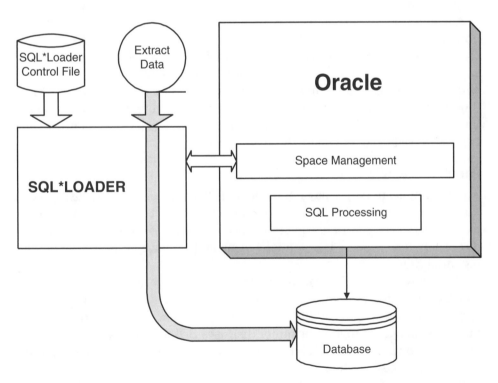

Figure 6.6 SQL*Loader direct path.

The answer is that direct path operations do not take place in the currently utilized space of a table or index. With direct path, space above the table's high-water mark is used. This is space that has already been allocated for use by the table but into which data has not yet been inserted by the normal SQL layer. Thus, space above the high-water mark is unused and can therefore be restricted for use by one process alone.

When the direct path load is finished, the high-water mark of the table is moved so the data loaded in direct path is now below the high-water mark and is now accessible by all users.

Triggers are disabled for all rows added via direct path. Integrity constraints are not validated until after completion of the load. SQL functions are unavailable to the load. Tables in clusters may not be loaded in direct path mode. No other transactions (INSERT, UPDATE, or DELETE) may be active in the table (or specified partition) during the load although queries may be executed on the existing table data.

If direct path loading to a single partition of an Oracle8 partitioned table, no global indexes on the table may exist and no referential integrity or check constraints may be enabled on the table. Also, all triggers on the table must be disabled.

As you can tell from the description, the direct path mechanism does place restrictions on concurrent access of the table. No other transactions may obtain locks to do DDL or DML operations. Constraints and database triggers will be disabled. Thus, only SELECT operations can proceed against the table while the load is running, but even SELECT statements may cause problems when the direct path load finishes and must rebuild the table's indexes. While direct path loads are occurring, a table should be considered pretty much unavailable. We see a little later in this chapter how to use Oracle8 partitioning features to reduce or eliminate these concerns.

Parallel Loading

Another implication that may not be obvious from the description just given is that only one direct path load can occur on a table at a time because of its exclusive locking. After all, each table has only one high-water mark, and one direct path load process is potentially using all the space currently above that high-water mark.

Starting with Oracle7, release 7.1, the PARALLEL parameter was added to SQL*Loader. This pertains only to direct path because conventional path SQL*Loader has always had the ability to perform "parallel loads" on the same table, just like any program or utility that uses SQL INSERT statements. This ability is shown in Figure 6.7, where multiple direct path SQL*Loader sessions are simultaneously writing to the database files.

If parallel direct path SQL*Loader is going to be used for a table, then all

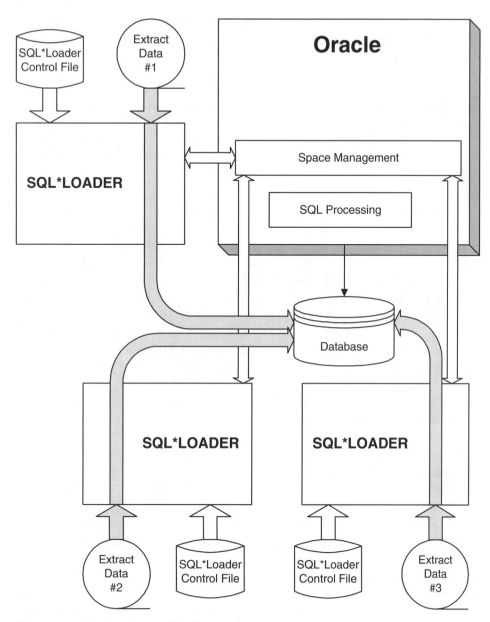

Figure 6.7   SQL*Loader parallel direct path.

SQL*Loader processes need to set the PARALLEL parameter to TRUE. Thus, instead of simply using currently allocated space above the high-water mark, parallel direct path processes actually allocate new, separate temporary segments in the same tablespace, and load data into the temporary segments.

Therefore, the space above the existing high-water mark is not touched, and multiple processes can work concurrently. When each parallel direct path process finishes its loading, it merges its temporary segment into the table being loaded.

> **NOTE** An index-organized table cannot be loaded in parallel direct path mode. Only the APPEND option for adding rows is valid; you may not specify REPLACE, TRUNCATE, or INSERT options. The SORTED INDEX option has no meaning. No indexes, either global or local, are automatically maintained by the load processes.

To minimize I/O contention, each parallel direct path load process should, ideally, be loading into a part of the table that is located on a separate disk. This requires that the table be striped across as many disks as there are concurrent direct path load jobs. This striping can be performed by creating multiple data files in the tablespace and then manually allocating extents in each file. Alternatively, the striping may be done "beneath the covers" at the hardware or logical volume management (LVM) software levels. If manual striping of the tablespace has been done (as would be appropriate in Oracle Parallel Server environments—see Chapter 11, "Warehousing with Oracle Parallel Server") then each parallel load control file should also specify the FILE parameter to determine where its data will be loaded.

Parallel direct path loads are ideal for loading data into a single partition of an Oracle8 partitioned table. This is facilitated by partitioning along the same keys that will be used to separate load jobs. Usually loads are performed based on time—each month or each week a new set of data needs to be loaded. This presents a strong recommendation for partitioning by time as well.

If partitioning is done by some other value, such as by ORGANIZATION, then performing a full table parallel load (each parallel job can load to more than one partition) requires that all partitions be located in the same tablespace in order to specify the FILE keyword. Generally, however, we will want to separate partitions into their own tablespaces. This complication can be avoided by partitioning the input data into separate load files that correspond with the table partitions. In this way, each partition can be loaded independently from the others, and you can use the FILE keyword to control exactly where the data will be placed.

For more information on the benefits and usage of parallel direct path SQL*Loader, see the appropriate section in Chapter 10, "Parallel Execution in the Oracle Data Warehouse."

Unrecoverable Option

Another nice feature important to data warehousing debuted in Oracle7, release 7.1—the UNRECOVERABLE option of SQL*Loader.

UNRECOVERABLE OPTION IN OLTP DATABASES

The unrecoverable option of SQL*Loader was actually included in the initial release of Oracle7. For some reason, however, it was not documented until release 7.1. Use of this option became critical at one client site in which several hundred gigabytes of data needed to be loaded into an early Oracle7 production database as part of the conversion from a legacy mainframe system. Without the unrecoverable option we found that our load processing filled 300 MB log files in about an hour. Unfortunately, the archiving process was taking about 80 minutes to copy each log. This quickly became a bottleneck to the loads. Starting multiple archiver processes helped, but the final solution was to get special permission to utilize the undocumented unrecoverable parameter, which completely eliminated the bottleneck and allowed the large loads to proceed unencumbered.

It was noticed quite early on that data warehouse data was not like data in operational databases. The data in data warehouses originates somewhere else and is copied to the data warehouse. Frequently, this happens in huge volumes. Oracle's redo logging mechanism faithfully copied all this data to the redo log files. In turn, this meant that the log writer (LGWR) process became very busy, as the huge volumes of data being loaded meant that sometimes LGWR was hard pressed to keep up. As you are aware, a database COMMIT does not complete until the LGWR process finishes writing redo information safely to the redo log files, so frequently a data warehouse would become bottlenecked on the redo logging subsystem.

This might not have been so terrible if the information being stored in the redo logs was important, but as we just mentioned, the data being loaded into a data warehouse is generally a *copy* of operational data that originated elsewhere. Therefore, saving this information in the redo logs is unnecessary. If something were to happen to the Oracle database, the data warehouse could be rebuilt relatively easily and reloaded; restoring from backups and recovering from the redo logs may not be the most expeditious way of recovering.

As a result, the UNRECOVERABLE option was first added to SQL*Loader circa 1994, and over the following years it was added to other features of Oracle, such as CREATE INDEX, CREATE TABLE AS SELECT, and parallel DML in Oracle8. Even though the Oracle7 keyword UNRECOVERABLE was generally changed to NOLOGGING in Oracle8, this updated syntax has not yet made it into SQL*Loader.

When the UNRECOVERABLE option is used, it does not mean that the table in question can never be recovered in the event of media failure (i.e., disk drive failure). Rather, it means that data loaded during the SQL*Loader session was not logged to the redo logs and therefore cannot be recovered from there. This option is available only with the direct path mechanism in Oracle7 and may still be specified in Oracle8 SQL*Loader, or it can be inherited from the NOLOG-GING table option in Oracle8.

The standard (and wise!) recommendation from Oracle Corporation is to perform a backup of the appropriate tablespace immediately after completing an UNRECOVERABLE load. This is to ensure that a restore operation is possible even if recovery using redo logs is not. The important point is that there is nothing wrong with the data loaded using UNRECOVERABLE, but that the normal methods of recovering data in the event of media failure have been disabled in the interest of speed. If media recovery is required for a tablespace with tables loaded UNRECOVERABLE before the tablespace is backed up, the tables in question will have to be truncated and fully reloaded.

Initial versus Periodic Loads

A very common mistake committed by many project teams is to forget the difference between an *initial load* and the *periodic loads* that will occur during the lifetime of the data warehouse.

Take, for example, the idea that SQL*Loader will be used to periodically (i.e., every day) load data from an operational source system into the data warehouse. Due to availability requirements, this load should not cause any interruptions in service.

Nonpartitioned Tables

Some of the choices here are straightforward. With smaller, nonpartitioned tables, SQL*Loader conventional path should be used for this type of load because conventional path uses "normal" SQL INSERT statements. Thus, if there are any triggers on the tables being loaded, they will fire. If there are any constraints on the table or its columns, they will be enforced. Indexes on the table will be maintained automatically and not be invalidated. The volume of data to be loaded is not excessive, so the periodic loads should be completed in an acceptable time. All in all, this is the kind of situation for which conventional path SQL*Loader may be ideally suited. These small loads, however, are not the primary performance issue facing the warehouse administrator.

When the data warehouse is initially loaded, the volume of information to be loaded is orders of magnitude greater. While this load is occurring, there are no availability requirements because there are no users on the system until the loads are completed. In this situation, the use of conventional path SQL*Loader would be a mistake, as the amount of overhead incurred by using INSERT statements, maintaining indexes, firing triggers, and checking constraints would result in what would probably be a prohibitively slow rate of loading. Obviously, the best idea here is to change the SQL*Loader parameter values from DIRECT=FALSE to DIRECT=TRUE, and possibly set PARALLEL=TRUE as well, and make use of the "direct path" insert mechanisms in SQL*Loader.

Now, using the exact same SQL*Loader control files and scripting routines developed for the periodic loads, the rate of loading should be sufficient to meet the higher volume demands of an initial load. In this way, by flipping a few switches (as a command-line parameter override), SQL*Loader can cover the needs both of high-volume initial loads and lower-volume, high-availability periodic loads.

What about the reverse situation? Should the high-performance "direct path" be used for periodic loads, so they are completed faster? Perhaps not. Remember that the direct path mechanism does not fire database triggers, does not maintain constraints during the load, and (in parallel mode) does not maintain indexes during the load. You must decide whether any of these features are needed and are more important than loading speed.

Additionally, because direct path SQL*Loader always writes its blocks above the table's current high-water mark, it can never reuse space that might have been available below the high-water mark. Managing the space consumption of a nonpartitioned table being periodically loaded in this way becomes more complex, especially when regular data archival or purges are being performed.

This is yet another valid illustration of a basic trade-off inherent throughout computing: speed versus flexibility. When you opt for speed, you typically give up something in terms of flexibility. When you choose maximum flexibility, you typically give up something in terms of speed.

Partitioned Tables

The use of Oracle8's partitioning features can allow us to get around these trade-offs by making each periodic load into an initial load! We see, later in this chapter, that the very large fact or detail tables that are common warehouse bottlenecks can exploit partitioning. We can use direct path loading of stand-alone tables that, after indexing and validating, can be quickly *exchanged* with an empty partition of our large fact table. We will use the term "PUBLISHING" to describe our combined use of these various features while minimizing the availability impact to our users.

Even if you elect not to take advantage of the exchange capability, it is possible to load into a specific partition. SQL*Loader syntax allows you to name the partition to be loaded and will reject any data rows that don't belong in that partition. Naming a specific partition for direct path SQL*Loader also provides another potential benefit in allowing DML operations and other direct path loads to other partitions of the table. While this may not be a frequent need within the warehouse, it does remove a restriction normally imposed by direct path SQL*Loader.

Loading to a specific partition is accomplished by using slightly extended syntax to the ordinary LOAD statement:

```
LOAD INTO TABLE table_name partition (partition_name) VALUES ...
```

Multiple Step Loads

In many cases it is not possible to simply load new data into a table or partition and then make it visible to warehouse users. In Chapter 4, "Designing the Oracle Data Warehouse," we discussed the transformation steps necessary for preparing data for the warehouse environment. We saw that some transformations are done during the extraction of data from its source. Other transformations might be performed during the movement from source to warehouse, and still others may have to be performed after the data is in the warehouse database.

A common example of this final option is in the processing of surrogate keys. If I'm loading data from a source system into a warehouse fact table that was designed using artificial keys that are unknown to the source system, they will have to be assigned as data is presented to the warehouse. The natural keys within the source data are used to look up the equivalent surrogate key being used in the warehouse. It is possible to handle them as part of a custom load program or even through database triggers, but both of these approaches generally prevent the highest load rates available through direct path SQL*Loader. Another alternative is to use direct path SQL*Loader to rapidly load the data into a temporary work area in the database. Then, as a second step, SQL (such as CREATE TABLE AS SELECT) or PL/SQL procedures can be executed in parallel to complete the transformation processing. Once the transformed data is completely inserted into its proper destination, the temporary work table can be dropped or truncated in preparation for the next load.

This is the primary transformation model used, for instance, by the Oracle Warehouse Builder product. It generates the work area tables and the direct path SQL*Loader control files to load them. It further generates the PL/SQL packaged procedures (including error handling and run-time audit entries) to perform the transformation requested by the warehouse designer.

Using Custom Load Programs

It is possible to write custom programs to handle the reconciliation and loading of data. There are only a few cases when this choice would be chosen instead of using SQL*Loader:

■ When data must be loaded into clusters. You cannot use the direct path mode of SQL*Loader. This is rarely an issue in data warehousing as clusters are not widely used or recommended.

■ When data being loaded must be processed using data already in the database or in some other source. SQL*Loader does not have the ability to do procedural logic involving looking at data outside of the individual input record being processed. An example would be to include decoded data in a row being inserted by looking up the value for the code supplied in the raw data. A similar decoding capability could be implemented using conventional path SQL*Loader and either database triggers or functions, but this approach is likely to have performance problems if large amounts of data must be processed. Another alternative used in many situations is to quickly load the raw data using direct path SQL*Loader into a temporary table and then post-process the data using custom-coded PL/SQL stored procedures. The post-processing step would perform whatever lookups and reformatting were needed and then insert the data into the proper permanent table or partition. Another possibility, if the transformations allow it, is to post-process the data using complex SQL subqueries, such as INSERT (SELECT).

■ When loading object data types prior to Oracle8*i*. Note that in the initial Oracle8 release, object data types are incompatible with SQL*Loader and several of the large database features, such as partitioning and parallel query, which are commonly required for data warehousing.

In short, there are relatively few cases when data warehousing teams have to write custom programs for loading their data. Whenever possible, attempt to take advantage of the bulk-loading speed provided by SQL*Loader's direct path mode. As a second choice, exploit the many parallel capabilities of Oracle, such as parallel CREATE TABLE . . . AS SELECT (and parallel INSERT and UPDATE in Oracle8). Only as a last resort, choose to write custom load programs.

Direct Load APIs

Since the introduction of the direct path option in Oracle7, only SQL*Loader has been able to exploit this streamlined way of adding large amounts of data to an Oracle database. In Oracle8*i*, however, the door has been opened for others to use the same direct path. The application programming interface calls necessary to use this capability have been made public and available for use. They are documented in the *Oracle Call Interface Programmer's Guide*. In theory, this would allow individual shops to include direct path load features in their custom load programs. It is more likely, however, that these API calls will be used by independent software vendors of ETT/ETL tools to directly load data from their tool into an Oracle database.

Using Oracle's Gateway Products

Oracle provides a series of gateway products that allow Oracle to access data maintained by a foreign database management system or file system. In Oracle8*i* these are now known under the new title of Heterogeneous Services that will, over time, include additional products beyond the gateways available today.

Some of these gateways allow for read-only access to the foreign data; others allow for read-write access and even the coordination of distributed transactions. Oracle also provides procedural gateway products that allow an Oracle PL/SQL call to invoke procedural logic on the remote site. Depending on the specific data source you wish to reach, you may find that an Oracle Transparent Gateway product exists that can make your remote data appear to the Oracle data warehouse just as if it were another Oracle database. For less common data sources, you may be able to "roll your own" using Oracle's Procedural Gateway Developer's Kit (PGDK). Figure 6.8 shows the relationship between the Oracle Open Gateway and the source system and the Oracle data warehouse.

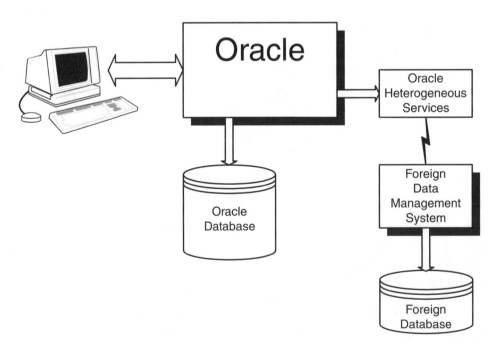

Figure 6.8 Oracle Open Gateway.

Most Oracle data warehouses are fed through the extract and load model we have discussed throughout this chapter. Occasionally, there may be a need to directly access data from a non-Oracle database. When relatively small amounts of data need to be retrieved from a remote site, issuing a SQL SELECT statement may be much simpler than performing extract, transfer, and load processes. Selecting data from a foreign source using a gateway should not be considered a replacement for extracting and loading when large amounts of data need to be transferred.

The other potential use for gateways is to develop a distributed data warehouse in which one or more sites are implemented using a DBMS other than Oracle. Distributed data warehouse architectures will be discussed in Chapter 12, "Distributing the Oracle Data Warehouse."

One final consideration about using gateways or operational Oracle databases requires mention. The ease with which remote queries can be constructed may tempt warehouse designers to provide "real-time" access to operational data. Just because it is possible to provide such access doesn't mean it is wise. Be wary of allowing the data warehouse to become a portal through which users attempt to perform operational processing and reporting. There are two negative consequences of allowing a "tunnel" from the warehouse into various operational systems. First is that data accessed in this manner will not have been subjected to the warehouse's thorough integration process and may lead to incorrect conclusions. Second, the performance of the operational system (and even of the warehouse) can be destroyed through uncontrolled ad hoc access in this manner.

Executing queries against the remote data should, in general, be limited to the administrators of the warehouse who will use the facility to load portions of the warehouse. The only exceptions should be to enable access to a different level of a distributed warehouse when it may be appropriate for users to issue queries directly or for administrators to perform modifications to data on the remote site.

Extracting Data from Oracle Sources

There are several alternative means for moving data from one Oracle database to another. This section discusses the following:

- The export/import of entire tables
- Using triggers to identify changed rows
- Using an unload/reload utility
- Using CREATE TABLE . . . AS SELECT
- Using the SQL*Plus COPY command
- Implementing advanced queuing

- Handling replication
- Working with transportable tablespaces

Each of these alternatives has relative merits and drawbacks that make it useful in different situations. In some cases, the best solution may be a combination of these techniques. For instance, if a subset of the rows in a large table needs to be identified and copied, you might choose to use triggers to time-stamp changed rows, use CREATE TABLE . . . AS SELECT in parallel to extract the selected rows to a local temporary table, then export that table for transport and import into the warehouse. The last option on the list, transportable tablespaces, is a new feature in Oracle8i but may eventually become the most widely used of all.

Using Export/Import Utilities

Oracle has provided special-purpose export (EXP) and import (IMP) utilities. Originally, these utilities were used for backup and recovery purposes. More recently, with the much larger databases and enhanced backup capabilities introduced in Oracle version 6, EXP/IMP have been used more for table reorganizations and for moving small amounts of data from machine to machine. One of the advantages of EXP/IMP is that it allows data to be exported from an Oracle database on one operating system and then imported to an Oracle database on a completely different operating system. It will, for instance, allow migration of data between a mainframe EBCDIC Oracle7 database and an ASCII Oracle8i database on a UNIX or Windows NT machine. Figure 6.9 illustrates the use of the EXP and IMP utilities to move data from one Oracle database to another.

NOTE The EXP and IMP utilities are documented in the *Server Utilities* manual.

EXP writes out a single file that contains the data definitions and data for all the data being exported. This file is commonly referred to as a "dump" file and is written with a default file extension of ".dmp." The dump file's format is not documented, is designed to be readable only by the IMP utility, and should not be processed by any user-written programs. The Oracle8 IMP utility is able to read an export file created by the Oracle7 version of EXP. This may be used to assist in copying a portion of an Oracle7 database while migrating to Oracle8, although the Oracle8 migration utility will generally be used if an entire database is to be converted.

Similarly, Oracle8i IMP can work with a dump file from an Oracle8 (or earlier) database. The reverse, however, is frequently not true. Exporting data from one release and then importing to an earlier release may not work. There are sometimes file format changes between releases and often there are new

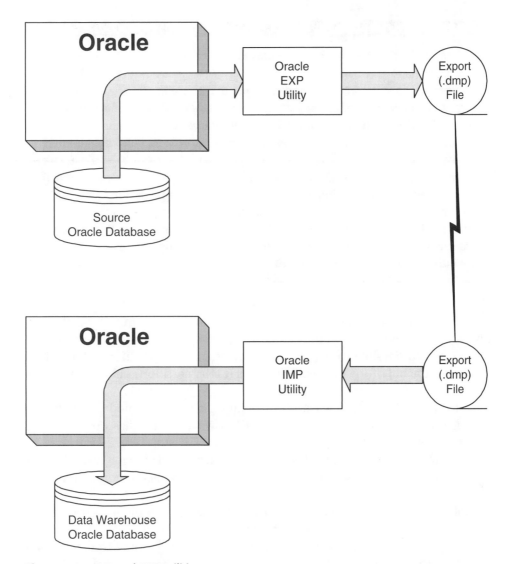

Figure 6.9   EXP and IMP utilities.

database object types included in the later release for which no capability exists in the earlier release's IMP utility. If you find yourself needing to move data to an earlier release with EXP/IMP, use the version of EXP from the earlier release to connect to the later release database.

LINKING AS SINGLE-TASK

EXP and IMP utilities and other programs are generally linked in "two-task" configuration for execution on UNIX platforms. This means that EXP or IMP run as a separate process and communicate with the Oracle kernel processes through an interprocess communication facility. This configuration is safer in that a client application is separated from the Oracle SGA and cannot accidentally corrupt these critical shared memory structures. This configuration does exact an additional cost for the extra communication. It is possible to link client programs "single-task," in which case they will include the Oracle kernel code and will be able to directly access the SGA. This configuration is not recommended for any user-developed programs but is frequently done with Oracle utilities such as EXP and IMP. IMP especially benefits from the speed-up associated with linking single-task. Instructions for linking utilities single-task are included within the operating-specific Oracle documentation.

EXP can back up data from a single table, a named series of tables, all of the objects in a schema, or all of the database objects in the entire database. In Oracle8, it is also possible to export single partitions of a partitioned table. IMP allows for the importing of specific objects (table, partition) out of a dump file created from an entire schema or database.

EXP was enhanced in release 7.3 to include a direct read mode. This greatly speeds the process of exporting data. IMP, however, still relies on doing SQL inserts to reload the data.

Because the individual table (or individual partition in Oracle8) is the lowest granularity of data access supported by EXP/IMP, it is uncommon to use these tools in data warehousing.

Full table copies between the operational database and the data warehouse are uncommon. Usually we need to reformat, rename, and filter data before it enters the data warehouse. Also, in most cases, we wish only to extract and load data that has been entered or modified during the period since the last refresh. EXP/IMP will transfer an entire table's contents.

Because of processing constraints on the operational Oracle database, it may not be feasible to perform complex selection and extraction processing on that database. We have seen one situation in which the administrator of a small OLTP database was willing to provide only a copy of an export dump file. In such a case, the warehouse administrator may have to use IMP to load a copy of the relevant tables into a temporary (nonpublic) area of the data warehouse and then perform necessary selection and reformatting processing in the warehouse.

It is possible to export from an Oracle7 database and then import into an Oracle8 warehouse. Moving data in the opposite direction is a bit tougher. This may not be much of an issue because most shops are more likely to use Oracle8 to build (or migrate) their data warehouse before operational systems. To import data into an Oracle7 database, it needs to be exported from an Oracle8 database using the Oracle7 version of EXP. If you have both Oracle7 and Oracle8 on the same server this will require only pointing to the Oracle8 database by specifying its SID when invoking the Oracle7 EXP utility.

NOTE If you are upgrading from Oracle7 to Oracle8, you may wish to retain a copy of the Oracle7 EXP executable before removing the original ORACLE_HOME directory tree. This will facilitate exporting data from the Oracle8 database should you ever need to IMP into Oracle7 on another server. Note that Oracle7 IMP will not be able to export new Oracle8 database objects such as partitioned tables or those with object data types.

If, however, you are running Oracle7 and Oracle8 on different servers, particularly with different operating systems, you will have an additional problem. Because the EXP executable from one operating system cannot be moved and executed on a different platform, it will be necessary to run EXP over the network. This is done by specifying the appropriate SQL*Net service name for the remote Oracle8 database when invoking EXP. Be advised, however, that performance of EXP over the network will be significantly slower than EXP run locally and linked single-task.

SPECIFYING SQL*NET OR NET8 SERVICE NAMES

How SQL*Net (Net8 with Oracle8) service names are specified varies by operating system and telecommunications protocol. In general, the name is provided by the user either through an operating system environment variable or as part of the command-line invocation of a specific program or tool. The provided name is translated into the necessary network routing and connection information through an entry in a local TNSNAMES.ORA file or through a lookup on a centralized Oracle Names Server. Additionally, Net8 provides new alternatives for using other naming services provided through network operating system facilities. To verify how to connect to a remote database, check your operating system-specific Oracle documentation or with the local administrator who has configured your Oracle network.

Uses for EXP/IMP in the Warehouse Environment

For performance reasons IMP is not the right tool for adding large amounts of data to a database. EXP/IMP may be of value in copying full summary tables from the warehouse to one or more data marts if the data volume is manageable.

Replication and transportable tablespaces (in Oracle8*i*) may prove both simpler and more efficient, however.

Invoking EXP

EXP can be run interactively by just invoking EXP from the command line. It will then prompt the user for values of the most commonly used parameters. Run in this manner, EXP will not give you the ability to change some of the less commonly used parameters, but for most types of export this is the easiest way to get started.

For example, if we need to copy data from an existing database:

```
$ exp

Export: Release 8.1.6.0.0 - Production on Sat  Jan 29 06:02:00 2000
Copyright (c) Oracle Corporation 1999.  All rights reserved.

Username: joebob
Password:                       <-- note that the password is not displayed

Connected to: Oracle8i Server Release 8.1.6.0.0 - Production Release
JServer Release 8.1.6.0.0 - Production

Enter array fetch buffer size: 4096 >   <-- default taken

Export file: expdat.dmp >    <-- full path-name of file to be exported

(1)E(ntire database), (2)U(sers), or (3)T(ables): (2)U >   <-- default
taken

Export grants (yes/no): yes >         <-- default taken

Export table data (yes/no): yes >        <-- default taken

Compress extents (yes/no): yes > no     <-- see COMMENTS below

Export done in US7ASCII character set

About to export specified users ...
User to be exported: (RETURN to quit) > joebob

About to export JOEBOB's objects ...
. exporting snapshots
. exporting snapshot logs
. exporting job queues
. exporting refresh groups and children
. exporting database links
. exporting sequence numbers
. exporting cluster definitions
. about to export JOEBOB's tables via Conventional Path ...
. . exporting table                GUN_COLLECTION      1,584 rows
exported
```

```
. . exporting table                  FAVORITE_BEERS           966 rows
exported
. . exporting table                   PICKUP_TRUCKS            23 rows
exported
. . exporting table                 SAT_NIGHT_DATES             0 rows
exported
. exporting synonyms
. exporting views
. exporting stored procedures
User to be exported: (RETURN to quit) >  <-- press RETURN to quit

. exporting referential integrity constraints
. exporting triggers
. exporting posttables actions
Export terminated successfully without warnings.
```

If you don't want to run EXP interactively this way, you can specify all these options from the operating system command line and possibly run EXP as a "batch" job. A complete reference on using the EXP utility is in the *Server Utilities* guide. To get online help on the command-line parameters available, enter the following:

```
$ exp help=y
```

from the UNIX shell command-line prompt. The method is the same on Windows NT platforms, but the executable name varies depending on which Oracle release you are running. EXP for Oracle7, release 7.3 was named *exp73.exe*. For Oracle8, the utility was named *exp80.exe*. Version-specific naming was done because of some limitations in the Windows NT environment that made it very difficult to create two Oracle Home directories to store multiple releases. Now, with the introduction of Oracle8*i*, we are back to a more consistent name of *exp.exe*.

Whichever version you invoke, you'll see something like the following display:

```
Export: Release 8.1.6.0.0 - Production on Tue Feb 22 19:53:08 2000
© Copyright 1999 Oracle Corporation. All rights reserved.
```

You can let export prompt you for the most common parameters by entering just the EXP command:

```
$ exp
```

Or, you can control how Export runs by entering the EXP command followed by various arguments. To specify parameters, you use keywords:

```
Format:  EXP KEYWORD=value or KEYWORD=(value1,value2,...,valueN)
Example: EXP SCOTT/TIGER GRANTS=Y TABLES=(EMP,DEPT,MGR)
```

The available parameters are as shown in Table 6.2.

Table 6.2 Parameters to the EXP Utility

PARAMETER NAME	DESCRIPTION	DEFAULT VALUE	COMMENTS
USERID	ORACLE account username and password.		Required
BUFFER	Size of the data buffer (in bytes) internal to the EXP process.	4096	
FILE	Name of the file to be written.	expdat.dmp	
COMPRESS	When exporting CREATE statements, should STORAGE parameters be recalculated to compress all allocated extents into one INITIAL extent?	Y	Choosing "N" for this option preserves the STORAGE parameters assigned to the segment at CREATE. Many DBAs prefer not to compress; see Chapter 8, "Administering and Monitoring the Oracle Data Warehouse," on administering and monitoring.
GRANTS	When exporting tables, should all GRANTS for those tables be exported as well?	Y	It is wise to accept the default, as GRANT statements typically do not take much room.
INDEXES	When exporting tables, should CREATE INDEX statements be exported as well?	Y	It is wise to accept the default, as CREATE INDEX statements do not take much room.
ROWS	When exporting tables, should the data in the tables be exported along with the table definitions?	Y	Sometimes you just want to export the table structure, instead of the table data.
CONSTRAINTS	When exporting tables, should table constraints (such as PRIMARY KEY and FOREIGN KEY) be exported as well?	Y	It is wise to accept the default, as ALTER TABLE statements do not take much room.
LOG	Log output from the EXP session to the specified file.		

PARAMETER NAME	DESCRIPTION	DEFAULT VALUE	COMMENTS
DIRECT	Use "direct path" EXP?	N	
FULL	Export the entire database?	N	Only available to privileged accounts (i.e., with EXP_FULL_DATABASE role).
OWNER	Export the indicated ORACLE accounts.		Unless this is the same account as specified in userid, this requires special privileges.
TABLES	Export the indicated tables and/or partitions.		Unless these tables are owned by the account specified by userid, this requires special privileges and each table must be specified as OWNER.TABLE. If exporting specific partitions of an Oracle8 partitioned table, use TABLE:PARTITION.
RECORDLENGTH	Length of I/O buffers used during writing.		
INCTYPE	When FULL=Y, INCTYPE=COMPLETE exports everything, INCTYPE=CUMULATIVE exports everything changed since the last COMPLETE or CUMULATIVE export, and INCTYPE = INCREMENTAL exports everything changed since the last COMPLETE, CUMULATIVE, or INCREMENTAL export.	COMPLETE	Requires EXP_FULL_DATABASE role.
RECORD	Track the incremental export.	Y	To use "N" would imply that the subsequent incremental exports would be unaware of this EXP session.
PARFILE	Retrieve EXP command-line parameters from the indicated file.		Can be used to safeguard the password for the userid by setting file permissions for the parameter file appropriately.

continues

Table 6.2 Continued

PARAMETER NAME	DESCRIPTION	DEFAULT VALUE	COMMENTS
CONSISTENT	All tables exported will be read-consistent to the exact same point in time.	N	Setting this parameter to "Y" causes EXP to issue the SET TRANSACTION READ ONLY command.
STATISTICS	Copies cost-based optimizer statistics to export file and also places ANALYZE commands to be executed by IMP. Values are COMPUTE, ESTIMATE, or NONE.	ESTIMATE	In environments where the Oracle cost-based optimizer is in use, it would be wise to accept the default or specify COMPUTE for smaller tables. There are many restrictions on the export of current cost-based statistics, so check the *Oracle8i Server Utilities* manual, Chapter 1, for more information.
TRANSPORT_ TABLESPACE	Are we exporting only data dictionary *metadata* related to the Oracle8i *transportable tablespace* feature?	N	Available starting with Oracle8i.
TABLESPACES	Comma-separated list of tablespace names to be transported.		TRANSPORT_TABLESPACE must be Y.
QUERY	Fragment of a WHERE clause of a SQL statement, applied against all tables in TABLES clause, used to restrict the rows exported.		

Using all these command-line options, the EXP session performed interactively previously could be performed in batch using the following:

```
$ exp userid=joebob/jimmyray compress=n owner=joebob
```

because defaults for all the other parameters are acceptable. As mentioned previously for SQL*Loader, it may be dangerous for security reasons to leave the password for the Oracle account JOEBOB on the UNIX command line like this because anybody running the UNIX utility *ps* could view it. Instead, using a parameter file as a standard method of operation would help here, as follows:

```
$ exp parfile=exp_profile.par owner=joebob
```

The contents of the parameter file *exp_profile.par* would look like this:

```
userid=joebob/jimmyray
compress=n
```

Then, read permissions can be set on this file so that only appropriate people can read it or edit it.

Direct Path EXP

Like SQL*Loader, EXP has both a *conventional path* and a *direct path* mechanism. The conventional path mechanism is implemented using normal SQL SELECT statements, generated dynamically using the Oracle Call Interface (OCI).

The much faster direct path mechanism bypasses SQL and reads directly from the data files in the Oracle tablespace. Because SQL statements are not generated to do this, the Shared SQL Area in the Shared Pool in the System Global Area (SGA) is not used. Also, the data queried for the export bypasses the shared buffer cache in the SGA. All in all, this can significantly reduce contention in a very busy system, making the direct path export much faster just by itself and, by reducing contention in the SGA, allowing the database instance overall to perform much faster.

Although using DIRECT=Y on EXP is essentially a transparent performance boost, not affecting the exported data in any way, there are (of course!) a few restrictions on direct path export. One is that direct path export is unable to translate from one character set to another.

Be sure to read the section on other dependencies for using direct path export in the Oracle7 or Oracle8 *Server Utilities* guides.

Invoking IMP

Just like EXP, the IMP utility can be run either interactively or entirely from the operating system command line. Once again, the relevant documentation in the standard Oracle documentation set is the Oracle7 or Oracle8 *Server Utilities* guide.

Running IMP interactively from the operating system command line and allowing it to prompt for parameter values would look something like this:

```
Import: Release 8.1.6.0.0 - Production on Tue Feb 22 21:55:58 2000
(c) Copyright 1999 Oracle Corporation.  All rights reserved.

Username: joebob
Password:

Connected to: Oracle8i Server Release 8.1.6.0.0 - Production Release
JServer Release 8.1.6.0.0 - Production

Import file: expdat.dmp >                               <-- default taken

Enter insert buffer size (minimum is 4096) 30720>      <-- default taken

Export file created by EXPORT:V07.03.03 via conventional path

List contents of import file only (yes/no): no >

Ignore create error due to object existence (yes/no): no >

Import grants (yes/no): yes >

Import table data (yes/no): yes >

Import entire export file (yes/no): no >
Username: joebob

Enter table names. Null list means all tables for user
Enter table name or . if done:                         <-- default taken

. importing JOEBOB's objects into JOEBOB
. . importing table                 GUN_COLLECTION        1,584 rows
imported
. . importing table                 FAVORITE_BEERS          966 rows
imported
. . importing table                 PICKUP_TRUCKS            23 rows
imported
. . importing table                 SAT_NIGHT_DATES           0 rows
imported
Import terminated successfully without warnings.
```

Just like the EXP utility, online help for the command-line parameters can be obtained by running

```
$ imp help=y
```

from the UNIX shell command-line prompt. Also just like EXP, on Windows NT the executable name depends on the Oracle release: For Oracle7, release 7.3, use *imp73.exe*, for Oracle8, you will use *imp80.exe*, and you'll use *imp.exe* for Oracle8*i*. In return, you'll receive a list of the available parameters that can be specified.

You can let import prompt you for parameters, as in the example at the start of this section, by entering the IMP command:

```
$ imp
```

Or, just like EXP, you can control how import runs by entering the IMP command followed by various arguments. To specify parameters, you use keywords:

```
Format:  IMP KEYWORD=value or KEYWORD=(value1,value2,...,valueN)
Example: IMP SCOTT/TIGER IGNORE=Y TABLES=(EMP,DEPT) FULL=N
```

The parameters for IMP are explained in Table 6.3.

From this list, it can be seen that the previous interactive IMP session can be run using the following command-line parameters:

```
$ imp userid=joebob/jimmyray fromuser=joebob
```

This occurs because all the other parameter value defaults were used. As mentioned previously, for SQL*Loader and for the EXP utility it may be dangerous for security reasons to specify the password for the Oracle account JOEBOB on the UNIX command line like this because anybody running the UNIX utility *ps* can view it. Instead, using a parameter file as a standard method of operation would help here, as follows:

```
$ imp parfile=imp_profile.par fromuser=joebob
```

The contents of the parameter file *imp_profile.par* would look like this:

```
userid=joebob/jimmyray
```

Then, read permissions can be set on this file so that only appropriate people can read it or edit it.

One important point should be made about importing and IMP. Database objects are imported in the exact same order as they were exported. In the case of the EXP and IMP of the Oracle account JOEBOB, the tables GUN_COLLECTION, BEERS, PICKUP_TRUCKS, and SAT_NIGHT_DATES were all imported in the same order as they were exported. This is fine if there are no referential integrity constraints between these tables, but just suppose that the table GUN_COLLECTION had a FOREIGN KEY to the table PICKUP_TRUCKS,

Table 6.3 Parameters to the IMP Utility

PARAMETER NAME	DESCRIPTION	DEFAULT VALUE	COMMENTS
USERID	ORACLE account username and password.		Required
BUFFER	Size of the data buffer (in bytes) internal to the IMP process.	30720	
FILE	Name of the file to be read from.	expdat.dmp	
SHOW	Just list the contents of the export file without writing anything to the database.	N	
IGNORE	Ignore any errors caused by the prior existence of objects when IMP tries to CREATE them?	Y	Set to "N" only if you are certain that the tables, indexes, sequences, and related PL/SQL objects do not already exist.
GRANTS	Should the GRANT statements exported and saved in the export file be imported?	Y	
INDEXES	Create indexes on import?	Y	Sometimes you just want to import the table structure and its data, without incurring the overhead of index maintenance.
ROWS	Import table data after tables are created?	Y	Sometimes you just want to import the table structure, instead of the table data.
FULL	Import the entire database from the FULL database export?	N	Only available to privileged accounts (i.e., with IMP_FULL_DATABASE role).
FROMUSER	List of ORACLE account names to which objects in the export file are going to be imported.		
TOUSER	List of ORACLE account names to be imported into.		

PARAMETER NAME	DESCRIPTION	DEFAULT VALUE	COMMENTS
TABLES	Import the indicated tables and/or partitions.		Unless these tables are owned by the account specified by userid, this requires special privileges and each table must be specified as OWNER.TABLE. If importing specific partitions of an Oracle8 partitioned table, use TABLE:PARTITION.
RECORDLENGTH	Length of I/O buffers used during reading.		
INCTYPE	When FULL=Y, INCTYPE=COMPLETE imports everything, INCTYPE=CUMULATIVE imports everything changed since the last COMPLETE or CUMULATIVE import, and INCTYPE = INCREMENTAL imports everything changed since the last COMPLETE, CUMULATIVE, or INCREMENTAL import.	COMPLETE	Requires IMP_FULL_DATABASE role.
COMMIT	Commit after each array INSERT?	N	COMMIT=N will perform a commit only after the entire import is completed.
PARFILE	Retrieve EXP command-line parameters from the indicated file.		Can be used to safeguard the password for the userid by setting file permissions for the parameter file appropriately.
LOG	Log output from the IMP session to the specified file.		
DESTROY	Recreate the data file in the tablespace?	N	Only with FULL database import.
INDEXFILE	Write DDL commands, such as CREATE TABLE and CREATE INDEX, to the specified file?		Ideal if you want to edit any DDL for the exported objects prior to importing.

continues

Table 6.3 Continued

PARAMETER NAME	DESCRIPTION	DEFAULT VALUE	COMMENTS
CHARSET	Specifies the National Language Support (NLS) character set used during the export of the export data file. IMP will automatically translate from that character set to the one used by the database.		
TRANSPORT_TABLESPACE	Are we importing only data dictionary *metadata* related to the Oracle8*i* *transportable tablespace* feature?	N	Available starting with Oracle8*i*.
TABLESPACES	Comma-separated list of tablespace names being transported.		TRANSPORT_TABLESPACE must be Y.
TTS_OWNERS	Comma-separated list of owners of segments in set of tablespaces being imported.		TRANSPORT_TABLESPACE must be Y.
TOID_NOVALIDATE	List of TYPEs to exclude from *type ID* validation checks.		
SKIP_UNUSABLE_INDEXES	Should indexes previously marked UNUSABLE be automatically maintained by this IMP session?	N	Available starting with Oracle8.
ANALYZE	Should an ANALYZE to generate cost statistics be run during import of the exported data, provided that the EXP parameter STATISTICS was set to either COMPUTE or ESTIMATE during the export?	N	See the explanation for the STATISTICS options for the EXP utility.
RECALCULATE_STATISTICS	Should IMP run ANALYZE to generate statistics, or should IMP simply use the precalculated statistics exported by EXP?	N	See the explanation for the STATISTICS option for the EXP utility.

implying that each pickup truck can have zero, one, or more guns stored in it. If this were the case, a straight import like those illustrated would fail.

Instead, it may be necessary to structure the running of IMP to accommodate these relationships. For example, it would work better if all tables that do not have any FOREIGN KEYS were imported first:

```
$ imp parfile=imp_profile.par fromuser=joebob \
                    tables=beers,pickup_trucks,sat_night_dates
```

Then, once that first import is complete, a *second pass* from the same export file can be run as follows:

```
$ imp parfile=imp_profile.par fromuser=joebob tables=gun_collection
```

Obviously, this kind of thing can grow quite complicated. You may find it useful to use the Oracle data dictionary view DBA_DEPENDENCIES to help find each layer of tables in a referential integrity hierarchy, if this has not been otherwise documented already.

Using Database Triggers in Operational Systems

At minimum, EXP copies all data from a table (or Oracle8 partition). In most cases, our real need is to copy only the data that has been entered or changed since the last copy. This requires some means of identifying the modified rows. This is an issue for all source systems, not just Oracle-based ones. In some cases, this identification will require keeping a copy of the database or files at each extract cycle and comparing data between the current copy and the previous one. For sequential files this "file rubbing" works well. For large databases, however, this may be expensive in terms of disk space and processing time. If only a small percentage of the rows have been touched, it is inefficient to have to examine every row and compare it to the previous database copy.

Another means of capturing data from an Oracle operational system is to use database triggers either to flag data rows that have changed or to copy the changed data into a temporary table for later movement to the warehouse. An Oracle database trigger is procedural logic, coded using Oracle's PL/SQL language, which is attached to a particular table. The trigger defines additional processing that should be performed each time a row in the table is acted on by SQL data manipulation language (DML) commands such as INSERT, UPDATE, or DELETE.

Triggers and Time-Stamp Columns

Some Oracle applications have already been written to use a trigger to flag each row with a time when it was last modified. If this is the case, it may be possible to build your extraction based on these time stamps. The extract SELECT statement for each table in the operational system would include a WHERE clause condition similar to the following:

```
SELECT *
  FROM EMPLOYEES
 WHERE DEPARTMENT= 'CONSULTING'
   AND LAST_CHANGED >= '1-NOV-99'
   AND LAST_CHANGED < '1-DEC-99';
```

TIP   **By default, all Oracle DATE columns include both a date and time portion. Unless the trigger maintaining the LAST_CHANGED column were specifically coded to store only the date, the time of day would be stored in the LAST_CHANGED data as a fractional portion of a day. Coding the conditions as shown will retrieve all transactions time-stamped starting just after midnight on the morning of November 1 and up through midnight on the evening of November 30.**

This example would let us retrieve the current information about any consultants who were hired, promoted, reassigned, and the like during the month of November. This data can then be added to the warehouse. (Of course, in this example it might be more appropriate to select data based on a transaction effective date, which is stored as part of the CONSULTANTS' data as opposed to the transaction's processing date. This is one of several design issues that must be evaluated by the warehouse analyst in determining extract strategies.)

Other Oracle applications (or other tables within the same application) may not already have time-stamp columns that are being maintained. It may be necessary to add such triggers in order to assist the regular extract process in finding the appropriate data. This will likely be a touchy point of negotiation between the warehouse team and the application maintenance teams. Such a change will require adding a column to the tables of interest that will affect storage requirements, and it will involve creating a simple trigger to those tables. The logic for each table's trigger can be identical and similar to the following:

```
CREATE OR REPLACE TRIGGER TIMESTAMP_TABLE_X
      BEFORE INSERT OR UPDATE OR DELETE
    ON TABLE_X
   FOR EACH ROW
BEGIN
    if inserting or updating then
        :new.last_update := SYSDATE;
    else if deleting then
        INSERT INTO TABLE_X_HISTORY (<column-list>,÷, LAST_UPDATE)
```

```
         VALUES (<column-list-values>, ÷, SYSDATE);
    end if;
END;
```

TIP Making such changes to a production OLTP application is not likely to be enthusiastically embraced by the team responsible for ensuring the performance of that application. This is another reason for a close cooperative involvement between the warehouse team and the application maintenance teams! Generally, the only way to invoke that cooperation is to have an executive sponsor from the user organization responsible for both the online application and the decision-support function. He or she can help reinforce the shared commitment to successfully implementing the warehouse as a supplement to the traditional application functions.

The extra processing load required by such a trigger is minor for each row (except when deleting!), but it may be significant when considered in terms of the total load of many rows being inserted or updated by the application. The processing load may be further increased if it is determined that an index is required on the column to efficiently locate the rows. Such an index will have to be updated every time a row in the table is inserted, updated, or deleted.

LOCATING A SMALL SUBSET OF ROWS IN A TABLE

An Oracle B*Tree index stores only nonnull values. Before the introduction of the Parallel Query Option in release 7.1, we frequently used this characteristic to our advantage when we needed an index to locate a small subset of rows from a larger table. Rather than keep a LAST_CHANGED value in every row, we would reset the column value to null in every row once it was extracted. Then the only rows included in the index at the time of the next extract were those that had been touched during the period between extracts. The index remained smaller and was more easily rebuilt.

As another approach, because of the speed-up provided by parallel query, it may be possible to eliminate the index entirely. Testing will determine whether the performance of the parallel full table scan is acceptable. If so, then there may be no need to maintain the index. Each extract reads the entire table in parallel to find the rows changed during our period of interest.

There is an additional issue with respect to using triggers to update a time-stamp column within application tables. This technique works well for identifying rows that are inserted or updated, but it fails to capture information about delete rows because the DELETE command also deletes our time-stamp column! Whether deleted rows need to be recorded in the data warehouse is a very specific design issue. For example, our warehouse might need to receive information about each order when it is taken, modified, shipped, and so on. There may be no value, however, in recording the fact that a completed order was purged from the operational system at some later point. The purge is not a business transaction of interest to us; it is an administrative transaction used to keep the online operational database to a manageable size.

In other cases, however, the delete may be part of a business transaction that is needed in the warehouse. If so, we'll need to use a different recording technique for these two different situations.

Triggers and Change Log

Rather than having our database trigger perform an update of a time-stamp column within the modified row, we can have the trigger insert a row into another table that we will create just for this purpose. That table becomes a log of changes made to our application's base table. This is the basic underlying concept used by the Oracle materialized view and replication facility. A simple example of a change log table based on primary key values might be designed as follows:

```
CREATE TABLE CONSULTANTS_CHANGES
     (EMPLOYEE_ID       NUMBER(7),
     LAST_CHANGED       DATE,
     CHANGE_TYPE        CHAR(1)
         CONSTRAINT CONS_CHANGE_TYPE_CK CHECK CHANGE_TYPE IN
('I','U','D'),
     CONSTRAINT CONS_CHANGE_PK PRIMARY KEY (EMPLOYEE_ID, LAST_CHANGED);
```

An example PL/SQL trigger to populate this change log might look like this:

```
CREATE OR REPLACE TRIGGER LOG_CONSULTANT_CHANGES
      BEFORE INSERT OR UPDATE OR DELETE
    ON CONSULTANT
   FOR EACH ROW
DECLARE
   v_change_type    VARCHAR2(1);
BEGIN
   --
   IF INSERTING THEN
        v_change_type := 'I';
   ELSIF UPDATING THEN
        v_change_type := 'U';
   ELSE
        v_change_type := 'D';
   END IF;
   --
```

```
    INSERT
      INTO consultant_changes (employee_id, last_changed, change_type)
    VALUES (:old.employee_id, SYSDATE, v_change_type);
      --
END;
```

Several variations on this approach may be considered. In the example just given we used the primary key of the base table (EMPLOYEE_ID) to track which row was modified. Some DBAs or programmers may suggest we use the ROWID of the base table row as the identifier of the source row. This is tempting because finding a specific row during the extract process will be faster using the ROWID than an index lookup based on the primary key. This minor performance benefit should be avoided, however, for several reasons:

■ Although ROWIDs do not change as long as a row exists in the database, they do get modified if the DBA does a table export/import to reorganize the table. Should this happen, the originally recorded ROWID will be useless.

■ Using ROWIDs raises the same problem with DELETEs that we saw using time-stamp columns—the ROWID will no longer point to a row after the row is deleted. (It may well even point to a new row that may have been inserted into the same block after the delete was completed!)

■ In the data warehouse, we will store data based on real-world primary key values, not on the Oracle physical storage convenience of ROWID. We should make our connections to the source data based on the same real-world key.

■ The ROWID format changes between Oracle7 and Oracle8. Building your extract process on an Oracle7 ROWID will present additional difficulties for the applications team when they someday need to migrate the source database to Oracle8. Of course, there is also the possibility that the ROWID format will change again in some future release of the Oracle RDBMS.

Another option in using a change log table is to copy additional source data into the change log in order to avoid having to look it up at extract time. This approach has the disadvantage of requiring additional storage in the change log table. It has, however, several advantages to recommend it:

■ If a row changes more than once during the period between extracts, we will be able to capture each of those successive changes in the warehouse. In our example, it may well be important for us to know that a particular consultant was promoted on the fourth of the month and then transferred to a new organization on the twenty-seventh of the month. For time reports entered for days between the fourth and the twenty-seventh, we would want to properly summarize his activity into the proper organization and job title. Recording only a primary key "pointer" to the row would provide us with only the final image when we try to capture the change made on the fourth.

- Having all the necessary warehouse data stored in the change log makes our extract process more efficient because we don't have to individually look up the original source rows. We can obtain all our data through a simple table scan of a relatively small table. In either case, we may have to make a second scan of the table to purge the rows that have been extracted.

- Data from deleted rows can be retained. In some uncommon situations, the warehouse may need the data after the DELETE even though it might not have been captured when inserted. This might occur when the operational inventory system's transaction removes a stock record rather than setting the quantity on hand to zero when inventory is depleted.

- Once we've found a way to identify which rows need to be extracted, we need to copy them to our data warehouse. We can do that in a variety of ways. We examine three methods, all of which allow the specification of a qualified query to retrieve specific rows from the source database and transfer them to the data warehouse for loading.

Unload and Reload

The import utility is notoriously slow in loading large volumes of data. IMP cannot be automatically parallelized and uses standard INSERT SQL processing. As we discussed earlier, the direct path mode of SQL*Loader processes large volumes of data much more efficiently by bypassing most of the work involved in SQL processing. In some cases, you may wish to move a large amount of data from one Oracle database to an Oracle data warehouse and may find that IMP is too slow for the volumes involved. Import also processes entire tables rather than a selected subset of rows.

We can use another variation on the SQL-to-generate-SQL technique to generate a SQL*Plus script that will extract data from an Oracle database, using parallel query processing when appropriate, and then generate a SQL*Loader control file to load the extracted data into the warehouse. Figure 6.10 illustrates this using a script to generate and execute the unload and reload tasks.

The generated unload script will probably run more slowly than EXPORT (especially direct path EXPORT) even when run with parallel query. The direct path SQL*Loader portion will, however, run in a fraction of the time required to IMPORT the same amount of data. Performance is related to the length of the records written to the intermediate file. A table with many columns defined with very long VARCHAR or VARCHAR2 specifications but that actually con-

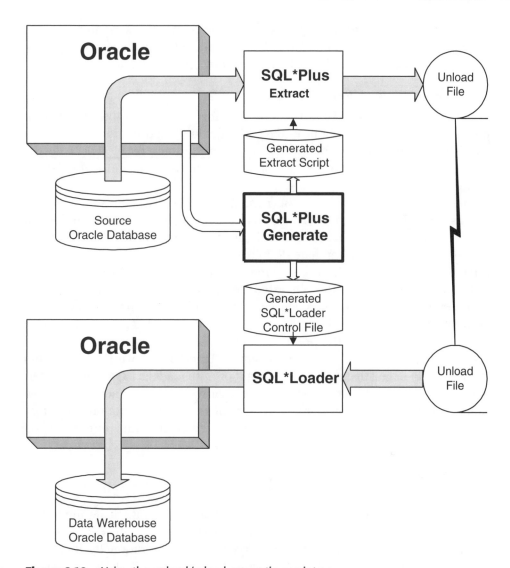

Figure 6.10 Using the unload/reload generation script.

tain relatively little data will involve writing out lots of spaces in this fixed format file.

Similar wasted bytes (and decreased performance) arise from NUMBER columns specified without precision and scale. In an ideal Oracle world, tables would not be defined with unspecified NUMBER columns, but there are certainly Oracle systems around that do not constrain the size of numbers. Oracle stores up to 38 digits of precision in such columns. To avoid writing out all such columns' data using 38 bytes, the script prompts the user for different default lengths to use for unspecified precision and scale. When responding to these prompts, the user needs to know the data well enough to avoid artificially trimming the precision of actual data being extracted in any column.

Executing the Unload/Reload Script

When you execute this script, it will prompt for the name of the schema that contains the table and the name of the table (or view). In order to deal with any NUMBER columns that might have been defined without precision or scale, the script will prompt you for a default value to use for precision and scale of these fields in the unload file.

The generated SQL*Loader script (named unload2.sql) assumes that fields of blanks should be loaded as NULLS—if the table has columns for which SPACES are valid values, then it will be necessary to edit the generated unload2.sql script to concatenate double quotation marks before and after the affected column(s) as well as change the length (linesize in unload2.sql and the individual field's length in the generated .ctl file) by 2 bytes.

If a numeric column is encountered that has no defined precision or scale, then this script will use default values (prompted for). This poses three risks: (1) you may overspecify the precision and thereby waste space in the unload file; (2) you may underspecify the precision and thereby get overflow indicators in the unloaded data that may not be caught prior to loading; (3) you may underspecify the scale and introduce truncation that will not be found by either the unload or load processes. For this reason, it is strongly recommended that numeric table columns be defined in the source database with appropriate precision and scale values.

Advantages of the Unload/Reload Script

This unload/reload utility has some other advantages besides speed. The unload can easily select a subset of the original table (for statistical sampling or retrieving rows for a particular department or range of business dates), whereas EXP/IMP deal with entire tables or partitions. Additionally, if desired, the unload script can be easily enhanced with an ORDER BY clause to sort the output in order to speed index builds and/or increase buffer cache hits on the reloaded data based on loading frequently used rows contiguously.

Finally, the generated unload script might have a GROUP BY appended to the SELECT statement that would facilitate initial loading of summary tables. In the project accounting case study used in this book, each week actual timecards are entered with data keyed down to the day, but we load data into the data warehouse based on a calendar month. At some point (during the extract, during the load, or in a summarization step after the initial load), this data will have to be summarized. The following script could be used to perform that level of summarization while unloading the data from the Oracle-based project accounting system.

One big advantage of using this utility is that it can also unload data from a view, which is not possible using EXP. By unloading data as defined in a view, this facility may be used to do subsets—selection (specific rows), projection (specific columns), joins, GROUP BY summaries—or to apply functions (either Oracle built-in or user-defined) during the selection without having to edit this script or its generated output scripts, other than possibly changing the name of the table in the SQL*Loader control file.

Finally, by manually editing the generated unload2.sql and SQL*Loader control files, it is possible to remove columns or modify them with SQL or PL/SQL functions during the extract. In general, however, you should avoid manually editing the files by using the capability of unloading from a view.

Limitations of the Unload/Reload Script

This script is not a complete replacement for the Oracle EXP and IMP utilities or for replication. In addition to being slower on the unload step than EXP, it has other limitations. This script moves data from only one table or view at a time. EXP/IMP can export database objects other than tables (such as indexes, synonyms, views, users, and roles). Use this tool only to help move data from an Oracle source system to the data warehouse.

It doesn't handle LONG, RAW, LONG RAW, ROWID, MLSLABEL, or any of the new Oracle8 object data types. These data types are not widely used in data warehousing but may be part of the source system from which you unload data. If the data you need to move includes "exotic" data types, EXP/IMP, or the SQL*Plus, the COPY command may provide a better solution.

This unload/reload script will not automatically make translations when the unload file is moved between Oracle databases running on machines with different data encoding schemes, such as ASCII and EBCDIC. Only a relatively small number of shops run Oracle in MVS or VM, so moving to or from EBCDIC is not a large concern. Other translations may be necessary for organizations with operations in multiple countries where various machine-encoding schemes are commonly used. Because all data is written in external formats, one should expect that file transfer utilities that do such conversions should work. SQL*Loader allows for specification of the data encoding used in the input file so, as an alternative, one could edit the SQL*Loader control file to specify the alternative encoding scheme.

The Unload/Reload Script

```
set tab off heading off heading off feedback off echo off verify off
set space 1 pagesize 0 linesize 120
ACCEPT owner            PROMPT 'What schema owns the table to be unloaded? '
ACCEPT table_name       PROMPT 'What table is to be unloaded? '
ACCEPT default_precision PROMPT -
    'How many TOTAL digits for numbers without defined precision? '
```

```
ACCEPT default_scale PROMPT -
    'How many DECIMAL digits for numbers without defined scale? '
--------------------------------------------------
--  Generate the unload script
--------------------------------------------------
SPOOL unload_fixed2.sql
Select 'SET HEADING OFF FEEDBACK OFF ECHO OFF VERIFY OFF SPACE 0 '
            || 'PAGESIZE 0 TERMOUT OFF'
  FROM dual
/

--  Calculate the sum of all output field lengths and set the output
record size
SELECT 'SET LINESIZE '
        || (SUM(DECODE(data_type,
                        'CHAR',data_length,
                        'VARCHAR',data_length,
                        'VARCHAR2',data_length,
                        'DATE',14,
                        'NUMBER',DECODE(data_precision,
                                        '',&default_precision+2,
                                        GREATEST(data_precision-
data_scale,1)

+DECODE(data_scale,0,0,1)+data_scale)+1,
                        'FLOAT',&default_precision+2,
                        data_length)))
  FROM dba_tab_columns
 WHERE owner=UPPER('&&owner')
   AND table_name=UPPER('&&table_name')
/
--  Generate a SQL*Plus COLUMN command to control formatting of each
output field
SELECT 'COLUMN ' || rpad('"'||column_name||'"',32)
        || ' FORMAT '
        || RPAD(DECODE(data_type,
                    'CHAR','A'||data_length,
                    'VARCHAR2','A'||data_length,
                    'VARCHAR','A'||data_length,
                    'DATE','A14',
                    'NUMBER',DECODE(data_precision,'',
                                RPAD('0',&default_precision-
&default_scale,'9')

||'.'||RPAD('9',&default_scale,'9'),
RPAD('0',GREATEST(data_precision-data_scale,1),'9')
                                        || DECODE(data_scale,0,'','.')
                                        ||
DECODE(data_scale,0,'',RPAD('9',data_scale,'9'))),
                    'FLOAT',RPAD('0',&default_precision-
```

```
&default_scale,'9')
            ||'.'||RPAD('9',&default_scale,'9'),
                    'ERROR'),40)
        || ' HEADING ''X'''
  FROM dba_tab_columns
 WHERE owner=UPPER('&&owner')
   AND table_name=UPPER('&&table_name')
 ORDER BY column_id
/


--  Generate the actual SELECT statement to unload table data
SELECT 'SPOOL /tmp/&&owner..&&table_name..DAT'
  FROM dual
/
COLUMN var1 NOPRINT
COLUMN var2 NOPRINT
SELECT 'a' var1, 0 var2, 'SELECT '
  FROM dual
UNION
SELECT 'b', column_id, DECODE(column_id, 1, '      ', ' , ')
                    || DECODE(data_type,'DATE',
'TO_CHAR('||''''||column_name||''''
        ||',''YYYYMMDDHH24MISS'') '
        ||''''||column_name||''''',
                          '''''||column_name||''''')
  FROM dba_tab_columns
 WHERE owner=UPPER('&&owner')
   AND table_name=upper('&&table_name')
UNION
SELECT 'c', 0, 'FROM &&owner..&&table_name'
  FROM dual
UNION
SELECT 'd', 0, ';'
  FROM dual
 ORDER BY 1,2
/
SELECT 'SPOOL OFF'
  FROM dual
/
SELECT 'SET TERMOUT ON'
  FROM dual
/
SPOOL OFF
---------------------------------------------------------------------
--  Generate the SQL*Loader control file
---------------------------------------------------------------------
SET LINES 120 PAGES 0
SPOOL &&owner..&&table_name..CTL
SELECT 'a' var1, 0 var2, 'OPTIONS(DIRECT=TRUE)'
  FROM dual
```

```
UNION
SELECT 'b', 0, 'LOAD DATA'
  FROM dual
UNION
SELECT 'c', 0, 'INFILE  ''/tmp/&&owner..&&table_name..DAT'''
  FROM dual
UNION
SELECT 'd', 0, 'BADFILE  &&owner..&&table_name..BAD'
  FROM dual
UNION
SELECT 'e', 0, 'DISCARDFILE  &&owner..&&table_name..DSC'
  FROM dual
UNION
SELECT 'f', 0, 'DISCARDMAX 999'
  FROM dual
UNION
SELECT 'm', 0, 'INTO TABLE &&owner..&&table_name'
  FROM dual
UNION
SELECT 'n', column_id,
           RPAD(DECODE(column_id,1,'(',',')||'"'||column_name||'"',31)
              || DECODE(data_type,
                      'CHAR','CHAR('||data_length||')',
                      'VARCHAR','CHAR('||data_length||')',
                      'VARCHAR2','CHAR('||data_length||')',
                      'DATE','DATE(14) "YYYYMMDDHH24MISS"',
                      'NUMBER','DECIMAL EXTERNAL('||
                             DECODE(data_precision,
                      '',&default_precision+2,
                      GREATEST(data_precision-data_scale,1)

+DECODE(data_scale,0,0,1)+data_scale+1)||')',
                      'FLOAT','DECIMAL EXTERNAL('||
TO_CHAR(&default_precision+2)||')',
                      'ERROR-'||data_type)|| ' NULLIF ("' ||
                             column_name||'" = BLANKS)'
  FROM dba_tab_columns
 WHERE owner = upper('&&owner')
   AND table_name = UPPER('&&table_name')
UNION
SELECT 'z', 0, ')'
  FROM dual
 ORDER by 1, 2
/
SPOOL OFF
-------------------------------------------------------------------
-- Cleanup
-------------------------------------------------------------------
```

```
CLEAR COLUMN
CLEAR BREAK
CLEAR COMPUTE
UNDEF owner
UNDEF table_name
UNDEF default_precision
UNDEF default_scale
```

Incidentally, this same script can be used for reorganizing a table that, due to improper PCTFREE and PCTUSED parameters coupled with unexpected patterns of UPDATE, INSERT, and DELETE processing, has become internally fragmented with many blocks with unnecessary and unusable free space.

Copying Data with CREATE TABLE . . . AS SELECT

It is possible to use the SQL CREATE TABLE command with a subquery to retrieve data from an existing table (or join of multiple tables). For small amounts of data, this feature can be used directly across a database link to retrieve data from a remote database and use it to create a table in the data warehouse. The following is an example:

```
CREATE TABLE NOV_ACTIVITY
      (consultant_id,
       project_id,
       function_code,
       revenue,
       hours,
       expenses)
   TABLESPACE temp_loads
      STORAGE (INITIAL 50M NEXT 50M PCTINCREASE 0)
AS
SELECT t.employee_id, t.project_code, t.function_code,
       sum(t.labor_hrs * p.rate) sum(t.labor_hrs), sum(t.expense)
  FROM TIMECARD@TEAM T, PROJECT_ASSIGNMENTS@TEAM P
 WHERE t.project_code = p.project_code
       t.employee_id = p.employee_id
   AND t.timecard_dt BETWEEN p.start_date AND p.end_date
   AND t.timecard_dt >= '1-NOV-97'
   AND t.timecard_dt <  '1-DEC-97'
 GROUP BY t.employee_id, t.project_code, t.function_code;
```

This will create a local table (called NOV_ACTIVITY) in our data warehouse that will be populated with the lightly summarized timecard records from the source system (identified by the database link named TEAM) for days worked during November 1997. (The specifics of the query and how it found the needed data in the TEAM database are not important. The key is that the subquery executes entirely in that remote database and performs the necessary join to find the data needed for the data warehouse.)

In many cases, however, the extracted data volume will be too large to pass over a SQL*Net connection efficiently. CREATE TABLE . . . AS SELECT can still be used, however, to extract the data from the source system and create a temporary table. Once the subset of data is extracted, the resulting temporary table can be exported (or unloaded) for transport to the warehouse for importing or loading. In this situation, the CREATE TABLE would be executed entirely on the source system.

Parallel CTAS (pCTAS)

When sufficient CPU and I/O resources are available, the CREATE TABLE . . . AS SELECT can be performed much more quickly using the parallel query capabilities of Oracle7 or Oracle8. Use of the NOLOGGING option on this command is especially useful for this type of task. There is no reason to endure the additional overhead of redo logging each of the INSERTs into our new temporary table. We expect to immediately back up (via the export) the data in this table as soon as it is created. Should the CREATE TABLE command fail to complete we can simply reexecute it when the system is available. In no event would we expect to recover an incomplete CREATE TABLE, so NOLOGGING costs us nothing.

Much more information on the specifics of Parallel CREATE TABLE . . . AS SELECT (pCTAS) is provided in Chapter 10. This command is frequently the fastest means of extracting a compact subset of Oracle data from a very large table to make the selected data available for transport to the data warehouse.

Using the SQL*Plus Copy Command

SQL*Plus includes a command called COPY that provides a means of copying data from one database to another or from one table to another within the same database. Note that COPY is not a SQL command and cannot be used from within an Enterprise Manager WorkSheet or other SQL interface. In most cases, it is preferable to use CREATE TABLE . . . AS SELECT or INSERT . . . SELECT SQL syntax. There are several reasons for this preference. SQL language commands should be used whenever possible over the proprietary syntax of any tool. Additionally, Oracle8 allows for parallelizing both of the alternative SQL commands (Oracle7 can parallelize the CREATE TABLE . . . AS SELECT), but COPY cannot.

There is one particular situation in which the SQL*Plus COPY command is valuable. Oracle has provided a LONG data type as a way of storing character data that would not fit within the allowable storage of the character data types

(CHAR, NCHAR, VARCHAR2, NCHAR2, and VARCHAR), which have been variously limited to 255, 2,000, or 4,000 bytes, depending on the Oracle release. LONG (as well as LONG RAW, which is used for noncharacter data) has been allowed to store from 64 KB (through version 6) to 2 GB in Oracle7 and Oracle8. LONG data is further limited to only 32 KB when referenced in PL/SQL.

Along with the greater storage capacity, the Oracle LONG data type has always had several limitations, which are documented in the Oracle7 and Oracle8 *SQL Reference* manuals. Among these limitations is a prohibition against including a LONG column in the SELECT list of CREATE TABLE . . . AS SELECT or the subquery of INSERT . . . SELECT. Incidentally, the Oracle replication facility also shares this inability to directly move LONG data between databases.

In general, we've traditionally recommended avoiding the use of LONGs when designing Oracle systems except when absolutely required. Oracle8's new CLOB and BLOB data types have been created to provide the capability to store long data without the severe limitations imposed by the LONG data type. Unfortunately, there are many systems around that have included LONG columns, often unnecessarily. We recently worked with a client who needed to copy data from a purchased application to a reporting database. The vendor of this particular application included LONG columns in several tables to store "memo" data. No row in this client's database ever stored more data than could have been accommodated by the Oracle7 VARCHAR2 data type, but the chosen design severely constrained our ability to replicate data for the client.

If your source data includes data stored in LONG columns that you need to move to the data warehouse, your solutions are generally limited. The EXP/IMP utilities will work with LONG data, providing you wish to copy entire tables. PL/SQL procedures can work with LONGs providing none of the data exceeds PL/SQL's 32-KB size limitation on character variables. Of course, writing custom programs (e.g., in Pro*C) is another option that offers the most flexibility but also requires the most effort. The SQL*Plus COPY command is a simple means of copying data, including LONGs, between databases with the flexibility to specify particular columns and conditions for row selection.

NOTE Define the maximum size of LONG data for COPY to transmit through the SQL*Plus SET LONG command. The value of this variable defaults to only 80 bytes. Any LONG data that exceeds the set value will be truncated by SQL*Plus.

The basic syntax of COPY has four basic parts:

```
COPY FROM source_db_connection
    TO destination_db_connection
    ACTION destination_table_specification
    USING query
```

You must specify either the FROM or TO database connection. If you omit one or the other then SQL*Plus will default that connection to the currently connected database. For example, if you are connected to the warehouse database and need to copy data from the PROD instance, you would specify the FROM connection to point at PROD and let the TO connection default to the warehouse. *source_db_connection* and *destination_db_connection* are of the form *userid/password@database_spec*. You must provide a valid Oracle userid and password in the database specified by *database_spec*. *database_spec* must be a valid SQL*Net (or Net8) connection, which can be resolved by SQL*Net's Transparent Network Substrate (TNS) facility. In general, this means it will be specified either in Oracle Names or your local TNSNAMES.ORA file.

The ACTION must be one of four keywords: CREATE, APPEND, REPLACE, or INSERT. The chosen keyword determines how SQL*Plus treats the destination table into which data is to be copied.

- CREATE creates a new table in the database schema specified in the TO clause (or defaulted to current database connection). If a table of the specified name already exists in the destination database schema then COPY . . . CREATE returns an error.

- APPEND acts just like CREATE except that, if the table already exists, COPY then inserts rows into the existing table rather than return an error.

- REPLACE drops an existing table of the name specified, if it exists. Then it creates a new table of the *destination_db_specification* using data retrieved via the *query*.

- INSERT copies the rows into an existing table in the destination database schema. The column list specified in the *query* must match the columns of the destination table. An error is returned if the table does not already exist.

destination_table_specification is of the form *table_name* (column name list). The *destination_table_specification* must provide a valid *table_name* for the destination database schema. Although it is not documented, you may specify an existing view name in *destination_table_specification* if doing an INSERT or APPEND. The column name list is optional syntax and allows for changing the names of columns retrieved by query when creating a new table through CREATE, REPLACE, or APPEND. The columns must match the order of columns specified in query and will be created with corresponding data types. If rows will be added to an existing table then the data types of the columns in the destination table must match those specified in query. SQL*Plus will allow minor data type translations, for instance, between CHAR and VARCHAR2 columns, but it will not allow you to change a LONG data type in the source to a VARCHAR2 in the destination. It will allow you to copy data into a column with a smaller maximum size provided the actual data is short enough to fit. Thus, you can copy from a column defined as VARCHAR2(20) into a column defined as VARCHAR2(10) as long as no row contains data longer than 10 characters. Copying data from a CHAR column, incidentally, into a VARCHAR or VARCHAR2 column requires the destination to be at least as long as the original CHAR column.

The USING clause specifies a query that will retrieve data from the *source_db_connection*. This is in the form of a standard SQL SELECT statement embedded in the SQL*Plus command. If you wish to add rows to an existing table using INSERT or REPLACE, then the column names of the destination table must match those in the query. You may use column aliases in the query to force the names to match.

The COPY command is not, however, an efficient way of moving very large volumes of data. It does not take advantage of any parallel capabilities (other than the possibility of performing a full table scan in the query). The total volume of rows will be transmitted from the source database to the destination database in a serial manner over SQL*Net, although it can bundle multiple rows together for transmission. The number of rows handled in each "batch" is controlled by the SQL*Plus SET ARRAYSIZE command.

Consider using COPY only when you must move a modest amount of data, particularly when it contains a column defined as LONG.

Advanced Queuing

Oracle8 introduced the Advanced Queuing (Oracle AQ) facility. It provides a very robust facility for communicating asynchronously between different Oracle processes. The application architect has a lot of flexibility in defining multiple queues, the structure of the message content (the "payload"), and any appropriate mix of writers and readers. The readers may be connected to the same database as the writer, or they may be on different servers.

The message can be defined to carry the full set of data needed by the reading transaction (the warehouse loading process in our case), or it can be used to just send a notification that a particular event has occurred. The reading process could then initiate a complex set of activities based on that notification.

This process could be a very effective tool for communicating between our source systems and our warehouse. The power and flexibility of the tool, oddly enough, become the limiting factor to its adoption. Because implementing this kind of communication requires modification to the operational system's transactions the programmers and administrators of that system are going to resist making these changes just to send a message to the warehouse. They are much more likely to provide a regular query or even a simple trigger.

Even though the effort to retrofit AQ into an existing system may not be justified by the warehouse's need, we believe that over time this facility will become an important means of capturing warehouse data. That will happen as more Oracle operational systems begin to use this method of communicating with each other. If, for instance, the order processing system sends notification to the inventory and shipping systems using a message queue, it will be a relatively easy task to add the warehouse as an additional consumer of that same message queue. New Oracle8*i* systems being developed in your organization may already be exploiting this feature. With only minor additional effort it may be possible to provide the warehouse with key transaction information using the same message queues.

Replication

Although we've never found occasion to do so, it is possible to use Oracle's replication facilities to bring a copy of operational data into the warehouse. This might be handy for copying new dimensional data from the source system to the warehouse.

From our case study introduced in Chapter 4, whenever we hire a new consultant or open a new project, it would be very helpful if an automated facility could give us a record of that change. If the administrator of the operational system is willing to allow snapshots to be defined on the appropriate tables, we could have that facility. The biggest problem that we face is that the operational systems commonly perform updates and deletes against the data we are thinking of replicating. We can't allow rows to be deleted from our dimension tables when a project ends or an employee resigns! Changes to these source tables commonly need to be reflected as a new row in our dimension tables, leaving the original row historically true.

In the early days of Oracle7 snapshots, the triggers that performed the replication were visible PL/SQL. Although it wasn't supported to do so, it was at least possible to edit the trigger code to change its behavior. As part of the performance improvements of Oracle8 replication, these triggers were internalized, preventing us from seeing or altering their code. This means that a snapshot can be used to keep a "current" copy of the data in our warehouse, but it will still be our responsibility to recognize changes in the snapshot and then apply those changes to our actual dimension table. This isn't really much better than the original situation of having query access to the original source table.

So, in the final analysis, replication is probably not a good general purpose tool for copying data into the warehouse. There are other valuable uses of replication, such as automatically maintaining data marts as subsets of our warehouse data, which will prove more practical. These are discussed in Chapter 12.

Transportable Tablespaces

The fastest way to move a large amount of data from one Oracle8*i* database to another is through the new transportable tablespace feature. Chapter 5 introduced the steps required to use this feature. If the nature of the source system allows the tablespace to be made read-only (even briefly) then this is an option to consider. By quickly exporting the metadata describing the contents of the tablespace and then copying the complete data files, then importing the metadata into the warehouse, the complete contents of the tablespace can be almost instantly be made part of the warehouse. This can be equivalent to loading several hundred gigabytes per minute!

Of course, there are issues that need to be considered. First, copying entire tablespaces may or may not be convenient, depending on how the source system's tablespace design was performed. Taking 100 times more data than necessary because of a poor design that stored everything in a single tablespace might not be feasible. It might turn out to be easier for the administrators of that source system to redistribute their tables and indexes than to have to build traditional extract programs that will have to be maintained and executed regularly for the lifetime of that system.

The second consideration is for the source system tablespaces that can't be made read-only long enough to perform the metadata export. Obviously, we can't shut down order processing or reservations for several minutes every night! And what about extracting from partitioned tables—you can't make a tablespace transportable if it contains only a subset of an object's partitions.

Well, all of these situations are pretty easily accommodated. By using the unrecoverable parallel CREATE TABLE AS SELECT construct, you can very rapidly extract whatever data you need into a special table in its own tablespace that can then be transported to the warehouse. This approach allows appropriate transformations to be performed efficiently as part of the extract process. Additional transformations can be applied to the data after it is made part of the warehouse. Overall, considerable time and effort can be saved during the extract phase, compared to extracting to a flat file, by exploiting Oracle8*i* parallelism inside the database. Far more time is saved during the "load" phase by avoiding the need to load rows at all.

Post-Processing of Loaded Data

In some cases, it is possible to complete all reformatting and cleanup of data during the extract and load processes. In such cases, the data can be directly loaded into the actual warehouse tables that will be accessed by users. When completely reformatted and scrubbed, data can be extracted (or preprocessed) via an ETT tool or customized extract programs; then direct loading will be extremely easy and fast.

In other cases, some additional processing will be needed on the warehouse side. If the volume of data to be loaded is not too large, database triggers on the warehouse tables can complete data validation and reformatting on data being entered via SQL*Loader's conventional path.

In many cases, however, the data being extracted will require some level of additional processing. Frequently, the volume of data to be loaded requires the use of SQL*Loader's direct path, which precludes trigger processing during the load. In such cases, it is common to load the data initially into a temporary table and then use PL/SQL to further massage the data and insert it into the final warehouse table.

Validating the Loaded Data

In the words of the old foreign policy maxim, "Trust but verify." We need to ensure that the data we have loaded is accurate. A huge variety of problems might occur in any given warehouse situation. It is impossible to anticipate all possibilities here, but we can discuss several ways of performing the necessary validation.

In earlier chapters we discussed the use of database constraints and came to the conclusion that enabling constraints on very large tables is frequently too expensive. One alternative solution that we have suggested many times is to load into a standalone table that can be exchanged into the large (partitioned) table when we are sure that the data is ready. Enabling constraints on this standalone table will be much more efficient because only the newly loaded data needs to be validated.

You may find, however, that enabling constraints, especially with the EXCEP-TIONS INTO clause, may still require too much time. Another road to the same destination is to use a SQL query to find and record all offending rows. Here is an example of validating a foreign key relationship that, using the table's default parallelism, performed more quickly than the equivalent constraint:

```
CREATE TABLE bad_empids
      TABLESPACE DBA_WORK
      NOLOGGING
   AS SELECT act.employee_id
        FROM activity_temp act, consultant_dim c
       WHERE act.employee_id = c.employee_id(+)
         AND c.employee_id is null
```

Of course, your mileage may vary, and you should try multiple alternatives before determining the best approach for your situation.

A third option for performing validation allows enforcement of more complex rules than those handled by constraints. When you have many rules to enforce on each row or you additionally must perform transformations on the data, it may be more efficient to use a PL/SQL procedure to open a cursor and read and process each row. This is the general method used by the new Oracle Warehouse Builder product.

Index Builds and Rebuilds

One of the frequently executed steps after loading data is to create the necessary indexes on that data. Whenever you are loading data to an empty table (or partition), it will be faster to build the indexes after the data is loaded than to incur the overhead of maintaining the indexes with each row inserted.

> **NOTE** When an index is needed to provide uniqueness (indexes created to support a PRIMARY KEY or UNIQUE constraint), it may be appropriate to incur this overhead to ensure that no duplicate rows are encountered. If you have confidence that the data has been properly cleansed before loading, even these indexes can be built after the load. Do this by disabling the constraint (with the ALTER TABLE command), then loading the data and enabling the constraint. If duplicates are discovered during the rebuild of the index, an error will be returned and the index build terminated. You can use the EXCEPTIONS INTO syntax on the CREATE INDEX and ALTER TABLE commands to obtain a listing of duplicate values.

The direct path mode of SQL*Loader generally avoids this overhead by deferring the index maintenance until after completing the load. Before making the new data part of the table (raising the table's high-water mark) it builds a mini-index on just the newly added data. It then merges this mini-index with the existing table index to create a new index that covers all the table's data. This means that at the completion of the load each index on the table will require roughly double its normal storage allotment. Ensure that index tablespaces have sufficient space to accommodate the original, the mini-index temporary segment, and the final merged index.

There is one exception to this process of performing an index merge. By specifying the SINGLEROW option on the direct path load, you can cause SQL*Loader to maintain indexes on a row-by-row basis. This will, of course, slow the load process, especially if there are several indexes to be maintained. This option should be used when there is a shortage of space in the tablespace and the number of rows to be loaded is relatively small compared to the current size of the table. In this case, the choice is made to slow the load in order to save space or the time needed to perform a complete rebuild of the index.

If any problem occurs during the index merge (such as running out of space or an instance failure) Oracle8 will leave the index in the index unusable state (in Oracle7 this was called the direct load state). No SQL statements will be able to use or maintain an index left in this state. Therefore, one of the necessary steps in post-load processing will be to examine all indexes and verify that they are usable. Any that are not usable must be dropped and re-created.

TIP To determine whether an index has been left in the index unusable or direct load state, look at the STATUS column within DBA_INDEXES table.

Another restriction when using SQL*Loader direct path is that when loading data into a partition of an Oracle8 no global indexes on the table may be in place. Drop all global indexes before loading, and rebuild them after completing the load. In practical terms, this really means that your design of large, partitioned tables should use only local indexes. In most cases, the effort required to re-create very large global indexes will exceed the potential savings in query effort.

Finally, parallel direct path SQL*Loader always leaves indexes in an unusable state. All indexes (both global and local in the case of an Oracle8 partition) on the segment being loaded will need to be dropped and re-created after each parallel direct path load.

Creating indexes on very large tables (including global indexes on Oracle8 partitioned tables) can be a very time-consuming effort. An index build consists of three steps:

1. Scanning the table (or partition) to determine the values of the indexed columns

2. Sorting the values (unless the NOSORT option is specified)

3. Building and loading the hierarchical B*Tree or bitmap structure

The first two of these steps are the most resource intensive, but luckily they lend themselves nicely to parallel operations. In almost every case, indexes for the data warehouse should be built with the PARALLEL and NOLOGGING (UNRECOVERABLE in Oracle7) options. Details for performing parallel index builds are presented in Chapter 10.

"Publishing" Data

It is important that users see a consistent view of data within the warehouse. It is not appropriate for a user to see some data that updated as of April and other data within the subject area that was current as of May. Running the same query a day later, when the May update had been completed, would give different results. A similar inconsistency could occur when new detail is loaded but the summarizations based on that detail have not been updated. Users attempting to drill-down from one layer to another will receive conflicting results.

To avoid these situations, the warehouse administrator should prevent access to the data from the time that periodic loads start until the entire process is verified as complete. When the entire load, index, and summarize process can be completed in the available batch window, then "closing" the warehouse may be appropriate. This can be done on a subject area basis through the use of the ROLE features of Oracle security. As described in Chapter 3, "Oracle Server Software Architecture and Features," each group of users should be assigned a role. The SELECT privilege on each subject area's data should be granted to a different role. To make access temporarily unavailable, the second role is revoked from the first. To make the subject area's data available to the group of users after the data is completely updated, only a single GRANT statement is executed.

The revoke, load, and grant approach works well when users are able to wait while the load and associated processes complete. This approach breaks down, however, when the load process takes a very long time or when loads are performed frequently (hourly, for instance) or when users have a very high availability requirement, perhaps due to global access. An additional problem arises in warehouses in which some queries might take many hours or even days to complete. In these situations it is important to find a way to perform the most time-consuming parts of the periodic maintenance while still allowing the users to access the existing warehouse data in a consistent manner.

There are four techniques, all of which have been introduced already, to perform this sleight of hand:

- The first is to divide the data warehouse into multiple subject areas and update each of the areas under a different schedule. This might mean delaying part of the weekly warehouse maintenance to Monday, Tuesday, and Wednesday evenings even though the source data is all made available over the weekend.

- The second technique is to work with temporary tables. If extensive processing of the new data is necessary, perhaps through trigger processing or other procedural code, then load the data into tables that users can't access. Complete as much massaging of the data as possible, including generating summarizations into additional temporary tables. Then close the warehouse (or individual subject area) long enough to add the processed data and new summary rows into their permanent tables.

- A third technique is to maintain two copies of the warehouse tables and switch between them using synonyms. Users continue to access the first copy while the second copy is created. When the second copy is ready for access, public synonyms are re-created to direct queries to those new tables. Currently executing queries will continue to access the first set of tables to completion. New queries will immediately access the new tables. This technique actually works very well, but it has two major drawbacks. First, the storage requirements are nearly double the real requirement, and second, this involves moving a lot of existing data during every load cycle. These two expenses obviously grow as the warehouse grows.

- The fourth (and most useful) technique for limiting the time that the warehouse needs to be closed is partitioning. Working with a separate table and then adding it to an existing Oracle8 partitioned table is an ideal way to minimize the time required to make data available in a coordinated, controlled manner. Even though partitioning is an extra-cost option to the Oracle8 RDBMS, no serious data warehouse should be built without this powerful capability. This is one of the few absolute recommendations made within this book. Of all the technical difficulties faced by designers and administrators of Oracle7 (or other RDBMS) warehouses, easily 80 percent are solved using this one key feature.

Figure 6.11 illustrates this last means of adding data to a very large Oracle8 partitioned table. The data is initially loaded into a standalone table. Data validation, reformatting, and other processing can be completed while users continue to access the partitioned table. Indexes on the standalone table can be created. When the entire process is complete and verified (which might even take several days) the administrator swaps the standalone table with an empty partition of the permanent table. Each index is also swapped and becomes a local index on the partition. As long as no global indexes need to be rebuilt, the entire process can be completed with only a few minutes of downtime. This allows several partitioned tables to be maintained in what seems, to the user community, a very short window. In fact, most of the difficult work was done while they were able to access the warehouse but in an area they can't see.

For related tables that are not large enough to warrant partitioning, such as many summaries or dimension tables, the effort required to INSERT new rows from their temporary "staging areas" is usually manageable. Oracle can easily copy hundreds of thousands of rows from one table to another within a few minutes. To further shorten the required time, it is possible to unload the data in the temporary table and then add it to the permanent table using direct path SQL*Loader. Keep in mind the cautions mentioned earlier for performing periodic loads with direct path, but this approach does provide a means for buying processing time at the cost of some additional space management and index maintenance concerns. (The other issues regarding triggers and constraints should not be a problem because the data is preprocessed before being added to the table. No triggers or constraints would be used on the permanent table.)

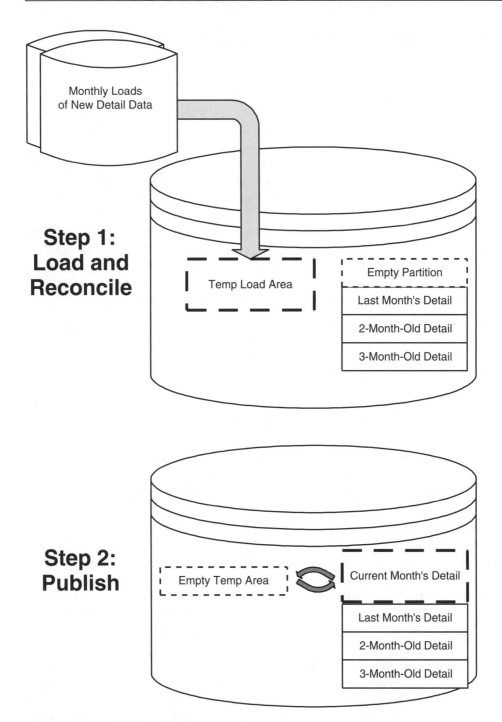

Figure 6.11 Publishing data in the Oracle8 warehouse.

Purging and Archiving Warehouse Data

It is impossible to keep all detailed data in the data warehouse forever. The cost of storing and administering the data goes up as the data volume grows. The cost of accessing data also goes up as the total volume increases. Luckily, the value of individual transaction data diminishes over time. This relationship—increasing cost and decreasing value—leads us eventually to start removing data from the data warehouse. Typically, we will want to retain the rows for old data in our summary tables as queries that span multiple years will need only summarized data for comparison. The details that fed those summaries become far less important as they age.

The warehouse team must evaluate the potential future value of the old detailed data. When we recognize that old data is no longer being used for online queries, we must consider whether there may be other uses. Sometimes we may anticipate a need to someday build a new summary that will require the old details. In some cases, it will be determined that there is no chance of ever needing to access the data again. In the former case, we will want to archive the data—copy it to a low-cost storage location outside the online data warehouse—so it may be made available again at some future time or through a different means. In the latter case, we may feel safe in purging the data—removing it from the warehouse without retaining a copy. When in doubt, it is much safer to retain the data in archival form. The cost of a few tape volumes each month is negligible compared to the cost of data that is needed but unavailable.

Figure 6.12 illustrates the conceptual process for archiving and purging data from the data warehouse. Multiple techniques exist for actually performing the archival and purge tasks.

The warehouse is, among other things, an archive of data that would otherwise be lost from our operational systems. But why think of archival as only a single step? Don't you archive your personal financial records in multiple steps? At the end of the month, when the checkbook is balanced, some of the records are "put away" where they can be retrieved easily if needed—perhaps to return a purchased item. At the end of the year (or when taxes are completed) some of those financial records get moved to a deeper level of archiving—where they can still be retrieved in case the IRS auditors come calling, but sufficiently out of the way of our current household expenses.

When considering archiving strategies, it is important to evaluate the possible future benefits of being able to access very old data. But, another benefit should not be overlooked. Without an archiving plan, there will be a tendency to keep unused data in the main warehouse perhaps longer than necessary. Retaining unused data in the warehouse is, one could say, a form of archiving—just a very expensive one.

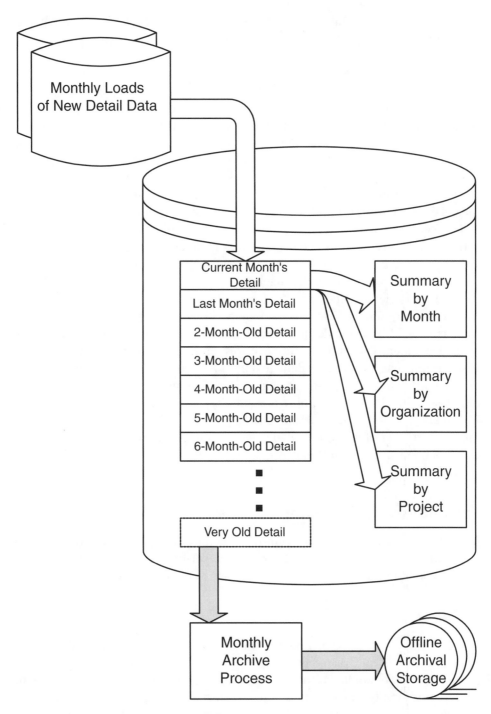

Figure 6.12 Archiving warehouse data.

Having considered the two categories of benefits to archiving data when it has a low probability of being accessed, let's also consider two categories of costs. The first is the cost of moving and storing the data outside the warehouse. The second is the cost of retrieving the data if and when it is needed. The first category of costs will be incurred on a regular basis, generally every month, once the warehouse retention period has been reached. Regardless of the residual value of the data (that is, the probability that someone will need it) we will pay the cost of unloading the data and storing it on tape, CD-ROM, or other low-cost medium. Because we will need to pay this price so frequently, we should try to minimize this cost to justify its potential benefits. As we'll see, the Oracle8*i* transportable tablespace feature provides the most cost-effective means of moving data from the warehouse database to archival storage.

The second category of cost associated with data archival, the cost of retrieval, is determined by the probability of someone needing the data. If we archive too soon, we will have more requests to restore data than if we retain the data in the warehouse for a longer period of time. If restoral of the archived data is very difficult (expensive) then we will want to postpone archival longer than if it is very simple. Prior to Oracle8*i*, archival required writing the data out to an external file and restoral required reloading it, either with the IMP utility or SQL*Loader. The administrative effort and processing time required to restore some past year's sales data, in many cases, exceeded the value of almost any query that might be posed against it. Hence, in many warehouses, data was either kept indefinitely or simply purged after a specified number of months. Fortunately, with the introduction of transportable tablespaces in Oracle8*i*, the cost of restoring older data is also greatly reduced. Remounting a tablespace that has been archived in this way can be as simple as a file copy and a single SQL statement.

Techniques for Archiving Data

Making the archival copy before removing data from the data warehouse can be accomplished using the same techniques described earlier for moving data from an operational system's Oracle database to the data warehouse.

EXP/IMP

The EXP utility works well enough if the data to be archived is stored in a separate partition of an Oracle8 partitioned table or is segregated into a complete table that can be handled as a unit. Data from the single table or partition can be exported simply and quickly. So far, Oracle has made a commitment to maintaining upward compatibility between earlier releases of EXP and newer versions of IMP. Of course, there may be some future change to that strategy, so if you choose to use EXP as your archival strategy be sure to verify each new version's capability for importing data from all prior versions during your testing and acceptance phase for each upgrade.

NOTE Downward compatibility is not guaranteed. You may not be able to use the export feature of a new version of Oracle to move the data to a previous release. You can generally fall back to a previous release by exporting data using the EXP version from the earlier release.

If you use EXP you will have the additional benefit of having the data dictionary metadata needed to reload the data later automatically included. Other user metadata will, however, need to be copied along with the archival data. If the archived data needs to be reloaded in a year or two, it will be important to know the structure and meaning of the data as of the time it was exported. If metadata is stored in tables within the database, then those tables can be included in the export. If only the pertinent metadata for the specific table(s) being archived is desired, then copy just that data into new temporary tables using CREATE TABLE . . . AS SELECT, include those temporary tables in the data export, and then drop the temporary tables.

Problems with EXP/IMP for Archiving Data

If the data to be archived is stored in a nonpartitioned state with a larger volume of data that is not going to be removed, then exporting the entire table may be time-consuming and wasteful. An export of 20 million rows (of which only 500,000 are about to be removed) will consume 40 times as much space on tape, which may not be a major concern. A greater concern is likely to be the space in the database required in the future if those 500,000 rows are needed again; importing all 20 million to get them back will be a problem especially if several successive archival data sets are required and each requires that another 20 million rows be imported! Therefore, it is critical to ensure that the archival data size is minimized.

This hints at the more general problem with using EXP as an archival method. If the archived data has to be restored, it will have to be reloaded using the IMP utility. As we've mentioned earlier, IMP is not known for blazing speed. The expense of having to import the data may exceed the value of the analysis that needs it.

Other Archival Techniques

If a subset of data must be archived from a very large table, an alternative archival method is required. The unload/reload script provided earlier in this chapter may be used for this purpose. This technique allows that specific rows be selected, as specified in the WHERE clause of the generated unload script. Remember that the primary performance benefit of the unload/reload is during the reload process. For archival purposes, where reloads are anticipated to be infrequent; optimizing the unload process is far more important.

Another useful technique for archiving a small subset of data from a very large table is to use CREATE TABLE . . . AS SELECT to copy the subset of rows into a new temporary table. This table can be exported efficiently and then dropped.

Once a permanent copy of the data has been archived, you can remove the data from the database using any of the techniques for purging data described next.

Note that these approaches require some manual involvement on the part of the administrator whenever the data might be needed in the future. This is the second category of cost discussed in the introduction to this section. The DBA will have to allocate enough room in a new or existing tablespace, then create a new table (or partition) to hold the restored data and then run the IMP or SQL*Loader utility to load the data back in. For a large volume of data, this process might take many hours to complete. Let's hope the user hasn't decided to forget about that query by the time we get the data restored!

Transportable Tablespaces

Transportable tablespaces (Oracle8*i*), in conjunction with range partitioning (Oracle8), make both the archival and restoration of data much less painful. When a partition of the large detail/fact table has reached its retention threshold, the DBA (or, better still, an automated script) will ALTER TABLE . . . EXCHANGE the partition to make it a standalone table in its current tablespace. (Typically the tablespace containing the data and one or more tablespaces containing the corresponding local index partitions will be archived as a complete set.) The tablespace is made read-only (if not already done), and the metadata describing its contents are exported. Two special parameters will have to be provided to the EXP utility:

```
EXP TRANSPORT_TABLESPACE=y TABLESPACES=ts_name1,tsname_2
```

The data file(s) associated with the tablespace are then copied to low-cost storage along with the small dump file from the export. Note that no time-consuming, individual movement of data rows is needed. The entire tablespace is archived just by copying entire files. This is very fast and efficient, and it provides a low-cost means of doing a regular archival of the oldest data from our warehouse's partitioned tables. Once archived, the tablespace may be dropped to free that amount of disk space for creation of tablespaces to house newer partitions. Likewise, the empty partition created during the exchange should be dropped to complete the archival process.

Retrieval is only slightly more complex. The data files and the small dump file created by the export will need to be returned from secondary storage to a location where they can be read by Oracle8*i*. If they were archived to tape, then the files will need to be recopied from tape back to disk. Alternatively, if the files were moved to CD-ROM for long-term storage, the data can be accessed directly once the CD-ROM volumes have been mounted.

Once the data files are available, the DBA will run the IMP utility, specifying the new location of the restored datafiles, again using some new keywords:

```
IMP TRANSPORT_TABLESPACE=y
    DATAFILES='ts_file1,'ts_file2'
    TABLESPACES=ts_name1,ts_name_2
    TTS_OWNERS=dwowner
```

The final parameter in this example (TTS_OWNERS) is optional and provides a means of verifying the specific schemas that own objects to be included in the IMP. Any mismatch to the objects' actual owners will cause an error. If not specified, no schema verification is performed. Of course, the FROM_USER and TO_USER parameters can be used to return objects to a schema other than the owner at time of export.

All of this is very straightforward for the warehouse because the owning schema names are likely to be very stable. Remember, though, that during archival the partition of data was first exchanged to become a standalone table. After the import process is run, this standalone table will be in place for user access. Remember to GRANT select privileges to users (or roles) that will query this table.

Issues with Archiving

When it meets the users' needs, this approach of restoring a standalone table containing the archived data is administratively simplest. The next level of complexity might occur when a user needs access to an entire year's data that was archived on a monthly basis. This need can be accommodated by retrieving the 12 monthly archival tables and then combining them into a single partitioned table through additional ALTER TABLE . . . EXCHANGE commands. In this case the DBA would create a table with 12 small placeholder partitions and then swap each with the restored tables. This approach still allows the restored data to be isolated from the current warehouse data to make it available for the one requesting user without potentially affecting other users' queries against the current table.

In some cases, however, it may be necessary to restore the data into partitions of the original warehouse table. There is some risk in doing this—not a technical risk that things will break, but a risk that other users of the table may issue queries that do not limit the range of data because they depend on the expectation that the table will always contain the most recent 36 months of data. There is no single, simple answer to this potential problem. The best solution is avoidance. Users need to be instructed regarding the archival process even before the first archival is executed. They should be sure to always include time-range conditions in each query's WHERE clause that accesses the date partitioned table. This condition might be a direct specification of the range of dates from the partitioned table or a restriction placed on the time dimension that is then joined to the fact table. This is good query design practice in almost every warehouse anyway, and certainly in any warehouse situation that warrants archiving data by date in the manner suggested.

This final approach (constraining the query through the time dimension) opens a new means of controlling the environment even if the DBA has to restore older partitions to the fact table. If, as part of the archival process, the entries in the time dimension that correspond to the archived data are removed (as they should be) then users who always join to the fact table using the time dimension are safe. The time dimension will not have any rows that join with the newly restored fact data so their queries will never attempt to access the restored partitions. But what about the one user who needed the restoration of the old data? A new private copy of the time dimension can be created for that user that includes the restored dates! Because time dimensions tend to have only a few thousand rows (unless the granularity of the time dimension is very fine—intervals shorter than hourly) this is not likely to be a major space consumption issue.

One other issue can arise during the restoration of archived data. As we all know, the definition of warehouse tables does not conveniently stay static forever. Some simple changes, like the addition of a column, are likely to occur at some time. More complex changes that completely redefine a table are occasionally required. How do we handle this? There are two general possibilities: (1) proactively restructure all your archived data as part of making the change or (2) deal with it when (or if) the data needs to be restored.

Proactive Restructuring of Archived Data

The large volume of archived data may make this a nontrivial process. Here are a few suggestions that can help if your shop elects this proactive approach. When a change is performed to the structure of a table that has been partially archived, begin scheduling the same change against each archived period. It is probably not necessary to implement the change simultaneously against all of the archived data, but one by one, each partition should be restored and reformatted using the same scripts that restructured the current table. This will involve restoring each standalone table's tablespace, changing the tablespace from read-only to read-write, making the changes, resetting the tablespace back to read-only, reexporting the metadata regarding the tablespace contents, and backing up the tablespace data files. Consider scheduling one partition per day (or whatever additional volume your system can handle) until all are rebuilt and rearchived.

One final suggestion to consider: The proactive reformatting of archived data does not necessarily have to occur on the same machine that houses your warehouse. One of the beauties of transportable tablespaces is that they can be "replugged" into another database on the same operating system. Perhaps your warehouse development server has spare cycles available at night that can be put to use!

Restructuring of Archived Data as Needed

Not every shop has the discipline (and computing cycles) necessary to perform the proactive restructuring of its archived data. In many cases, the probability of needing to access the archived data in a hurry may be judged very low. If we elect to retain the archived data in its original form and expect to be able to restructure it when we restore it, we need to retain every script (and whatever transformation data was used by the script) forever. Losing track of one ALTER TABLE can make a future restoral very difficult or even impossible. That, in turn, puts the entire archival strategy at risk. Hence, this approach may actually require more discipline than the proactive one!

Finally, in still other cases, it may be determined that the need to access the older data will be adequately met without making the changes. Think this through very carefully, however, before accepting this decision. It assumes that we can anticipate the reasons for a request that hasn't even been made yet. It also assumes that the data can be accessed in a standalone table to answer the request because we won't be able to exchange the table back into a partition if the layouts, indexes, constraints, etc. are not identical. Finally, it assumes that all future changes to the structure of this same table can also be ignored. We can't change our minds later and start applying changes to a structure that doesn't match the warehouse's base table.

That's a lot of assumptions about things that haven't even been thought of yet! If you are going to archive, do it effectively and with proper dedication and control.

If your shop doesn't have the appropriate organizational discipline (and the corresponding checks and balances of a thorough testing function) then perhaps it is best not to promise users that you will be able to restore their data in case of some future emergency. Perhaps you should just set the proper expectations and simply purge the data.

Techniques for Purging Data

The ability to retain and manage large amounts of detail data has been greatly enhanced with each major release of Oracle. Very large databases in Oracle version 5 were typically measured in a few hundred megabytes of data. Large version 6 databases might consist of several gigabytes. One early Oracle7 database that we helped develop in 1992 was considered very large at 300 gigabytes. Oracle8 has removed many of the explicit and implicit limitations of Oracle7. Today, there are many Oracle8 warehouses that exceed a terabyte in size. We will certainly see Oracle8*i* databases exceeding 100 terabytes within a few years.

Each Oracle7 database could include a maximum of 1,022 files. In Oracle8, each tablespace of the database is now individually subject to the 1,022 file limit. Of course, in addition to relaxing such limitations, Oracle8 and Oracle8*i* have added several new enhancements that make it possible to administer the much larger databases that are now physically possible. The most significant of these is the ability to partition tables and indexes. We've discussed the use of partitioned objects extensively throughout this book in relation to the performance benefits of loading, indexing, and querying individual partitions rather than entire very large tables.

Drop/Exchange Partition

Partitioning is also one of the key tools to help you move data back out of the Oracle8 warehouse when its value has faded. If the detailed data has been partitioned based on transaction dates, as is most common, then removing an old partition is as simple as adding a new one. A single partition may be dropped with the syntax

```
ALTER TABLE table_name DROP PARTITION partition_name;
```

This single statement quickly and efficiently purges the data from the oldest partition of our time-partitioned warehouse table.

Another partitioning alternative aids in archiving the data. It is possible to switch the partition with an empty table, then drop the now-empty partition, and if needed, back up the standalone table using the techniques just discussed for archiving. This is the same technique described earlier regarding publishing the newly loaded data, but with the opposite effect. The syntax is as follows:

```
ALTER TABLE partitioned_table_name
    EXCHANGE PARTITION partition_name WITH TABLE unpartitioned_table_name;
```

Figure 6.13 illustrates the exchange of a partition.

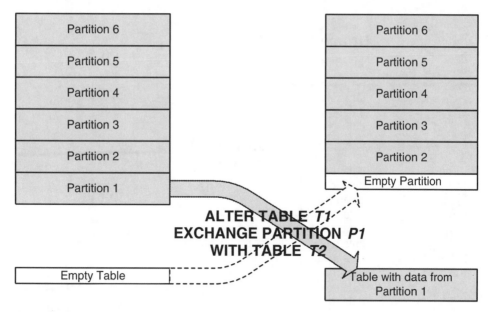

Figure 6.13   Exchange of a partition.

Once the data has been moved to a standalone table, unavailable to the warehouse users, the administrator may archive the table at his leisure.

TRUNCATE

When the entire contents of a table (or cluster) are to be removed, the SQL TRUNCATE command is the fastest way to accomplish the task. TRUNCATE immediately resets the table's high-water mark to indicate an empty table. No undo or redo information is generated for the individual rows, which are, in effect, deleted so this command is permanent and cannot be rolled back! Truncate is most useful for emptying a temporary table that will be used repeatedly as part of a regular load or summarization process. Any indexes on the table are also truncated simultaneously. Figure 6.14 illustrates the effect of TRUNCATE on a table.

The syntax for truncating a table is simple, with only one significant option:

```
TRUNCATE TABLE table_name [REUSE STORAGE];
```

If you do use the REUSE STORAGE option, then the entire table's current storage will be retained. Without this optional syntax, the truncated table will release all additional extents allocated beyond the extents originally allocated.

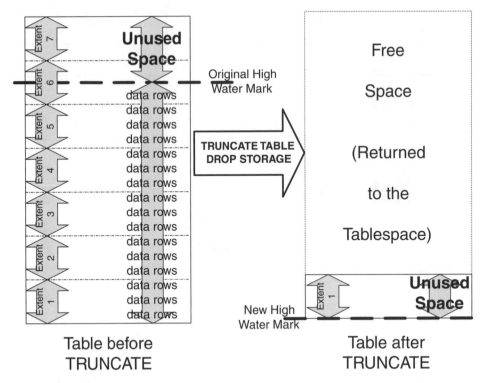

Figure 6.14 Truncating a table.

Unfortunately, it is not possible to directly truncate a single partition from an Oracle8 partitioned table. If you have this need, the ALTER TABLE . . . EXCHANGE PARTITION facility will provide a suitable substitute. Simply create a small table of the same layout as your partitioned table, exchange the table with the partition whose data you want to remove, then truncate the standalone table (the former partition) and exchange the empty table back to its original partition, and, finally, drop the little temporary table. A script to perform these few DDL statements will run within a few seconds. A sample script to perform this task can be downloaded from the Web sites described in the Introduction.

SQL DELETE

If the data has not been partitioned (or has been partitioned by criteria other than those used for purging) the data to be purged will need to be removed from the table with the SQL DELETE command. The syntax for deleting rows from a table is straightforward:

```
DELETE
  FROM table_name
 WHERE conditions;
```

Undo information (in a rollback segment) and redo information (in the redo logs) will be generated for each row deleted. It will be necessary to properly size these structures to accommodate large purge jobs. The NOLOGGING attribute, discussed earlier for parallel INSERT to a partitioned table, does not apply to DELETE (or UPDATE) activities.

The SQL DELETE command was not parallelized in Oracle7. Beginning in Oracle8 it is parallelized only for partitioned tables and only to the limit of one parallel process per partition. To utilize parallel DELETE the partitioned table may have only local indexes and no enabled triggers.

NOTE Oracle8 syntax allows you to specify the name of a partition in a DELETE statement. This is useful when some, but not all, data from a single partition of a partitioned table needs to be deleted. This provides a shorthand method to avoid having to specify the additional WHERE clause conditions that would limit the DELETE to data within that partition. The syntax is as follows:

```
DELETE FROM table_name PARTITION (partition_name)
           WHERE conditions;
```

When rows are deleted from a table, the space they occupied in each data block is theoretically made available for additional rows to be inserted. If new rows are added by direct path SQL*Loader, however, the new rows cannot use space in data blocks that have been used before. Direct path only writes to new blocks above the table's high-water mark that it can initially format and fill. Also, depending on the value of the PCTUSED parameter defined for the table, the space in individual blocks might actually never be used for regular SQL inserts either. The default value of PCTUSED is 40 percent, meaning that new rows will be inserted into a block, provided that at least 40 percent of its available space is emptied by the DELETE statement. Generally, this value will work well to ensure that blocks are reused efficiently. Should PCTUSED be set to a higher value of, say, 80 percent, then the table could end up with a significant amount of wasted space within its allocated storage.

PCTFREE controls when new inserts should stop adding rows to a table. In OLTP systems where rows are expected to be UPDATED, it may be appropriate to reserve a significant portion of each block for future growth of existing data rows. Within a data warehouse it is rare that this type of activity would occur on detail tables, so generally the PCTFREE should be set to 0. The default value of 10 percent would lead to an automatic 10 percent wastage in each block of a table. For data warehouse tables in which no UPDATEs will be performed, it is appropriate to set PCTFREE to 0 when creating the table.

PL/SQL

In some cases, a single DELETE statement might not be able to remove data rows in the manner desired. This may be because a very large number of rows must be deleted, which generates more undo information than can be accommodated by one of the available rollback segments. It may be because the archive process needs to do more than just delete each row; for instance, it may need to reformat and move a portion of the rows to an archival area while purging some other rows.

With any exotic requirements (and relatively low volumes!) it may be appropriate to write some procedural code to handle the archival and purge of a table. The procedural code should be written in PL/SQL and stored in the database as either a database "ON DELETE" trigger or a stored procedure. If the extra procedural work affects a small number of rows out of the total number to be deleted, then with an appropriate trigger in place, a SQL delete statement will cause the extra logic to be invoked for the appropriate rows. This approach will be most efficient when the identification of appropriate rows can be performed as part of the trigger's WHEN clause. The WHEN clause of a row-level trigger specifies the data conditions under which the rest of the trigger logic will be invoked. For each row that does not meet the WHEN conditions, the row is simply deleted with no additional action. WHEN clause conditions may not include a subquery or any user-defined PL/SQL functions.

If the objective is to avoid the undo associated with a massive DELETE then it may be more appropriate to write a "purge" procedure. Within the procedure you may open a cursor defined on the set of rows to be deleted. The procedure can then delete a specific number of rows, say 10,000, from the cursor and then COMMIT WORK to release the rollback segment. The cursor can then be repeatedly reopened and another 10,000 rows deleted and committed until all the rows have been removed.

The primary disadvantage of using a PL/SQL trigger or procedure is the performance decrement when compared to a simple SQL delete, which, in turn, is far more expensive than a table TRUNCATE or drop of a partition.

Indexing Issues When Purging Data

Whenever you delete rows from a table, the corresponding entries in every index on the table must also be removed. This has an immediate performance impact on the DELETE. It may also have a negative effect on the organization of the index. A common problem with B*Tree indexes occurs when new entries are consistently made at the "high" end of the indexed range and subsequently removed from the "low" end. Figure 6.15 illustrates this phenomenon. In this example, the CUSTOMER table has a large number of rows grouped within a tight range of sequenced values. The index has become disorganized and has split to a fourth level even though the left side is mostly empty. This suggests that there were once many rows before the current range that have since been deleted.

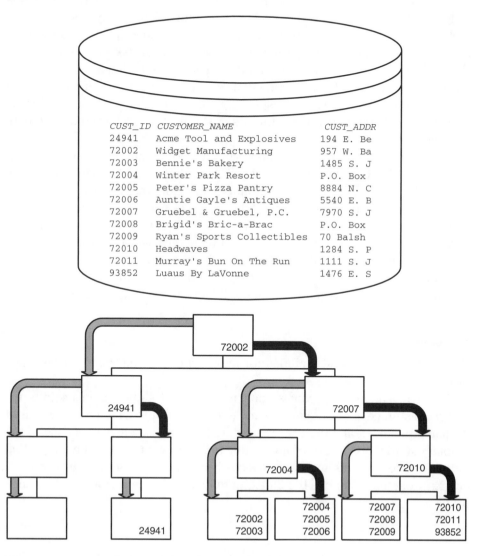

Figure 6.15 Normal B*Tree index after sequential inserts and purge.

This situation commonly occurs in indexes built on date columns and numeric columns that get their value from a sequence generator. In these cases, new rows are always of a higher value than the previous entry, and deletes are usually done of the oldest data—and the lowest values in the index.

Over time the structure of the index can become lopsided—the blocks that were originally built to hold the early data are now empty, but new blocks continue to be built for new data. The index continues to grow even though the number of rows may remain relatively constant. The administrators of the warehouse database should anticipate this behavior in indexes that have this usage pattern. By running the ANALYZE command regularly, the DBA can monitor a few key statistics to determine when an index needs to be reorganized. The primary statistic to observe is the BLEVEL column in the DBA_INDEXES view. This indicates the number of levels in the index hierarchy that must be read to reach the leaf node that points to a specific data block. When the value of BLEVEL increases (especially when the value of NUM_ROWS has remained relatively unchanged) the index should be considered a candidate for rebuilding.

Even more specific statistics can be obtained for an index by performing an ANALYZE INDEX . . . VALIDATE STRUCTURE and then observing the values displayed in the INDEX_STATS dictionary view. Note that this view shows the statistics only for the last index validated. Make sure to capture the values before analyzing the next index! The PCT_USED column will tell you the percentage of space in the index that is currently being used. The DEL_LF_ROWS statistic will tell you how many values have been deleted from the index, while DEL_LF_ROWS _LEN will provide the number of bytes of those deleted entries. Monitoring these statistics for changes will indicate when a rebuild is required.

Solutions

Oracle8 provides several facilities for avoiding or solving this out-of-balance problem.

First, when an index becomes unbalanced enough to be expensive in terms of wasted storage or wasted I/O, it can be rebuilt. Prior to Oracle8, this required dropping the index and then re-creating it. This was expensive because of the work involved in reading the data, sorting the data, and then building the actual index. Additionally, this approach was costly because, during the entire process, queries were unable to use the index, potentially causing serious performance problems.

With Oracle8, however, we got the capability to rebuild an index without first dropping the original, unbalanced index. This capability addresses both issues with the manual drop-and-create scenario. First, the index rebuild is far less expensive than creating an index from scratch. Rather than having to scan the entire table, only the existing index needs to be read. This requires far less I/O and is already in the sorted order so we avoid the second (and most costly) part of an index build. Second, the original disorganized index is available for queries while the rebuild occurs. When those queries complete, Oracle8 then removes the original structure, freeing that space for other uses. This is done with the ALTER INDEX REBUILD command. Be sure to specify an appropriate tablespace for the newly created index—otherwise, it will attempt to build the index in the user's default tablespace!

ALTER INDEX REBUILD is the mechanism for solving the problem of disorganized indexes. What about ways of avoiding the situation that makes reorganization necessary? Oracle8 provides two features to help us here. The first and primary tool to avoid reorganizations is partitioning. If our large fact tables and their indexes are partitioned, we can avoid doing SQL DELETE commands to purge old data. Index partitions are initially built as we load data, and then they are never modified. Therefore, they remain perfectly organized! When we drop the oldest partition from our table, Oracle8 automatically drops the corresponding index partitions as well. Voilà!

Another Oracle8 feature that may help in this area is the reverse-order index. When a B*Tree index is created with the REVERSE keyword, Oracle stores the bytes of each index value in reverse order. Figure 6.16 illustrates this concept. By storing the bytes in reverse order, the low-order bytes that change most frequently get stored in the leading edge. Thus, when successive rows are entered they will be distributed evenly over all the branches of the B*Tree. When older rows are deleted they, too, will be evenly distributed. Thus, regular insert and purge cycles will tend to balance each other and maintain a stable structure.

When the Oracle8 DBA identifies an index that will grow in one direction while being purged from the other (older) end, rebuilding the index with the REVERSE keyword may be in order. This will greatly reduce the future need for index rebuilds. The disadvantage of reverse-order indexes is that they cannot be used to perform range scans. Thus, this feature is of primary value to the OLTP systems designer where it may be known that the index will be used only for single-row, equality retrievals. This means that, in most warehouses, the proper solution will be to partition large tables with locally partitioned indexes and to be prepared to rebuild other indexes when they become lopsided after large purges.

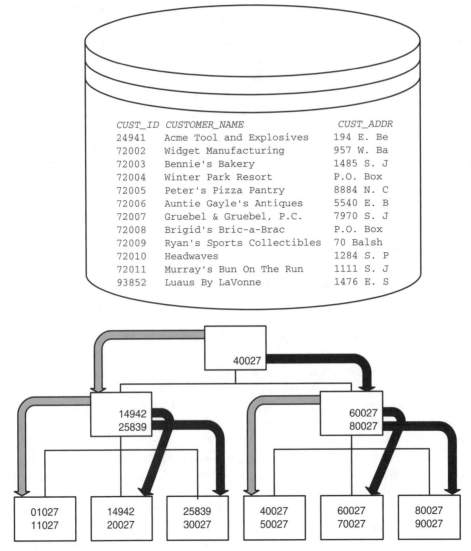

Figure 6.16 Reverse-order index after sequential inserts and purge.

Summary

Once the data warehouse has been designed and built, it is necessary to load data and make the warehouse available to users. Typically, the warehouse will be loaded with data from multiple sources including various corporate transaction processing systems and purchased external data. Frequently, this data suffers from problems with quality or consistency, particularly when it has been combined with data from other sources. Reconciling data quality problems may be performed during the extract from the operational system, during the load into the warehouse, or sometime in between.

We examined several alternative methods for loading data into the warehouse, including SQL*Loader, custom-written load programs, and Oracle's gateway products. We discussed several special ways of moving data from one Oracle database to another.

After data is loaded it must be verified, indexed, and "published" to make it available to users. Finally, we presented the need and techniques for archiving and purging—that is, removing data from the warehouse when it is no longer needed. We saw how Oracle8's range (or composite) partitioning is especially helpful to making these administrative chores very painless.

Post-Load Processing in the Data Warehouse

*"Rolling, rolling, rolling! /Though the streams are swollen,/
Keep them dogies rolling! /Rawhide!"*

***Theme song to the TV series* Rawhide**

Populating with detail data from the operational systems, which was described in the previous chapter, is by far the biggest ongoing task in the building and running of a data warehouse. Without this grist for the mill that is the data warehouse, nothing further can happen.

Many data warehouse initiatives run into serious problems early on because the task of populating the data warehouse was not given the emphasis it was due. Other aspects of building the data warehouse may occupy the attention of the project management, such as data model design and query/analysis tools. The ability to populate the data warehouse with data and then manipulate that data into the desired format is often dismissed as an easy-to-solve technical problem. We hope the previous chapter shed light on that misconception.

Simply populating the warehouse with data may well be only the first half of the story. Often, the processes that populate the data warehouse cannot load the data into a format that is ready for use. This involves transforming the data from one (or more) operational data models into the data warehouse data model.

Tactical versus Strategic

It is useful to think in terms of *tactical* and *strategic* data and reporting.

The operational data models, with their emphasis on detailed transactional data and enforcing the rules of data integrity during transactions, are suitable for answering *tactical* business questions. Questions like "What are total sales for the week?" or "Which stock items need to be replenished?" are tactical, and are of more interest to lower- and middle-management.

The data models used in data warehouses, however, are generally intended to answer more *strategic* business questions, such as "What are the trends for revenue and margin over the past three years?" or "What is the correlation between sales volumes and advertising efforts?"

While it is possible to answer *strategic* as well as *tactical* questions using the operational data model and its *transactional level of data granularity*, it will take a lot longer! Continually transforming the data, with every single query, from this low level of data granularity to a more summarized view will take a lot of processing horsepower. The data warehouse data model is optimized for answering strategic business questions by performing much of this initial processing up front and saving the data in this more useful format.

It is not necessary, of course, to have multiple levels of data granularity in the data warehouse. The transformation from *tactical* to *strategic* could possibly take place during ETT, during the loading of data into the data warehouse. But, in order to minimize effort during data extraction from operation systems, it is very common to perform a minimum of transformation on data load (see Figure 7.1).

One reason could be that the utilities used to load the data are simply not capable of completing this transformation. The Oracle import utility (i.e., IMP) is a good example of this. IMP will import exactly what resides in the exported "dump" file. SQL*Loader, while it has some very powerful capabilities for transforming data, is also not capable of performing a radical transformation of the data.

Another reason may have to do with the complexity involved in performing the transformation. Radical transformation may best be done in several discrete simplified stages, rather than in one complex step.

Another consideration is performance. According to the old saying—and with all due respect to animal lovers everywhere—"there is more than one way to skin a cat, but some are faster than others." Each utility can perform the required task, but some do the job faster. An example might be the use of Oracle snapshots or SQL*Loader in conjunction with database triggers. Each of these mechanisms can do the required tasks. But both these particular methods do the job *transactionally* rather than in *mass*. Neither of these methods is built primarily for speed, but rather for transactional integrity and transparency of operation. If performance is a major consideration because of the amount of data to be transferred, then certain methods quite simply cannot be considered, even if they do the job correctly.

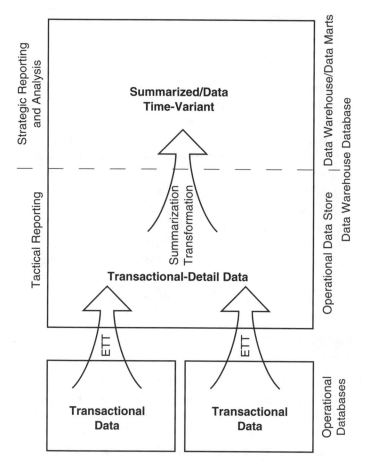

Figure 7.1 Data granularity in the data warehouse.

Last, having the detailed operational data complete with the original operational data model has the added advantage of potentially offloading some of the *tactical* reporting from the operational systems. By freeing the operational systems from this kind of reporting, you are freeing up CPU and memory resources as well as disk space in the operational environment. If the operational environment has a purge capability, it can now be used after the data is extracted to the operational data store in the data warehouse.

Operational Data Stores and Data Warehouses

As we mentioned in Chapter 1, "Data Warehousing," and Chapter 4, "Designing the Oracle Data Warehouse," there is no reason why a data warehouse should not hold detailed operational data. But if the true purpose of the system is to process and produce tactical reports, then we have an *operational data store*, not a data warehouse. The distinction is important, and recognizing it at an early stage can be the difference between success and failure for a project. Designing and implementing an *operational data store* to answer *strategic*, high-level business questions starts with poorly set expectations and leads to ultimate frustration as the finished systems prove incapable of performing adequately. Likewise, imposing mission-critical *tactical* reporting requirements on a *data warehouse* is an expensive mistake that can lead to conflicts of priority and political clashes. Answering strategic business questions may not require 24×7 availability, but answering tactical business questions will indeed have this requirement. Imposing high availability requirements on a system not originally implemented for this can lead to some expensive and unexpected complications, much like a line of dominos falling.

For a detailed discussion on the *operational data store* versus the *data warehouse*, please review Bill Inmon's books, *Building the Data Warehouse* (second edition, 1996, ISBN 0471141615) and *Building the Operational Data Store* (second edition, 1999, ISBN 047132888X), both published by John Wiley & Sons.

Post-Load Processing

Thus, the second half of the load phase is manipulating this data into a level of detail appropriate for analysis, strategic reporting, and data mining. Typically, this processing is treated as *post-load* functionality in the final step of the load phase.

Once the original detail data has been loaded into the data warehouse database, there are three basic kinds of post-load processing to be performed:

- Summarization and aggregation
- Filtering
- Merging and denormalization

The reasons for these operations are quite well documented in this book and in others. Decision support systems such as data warehouses and data marts generally produce *strategic* reports, not *tactical* reports. Tactical reporting is operational in nature and generally shows operational levels of detail. Strategic reports cover large volumes of data over wide ranges of time. Also, the people who read strategic reports are simply not looking for details. They are looking for the "big picture."

For more detail, we discuss the following mechanisms for performing the three previously-mentioned kinds of post-load processing:

- Oracle8*i* materialized views
- Refresh

- Query rewrite
- Dimensions and constraints
- Parallel CREATE TABLE . . . AS SELECT (pCTAS)
- Parallel DML
    - Parallel INSERT with APPEND hint
    - Parallel INSERT with NOAPPEND hint
    - Parallel UPDATE
    - Parallel DELETE
- PL/SQL or Java functions used with parallel DML or pCTAS

Summarization and Aggregation

It is easy to think of rollup summarization as a *saved intermediate step* (see Figure 7.2). There may be dozens or hundreds of queries that first perform a summarization or aggregation on the way to the final result. Creating tables with this summarized information essentially allows programmers to skip this initial step and start querying using the intermediate information.

This can have an enormous positive effect on query performance. Although many database vendors (including Oracle) may tout their parallel capabilities as able to substitute for indexing, it is not always a wise strategy to depend on this capability. Although it is true that the parallel queries against huge tables can indeed rival the performance of a nonparallel scan against a smaller table

IS SUMMARIZATION NECESSARY?

The use of any of these techniques is, in a very strict sense, completely superfluous. There isn't any real business need to summarize or aggregate, for example, because the summary data can always be reconstructed from the detail data. A purist might sniff that such activities are simply intermediate steps, imposed because of the limitations on performance and capacity set by existing hardware and software.

This is true, but the limitations on performance and capacity are nonetheless real. If a data warehouse is tasked with storing 5 to 10 years of historical data, it may be unrealistic to expect the entire 5 to 10 years to be stored in detail. The costs in storage capacity might significantly reduce the return on investment of the data warehouse, and we can't have that!

Similarly, the performance implications of constantly reaggregating detail data to answer basic questions are staggering. Why waste the resources to perform an operation thousands or millions of times when you can perform it once a month and save the results for later use?

for some queries, consider *scalability*. Parallelized full table scans against huge tables may indeed be able to rival nonparallel scans against smaller tables when the system is virtually empty, but it is unlikely that *100* simultaneous parallel queries can match the performance of *100* simpler nonparallel queries. Parallel queries on huge tables simply consume too many resources to scale effectively. Rollups eliminate that problem.

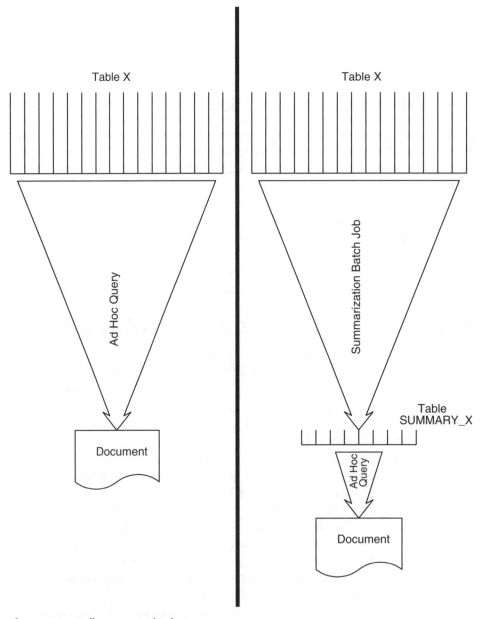

Figure 7.2   Rollup summarization.

For example, take our example schema for a project accounting application, specifically the two tables, ACTIVITIES and PROJECTS.

```
CREATE TABLE PROJECTS
(    PROJECT_ID          NUMBER(10),
     PROJECT_NAME        VARCHAR2(40),
     SERVICE_LINE        VARCHAR2(40),
     INDUSTRY            VARCHAR2(40),
     TYPE                VARCHAR2(40),
     CLIENT              VARCHAR2(60),
     START_DATE          DATE,
     CLOSE_DATE          DATE,
     STATUS              VARCHAR2(5),
     CONSTRAINT PROJECTS_PK PRIMARY KEY (PROJECT_ID)
)
CREATE TABLE ACTIVITY
(    PROJECT_ID          NUMBER(10),
     ORG_ID              NUMBER(10),
     EMPLOYEE_ID         NUMBER(10),
     FUNCTION_ID         NUMBER(10),
     FISCAL_YR           NUMBER(4),
     FISCAL_MONTH        NUMBER(2),
     HOURS               NUMBER(11,2),
     EXPENSES            NUMBER(11,2),
     REVENUE             NUMBER(11,2)
)
```

In terms of an entity-relationship diagram, these two tables belong to the relationship illustrated in Figure 7.3.

A large number of decision-support queries are likely to be at the PROJECTS level as opposed to the ACTIVITIES level. Instead of forcing each user to query the detailed table ACTIVITIES, it would make sense to use the following:

```
SELECT  SUM(HOURS)  SUM_HOURS,
        SUM(EXPENSES)  SUM_EXPENSES,
        SUM(REVENUE)  SUM_REVENUE
  FROM ACTIVITIES
 WHERE PROJECT_ID = 9999999
 GROUP BY  PROJECT_ID;
```

Figure 7.3 Relationship between ACTIVITIES and PROJECTS.

The new columns SUM_HOURS, SUM_EXPENSES, and SUM_REVENUE could be added to the PROJECTS table and modified whenever new data is added to the ACTIVITIES table.

Filtering

Data marts are generally differentiated from data warehouses by being focused on specific subject matter, such as financial, sales and marketing, or product service history. Creating each of these subject-matter specific subsets involves filtering information from the greater mass (see Figure 7.4).

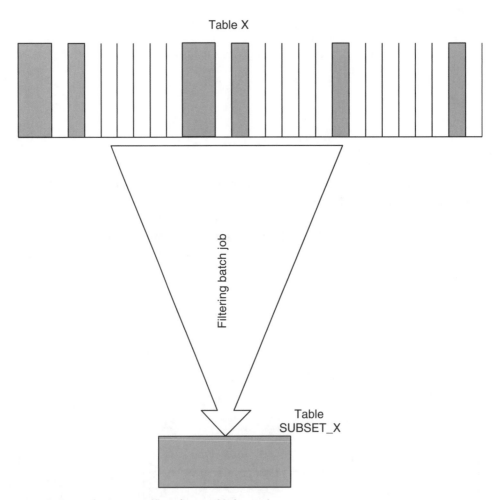

Figure 7.4 Filtering specific subsets of information.

For example, using our example of the ACTIVITIES table we have:

```
CREATE TABLE ACTIVITY
(      PROJECT_ID         NUMBER(10),
       ORG_ID             NUMBER(10),
       EMPLOYEE_ID        NUMBER(10),
       FUNCTION_ID        NUMBER(10),
       FISCAL_YR          NUMBER(4),
       FISCAL_MONTH       NUMBER(2),
       HOURS              NUMBER(11,2),
       EXPENSES           NUMBER(11,2),
       REVENUE            NUMBER(11,2)
)
```

We may want to extract just revenue information for the business purpose of analyzing revenue separately.

We may also wish to extract information about projects based within certain geographies or employees with specific job titles.

Filtering is a way of reducing a complex question into easily answered components. If we can create a set of information composed of data that has already been filtered against several initial criteria, then the complexity involved in reaching the final answer can be reduced.

Also, filtering can be a way of ensuring that disparate organizations or end users see only the data that they are supposed to see.

```
CREATE TABLE EAST_REVENUE
AS
SELECT org_id
       revenue
  FROM activities
 WHERE org_id IN
       (SELECT org_id FROM organizations WHERE region = 'EAST')
```

Because organizations in the West may not need to know about issues in the East, we now have a smaller set of data for each region to query.

Merging and Denormalization

Often, strategic data is created by the act of merging data. For example, merging customer service history with invoicing and customer billing information produces a more complete picture of the customer. Further merging of this customer information with demographic data or psychographic data can yield a completely unexpected portrait of the customer. This process is illustrated in Figure 7.5.

For instance, with the addition of demographic data you could realize that all customers with specific buying patterns live within a certain area, close to one

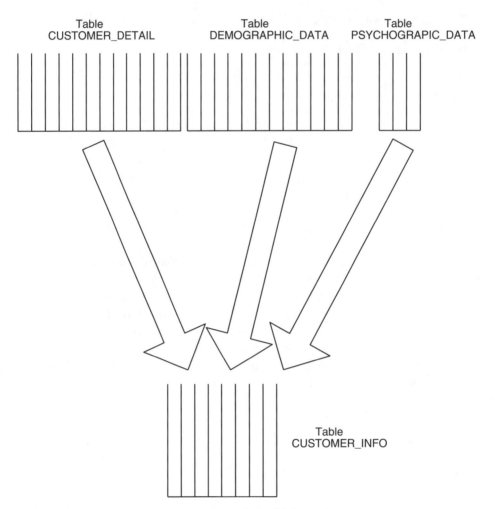

Figure 7.5 Merging information to create derived information.

another. This could lead to insights in focusing marketing efforts as well as shifting inventory to meet demand that could pay for the cost of the entire data warehouse with a single decision.

Oracle8*i* Materialized Views

Easily the most significant new feature of Oracle8*i* for data warehousing is *materialized views* and the breadth of new features to support their use.

Materialized views are in fact a reuse of the Oracle SNAPSHOT, which was originally introduced in Oracle7 version 7.0. For the most part, the terms *materialized view* and *snapshot* have become synonymous within the Oracle RDBMS, such that the documentation in the *Oracle8i SQL Language Reference* manual combines the CREATE, ALTER, and DROP commands for both commands.

There is more to the concept of a materialized view that differentiates it from the snapshot, which has been in use for almost 10 years. The cost-based optimizer (CBO) in the Oracle RDBMS has been enhanced to recognize conditions when a query might benefit from using a materialized view instead of executing the way it was written. If this is detected, the CBO can actually *rewrite* the query to use the materialized view instead.

The power of this *query rewrite* feature cannot be underestimated. Why?

It is common for an alert application developer or database administrator to detect that it would be more efficient for a query to use a *rollup* or *summary table*, instead of spending resources summarizing from detailed data repeatedly. It is a relatively small matter to prove that the query should be changed, to create the rollup or summary table if necessary, to create the jobs to populate them with data. Depending on circumstances, it is possible to have a new summary table in place in a matter of hours or days.

None of these things is trivial, but their cost pales beside the task of somehow getting the original SQL statements themselves modified to use the new table. Think about it: You've recognized the problem and implemented the fix, but nobody has the time to modify applications and reports to use it.

Change is not easy, and changing code (even a fourth-generation language like SQL) can be time-consuming and tricky. New bugs may be introduced, causing further problems. If the SQL is *generated* using a browsing or OLAP utility, it might be completely impossible to cause the utility to generate its SQL statements differently.

Consider the Year 2000 problem: Fixing it was never a complex technical issue. It is the task of finding all the places in billions of lines of code in which it resided, of applying the changes without causing side effects in scrambled and undocumented spaghetti-code, and of simply finding competent people to effect the fixes.

Sometimes, the technical issue at hand is the easiest to resolve; it is infinitely more difficult to handle all the side effects. The Y2K bug is one example. Shifting data warehouse workload from one table to a summary table is another example. The decentralized, free-format, *buy-some-software-at-the-dime-store-plug-it-in-and-use-it* nature of data warehouse end users has its benefits, but this is one of the drawbacks.

Having a SQL optimizer that can perform this redirection automatically, without the end user (or the OLAP utility he is using) getting involved is quite simply a stroke of genius.

Of course, you have to jump through some hoops to provide the cost-based optimizer with all of the information it needs to perform this magic, but it is undoubtedly worth it. The purpose of this chapter is to help you decide whether you should jump through those hoops, and determine where they are if you decide you want to.

Rollup and summary tables have been around since the beginning of computing. In the world of Oracle, you were required to write most of the data refresh logic outside of the RDBMS, and you were required to alter application code to take advantage of it.

With Oracle8*i* materialized views, you have the capability to put together rollups and summary tables completely within the Oracle RDBMS, without needing any outside help from the operating-system or other software packages. Even more importantly, you can ensure that your efforts bear fruit by using the *query rewrite* feature to redirect workload automatically.

Gee, I wonder if Oracle does windows, too . . .

Snapshots and Materialized Views

Snapshots have been a feature of the Oracle RDBMS for almost 10 years now. They were originally intended for data replication between two Oracle databases connected by a database link (see Figure 7.6). By copying data across the

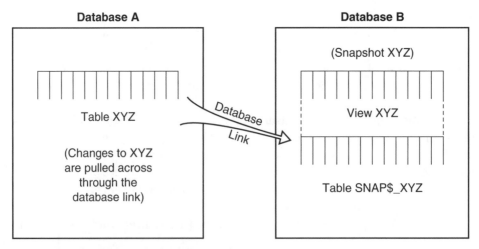

Figure 7.6 Snapshots introduced in Oracle7.

link asynchronously and caching it locally, SQL statements could avoid the costs of pulling data through the network repeatedly while also avoiding the possible loss of service in the event the network failed.

Snapshots were the first of a deluge of data replication features. With the concept of *distributed databases* effectively discredited for mission-critical systems due to issues with the network, data replication provided the perfect compromise, providing reliable access to distributed data while enforcing *ownership* or *mastery* of the data.

Oracle's data replication schemes have moved far beyond the original concept of the read-only snapshot. Updateable snapshots and N-way mastering of data have greatly improved the range of capabilities of Oracle. Replication is now a huge area of interest that can take years to master.

Materialized views are implemented exactly the same way as read-only snapshots (see Figure 7.7). They are usually located in the same database and schema as their source data. They are not updateable as of version 8.1 of Oracle8*i*, but for data warehousing applications, that is certainly not an issue.

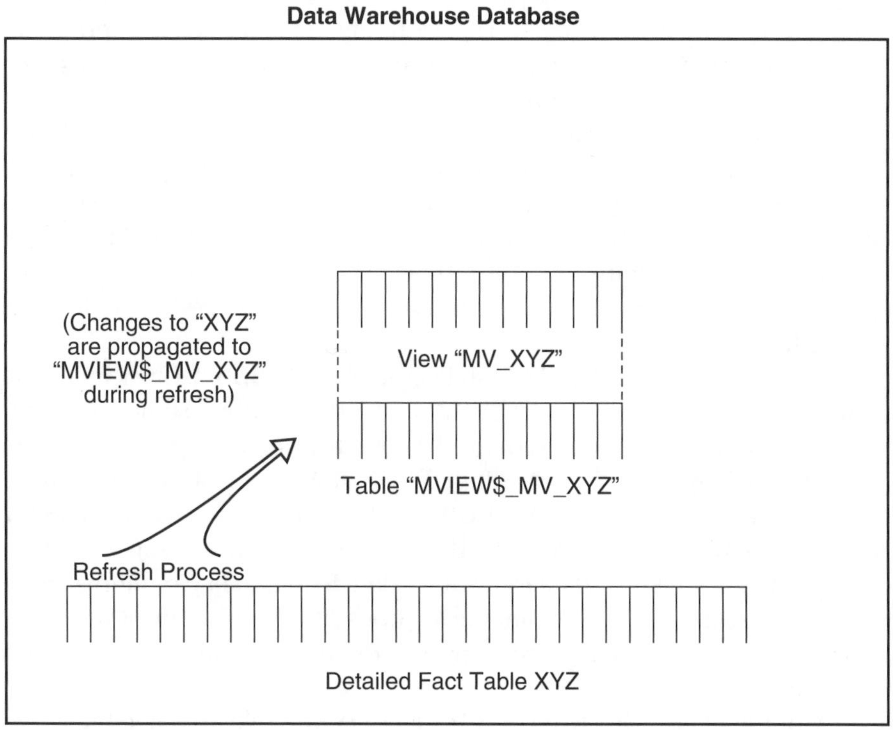

Figure 7.7 Oracle8*i* materialized views.

A materialized view, like a snapshot, consists of a table that is populated according to a query. The query is defined in the CREATE MATERIALIZED VIEW command:

```
CREATE MATERIALIZED VIEW ACTIVITIES_PROJECTS_MV
       STORAGE (INITIAL 128K NEXT 128K PCTINCREASE 0)
       TABLESPACE FOOBAR_DATA01
       BUILD IMMEDIATE
       REFRESH FAST ON COMMIT
       ENABLE QUERY REWRITE
    AS
SELECT PROJECTS.ID,
       PROJECTS.NAME,
       COUNT(*) CNT,
       SUM(ACTIVITIES.HOURS) HOURS,
       SUM(ACTIVITIES.EXPENSES) EXPENSES,
       SUM(ACTIVITIES.REVENUE) REVENUE
   FROM ACTIVITIES,
       PROJECTS
 WHERE ACTIVITIES.PROJECT_ID = PROJECTS.ID
 GROUP BY  PROJECTS.ID
          PROJECTS.NAME;
```

The query is simply a join between the PROJECTS and ACTIVITIES table, summarizing activities by project. The resulting table is given appropriate STORAGE parameters in tablespace FOOBAR_DATA01. Now, let's discuss the other clauses in this CREATE statement.

The BUILD IMMEDIATE clause indicates that the materialized view should be populated with data immediately when this CREATE command is executed. The other alternative is to BUILD DEFERRED, which would define the materialized view in the data dictionary and create the necessary table, but not populate the table with data until the first refresh. Thus, the BUILD clause affects only the initial population of the materialized view; for the rest of its lifetime this clause has no effect.

In most cases, choosing BUILD IMMEDIATE or BUILD DEFERRED can come down to a matter of style, but BUILD DEFERRED offers some additional options when two or more materialized views are logically related to one another. The DBMS_MVIEW.REFRESH_DEPENDENT procedure can be used to refresh all materialized views that are dependent on a list of source tables, or the DBMS_MVIEW.REFRESH_ALL_MVIEWS can be used to refresh all materialized views that have "stale" data following a data load into one or more source tables. Using BUILD DEFERRED and these procedures may allow new materialized views to be populated at once, thereby *publishing* the materialized views in a coherent fashion.

Next, with the clause REFRESH FAST ON COMMIT, we are specifying two different properties of the method by which data will be propagated—or *refreshed*—from the source tables (i.e., ACTIVITIES and PROJECTS). First, REFRESH FAST means that we will use one of two fast refresh mechanisms: a direct-path operation (i.e., INSERT APPEND) or *materialized view logs*.

Besides the REFRESH FAST clause, which will succeed only if several restrictions are resolved, one can always perform a REFRESH COMPLETE. For a complete refresh, the defining query of the view is reexecuted, and all of the data in the materialized view is replaced completely. While this option has no restrictions on it, you can tell that it will likely be too slow in the vast majority of situations. If one or more of the source tables are large, then there simply might not be enough hours in the day to perform a COMPLETE REFRESH! It's another example of the perpetual trade-off in computing: *speed* versus *flexibility*. One method of refresh is fast but relatively inflexible, with many restrictions. The other method of refresh is as flexible as the SELECT command but may not be very fast.

If you don't want to choose between FAST and COMPLETE immediately, then you can try the REFRESH FORCE clause. Here, if a fast refresh is possible, it is used. If not, then a complete refresh is used. This might be useful if the restrictions preventing the use of fast refresh are in place at the present time, but in future they may be resolved.

And, if for some reason you don't wish the materialized view to be refreshed, there is always the option REFRESH NONE, which should be self-explanatory!

Because the ON COMMIT clause is also specified, it means that we want the materialized view to be updated with each committed transaction against the source tables. Every time someone commits an INSERT, UPDATE, or DELETE from the tables ACTIVITIES and PROJECTS, we want the materialized view ACTIVITIES_PROJECTS to be refreshed with the same information as part of the same transaction. Specifying ON COMMIT implies that we always want the materialized view to be precisely synchronized with its source tables. In other words, one of our business requirements is that we have no tolerance for the data in the materialized view to be *out-of-date* in any way.

The alternative to ON COMMIT is ON DEMAND, which indicates that refresh will be performed explicitly by the DBMS_MVIEW package. The procedures in this package can be called manually (via SQL*Plus, for example), from the DBMS_JOB scheduling package, or from an external job-control utility (such as Oracle Enterprise Manager or CA-Unicenter).

When should ON COMMIT be used instead of ON DEMAND?

- When changes to the source tables(s) come from transactions, not batch loads or discrete "load cycles"

- When changes to the source table(s) must be reflected immediately in the materialized views and "stale" data cannot be tolerated

- When changes to the source table(s) are relatively sparse or few

CHECK *ALERT.LOG* AND *.TRC* FILES IF USING ON COMMIT

If you have specified ON COMMIT as part of the refresh policy for your materialized view, then be sure to check the database instance's "alert.log" for any errors that may occur during refresh. In the event that a failure happens during the refresh, it will be logged to the "alert.log" file and trace (".trc") files will be created in the USER_DUMP_DEST directory.

  If the refresh of a materialized view fails, then refreshes will no longer be performed ON COMMIT. It will be necessary to correct the problem and then continue the next refresh successfully using the DBMS_MVIEW package before ON COMMIT refresh will be enabled again.

When should ON DEMAND be used instead of ON COMMIT?

- When changes to the source table(s) are applied in bulk, in large quantities
- When there is complex logic in the load cycle, involving intermediate steps where changes to source tables should not be propagated to the materialized views immediately
- When the data in the materialized views is allowed to be out-of-synch with the data in the source tables

Overall, it is most common to use the ON DEMAND method of refresh in most data warehousing applications. ON COMMIT involves less intervention from humans (thus less care and feeding), but the costs implicit with it can make it troublesome. If data changes to the source tables are applied in large quantities with frequent commits, then appending the changes to materialized views to each transaction can significantly slow each transaction, for example. Also, a business requirement to transactionally modify a table does not fit well with most decision support systems; this is likely a requirement for an *operational system*, and it might be worthwhile to reexamine this requirement. Such a requirement would indicate an *operational data store* instead of a *data warehouse* or *data mart*, quite possibly. An *operational data store* can still be a part of a decision support system, but it might be wise to mark a clear dividing line between the ODS and downstream data warehouses and data marts to prevent conflicting requirements.

It may not be necessary for the source tables and the materialized view to be perfectly synchronized with each other. It simply may not be a business requirement. In a data warehouse, it is more common for large bulk operations to be performed according to a scheduled *load cycle* (rather than *transactionally*), so that data from many tables and materialized views is "published" for end-user use all at once. It is quite common for end users to understand that there may be a time delay of hours or days between the appearance of changes in detail-level source tables and the summarized materialized views. Given these facts, it is more common practice to create the materialized views as follows:

```
CREATE MATERIALIZED VIEW ACTIVITIES_PROJECTS_MV
        STORAGE (INITIAL 128K NEXT 128K PCTINCREASE 0)
        TABLESPACE FOOBAR_DATA01
        BUILD DEFERRED
        REFRESH FAST ON DEMAND
        PARALLEL
        ENABLE QUERY REWRITE
AS
SELECT PROJECTS.ID,
        PROJECTS.NAME,
        COUNT(*) CNT,
        SUM(ACTIVITIES.HOURS) HOURS,
        SUM(ACTIVITIES.EXPENSES) EXPENSES,
        SUM(ACTIVITIES.REVENUE) REVENUE
   FROM ACTIVITIES,
        PROJECTS
  WHERE ACTIVITIES.PROJECT_ID = PROJECTS.ID
GROUP BY  PROJECTS.ID
           PROJECTS.NAME;
```

This materialized view is defined with exactly the same query as the previous one. The only differences are in the REFRESH specifications. We are using BUILD DEFERRED to populate the view at the first refresh. Also, we are using ON DEMAND to specify that refresh occurs through the use of the DBMS_MVIEW package. Also, the PARALLEL clause is specified to enable the use of parallelism wherever possible to speed refreshes.

Last, the materialized view mechanism can apply to summary tables or rollups created under previous versions of Oracle. These are known as PRE-BUILT materialized views, and they can be created as follows:

```
CREATE MATERIALIZED VIEW ACTIVITIES_PROJECTS_MV
        ON PREBUILT TABLE
        WITHOUT REDUCED PRECISION
        REFRESH NONE
        ENABLE QUERY REWRITE
AS
SELECT PROJECTS.ID,
        PROJECTS.NAME,
        COUNT(*) CNT,
        SUM(ACTIVITIES.HOURS) HOURS,
        SUM(ACTIVITIES.EXPENSES) EXPENSES,
        SUM(ACTIVITIES.REVENUE) REVENUE
   FROM ACTIVITIES,
```

```
         PROJECTS
  WHERE ACTIVITIES.PROJECT_ID = PROJECTS.ID
  GROUP BY   PROJECTS.ID
             PROJECTS.NAME;
```

The ON PREBUILT TABLE clause indicates that the table of the specified name already exists, built according to the query specified in the CREATE command. The clause WITHOUT REDUCED PRECISION indicates that the table that is already defined must be able to store all column values without any loss of precision, or the CREATE command will fail. The alternative, WITH REDUCED PRECISION, will allow the CREATE command to succeed even if some form of numeric rounding or string truncation would be necessary to store data from the specified query.

The REFRESH NONE clause indicates that this prebuilt materialized view will not be populated with data using Oracle's refresh mechanisms. Rather, other arrangements (presumably a prebuilt batch process) will populate the table with data. It is possible to specify COMPLETE, FAST, or FORCE for prebuilt materialized views, if you wish the view to be maintained that way from here on.

These three brief examples illustrate some of the choices that need to be made when creating materialized views.

> **TIP** It is strongly advised that the reader consult the *Oracle8*i *Server Tuning* manual, Chapter 28. "Data Warehousing with Materialized Views" and Chapter 29, "Materialized Views" for more detailed explanations of concepts. If you do not have access to these manuals in hard copy, then soft-copy versions in HTML and Adobe Acrobat format are available online at http://technet.oracle.com/.

Now, we'll discuss some guidelines for successfully using materialized views.

Guidelines for Creating Materialized Views

We'll first discuss some guidelines for creating materialized views. This is followed by issues surrounding *refresh* and *query rewrite*, and as we do so we discuss how each of the features found in Table 7.1 (some new with Oracle8*i*) relate to and affect materialized views.

The purpose of materialized views in data warehouses is to improve query performance by precalculating expensive and time-consuming aggregations, prejoining complicated and expensive table joins, or both of these together.

Thus, it's important to remember that materialized views are intended for the following situations:

Table 7.1 Related Features and Their Effects on Materialized Views

RELATED ORACLE FEATURE	MV OPERATION AFFECTED
DBMS_JOB supplied package	Refresh
DBMS_MVIEW supplied package	Refresh
DIMENSIONS	Query Rewrite
RELY constraints	Query Rewrite

- Preaggregation on a single table
- Prejoining two or more tables
- Preaggregation resulting from prejoining two or more tables (combination of the above)

Each of these situations presents different challenges to the Oracle cost-based optimizer during refresh and query rewrite, so it is important to note what category you are working with, in the event that there is a problem and something is not working correctly. If you determine that your situation does not fall into one of these situations, then it may help explain why problems with fast refresh or query rewrite may be occurring!

Best Practices

But first, let's discuss some *best practices* to help ensure the successful implementation of materialized views:

When joining, make sure PRIMARY KEY and FOREIGN KEY constraints are defined. The constraints are intended mostly as *data dictionary documentation* for use by the cost-based optimizer. Also, they can ensure that each child record has one and only one row for a parent. If you do not wish to incur the overhead of enforcing the constraints, then use the NOVALIDATE and RELY options.

When loading source tables, use direct-path SQL*Loader or direct-path INSERT APPEND where possible, to enable *fast refresh*. The Oracle8*i* RDBMS creates a *direct-path log* during a direct-path insert. This log is invisible to users and is created automatically, marking database blocks loaded with direct-path. Materialized views can subsequently use this direct-path log for incremental refresh during a fast refresh.

If source tables will be modified with conventional INSERT, UPDATE, or DELETE statements, create materialized view logs on the source tables, to enable *fast refresh*. If direct-path cannot be used, then materialized view logs will track any changes. Database triggers trap all conventional-path INSERT, UPDATE, and DELETE statements and log the rows affected. Then, during an ON COMMIT or ON DEMAND refresh of a materialized view, these logs can be replayed to propagate the changes incrementally.

If source tables are partitioned, try to partition the related materialized view similarly. Quite often, one of the reasons for partitioning the source tables is to optimize the loading of data. If this is the case, then partitioning the materialized view similarly can also simplify refresh.

If the materialized view is a join of two or more partitioned tables and the partitioned tables are not partitioned similarly, then try to choose the partitioning scheme that is time-based and that most closely matches the frequency of refreshes.

After loading the source tables and before refreshing the materialized view, use DBMS_OLAP.VALIDATE_DIMENSION. Avoid trouble before it happens. If the VALIDATE_DIMENSION procedure fails, then don't perform the refresh. Fix the problem, and then continue. We talk more about dimensions later in the chapter.

Create a concatenated index across all of the non-aggregated key columns on the materialized view's underlying table. This approach aids fast refresh. If a change to the source table might cause an INSERT of a new row in the materialized view or UPDATE of an existing row, the fast refresh mechanism will look for a concatenated index across all of the nonaggregated columns in the SELECT list of the defining query. Lack of such an index would disable fast refresh.

Initialization Parameters

For more information about these (and other) parameters, please see the *Oracle8i Server Reference* manual. These parameters have direct effect on the use of materialized views:

- COMPATIBLE
    - Should be at least 8.1.0; best if it matches the first three numbers of the actual version.
- OPTIMIZER_MODE
    - Should be either CHOOSE (the default), ALL_ROWS, or FIRST_ROWS. The default should be sufficient for most cases, but there is a more detailed discussion in Chapter 9, "Data Warehouse Performance Tuning," on the behaviors of each option.

- QUERY_REWRITE_ENABLED

  - Should be set to TRUE. If not, it can be overridden at the session level by ALTER SESSION SET QUERY_REWRITE_ENABLED = TRUE or at the statement level by the hint REWRITE.

  - Conversely, if this parameter is set to TRUE, it can be overridden at the session level by ALTER SESSION SET QUERY_REWRITE_ ENABLED = FALSE or at the statement level by the hint NOREWRITE.

  - Be aware that each materialized view must have been created or altered with ENABLE QUERY REWRITE as well and that the user executing the query must have been granted QUERY REWRITE permission. That makes a total of three *circus hoops* you have to jump through to enable query rewrite.

- QUERY_REWRITE_INTEGRITY

  - Can be set to ENFORCED (the default), TRUSTED, or STALE_TOL- ERATED. These settings indicate how synchronized the data in the materialized view can be in order to allow query rewrite.

  - The default setting of ENFORCED is the safest setting, as it will allow query rewrite only when referential-integrity constraints among the source tables are enabled and validated and if the data in the materialized view is fully refreshed and synchronized with the source tables. It may be the safest setting to use, but it may also be the least realistic. Most data warehouses do not validate using con- straints, due to the processing overhead. Instead, many times the constraints are declared but set to NOVALIDATE RELY, which dis- ables enforcement.

  - TRUSTED represents a slightly more lax attitude toward the accu- racy of data in the materialized view. It is a trade-off between the processing-overhead benefits of using NOVALIDATE RELY con- straints and the accuracy costs of possibly returning erroneous data. TRUSTED still requires the data in the materialized view to be fully up-to-date on refreshes, but it allows the use of NOVALIDATE RELY constraints regardless. If there are referential-integrity prob- lems in the data, the setting of TRUSTED will allow query rewrite using the materialized views. This is actually not a serious issue, as referential-integrity problems in the source tables will affect queries that go directly against the source tables anyway. In one respect, TRUSTED might allow those problems to be detected sooner, as query rewrite using materialized views provides faster query response.

- STALE_TOLERATED takes an even more lax attitude toward data accuracy in the materialized views. STALE_TOLERATED has the same attributes as TRUSTED, with regards to constraints. In addition, STALE_TOLERATED will allow query rewrite regardless of the "freshness" of the data in the materialized views.

- JOB_QUEUE_PROCESSES

    - By default, this is set to 0, indicating that there are no background processes to push the job queues used by the DBMS_JOB package. While the use of the DBMS_JOB package to perform materialized view refreshes and other maintenance is not a requirement, it is a very good practice.

    - External job processing systems (such as Oracle's Enterprise Manager, UNIX's *cron*, NT's *at*, or more elaborate packages such as CA-Unicenter and Tivoli) would need to handle the situation where the database instance is not running or is unavailable due to network failure. Using the internal DBMS_JOB package would not need to make such checks or handle such errors because it would run only when the database was available.

    - The setting of JOB_QUEUE_PROCESSES represents the number of jobs that can execute concurrently.

- JOB_QUEUE_INTERVAL

    - This is the number of seconds between checks for newly submitted jobs from DBMS_JOB. The default of 60 is usually sufficient, but certain requirements might provide a good case for resetting it to a lower value. For example, if the parameter QUERY_REWRITE_INTEGRITY is set to ENFORCED or TRUSTED and materialized views that are being refreshed through DBMS_JOB are frequently failing to use query rewrite, it might make sense to initiate refreshes more often.

- UTL_FILE_DIR

    - The file-system directory in which log files (in ASCII text) that chronicle errors during ON DEMAND refreshes using the DBMS_MVIEW package will be located. If a list of directories is specified, then the first will contain the log text files.

Permissions

At least up through Oracle8*i* version 8.1.5, it is highly recommended (to the point of being a requirement) that the materialized view be created in the same schema as its source tables. This eliminates possible complications due to lack of SELECT permissions on source tables, their materialized view logs or direct-path logs, the database triggers that are implicitly created, and so on. Listed in Table 7.2 are permissions related to materialized views which must be GRANTed or REVOKEd:

Data Dictionary Views

As with most data dictionary views, there are three levels: USER, ALL, and DBA. Each of the views described in Table 7.3 has USER-level views that describe information for the current Oracle schema or account, ALL-level views that describe information for which the current Oracle schema or account has privileges, and DBA-level views that describe all information for all Oracle accounts. Replace the "xxx" in the view names with "USER," "ALL," or "DBA" as appropriate.

Refresh

Materialized views are like the perfect household pet. Real household pets require care and feeding, with frequent litter-box cleanings (depending on the species and diet of your pet). So, too, in a way, did summary tables and rollups prior to materialized views. Now, with materialized views, all of that care and feeding can be dealt with up front. But they are not without cost. They do consume disk space, and they do need to be properly planned to take advantage of refresh and query rewrite. It's sort of like arranging to have your pet fed,

Table 7.2   Security Permissions Related to Materialized Views

PERMISSION NAME	DESCRIPTION
CREATE MATERIALIZED VIEW	Create or replace a materialized view in the current schema.
CREATE ANY MATERIALIZED VIEW	Create or replace a materialized view in another schema.
QUERY REWRITE	Be aware that the database initialization parameter QUERY_REWRITE_ENABLE must be TRUE or that ALTER SESSION QUERY_REWRITE_ENABLE = TRUE or the SQL statement must use the hint REWRITE to enable query rewrite. Of course, the materialized view must also have been created or altered with the ENABLE QUERY REWRITE clause.
GLOBAL QUERY REWRITE	Enable query rewrite when using a materialized view in another schema.

Table 7.3 Data Dictionary Views Pertaining to Materialized Views

VIEW NAME	DESCRIPTION
*xxx*_SNAPSHOTS	Describes materialized views (snapshots), including refresh methods.
*xxx*_MVIEW_AGGREGATES	Describes aggregation expressions within materialized views, one row per item in the SELECT-list.
*xxx*_MVIEW_ANALYSIS	Populated from the DBMS_OLAP package, this view contains information about materialized views that are eligible for query rewrite. Contains information about: last refresh, whether data is stale or not, whether incremental refresh is possible, and other useful facts for debugging refresh and query rewrite failures.
*xxx*_MVIEW_DETAIL_RELATIONS	Describes the tables and views in the FROM clause of the query defining a materialized view. Does not include entries for inline views (e.g., subqueries in the FROM clause).
*xxx*_MVIEW_JOINS	Describes the columns used for joins in the WHERE clause of the query defining a materialized view.
*xxx*_MVIEW_KEYS	Describes the columns referenced in the SELECT (and GROUP BY) clauses of the query defining a materialized view.

watered, and walked for several years in advance; best to set it up correctly in the beginning to avoid a malnourished or under-exercised pet after time passes. But once they've been set up, materialized views very much take care of themselves. As much as you love your Labrador Retriever or Siamese, think how much fonder you would be if Brutus or Tabitha could take care of his or her own adorable self. It is probably not wise to take this analogy too far, but the point to be made is that materialized views reduce care and feeding.

Although the technique of rollups and the like has been around for decades, and has certainly been a part of Oracle-based applications since the very beginning, the technique has always involved pulling together many disparate parts to accomplish everything. The database (and database administrators) must provide the storage of and access to the tables. A job-control system (and system administrators and operations staff) must provide the processes to refresh data in the tables. Developers must provide changes to application program modules to make use of the new data. With all the coordination necessary to mesh all of the moving parts, staging the Summer Olympics begins to look comparatively simple, and it becomes quite easy to talk yourself out of the whole thing.

Materialized views, with automatic refresh, can eliminate much of the need for working with a job-control system. Query rewrite can avoid the need to rewrite application code.

First, let's start with the refresh mechanisms. As previously mentioned, there are two primary methods for refresh: *complete* and *fast*.

Complete refresh simply means that the underlying table of the materialized view is truncated and the defining query is reexecuted to populate it. As you can imagine, you might want to consider if this could occur fast enough to suit your purposes. If it does, then there is nothing further to consider. If not, then we must consider fast refresh.

Fast refresh implies some form of *incremental refresh*, and this is done two ways: using a *direct-path* mechanism or using *materialized view logs*.

Ideally, we would like to use fast refresh, in much the same way most people prefer first-class seating on airplanes. Coach seating still gets you there, but as I'm writing this sentence on a laptop in seat 32B (middle) at this very moment, I can vouch for the fact that first class is better in every possible way. Sometimes just getting there is not good enough! So, because *complete refresh* is generally less desirable, let's concentrate on getting *fast incremental refresh* to work.

Fast refresh can occur using either *direct-path logs* or *materialized view logs*. Let's discuss direct-path first, then materialized view logs.

Fast Refresh from Direct-Path Load Logs

The direct-path mechanism in Oracle was originally written for the MVS mainframe port of the Oracle RDBMS in the version 6.0 timeframe. It was intended to compete with fast data loading utilities provided by IBM's DB2 product. The direct-path mechanism bypasses many of the shared and cached facilities of the Oracle RDBMS, permitting individual processes to insert data directly to data files, resulting in bulk insertion of rows that is orders of magnitude faster than *conventional-path* inserts. The direct-path mechanism can be used only for the insertion of rows; no direct-path mechanism exists to update or delete rows.

As of Oracle8*i* version 8.1, the only methods of utilizing direct-path to append additional rows to an existing table are those listed in Table 7.4.

Whenever one of these loading methods is used against a source table, a direct-path log is created within the table in question, identifying the database blocks created in this manner. As long as no "conventional" DML takes place against these blocks, then the materialized view fast refresh mechanism can use this log to identify recently inserted rows. This data can then be propagated to the materialized views according to their defining queries.

Table 7.4 Direct-Path Interfaces

NAME OF INTERFACE	DESCRIPTION
SQL*Loader direct=TRUE	Introduced in Oracle7 version 7.0. See the *Oracle7 Utilities* or *Oracle8i Utilities* manual.
SQL*Loader direct=TRUE parallel=TRUE	Introduced in Oracle7 version 7.1. See the *Oracle7 Utilities* or *Oracle8i Utilities* manual.
INSERT /*+ APPEND */	Introduced in Oracle8*i* version 8.0. See the *Oracle8i Tuning* manual.
OCI	Introduced in Oracle8*i* version 8.1. See the *Oracle Call Interface Programmer's Guide*, Chapter 9, "OCI Programming Advanced Topics," for a description of the direct-path API for 3GL programming languages such as C, C++, or COBOL.

Fast Refresh from Materialized View Logs

Materialized view logs are exactly the same as *snapshot logs* from earlier versions of Oracle. In Oracle8*i*, these two features are really one and the same, just as *snapshots* and *materialized views* are one and the same. Materialized view logs are additional tables that are populated by means of database triggers recording all *conventional-path* INSERTs, UPDATEs, and DELETEs to a table. For example, the source tables ACTIVITIES and PROJECTS might have materialized view logs associated with them. When the materialized view logs are created, database triggers are also created on these tables that record all INSERT, UPDATE, and DELETE operations against them (see Figure 7.8).

General Restrictions on Fast Refresh

You should be aware of some restrictions on fast refresh for all types of materialized views:

- Tables cannot appear more than once in the FROM list.
- Tables cannot be remote (no database links).
- Nonrepeatable expressions such as ROWNUM, SYSDATE, or user-defined PL/SQL functions that are not created with the DETERMINISTIC clause are *verboten*.
- No RAW or LONG RAW columns are allowed.
- No HAVING clause is allowed.

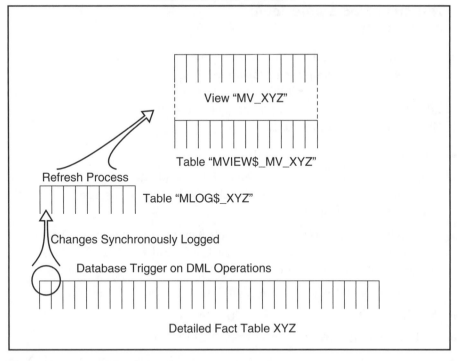

Data Warehouse Database

Figure 7.8   Materialized view logs.

- No CONNECT BY clause is allowed.
- No subqueries are allowed.
- No inline views in FROM list are provided.
- No set operators (i.e., UNION, MINUS, INTERSECT) are used.

In addition to these restrictions, which are common for all types of materialized views that allow fast refresh, there are other restrictions to be aware of. Be sure that you classify your materialized view into one of the three following categories if you intend to use REFRESH FAST with them:

- Preaggregation on a single table.
- Prejoining two or more tables.
- Preaggregation resulting from prejoining two or more tables (combination of the above).

Remember: You can create materialized views that do not fall into one of these categories, but you will only be able to REFRESH COMPLETE.

Additional Restrictions for Fast Refresh of Presummarized Single-Table Aggregate Views

Just as with most advanced features, there is a fairly extensive list of things that you either *must do* or simply *cannot do*. Sometimes, these restrictions seem like the incantation for a witch's brew. For materialized views which are defined with a query that is a simple single-table aggregation (i.e., it includes a GROUP BY clause), we have the following:

- No WHERE clause is permitted.

- Nonaggregated expressions in the SELECT and GROUP BY clauses must be simple column references; no single-row functions (i.e., DECODE, NVL, etc.) are permitted.

- Arithmetic operators (i.e., +, −, *, /, etc.) and string operators (i.e., "||" for concatenate) are permitted in the SELECT and GROUP BY clauses for nonaggregated columns, but they must be the same in both places.

- Aggregate functions (i.e., SUM, COUNT, etc.) cannot be nested.

- No MIN and MAX functions are permitted.

- COUNT(*) must always be present in SELECT list.

- SUM *(column-name)* must be present in SELECT list if either VARIANCE *(column-name)* or STDDEV *(column-name)* is used.

- Materialized view logs must be created on source table with the INCLUDING NEW VALUES clause. Also, in the WITH *(column-list)* clause, every column referenced in the defining query's SELECT list must be listed.

Additional Restrictions for Fast Refresh of Prejoin Views

For materialized views that are defined by a query that is a simple join between two or more tables, please be aware of the following restrictions to consider:

- No GROUP BY clause is allowed.

- ROWIDs of all source tables must appear in the SELECT list of the defining query.

- Materialized view logs must exist on all source tables using the WITH ROWID clause.

- IN or OR cannot be used on *join predicates* in the WHERE clause of the defining query; they can be used only for single-table *filter predicates*.

- If the defining query contains an outer-join, then a UNIQUE or PRIMARY KEY constraint must exist on the join columns of the inner table of the join.

Additional Restrictions for Fast Refresh of Prejoined and Preaggregated Views

Last, for materialized views that are defined by a query that involves both joins and aggregations, it takes no great leap of imagination to realize that the list of restrictions will look like:

- Arithmetic operators (i.e., $+$, $-$, $*$, $/$, etc.) and string operators (i.e., "ll" for concatenate) are permitted in the SELECT and GROUP BY clauses for nonaggregated columns, but they must be the same in both places.

- Aggregate functions (i.e., AVG, COUNT, etc.) cannot be nested.

- IN or OR cannot be used on *join predicates* in the WHERE clause of the defining query; they can be used only for single-table *filter predicates*.

- If SUM *(column-name)* is used, then COUNT(*) must be specified.

- COUNT(*) and SUM *(column-name)* must be present in SELECT list if either VARIANCE *(column-name)* or STDDEV *(column-name)* is used.

Quite a list of restrictions! It may take a bit of trial and error to determine whether fast refresh is working, but we hope that these lists will help explain why when it is not.

Remember first to classify your materialized view into one of the three categories of views eligible for fast refresh, then work through the relevant lists of restrictions. It is not necessary to actually attempt a fast refresh to determine whether your view is eligible. Either the CREATE MATERIALIZED VIEW command or the ALTER MATERIALIZED VIEW command with the REFRESH FAST clause will fail outright. Also, querying the data dictionary view *xxx*_MVIEW_ANALYSIS for the materialized view can provide insight on whether the view is eligible for fast refresh, particularly the value (either "Y" or "N") in the column INC_REFRESHABLE.

To help debug refreshes, remember that any errors resulting from ON COMMIT refreshes will be logged in ".trc" files in the USER_DUMP_DEST directory and also in the "alert.log" file in the BACKGROUND_DUMP_DEST directory. If you are using the DBMS_MVIEW package for refreshes, be sure to set the UTL_FILE_DIR parameter so that log files can be written to record errors if they occur. If UTL_FILE_DIR is not set or if the specified directory cannot be written to, then valuable debugging information will be lost.

NOTE It is strongly advised that the reader consult the *Oracle8*i *Server Tuning* manual, Chapter 29, "Materialized Views" for more detailed explanations of the subject of REFRESH FAST and REFRESH COMPLETE. If you do not have access to these manuals in hard copy, then soft-copy versions in HTML and Adobe Acrobat formats are available online at http://technet.oracle.com/.

Query Rewrite

If automatic refresh is what reduces the costs of care and feeding of materialized views, then query rewrite is the sizzle that makes them absolutely indispensable. After all, most people don't mind cleaning up after their pets (to a certain extent); in the same way, most data warehouse implementers do not mind handling and coordinating all the details involved with the refresh of their summary tables and rollups. Automatic refresh can be handy, but it's not all that indispensable.

But now imagine a pet that not only takes care of itself but is also eager to help out in some way that truly relieves your workload. Not just fetch the paper, but do the weekly grocery shopping. Not just clean up after itself, but clean up after you as well. Not just provide love and companionship, but to . . . wait a minute, let's not go there! I knew that it would be a mistake to take that analogy too far!

Query rewrite simply means that the Oracle cost-based optimizer, using information in the static data dictionary views, can recognize the relationship between a materialized view and the tables that compose it. Under some circumstances, the optimizer can then subtly rewrite the query to use the more efficient materialized view, instead of the table originally specified in the original query.

This kind of transformation can happen with SELECT statements, with CREATE TABLE . . . AS SELECT statements, and with INSERT INTO . . . SELECT statements. It can also be performed on the individual SELECT statements within set operators such as UNION, UNION ALL, MINUS, and INTERSECT. Unfortunately, it is performed neither for other subqueries including inline view subqueries.

The cost-based optimizer always chooses what it sees as the least-cost alternative. When query rewrite is enabled, the optimizer will evaluate the least-cost alternative with and without the materialized view and choose the most efficient access path.

Factors Affecting Query Rewrite Eligibility

Many factors control whether a particular query in a particular session is eligible for query rewrite:

- If the database instance is running at the proper version of Oracle software compatibility. The initialization parameter COMPATIBLE must be set to 8.1.0 or above.

- If the cost-based optimizer is in use. The parameter OPTIMIZER_MODE must be set to ALL_ROWS, FIRST_ROWS, or CHOOSE (not RULE). This can be set either globally for the entire database instance (via initialization parameter), or for the current session (via ALTER SESSION), or using the ALL_ROWS, FIRST_ROWS, or CHOOSE hints on the SQL statement.

- If the parameter QUERY_REWRITE_ENABLED is TRUE. This can be set either globally for the entire database instance (via initialization parameter or ALTER SYSTEM), or for the current session (via ALTER SESSION), or using the REWRITE hint on the SQL statement.

- If the Oracle account executing the query has been granted QUERY REWRITE or GLOBAL QUERY REWRITE permissions.

- If the query references a table related to a materialized view with ENABLE QUERY REWRITE specified during CREATE or ALTER.

- If the current refresh state of the materialized view matches the setting of the initialization parameter QUERY_REWRITE_INTEGRITY. This can be set either globally for the entire database instance (via initialization parameter or ALTER SYSTEM) or for the current session (via ALTER SESSION).

- If the materialized view under consideration has been analyzed with COMPUTE STATISTICS; the cost-based optimizer will not rewrite a query to use a materialized view whose statistics were gathered using ESTIMATE STATISTICS.

Query Transformation Methods

If all of these tests are passed successfully, then the query might be eligible for query rewrite. To determine this, the cost-based optimizer will first attempt the two simplest forms of transformation.

With *full SQL text comparison*, the optimizer will simply compare the text of the query being executed against the text of the query that defines the materialized view. White space will be removed for the comparison. If this simplest of transformations does not work, then it will attempt *partial SQL text comparison*. For this, the optimizer will compare only the FROM and WHERE clauses of the query to be executed with the corresponding clauses of the query that defines the materialized view. If a match is found in the basic components of these clauses, then the query being executed can be transformed.

If neither *full* nor *partial SQL text comparison* works, then the cost-based optimizer rolls up its sleeves and really gets to work. It parses the SQL statement to be executed into its base components, the SELECT, FROM, WHERE, and GROUP BY clauses, and further decomposes each clause by columns, tables, join predicates, and filter predicates.

Once the query has been decomposed to this point, it can then be compared in detail against the components of the query defining the materialized view. This information is visible in the data dictionary and in the views *xxx*_MVIEW_ AGGREGATES, *xxx*_MVIEW_DETAIL_RELATIONS, *xxx*_MVIEW_JOINS, and *xxx*_MVIEW_KEYS (where *xxx* can be replaced by the words DBA, ALL, or USER).

If the query can be decomposed to match the information in these views, then the query falls into the same three categories used for determining suitability for fast refresh:

- Preaggregation on a single table

- Prejoining two or more tables

- Preaggregation resulting from prejoining two or more tables (combination of the above)

If the query does not fall into one of these three categories, then query rewrite will not be possible. If it does, then we continue.

Next, the Oracle cost-based optimizer must perform yet another series of checks, known as *general query rewrite methods*:

Join compatibility. Necessary only for *prejoin* and *prejoin/preaggregated* views, this check uses information in the ***xxx*_MVIEW_DETAIL_RELATIONS** and ***xxx*_MVIEW_JOINS** data dictionary views to determine whether the query and the materialized view perform the same joins to the same tables.

Data sufficiency. Necessary for all three types of materialized views, this check uses information from all of the ***xxx*_MVIEW_*xxx*** data dictionary views to determine whether the data requested by the query to be transformed can be satisfied solely from the materialized view. The optimizer can also use additional *dimension* and *relational-integrity constraint* information from the data dictionary to perform joins to additional tables to obtain the requested data.

Grouping compatibility. Necessary only for *preaggregated* and *prejoin/preaggregated* views, this check uses information from the ***xxx*_MVIEW_KEYS** data dictionary view to determine whether both the query to be transformed and the query defining the materialized view share the same GROUP BY clause.

Aggregate computability. Necessary only for *preaggregated* and *prejoin/preaggregated* views, this check uses information from the ***xxx*_MVIEW_AGGREGATES** data dictionary view to determine whether both the query to be transformed and the query defining the materialized view share the same aggregate columns in the SELECT clause. For aggregates such as AVG, VARIANCE, and STDDEV, returned values are derived from additional required aggregates such as COUNT and SUM.

Each of these checks is intended to prove that the prejoined or presummarized information stored in the materialized view can indeed be substituted for the information in the tables actually specified in the query's FROM clause.

Referential-Integrity Constraints

Normally, referential-integrity constraints are avoided in data warehouses because of the overhead involved in maintaining them and because decision support systems are generally unconcerned with referential integrity. After all, the operational systems, which are the actual systems of record, are responsible for ensuring referential integrity; it is not truly the responsibility of a decision support system to double-check or second-guess the system of record.

On the other hand, referential-integrity constraints have been used in data warehouses. One reason is to ensure that mistakes are not made while transporting, cleansing, or transforming the data. For the volumes of data stored in most data warehouses, it is most effective to ensure this during transportation, cleansing, or transformation.

The most prevalent reason that referential integrity constraints have been used in decision support systems is because of the *metadata documentation* that they provide for querying tools and online analytical processing (OLAP) tools. Without declarative referential integrity constraint information available inside the database, these tools would require administrators to manually reenter this metadata.

And so it is with the query rewrite feature of materialized views. The cost-based optimizer uses the metadata documentation provided by referential-integrity constraints, such as PRIMARY KEY, UNIQUE, FOREIGN KEY, and NOT NULL, to help it with some of the general query rewrite methods described here.

In particular, referential integrity constraints are required for query rewrite against any materialized view that contains joins. In particular, the *join compatibility*, *data sufficiency*, and *grouping compatibility* checks are not possible on views containing joins without referential integrity constraints.

The constraints do not necessarily have to be enforced; they can be created as RELY NOVALIDATE, which indicates that they are not enforced or validated by the database at all. They truly exist only as metadata documentation in this case. But the decision of whether the constraints are enforced is determined by the setting of the QUERY_REWRITE_INTEGRITY parameter, which is discussed in greater detail in the text that follows.

For now, simply be aware that if the materialized view contains joins, then proper referential integrity constraints must exist.

Dimensions

While referential integrity constraints enforce the relationship between tables, the concept of aggregation inherent to materialized views adds (quite literally) another dimension to referential integrity. Prior to Oracle8*i* release 8.1, there was no construct in the Oracle data dictionary to depict relationships between different levels of aggregation. Now we have dimensions.

Dimensions in Oracle mean much the same as described by Ralph Kimball in his book *The Data Warehouse Toolkit* (second edition, John Wiley & Sons, 1996) when he describes *fact* tables and *dimension* tables as components of a *dimensional* data model.

The *fact* table contains the lowest-level dimension of data, sometimes at the level of granularity of a single transaction, sometimes even finer. The *dimension* table or entity contains a specific group of attributes, known as a *dimension*. Data is typically aggregated along one or more dimensions, sometimes to multiple levels.

Take the most common dimension, *time*. A fact table, with its low level of granularity, may contain an attribute (column) called TXN_DATE, which contains the time-stamp when the transaction occurred. Within the time dimension, time-stamps (which could resolve to hundredths of seconds within Oracle) can summarize to days, which can then summarize to weeks, which can then summarize to months, to quarters, and to years. Moving upward from the lowest dimension (on the fact table) to the highest is traditionally called *rolling up*, while moving from the highest dimension (i.e., years) to the lowest is traditionally called *drilling down*. These terms have been used freely for decades, and everybody is familiar with these concepts . . .

. . . everybody except the Oracle RDBMS! Now, with dimensions, these concepts can be represented in ways that can be stored and used by the Oracle cost-based optimizer, as well as other query tools.

For example, let's take a fact table defined as follows:

```
CREATE TABLE FACT
(
     TXN_DATE            DATE          NOT NULL,
     TXN_DAY             NUMBER(3)     NOT NULL,
     TXN_WEEK            NUMBER(2)     NOT NULL,
     TXN_MONTH           NUMBER(2)     NOT NULL,
     TXN_QUARTER         NUMBER(1)     NOT NULL,
     TXN_YEAR            NUMBER(4)     NOT NULL,
     TXN_TYPE            VARCHAR2(8)   NOT NULL,
     TXN_AMOUNT          NUMBER(10,3)  NOT NULL
);
```

The columns TXN_DAY, TXN_WEEK, TXN_MONTH, TXN_QUARTER, and TXN_YEAR are redundant with TXN_DATE, but this is a purely denormalized fact table, so bear with us.

We can now declare a dimension named TIME as follows:

```
CREATE DIMENSION TIME
```

```
LEVEL timestamp     IS fact.txn_date
LEVEL day           IS fact.txn_day
LEVEL week          IS fact.txn_week
LEVEL month         IS fact.txn_month
LEVEL quarter       IS fact.txn_quarter
LEVEL year          IS fact.txn_year
HEIRARCHY time_rollup
(
    timestamp       CHILD OF
    day             CHILD OF
    week            CHILD OF
    month           CHILD OF
    quarter         CHILD OF
    year
);
```

Now the exact nature of the time dimension in the FACT table is known by Oracle, and it is available through data dictionary views to query and OLAP utilities, as well as the cost-based optimizer.

Setting up dimensions requires additional work on the part of the data modeler, but (like any documentation) it is well worth doing.

In the case of the query rewrite feature of materialized views, creating and maintaining DIMENSIONs is required for the *data sufficiency* and *grouping compatibility* checks performed by the cost-based optimizer on any materialized views with aggregates functions.

It is important to remember that neither dimensions nor referential integrity constraints are required for query rewrite. It is still possible to use the simple *full* and *partial SQL text comparison* transformation methods to determine if query rewrite is possible.

But if these simplistic transformation methods do not work, and if the cost-based optimizer is unable to find the additional metadata documentation provided by dimensions and constraints, then it will be unable to perform the more complex methods of query transformation.

NOTE It is strongly advised that the reader consult the Oracle8*i* *Server Tuning* manual, Chapter 30, "Dimensions," for more detailed explanations on this subject. If you do not have access to these manuals in hard copy, then soft-copy versions in HTML and Adobe Acrobat formats are available online at http://technet.oracle.com/.

Data Accuracy

Last, if all of these checks and tests indicate that rewrite is indeed possible, then the cost-based optimizer must make one final check for data integrity.

According to the current setting for the parameter QUERY_REWRITE_
INTEGRITY, the cost-based optimizer must determine whether the data in the
materialized view is sufficiently up-to-date to be used. QUERY_REWRITE_
INTEGRITY can be set globally, across the entire database instance, either by
setting the initialization parameter at instance startup time or by using the following command:

```
ALTER SYSTEM SET QUERY_REWRITE_INTEGRITY = xxx
```

Here *xxx* has the value of ENFORCE, TRUSTED, or STALE_TOLERATED.
Alternatively, the parameter can be set for an individual session using the following command:

```
ALTER SESSION SET QUERY_REWRITE_INTEGRITY = xxx
```

Here *xxx* has the same three possible values.

If the value is ENFORCE (the default), then query rewrite is possible only if
the data in the materialized view is completely up-to-date with the source
table(s). Also, all referential-integrity constraints (i.e., PRIMARY KEY, UNIQUE,
and FOREIGN KEY) must be enforced and validated. This guarantees complete
accuracy for results returned using the materialized view. If one of the source
tables has a lengthy or complex data load cycle that must be completed prior to
the view being refreshed, then certain materialized views may be ineligible for
query rewrite for a substantial period of time. Additionally, in many data warehouses it is completely impossible to enforce referential integrity constraints,
particularly FOREIGN KEY constraints, due to the volumes of data in the tables.
Last, in this mode, the optimizer will not use PREBUILT materialized views for
query rewrite at all. In some situations, it might be impossible to use the
ENFORCE setting, and in others, quite impractical.

The value of TRUSTED is intended primarily to allow the use of PREBUILT
materialized views. Because these were built and are usually refreshed using
mechanisms separate from Oracle's normal refresh mechanisms, the setting of
TRUSTED allows the optimizer to *assume* that PREBUILT materialized views
have up-to-date data. Also, dimensions defined for PREBUILT views are
assumed to be valid, and referential-integrity constraints that use the RELY
clause (i.e., are completely unenforced) can be used. Otherwise, for normal
(i.e., not PREBUILT) materialized views, the setting of TRUSTED is similar to
ENFORCED. This setting is appropriate to allow the use of PREBUILT views
while still guaranteeing accurate results from normal materialized views.

The most lax setting for data accuracy is STALE_TOLERATED, where the
optimizer does not even check for data "freshness" or "staleness." Dimensions
are used as are referential-integrity constraints, but constraints can be RELY
NOVALIDATE. This setting allows maximal use of query rewrite, but (obviously!) it could result in inaccurate query results.

Quite a few things have to go right for query rewrite to be possible. To summarize, the Oracle cost-based optimizer first does a complete cost-based analysis of the query as it is submitted. If it detects that one or more of the tables in the FROM clause are also referenced by materialized views and if query rewrite is enabled for the view, for the session, and for the user account, then it attempts some simple query transformations. If these simple transformations do not work, then the optimizer will perform more complex transformations where data dictionary information from *dimensions* and *referential integrity constraints* can prove vital.

> **NOTE** It is strongly advised that the reader consult the *Oracle8i Server Tuning* manual, Chapter 30, "Dimensions," and Chapter 31, "Query Rewrite," for more detailed explanations of these subjects. If you do not have access to these manuals in hard copy, then soft-copy versions in HTML and Adobe Acrobat formats are available online at http://technet.oracle.com/.

Life before Materialized Views

As useful as materialized views are, they are still new. Like all new features, it will take time for them to "catch on." Additionally, for decision support systems that have been around for awhile, as well as systems not yet using Oracle8i release 8.1, there are other ways to achieve the same goals.

Automatic query rewrite is not possible outside of materialized views, so it might be prudent to carefully consider registering existing summary tables as PREBUILT materialized views to take advantage of query rewrite.

Also, the refresh of some summary tables may not abide by the rules imposed by fast refresh of materialized views, so it might be necessary to custom-build a fast refresh mechanism. An example might be a refresh that cannot be accomplished with a single SQL statement. In this case, you can still register the summary table as a PREBUILT materialized view to take advantage of query rewrite, but you may want to specify REFRESH NONE so that you handle refresh your own way.

The remainder of this chapter covers some of the features you may want to use to perform this kind of processing. These features are as follows:

- Parallel CREATE TABLE . . . AS SELECT (a.k.a. pCTAS)
- Parallel INSERT APPEND
- Parallel INSERT NOAPPEND
- Parallel UPDATE

- Parallel DELETE
- Custom-written PL/SQL or Java functions for complex logic

Parallel CREATE TABLE . . . AS SELECT (pCTAS)

The pCTAS command is one of the most useful commands in Oracle's arsenal for performing summarization, aggregation, filtering, and merging (see Figure 7.9). It is explained in much greater detail in Chapter 10, "Parallel Execution in the Oracle Data Warehouse," but for our purposes here its advantage is that it can quickly create an entire table based on the results of a parallel query. Although the actual table creation operation is not performed in parallel (it is not necessary), both the INSERT phase and the SELECT phase of the command are completely parallelized in an efficient *consumer-producer* relationship.

The query inside the pCTAS command can be an aggregation or summarization, making it ideal for re-creating summary tables after a complete refresh of the detail data.

The parallel CREATE TABLE . . . AS SELECT command can query from partitioned tables, but it cannot be used to create Oracle8 partitioned tables or their individual partitions, at least not directly. Using the ALTER TABLE . . . EXCHANGE PARTITION command, a "standalone" table created by pCTAS can be merged into a partitioned table as a new partition. This is an extremely powerful technique for data warehousing, as it allows the new partition to begin life separate from the table in which it will eventually reside. While it is being loaded, indexed, and analyzed, it remains separate from the partitioned table. Then, it can be *published* for end users by the EXCHANGE PARTITION operation, which simply alters the Oracle data dictionary to swap places between the standalone table and the named partition. Because the data segments themselves are not being moved, and only data dictionary entries are being modified, this can be a very swift operation, usually requiring only seconds. Be aware, however, that the size of the segments being swapped does seem to affect the duration of the EXCHANGE PARTITION command, and we have seen cases where the operation may require several minutes to complete for segments with several hundred thousand database blocks or more.

Parallel DML

As we describe in Chapter 10, there are a variety of parallel Data Manipulation Language (DML) operations. All of these operations are available starting with Oracle8.

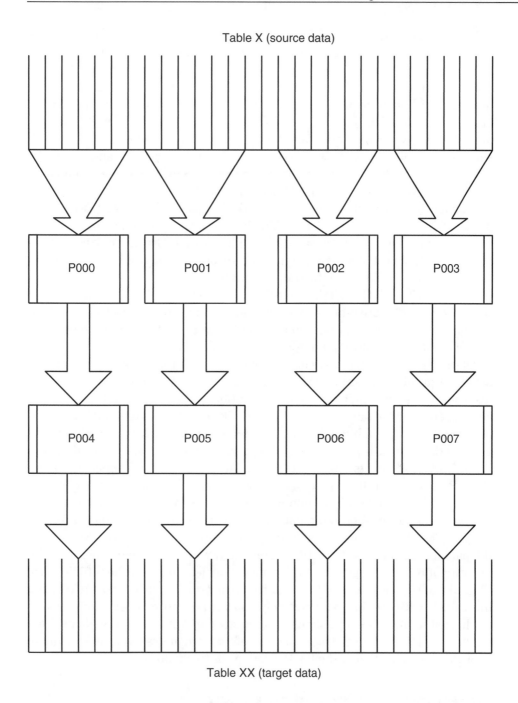

Figure 7.9 Parallel CREATE TABLE . . . AS SELECT.

Parallel DELETE, UPDATE, INSERT (using the NOAPPEND hint) statements can be performed on both partitioned and nonpartitioned tables; only the parallel INSERT (using the APPEND hint) statement can be performed on both partitioned and non-partitioned tables. Each of these operations must be enabled using the ALTER SESSION ENABLE PARALLEL DML command immediately prior to the DELETE, UPDATE, or INSERT. Also, a COMMIT or ROLLBACK must be issued immediately after the DML completes, before any other SQL statement (even a SELECT) is issued, to close the parallel DML transaction. The reason for these conditions, the initial ALTER SESSION and the terminating COMMIT or ROLLBACK, is that Oracle implements parallel DML commands very similarly to distributed transactions. Each separate process or thread (i.e., parallel DEGREE) is managed as an individual transaction within Oracle. When these multiple, individual transaction complete within Oracle, they use a two-phase COMMIT protocol (very similar to distributed-database DML) to coordinate the completion of all of the transactions together.

Parallel DELETE, UPDATE, and INSERT (using the NOAPPEND hint) are all *conventional SQL* operations that can cause database triggers to fire, which maintain indexes with full normal availability, and which create both rollback (or *undo*) and redo information for full recoverability.

Alternatively, the direct-path mechanism used with the pCTAS operation can also be utilized with parallel INSERT, using the APPEND hint. This operation becomes exactly like pCTAS with the exception of the nonparallel operation of actually creating the table prior to INSERT. Like pCTAS, it is blindingly fast, and because the direct-path mechanism is being used, rollback information is not generated. Instead, because the direct-path mechanism loads data first into TEMPORARY segments, rollback can be achieved simply by dropping the TEMPORARY segment, rather than unapplying changes to table and index blocks. Of course, if the operation commits, then the TEMPORARY segments are appended to the existing table data segment itself, hence the reason for the term APPEND. And, when used in conjunction with the NOLOGGING option, the parallel INSERT /*+ APPEND */ command will also forego generating the majority of redo information for the transaction, leading to further efficiencies. Please be aware, however, of the negative impact on database recovery of using the NOLOGGING option. You certainly can't expect to recover data that was not logged to the redo logs, should a failure occur! You are automatically buying into a philosophy of *reload* instead of *recover*, unless you are fortunate enough to get a backup of the loaded data prior to a failure.

Procedural Code for Complex Logic

Quite frequently, it is difficult to perform all the necessary logic in a single nonprocedural SQL statement such as a parallel CREATE TABLE . . . AS SELECT or a parallel INSERT, UPDATE, or DELETE. What is occasionally needed is procedural logic, with familiar programming constructs such as IF conditionals or looping. PL/SQL can be incorporated into parallel operations through the use of stored PL/SQL functions and packaged PL/SQL functions.

By creating stored functions in PL/SQL or Java, it is possible to extend the Oracle SQL language, to effectively customize it. This is done by using these custom-built functions in SQL statements, in the SELECT clause of queries, in the SET clause of UPDATE statements, or in the WHERE clauses of queries, UPDATE, or DELETE statements.

There are some restrictions on this functionality:

- Functions used within SQL statements (SELECT, VALUE, SET, and WHERE clauses) cannot perform DML on database tables. They must be created with PRAGMA EXCEPTION_INIT to the WNDS (i.e., "Write No Database State") level of "purity."

- Only IN arguments are allowed. The only output from the function is through the RETURN value.

- Functions to be executed remotely or in parallel may not read or modify the values of package variables. They must be created with PRAGMA EXCEPTION_INIT using all four levels of "purity" (see the notes on "purity" that follow).

- Functions that modify the values of package variables may be called only within the SELECT, VALUE, and SET clauses, but not within the WHERE clause. They also must be created with PRAGMA EXCEPTION_INIT using all four levels of "purity" (see the notes on "purity" that follow).

NOTE These restrictions are enforced on packaged functions using the PRAGMA operator in PL/SQL while the package or function is being compiled. The PRAGMA operator is a package compile-time construct very similar to PRAGMA in the Ada programming language. PL/SQL was closely modeled after the Ada programming language.

Outside of these restrictions, however, developers are permitted to use PL/SQL package variables and PL/SQL tables, which provide a broad and powerful range of possibilities.

For example, suppose that a value to be inserted into a table created with pCTAS could be retrieved from one of several different tables, depending on the data value in a certain column. For example, if the value in column TYPE was "REVENUE," then a table named REVENUE would be queried for the value to be inserted. If the column TYPE contained the value "MARGIN," then a table named MARGIN would be queried. If TYPE = "COST," then the table named COST would supply the value to be inserted. Last, if the column TYPE had a NULL value, then the value would come from a table named OTHER multiplied by a value from the table named MISCELLANEOUS.

As you can imagine, this could become a very complex SQL statement. It would be possible to process using outer-joins:

```
CREATE TABLE big_mess
           PARALLEL (DEGREE 8)
AS
SELECT f.key_value,
       DECODE(f.type,
               'REVENUE', r.value,
               'MARGIN', m.value,
               'COST', c.value,
               NULL, o.value * x.value,
               NULL) VALUE
  FROM fact f,
       revenue r,
       margin m,
       cost c,
       other o,
       miscellaneous x
 WHERE r.key_value (+) = f.key_value
   AND m.key_value (+) = f.key_value
   AND c.key_value (+) = f.key_value
   AND o.key_value (+) = f.key_value
   AND x.key_value (+) = f.key_value;
```

Although both the pCTAS command and the parallel DML commands fully support and parallelize outer-join operations, you can see how this overly simplified, but not so far-fetched, scenario can quickly become a nightmare in nonprocedural SQL programming.

Compare this with the following:

```
CREATE OR REPLACE PACKAGE example_package
AS
     PRAGMA RESTRICT_REFERENCES(example_function, WNDS, RNPS, WNPS);
     FUNCTION example_function
         (in_key_value     IN NUMBER,
          in_type          IN VARCHAR2)
         RETURN NUMBER;
END example_package;
/
CREATE OR REPLACE PACKAGE BODY example_package
AS
     FUNCTION example_function
         (in_key_value     IN NUMBER,
          in_type          IN VARCHAR2)
         RETURN NUMBER
     IS
          v_rtn_value      NUMBER;
     BEGIN
```

```
                    IF in_type = 'REVENUE' THEN
                        SELECT value
                          INTO v_rtn_value
                          FROM revenue
                         WHERE key_value = in_key_value;
                    ELSIF in_type = 'MARGIN' THEN
                        SELECT value
                          INTO v_rtn_value
                          FROM margin
                         WHERE key_value = in_key_value;
                    ELSIF in_type = 'COST' THEN
                        SELECT value
                          INTO v_rtn_value
                          FROM cost
                         WHERE key_value = in_key_value;
                    ELSIF in_type IS NULL THEN
                        SELECT o.value
                          INTO v_rtn_value
                          FROM other o,
                               miscellaneous m
                         WHERE o.key_value = in_key_value
                           AND m.key_value = o.key_value;
                    END IF;
                    RETURN V_RTN_VALUE;
            END;
    END example_package;
    /
```

Please note the PRAGMA statement used during the creation of the package header. The "purity levels" are as follows:

RNDS	Read No Database State (includes no SELECT statements)
WNDS	Write No Database State (performs no DML statements)
RNPS	Read No Package State (does not reference PL/SQL package variables)
WNPS	Write No Package State (does no updating of PL/SQL package variables)

As we mentioned earlier, in order for it to be used in a nonparallelized SQL statement's SELECT clause, the PL/SQL function must be able to pass the WNDS purity level as a requirement. It does not have to pass any of the other purity levels, although it does not hurt to do so. To allow the function to be used in a parallelized SQL statement, it must also pass the WNPS and RNPS purity levels.

Using the PL/SQL function inside an SQL statement then becomes as easy as this:

```
CREATE TABLE big_mess
        PARALLEL (DEGREE 8)
```

```
AS
SELECT key_value,
       example_package.example_function(key_value, type) value
  FROM fact;
```

This simple example doesn't begin to delve into the power of this technique. It allows very complex programming logic to be encapsulated inside easy-to-use program units and is also fully parallelizable.

Summary

With few exceptions, data requires a great deal of transformation during the journey from its source operational system to the destination data warehouse. Some of the transformation may occur during extraction from the source operational systems. Some transformation may occur during the actual transportation, or transfer, from the source system to the data warehouse. Some may occur during the load into the data warehouse. But, based on past experience, it is likely that the majority of data transformation will occur after the detailed operational data has been loaded into the data warehouse, making data load a two-stage process.

Materialized views are the single most significant new feature for data warehousing introduced in Oracle8i. The query rewrite feature is a stroke of genius, and any headaches due to encountering glitches in early releases will be more than amply repaid as the feature matures. Oracle's cost-based optimizer, despite its rocky start in Oracle7, has stabilized its core functionality, and it is now becoming capable of making almost sentient decisions.

Wherever the restrictions on materialized views become more intense, Oracle has provided a robust set of bulk-mode operations, featuring the direct-path mechanism as well as sophisticated and effective parallelism.

Using these techniques and features should enable you to handle almost any eventuality in the Oracle data warehouse, quickly and elegantly.

Administering and Monitoring the Oracle Data Warehouse

SURLY PEASANT: Strange women lying about in ponds distributing swords is no basis for a system of government. Supreme executive power derives from a mandate from the masses, not from some farcical aquatic ceremony.

KING ARTHUR: Be quiet!

SURLY PEASANT: Well, but you can't expect to wield supreme executive power just 'cause some watery tart threw a sword at you!

KING ARTHUR: Shut up!

SURLY PEASANT: I mean, if I went 'round saying I was an emperor just because some moistened nymph had lobbed a scimitar at me, they'd put me away!

KING ARTHUR: Shut up, will you? Shut up!

SURLY PEASANT: Ah, now we see the violence inherent in the system.

KING ARTHUR: Shut up!

SURLY PEASANT: Oh! Come and see the violence inherent in the system! Help! Help! I'm being repressed!

Monty Python and the Holy Grail—*Python (Monty) Pictures, Ltd., 1974*

Lights out.

That's how we want all our systems to run: off by themselves in a darkened machine room, humming away busily. Running themselves. Monitoring themselves. Calling for help only when absolutely necessary. Not demanding help from people unless something is about to go wrong.

Technical people like this idea because they hope it will allow them a utopian existence: working from home, playing golf, coaching Little League, surfing the Web, or reading Dilbert comics. Management likes the idea because it also conjures up pleasant images of trouble-free 24×7 operation, playing golf, bonuses and kudos from the CEO, a guest column as management guru in *Business Week,* and perhaps a fellowship at the Harvard Business School.

Well, maybe, but there's no doubt that is the goal. Existing systems running themselves, freeing everybody to create newer and better systems. The path to this utopia starts with *responsibility.*

Occasionally, as Oracle consultants, we teach classes for customers through Oracle Education Centers. Recently, while teaching the class on database administration, we asked the students the standard question, "Who are you, and what do you hope to gain from this class?" The majority of folks in the class were either application developers or programmer/analysts who wanted to find out more about how the Oracle RDBMS works. Another large segment were information systems (IS) managers tasked with leading a development effort involving Oracle who wanted to know what their team members should be doing.

Only a small handful of people were actually database administrators (DBAs), about one-quarter of the class. After the first two or three days of the class, it was clear that there were two mind-sets in the class: conservative and "put the pedal to the metal." The former seemed more interested in nailing down the core concepts; the latter were most interested in probing the outermost reaches of the features of the RDBMS. Without formally polling the class, it seemed clear that the folks who were already administrators fell into the conservative category, and the application developers and programmer/analysts fell into the aggressive category.

After a lively discussion that pitted the two mind-sets against one another, the instructor commented, "You know, the most important thing about being a DBA is not so much what you know but being able to stare at anyone, including the company CEO, and growl, 'Not on my production database, you're not!' And mean it."

Most of the class laughed, thinking it was a recommendation that DBAs be obstructive and possessive. The conservative faction in the class nodded grimly. They understood that the instructor's comment did not imply that the identifying characteristics of a DBA are inflexibility, sociopathic tendencies, and a penchant for career-limiting moves. The issue is not *power* or *authority,* but *responsibility.* The DBA should always hold the goal of meeting the business and systems requirements of his database above all else and emphatically defend against the erosion of the database's abilities to meet those requirements. In practical terms, DBAs simply don't want to be paged at 2:00 A.M. with a downed system. In short, they are *responsible.*

For example, take the case of the DBA of a mission-critical order entry system who is in a meeting regarding a proposed new data warehouse that will extract from the order entry database. The team tasked with loading data into the data warehouse has just requested a read-only logon to the order entry system for the purpose of developing and testing extract programs. The CIO of the company has just unthinkingly said, "Sure, why not?" in the interests of keeping the momentum of the data warehouse project, which is enthusiastically sponsored by the company's CEO and CFO.

But hold it—stop right there. In this example, the DBA knows that this particular order entry system has very strict performance requirements. If a certain EDI transaction takes longer than N number of seconds, the system sending the transaction cancels it and routes it elsewhere. Essentially, if response time is too slow, the company loses the transaction. If X number of transactions are lost in this manner within an hour, then the reservation company feeding the transactions decides that this company is having problems and disconnects. Reconnections won't happen until after the following midnight, meaning the company is effectively shut down until then.

Should a team of people unfamiliar with the order entry system be blindly consuming resources, even if they have just read-only privileges? Although it's true that they can't harm the existing data, should they be allowed to even consume resources? Even if the upper-level management team makes a decision, the DBA may be in a position to educate everyone about the potential impact of the decision. Those who made the request and those who made the decision may not have realized the importance.

Obviously, the answer in this case is not to emphatically deny access. But because of the importance of maintaining the response time on transactions, a great deal of care should be taken to ensure not only that the data is safe but also that system resources are consumed modestly and in a controlled fashion, in a way that does not jeopardize the primary function of the system.

The issue is responsibility. It's not that other people are irresponsible; it's just that they may have many or conflicting priorities. The DBA has one priority: to keep the production database up and running and serving the business. It doesn't make sense to take responsibility for something without having a plan. That is where this chapter is intended to help—in developing a plan for administering an Oracle data warehouse. It also doesn't make sense to establish a plan that can't be adjusted to meet changing conditions. That is the other area in which this chapter provides guidance—monitoring the system to prevent surprises.

Who Are We? Why Are We Here?

To paraphrase James Stockdale's famous statement in the 1992 vice presidential debates, we have to focus on basic issues. Because of Vice Admiral Stockdale's somewhat strained oratorical abilities and nervous delivery, his opening statement, "Who am I? Why am I here?" came out sounding like the words of a confused (possibly senile) old man asking where he was, rather than an attempt to establish a logical base from which to proceed in a reasoned discussion.

ADMINISTRATION TOOLS

There are tools provided by Oracle Corporation and many other vendors for administering Oracle8*i* databases, including Oracle Enterprise Manager. This chapter does not provide a tutorial on using any specific tool. The official documentation for each product can do a more complete job of that task. Repeating that material here would waste your time as well as ours.

We do, however, provide a realistic discussion of the real-life role of a DBA and some very specific practical techniques to allow the DBA to do a better job of avoiding and, if necessary, solving problems that can occur in the very large Oracle database arena. All of the example code is provided in generic SQL and PL/SQL (with occasional minor SQL*Plus formatting commands) scripts that can be readily adapted to whichever administration tool you are using.

Although it is seems like a good idea to establish basic principles and work forward from there, it is possible to be boring or condescending in the process. In many IS and DP shops, it is possible (even necessary, in the interests of time) to skip over basic principles and address the questions at hand. Unfortunately, a surprising number of people walk into a data warehousing project believing that the objective is to do cool new things using neat new technology, to learn new techniques, and to gain marketable new skills. All that is possible and desirable, but only if it meets the objectives of the business.

It is not possible to make rational technical decisions without having a complete understanding of business requirements. Once the business requirements are understood, then system requirements can be defined.

Business Requirements

As countless texts and articles on data warehouses have made clear, the primary purpose of the data warehouse is to provide the most efficient reporting on tactical and strategic data. Because this book is a practical guide to implementation, we should assume, at this point, that all business requirements have been dealt with, especially with respect to designing the data warehouse in the first place. Other business requirements that affect administration and monitoring mainly have to do with expectations. These requirements were described in Chapter 2, "Hardware Architectures for Oracle Data Warehousing," as some of the evaluation criteria for the selection of a hardware architecture. They include the following:

- Reliability and availability expectations of the data warehouse

- Overall performance expectations by end users or downstream data marts

- Mean-time-to-repair (MTTR) expectations, defined as the business's expectations for repair should an outage occur

- Maximum-time-to-repair (XTTR) requirements, defined as the absolute maximum amount of time to repair a problem should an outage occur, after which the business is in serious jeopardy

These expectations may not have been set down explicitly, and, as a result, different people may have different expectations. It is important to document these expectations so that everyone is clear on them, from the top of the organization chart to the bottom. Once these expectations are understood, then the technical team can start turning these expectations into system requirements.

Let's discuss *reliability* and *availability* expectations for the warehouse. Most of the time, this is defined in terms of a percentage, such as *99 percent uptime*. Implicitly, this is construed to mean that the data warehouse is expected to be unavailable 1 percent of the time. One percent of a single year is 87 hours and 40 minutes (if you consider a year to be 365.25 days); that's about three and a half days. What is not specified is how do you want that downtime? One long weekend, once a year? One 22-hour day, once per quarter? One 7-hour period, once per month? Or perhaps one 30-second outage every hour? They all represent 99 percent uptime. But the 30-second outage every hour is not going to allow you to get very much done.

How about a system that is supposed to be available 100 percent of the time? Never mind that no such system exists; how are you going to apply upgrades and patches? The application software needs to be upgraded and patched, the Oracle RDBMS needs to be upgraded and patched, the operating system and all of its subsystems need to be upgraded and patched, and hardware wears out. Redundancy can help *theoretically*, but the mind-boggling complexity and sheer bleeding-edge *newness* of clustered and massively parallel systems can cause availability to *drop* rather than *increase*.

How do you define availability? Is it the fact that the server is running and the Oracle RDBMS is available? What if this is true but performance is so abysmal that nobody can get his jobs done? Clearly, adequate performance is a factor in availability.

So, the business has, likely arbitrarily, decided that the data warehouse must be available 99 percent of the time, and it has agreed to schedule one six-hour *scheduled outage* every month for maintenance. With such a schedule in a perfect world, this means 99 percent availability. But, in the event of an *unscheduled outage*, how quickly must the data warehouse be repaired and brought back into service?

There are two metrics crucial to this consideration. The first, *maximum time to repair*, or XTTR, is the absolute, utmost period of downtime before the business suffers serious, irreparable harm. This is the absolute drop-dead repair time. It could be two hours, or it could be two weeks. But the data warehouse must be back online after such an outage or else it's time to go home. The amount of time specified for XTTR tells the data warehouse systems implementation exactly how robust the system must be, at a minimum. This prevents the procurement of an inadequate and obsolete system, and it sets minimum requirements for systems staff coverage and responsibility.

But no human wants merely to survive! Basing policy on only the worst-case scenario takes all the fun out of it. So the *mean time to repair*, or MTTR, is intended to express the business's *expectations* for the average amount of time for the restoration of service. It is that metric that the data warehouse systems implementers are really striving for, the metric most often cited in *service-level agreements*, or SLAs.

Before embarking on a data warehouse, it is important to have these expectations and requirements clearly defined and *agreed on* at the very beginning.

System Requirements

These expectations, once quantified, can then be translated into system requirements. For example, let's assume that the development team for a proposed data warehouse has been told the following:

- The data warehouse needs to be available only five days a week (Monday through Friday) for eight hours a day.

- Response-time expectations are 30 seconds for formal reports and "canned queries" and no more than 4 hours for *ad hoc* queries.

- Should the system crash, a day of downtime would not cause the world to stop.

Sound familiar? Let's examine this further.

So-called 8×5 availability (i.e., eight hours per day, five days per week) implies that the system need be up and running only between 9:00 A.M. and 5:00 P.M. Suppose the company operates in several time zones, say, just in the continental United States (i.e., four time zones). This means that the system will need to be available from 6:00 A.M. Pacific Time (which is 9:00 A.M. Eastern Time) until 5:00 P.M. Pacific Time, which spans 11 hours. So the requirement should expand from 8×5 to 11×5. But wait.

The response-time expectations indicate at least four hours for *ad hoc* queries. Based on the habit of some end users of composing last-minute queries and firing them off at 5:00 P.M., this means that the system should probably remain available until 9:00 P.M. Pacific Time. If this is, in fact, the business user's expectation, then the hours of required availability just expanded from 11×5 to 15×5.

By asking a few questions, we've found that the uptime expectations are double what was originally stated. Let's keep going.

Given the expected size of the data warehouse, how likely is it that reports and queries could run longer than four hours? Will data mining techniques be used on the system? Will online analytical processing (OLAP) tools be used, or will end users have unrestricted access to *ad hoc* queries using SQL? If they will have unrestricted *ad hoc* access, how proficient are they in tuning SQL statements on Oracle?

Depending on the answers to these, and other, questions, it is probably reasonable to at least double the expected duration of some reports and queries from four to eight hours (or more). Now, because the system has to stay up eight hours after 5:00 P.M., this means we now have a 19×5 system supporting four time zones.

Think again about time zones. Aren't we expanding into Europe and Asia? If not, should we be? There goes the remaining downtime during the week: We're now at 24×5. Now let's look at those weekends.

It seems clear that no matter what anyone says, you should try to plan for the effects of globalization, which implies a 24×7 operation. But before you tell anyone you're going to try to run a 24×7 operation, let's look at the record. On planet Earth (and, to our knowledge, throughout the neighboring worlds), there is not a single computer system that truly runs 24 hours a day, 7 days a week, and 52 weeks a year, year after year. There are some that come excruciatingly close, but they do shut down once a year for something like 45 minutes. While this seems close to 100 percent uptime, it is in fact 99.9914 percent uptime.

Systems like this (American Airline's SABRE computerized reservations system is an example) have been in existence for several decades. It has literally taken billions of dollars of investment in equipment, people, training, research, and experience to get to this level of availability. Is your company prepared for this level of investment? Is an investment of this magnitude appropriate for a decision support system?

At the beginning stages of any project, it is probably prudent to consider more attainable goals. It makes a lot of sense for a data warehouse to have a significant chunk of time set aside for the load phase, backups, and other maintenance in the form of patches, upgrades, and card swap-outs. During these time periods, the end-user community should expect the data warehouse to be unavailable for their use. The administrators can then perform whatever maintenance actions are necessary during this time. If the administrators do not have anything to do, or if they complete their tasks early, then they can "give back" the time to the end-user community.

If this can be agreed on, then the end-user community can be assured that the data warehouse will remain available during the time periods allocated to them. The administrative staff can also be assured they will have scheduled downtime available to them in order to perform necessary maintenance on the systems.

Given the initial requirements mentioned earlier (i.e., 8×5 availability, one day mean time to repair), it is likely that this technical implementation team should stake out one or both days of every weekend as "owned" by them. Over time, this scheduled downtime could be renegotiated to become less and less frequent, until some point of equilibrium is reached.

Administration Roles

There are many distinct roles in administering an Oracle data warehouse. Quite often, all these roles will be performed by 1 or 2 people, but regardless of whether the IT department is 1 person or 500, it is important to understand the roles that must be fulfilled.

Understanding these roles and keeping them separate, distinct, and private are not matters of authority or power. It is a matter of responsibility. Should a problem occur, it is best that the resolution of that problem be routed to the person most capable of handling it.

Data Warehouse Administrator (DWA)

The data warehouse administrator is a relatively new concept, and one frequently overlooked or possibly regarded as redundant. This is the person who understands the business requirements of the data warehouse and is responsible for the decisions that make the data warehouse continue to meet those requirements, even as they change.

While a project is underway for the initial development of a data warehouse, the project manager fills the role of data warehouse administrator. But when that initial development is completed successfully, the project manager is often deemed worthy of *bigger and better things* and is rolled onto another project. Because the data warehouse is now up and running, it would seem silly to devote a project manager to something that is no longer a project, and so a leadership void is created. At first, this may not present a problem, but over time, the lack of a single informed decision maker will contribute to the data warehouse's increasing irrelevance.

It is not strictly necessary to dedicate a person as the DWA; often such a person is elected spontaneously or recognized de facto. It is not wise to risk this to an organic process. Rather, it is vital to either formally designate someone as the DWA as an adjunct to his current role (i.e., DBA, data modeler, or director) or appoint someone to take the job on as a full-time commitment.

The job description might include the following roles:

- Liaison between business owners and IT

- Decision maker for all strategy, design, and implementation issues affecting the data warehouse

- Single point of contact for enhancements and fixes

Once again, it comes down to *responsibility*. After the initial implementation project is complete and the project leads move onto other, newer projects, they cannot leave a void.

Database Administrator (DBA)

The database administrator (or DBA) is responsible for the Oracle database. The configuration, growth, and well being of the database and its software are the responsibility of the DBA. Most of the discussions in this chapter (indeed, in this entire book) center on this role.

System Administrator

The system administrator (or "SysAdmin," "SyAd," "SA," or whatever) is generally responsible for the computer machinery itself, along with system software. The computer, its subsystems, and most of its peripheral devices fall under this jurisdiction. In a UNIX environment, the SysAdmin "owns" the password to the "root" superuser and should not share it with anybody else.

Security Administrator

The security administrator is responsible for setting up access to system resources (i.e., operating system logons, Oracle accounts, network logons, etc.) for developers, administrators, and end users. In some organizations, this role can occupy several full-time people; in others, it is a small part of the other administrative roles.

Network Administrator

The network administrator is generally responsible for network devices, peripherals, and client machines outside the data centers. Frequently, this person is the first line of support to the end users.

Help Desk and Problem Resolution

This is perhaps the most important, yet most overlooked, role of all. The help desk is the single point of contact for the end-user community when something goes wrong. Help desk personnel need to be able to route the problem to the appropriate administrator after recording pertinent facts. An effective help desk allows you to control the amount of work that flows to the various administrators. An ineffective, poorly trained help desk can make a bad situation worse, and a well-trained help desk can ensure that the system runs smoothly.

The reasons go beyond the obvious. The obvious reason is that an effective help desk can understand and resolve problems faster, handling many of the problems without involving the rest of the IT organization.

The less obvious costs of an ineffective (or nonexistent) help desk lie in the resolution of more complex problems. If no help desk exists, end users and developers alike tend to resolve their problems using their own personal network. Using a personal network of "gurus," "power users," and system administrators can be an effective way to resolve problems when the number of problems is few, but if there are a great many problems to be resolved, it has a disastrous effect.

As the most highly trained people spend time resolving problems that are not their normal tasks, they become unable to perform their own jobs during a normal workday. As a result, their own productivity suffers, and they become frustrated and disgruntled. Management, unable to record, track, or react to problems handled in this manner, notices only the decreased productivity and may take steps that do not address the real problem.

Most other types of applications, such as ERP (enterprise resource planning) systems, have extensive documentation or vendor support that end users can use when they have questions. Very few data warehouses have this kind of infrastructure. As a result, a help-desk function is vital to the success of the data warehouse, to ensure that end-user problems are dealt with effectively.

Data Warehouse Security Issues

Security administration is just one of the many facets of warehouse administration. In some IT shops security is assigned to a special individual or team. In others it is one of the responsibilities of the DBA. Even the shops that do a thorough job of controlling access to their operational systems may be tempted to overlook security issues when planning and implementing the data warehouse. This is probably because of the mistaken perception that read-only access has less potential for abuse than other types of access. This is only partly true. True, a user of the warehouse cannot misuse the tool to enter fraudulent invoices into accounts payable. But the value (and risks) of an organization's computing resources are not limited to fraud and sabotage. Information is a key resource of the corporation—that is the justification for building the warehouse, isn't it? If a user prints out a customer list and takes it to a competitor, has the corporation been damaged? Probably. Would the fictitious "Consultants 'R' Us" company in our case study want the effective billing rates and project profitability numbers of its warehouse distributed to other consulting companies in its market? I doubt it. Would you like your competitor to have a copy of your standard pricing and volume discount policy? If not, then you probably don't want to make it available to every employee of the company. Whatever information is considered strategic to your organization's success is potentially just as valuable to someone else (and damaging to you if they get it).

Unfortunately, a common opinion of warehouse planners is that if everyone has access to everything they will be empowered to make better decisions. This attitude has fostered a very *laissez-faire* attitude toward security. Well, frankly, not everyone in the organization needs to make decisions about everything! Some thought needs to be given to who should be using the warehouse and what areas they should be allowed to investigate. A straightforward process needs to be created to allow for requesting, approving, and providing additional access when justified.

In designing the security plan for the data warehouse there are three objectives to balance. Security should be effective, unobtrusive, and simple.

Effective Security

Far too many warehouses have been built and delivered without consideration for the security of the information contents. It is simple, but inappropriate, to give every user access, SELECT ANY TABLE privilege, and unlimited resources. Each subject area in the warehouse should have one or more assigned owners who should specify guidelines for who may receive access (or even review and approve each specific user request for access). A particular subject area may need to be divided even more granularly to properly separate "public" information from potentially sensitive data.

One frequently ignored element of an effective security policy (for any system) involves education. Each user, as part of obtaining access to the warehouse, should be instructed on the value, confidential nature, and need for securing the information in the warehouse. They should be taught how (and why) to change their passwords regularly. They should also be made aware of the specific policies for accessing and distributing that information and the potential penalties for violating security policies. Finally, each user needs to understand the process for obtaining additional access where warranted.

Unobtrusive Security

Applying the security plan to the warehouse should not impair the user from doing legitimate operations. They should be generally unaware that certain operations are forbidden. Other than having to remember and occasionally change their passwords, users should be generally unaware of the existence of security measures. They should be trained in the process of requesting additional privileges, however, if they find legitimate reasons for access to objects in a part of the warehouse not currently available to them. The security administrator should be prepared to quickly obtain the necessary authorization from the "owner" of that new subject area.

Simple Security

Just as security should not be obtrusive on the users' legitimate pursuit of business decisions, it should also not become a burden on the DBA or security administrator. Oracle has provided excellent features for simplifying the administration of security once an effective and unobtrusive plan has been designed. Three of these features (roles, auditing, and password management) meet this need for administrative simplicity particularly well.

Roles

It is common for any particular user of the warehouse to need a wide variety of privileges—both system level and object level—to perform their analysis. As introduced in Chapter 3, "Oracle Server Software Architecture and Features," there may be hundreds or thousands of privileges to be granted. The roles feature allows a common set of privileges to be grouped together as a role, assigned a name, and then distributed as a unit with a single GRANT or REVOKE statement. Two levels of roles are recommended for the data warehouse. One role is defined for each group of users who will need the same privileges. This is frequently done on the basis of department and SQL sophistication. You may wish to limit new or untrained users to summary tables rather than allowing them to plow through large detail tables.

A second set of roles is then created, one per warehouse subject area (or portion of subject area if the owner has decided that access to some data needs additional restriction). Finally, the subject area roles are granted to the appropriate user group roles. This provides a simple network of grants between the two levels of roles (as depicted in Chapter 3, Figure 3.13). When a section of the warehouse needs to be made unavailable for maintenance, only the handful of grants between roles needs to be revoked and later restored. This is far simpler than having to revoke privileges on dozens of objects or hundreds of individual users.

Auditing

Later in this chapter we recommend that session level auditing be used to track warehouse usage. There is very little overhead involved in recording when users connect and disconnect from the database. The advantage, from a security perspective, is an easy means to identify when unauthorized access is attempted. If auditing is not used for any other purpose, it should be enabled to record each unsuccessful attempt to access the Oracle7 warehouse database (Oracle8's new account locking feature, described in the next section, is an alternative solution). This is done by enabling auditing with the AUDIT_TRAIL initialization parameter and then specifying particular objects or actions to be tracked using the following AUDIT command:

```
AUDIT SESSION WHENEVER UNSUCCESSFUL;
```

This command will ensure that every unsuccessful attempt to log on to the database is recorded in the audit trail. You should expect to see an occasional entry when a user misspells a password. Your concern should be for situations where dozens or hundreds of entries appear, which indicate someone is attempting to "crack" a password. The audit trail will tell you what username(s) were being attempted. You should contact that user (assuming a valid username was being entered) to find out whether he was having trouble or to have him change his password in case it was eventually guessed.

Gathering usage statistics would use the same AUDIT SESSION command, but without the WHENEVER UNSUCCESSFUL restriction. This usage, along with relocation and maintenance of Oracle's internal audit trail table, is described later in this chapter.

Password Management

This topic is mentioned last not because of limited value but because it is a new set of features in Oracle8. For instance, in earlier releases there was no automatic means of ensuring that users changed passwords regularly or that they selected a password of some minimum length or complexity. These features are described in depth in Chapters 19 and 20 of the Oracle8 *Server Administrator's Guide* so they are presented very generally here.

Password expiration. The administrator may define how long a password may remain valid before the user is required to change it.

Password history. Oracle can maintain a list of the previous passwords used by the user to prevent him from immediately resetting his current password.

Password complexity verification. The administrator may develop a PL/SQL script that will be executed whenever a user password is changed.

This routine can ensure that passwords are of sufficient length, that they contain an appropriate mix of special characters, that they are not the same as the username or other common words (such as "welcome" or "oracle").

Account locking. This feature can cut off access to a particular user account for a designated length of time whenever a specified number of unsuccessful logon attempts are made. This is a preemptive measure to prevent unauthorized access, in contrast to the auditing approach described earlier that only detects attempted breaches.

All four of these new features are implemented through entries in the user's resource profile. Profiles were introduced in Oracle7 for controlling the resource usage by groups of users. Using profiles is a two-step process. First, the administrator creates a profile with a specific list of resource limits or any of these new password management features. This is done with the CREATE PROFILE command or modified later with ALTER PROFILE. Then the profile is assigned to users using the ALTER USER command. Different profiles may (and should) be created to control different groups of users who have different responsibilities. Resource limits (especially on logical I/O per call) should be assigned based on a user's training, experience, and awareness of SQL performance issues.

More Sophisticated Security Tools and Techniques

Roles, auditing, and password management are the bare minimum for database security. The infrastructure of security may require complete omniscience into all the goings-on in the data warehouse. Also, it may be necessary to regulate data access to a very fine level. Roles and privileges control access to the level of the table or view, but fine-grain security may require that access be controlled by specific columns or rows. Oracle has always been able to employ database views for filtering specific columns from specific users, but until Oracle8*i* it has been extremely difficult to specify how rows can be restricted at any specific time by any specific user in any specific situation. Also, the integration of database authentication with middleware such as object-request brokers, Web application servers, and transaction processing monitors may be necessary. Requiring end users to provide passwords at every tier of a multitier application architecture is neither manageable nor ergonomic. Net8 provides integration features for these vertically integrated environments, allowing *single-signon* authentication.

Usage Tracking

A variety of techniques and products are available that monitor and analyze *usage* of the data warehouse. Such techniques seem unnecessary for operational systems, due to the rigid ways in which end users are permitted to access those systems. Interactive access is never *ad hoc* and free-format; it is always provided through *forms* and *reports*. Large-scale data manipulation to operational systems is always provided through *batch processes* using *job-control systems*, and modifications to all these methods of access are controlled by *change management, version control,* and *QA testing*.

This is not the case with many data warehouses.

The battle cry of the data warehousing revolution has been *More Power to the Users!* Ad hoc access is common and jealously guarded. Change management of ad hoc access is a contradiction in terms. Intrusive security methods are also incompatible with effective ad hoc access.

In such a situation, where being *proactive* is not possible, the best approach is being reactive. We may not be able to proactively stop a security violation, in which case it becomes absolutely vital that we be ready to recognize and react quickly to odd usage patterns. If we cannot use change management techniques and QA testing to prevent problems, we can at least be *omniscient, all seeing,* and *all knowing*. Usage tracking and analysis provide this omniscience and the ability to react quickly. Making *usage tracking* products and techniques part of the infrastructure underlying a data warehouse is as vital as making change management products and techniques part of the infrastructure of an operational, mission-critical system.

Usage tracking techniques include polling the V$SESSION and V$SQLAREA views and saving the information in a time-series data mart for later analysis. One of the authors, Tim Gorman of SageLogix, Inc., has such a package implemented in PL/SQL available on the Web at www.evdbt.com/library.htm. The package is implemented in PL/SQL packages and SQL*Plus scripts in an archive called "usage.zip." This is a nonsupported and rudimentary package intended to help you get started in usage tracking in your database. It's free and rather effective for all releases of Oracle7 and Oracle8, as it is capable of trapping any and all SQL statements issued against the data warehouse. It is intended not as a true solution for usage tracking, but rather as a demonstration that can whet the appetite for such information. In fact, it is best used as an illustration for more complete, supported products.

More impressive (and supported) products for usage tracking are available from Pine Cone Systems (www.pine-cone.com/), Precise Software (www.precis-esoft.com/), Cyrano (www.cyrano.com/) and Teleran Technologies (www.teleran.com/). There are almost certainly others, and we apologize for not mentioning them as well.

It should also be noted that, over time, it is probably inevitable that Oracle will enhance its own Net8 and RDBMS products to encompass this type of functionality. So far, the use of Oracle Trace by the DBMS_OLAP package in Oracle8*i* to gather "workload" information related to materialized views seems to indicate that the Oracle Trace product may be the start towards filling this functionality gap. The authors certainly do not speak for Oracle Corporation in any way, shape, or form, but this gap in administrative functionality for data warehousing systems is ripe to be bridged, and Oracle's product marketing must certainly have plans to do so, we feel.

Additionally, many ROLAP and MOLAP query and analysis packages, such as Oracle's Discoverer product and DSS MicroStrategy, to name a few, have the ability to capture all queries submitted from that tool and store it for analysis. This capability should probably be considered one of the criteria for selecting such products, unless you are going to handle usage tracking using one of the previously mentioned methods.

Fine-Grain Row-Level Security

New with Oracle8*i*, fine-grain access control allows you to embed *security policies* in stored functions or packaged functions, then associate those functions with tables and views. The intent is to use the logic in those embedded functions to implement security for each row, for SELECT, INSERT, UPDATE, or DELETE. Fine-grain access controls provide complete flexibility, allowing different security policies for insertions as opposed to updates, deletes, or selects. It also allows different security policies for a user depending on environment, time or date, enabled roles, and manner of connection.

The Oracle-supplied PL/SQL package DBMS_RLS provides the ability to add, drop, enable, and disable security policies against tables and views. This package is documented in the *Oracle8*i *Supplied Packages Reference* manual.

Net8 Advanced Security

Oracle provides access to the database based on several possible authentication methods:

- Authentication by the database (i.e., passwords on the Oracle account)
- Authentication by the operating-system (i.e., externally authenticated "OPS$" accounts)
- Authentication by a network service
- Authentication by middleware in a multitier architecture

The first two authentication methods are familiar to most Oracle users. The latter two authentication methods are available through additional Net8 options.

Network services such as DCE and Kerberos as well as middleware such as Tuxedo or CICS can be integrated with Net8 if you are using the *Enterprise Edition* of the Oracle8*i* RDBMS. See the *Oracle8*i *Advanced Security Administrator's Guide* for more information.

Data Warehouse Configuration Issues

The following issues are covered in this section:

Optimal Flexible Architecture (OFA). This is a file directory structure for successful growth.

Build/rebuild documentation. *Semper paratus.*

Identifying all inbound data and its sources. This demonstrates the importance of easily available metadata.

Job scheduling. Give yourself a fighting chance to prevent being overwhelmed.

Identifying all outbound data and its destinations. Know thy users.

Capacity planning. This refers to space capacity planning and resource capacity planning.

Development, test, and training environments. Despite what you may have read or heard, data warehouses are serious business too, and they require separate development and test areas.

Backup and recovery. Data warehouses *are* mission-critical.

Analyzing statistics. The cost-based optimizer requires it, and many tools require the cost-based optimizer.

Enabling and optimizing auditing. It's not just for security any more; it can help track resource utilization, too

Optimal Flexible Architecture (OFA)

As of release 7.3 of the Oracle7 RDBMS, the Oracle Installer will enforce the OFA's directory structure. This means that users of Oracle products will either have to comply with OFA or fool the Installer into believing that there is compliance. It is probably a good idea to become OFA compliant, as long as you understand the reasoning behind it.

As briefly introduced in Chapter 4, "Designing the Oracle Data Warehouse," in the context of tablespace design, OFA was developed primarily by Oracle Consulting Services' System Performance Group (SPG), led by Cary Millsap in the early 1990s, to help manage the increasingly large databases being developed using Oracle version 6. Although the documentation on OFA (available from www.orapub.com) describes the purpose of OFA in detail, the guidelines of OFA have three main objectives:

- Separate software from database and configuration/log/trace files
- Allow easy load balancing across disk devices as well as systems
- Establish a cross-platform standard for directories and files for Oracle (and other) products

Understanding these goals is key to understanding why the OFA standards are what they are. To attempt to implement them without this understanding would be an exercise in jumping through hoops for no purpose.

In versions of Oracle prior to version 7.3, the Oracle Installer would attempt to perform the simplest possible install. This usually meant that, unless nondefault directory locations were specified, all the Oracle software files went into a single directory tree, usually known as ORACLE_HOME. The Oracle software; the database; and all configuration files, log files, and trace files would reside underneath this directory structure (see Figure 8.1).

As you may expect, this works well in very simple environments that remain small and simple. But as the environment grows, managing this single directory tree becomes more and more complex (see Figure 8.2). In fact, because the maximum size of most UNIX file systems is 2 gigabytes, it's clear that the database itself will need to be relocated to another directory structure almost imme-

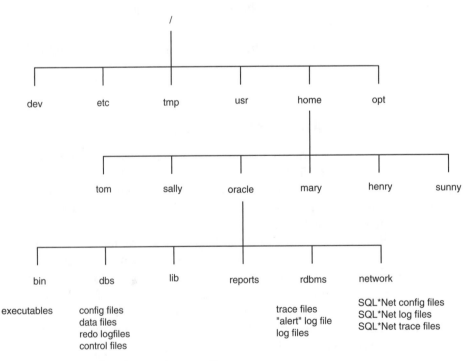

Figure 8.1 Everything in ORACLE_HOME.

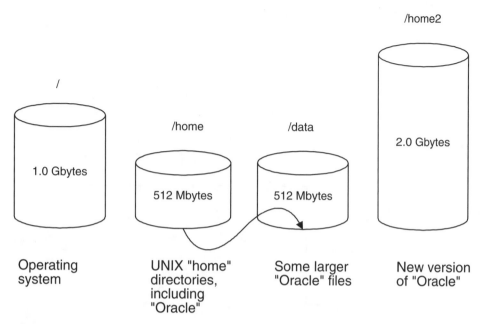

Figure 8.2   Growing pains.

diately. Archived redo logfiles also represent another growth risk, as they can accumulate rapidly in very busy database environments. Last, even log files (such as "alert.log") and trace files can exceed the available space quite rapidly.

So, it makes sense to plan for this kind of growth right from the beginning, so it can be planned properly. OFA guidelines therefore provide direction for creating similar directory structures under several similar *mount points*, where each mount point represents a separate file system or disk drive (see Figure 8.3). This scheme has the dual advantage of allowing the installation to exceed one file system and of balancing the I/O load across the multiple mount points.

One other fact of life that OFA enables is upgrades. Unless OFA (or some similar guidelines are utilized), a software upgrade may prove more exciting than it needs to be. An upgrade should just replace the software without changing anything else. Ideally, it should also allow the DBA to schedule independent upgrades to multiple databases on the same server to allow for testing and controlled migration. If the software, database files, configuration files, log files, and trace files are all mixed up in the same directory structure, then it would be very difficult to accomplish an upgrade without affecting (even jeopardizing) everything else. Because OFA separates the software from everything else, upgrades under an OFA-compliant installation are quite uneventful affairs.

Also, this standard can easily be adapted across platforms: UNIX, NT, and VMS. In place of the UNIX mount points named in Figure 8.3, just replace those

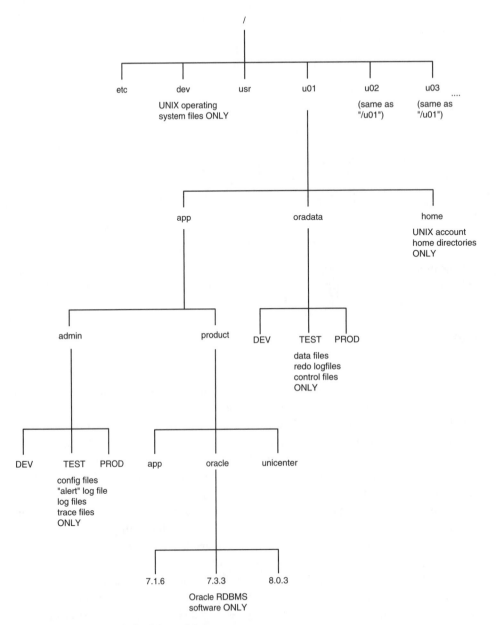

Figure 8.3   Optimal Flexible Architecture.

names with NT or VMS drive specifications. If a single group of DBAs has to manage Oracle databases on many platforms or if Oracle Support is dialing into your system to work on a problem, using OFA makes everyone's job easier.

Build/Rebuild Documentation
and Scripts

For a number of reasons, at any time it may be necessary to rebuild all or part of your database. Restores from backups can prevent this from being necessary, but in certain situations sometimes the best approach is to simply rebuild. Situations where this is true aren't necessarily due to mishaps or failures; you may be rebuilding the data warehouse environment on a different platform, either for migration or testing purposes or even to train new DBAs.

There are some situations, though, where rebuild scripts and documentation may be useful as a recovery strategy instead of restoring from backups.

To illustrate this, let's consider some typical data warehousing environments. In many situations, a significant portion of the data is downloaded regularly as "complete refreshes" of the data. Sometimes, the frequency between refreshes is weekly or even daily. Does it make sense to back this data up regularly? Or, because this data is short lived on the system anyway, should the affected tablespaces simply be dropped, re-created, and reloaded in the event of media failure or corruption? This is known as the *restore-versus-rebuild* debate.

There are many things to consider when deciding which recovery strategy (i.e., restore from backups or rebuild and reload) to implement.

First, Oracle tablespaces such as SYSTEM and the tablespace(s) containing rollback segments should always be backed up with ARCHIVELOG mode enabled with the archived redo logfiles backed up as well. Losing SYSTEM (which contains the data dictionary) and the rollback segments can cause problems that may necessitate a complete database rebuild. Because of this, always implement the RESTORE FROM BACKUP strategy for these tablespaces.

If database auditing is enabled and you have relocated the SYS.AUD$ table to another tablespace outside of the SYSTEM tablespace, you may also want to use the RESTORE FROM BACKUP strategy here as well. While the loss of auditing data will not threaten structural integrity of the database, it should seem obvious that if auditing information is worth recording, it is worth restoring completely rather than losing it completely.

What about data that cannot be reloaded easily? Of course, it can be argued that even historical tables that contain aggregated data accumulated over many years could eventually be reloaded, but who would want to go through the effort? And who could decide whether the reloaded and reaggregated data is accurate? If a mistake were made, how would it be verified? As a rule of thumb, any data that cannot be reloaded in one step should not be considered for a REBUILD THEN RELOAD strategy but instead should be RESTORED FROM BACKUP.

Always consider the mean time to repair. If you are not sure that you can quickly and reliably recall the data for reload, then don't consider REBUILD

THEN RELOAD. What you may not be aware of is that data from legacy systems used to load a data warehouse one day may be overwritten with new data the next. Or it may be sent to deep off-site storage. Or it may be misplaced.

If the tablespace contains an end-user layer for a development tool such as Oracle Forms Developer, Oracle Designer, Oracle Warehouse Builder, or Oracle Discoverer, don't assume that it will be acceptable to simply reinstall the tool. Developers using the tool may have many months of work stored in these tables and may not share a laissez-faire attitude toward this data.

Altogether, probably the only kind of data that is well suited for a REBUILD THEN RELOAD strategy is short-lived data that is frequently refreshed completely anyway. In this situation, which can sometimes consume several hundred gigabytes in a data warehouse, the idea of not performing backups has great appeal. If a media failure situation should occur, it can be quite easy to drop and re-create the affected tablespaces and then simply restart the normal load processes to reload them.

Tablespaces that have been made READ ONLY are ideal candidates for RESTORE FROM BACKUP. These files can be truly restored from backup and immediately made available. No roll-forward recovery from archived redo logs is necessary, provided they are backed up once after being altered to the READ ONLY state. Partitioning of large tables can frequently allow the majority of the table's data to be maintained in READ ONLY tablespaces.

Many DBAs and SysAdmins like the idea of REBUILD THEN RELOAD because they think it implies less work for them. But REBUILD THEN RELOAD really implies a custom-built recovery solution that must be as reliable and as easy to perform as RESTORE FROM BACKUP. Although a DBA will likely be performing the recovery, it might not necessarily be the DBA who is intimately familiar with the database in question.

Identifying All Inbound Data and Its Sources

The need for metadata is well documented in all references on data warehousing. More than other kinds of systems, data warehouses must make all metadata, both for the data warehouse itself and for its sources, easily and readily available to everyone. End users, developers, and administrators alike need to understand what data is available, where it came from, and what transformations (if any) were performed in bringing it on board.

The administrators of a data warehouse must be able to accurately describe the source of all the data being loaded into the data warehouse. At one basic level, this documentation could simply be a listing of all the load jobs, their frequencies, how they are invoked, the primary contact for the load jobs on the data warehouse system, and the contact who maintains the extract programs on the source system. This could then be expanded using CASE tools to be composed of complete metadata repositories of the source systems and the data warehouse.

Whatever the depth and degree of this documentation, it should be made accessible to all systems and end-user personnel using the data warehouse. Access mechanisms can include intranet Web sites, documentation on network drives, CASE repositories, or hard copy in binders in libraries.

Metadata can be integrated into the tools that users will use for reporting and analysis. As an *ad hoc* query and report tool, Oracle's Discoverer is an excellent choice for this reason. Most OLAP tools such as Oracle Express, Cognos Impromptu, and Business Objects come with extensive metadata facilities.

Metadata could also be a separate, nonintegrated part of the tool set; for example, an intranet Web site. Providing metadata in this manner could allow end users to share a common repository instead of having to learn how to navigate through each tool's metadata facilities. Naturally, this option implies (at the least) purchasing another product or (at the most) extensive additional development effort to develop this Web-based documentation. But with a diverse and dispersed end-user community utilizing many different tools (not to mention different versions of tools!), a Web-based metadata repository may prove extremely cost-effective in the long term as a common repository.

Job Scheduling

It has been said that 80 percent of the work of a data warehouse is getting the doggone thing loaded, day after day, week after week, month after month. The queries and reporting, while they represent 100 percent of the work performed by end users, pale in comparison to the amount of human and computer effort involved in keeping the data warehouse up-to-date and functional.

It stands to reason that this work should be automated rather than depend on human intervention to initiate, track, and sequence job submissions. It is fairly common for data warehouse developers and administrators to perform job scheduling and submission manually, purportedly until the development phase transitions into production. Unfortunately, during the transition there never seems to be enough time to automate the process, and by that time extra software cannot be purchased anyway as the budget has been exhausted until the next budget cycle.

There is an old adage that has been attributed both to Confucius and Murphy: "Things that are temporary are permanent, and things that are permanent are temporary." In this spirit, the bad habits and inefficiencies acquired during development and initial implementation cannot be corrected at a later date because the bad habits themselves leave no time to implement the correction. This serves to demonstrate the first half of the adage. The second half of the adage is a cynical commentary that over-engineered solutions often collapse under their own weight, prompting replacement by less elegant, more expeditious solutions.

Although some environments such as VMS, MVS, and AS/400 have very well-developed job-scheduling facilities built in, it is unfortunate but true that most Unix and NT platforms have extremely primitive job scheduling facilities—namely, "cron" and "at." Without a significant amount of custom development, these utilities are not sufficient for production job scheduling.

Therefore, it is highly recommended that a full-featured job-scheduling package be obtained for the data warehouse right from the beginning of the development phase. Job scheduling is not something that should be retrofitted in at a later date, nor would it be easy to convert manual processes over to automated job scheduling. When people develop manually initiated jobs, they generally implement them in a highly personalized fashion. This alone makes it very difficult and labor intensive to convert to the single format expected by an automated job scheduling system.

Automated job scheduling software should have at least the following features:

- Time-based job submission
- Event-based job submission
- Job-dependency submission
- Reporting on job schedules
- Queue management (queue creation and removal, queue quiesce/pause, queue bandwidths, queue workshifts, job assignments to queues, job viewing, job resubmission to different queues, job prioritization/reprioritization within queues, job hold/release/termination)
- Job history (log files, output files, records of elapsed time, queue, submitted by, scheduled at, began at, finished at, management reports, performance trend reports by queue, job, job type, user, time of day, etc.)

Additional desirable features include the following:

- Cross-platform support
- Integration with other job scheduling systems
- Unified console management of distributed heterogeneous systems
- Records of resources consumed

Job scheduling is not something that should be limited to administrators, however. End users should be encouraged to utilize the job scheduler for their repetitive jobs as well. Most data warehouse query tools, analysis tools, and OLAP tools do not have the ability to submit "batch jobs" or interface with job scheduling systems. They are generally designed to be executed interactively from a console or workstation.

Nonetheless, when evaluating such tools during the purchasing cycle, it would be wise to consider whether the query tool, analysis tool, or OLAP tool is capable of integrating with a job scheduling system, especially in the event of long-running queries. In this manner, the load on the system can be controlled to some extent, jobs that fail can be resubmitted automatically, and usage trends can be tracked more readily.

Identifying All Outbound Data and Its Destinations

Without prior planning, outbound data can be very difficult to document, and once documented it can be very difficult to keep up-to-date. Outbound data that is extracted from the data warehouse by means of batch jobs is not the problem. If a job scheduling package is used, batch jobs that extract data for reporting or transportation to other destinations such as data marts are quite easy to document and keep documented. With the job control features specified in the previous section, it is also very easy to restrict jobs running on the system and to terminate them if needed.

The real problem is potentially the *ad hoc* access to the data warehouse. More often than not, it is access via *ad hoc* tools (such as SQL*Plus) that causes performance degradation and security breaches in data warehouses. To guarantee the response time on specific load jobs, queries, and reports in a data warehouse, the administrators of the warehouse must be able to account for everything that is happening on the system. While Oracle DBAs can accomplish this after the fact using internal views such as V$SESSION and V$SQLAREA, it is far more effective to invest some planning into how *ad hoc* jobs will be submitted, tracked, and accounted rather than react to situations on an as-needed basis.

One way to document all outbound data is to restrict the tools being used, if possible. SQL*Plus allows rather unrestricted and completely *ad hoc* access to the database. This kind of access is very difficult to monitor and almost impossible to control.

Tools such as Oracle Discoverer and Oracle Express provide additional levels of security, the ability to restrict what queries are running, and the ability to analyze those queries that do run (see Figure 8.4).

See Chapter 13, "Analytical Processing in the Oracle Data Warehouse," for a more detailed explanation of Oracle Express and its capabilities.

In short, both batch and *ad hoc* activity should be tracked to effectively regulate resource consumption in the warehouse. Toward this end, you should favor tools, such as Discoverer that have features to predict resource consumption and cache data on the client side and that store submitted SQL statements for later analysis and optimization. Simplistic tools such as SQL*Plus should be used only very rarely, using lockout features (such as the PRODUCT_USER_PROFILE table) provided by the vendor.

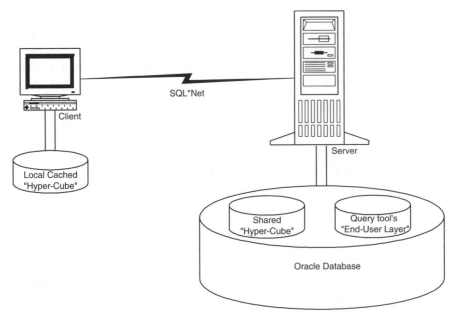

Figure 8.4   Query tools and OLAP tools: end-user layers.

CONTROLLING SQL*PLUS ACTIVITIES

If *ad hoc* access using SQL*Plus is a problem in your data warehouse, then consider selectively disabling the functions that can be performed from SQL*Plus using the SYSTEM.PRODUCT_USER_PROFILE table in Oracle7 or the SYSTEM.SQLPLUS_USER_PROFILE table in Oracle8. The use of these two tables is documented in the SQL*Plus *User's Guide and Reference*. They won't prevent a user from connecting to the database with SQL*Plus, but they will prevent a user from executing the commands you specify (i.e., SELECT, INSERT, UPDATE, DELETE, HOST, SPOOL, EXECUTE, etc.) from SQL*Plus. Please note that this feature pertains to SQL*Plus only and does not have anything to do with object permissions, system permissions, and roles granted and revoked using the GRANT and REVOKE commands. This is an entirely different level of security particular only to access to the database through SQL*Plus.

This is not to say that SQL*Plus does not have its place in a data warehouse environment; it simply lacks facilities to allow its usage to be moderated. It is a simple interface into the Oracle database, and as such it will allow careless end users to *code-and-fire* some truly resource-intensive SQL statements (affectionately referred to by DBAs as "queries from hell"). Make sure that only knowledgeable developers and users are using SQL*Plus by using the PRODUCT_USER_PROFILE table to limit SQL*Plus access to certain Oracle accounts.

Also, SQL*Plus is a worthy batch-processing tool for running reports and updates against the data warehouse. It is a good idea to have Oracle accounts for batch processing separate from developers' normal logon accounts.

For example, take the case of a developer who has an Oracle account named SALLY on a production data warehouse for the purpose of testing and analysis. This account is set up to allow read-only access to most of the data warehouse, and it has a *resource profile* that prevents intensive queries from consuming too many resources (resource profiles were described in the "Security Issues" section earlier in this chapter). In this account, Sally can develop, test, and play around without consuming too many resources and without damaging any data. If she is doing anything that temporarily requires more resources, the DBAs can change her resource profile to something less restrictive, temporarily or permanently.

The batch jobs that Sally develops are never executed under the account SALLY. Rather, the DBAs have set up another account named SALLY_BATCH that is entirely under their control. Sally can develop the batch processes, specify a schedule for their submission, and receive the results of the jobs, but access to this account is limited to the warehouse administrators. The reason for this is to give the people responsible for keeping the data warehouse up and running efficiently more control over how and when the data warehouse's resources are consumed.

Capacity Planning

There are two kinds of capacity in a computer system: space and resources. *Space* refers to storage—how much data can be stored in the data warehouse. *Resources* refers to the amount of work that can be performed on the data stored in the data warehouse.

Space Capacity Planning

Many formulas can be used to predictably calculate the amount of space that will need to be allocated in order to store a set of data in an Oracle database. Appendix A in the Oracle *Server Administrator's Guide* has formulas for predicting the sizes of tables, indexes, and clusters given the average sizes of each column in these objects.

But herein lies the rub: The formulas are based on *average sizes* and will therefore produce size estimates that will accumulate any errors made in estimating average column sizes. Thus, if you inaccurately estimate the average size of the data in a VARCHAR2(20) column as 10 characters instead of 11 for a table that will hold 1 million rows, you are going to be off by 1 MB, just on the basis of that one column. In data warehousing, tables are frequently denormalized and contain dozens or hundreds of columns. Now the margin of error will be larger unless scrupulously accurate values are used.

Can scrupulously accurate sizing data be obtained? The answer, frequently, is no. The only way to obtain accurate sizing data is from existing data, and frequently the existing data itself or the ability to analyze it is not available. For example, imagine making the request to find the average size of all fields in all files to the administrators running a legacy order entry system. You can imagine that there are many good reasons, as well as a few equally frivolous ones, why this task will never even be initiated, never mind completed. Therefore, database designers, in order to use these predictive formulas, must guess. Try to imagine the margin of error now.

While these documented formulas are useful in helping one understand Oracle data block formats and the factors involved in data storage, they are rarely useful in actual practice. As a matter of fact, there is a much faster, easier, and more accurate way to predict storage needs: data sampling and extrapolation.

The idea is this: obtain a few thousand data records. Create a table in Oracle and load the data. Observe how much space is consumed. Because you know how many records occupy this space, you can now calculate how many rows are in each database block. From this value (i.e., rows per block), you can now extrapolate how many database blocks would be necessary to hold N number of rows, where N is your estimated total table size. In addition to normal statistical sampling error, the maximum error introduced by this approach is an overestimate of nearly one Oracle block (assuming the worst case of only a single row being loaded into the final allocated block). Both forms of potential error are reduced by using larger sample sizes.

Of course, if you cannot obtain any of the data in the first place, this method is useless. In this event, where you can neither obtain data for extrapolation purposes nor obtain detailed and exhaustive information on size averages, you may as well just make simple guesses at space requirements. Simple guesses are faster than plugging guessed-at values into the sizing formulas, and either way the results are irrelevant to some extent.

It is somewhat reasonable, though, to expect that a data warehousing effort would be able to acquire some data to test. Submitting a request to the harried administrators of a legacy order entry system for a certain number of records from each file might be treated more kindly than a request to analyze the data itself, which will likely entail extra effort on their part. Additionally, because some test data will be required at an early stage of the data warehouse project anyway, obtaining data samples for the purpose of sizing will kill two birds with one stone.

Next, create the sample table using reasonable parameters reflecting the expected behavior of the table. The Oracle *Server Administrator's Guide* has chapters entitled "Managing Tables" and "Managing Indexes" that describe the use of PCTFREE and PCTUSED and INITRANS and MAXTRANS. In a largely read-only environment like a data warehouse, it is doubtful that the values of INITRANS and MAXTRANS will need to be changed from their defaults, but it might be possible if the loads of the data warehouse incur contention for data blocks. Altogether, it is likely that the settings for PCTFREE and PCTUSED will require the most consideration for this exercise. It is completely valid to perform this extrapolation multiple times, each time using different values of PCT-FREE, PCTUSED, INITRANS, and MAXTRANS, to observe their effect on storage. As described in Chapter 5, "Building the Oracle Data Warehouse," PCT-FREE should generally be set to 0 for most warehouse tables. The value of PCTUSED will depend on whether you will ever DELETE rows from the table.

When the data has been loaded, you can run the following query in Oracle7:

```
SELECT AVG(COUNT(SUBSTR(ROWID,10,4))) avg_rows_per_blk
  FROM <name-of-the-table>
 WHERE ROWNUM <= <total-#-rows-minus-some>
 GROUP BY SUBSTR(ROWID,1,8),
          SUBSTR(ROWID,15,4);
```

Or, for Oracle8:

```
SELECT AVG(COUNT(DBMS_ROWID.ROWID_ROW_NUMBER(ROWID))) avg_rows_per_blk
  FROM <name-of-the-table>
 WHERE ROWNUM <= <total-#-rows-minus-some>
 GROUP BY DBMS_ROWID.ROWID_OBJECT(ROWID),
          DBMS_ROWID.ROWID_RELATIVE_FNO(ROWID),
          DBMS_ROWID.ROWID_BLOCK_NUMBER(ROWID);
```

Knowing something about the meaning and contents of a ROWID is helpful. In Oracle7, a ROWID is stored internally as a *block number*, a *row number within block*, and a *file number*. In Oracle8, the ROWID has been expanded to include an *object number* as well.

Of course, you need to substitute *<name-of-the-table>* with the name of the table itself, and you should substitute *<total-#-rows-minus-some>* with a value that is at least a couple of hundred or thousand rows less than the actual total number of rows in the table. The reason for this is to avoid counting partially filled database blocks, which would normally reside near the "end" of the table. These blocks may have been left partially filled when the load ended, and including them in this calculation may skew the average, however slightly.

Depending on the size of the database blocks, the settings of PCTFREE and INITRANS, and (of course) the characteristics of the data itself, you will get a value that can be used when extrapolating the eventual full size of the table. For example, if one of the queries just shown returned a value of 48.3, this means that—on average—each database block will hold 48.3 rows. Therefore, if you know that you'll need to store 100 million rows, then it will take just over 2 million (2,070,394, to be exact) database blocks to store this. If each database block is 8 KB, then this table should require 15.8 gigabytes.

Don't forget indexes. Again, it may be simplest to extrapolate: create the proposed indexes, see how big they are, and project their final size. If the sample version of the table contains 100,000 rows, and an index created against that consumes 1,000 blocks (according to the USED_BLOCKS column in the USER_INDEXES view following an ANALYZE INDEX), then it stands to reason that when the table is at its full size of 100 million rows the index will also be approximately 1,000 times larger as well (1 million blocks at 8 KB, which is about 7.6 gigabytes). (Index growth is not exactly linear because of the hierarchical nature of B*Tree indexes, compression in the branch blocks, and the capability of storing multiple ROWIDs for each key value.)

There is another issue regarding index space utilization that must be considered. When using parallel CREATE INDEX, each parallel slave temporarily allocates space according to the INITIAL and NEXT parameters specified in the STORAGE clause. During the course of the CREATE INDEX, the amount of space consumed will briefly equal about twice the eventual size of the final index segment. This is due to a merge operation in which all the results of each parallel slave are merged into a single index structure. In essence, this is a kind of trade-off between *speed* and *space* during the CREATE INDEX operation: The nonparallel CREATE INDEX operation consumes less space during index creation, but it's slower; the parallel CREATE INDEX operation completes the index creation faster but uses lots of "scratch space" while doing so.

Because data warehouse environments are generally large enough to make the use of Oracle parallel execution features such as parallel CREATE INDEX (pCI), always remember that enough space should be left unused in a tablespace to accommodate the parallel creation of the largest index. This same allowance needs to be made in anticipation of reorganizing indexes using ALTER INDEX . . . REBUILD. For example, say you have sized four indexes at 8 gigabytes, 9 gigabytes, 10 gigabytes, and 12 gigabytes, and they are all going to reside in the same tablespace. Should you size the tablespace at 40 gigabytes (9 + 10 + 11 + 12 = 39)? Only if you intend to create these huge objects using regular old nonparallel CREATE INDEX. If you intend to make use of parallel CREATE INDEX, you should plan on leaving at least the equivalent of the largest index as unused space (see Figure 8.5); in this example, this implies that the tablespace should be sized at around 52 gigabytes! If disk space is at a premium, you could get away with sizing this tablespace with the equivalent of the smallest index as unused space, but that would imply that if you wished to re-create the largest (12 gigabyte) index, you would have to drop the two smallest indexes as well and re-create them after the large one had been re-created!

So far, we have discussed table and index space capacity planning, but there is more to an Oracle database than just the tables and indexes that make up your data warehouse applications.

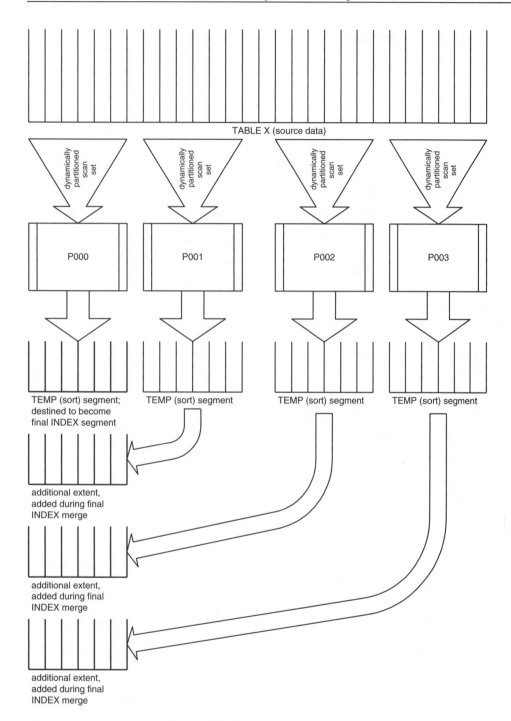

Figure 8.5 Leaving room for parallel CREATE INDEX.

Oracle Database Space Requirements

Within the Oracle database, there are several types of special "internal use" tablespaces to consider (see Figure 8.6).

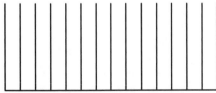

SYSTEM tablespace (the only required tablespace, and the only one whose name is unchangeable) contains:

* Oracle data dictionary
* one rollback segment named SYSTEM
* SYS.AUD$ table (by default)

Expected I/O characteristics:

* most of Oracle data dictionary should be buffered in the SGA; heavy I/O should be a cause for concern

TEMP tablespace (an arbitrary name) contains:

* temporary segments used during sorting

Expected I/O characteristics:

* expect high volumes of I/O during normal operation and during the load phase when indexes are being created

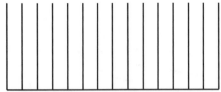

TOOLS tablespace (an arbitrary name) contains:

** **end-user layer** for Oracle tools (i.e, Developer, Designer, Discoverer)*

Expected I/O characteristics:

* should be low, if the tools in question are tuned properly. If the tool in question creates "sharable hyper-cubes", I/O volume could be high on occasion

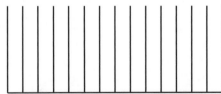

RBS_1 tablespace (an arbitrary name) contains:

* rollback segments for one instance of Parallel Server
or
* rollback segments for entire "exclusive" database

Expected I/O characteristics:

* expect high volumes of random, single-db-block I/O during the load phase

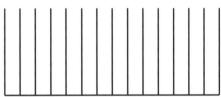

USERS tablespace (an arbitrary name) contains:

** **scratch area** for Oracle accounts*

Expected I/O characteristics:

** dependent on the nature of the Oracle accounts. **Developer** accounts might generate high volumes of I/O...*

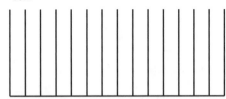

AUDIT tablespace (an arbitrary name) contains:

* SYS.AUD$ table and any user-defined tables and indexes used for database auditing

Expected I/O characteristics:

* dependent on the level of auditing, but anticipate high levels of I/O . . .

Figure 8.6   Oracle "internal use" tablespaces.

LOCALLY MANAGED TABLESPACES

New with Oracle8*i*, *locally managed* tablespaces provide an alternative to the way that the Oracle RDBMS has managed space in the database since the product was introduced.

Until Oracle8*i*, space was managed in the data dictionary, specifically two tables named SYS.UET$ and SYS.FET$. These tables, which are clustered with the SYS.SEG$ and SYS.TS$ tables, respectively, contained information about extents, whether *used* by a segment or *free*. Thus, every time an extent is added anywhere in the database, due to an explicit CREATE or ALTER command or automatic space allocation, rows would be added to the UET$ table and removed from the FET$ table. When extents were dropped, whether due to explicit DROP or TRUNCATE commands or due to automatic rollback segment shrinkage, rows would be added to the FET$ table and removed from the UET$ table.

Because there are actually many steps to space management besides adding and removing rows from these tables, any session performing space management must first acquire the "ST" (space-management transaction) enqueue or lock in *exclusive mode*. This means that space-management activities are essentially *single-threaded* in the Oracle RDBMS for *dictionary-managed* tablespaces.

The new *locally managed* tablespaces decentralize space management operations. Each data file in a locally managed tablespace has the first few blocks dedicated as a *bitmap segment*. Each bit in this segment represents one extent: A bit-value of 1 means that the extent is *used*, and a bit-value of 0 means that the extent is *free*.

Because extent information is now decentralized, there is no longer need to acquire the "ST" enqueue for space-management activities, which can significantly reduce contention in very active environments. Reducing dependencies on enqueues is especially important in Oracle Parallel Server.

Moreover, using locally managed tablespaces is simply more efficient; bitmap operations are faster than inserting and removing rows from tables. Also, because locally managed tablespaces employ uniformly sized extents, the possibility of tablespace fragmentation is completely eliminated forever.

Any tablespace in the database, excluding SYSTEM, can be created as *locally managed* using the EXTENT MANAGEMENT LOCAL clause in the CREATE TABLESPACE command. Also, be aware that any tablespaces containing rollback segments cannot be locally-managed either, at least through version 8.1.6 (Oracle8*i* Release 2). Also, locally managed tablespaces for *temporary* tablespaces further enhance the performance of sorts during SQL statements, as well as the new *global temporary table* functionality introduced with Oracle8*i*. The new syntax for CREATE TEMPORARY TABLESPACE can be used here; check the *Oracle8*i *SQL Language Reference* manual for more information.

Using locally managed tablespaces for any tablespace with large volumes of transactions is a big win. Use it wherever possible.

SYSTEM Tablespace

The *data dictionary* resides within the SYSTEM tablespace and is owned by the SYS account. The size of the data dictionary is generally quite fixed and usually starts at around 10 MB at initial configuration. The space required by the data dictionary after that initial configuration is affected by the number of schema objects in the database and the number of PL/SQL packages and triggers in the database. Generally, typical data warehouse applications will not include a large number of tables and indexes or PL/SQL stored procedures. Numbers of tables and indexes in the low hundreds is considered small, as is a couple of dozen PL/SQL stored packages or procedures. By contrast, prepackaged software (such as Oracle Financials or Oracle Manufacturing) can sometimes consist of many thousands of tables, twice or four times that number of indexes, and hundreds or thousands of PL/SQL stored objects. For situations like these, it is not uncommon to see the data dictionary require up to 500 to 700 MB. Size your SYSTEM tablespace accordingly. If you think you may have a couple of hundred tables and indexes, then sizing SYSTEM at 30 to 100 MB is not unreasonable, regardless of the amount of space those tables and indexes will consume. The data dictionary does contain extent and freespace information, which is affected by object size, but in general the sizing needs of the data dictionary are more dependent on the number of objects than the size of the objects (other than stored packages, procedures, and functions, which are stored in SYSTEM). If you think that your database will eventually hold thousands of tables and thousands of indexes and will be heavily dependent on PL/SQL-stored packages and procedures, then sizing your SYSTEM tablespace from 500 to 1,000 MB is not unreasonable.

NOTE If needed, additional space can be added to the SYSTEM tablespace using ALTER TABLESPACE SYSTEM ADD DATAFILE to add another data file or ALTER DATABASE DATAFILE *xxx* RESIZE to expand an existing data file.

Tools Tablespace

Objects belonging to the SYSTEM schema (not to be confused with the SYSTEM tablespace) are not part of the data dictionary. Generally, the SYSTEM account owns the *end-user layers* for such tools as Oracle Forms Developer. The Oracle Universal Installer program creates a tablespace named TOOLS as the default tablespace for the SYSTEM account, and the size of the TOOLS tablespace should take into consideration whether tools such as Oracle Forms Developer will be installed and used, now or in the future.

Rollback Segment Tablespace

It is also a good idea to keep all rollback segments in one or more tablespaces named RBSnn (i.e., RBS01, RBS02). There are no specific rules as to whether one tablespace is better for rollback segments or several. Losing any tablespace (due to disk failure) that contains an online rollback segment may make the database unusable. For this reason, if you have extremely strict mean time to repair (MTTR) expectations, it might be wise to make sure that there are at least two tablespaces in your database devoted to rollback segments. That way, if anything happens to one tablespace, it can be recovered or re-created while the other tablespace allows the database to continue at least some processing. Of course, disk mirroring should make such a possibility extremely remote, but even mirroring can be defeated by extremely bad luck, and nothing can stop corruption, as corruption is by nature unpredictable and not predictable. Corruption of rollback segments is the absolute worst predicament for an Oracle database administrator, and the safest approach to resolving corruption is to treat it like media recovery; that is, restore from a backup taken prior to the corruption and roll forward recovery until the current point-in-time. If all rollback segments are in one tablespace, then doing this means keeping the system unavailable. If there are two tablespaces devoted to rollback segments, then it is possible to keep the database up and available while this recovery is in progress. Of course, the transactions whose rollback segment entries were affected by the corruption cannot continue, but perhaps others can.

The size and number of rollback segments has provided fodder for a great many books, white papers, and presentations, but we tend to follow these general guidelines for starters:

- Each rollback segment should have a minimum of 20 extents, perhaps 40 for very busy transactional systems. This means MINEXTENTS should be set between 20 and 40.

- The OPTIMAL setting for each rollback segment should be set to the size implied by MINEXTENTS times NEXT. For example, MINEXTENTS 20 and NEXT 1M should indicate an OPTIMAL 20M.

- The size of extents in rollback segments should reflect the anticipated duration of the "average" transaction. If you are running an OLTP-type system where there are hundreds or thousands of transactions concurrently active, but each is very small, then size rollback segment extents smaller (i.e., 64 to 128 KB). If the average transaction is larger, tending more toward batch and less toward online operations, you should size extents larger (i.e., 1 MB to 4 MB). Most data warehouse applications tend toward the latter.

- Extremely large transactions require more rollback space. If a large transaction cannot be split into smaller pieces or modified to run UNRECOVERABLE (Oracle7) or NOLOGGING (Oracle8), it may be necessary to create one or more very large rollback segments. The large transaction will need to specifically request the large rollback segment using the SET TRANSACTION USE ROLLBACK SEGMENT command.

HOW MANY ROLLBACK SEGMENTS ARE NEEDED?

We like to follow the Oracle guidelines of 1 rollback segment for every 4 concurrently *active* DML (data manipulation language, such as INSERT, UPDATE, or DELETE) transactions on the system, with a minimum of 4 and a maximum of 50 to 60. In an online application, it is not uncommon for 90 to 95 percent of all sessions to be *inactive*, leaving only 5 to 10 percent of all connected sessions *active* at any point in time. Thus, when there are 200 connected users, only 10 to 20 user sessions might actually be actively performing DML at any one time. This implies the need for 4 to 5 rollback segments. In a mostly batch-oriented application, it is likely that 90 percent of all sessions are *actively* running DML operations at any one time, with only 5 to10 percent *inactive* or read-only (i.e., non-DML). This is the exact reverse of online applications. So, if you have a batch-oriented system with 30 connected sessions, this might also imply that 25 or more of those sessions are active, which implies 6 to 8 rollback segments for starters. Again, most data warehouses tend toward the latter during their load phase. During their read-only phase, most data warehouses provide few issues involving rollback segments whatsoever because read-only operations involve read-consistency issues only when there is simultaneous DML in the database.

Next is an example of rollback segment sizing:

Jane is building an Oracle database for a data warehouse that is expected to have about 200 gigabytes in data and 300 gigabytes in indexes at initial load. The nature of the application is that half that data will be reloaded completely (a complete refresh) every week (on Sunday); the other half will grow at a rate of 100 percent per year.

Outside the Sunday load phase, tablespaces will be "locked down" into READ ONLY mode to prevent any updates. The complete refreshes will utilize parallel SQL*Loader direct path, and the remaining loads will use SQL*Loader conventional path and PL/SQL and PRO*C programs to massage the data into its final form.

The Sunday load phase is allowed to take a full 24 hours if absolutely necessary, but if hardware maintenance is scheduled or if software upgrades or patches are necessary, they will also have to be accomplished during Sunday. Therefore, it is in everybody's best interests to make the utmost use of the parallel capabilities of the hardware platform to finish the load phase in as short a time as possible.

Given this information, it is difficult to anticipate sizing needs for rollback segments. But let's assume that Jane knows she has 20 to 30 tables to load via complete refresh. Using SQL*Loader direct path means that rollback segments are not utilized at all. She has another 20 to 30 tables that will be loaded using SQL*Loader conventional path, PL/SQL, and PRO*C. Assuming that parallelism will allow her to run at least two separate processes (SQL*Loader, PL/SQL, or PRO*C) against each table, about 40 to 60 load processes requiring rollback segments will result. Using the basic formula of TRANSACTIONS / 4, this gives about 10 to 15 rollback segments. Because these are batch load transactions, Jane decides to size extents at 1 MB apiece for starters. Taking the conservative route of using MINEXTENTS 20, this means that Jane has 15 rollback segments, each requiring 20 MB at OPTIMAL, which means a minimum of 300 MB. Figuring also that each of these rollback segments can triple (or more) in size, Jane decides to double the minimum size figures and create an RBS01 tablespace of 600 MB.

Temporary Segment Tablespace

Most Oracle databases also have a tablespace set aside strictly for use by TEMPORARY segments during sorting operations. These tablespaces, which beginning with Oracle7, release 7.3 should be marked as TEMPORARY, are usually named TEMP or TEMP_DATA, and all Oracle accounts should use this tablespace as the account's TEMPORARY TABLESPACE. The amount of temporary space a database will require for sorting is, again, dependent on the application. Many online (OLTP) systems don't do much sorting; they may generally do short, quick queries. They use queries that utilize indexes and retrieve only one or a few rows at a time. Although such systems also usually have reporting processes that may perform a great deal of sorting, overall they do not require much in the way of space in the TEMP tablespace.

On the other hand, data warehouse applications may require enormous amounts of sort space. Many data warehouses do not have large numbers of users logged in at any one time, but each user who is connected might very well be running enormous queries that are either sorting due to explicit ORDER BY or GROUP BY clauses, or they may be requiring temporary segments because they are using join methods that imply sorting or temporary space (i.e., SORT-MERGE joins). Additionally, the use of Parallel Execution may increase these needs many times. If the typical large query in a data warehouse utilizes Parallel Execution to a DEGREE of 8, this means that up to 16 parallel query slave processes are working simultaneously on a query where previously only 1 process may have worked (8 for data retrieval and 8 for sorting). This may mean that the demands for sorting space may have just increased eightfold (although for only one-eighth of the time as a nonparallel query, we hope). It is not uncommon for a data warehouse application that is going to make heavy use of Parallel Execution to require a significant percentage of its space in the TEMP tablespace. Ratios of 10 to 25 percent of total database size may be valid. We recommend starting with 5 to 10 percent of total data size (i.e., 10 to 20 gigabytes in

Jane's example, based on 200 gigabytes of data) at initial configuration. If during the development of the data warehouse that proves insufficient, feel free to dedicate more space to the TEMP tablespace, especially if Parallel Execution is in use. If the ratio starts to approach 15 to 20 percent of total data size (i.e., 30 to 40 gigabytes in Jane's example) and the demands for more sort space do not abate, start to question the validity of what the query developers are doing. Maybe they can make use of indexing rather than Parallel Execution. Maybe they should be using summary tables or materialized views to *preaggregate* data, instead of aggregating "on the fly" all the time.

Other Tablespaces

In addition to the SYSTEM, tools, rollback and temporary tablespaces, it is common to create another special tablespace generally called USERS. Create a USERS tablespace if any of the warehouse users will be allowed to create their own objects, perhaps to store temporary results between multiple analysis steps.

Also, if you will be using the Oracle auditing features (as described later in this chapter) you may wish to move the audit trail table (SYS.AUD$) to its own tablespace to avoid interfering with the other operations of the SYSTEM tablespace.

Redo Log Space Requirements

Last, but certainly not least, is the need to provide space for online redo logfiles. Think of these structures almost as representing a second copy of the database. The data files contain the *current* image of the database. The redo logfiles (online and archived) represent an *historical* image of the database, every action ever taken, in sequential order. While this image of the database is not useful for general use, it serves an extremely important function: In the event of some kind of failure, actions recorded in the redo logfiles can be replayed against the data files to bring them up-to-date. The sizing of redo logfiles is important mainly for controlling checkpoints and the archiving process.

Because we can control the frequency of *checkpointing* using initialization parameters such as LOG_CHECKPOINT_INTERVAL and LOG_CHECKPOINT_TIMEOUT, the size of redo logfiles should provide only an upper boundary for checkpoint frequency; checkpoints must occur during the switch of online redo logfiles. If redo logfiles are sized too small, then database activity will cause *redo switches* every few seconds or minutes. As a rule of thumb, you don't like to see redo logfile switches more frequently than every 30 minutes on a consistent basis. Occasionally, "freak" high volumes of transactions may cause redo logfile switching to occur more often, but if this occurs frequently and regularly, then it is not a "freak" occurrence. In this event, you want to size your redo logfiles larger. As a starting point, you should not be uncomfortable to size the redo logfiles at 50 to 100 MB.

Of course, there is an upper limit to the size of redo logfiles. When archiving (and there are very few reasons not to enable ARCHIVELOG mode in Oracle!), the destination for archived redo logfiles is typically a file system directory. In many versions of UNIX, the maximum file system size is 2 gigabytes (although several ports now allow much larger sizes). If you sized redo logfiles at close to or larger than 2 gigabytes, you run the risk of overwhelming the LOG_ARCHIVE _DEST directory and file system. This would cause your Oracle database to halt dead in its tracks. No data would be lost, but any activities causing updates to the database would freeze until space for redo logfile archiving is opened up.

Another consideration is tuning the ARCH background process. You want ARCH to promptly archive the online redo logfiles as quickly as possible, but you do not want the effect of the ARCH process while it is working to cause a system "brownout," or temporary performance degradation. Ideally, the ARCH process should be able to finish copying the redo logfile to the archive log destination in less than one-third the time it takes the LGWR process to fill up a redo logfile, on average. If LGWR is filling up a redo logfile every 30 minutes, then it should be quite easy for the ARCH process to accomplish the simple task of copying the file off to the archive log destination in 10 minutes or less.

Try to size the redo logfiles so that it takes the LGWR process at least 30 minutes *at a minimum* to fill one up. The "alert.log" file records the times of redo logfile switches, as does the V$LOG_HISTORY view.

If the ARCH process cannot finish archiving one of the logfiles in less than 10 minutes, then add more redo log groups. By default, the Oracle Installer will create a database with the minimum of 2 redo groups; most DBA handbooks recommend at least 3. If the ARCH process cannot finish its job quickly enough, adding more redo logfile groups will provide additional time for ARCH to finish its job before the circular redo logging once again needs to reuse the file being archived. Of course, be sure that some kind of I/O bottleneck is not slowing down either ARCH or LGWR; the I/O subsystem underneath the redo logfiles should be optimized for sequential writes (by LGWR) and sequential reads (by ARCH). Be aware also of the I/O characteristics of the file system to which the ARCH process is writing; if I/O performance is slow there due to contention, then it would be more efficacious to remove the contention instead of adding more redo groups.

As a starting point for Oracle data warehouses, try three groups of redo logfiles of 100 MB apiece. Even if RAID 1 volume mirroring is available, it makes sense to use multiple redo logfile members (i.e., mirroring at the Oracle level) to protect against some additional failure scenarios. These recommendations imply 600 MB of space optimized for sequential writes and reads. Start with these guidelines, make sure that neither LGWR nor ARCH are being overwhelmed, and tune checkpoints separately using LOG_CHECKPOINT_INTERVAL and LOG _CHECKPOINT_TIMEOUT. Set the LOG_CHECKPOINTS_TO_ALERT initialization parameter to TRUE to have a message inserted into the "alert.log" file when each checkpoint occurs, so that you can tune the frequency of checkpoints.

Resource Capacity Planning

What kind of platform should you get for your data warehouse?

We hope that the discussions in Chapter 2 have helped you decide which architecture might be best suited for your needs. Once you have chosen a platform architecture, once you have designed your data warehouse, and once you have sized your database, you will need to forecast how much CPU, memory, and network resources you will require. Typically, this answer is easy: as much as you can afford! Your hardware vendor will help you size the CPU and memory resources for your environment; with the variety of platforms and the pace of advances in hardware, this book can't delve into that subject.

As an administrator, the best thing you can do is try to anticipate what kinds of operations will be running on the data warehouse. This analysis is a direct offshoot of requirements analysis: What kinds of things are end users expecting to do in the warehouse? This is also a result of system requirements analysis: What kinds of batch processing are necessary to load and prepare the data warehouse for end-user access?

Because the story always changes (usually for the worse) after the analysis and design phases of a software project, the next best thing an administrator can do is plan system management for the new system, at as early a stage as possible. For this reason, the best approach to planning resource capacity might be to ensure that, during full production usage, all utilization can be monitored, understood, and controlled.

Monitoring is not difficult: Many system management tools (including Oracle Enterprise Manager's Performance Pack) provide the ability to find the "top 10" or "top NN" processes in terms of resource consumption, to monitor locks and "waits" in the database, and to monitor space utilization in the database easily and graphically.

The understanding may be trickier, depending on your level of expertise. If a process is the top consumer of CPU resources on your system for 60 seconds, is that necessarily a problem? What if it is one of the top consumers of CPU resources for an hour? If someone is running some SQL statements that are continuously running out of rollback segment space, what can be done about it? What *should* be done about it?

Control involves the ability not only to run and cancel execution but also to limit resource utilization and queue execution. So, once again, we begin a discussion of system management tools, especially job control packages and end-user tools that are integrated with some sort of queuing system.

Queuing

What role does queuing play in controlling the utilization of resources? Consider the standard textbook depiction of queuing theory. The classic case is an airline ticket counter. There are only a few ticket agents ready to serve, but potentially hundreds of passengers desiring service. One approach is to set up a single queue, allowing each ticket agent to service the next passenger at the head of the line.

But consider the fact that not all passengers are equal. Some belong to the frequent-flier program, and the airline wants to treat them well. First-class passengers should also be given priority. Also, some passengers have long transactions (to purchase tickets), and others will require only a few minutes to check in and receive their boarding passes. Clearly the airline can accomplish a lot by setting up multiple queues and devoting different levels of resources (i.e., agents) to each queue. On the other hand, the airline may be guaranteeing customer unhappiness if it can't react quickly to changing volumes of passengers in the various queues.

The same situation confronts Oracle data warehouse administrators. Most data warehouses are opened with no consideration for limiting the access of end users to system resources. As a consequence, many warehouses resemble a free-for-all melee with each transaction vying for resources as soon as it is submitted. Oracle8*i* introduces the new Database Resource Manager that allows the DBA to control the allocation of resources such as CPU and parallel execution slaves across multiple *consumer groups*. Using the DBMS_RESOURCE_MANAGER package however requires using a command-line facility for managing something that is best visualized using a graphical tool. Unfortunately, no such graphical tool yet exists, but undoubtedly Oracle Enterprise Manager will fill this gap in a future release. For now, using the Resource Manager product requires careful graphing by hand (on paper or using something like PowerPoint or VISIO) and then carefully scripting calls to the DBMS_RESOURCE_MANAGER package inside a SQL*Plus script. Earlier Oracle releases, however, do not provide any scheme for assigning different processing priorities to different users or jobs. The administrator must attempt to control demand by limiting the number of simultaneous users, the degree of parallelization, and the scheduling of batch operations. The best approach is to plan for a crushing volume of demand for system resources and to line up the appropriate end-user tools and system management facilities to deal with the demand during the earliest phases of planning.

Development, Test, and Training Environments

A data warehouse is a production environment, generally with availability requirements similar to a production OLTP system. As such, developers and end users should not be performing development activities inside the production environment, and there needs to be a separate "QA test" environment for new applications, software versions, and tools, just as in "real" system environments. Finally, new end users need to be trained in the data warehouse, so a training area separate from the development, test, and production areas should be available.

This, however, begs the question: Because data warehouses are so often huge, how do we support not one but *four* copies of this huge database?

The best answer probably is this: We don't. The best approach is to use sampling techniques to extract subsets of the production data to populate smaller versions of the database. This can be done in two ways: load sampling or data sampling.

Load sampling occurs when a filtering process is performed against the original data to be loaded (see Figure 8.7). This filtering process is inserted ahead of the load process and feeds the load process a subset of the original records to be loaded.

Data sampling (see Figure 8.8) is similar in that instead of extracting the subset from original load data, the subset is extracted from the data warehouse database after the loads are completed. As such, the data sampling becomes yet another extract from the data warehouse.

Samples can be chosen at random using new Oracle8*i* feature the SAMPLE clause for SELECT statements, or it can be chosen by some well-known non-random attribute, such as geography (see Figure 8.9).

Take the example of a national retailer that does business in all 50 states in the United States and all the provinces and territories of Canada. It may decide that a valid sample would be to select from 5 geographically distributed states and 2 provinces, effectively selecting about 10 percent of the total production population.

Or, it may be equally valid to select from particular months, weeks, or days (see Figure 8.10). This may be easier to perform while you are data sampling as opposed to load sampling, as most load processes involve data from a certain recent period of time.

Or, the sampling can be random, using the new SAMPLE clause of Oracle8*i*. This clause externalizes the same random sampling algorithms that have been used by the ANALYZE . . . ESTIMATE STATISTICS command since Oracle7. There are two ways to sample. You can use a more expensive sampling method to ensure that an exact number of rows are returned:

```
SELECT      *
FROM        TABLE_X
SAMPLE (2)
```

This method continues to randomly request rows until exactly 2 percent of the number of rows (according to the latest ANALYZE statistics) have been retrieved. Or you can use a faster but less exact method that may not return the exact sample size you had requested:

```
SELECT      *
FROM        TABLE_X
SAMPLE BLOCK (2)
```

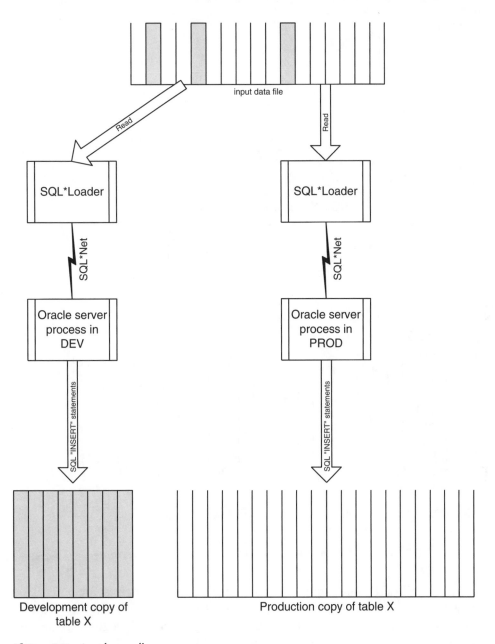

Figure 8.7   Load sampling.

This method will sample rows from approximately 2 percent of the blocks in the table, randomly selected. It is faster but less accurate. Sometimes, that's good enough!

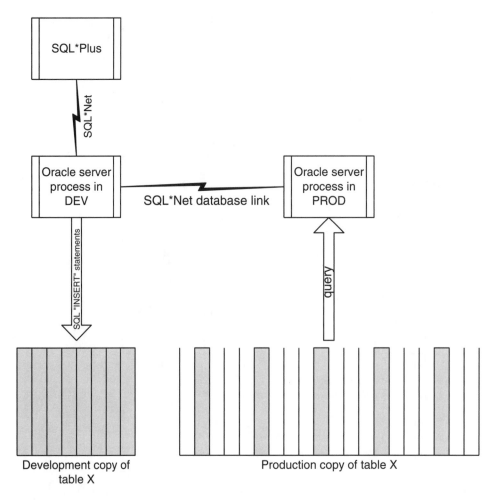

Figure 8.8   Data sampling.

These SELECT statements can now be used as subqueries for pCTAS, as described in Chapter 7, "Post-Load Processing in the Data Warehouse." Be sure to test this first, to ensure that the returned sample size is close to the requested size and that the returned sample is fairly random.

Backup and Recovery

There are already several terrific books on this subject:

■ *Oracle8 Backup & Recovery Handbook* by Rama Velpuri, published by Oracle Press in 1998 (ISBN 0-07-882389-7).

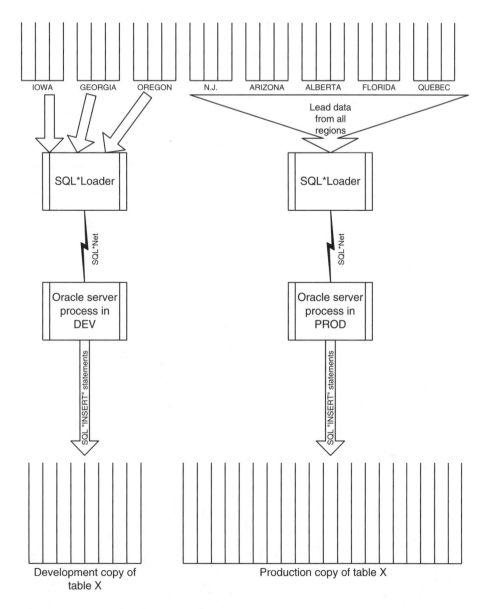

Figure 8.9 Sampling by geography.

- *Oracle7 Server Administrator's Reference*, part of the standard Oracle documentation set. This book has several chapters devoted to backup and restore.

- *Oracle8i Server Backup and Recovery Guide*, part of the standard Oracle documentation set, an entire book devoted to the subject in general and the new features of Oracle8 and Recovery Manager in particular.

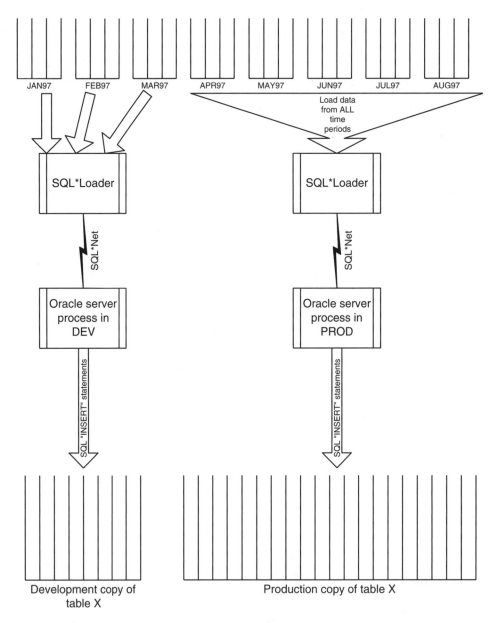

Figure 8.10 Sampling certain months, weeks, or days.

Get your hands on at least one of these books and read it thoroughly. This book is not going to repeat what is covered so thoroughly in these standard references, especially the Oracle8*i* *Server Backup and Recovery Guide*.

While none of these three books is explicitly devoted to data warehouses in particular, they still do an excellent job presenting the technical details related to backup and restore, and they also map to the business requirements behind each option.

> **NOTE** Contrary to common opinion, a DBA does not have a responsibility to back up a database. The DBA's real responsibility is to be able to *recover* the database. In most cases that will require a program of regular backups and archive logging.

All in all, the *how* of backup and recovery is already very well covered, and this chapter will not delve far into the basic details of backup and recovery. We skim briefly over the basics of backup and restore and then concentrate on the main issues: *what*, *when*, *how often*, and *why* to back up.

First, let's understand the basics of backup and restore in the Oracle environment.

Backup and Restore Basics, or What to Back Up?

The most minimal backup strategy for Oracle databases involves the use of the Oracle EXP (export) utility. The use and capabilities of EXP are described in the Oracle *Server Utilities Guide*, part of the standard Oracle documentation set. Doing a *full database export* using EXP allows you to perform a complete restore of a database, but you may have to re-create the database from scratch, and you cannot recover to the point in time of the failure. A restore using the Oracle IMP (import) utility will restore only to the points in time while the export was running. It is quite possible that there will be referential integrity problems with the restored data unless either the EXP utility's CONSISTENT=Y option was used or access to the database is limited from users by RESTRICT mode. Last, the EXP and IMP utilities are each *single-threaded* processes writing to and reading from a single file. Because of this, they are both slow and constrained by file size limits. Relying on EXP and IMP as the sole components of a backup strategy is feasible only for smaller, unimportant databases. EXP and IMP should be considered only as a complementary part of backup strategy for a database with any kind of importance.

The next level in backup strategies involves "cold" backups with ARCHIVE LOG mode disabled. Backup (both "hot" and "cold") are explained in more detail in the Oracle7 *Server Administrator's Reference* and the Oracle8 *Server Backup and Recovery Guide*. This means that the database instance is shut down successfully and all the files making up the database are simply copied to backup media while it is down. The files that need to be copied are as follows:

- All data files (see V$DATAFILE), control files (see V$CONTROLFILE), and online redo logfiles (see V$LOGFILE)
- Configuration files (i.e., all "*.ora" files, including those for SQL*Net) and password files (i.e., "orapwd.dat")

What does a "cold" backup in this manner buy you over full exports? First, there is no risk of referential integrity problems; because the database is shut down successfully while the backup is happening, the state of the database is completely consistent. Also, because a "cold" backup is done with operating system utilities, it is likely that many file copies can be done in parallel, making "cold" backups and restores quicker. Last, because each file in the database (just listed) is being copied separately, "cold" backups are not constrained by file size limits resulting from trying to pack the entire database into a single file.

Beyond those substantial advantages, however, "cold" backups still require a complete restoration of the database, and recovery is only to the point in time of the backup, not to the point in time of the failure. Also, if there are any failures at all in the backup media (i.e., bad tape), the entire backup is useless, and you will have to restore from a previous backup. This is true both for full database exports as well as "cold" backups. Last (but not least) a "cold" backup means that the database is unavailable, as does performing an export with the database in RESTRICT mode.

How do we get past these limitations?

Enabling ARCHIVELOG mode means that the Oracle database instance will now save all the information kept in the redo logs. To visualize why this is important, think of the redo logs as one of two databases kept by Oracle. The first database is, of course, the database itself. This database shows the current image of the data and is useful to humans. The second database is a different view of the same data and is the redo logs. The redo logs are also a database, but they do not have the same image of the data, the *current image* of all the data, that the regular database has. Rather, the database of the redo logs is a sequential record of every action (with a few notable exceptions when the actions are run in NOLOGGING mode!) against the database. If you are looking for a blow-by-blow account of what has changed in the database, the redo logs have that information readily available. If you are looking for the current state of all the data in the database at the current time, the database in the data files (and SGA database buffer pool) has that information.

Of course, nobody actually accesses that second database, the redo logs, directly. Rather, the Oracle instance uses that second database to provide recoverability for the data files.

The *online redo logfiles* provide the basic required level of recoverability, which is the ability to recover from *instance failure*. Should a running database instance fail for any reason, the online redo logfiles contain enough of the sequential history of changes to rebuild the database. This is known as *instance recovery*, and it happens automatically and transparently during the next startup after the database instance is shut down with SHUTDOWN ABORT or is terminated due to a system failure.

The online redo logfiles represent a circular buffer. There are a finite number of them, and when the last logfile is filled up the database *circles back* and overwrites the first logfile. When the database is not in ARCHIVELOG mode, this means that the historical data that was overwritten is now lost forever. When ARCHIVELOG mode is enabled, this overwrite will not be allowed to occur until the online redo logfile is *archived* or copied to an offline destination. In ARCHIVELOG mode, the combination of the archived redo logfiles and the online redo logfiles represents a solid, continuous history of all changes made to the database.

This means that if one or more data files are restored to points in time that are not consistent, the history of all changes in the redo logfiles can be used to bring all the data files to the same, consistent point in time. This mechanism is known as *roll-forward*.

Why doesn't everyone use ARCHIVELOG mode? There are some extra responsibilities that come with enabling ARCHIVELOG mode, namely, ensuring the safety of the archived redo logfiles. This is not a trivial task, as a busy Oracle database can generate several gigabytes of archived redo logfiles per day, requiring continuous backup to tape or other backup media. Additionally, tapes containing archived redo logfiles should be kept available for several weeks or months (depending on the frequency of backups), so the demands for proper tape handling and storage procedures can grow quite expensive for smaller IT departments.

However, adding ARCHIVELOG mode to a regimen of "cold" backups resolves most of the drawbacks associated with the other methods of backup. In addition to backing up all the files for a standard "cold" backup, you must now do the following:

- Provide a "staging" area for redo logfile archiving, specified with the initialization parameter ARCHIVE_LOG_DEST or archive logfile destination.

- Make sure that this staging area always has sufficient freespace to archive newly filled redo logfiles.

- Ensure the safety of archived redo logfiles by copying them to backup media as soon as possible.

In return, you get the following advantages:

- Recovery to the point in time of failure or until a specified point in time between the time of backup and the failure.

- The ability to perform a partial restore of an individual tablespace or data file instead of having to restore the entire database.

- Fault tolerance for backup media failures—if one tape from a backup set is bad, you need to fall back to a previous backup set for just the bad tape rather than the entire backup set.

For a production, mission-critical database application, these features address almost all availability concerns, except one: the downtime required to perform a "cold" backup. The remedy? Online or "hot" backups, which are performed while the database instance is "up," running, and fully available for all functions. The ability to perform "hot" backups is possible only when ARCHIVELOG mode is enabled, and it implies a little more administrative complexity for DBAs, as each tablespace must explicitly be placed into and out of BACKUP mode.

All in all, a complete backup/restore strategy for an Oracle database includes the use of ARCHIVELOG mode to enable "hot" (or online) backups if desired, point-in-time recovery, incomplete recovery, and partial restores of specific data files and tablespaces as opposed to full restore of the complete database. Without ARCHIVELOG mode enabled, the only possible way to back up the database is "cold," or while the database instance is shut down or offline. The use of "cold" backups affects uptime right away, as it implies regularly scheduled downtime or unavailability. Not enabling ARCHIVELOG mode also forces any database restore to be a complete restore of the entire database rather than of only those data files that were corrupted. Thus, for a database sized over 1 terabyte, corruption (due to media failure or some other reason) to a single data file in a critical place—underneath the SYSTEM tablespace or underneath the primary *fact table* in the data warehouse—can be recovered by restoring the one lost file and then replaying the changes to that file from the archived and online log files.

A complete backup strategy for an Oracle database may also include the use of Oracle EXP (export utility) to save "snapshots" of specific tables or schemas for selective restore of those tables or schemas, if desired. The advantages of having exports to supplement backups include the following:

- Ability to restore individual tables or schemas within tablespaces; backups and restores have a minimum granularity of databases, tablespace, or data files.

- Ability to restore indexes, constraints, and triggers related to individual tables or schemas.

- Ability to restore PL/SQL packages and stored procedures related to individual schemas.

While the ability to restore these objects is certainly included with a standard backup scenario, there are many advantages to being able to do it at the level of granularity made possible by the IMP utility. When an object is lost or damaged through a user (or administrator!) error, IMP can allow that single object to be restored to its condition at the time of the export.

When and How Often?

How frequently should backups occur?

The only correct answer is derived from the business's required mean time to repair, or MTTR. The basic formula is quite simple: the more frequent the backups, the quicker the recovery. This is due to the fact that the *roll-forward-then-rollback* phase of Oracle database recovery can be shortened by restoring from a more recent backup. If a month-old backup is used for restore, then the recovery process will have to roll forward through a month's worth of archived redo logfiles. Certainly, this takes longer to accomplish than restoring from a day-old backup and doing a roll-forward through only a day's worth of archive redo logfiles.

In a data warehouse environment, there are some additional considerations that affect this simple formula.

In a data warehouse, there might be a *load phase* during which data is refreshed completely or during which data is appended to existing data (see Figure 8.11). Quite often, this load phase is not continuous but rather happens at certain predefined times. Data changes to the data warehouse occur quite rapidly during a load phase, after which the data warehouse is used primarily in a *read-only* manner, when queries are run, reports are generated, and analysis is performed. It makes sense to schedule backups to occur *after* such a load phase, on completion of the loads, data cleansing, and aggregations. This provides the additional benefit of immediately capturing data loaded or summarized with the UNRECOVERABLE or NOLOGGING options.

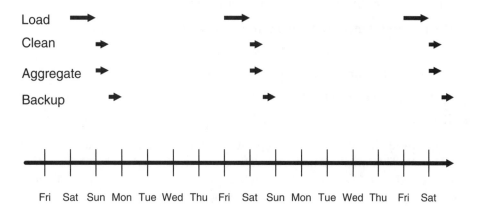

Figure 8.11 Weekly load phases and backups.

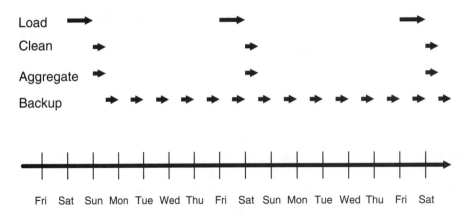

Figure 8.12 Daily backups with weekly load phases.

Because the numbers of changes and updates to the database are minimal following the backup, a restore followed by a media recovery roll-forward can proceed quite quickly for the simple reason that the number of archived redo logfiles is likely to be relatively small. If the backup were taken prior to the load phase, you might see that a roll-forward from that point would have to use over a hundred archived redo logfiles. On the other hand, imagine scheduling backups according to the timetable shown in Figure 8.12.

Although the simple formula of increasing frequency to reduce roll-forward still holds true, the cost-benefit ratio is not as clear. Having to roll forward through 2 archived redo logfiles as opposed to 10 is not as dramatic a difference as rolling forward through 10 archived redo logfiles instead of 100.

Backup Utilities

In general, there are five methods for performing backups:

- Operating system (UNIX *dump, tar, cpio,* and *dd, NT COPY*)
- Third-party packages (i.e., BMC Software's SQL-BackTrack)
- Enterprise Backup Utility (Oracle 7.3 only)
- Recovery Manager (Oracle8 and up only)
- Export

Backups from the *operating system* are by far the most prevalent backup method in use. This involves using operating system utilities such as *cp, dd, tar,* or *cpio* on UNIX or *COPY* or *EXCHANGE* on VMS. For Windows NT, Oracle supplies *ocopy73.exe,* or *ocopy.exe,* depending upon release.

The basic method for such backups was to copy the data files, logfiles, and control files to tape using one or more of these operating system utilities. If database was in ARCHIVELOG mode, then *hot* backups would be possible if the file copy occurred while the tablespace involved was in BACKUP mode, using ALTER TABLESPACE . . . BEGIN/END BACKUP.

The third-party packages such as Datatools' SQL*BackTrack and Oracle7's own short-lived Enterprise Backup Utility (OEBU) essentially provide a more user-friendly layer to operating system backups. Additionally, they document backups and provide assistance during restores by recording backup details in a *recovery catalog*. EBU interfaces with underlying tape management software such as Hewlett-Packard's OmniBack.

All three methods described so far perform only *image backups*. Image backups are exact copies of the original physical data files, logfiles, and control files. Oracle8 Recovery Manager (RMAN) is capable of creating both image backups as well as incremental backups that copy only the blocks within the file that have been changed since the last backup. Although third-party utilities such as Datatools' SQL*BackTrack are also capable of performing incremental backups, Oracle Worldwide Support may not support a database that has been restored by a third-party product that has modified the contents or structure of the data files. RMAN is the only supported incremental backup/restore utility.

Recovery Manager can store the information from multiple data files (or archive logs, but not both) in a *backup set*. Backup sets are stored in a proprietary format that can't be processed directly. Backup sets are strictly for use by RMAN when database recovery is needed.

RMAN will perform either *cold* (offline) or *hot* (online) backups. It uses Oracle server processes known as backup I/O slaves instead of operating system utilities to perform the backups. If the backups will be written to tape, then RMAN will require that an approved *media manager*, such as Legato Systems' NetWorker product or IBM's ADSTAR Distributed Storage Management (ADSM), be linked to Oracle.

RMAN has three major features shared by no other backup and recovery option. If you are serious about high availability, these features make the use of RMAN completely unassailable:

- Incremental backups. You can reduce the volume of data backed up by 50 percent or more. For very large databases and backup media costing hundreds of dollars per backup set, this ain't chopped liver!

- Corrupt block detection. The primary method to correct data corruption is to restore from an uncorrupted backup and recover. RMAN can prevent corrupted blocks from being backed up, and can provide early detection of corruption problems.

- Hot backups. These backups do not require ALTER TABLESPACE BEGIN/END BACKUP, which means that additional redo information is not written to the redo log files. RMAN eliminates the most serious impact of hot online backups.

RMAN may still be a pain in the neck to install and integrate with a media-management package, but its ease of use and especially these three important features make it a must-have.

IS COMPLETE RECOVERY EVEN NECESSARY?

Even if the database is not in ARCHIVELOG mode, thus eliminating the possibility of recovering the database to the point in time of the failure, the use of incremental backups may facilitate more frequent backups, allowing complete restoration of the database to a point in time close to the failure. In a data warehouse environment, this might even be *good enough* under some circumstances. Data warehouses, because they are generally composed of data originating from other systems, may not jeopardize the organization's ability to run the business if they are not fully restored after a failure. This decision can only be made based on the documented business requirements for the warehouse. Don't make this call unless all users are aware and in agreement.

Incremental backups are extremely useful in data warehouse environments. This is due to the nature of load phases in data warehouses and the fact that the majority of data in the warehouse remains static between load phases. Thus, with incremental backups, it will be possible to take a full (incremental level 0) backup immediately after the completion of a load phase and then take frequent higher-level incremental backups after that, to record only the changes since the level 0 backup. In a recovery situation, it is likely that any corrupted data files will be able to be restored to a point in time very close to the failure. As a result, the *roll-forward* recovery from the redo logfiles would complete very quickly, as relatively few transactions would need to be replayed.

Export (using the Oracle utility, EXP) provides a logical backup of the data. EXP has very little value in the backup strategy for the large objects typically found in a data warehouse. This utility was discussed in Chapter 6, "Populating the Oracle Data Warehouse," and is fully documented in the Oracle7 and Oracle8 *Server Utilities* manuals.

Why? And Why Not? Rebuild versus Restore

Many people point out that a data warehouse is composed of derived data and therefore does not need backup and restore to recover from failure. For databases sized in terabytes and mainly composed of data derived from other sources, performing regular backups to offset the seemingly remote possibility of media failure might seem unnecessary.

If you ask people how quickly a mission-critical order entry system should recover after a failure, the reply is likely to be instantaneous as well as non-negotiable: "Recovery must be as brief as possible and it must be to the point in time of the failure." At least that would be the response from the technical people; the business unit being supported by the order entry system is likely to respond with: "What?! The system is down? Nobody told me the system is down! Find out when it's going to be back up! AND DON'T LOSE ANY ORDERS!"

When the same question is asked regarding a DSS, data mart, or data warehouse system, the response is much less predictable. All too often, a decision support system is viewed as not being mission-critical, as in the statement, "Well, if the data warehouse goes down, the company doesn't grind to a halt." Or, "If my boss doesn't get those reports today, tomorrow will do." This perception, plus the scale of most data warehouses, leads project managers, system administrators, and DBAs to try to implement something less than a complete backup strategy.

The arguments against a complete backup strategy can be compelling:

- Availability requirements for decision support systems are not as stringent as those for operational systems.

- Data can be reloaded and reaggregated as quickly as it can be restored.

- We invested in redundancy and fault-tolerance features (such as "mirroring" or RAID 5) to drastically reduce the probability of media failure.

- ARCHIVELOG mode is "overkill" for decision support systems because they're read-only.

- Capacity and throughput of backup media are insufficient for regular backups.

In summary, this debate, which is generally discussed (at one point or another) during every large-scale data warehouse implementation, can be described as *rebuild versus restore*.

The arguments in favor of *rebuild* were just itemized. While they have some clear elements of truth, it is important to discuss the pros and cons of each thoroughly.

Availability Requirements for Decision Support Systems

Each of the following paragraphs is formatted as an individual reflection on this subject, intended to help stimulate points of view counter to the opinion that data warehouses are not mission critical.

- Be sure to stay focused on the purpose of the decision support systems. If they are perceived as not being mission critical, then imagine what life would be like without them. Strategic reporting and analysis are mission critical. Being able to accept orders does not guarantee business success if your products and services are not priced correctly.

■ The stated mean time to repair (MTTR) is sometimes based on a presumed favorable mean time between failures (MTBF); should the MTBF worsen for any reason, the MTTR is likely to tighten significantly. For example, if the end-user community had agreed to an MTTR of 12 hours, it may not be bothered if the MTBF is 6 months. However, if the MTBF becomes 3 days, an MTTR of 12 hours will undergo reconsideration; count on it!

■ Be sure to define precisely what constitutes downtime. Certain parties may consider downtime to mean that the machine is not powered on. Other parties may define downtime as the inability to log on to the machine due to operating system problems, database problems, or network problems. Yet other parties may define downtime as absolutely any condition that prevents them from getting their work done in a timely manner, such as any of the conditions listed earlier, and including performance degradation beyond 50 percent. In this last case, the line between performance and availability blurs, and who can argue with that?

■ Generally, the end users of a data warehouse are senior management or their designees. Who else uses or needs strategic reporting? While it is true that the promptness of strategic reports will not cause a business to shut down, frequent unavailability of a data warehouse will erode confidence in the data, cause reliance on alternative methods of obtaining the data, and essentially negate the purpose of the whole warehouse effort.

■ Analyzing strategic data is difficult enough without performance problems making it more difficult. Unavailability is the ultimate performance problem; a downed system is racking up zero MIPS, and strategic analysis is not happening.

Assertion: Reloading Is as Fast as Restoring

Because the data loaded into a data warehouse generally originates on one or more other "sources of record," there is an accurate perception that the database in a data warehouse can sometimes be rebuilt and reloaded as quickly as it can be restored from a backup. *Rebuild then reload* may take the same amount of time or even more than *restore from backup*, but at least you did not expend time, resources, and effort performing the backups.

It is tough to argue against this approach, but it is important to remember the following points if you choose to go this route:

■ Source data may not be available for reload after initial load. Make certain that the data used to load the data warehouse is not overwritten after use. Are those initial load files *really* still available?

- Rebuilding as a recovery strategy implies significant automation and testing of the rebuild procedures. This is not a trivial amount of development, and it is likely to require a lot of custom development as few (if any!) system management packages aid in automating the process of rebuilding tablespaces, tables, indexes, constraints, and triggers. This is not an activity to perform extemporaneously during a crisis!

- Only data that is completely refreshed is likely to be reloaded readily. Data that is accumulated over time may be difficult to restore in this manner, especially if it wasn't saved.

- Data that requires some form of post-processing (i.e., cleansing and/or aggregation) may be post-processed differently if the reference data or supporting data has been changed over time. For example, if data is aggregated using demographic or psychographic reference data that is refreshed on a monthly basis, chances are good that this reference data has changed over time. Aggregating 24 months of data against the current month's demographic data will not produce the same data that had been aggregated over the past 24 months, each against its own current demographic data. In brief, be ready to accommodate data dependencies for time-series data. This is a data warehouse design issue, not something that the DBA should be dealing with at three o'clock in the morning during a recovery. The prospect of storing reference data over time to facilitate reloads is not something that would necessarily occur to a data warehouse designer who hasn't been faced with a recovery situation.

Assertion: Investment in Fault Tolerance Eliminates the Need for Backups

Some people actually believe that an investment in fault-tolerant components (such as mirrored disk drives) actually eliminates the need for database recovery. In reality, corruption due to human mishap or some kind of software failure can occur just as easily as media failure. Fault-tolerant system components mitigate only one kind of risk—failure by one of the components that has been duplicated. And who is to say that simple disk mirroring cannot be defeated by bad luck? Who is going to guarantee that a raw partition won't be accidentally reallocated and destroyed? Who is to say that both a volume as well as its mirror cannot fail at the same time? Yes, it's unlikely, but . . .

Assertion: ARCHIVELOG Is Overkill

This sentiment is closely related to "reloading is as fast as restoring;" if we don't want to back up derived data, we also do not want to save archived redo logfiles that are full of this same data as it's being loaded into the data warehouse.

Once again, this is absolutely true. For reasons like this, Oracle has, since release 7.1, 7.2, and 7.3, successively implemented several UNRECOVERABLE

Table 8.1 History of UNRECOVERABLE/NOLOGGING Features

FEATURE	INTRODUCED IN VERSION
SQL*Loader direct path UNRECOVERABLE	7.1
Parallel CREATE TABLE ... UNRECOVERABLE ... AS SELECT	7.2
Parallel CREATE INDEX ... UNRECOVERABLE	7.2
Parallel ALTER INDEX ... REBUILD ... UNRECOVERABLE	7.3
Parallel INSERT /*+ APPEND NOLOGGING */ SELECT ...	8.0
Parallel ALTER TABLE ... MOVE PARTITION ... NOLOGGING	8.0
Parallel ALTER TABLE ... SPLIT PARTITION ... NOLOGGING	8.0
Parallel ALTER INDEX ... REBUILD PARTITION ... NOLOGGING	8.0
Parallel ALTER TABLE ... MOVE ... NOLOGGING	8.1
Parallel ALTER TABLE ... MERGE PARTITION ... NOLOGGING	8.1

(known as NOLOGGING in Oracle8) operations that minimize the generation of redo almost to the point of elimination (see Table 8.1). Loading using direct path SQL*Loader, CREATE TABLE . . . AS SELECT, and CREATE INDEX are all operations that can be run in UNRECOVERABLE mode, which generates virtually no redo and no rollback information. As a result, you can perform most of the data loads as well as much of the post-processing without generating any redo logging to be archived and backed up.

If this is the case, then what is the benefit of ARCHIVELOG mode?

It is this. There must be hundreds of other actions that take place in the data warehouse that have nothing to do with loading data. End users create "scratch" tables for holding their intermediate results from hours of work. Administrators create objects for testing. Our audit trail records user resource consumption, possibly for internal billing. Wouldn't it be inconvenient for them to be wiped out by re-creating the database? Wouldn't it just be easier to back them up and restore them if the need arises?

The problem with the rebuild-then-reload strategy is that it demands that every step of the recovery process be documented, understood, and performed during a recovery. Frankly, it may not be possible to do this. While it may be cost-effective to do this in a few areas, it can't possibly be cost-effective to do it for everything. Why not let the database remember all these actions and perform them during a restore? Life is too short to custom develop a duplication of one of Oracle's major features.

Assertion: It Is Too Big to Back Up!

It is not unusual to hear people say "That database is just too big to back up and restore." No matter how big a database gets, you really have to be able to move the whole thing to backup media and restore it in a reasonable amount of time. If you can't do that with your existing backup resources, invest in more hardware. If it is too big to be backed up, then the reload tasks are going to be even more overwhelming. Hot backups, incremental backups, and READ ONLY tablespaces can make the backup load more manageable.

If it seems too expensive to invest in more tape drives and in better backup media, then quite frankly you are out of your depth. You have no business creating a database that size. Hate to be so blunt, but there it is.

Summary of the Rebuild versus Restore Debate

Both strategies have their place. Because of all the flexibility and availability benefits it provides, the basic strategy should be a complete backup strategy as described previously. If circumstances warrant it, use READ ONLY tablespaces to reduce the amount of data that must be backed up. Use ARCHIVELOG mode, but also use UNRECOVERABLE options to reduce the volume of redo logging if the data can be backed up immediately afterward.

In circumstances where data is refreshed completely and not post-processed, consider using the rebuild-then-reload approach.

The two approaches are not mutually exclusive. But the rebuild approach should only selectively complement a backup strategy that protects key database structures using ARCHIVELOG mode.

Enabling and Optimizing Auditing

Auditing has a lot of benefits for a data warehouse environment. It can be used for its most obvious purpose: enhancing security by tracking what, when, and where people query or manipulate specific tables. But it also has usefulness in providing some other important functionality in a decision support environment:

- Information for usage chargeback
- Information for determining proper RESOURCE PROFILES for various types of users
- Failed connect or abnormal disconnect analysis
- Usage analysis of all or certain tables

A data warehouse environment is actually well suited for an option like Oracle database auditing even though it sometimes carries a relatively high cost in terms of overhead. For each operation being audited, Oracle can log an audit record to a database table (i.e., SYS.AUD$) or to an operating system file. If only session connections and disconnections are being audited, this is usually a very light price to pay because connections and disconnections are relatively infrequent. However, if SELECT statements against all objects are being audited, then it is possible that the impact of auditing might be noticeable, as each SELECT statement would generate an INSERT into the audit trail.

Enabling AUDIT SESSION, which audits session connections and disconnections, is a relatively low-cost but high-value form of auditing in a data warehouse environment. Among other things, AUDIT SESSION records the following:

- Operating system user name
- Oracle user name
- The machine or host from which the user had logged in
- The terminal from which the user had logged in
- The time of connection
- The time and manner of disconnection
- The number of logical reads, physical reads, and logical writes accumulated during the session

The duration of the connection or the I/O statistics could be useful in calculating accurate chargeback values. They could also be used for setting up valid and useful RESOURCE PROFILES for limiting resource consumption. The manner in which sessions were disconnected could be used to locate users who are having difficulties in a client/server environment, who think that CTRL-ALT-DEL is a valid way to log out of the data warehouse, for example.

Refer to the Oracle *Server Concepts* manual and the Oracle *Server SQL Language Reference* for more information on the breadth and depth of auditing.

If you choose to keep the audit trail in the database (a good choice, as it allows easy query of the audit information), there is one important thing to do. The audit trail in the database is a table named AUD$ owned by the Oracle account named SYS. By default, the table SYS.AUD$ is created in the SYSTEM tablespace. Depending on the amount of auditing activity, it is probably advisable to move this table out of the SYSTEM tablespace in case it grows large enough to "crowd" the data dictionary tables, indexes, and clusters in that tablespace. It is a common task, and simple enough, as Figure 8.13 illustrates.

```
CONNECT SYS/sys_password
CREATE TABLESPACE AUDIT_DATA DATAFILE 'file-specification';
CREATE TABLE new_aud$
     TABLESPACE AUD
     STORAGE (appropriate storage parameters)'
```

```
    AS SELECT *
        FROM aud$;
RENAME aud$ TO old_aud$;
RENAME new_aud$ TO aud$;
<test by connecting to database and then verify the entry in the new
table>
DROP TABLE old_aud$;
```

Sizing of the new audit trail table will be governed by how frequently you will report, summarize, and then delete from the table. If you are using audit extensively, such as monitoring each select against many tables, you should specify multiple freelists when constructing the NEW_AUD$ table.

As a starting point, plan to summarize usage each week or month into a series of permanent administrative tables. Depending on what you've elected to audit you may want to summarize activity by user, by day, by warehouse table, by time of day, and so on. After the summary is saved the detailed audit data may be deleted. You will want to support both the usage analysis and chargeback functions described earlier in this chapter. You will also want to use the historical record to monitor processing trends over time.

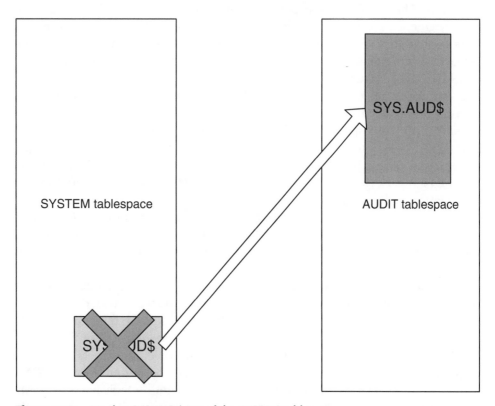

Figure 8.13   Moving SYS.AUD$ out of the SYSTEM tablespace.

Two important reminders:

1. Be very careful while connected to the Oracle SYS account. This is the equivalent of UNIX root, and accidents can cause irreparable harm to the database.

2. Also, be sure to monitor the growth of the AUD$ table and schedule regular purges. If you enable auditing and then forget about it, eventually AUD$ will consume all the available space (or number of extents) and all (audited) database activity will come to a halt.

Configuration Rules of Thumb

The following sections are not intended as "hard-and-fast" rules, but merely as suggestions based on experience. Like all repeatable exercises, building a data warehouse in Oracle tends to fall into common patterns. We think you will find these suggestions useful.

Locally Managed Tablespaces

Except for the SYSTEM tablespace and any tablespaces that will contain rollback segments, use the new Oracle8*i* feature of *locally-managed tablespaces*. In terms of CREATE TABLESPACE syntax, this feature is characterized by the replacement of the familiar DEFAULT STORAGE clause with the new EXTENT MANAGEMENT LOCAL clause.

Locally-managed tablespaces store all extent information for tables, indexes, and clusters in *bitmap header* segments in the beginning (blocks 2-8) of each datafile in the tablespace. The old method of managing extent information in centralized tables in the SYSTEM tablespace, renamed *dictionary-managed tablespaces*, uses tables named SYS.UET$ (a.k.a. view DBA_EXTENTS) and SYS.FET$ (a.k.a. view DBA_FREE_SPACE). Oracle has always stored extent information in the segment header blocks of each segment, but for the purposes of permitting fast space management, the information in each segment header is *replicated* to a more central location. Up until Oracle8*i*, that central location was the SYSTEM tablespace. With Oracle8*i*, this replicated extent information can now be less centralized.

Since each extent is now represented by a single bit, it is no longer possible to have differing extent sizes within a datafile. Instead, you can use the AUTOALLOCATE clause to allow the RDBMS to choose an extent size based on the size of the datafile, or you can specify the size yourself using the UNIFORM SIZE clause. This is the reason that the INITIAL, NEXT, and PCTINCREASE clauses in the DEFAULT STORAGE clause are not permitted with EXTENT MANAGEMENT LOCAL. Tables, indexes, and clusters which have INITIAL, NEXT, and PCTINCREASE clauses will not have any problems, since Oracle will simply allocate space using the datafile's single extent size to approximate the values for INITIAL and NEXT.

This new mechanism has several advantages over the old mechanism:

- Flipping bits in a bitmap mechanism is much more efficient that inserting and deleting rows from two clustered tables.

- Scanning for free space is much more efficient in a small (eight database blocks) bitmap segment than scanning for rows in a clustered table. The MAXEXTENTS UNLIMITED feature, introduced in v7.3, can now be used without the problems experienced in dictionary-managed tablespaces.

- Storing extent information in the header of the relevant datafile decentralizes storage management processing, relieving a potential I/O bottleneck in the SYSTEM tablespace

- Since locally-managed tablespaces do not utilize the "ST" enqueue to serialize space management operations, another serious performance bottleneck is minimized. This can be especially important when using Parallel Server.

- Uniform extent sizes means that tablespace fragmentation issues are *completely eliminated*. Throw away your "tablespace reorganization" software!

- The supplied package DBMS_SPACE_ADMIN provides diagnostic and repair features not available with the old *dictionary-managed* tablespace scheme. Repairing corruption to the SYS.UET$ and SYS.FET$ requires working closely with Oracle Support.

SYSTEM Tablespace

Data warehouse systems generally do not involve the creation of a great number of objects in the database. The data dictionary (i.e., objects belonging to SYS) of a basic installation of Oracle7.3 typically consumes about 20 to 30 MB initially; for Oracle8, this expands to 40 to 50 MB. The number of tables, columns, indexes, views, stored procedures, and packages created in the database will affect space consumption in the SYSTEM tablespace.

Large-scale packaged applications (such as Oracle Financial and Manufacturing applications) tend to create thousands of tables, indexes, synonyms, and stored procedures and packages. It is not uncommon for such databases to require as much as 1 gigabyte for the data dictionary alone. Data warehouses, by contrast, typically feature more simplistic, consolidated, denormalized data models. As a result, the number of tables, indexes, views, and stored procedures and packages tends to be relatively small.

A good starting point for a data warehouse is 100 MB for the SYSTEM tablespace. Even if the dictionary ends up needing only 60 MB, the "wasted" space is a very small percentage of the total warehouse usage. It is better to spend time on more profitable pursuits than trying to accurately estimate the SYSTEM tablespace needs in advance.

TEMP Tablespace

Use the new CREATE TEMPORARY TABLESPACE command for all tablespaces intended as areas for large sorts or for using the new *global temporary tables*. This new feature is an improvement on the CREATE TABLESPACE . . . TEMPORARY command introduced back in version 7.3. Like the previous TEMPORARY command, it does not allow any objects other than TEMPORARY segments to be created. TEMPORARY segments are created implicitly as the result of a sorting operation or when a global temporary table is populated with data.

TEMPORARY tablespaces in Oracle8*i* utilize locally-managed datafiles, permitting all of the benefits described above while we were discussing locally-managed tablespaces. Additionally, TEMPORARY tablespaces now also use TEMPFILEs instead of DATAFILEs, which have several recoverability benefits. First of all, TEMPFILEs are not involved in any recovery operations. They are ignored by the Recovery Manager and can be ignored by your own custom-written backup/recovery scripts, if you wish. If a TEMPFILE needs recovery, the database can start without error; corrupted TEMPFILEs do not prevent a database from being opened. They would still have to be repaired, but at least you can open the database.

Using the new CREATE TEMPORARY TABLESPACE command will make life much simpler, as space management and recovery are simplified. Please note, however, that you must use the UNIFORM SIZE clause with the required EXTENT MANAGEMENT LOCAL clause; you cannot use the alternative AUTOALLOCATE clause. Additionally, the UNIFORM SIZE clause must specify a size greater than 10M; anything smaller will be ignored in v8.1.5 and will generate an error message in v8.1.6.

Be aware that the use of Parallel Query or Parallel DML can greatly exaggerate the number of users from a sort space standpoint. If the single nonparallel query consumes 100 MB, then it is conceivable that the same query using a parallel degree of 8 could possibly consume 800 MB, although presumably for a shorter period of time. Multiply that value by 50 simultaneously executing queries, and you are now talking about needing 40 gigabytes for the TEMP tablespace. If you are using the Parallel Execution feature extensively, you will probably want to use a smaller value for SORT_AREA_SIZE than if all queries are being run serially.

Of course, these sizes are very dependent on the sizes of the tables, the "raw" data to be sorted. It's unlikely that any valid query would require 100 MB of sort space if the largest table in the database is only 40 MB. Because many data warehouses contain tables sized at hundreds of gigabytes, it is conceivable that some queries may require that much space for sorting. As a rule of thumb, use the following equation to set initial expectations for sizing the TEMP tablespace:

```
min((total-data-in-db * 0.5), (largest-table-size * 2))
```

If you have about 100 gigabytes of "raw" data in tables in your data warehouse and the largest table is 15 gigabytes, then sizing the TEMP tablespace at around 30 gigabytes is reasonable. If the largest table is 30 gigabytes, then sizing TEMP at 50 gigabytes would be reasonable. If the largest table is 55 gigabytes, then sizing TEMP to 50 gigabytes might still be reasonable because the best approach at this point would be to either partition this table or prevent most sorting operations during a full table scan. In other words, there is a limit to the amount of sorting you want to support. Beyond that, you should tune or limit the application.

Rollback Segments and the RBS Tablespace

Oracle gives some good rules of thumb for rollback segments. Use the following formula

```
4 <= #-of-rollback-segments <= 50
```

where the number of rollback segments is determined by dividing the number of concurrently active DML transactions by 4. It would be surprising if a data warehouse application ever needed more than 10 rollback segments using this formula. Don't forget to ignore UNRECOVERABLE or "direct path" operations as they do not generate rollback entries.

Because rollback entries for transactions occupy entire extents in the rollback segments, it is a good idea to preallocate plenty of extents for each rollback segment. For relatively "quiet" systems such as data warehouses, using MINEXTENTS 20 should be sufficient unless very large batch processes are going to be executed without the UNRECOVERABLE or NOLOGGING feature. For relatively busy OLTP-type systems, MINEXTENTS 40 should work.

The OPTIMAL parameter should be set to match MINEXTENTS. If MINEXTENTS implies 20 MB of space, then OPTIMAL should be set to 20 MB.

All that is left is to determine the extent sizes. Again, using basic rules of thumb, a starting value of 1 MB seems reasonable for data warehouse systems. For most OLTP-type systems, a starting value of 128 KB or 256 KB is reasonable.

When sizing the RBS tablespace, use the values determined earlier in the following formula:

```
((#-of-rollback-segments + 8) * MINEXTENTS * extent-size)
```

This would allow one of the rollback segments to grow to eight times its original size to handle long-running transactions. When possible, treat all the rollback segments the same. Define an appropriate value of OPTIMAL so that they can grow and shrink as needed. Then give them room to grow. If individual rollback segments have to grow and shrink frequently and dramatically then consider creating one or more very large rollback segments. This will avoid the additional allocation and deallocation overhead and also prevent the occasional "unable to extend rollback segment" error if one needs to grow very large but another has not yet shrunk.

> ### NAMED ROLLBACK SEGMENTS ARE NOT *DEDICATED* TO THE TRANSACTION
>
> While it is possible to dedicate a transaction to a particular named rollback segment using SET TRANSACTION, there is no way to keep other transactions from using that special rollback segment. Oracle attempts to balance the number of transactions active in every rollback segment (other than the SYSTEM rollback segment) regardless of their relative sizes. Thus, having one or more big rollback segments for long-running transactions does not guarantee that the rollback segment in question won't already be in use when the long-running transaction is assigned to it. Multiple transactions can share a rollback segment, so it is possible that even the special large rollback segment may need to grow.

DB_BLOCK_SIZE

For data warehouses, use 8 KB database blocks as an absolute minimum; 16 KB is common for data warehouses and is now accepted as a standard recommendation. Even larger block sizes are supported by only a few operating systems at this time (i.e., Compaq UNIX).

If you believe block contention (see "Monitoring Latch Contention and Locking," later in this chapter) is occurring, then increase INITRANS and FREELISTS to reduce contention. INITRANS controls how many simultaneous transactions can be active in a fully loaded data or index block. Multiple freelists avoid contention when doing simultaneous INSERTs to a table. The FREELISTS parameter can be set only at the time of table creation. If you are using Parallel Server and you expect to insert to the table through multiple instances, also set FREELIST GROUPS to at least the number of instances.

As a last resort, you can selectively simulate a smaller DB_BLOCK_SIZE for certain tables or indexes by setting PCTFREE high on certain heavily contended segments and/or partitions. This will essentially lower the amount of data per database block, simulating a smaller DB_BLOCK_SIZE. For example, to simulate PCTFREE 10 on 4 KB database blocks when DB_BLOCK_SIZE is 8 KB, set PCTFREE to 55. To simulate PCTFREE 0 on 2 KB database blocks when

DB_BLOCK _SIZE is 16 KB, set PCTFREE to 80. It should be noted that this trick is very infrequently needed in a data warehouse because it is extremely rare to ever have multiple transactions simultaneously modifying a table.

NEW ALTER FREELISTS COMMAND

As of the writing of this book, Oracle8*i* Release 2 (a.k.a. version 8.1.6) was just being released. The *Oracle8*i *Server Administration* reference manual mentions the existence of a new ALTER FREELISTS command, which modifies the number of freelists in an existing table or index without requiring a DROP then re-CREATE (in the case of indexes, a REBUILD). The *Oracle8*i *SQL Language* reference manual for the same version, however, makes no mention of this command. As it turns out, the command does not exist in the initial release of the version 8.1.6 software after all, which is a genuine shame. However, the new ALTER TABLE . . . MOVE command is almost as good, allowing the segment underlying a table to be rebuilt without necessitating a DROP then re-CREATE, with all of the attendant problems with dependencies.

Setting "init.ora" Initialization Parameters

Use the values supplied with the sample "initdw.ora" file provided as part of the Oracle install to start. Don't modify the values provided in this default file unless you have a good, empirically proven reason to do so. See the section on monitoring rules of thumb later in this chapter for some empirically proven reasons.

When you change a parameter, comment out the old value and leave comments with your initials and the date next to the new values. A brief explanation of the reason for the change is helpful, too. This allows you a backout route should the change prove harmful. Also, when attempting to tune performance it is helpful to change only one parameter at a time so that its effects can be measured. Of course, there are some parameters that work together and need to be changed together, but don't attempt to change a dozen parameters and then determine why an unexpected effect materialized.

Redo Logfiles

Use at least three redo log groups per instance, with the files of each group of at least 100 MB for a start. Each redo group should be multiplexed, mirrored, or both. If you need to resize the logs later, you can add new log file groups with files of the proper size using ALTER DATABASE ADD LOGFILE. Then switch logging to one of the newly added groups using ALTER SYSTEM SWITCH LOG-FILE. Finally, you can drop the old, smaller logs with ALTER DATABASE DROP LOGFILE.

Monitoring Rules of Thumb

In this section we cover guidelines for monitoring the following:

- The "worst" SQL statements
- The top consumers in the operating system
- Configurable resources
- AUDIT session statistics
- Rollback segment contention
- Latch contention and locking
- The number of extents
- Freespace
- Tablespace fragmentation
- Invalid compiled objects

NOTE Many of these situations can be monitored using facilities of Oracle Enterprise Manager and its optional packs. In this book we have chosen to demonstrate concepts and techniques using SQL queries. Understanding the direct access with SQL queries will make interpretation of Enterprise Manager outputs easier. Learning only the screens and graphs of Enterprise Manager (or other third-party administration tool) does not fully equip the DBA for understanding the underlying database operations.

Monitoring the "Worst" SQL Statements

Use the following query (borrowed from Oracle Consulting's System Performance Group APS toolkit) to determine the "worst" SQL statements being executed on your system:

```
SELECT hash_value "SQL Stmt ID",
       disk_reads "Physical Reads",
       buffer_gets "Logical Reads",
       sorts "Sorts"
       users_executing "Runs",
```

```
          loads "Cache Loads",
          ((((disk_reads*100)+buffer_gets)/1000)/users_executing "Load"
   FROM v$sqlarea
 WHERE disk_reads > 100000
    OR buffer_gets > 1000000
 ORDER BY (((disk_reads*100)+buffer_gets)/1000)/users_executing DESC;
```

This will identify the worst SQL statements, in descending order of horror. The query will consider only those SQL statements that exceed a threshold. In this example, that threshold is either 1 million logical reads against the buffer cache or 100,000 physical reads on disk.

The sorting emphasizes the physical reads, multiplying by a weighting factor of 100. To this number is added the number of logical reads, after which the total is divided by 1,000 to make it a more manageable number. Finally, to emphasize those statements that cost the most every time they are run, this total figure is divided by the number of executions. The result is a number that means little by itself but is useful for ranking the cost of various SQL statements.

Data in V$SQLAREA reflects the contents of the shared SQL area, cumulatively since database startup. Naturally, the shared pool is fixed in size, so seldom-used SQL statements do get cycled out, but they are of no concern to us. It is the statements that persist in the shared pool for long periods of time that are of interest.

Once the bad statements are identified, a DBA should strive to understand how it is being used. First, it is useful to know who is using it. The following query may help identify who is executing the statement, if it is currently in use:

```
SELECT username,
       osuser,
       machine,
       terminal,
       process,
       program,
       sid,
       serial#
  FROM v$session
 WHERE sql_hash_value = <SQL-stmt-ID-from-previous-query>;
```

The column USERNAME is the Oracle account name, the column OSUSER should show the operating system account name of the client executing the statement. The column MACHINE should show the IP host name of the machine from which the client is executing the statement. In the event these first three columns do not positively identify the end user executing the SQL statement, the remaining column values might be helpful.

Once the end user executing the SQL statement is identified, then more can be learned about the reasons why the SQL statement is running and why it is running as it is.

The tuning of SQL statements is discussed in greater detail in Chapter 9, "Data Warehouse Performance Tuning," but for now simply identifying these resource hogs will have the greatest impact on system performance. You can buy the biggest computer in the world, you can tune all of its subsystems until they scream, but if the application is simply doing too much work, it will still appear sluggish.

There are many ways to tune a SQL statement, and optimizing its execution plan is only one. Sometimes, the SQL statement is simply unnecessary and should not be executing at all. This would be the case if a query were being executed against too low a level of detail, when the same information could be obtained faster from a higher level of summarization or aggregation. Perhaps the higher level of aggregation does not yet exist, but it should.

Perhaps the SQL statement is joining too many tables, indicating a problem with the data model or with the end user's understanding of the data model. Perhaps it would be useful to create a denormalized version of a certain set of tables by *prejoining* these tables as a final step in the data warehouse's load phase.

It should be the job of the DBA to identify these questions and help drive them through to resolution. It does not make sense to tune the database and tune an operating system to handle more load than is necessary. Saying this in a slightly different way, it doesn't make sense to tune unnecessary work—eliminate it! Identification is the first step.

Identifying the worst three or five SQL statements and fixing them will have absolutely the most impact on overall system performance. Doing this iteratively, every week or several times per month, will virtually ensure that any Oracle system performs to the utmost of its capabilities. If anybody complains that an Oracle database is sluggish or performing poorly, this is the first place to look for the culprits.

Monitoring the Top Consumers in the Operating System

Most operating systems have a "top 10" utility, which will display information about the top 10 resource (usually CPU) consumers on the system. Such utilities are available for Sun Solaris, HP-UX, and Windows NT.

If you are on a UNIX system and such a utility is not available, you can use the following:

```
$ ps -eaf | sort -n +3 | tail
```

This uses the UNIX *ps* utility (i.e., *process status*) to display information about all processes on the system. This output is piped to the UNIX *sort* utility, which sorts numerically on the fourth column of the *ps* output. Finally, this output is piped to the UNIX *tail* utility, which displays only the last 10 lines of output. Thus, the last line should be the most active CPU consumer on the system.

The operating system process ID or PID (i.e., the second column in the output of the command just shown) is represented in Oracle in the V$PROCESS dynamic performance view if the name of the process is *oracle<ORACLE_SID>*. For example, if the name of the process starts with the string "oraclePROD," where the ORACLE_SID is "PROD," then this is an Oracle server process. In the V$PROCESS view, the operating system PID is stored in the column SPID. On Windows NT, it is stored in hexadecimal format, which is a shame because the NT Task Manager utility displays the PID as decimal. On UNIX, the representation of the PID both in V$PROCESS and in UNIX is decimal.

Once an Oracle server process is identified as a resource "hog" in this fashion, it would be worthwhile to determine what the process is doing. This can be done by joining from V$PROCESS to the V$SESSION, V$SQLAREA, V$SES-STAT, and V$SESSION_WAIT views as follows:

```
SELECT username, osuser, machine, process, terminal, program,
       sql_hash_value, sql_address, sid, serial#
  FROM v$session
 WHERE paddr IN
       (SELECT addr
          FROM v$process
         WHERE spid = 'O/S PID');
```

This information may help identify who the user of the Oracle server process is and (perhaps) what they are doing. For more definitive information on what they are doing, use the following:

```
SELECT sql_text, disk_reads, buffer_gets, sorts, loads, users_executing
  FROM v$sqlarea
 WHERE hash_value = <sql_hash_value-from-the-previous-query>
   AND address = <sql_address-from-the-previous-query>;
```

From this query, you will know exactly what SQL statement the user is executing at the moment. Additionally, you will see cumulative statistics (since database instance startup) on disk reads, logical reads, sorts, SQL cursor cache loads, and the number of times the SQL statement has been used.

But it would be interesting to know exactly what the SQL statement is waiting on. For this information, use the following query:

```
COLUMN p1 FORMAT A15
COLUMN p2 FORMAT A15
COLUMN p3 FORMAT A15
SELECT event,
       p1text || ' ' || p1 p1,
       p2text || ' ' || p2 p2,
```

```
        p3text || ' ' || p3 p3
  FROM v$session_wait
 WHERE sid = <SID-from-the-first-query>;
```

Each event indicates whether the session is waiting on network access, physical I/O, a latch or a lock, or some other kind of contention. See the table in Chapter 9 for a list of the most common events and a brief explanation of what they mean.

Last, it might be useful to know something about the kinds of run-time statistics that the session has been racking up. The following query can help:

```
SELECT n.name, s.value
  FROM v$sesstat s, v$statname n
 WHERE s.statistic# = n.statistic#
   AND s.value > 0
   AND s.sid = <SID-from-the-first-query>;
```

Monitoring Configurable Resources

Starting in Oracle8, the view V$RESOURCE_LIMIT allows database administrators to determine whether the database instance is about to run out of certain resources. Some of these resources include the following:

PROCESSES

SESSIONS

TRANSACTIONS

DML_LOCKS

ENQUEUE_RESOURCES

Each of these resources is represented by an initialization parameter of the same name. The view V$RESOURCE_LIMIT shows current utilization numbers for the resource, as well as the *high-water mark* of utilization or maximum utilization, in addition to the currently allocated value from the initialization file or ALTER SYSTEM commands.

Monitoring the AUDIT Session Statistics

Another way to find users who are using an inordinate amount of system resources is to periodically query the audit records produced by AUDIT SESSION. To find the worst offenders, use the following query:

```
    COLUMN os_username    FORMAT A10
    COLUMN username       FORMAT A10
    COLUMN userhost       FORMAT A10
```

```
COLUMN terminal          FORMAT A10
SELECT os_username, username, userhost, terminal,
       avg(logoff_lread + logoff_lwrite) l_io,
       avg(logoff_pread) p_io
  FROM dba_audit_session
 WHERE logoff_lread > 1000000 or logoff_pread > 100000
 GROUP BY os_username, username, userhost, terminal;
```

If this query identifies any particular person or group of people, it would be wise for the DBA to become familiar with what they are doing to offer assistance in tuning the SQL statements they are running. It may be that these are the power users who are legitimately exercising the warehouse. Or (more likely), they are submitting poorly tuned SQL statements. A third possibility is that they are doing legitimate work against detail tables that you, as the administrator, can make easier by creating additional indexes or summarizations.

Monitoring Rollback Segment Contention

The view V$ROLLSTAT contains run-time statistics on rollback segments since database startup. High values for the column WAITS indicate that transactions are being forced to wait for an available slot in that rollback segment. This is not an issue with end users' queries but with transactions that are updating the warehouse. If this is happening for all the segments, then consider adding more rollback segments or rescheduling some of the workload.

```
SELECT n.name,
       s.writes,
       s.waits
  FROM v$rollstat    s,
       v$rollname    n
 WHERE s.usn = n.usn;
```

What is a *high value*? There is no ready formula, but bear in mind the number of hours that the database instance has been running. Also keep in mind that your system probably has *off hours* as well as *peak hours*, so simply dividing these figures by the number of hours is bound to water down the rate during peak hours. Try to sample the table several times during peak periods of DML activity, and use the difference between the first sampling and the last sampling to calculate the current hourly rate.

If the value for WAITS is high on an hourly or daily basis, then consider adding some more rollback segments to create more *transaction table slots*. Each rollback segment has a fixed number of *slots* in the *transaction table* in its header block. If WAITS are occurring, then more slots are needed, which means more rollback segments. Another good approach is to simply use the Oracle-provided SQL scripts *utlbstat.sql* and *utlestat.sql*, which reside in the directory *$ORACLE_HOME/rdbms /admin*. Commonly called BSTAT/ESTAT, these scripts sample the majority of the V$ performance tables for a particular time period. To use them, connect as SYS and run *utlbstat.sql* at the start of the sample period. Then, at the end of the sample period, connect again as SYS and run *utlestat.sql*. Each script takes a "snapshot" of many of the critical V$ performance views at the time they are run. The *utlestat.sql* script then takes an ending snapshot of the same views and calculates the differences between the beginning and ending snapshot values. It then produces a report and spools it to the current working directory as a file named *report.txt*. The rollback segment statistics are easy to find in *report.txt*.

If the hourly rate of WAITS is into double digits at peak hours, then certainly there is a need to add more rollback segments. If the hourly rate is nonzero but in the single digits, then the choice is less clear. Certainly, if there is room readily available, add more rollback segments. If space is tight, then consider the risk incurred by cramming more rollback segments into the RBS tablespace and possibly not leaving enough space for each of the rollback segments to extend, causing long-running transactions to fail for lack of space.

Don't go overboard adding new rollback segments. If you already have 20 segments, don't double the number. Add 4 or 5 more, then monitor the effect on WAITS. If necessary, add more, until you feel that the number of WAITS has gone down to an acceptable value (i.e., only a handful of waits per hour or per day, relative to the volume of transactions in the system).

Make certain that all of the rollback segments have room to grow, if needed. Realistically, some growth is to be expected, and setting OPTIMAL should cause occasional "shrinkage" back to reasonable values. Ideally rollback segments should extend and shrink very seldom. The following query can help determine whether your rollback segments need to be larger:

```
SELECT n.name,
       s.extents,
       s.hwmsize/1024 hwmsize_kb,
       s.rssize/1024 currsize_kb,
       s.extends,
       s.shrinks,
       s.wraps,
  FROM v$rollstat    s,
       v$rollname    n
 WHERE s.usn = n.usn;
```

This query shows the current size of each rollback segment: the number of EXTENTS, and the current size in bytes (i.e., RSSIZE). It also shows the *high-water mark* size in bytes, which is the largest size to which the segment has grown since the database instance was started. But the most important information shown is EXTENDS and SHRINKS. These are counters of the number of times that the rollback segments have grown to accommodate transaction size and volume, and the number of times that they have been shrunk back to OPTI-MAL.

Ideally, EXTENDS and SHRINKS should be 0 or close to it. If not, raising OPTIMAL using ALTER ROLLBACK SEGMENT should help correct this. The activity performed by rollback segments is arduous enough; adding unnecessary space management to that workload is unreasonable. Set OPTIMAL high enough so that EXTENDS and SHRINKS are minimized. You cannot eliminate them, but you can minimize them.

The value of WRAPS is the converse of EXTENDS and SHRINKS. It should be a very high value.

Another place to look for rollback contention is the V$WAITSTAT view, using the following query:

```
SELECT class, count, time
  FROM v$waitstat
 WHERE class LIKE 'undo%';
```

This view provides more detail on contention for buffers in the Buffer Cache in the Oracle SGA. Each time a process is forced to post a "buffer busy wait" event to the Session Wait interface, while it is trying to access a buffer, this view is incremented. The contents of this view are almost useless without the time information, so setting the initialization parameter TIMED_STATISTICS to TRUE is important.

Again, bear in mind that the statistics in this table are cumulative since database instance startup. Raw numbers are meaningless; only differences are useful. Use that knowledge to come up with an hourly rate, especially during peak hours. Lots of waits on *undo header* (i.e., segment header for rollback segments) indicate the need for more rollback segments. This information can help confirm the values witnessed in the WAITS column of V$ROLLSTAT. Many *undo block* waits (i.e., blocks within rollback segments) can be solved by additional rollback segments or additional extents to the current rollback segments.

Monitoring Latch Contention and Locking

Yogi Berra once said, "You can observe a lot by watching." This is certainly true for Oracle databases, particularly if you know what you are looking for. The following query might be helpful for detecting various kinds of contention in your database:

```
SELECT * FROM V$SYSTEM_EVENT ORDER BY TIME_WAITED DESC;
```

The V$SYSTEM_EVENT dynamic performance view shows the cumulative total of *wait events* that Oracle server processes have waited on since the database instance was started. In Oracle8 Parallel Server, it would make sense to use the global version of this view instead:

```
SELECT * FROM GV$SYSTEM_EVENT ORDER BY TIME_WAITED DESC, INST_ID
```

Sorting this query by the TIME_WAITED column in descending order will effectively display all the *wait events* in the order of the amount of time we waited. Wait events were introduced in Oracle7 version 7.0, and they are a simple and effective way of detecting contention. The way they work is very simple: Whenever an Oracle server process is going to *relinquish the CPU* (i.e., go to "sleep") in order to wait for *something* (i.e., a system call, an I/O call, a "lock" of some kind, etc.), the process posts a "*gone fishing*" sign in the SGA, also known as a wait event. When the process returns from the wait event, it removes the "*gone fishing*" sign and increments some counters in the SGA. These counters can be seen cumulatively for the entire instance since startup in V$SYSTEM_EVENT and cumulatively for active sessions in V$SESSION_EVENT. The list of active "*gone fishing*" signs can be seen in the real-time view V$SESSION_WAIT. The initialization parameter TIMED_STATISTICS must be set to TRUE (default: FALSE) in order to populate columns like TIME_WAITED and AVERAGE_WAIT in the V$SYSTEM_EVENT and V$SESSION_EVENT views. The incalculable value provided by the information in these columns is the single greatest reason to always set TIMED_STATISTICS to TRUE. Don't listen to people who argue that "it's too expensive for Oracle to make calls to the system clock all the time." It's too expensive NOT to do this; the timing information associated with wait events is crucial.

Wait events are documented in the *Oracle8i Server Reference* manual, in Appendix A. Many wait events are harmless or innocuous, such as these:

- pmon timer
- smon timer
- rdbms ipc message

These wait events just describe normal events within the Oracle database instance. Other events, such as "*SQL*Net message from client*," describe a situation that accumulates a lot of time, but is not a contention issue; in this case, this wait event describes the Oracle server process waiting for the client process to do something. Think of what the Oracle server process does while the "SQL>" prompt is showing in SQL*Plus.

Two wait events in particular mean you should do extra investigation, if they show a lot of time spent waiting. If these wait events are not one of the "top 10" from the query above, it is probably not necessary to worry about them. But if they are in the "top 10," then pay attention!

One is the "*latch free*" event, which indicates excessive amounts of time spent waiting on latches in the Oracle instance. More information can be obtained with the following query:

```
SELECT * FROM V$LATCH ORDER BY SLEEPS DESC;
```

In parallel server, the corresponding global view to use is:

```
SELECT * FROM GV$LATCH ORDER BY SLEEPS DESC, INST_ID;
```

These queries will find the latches that are causing the longest waits, resulting in contention. There are some extremely brief descriptions of latches in the view V$LATCHNAME, and there is no documentation in any of the standard Oracle documents. Probably your best bet for finding descriptions of latches comes from the Web, in the form of your account in Oracle Support's *MetaLink* search function or `http://technet.oracle.com/` and its search function. What follows are some descriptions of commonly seen latches.

An *enqueue* latch means that there is a lock on an object. The V$LOCK view would have more information for the session identified by the value of SID.

The *cache buffers chains* latch is used by server processes to serialize updates to a specific block in the buffer cache. Several blocks in the buffer can get hashed to the same latch. Many waits on this latch typically indicate block contention. Verify this finding by querying V$WAITSTAT where CLASS = "data block." If block contention appears to be occurring, use V$SESSION and V$SQLAREA to try to determine on which table or index the contention is occurring. If the SQL statement is an UPDATE or DELETE, increase INITRANS. If the SQL statement is an INSERT, increase FREELISTS (which requires rebuilding the table). In either case, if increasing INITRANS or FREELISTS doesn't help, consider lowering the number of rows in the database blocks for this segment by re-creating the segment with increased PCTFREE.

The *cache buffer lru chains* latch is used for moving buffers around in the SGA buffer cache. Excessive contention on this latch may indicate either a buffer cache that is much too small or a buffer cache that is much too large. In the former case, an extremely small buffer cache is being updated rapidly because blocks are aging out of the buffer cache too quickly. In the latter case, the buffer cache is so large that manipulations of the LRU (least recently used) chain take an excessive amount of time. In either case, excessive waiting on this latch may indicate that DB_BLOCK_BUFFERS should be increased or decreased, respectively. As in all cases, DB_LRU_STATISTICS or DB_LRU_EXTENDED_STATISTICS should be used to determine the proper size for DB_BLOCK_BUFFERS; see the Oracle7 or Oracle8 *Server Tuning Guide* for more information. In an Oracle8 warehouse it is possible to manually tune the buffer cache for different types and sizes of tables by subdividing the buffer pool, as described in Chapter 3.

The *redo allocation* latch is used to allocate the redo buffers in the redo log buffer. It is also used during *checkpoints* to advance the System Commit Number (SCN). If anything, excessive waiting on this latch may indicate that database instance is checkpointing too frequently. This may be due to the redo logfiles being too small or LOG_CHECKPOINT_INTERVAL or LOG_CHECKPOINT_TIMEOUT is set too low.

The *redo copy* latch is used when the size of a redo entry is greater than the value of the configuration parameter LOG_SMALL_ENTRY_MAX_SIZE; the solution might be to raise this value. For Oracle7 and Oracle8*i* version 8.0 and before, use the following formula using statistics from the performance view V$SYSSTAT to determine this value:

```
(redo size / redo entries) * 1.3
```

The number of *redo copy* latches is set by the configuration parameter LOG_SIMULTANEOUS_COPIES, and the LGWR process will grab all these latches before writing from the log buffers to the redo logfiles. Thus, excessive waiting on this latch might also mean that LGWR is writing too often, which might mean that the application is committing too often or that the LOG_BUFFER value is too low.

In Oracle8*i*, the LOG_SMALL_ENTRY_MAX_SIZE and LOG_SIMULTA-NEOUS_COPIES parameters become obsolete, and the RDBMS calculates these values dynamically.

The *row cache objects* latch guards the data dictionary cache in the shared pool. When loading, referencing, or freeing any data dictionary objects in the shared pool, this latch must be obtained by the Oracle server process. If this latch is being waited on and a lot of *recursive SQL* is being generated by SQL statements, then the SHARED_POOL configuration parameter should be raised. If there is excessive waiting on this latch and not much recursive SQL is being generated by SQL statements, then it simply means that the data dictionary is effectively cached in the shared pool already and is simply being referenced often. There is nothing to be done in this case.

Oracle uses at least 70 other latches. Contact Oracle Worldwide Support for help if you believe you are having problems with latches.

If the query against the V$SYSTEM_EVENTS view shows that the "enqueue" wait event is accumulating a lot of time, then monitor the V$LOCK view to detect any sessions currently holding enqueues:

```
SELECT    TYPE,
          DECODE(LMODE,
                 0, '--Waiting--',
                 1, 'Null',
                 2, 'Sub-Share',
                 3, 'Sub-Exclusive',
                 4, 'Share',
                 5, 'Share/Sub-Exclusive',
                 6, 'Exclusive',
                    '<Unknown>') mode_held,
          DECODE(REQUEST,
                 0, '',
                 1, 'Null',
                 2, 'Sub-Share',
                 3, 'Sub-Exclusive',
```

```
                          4, 'Share',
                          5, 'Share/Sub-Exclusive',
                          6, 'Exclusive',
                              '<Unknown>') mode_requested,
            COUNT(*)
FROM        GV$LOCK
WHERE       TYPE NOT IN ('MR','RT')
GROUP BY    TYPE,
            DECODE(LMODE,
                          0, '--Waiting--',
                          1, 'Null',
                          2, 'Sub-Share',
                          3, 'Sub-Exclusive',
                          4, 'Share',
                          5, 'Share/Sub-Exclusive',
                          6, 'Exclusive',
                              '<Unknown>'),
            DECODE(REQUEST,
                          0, '',
                          1, 'Null',
                          2, 'Sub-Share',
                          3, 'Sub-Exclusive',
                          4, 'Share',
                          5, 'Share/Sub-Exclusive',
                          6, 'Exclusive',
                              '<Unknown>');
```

Certain enqueues are used by the Oracle instance internally and should be disregarded. An example is the MR (for Media Recovery) enqueue, one of which is held by the instance for each data file in the database. Another example is the RT (for Redo Thread) enqueue, one of which is always held by the instance for each online thread of redo in the database. So, this query excludes these enqueues, as they just get in the way!

Other enqueues are natural to the normal functioning of transactions in the database, such as the TM and TX enqueues. The TX enqueue corresponds to a row in the V$TRANSACTION view, and the TM enqueues are acquired to prevent DDL commands (such as DROP or TRUNCATE) against tables or indexes involved in the transaction. Another enqueue that could betray contention is the ST (space transaction) enqueue. There is only one ST enqueue for any Oracle database, and this enqueue must be acquired before any modifications by any session to the DBA_EXTENTS and DBA_FREE_SPACE views, which are the public representations of the SYS.UET$ and SYS.FET$ tables in the SYSTEM tablespace.

The important thing to watch for is when sessions are waiting for each other for long periods of time, regardless of the type of enqueue. If you run this query and find some sessions waiting, then run the query again, to ensure that the condition is not transient and quickly resolved. If so, seek further information about the sessions themselves by querying V$LOCK again, this time to retrieve the session ID or SID column. Once you have the SID, you can query V$SESSION view to learn more about the session (i.e., who it is, what program is being used). Once you know the session information, you can also query the V$SQLAREA view using the SQL_ADDRESS value from V$SESSION, to find out what SQL statement is currently being executed.

Enqueues are very briefly documented in the *Oracle8i Server Reference* manual in Appendix B. Again, your best sources of information might be the *MetaLink* Web site at http://www.oracle.com/support/ or the *TechNet* Web site at http://technet.oracle.com/. If this doesn't help, log a TAR with Oracle Support for an explanation.

Monitoring the Number of Extents

Although the MAXEXTENTS UNLIMITED clause became available in Oracle7.3, it is a mistake to use it. Always set a finite value for the number of extents, even if that value is 1,000. To explain, imagine receiving this particular wish: a table or index with hundreds of thousands of extents. In such a situation, it is virtually guaranteed that each extent is tiny because hundreds of thousands of any sizable extent would probably be obscenely large. Simply put, tens of thousands of extents, hundreds of thousands of extents, or millions of extents put an unnecessary burden on Oracle space management. There is no need for the data dictionary tables to grow this large. MAXEXTENTS UNLIMITED combined with inappropriate values of INITIAL, NEXT, PCTFREE, or PCTUSED can lead to this situation. Once the data dictionary tables (specifically SYS.UET$, the used extent table, and SYS.FET$, the free extent table) grow unnecessarily large, they will remain so for as long as the database exists.

PERFORMANCE IMPACT OF MANY EXTENTS

There has been unnecessary concern for years about the performance impact of working with tables with many extents. Random reads are not affected at all. Sequential reads (during full table scans) are impacted only when the extent size is very small. As long as Oracle can obtain DB_FILE_MULTIBLOCK_READ_COUNT contiguous blocks in a single I/O request the read will operate at full efficiency. Only when it receives a smaller number of blocks (at the end of an extent) will it be impacted. The worst case would be when each extent is one block larger than the value of DB_FILE_MULTIBLOCK_READ_COUNT. In this situation, every other sequential read would receive only a single block. If the extent size is any exact multiple of this parameter value then there is no adverse effect at all. If it is anything greater than four or five times this value then the performance impact will be minimal.

Also, be aware that all space management transactions in dictionary-managed tablespaces are single-threaded through the ST (space transaction) enqueue. Only one space management transaction can occur at any given moment in Oracle. Thus, if one or all space management operations begins to consume more time (by having to work with an unnecessarily large FET$ table, for instance), this means that the single-threading on the ST enqueue will become very noticeable.

This effect can be eliminated for certain tablespaces by making them *locally managed*. Instead of all the extent information being stored in the SYSTEM tablespace in the FET$ and UET$ tables, locally managed tablespaces store extent information in data file header blocks in a bitmap structure. Thus, extent information is decentralized, eliminating the database-wide single-threaded effect of the ST enqueue. Instead, extent information is maintained within each data file using far more efficient bitmap operations.

Plan on setting MAXEXTENTS to a manageable value like 200, 400, or 1,000. If your tables or indexes are located in the old-style, dictionary-managed tablespaces, then 1,000 should be the maximum for MAXEXTENTS. If your table or index is located in a locally managed tablespace, then setting MAXEXTENTS UNLIMITED is quite reasonable, and finding segments with more than 10,000 extents should not be a major cause for concern.

To find out if any segments are approaching their MAXEXTENTS using the following:

```
SELECT  s.owner,
        s.segment_name,
        s.partition_name,   /* only for Oracle8 */
        s.segment_type,
        s.max_extents,
        COUNT(distinct e.extent_id) nbr_extents
  FROM dba_segments    s,
       dba_extents     e
 WHERE s.segment_type <> 'CACHE'
   AND e.owner = s.owner
   AND e.segment_type = s.segment_type
   AND e.segment_name = s.segment_name
                            /* only for Oracle8 */
   AND NVL(e.partition_name, '~') = NVL(s.partition_name, '~')
GROUP BY s.owner,
         s.segment_name,
         s.partition_name, /* only for Oracle8 */
         s.segment_type,
         s.max_extents
HAVING COUNT(distinct e.extent_id) > (s.max_extents - 5);
```

It is really quite embarrassing for a DBA to be told that an application operation failed because a table or index exceeded its MAXEXTENTS. This query will warn of all segments within five extents of exceeding their current MAXEXTENTS.

The DBA_EXTENTS and DBA_FREE_SPACE views will include information from both locally managed and dictionary-managed tablespaces.

Monitoring Freespace

One of the surest ways for upper management to get the impression that a DBA is not doing his job is to find unexpected failures occurring because of a lack of space. This is the classic *unnecessary error*, and if it can't always be avoided it certainly can be anticipated.

To find out if any tables, indexes, or clusters are about to run out of space, use the following query:

```
SELECT tablespace_name,
       segment_name,
       initial_extent,
       next_extent,
       max_extents
  FROM dba_segments x
 WHERE NOT EXISTS
         (SELECT NULL
            FROM dba_free_space
           WHERE tablespace_name = x.tablespace_name
             AND bytes > x.next_extent);
```

Be aware that this query may take a long time for databases with a lot of segments. It may be useful to copy the full contents of each of these views into tables first (using CREATE TABLE . . . AS SELECT), index the table by TABLE-SPACE _NAME and BYTES, and run this query off those tables instead.

Monitoring Tablespace Fragmentation

Tablespace fragmentation occurs when segments within a tablespace each have their own customized storage parameters, causing each segment to have differently sized extents or, through the use of a nonzero PCTINCREASE parameter, extents that are successively growing or shrinking in size.

Tablespace fragmentation becomes harmful when DROPs occur in such tablespaces. Dropping segments will leave the formerly occupied extents as differently sized *free extents*. Newly created segments can reuse these free extents, but over time, as segments are added and dropped, the freespace in the tablespace will become "chopped up" into smaller and smaller widely scattered free extents. Eventually, what may happen is that a significant amount of freespace is available, but only in hundreds or thousands of tiny freespace extents, each too small to use. As a result, either more data files must be added to the tablespace, or all the segments in the tablespace will need to be dropped and re-created. This latter move is also known as a *tablespace reorganization*.

It is common to use the Oracle EXP and IMP utilities for this purpose, and there are several third-party utilities (such as Platinum's TSReorg product) to facilitate this activity. The sad fact is that it is all completely unnecessary.

Craig Shallahamer, president of Orapub, Inc., has written a paper entitled "Avoiding a Database Reorganization," which is available at his Web site, www.orapub.com. This document explains how to understand, detect, and eliminate all kinds of fragmentation in an Oracle database. There is another fine paper at the same Web site by Cary Millsap entitled "Oracle7 Server Space Management," which covers in fine detail all the issues and myths surrounding Oracle space management.

To supplement these documents, the following analogy can be used to picture what is happening when tablespace fragmentation occurs.

Think about tiling—specifically, tiling the floor of a kitchen. In this analogy, the floor of the room is the Oracle tablespace. The tiles themselves are extents. A tablespace is created out of one or more data files. Typically, determining the size of those data files did not take into consideration the size of the extents that would be contained within. The same is true for a kitchen. Chances are good that the kitchen was sized without any particular regard for the tiles that would be used on the floor.

In this analogy, laying tile down on the floor is similar to creating segments and their extents in a tablespace. There is one major departure from real life in this analogy: When segments and their extents are dropped or truncated, this would be similar to picking up and removing tile. Normally, that doesn't happen in real life unless a cracked tile has to be replaced.

Anyway, if kitchen floors were tiled the way most people create tables and indexes in Oracle tablespaces, then the floor would be composed of many differently sized tiles. Of course, our objective in both cases is to be able to cover as much floor as possible, but as you can visualize, this would start to become difficult when all the tiles are sized differently. Ultimately, there would be many situations where many of the tiles do not fit against one another neatly, leaving gaps. As the floor started to fill up, it would become progressively more difficult to find places to lay the remaining tiles.

The same is true of extents in Oracle tablespaces. In the beginning, there is no issue; finding space for all the extents is quite easy. But over time, as the tablespace fills up, it starts to become more difficult to find contiguous patches of open space in which to fit new extents.

Then, in Oracle we have the case of dropping extents, which in the analogy would be like removing some of the tiles previously laid down. That would potentially open new slots in which to place additional tiles, but the additional tiles would certainly have to be either the same size or smaller than the open slots.

Clearly, this analogy makes it easier to visualize how difficult this all becomes.

Now, using the same analogy, add one additional rule: All tiles will be either the same size or multiples of one another. Suddenly, the problem of covering every square centimeter of flooring becomes quite simple (except around the walls and cabinets, which we'll ignore for the sake of simplicity). Even when you throw in the additional scenario of removing tiles (to simulate dropping tables and indexes), what is left as gaps will be quite easy to refill. All the tiles are the same size or are sized as multiples of one another.

Next time you have to tile a floor, consider whether you will use uniformly sized tiles or randomly sized ones. Unless you are an artist, you almost certainly must choose the former. After all, unless you feel quite strongly about it, who has time to make artwork out of the kitchen floor? The same is true with Oracle space management. Who has time to make artwork about segments, extents, and freespace? Life is simply too short, and there are much more demanding issues on which to vent creative urges.

Coming up with sizes for INITIAL and NEXT for tables, clusters, and indexes should not be a matter of calculation at all. Rather, database objects should fit one of a very few profiles, such as SMALL, MEDIUM, LARGE, and HUGE. Tablespaces should be available for each profile, and each tablespace should use a small number of uniformly sized extents; only one extent size per tablespace is ideal.

Oracle8 introduced an option to help enforce this:

```
ALTER TABLESPACE . . . MINIMUM EXTENT nn;
CREATE TABLESPACE . . . MINIMUM EXTENT nn;
```

If MINIMUM EXTENT is specified for the tablespace, then all extents in that tablespace must be at least the size specified, and if they are larger they must be multiples of the size specified. For example:

```
CREATE TABLESPACE dw01_huge
     MINIMUM EXTENT 32M
     DEFAULT STORAGE (INITIAL 32M NEXT 32M MAXEXTENTS 400 PCTINCREASE
0);
CREATE TABLESPACE dw01_large
     MINIMUM EXTENT 4M
     DEFAULT STORAGE (INITIAL 4M NEXT 4M MAXEXTENTS 400 PCTINCREASE 0);
CREATE TABLESPACE dw01_medium
     MINIMUM EXTENT 128K
     DEFAULT STORAGE (INITIAL 128K NEXT 128K MAXEXTENTS 400 PCTINCREASE
0);
CREATE TABLESPACE dw01_small
     MINIMUM EXTENT 16K
     DEFAULT STORAGE (INITIAL 16K NEXT 16K MAXEXTENTS 400 PCTINCREASE
0);
```

In the tablespace DW01_HUGE, you would be able to create tables, indexes, or clusters with extent sizes of 32 MB, 64 MB, and so on. By setting MAXEXTENTS to 400, you are implying that the largest object you can have in that tablespace is at least 12.5 gigabytes, assuming the smallest extent size of 32 MB.

Oracle8*i* presents a complete solution to the issue of tablespace fragmentation in the form of *locally managed* tablespaces. Extent information for segments within locally managed tablespaces is stored in bitmap data structures located within several database blocks at the beginning of each data file in the tablespace. Because single bits in the bitmap structure represent each extent, locally managed tablespaces require same-sized extents. So, when a locally managed tablespace is created, you can choose the AUTOALLOCATE option to let the Oracle RDBMS choose the size of extents, or you can choose your own extent size using the UNIFORM clause. Either way, because all extents are the same size, there is no longer a fragmentation issue. Since tablespaces became available in Oracle version 6, it has always been possible to have same-sized extents, but it has never been possible to enforce this absolutely. The MINIMUM EXTENT functionality introduced in release 8.0 was a big step in the right direction, but locally managed tablespaces address the problem completely.

Databases that have their space managed in this manner will never have problems with tablespace fragmentation, and they will make extremely efficient use of the space they have available.

There is a myth in Oracle performance tuning that many extents present a performance problem. Proponents theorize that skipping from extent to extent must cost *something* in terms of performance. The truth is that this is absolutely false. All extents are equally available for random as well as sequential access; there is no "chaining" from one extent to the next. The *extent map* residing in the segment header contains the address of all extents.

Only in the extreme case of extents being sized small enough to impair multiblock reads for full table scans is this supposition true. Again, the floor tile analogy covers this scenario quite graphically. When you want to tile a floor with the minimum amount of trimming, you want to use as small a tile as possible, so you can fit into tight corners and get close to rounded edges. On the other hand, there is a limit to how small you want to make the tile. What if you had to count the tiles every day for as long as you live in the house? In effect, that is similar to what Oracle has to do during space management operations. If the extent size is too small, you are building a mosaic, and once again you are indulging in artwork. If you care to indulge in art in such a mundane area, simply be aware of the costs involved.

Visualize a tiled floor next time you are trying to determine the space management policy for your database.

Monitoring Invalid Compiled Objects

If your application is making heavy use of database VIEWs or PL/SQL stored procedures, stored functions, or packages, then there is the possibility that DROPs and re-CREATEs on tables or views or PL/SQL stored objects could cause *invalidations* of those objects. While this situation would usually cause applications to fail with an error message from the Oracle server, sometimes the server attempts to recompile the object at run-time, and sometimes the application disregards the error message. As a result, multiple sessions are constantly running into the same error situation repeatedly, and processing the error and/or trying to recompile the object on the fly is burdensome to the Oracle server.

Periodically running the following SQL*Plus script may help prevent this simple-to-fix but difficult-to-diagnose problem from occurring:

```
set echo off feedback off timing off pause off termout off
set pagesize 0 linesize 500 trimspool on trimout on
SELECT 'alter ' ||
        DECODE(object_type,
                'PACKAGE BODY', 'PACKAGE',
                object_type) ||
        owner || '.' || object_name ||
        ' compile' ||
        DECODE(object_type,
                'PACKAGE BODY', ' BODY;',
                ';') cmd
  FROM dba_objects
 WHERE status <> 'VALID'

spool tmp_recompile.sql
/
spool off
set echo on feedback on timing on termout on
spool tmp_recompile
start tmp_recompile
spool off
```

This script can even be run as a regular job, using a job scheduling utility such as the UNIX "cron" utility. Also, it can be rewritten as a PL/SQL stored procedure, which uses dynamic SQL to generate and execute the ALTER statements. If it is rewritten in PL/SQL or as a Java stored procedure, it can then be submitted using the internal DBMS_JOB package.

Monitoring "Stale" Optimizer Statistics

New with Oracle8*i* release 8.1 is the ability for the RDBMS to determine when data dictionary statistics become stale. The new MONITORING clause in the CREATE TABLE and ALTER TABLE commands specifies that the RDBMS collect modification statistics on the table. This information is stored in data dictionary views named DBA|ALL|USER_TAB_MODIFICATIONS, and this information can be used by the DBAs, by the DBMS_STATS package, and by the cost-based optimizer.

Instead of trying to schedule periodic ANALYZEs of tables based on guesses of the frequency of data modification, database administrators can now use estimates collected by the RDBMS. The GATHER_SCHEMA_STATS and GATHER_DATABASE_STATS procedures in the DBMS_STATS package have GATHER STALE options. GATHER STALE will analyze only those tables that are marked "stale" as a result of the modification statistics collected from the MONITORING option. So, if you can schedule these procedures to be executed periodically, using a job control system or the DBMS_JOB package, these procedures will analyze only those tables that have become "stale" and leave unmodified tables alone.

The MONITORING option is documented in the *Oracle8i SQL Language Reference* manual and the *Oracle8i Server Tuning* manual. The DBMS_STATS package and the GATHER_SCHEMA_STATS and GATHER_DATABASE_STATS procedures are documented in the *Oracle8 Supplied Packages Reference* manual.

Summary

There is much that has not been covered in this chapter. For example, we did not begin to cover system management or database monitoring tools, such as Oracle's Enterprise Manager or CA-Unicenter. Instead, this chapter covers most of the basic concepts outlining the administration and monitoring of an Oracle data warehouse—indeed, any Oracle database.

What this chapter did attempt to cover was basic configuration, tuning, and troubleshooting issues. In the very large database (VLDB) environments occupied by many data warehouses, these are the issues that could make or break an implementation.

The basic message is that Oracle provides application developers, end users, and project managers with a huge array of tools, some of which may be more harmful than helpful. The DBA needs to steer people toward the proper usage of these tools and away from the harmful uses of other tools. The administrators have the responsibility to keep the systems available for all users.

Most important is the leadership role of the DWA. The DWA must focus on the genuine issues facing end users as the data warehouse changes over time. After the initial data warehouse implementation project is completed, the leadership of the sort that a project manager provides is still necessary. Rarely can a data warehouse be "put into production" and then left to languish without major design changes on a frequent basis. The questions asked and answers expected by the business are constantly evolving, and change in the data warehouse is more of a continuous cycle than a project with a start and a finish. Data warehousing is a process, a project that never ends.

CHAPTER

9

Data Warehouse Performance Tuning

COLONEL SANDURZ: Prepare ship for light-speed!

DARK HELMET: No, no, no! Light-speed is too slow!

COLONEL SANDURZ: Light-speed is too slow?

DARK HELMET: Yes! We're going to have to go to . . . *ludicrous-speed*!

(*everyone gasps*)

COLONEL SANDURZ: Ludicrous-speed? Sir, we've never gone that fast before. I don't know if the ship can take it. . . .

DARK HELMET: What's the matter, Colonel Sandurz? Chicken?

Spaceballs, *MGM Pictures, 1987*

In the closing scene of the Indiana Jones movie *Raiders of the Lost Ark*, the legendary Ark of the Covenant is crated by U.S. government drones and stored in a vast, anonymous warehouse, presumably never to be seen again. That chilling scene seems to mirror the impression that people have of warehouses in general. This misconception carries over into data warehouses as well. There seems to be a wide misconception among people new to this arena that a data warehouse is a place where all data goes to die.

In reality, if you have ever worked in a real warehouse, the image couldn't be further from the truth. Warehouses are highly organized. Everyone knows where everything is located and how much is there. Real warehouses accept huge quantities of materials from one mode of transport, reorganize the materials for transshipment, and then reship huge quantities of material onto other modes of transport. For example, trainloads of product arrive from manufacturers; the products are restacked for shipment to retailers by truck or van. So, while the materials are in the warehouse, they are frequently transformed from homogeneous product shipments from wholesale manufacturers into palletized mixes of products, suitable for delivery to retail destinations. There are probably not many warehouses like the one portrayed in the Indiana Jones movie, where things are just stored for all eternity. At least, it's important to distinguish between warehousing for the purposes of *archival* and *retrieval*.

So, just as a real warehouse, a data warehouse is not a place in which old data is archived. It is not a *data graveyard* or a *data attic*. Like a real warehouse, it is a dynamic place, and it contains only stuff that is going to be used.

Think of the system underlying a data warehouse as a *data pump*, as illustrated in Figure 9.1. More than any other kind of database, data warehouses have to move larger volumes of data faster. Think about the size of most data warehouses: several hundred gigabytes or even many terabytes. Where do they get their data from and how regularly? The answer is that they get their data from other databases, and they get it quite often.

Going back to real warehouses, think of the view of a large warehouse from the air. Large warehouses are usually located near railroads, interstate high-

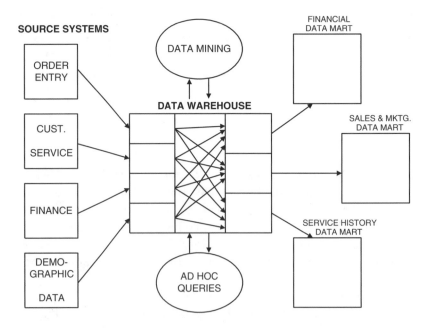

Figure 9.1 The data warehouse as pumps and pipelines.

ways, airports, and shipyards. Most of the outer walls of the warehouse building itself consist of loading docks to facilitate the fast simultaneous transfer of large amounts of material. On one side of the building may be a rail loading dock. On two or three other sides may be truck loading docks.

A data warehouse is not unlike its real-world counterpart. On one side of the data warehouse are the many data sources. Data enters the warehouse through tape drives, through network connectivity, through file transfers, and through direct connections to the operational data sources. On the other side of the data warehouse are the many outbound data destinations. Data leaves the warehouse using the same variety of media on which it arrived.

In the middle is the data warehouse system itself. Inbound source data is cleansed, transformed, and aggregated. Outbound data is sorted, subsetted, and aggregated—downloaded, spooled, and cubed. While all this is going on, certain enterprising souls may be performing *ad hoc* or tactical reporting or data mining.

Facilitating all this movement and activity requires a lot of attention to the foundation of the system, the I/O subsystem, the CPUs, the operating system, and the database itself. Let's investigate what it takes to tune this behemoth!

ORACLE ENTERPRISE MANAGER DIAGNOSTICS AND TUNING PACKS

This chapter, like much of this book, explains operations at the most basic level—usually as SQL interactions. To effectively use a graphical tuning tool, such as the OEM Tuning Pack, it is critical to understand what the tool is doing for you. Without an understanding of, for instance, the trace and TKPROF facilities, the output of an automated tuning tool seems mysterious and magical. Effective interpretation of the tool's recommendations can be performed only when you understand the underlying technology used by the tool. By avoiding coverage of these management packs, we are not saying that you shouldn't use graphical tools—just that you should first learn to do the task without them.

Sizing Your System

A complete refresh from the legacy operational data sources could involve several hundred gigabytes being loaded from a tape drive or across the network. Many complete refreshes occur on a monthly or weekly basis, and some data warehouses even deal with daily refreshes. Additionally, incremental loads may account for hundreds of megabytes or several gigabytes, and generally these take place on a daily or weekly basis.

That's only the start of it. Once data has been loaded, cleansing and aggregation must take place, which generally involve making extra copies of the data to preserve your ability to restart the cycle in case something goes wrong. It is not unusual for each row of the *raw* detail data that is loaded into the warehouse to be copied two or three times, doubling or tripling the amount of space needed to store it. Redundancy of data in a data warehouse is sometimes necessary, if the redundancy occurs as part of a process. Redundancy, in this case, also provides the ability to checkpoint and restart a long involved process of transforming raw detail data into clean, strategic, summarized data.

Not only is the amount of storage mindboggling, but the realization that every byte of this storage will be picked up and put back—perhaps two or three times—on a regular basis in the shortest amount of time should disabuse one of the notions that data warehouses are like quiet, serene libraries, where the only activity is reading. If you share this popular perception of a data warehouse as a "reading room" or "library," imagine the data warehouse as a public library where every week the entire inventory of books is removed and reshelved, in six or eight hours!

Once the loading, cleansing, and aggregation is complete, the overall *load phase* is complete, and the data warehouse must shift from a *read/write* application to a *read-only* application. *Ad hoc* reporting, operational and strategic summary reporting, online analysis, data mining: These are all activities that typically involve massive queries against the extremely large volumes of data.

Again, to debunk the image of a data warehouse as a quiet, serene "reading room" or "library," think of it not as a place where people calmly stroll among the aisles and pick out a book here and there to sit down with and read at leisure. Instead, think of it as a place where readers madly rush through the aisles, sweeping entire shelves of books into carts from which they will digest and read them. It is a place where every single book must be read because, in a week or in a month, the whole place is turned upside down and reorganized again.

Setting Up the I/O Subsystem

When people think about sizing their system, especially the I/O subsystem, they generally think in terms of disk space, in terms of capacity. The I/O subsystem may be described as being 100 gigabytes, 400 gigabytes, or 6 terabytes in size.

But try to imagine 100 gigabytes of disk drive attached to a 1985-era IBM PC AT. Plainly, the CPU of such a computer would be overwhelmed by the amount of data those modern-day disk drives would be able to pump at it. Such a configuration would be CPU-bound (i.e., bottlenecked at the CPU) right from the start. Conversely, imagine a Sun UltraSPARC E10000 with 100 gigabytes of disk space in the form of 5.25-inch, 10-MB drives manufactured in 1985. In this case, obviously we would be I/O-bound (i.e., bottlenecked at the I/O subsystem).

Invoking these images is not intended as an exercise in sado-masochism (well, not entirely!) but rather to illustrate the point by describing extremes. Each component of the system is a pump, and little good comes of mismatching the flow rates between the components. Another way of thinking of it is to remember the old adage that a chain is only as strong as its weakest link. In the same way, a pumping system will provide only as much throughput as its narrowest pipeline or its least capable pump.

In fact, it is very effective to think of the entire I/O subsystem (disk drives or DASD, tape drives, network) as pumps with which to drive data at the CPUs (see Figure 9.2). Thinking of the I/O subsystem as simply a repository in which to store data is terribly one-dimensional, and it doesn't help design a system capable of performing the tasks asked of it, nor does it aid in figuring out why a system is not performing up to expectations. Remembering that each component of the I/O subsystem has a *throughput rate* in addition to a *capacity* helps us construct a more useful picture of system components.

What do you see in Figure 9.2? Drives A, B, C, and D all have equivalent throughput. And the single CPU is able to handle eight drives with this throughput. If all these components are used to their maximum effectiveness, how is this system likely to bottleneck?

Now, add back in the concept of capacity, and see how the picture in Figure 9.3 changes.

Where will the bottleneck occur in this scenario? As you can see, the majority of the capacity is on drives A and B, but they have equivalent transfer rates to drives C and D. This means that all the data stored on drives A and B can be

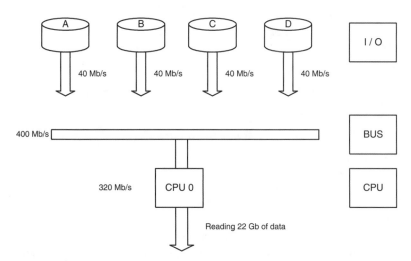

Figure 9.2   Subsystems as data pumps.

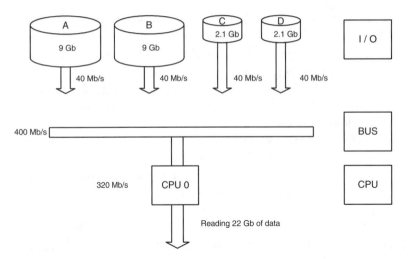

Figure 9.3 Subsystems as data pumps with capacities.

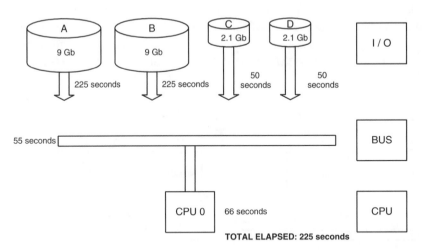

Figure 9.4 Retrieval times.

retrieved only 25 percent as quickly as all the data stored on drives C and D. All four drives have the same transfer rate, but the larger drives have four times as much data. If all the data on these four drives had to be read or written, it would take as long as the times shown in Figure 9.4.

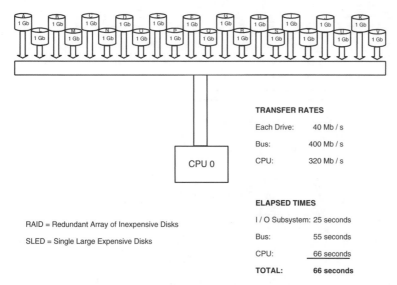

TRANSFER RATES

Each Drive:	40 Mb / s
Bus:	400 Mb / s
CPU:	320 Mb / s

RAID = Redundant Array of Inexpensive Disks

SLED = Single Large Expensive Disks

ELAPSED TIMES

I / O Subsystem:	25 seconds
Bus:	55 seconds
CPU:	66 seconds
TOTAL:	**66 seconds**

Figure 9.5 RAID versus SLED.

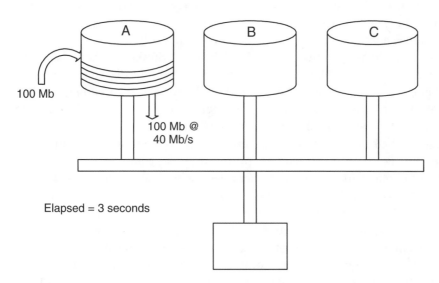

Figure 9.6 No striping of data.

In contrast, consider the configuration shown in Figure 9.5. Obviously, this I/O subsystem would perform better than the previous one.

Just as obviously, you're not always going to be dumping or loading all the

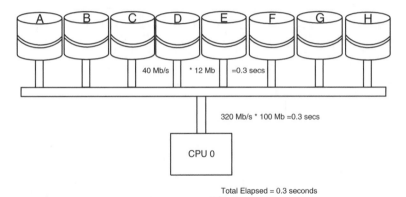

Figure 9.7 Data spread across eight drives.

data on all your disk drives as illustrated in these figures, but the same basic principle holds true for smaller amounts of data. For example, let's say that you have 100 megabytes of data to retrieve. Suppose that Figure 9.6 is the scenario.

The amount of time needed to retrieve the data is simply a function of the amount of data times the transfer rate. What if the data was organized on the disk as in Figure 9.7? It might then be possible to have all eight drives returning the data at once, making the read almost eight times faster. So far, so good. But *how* the data is spread across these eight drives is important, too.

Let's take a table of 1 gigabyte and eight disk drives. Spreading the data across these eight drives might mean dividing the table into eight distinct pieces and laying them down on the drives. This would fulfill the idea of spreading the data onto eight devices, but would a sequential scan of the data run any faster? The answer is no, for the reason shown in Figure 9.8.

As Figure 9.8 shows, each read operation scans 128 KB at a time, meaning that it should take about 8,192 read operations to read 1 gigabyte of data. Notice that each read operation is still being serviced by only one device at a time, as the scan will make 1,024 reads (of 128 KB apiece) across each disk drive before moving on to the next. Because the number of read operations is the same and each read operation takes the same amount of time, laying the data across many drives in this fashion will not cause a single scan to speed up.

Imagine that 10 such scans were going on at roughly the same time. Instead of a single disk drive device trying to service all 10 scans, you might now have 8 disk drive devices doing so. Depending on how the scans are distributed across the data, it may be possible for the 10 scans to concurrently complete in roughly the same amount of time as if each were running alone. Thus, spreading data across multiple devices, even in as rudimentary a manner as concatenation, may cause *scaleup* for multiple concurrent operations, even if it doesn't cause *speedup* for individual operations—see Figure 9.9.

1 Scan

Figure 9.8   Stripe width equal to partition, or concatenation.

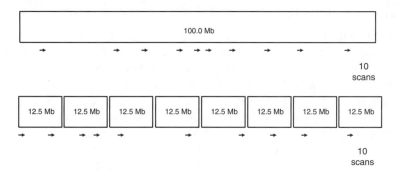

10
scans

10
scans

Figure 9.9   Ten concurrent scans experiencing scaleup.

Obviously, with stripe widths of 128 MB apiece, we would have to get quite lucky to experience this kind of scaleup. Who can say that 10 concurrent scans will each be called with enough time in between each so that all 8 drives are in use at once? Who can say that all 10 concurrent scans won't be seeking data on the same drive at the same time?

The solution is to reduce the size of the stripe widths, using RAID 0 striping. If the stripe width were reduced to 1 MB, then a new drive would be hit every 8 read operations (of 128 KB apiece) during a scan of 1 gigabyte. Again, each read operation would not speed up, and 1 scan running on the system would not run any faster than if the entire 1 gigabyte were on 1 disk drive. But now throw 10 or 20 concurrent scans at the system. Instead of 1 disk drive frantically trying to return 20 gigabytes (i.e., 20 scans of 1 gigabyte apiece), now 8 drives would be involved, almost certainly improving performance.

So, to build a data warehouse system that will meet the needs of not one solitary user but dozens or hundreds of concurrent users, keep in mind that the foundation of the system is in the I/O subsystem. If you buy your storage devices only for their capacity, you will lay the foundation for a data warehouse that may fulfill all expectations on paper, but it will quickly "hit the wall" on performance when several users start pounding on it.

Striping the data is important, not because the technique of striping necessarily provides any kind of speedup, but because it allows many concurrent operations to scale up. Spreading the I/O load across many devices doesn't improve any single device's transfer rate, but it helps each device sustain its own transfer rates without degrading. Chapter 2 provides a more detailed explanation of the issues surrounding RAID 0 striping.

ANOTHER WAY OF LOOKING AT IT

When teaching this concept in a classroom, we like to use an analogy to help clarify the ideas. You're all familiar with those bottled-water coolers that have the upside-down five-gallon jugs? Those jugs are sometimes referred to as *car-boys*. At least they might be called that if you happen to brew your own beer . . .

Anyway, for a moment visualize your disk devices as these *car-boys*, or jugs of water. Each has a capacity, five gallons, and because of its relatively small nozzle, each has a throughput. Let's say that by turning a car-boy upside down, you can empty it in 60 seconds, giving it a throughput of 0.08 gallons per second. 0.08 gallons is roughly the size of a drinking glass. For you beer drinkers, it would be little more than half a pint-glass.

Now, let's add a scenario to imitate disk devices in a large data warehouse database. Suppose you want a glass of water. Getting it from one car-boy would take about a second. Suppose you wanted a gallon of water. Getting it from a single car-boy would take about 12 seconds. Because you're always in a hurry, 12 seconds is too long. Suppose you can tap 12 car-boys at once? Then, you'd get your gallon of water in a second. From 24 car-boys at once? Then, it would only take half a second. And so on.

But now, suppose you're not the only person wanting water by the gallon. Suppose a dozen of your friends are always standing in front of two dozen upside-down car-boys, each wanting a gallon or more of water. If you are occupying all of those car-boys by yourself, then your friends will have to wait until you are done. Then, if the next person also uses all two dozen car-boys at once, then everyone else will have to wait.

One possible solution is a trade-off. Instead of allowing one person to utilize all of the car-boys at once, limit them to a certain number, say 6. That way, up to four people can get water. Sure, it may take 2 seconds instead of 0.5 seconds, but perhaps that's OK, since it may take several minutes for each person to use up whatever water they get and return for more.

If it helps, go back and reread the previous section on I/O subsystems and substitute *water jugs* or *car-boys* for disk devices in the discussion.

Pretuning the Data Warehouse

In Chapter 8, "Administering and Monitoring the Oracle Data Warehouse," we mentioned that the DBA must be aware of where and how all data is to be cleansed, transformed, and aggregated, as well as knowing when and how all data was going to be extracted to outbound destinations. The reason for this tall order is to make the most of proactive tuning opportunities. You can't be proactive unless you know exactly what is going on and when it is going on.

During the design phase of the data warehouse implementation, *star schemas* can be designed to optimize queries from huge *fact tables*. The *dimension tables* surrounding the fact table can either be completely *normalized* (i.e., containing only key and attribute information, as in Figure 9.10) or the dimensions can be *denormalized* (i.e., containing summarized information from the fact table, in addition to key and attribute information, as in Figure 9.11).

Naturally, there are major performance advantages to denormalization that have been extensively addressed in earlier chapters of this book. The data

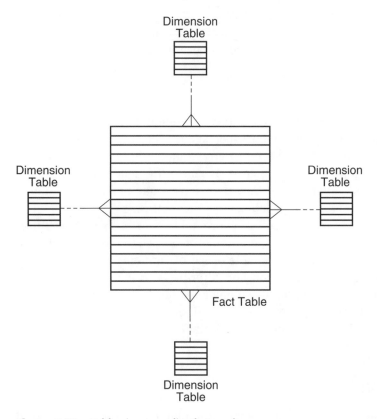

Figure 9.10   Tables in normalized star schema.

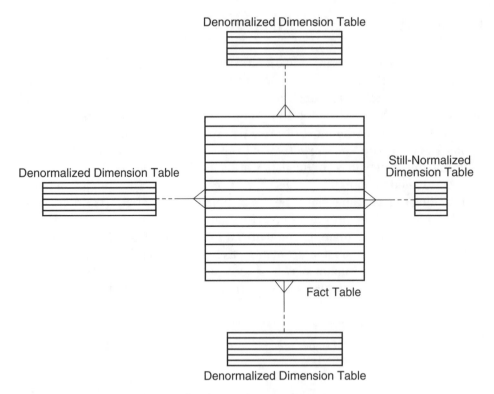

Figure 9.11 Tables in denormalized star schema.

warehouse designer can take advantage of these techniques based on his knowledge of the types of queries that will be issued against the star schema.

But denormalized star schemas tend to grow quickly in complexity, as the levels of summarization and filtering grow. Because the denormalized dimension tables are now so much larger, they themselves may need to be summarized to higher and higher levels of detail, as in Figure 9.12.

Also, if a particularly important set of reports must constantly retrieve information from a specific subset of data, it is sometimes wise to filter that specific subset of data into its own summary table or set of summary tables. The purpose of this additional summarization and filtering is to ensure a consistent level of query response-time for highly summarized queries.

The techniques of creating star schemas and snowflakes are discussed in detail in Chapter 4, "Designing the Oracle Data Warehouse," and Chapter 5, "Building the Oracle Data Warehouse."

Materialized Views

If possible, use Oracle8*i* materialized views for implementing the denormalized dimension tables. This will not only automate the refresh of the various tables

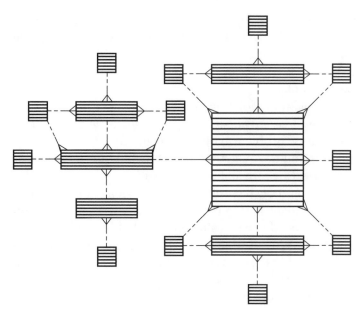

Figure 9.12   Snowflake becomes a blizzard.

of each dimension, but it will also utilize the new *query rewrite* feature of the Oracle Optimizer. Query rewrite will automatically and transparently redirect any queries written against the fact table or larger denormalized dimension tables to instead execute against the smaller, more highly summarized dimension tables, when appropriate.

Materialized views can be used for implementing the optimized elements:

- Preaggregated or presummarized *rollup* or *summary tables*
- Prefiltered *subset tables*
- Prejoined tables to disguise *complex joins*
- Prejoined tables to preprocess *large, time-consuming joins*
- All or some of the previous items

The techniques of *preaggregating, prefiltering,* and *prejoining* have benefited all types of computer systems for decades. As a feature, automated data refresh of materialized views may not provide anything new, except convenience for data warehouse administrators. But because the techniques themselves have been around for decades, so too have the methods and mechanisms for data refresh been around for decades.

What is new and exciting about materialized views is the fact that the Oracle optimizer is now equipped to automatically and transparently *rewrite* queries to make use of the most effective data source. If the optimizer determines that it costs less to execute the query as written, then it will do so. If the optimizer determines that a materialized view exists that could potentially return the same results, and if it compares the cost of using that materialized view to the original execution plan and determines that using the view is cheaper, it will execute the query using the lower-cost plan.

This has tremendous implications for tuning the warehouse. Previously, if you used the techniques of *preaggregating*, *prefiltering*, or *prejoining* to resolve a specific performance problem, you had to instruct the end users affected to edit their queries and now use the newly created tables instead of the tables they had been using. Now, we all know that getting end users to actually implement these instructions may be problematic. They may not know how to edit the queries because someone else may have originally written them, and that someone else is no longer available or willing to do additional editing. Perhaps the end user is using some type of whiz-bang data analysis utility that generates its own SQL to be executed, and there is no way the end user can encourage or instruct the whiz-bang utility to use the better tables. Perhaps the end users are *incommunicado*; they are on the Internet and you don't even know who they are.

Many SQL tuners shrug and say, "That's not my problem." Well, if you implement a fix and nobody uses it, is it a fix? Think of the classic question, "If a tree falls in the forest and nobody hears it, does it make a sound?" The answer to both is the same: Who cares?

A tuner's job is not complete until the fix is being used. The *query rewrite* feature is important to ensuring that this happens.

Materialized views and the specifics of automatic *fast refresh* and *query rewrite* are discussed in detail in Chapter 7, "Post-Load Processing in the Data Warehouse."

Usage Tracking

We discussed this in Chapter 8, on administering the data warehouse.

You have to know what kinds of SQL statements are being issued against the warehouse, by whom, and what effect they are having. Even if you designed the perfect data model for your data warehouse, which accurately anticipates and optimizes all types of reports that are envisioned, someone is going to come up with something new. That's actually one of the signs of success of a warehouse. Besides fulfilling its original objectives, new objectives evolve. A successful data warehouse is constantly evolving.

This evolution is not always centralized. You cannot leave the responsibility for managing the changes simply to a data modeler, charging him with the responsibility of keeping track with what all of the end users are currently doing and what they will be needing. You need to have the ability to monitor and analyze usage patterns in the data warehouse. Many data warehouses run into growing pains after their successful initial implementation because the patterns of usage change significantly, causing severe performance problems and out-of-control growth in storage. This usually leads to a special task involving a senior person or many people to find out what is going on, what is causing these unexpected stresses.

Because a data warehouse is subject to decentralized *ad hoc* use, it is generally not feasible to implement traditional *change control* methods. Familiar IT processes and methodologies such as *release management* and *source code version control* cannot exist in a decentralized *ad hoc* environment. Therefore, the documentation inherent to change control cannot be used to determine usage patterns in the data warehouse.

Monitoring and analysis of SQL usage in the data warehouse is called *usage tracking*. It is a *reactive* form of management, rather than a *proactive* one. As usage patterns change, a usage tracking utility will begin to detect excessive resource consumption. Usage tracking systems can also detect data that is never utilized at all or rarely. They can detect *dormant data*, which could be either archived or simply removed.

There are several usage tracking products on the market, most notably "Usage Tracker" by Pine Cone Systems, founded by data warehouse pioneer Bill Inmon. There are also data query and analysis utilities that include the ability to monitor and analyze SQL statements issued by those utilities, such as Oracle's *Discoverer* product. If neither of these options are suitable for you, some of the functions of usage tracking can be fulfilled by *polling* the internal Oracle V$SESSION and V$SQLAREA views and saving the polled information for later analysis. One of the authors, Tim Gorman, has such a utility (named the USAGE package) available on the Internet at www.evdbt.com/. The file "usage.zip" is located at the link to a free, shareware site of downloadable scripts.

However you choose to monitor and analyze usage patterns in your data warehouse, be sure that you do it. It should be part of the infrastructure of your database, not a periodic task performed by valuable senior people only after the situation becomes intolerable.

If you can comfortably claim omniscience of all that is running in your data warehouse, then you will be able to confidently control the evolution of your data warehouse as the end users, not the IT department nor the data modelers, steer it toward its destiny.

Optimizing the Load Phase

Here are some main issues concerning loading into the data warehouse:

- Use SQL*Loader direct path for large loads.
- Use SQL*Loader direct path parallel for very large loads.

- FOREIGN KEY constraints are unnecessary in the data warehouse.

- On UNIX, use *named pipes* to load data directly from another system without *staging* data on disk.

- Range partitioning can facilitate *publishing* of new data.

- Range partitioning can also facilitate *archiving* or *purging* old data.

SQL*Loader Direct Path versus "Conventional SQL"

Many people have a misconception that anything written in C or C++ has got to be faster than any other method. This may sometimes be true, but historically it has been distinctly untrue when loading data into Oracle.

Up until Oracle8*i*, both of the two *application programming interfaces* or APIs used for accessing Oracle databases from languages such as C, COBOL, or C++ were able to use only *conventional* INSERT statements, instead of the *direct-path* data loading operations. The only utility that could use the much faster *direct-path* mechanism was SQL*Loader. No matter how able the programmer, it is simply not possible for *conventional* INSERT operations to outperform *direct-path* load operations. As a result, until Oracle8*i*, nothing could load data into Oracle as rapidly as SQL*Loader.

But, at last, an API for direct path has been added to OCI with Oracle8*i*. Now, finally, programmers can use languages like C, C++, or COBOL to load data into Oracle using *direct-path* operations. Why is direct path so important?

In brief, as we explained in Chapter 6, "Populating the Oracle Data Warehouse," conventional-path SQL*Loader (see Figure 9.13) really operates against cached database blocks in the SGA buffer cache. At the time of the changes, the log writer process (LGWR) logs the changes. At a later time, the database writer (DBWR) process writes the changes in the buffer cache to the datafiles.

All in all, this buffering mechanism works very well for large numbers of processes simultaneously accessing and modifying the same database blocks. But this mechanism actually becomes a hindrance when one process simply wants to shovel data into a table. In this case, the need to manipulate buffers in a memory cache, about which all changes have to be logged and then flushed to disk by another process, can seriously stress the locks and latches designed to keep everything running smoothly. This buffered mechanism is designed for lots of different activities, not for a long-running, intensive activity like a bulk load. For a bulk load, all the locking, logging, and flushing becomes a bottleneck.

In response to this, Oracle introduced *direct-path* loads. In short, using the direct-path mechanism means that an SQL*Loader process bypasses the buffer cache and the rollback mechanisms, largely bypasses the redo log mechanism, and writes directly to the data file (see Figure 9.14). In one sense, the direct-

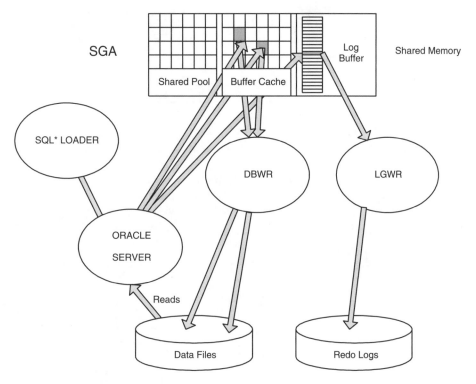

Figure 9.13   Conventional SQL.

path mechanism is very *sociopathic*, as it does not adhere to the general rules for cooperation and largely operates by itself.

The direct-path mechanism reserves space outside the area currently utilized by the rest of the Oracle processes. In that area outside the bounds, the direct path does its work, populating database blocks and writing them directly to disk. When a direct-path operation is complete, it notifies the rest of the Oracle instance and performs the necessary space management manipulation to add the formerly out-of-bounds area to the existing table data.

In fact, because it does almost pure I/O, SQL*Loader direct path is a very good testing mechanism for your I/O subsystem. It tends to read from the input data file very quickly, and when it's not reading it is writing Oracle database blocks directly onto the Oracle data files. Unless there is some kind of translation involved (like parsing variable-length, delimited input records or converting EBCDIC character sets to ASCII), SQL*Loader direct path spends all of its time reading or writing.

The direct-path mechanism was first introduced in Oracle7, version 7.0, in SQL*Loader only. Later, in version 7.1, it was expanded to include an UNRE-COVERABLE option, whereby logging to the redo logs can largely be disabled.

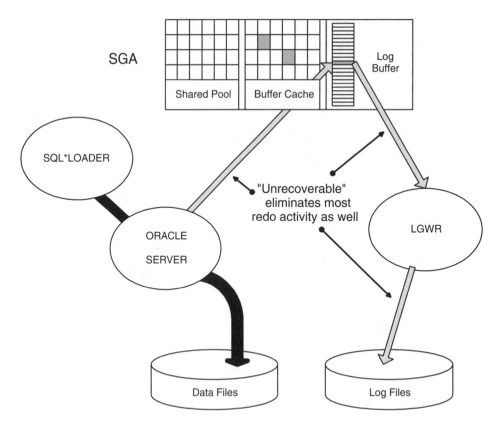

SGA

Shared Pool | Buffer Cache

Log Buffer

SQL*LOADER

ORACLE

SERVER

"Unrecoverable" eliminates most redo activity as well

LGWR

Data Files

Log Files

Figure 9.14 Direct-path mechanism.

Disabling redo logging is not necessarily a performance boost in and of itself. Only if the system on which the database is running is near capacity in terms of I/O throughput or CPU utilization will the lack of redo logging be immediately useful. But the other primary benefit of selectively disabling redo logging is to reduce the amount of redo being generated, archived, and backed up.

Using the UNRECOVERABLE option will certainly reduce demands on CPU utilization and I/O throughput; whether this translates into a performance benefit depends on if these subsystems are near capacity.

Of course, disabling redo logging has ramifications for the recoverability of the table. A table loaded with SQL*Loader direct-path UNRECOVERABLE can be restored only from a backup; it cannot be recovered by the roll-forward of redo logs. Therefore, unless you are prepared to reload a table (which is actually a common strategy—see Chapter 8), you should perform a backup after loading a table UNRECOVERABLE.

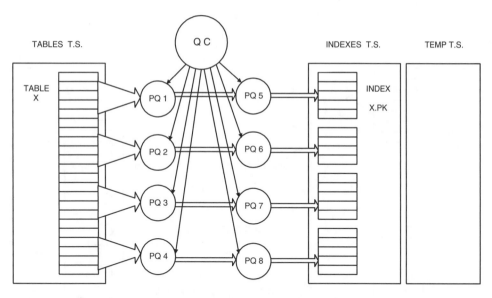

Figure 9.15 Parallel CREATE INDEX.

Oracle7, version 7.1, also saw the introduction of the Parallel Query Option (PQO), which included another use of the direct-path mechanism in the parallel CREATE INDEX (pCI) command (see Figure 9.15). Parallel CREATE INDEX also has an UNRECOVERABLE option.

Oracle7, version 7.2, saw the introduction of the parallel CREATE TABLE . . . AS SELECT (pCTAS), which also uses the direct-path mechanism and has an UNRECOVERABLE option as well (see Figure 9.16).

To load tables from a "flat file" fast, resist the temptation to assume that it is necessary to write a "screamingly fast" program in C or C++. Instead, try to use SQL*Loader with direct path. SQL*Loader has a dazzling array of capabilities, so please don't assume what it can and cannot do. Read the *Oracle8i Server Utilities* reference manual for complete descriptions of the types of loads SQL*Loader can do. Also, note that sample SQL*Loader control files (i.e., ".ctl" files) are available in soft copy in your Oracle installation. On UNIX systems, these files are located in the "$ORACLE_HOME/rdbms/demo" directory.

Direct-Path Loads without SQL*Loader

Suppose SQL*Loader is actually incapable of handling the data from your data sources for some reason, so you absolutely must resort to the use of a 3GL programming language.

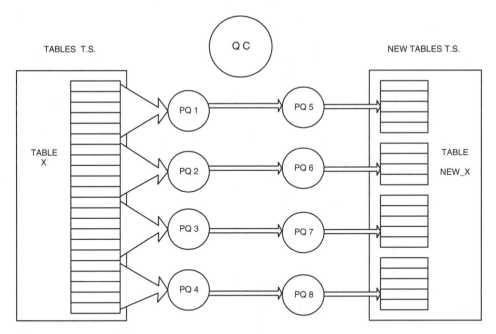

Figure 9.16 Parallel CREATE TABLE . . . AS SELECT.

There are two ways of dealing with this situation while still using the direct-path loading mechanism.

The older way of doing this, and still by far the simplest, is to write a *data preprocessor* utility in some other programming language, such as Perl, shell script, C, C++, or COBOL. The input to this preprocessor program would be the data whose format SQL*Loader cannot handle. The output from this preprocessor program would be data in a format that SQL*Loader *can* handle.

If you are on a UNIX system, the linkage between the preprocessor program and SQL*Loader does not need to be a file in the file-system. Instead, you can actually *pipe* data from one to the other using UNIX *named pipes*, a technique described later in this chapter.

The big advantages of using a preprocessing program in conjunction with SQL*Loader for its direct-path capabilities are *simplicity* and *segregation* of file-handling and Oracle data loading. Most 3GL programming languages have simple file handling features and all 3GL programmers are intimately familiar with them. Using either the PRO*Precompilers or the Oracle Call Interface (OCI) is a specialized expertise, and not many 3GL programmers are expert with these. Therefore, it may be far more efficient to simply direct the 3GL programmers to build a 3GL preprocessing program that does only file manipulation and does not include anything to do with Oracle. Even if the 3GL programmers are comfortable with Oracle PRO*Precompilers or OCI, it is a more modular programming design to separate file processing from data loading into Oracle. SQL*Loader does one thing and does it very well: It inserts rows into Oracle. Why not make use of this?

There are occasions, though, when this modular preprocessor-into-SQL*Loader approach is not suitable. For these situations, the Oracle Call Interface for Oracle8i has a new set of direct-path API functions, so that you can utilize the direct-path mechanism directly through OCI.

If you can't use SQL*Loader by itself, then consider using a preprocessor program or utility in conjunction with SQL*Loader. If that will not work, then you can write a 3GL program using the new direct-path API in OCI.

Parallel Loads

After SQL*Loader direct path was introduced in version 7.0, it became clear that even the direct-path mechanism was not fast enough. For one thing, on most multiprocessor platforms, a single SQL*Loader direct-path process would probably utilize only one CPU at a time. This can be unsatisfactory if you have 12 CPUs and most of them are sitting idle. Because the direct-path mechanism operated *outside the bounds* in terms of Oracle storage, the initial release of the direct-path mechanism did not allow more than one SQL*Loader process to operate on the same table at a time.

But, starting with the introduction of the Parallel Query Option (PQO) in version 7.1, it became possible to run more than one SQL*Loader direct-path process against the same table (see Figure 9.17). To enable this, set both the DIRECT= and the PARALLEL= parameters to TRUE either on the SQL*Loader command line or in the SQL*Loader control file. Running more than one SQL*Loader process to load into the same table implies that each process has its own input data file.

It is possible to "partition" an input data file into segments for multiple loader processes, using the SKIP= and LOAD= parameters, either on the SQL*Loader command line or in the SQL*Loader control file (see Figure 9.18).

Be aware that SQL*Loader direct-path processes can be so efficient at loading that they can cause a bottleneck on the input data file because the disk drive(s) on which they are located suddenly find not one but several processes intensively issuing read requests. The SKIP= parameter in SQL*Loader does not actually "skip over" or forego actually reading the records to be skipped; it just fails to load from them. When using the SKIP= parameter, SQL*Loader will actually read the skipped records but not load them.

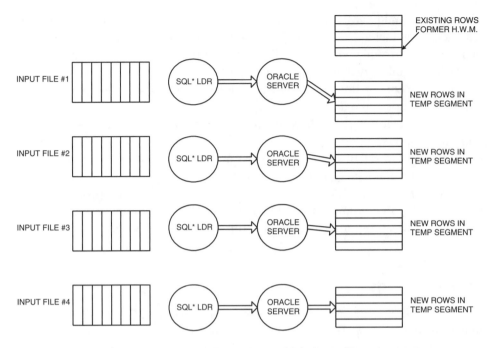

Figure 9.17 Multiple direct-path loaders using multiple input files.

Drop and Re-Create Indexes for Large-Volume Loads

Whether using conventional-path INSERT statements or direct-path loads for large-volume loads, the load will simply go faster if there are no indexes on the table during the load.

Dropping the indexes and re-creating them after the load is complete can boost load performance many times. Using parallel CREATE INDEX, the index could be rebuilt much faster than if it were maintained during the load. Also, the resulting index would be more compact than an index that has been inserted into, as each database block making up the index would be filled up to the point of PCTFREE—as opposed to being half full, as would inevitably be the case from index block splitting due to INSERTs.

The downside of dropping and re-creating indexes is, of course, that the table being loaded is unusable while it is being loaded. If this is not possible because of business requirements, consider using partitioned tables (Oracle8) or leaving the indexes in place and taking the performance hit.

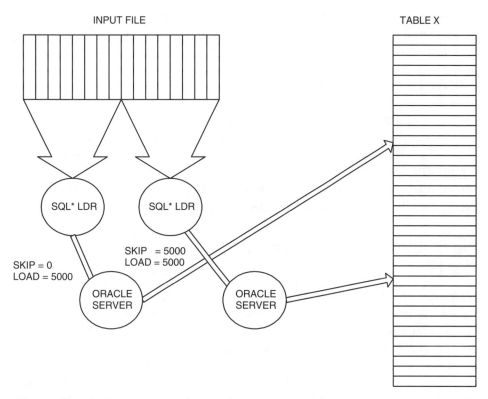

Figure 9.18 Partitioning an input file using SKIP= and LOAD=.

Constraints in the Data Warehouse

Many people new to data warehousing come from the world of "operational" systems. Inevitably, people who are used to creating data models for "operational" systems consider the use of integrity constraints such as PRIMARY KEY, UNIQUE KEY, and FOREIGN KEY to be mandatory for all relational databases.

This is not true, though, for data warehouses.

Think about it. A data warehouse should not need referential integrity constraints. The operational system from which the data is loaded needs referential integrity. This is to ensure that declared relationships between PRIMARY KEYs and FOREIGN KEYs are valid because a FOREIGN KEY in a "child" entity demands the existence of a PRIMARY KEY in a "parent" entity. Orphaned "child" records violate the relational model.

Data warehouses are not tasked with maintaining referential integrity. They exist to provide a reporting base for the data as it exists. If there is a referential integrity error on the source operational system, then this same error should be propagated to the data warehouse. This occurs because the operational system is *the source of record*, whether that data is *right* or *wrong*. If it is inappropriate for incorrect data to be in the data warehouse, then the correction should be made in the operational system, not in the data warehouse.

Of course, data cleansing routines and processes can be used to correct these errors in the data warehouse if desired, but referential integrity constraints are not a cost-effective mechanism to use in cleansing large amounts of data.

Data warehouses implemented in Oracle should use indexes to facilitate access. These indexes could be NONUNIQUE or UNIQUE, depending on which is more efficient at accessing the data. PRIMARY KEY and UNIQUE constraints should not arbitrarily be used to enforce entity integrity in a data warehouse because the terms are quite meaningless in this environment.

Pipelining Instead of "Staging" Flat Files

Frequently, the "flat files" used to load data into the data warehouse come from a remote system. Although it may be possible to run SQL*Loader from that remote system and use SQL*Net to connect into the data warehouse, this may not be optimal in terms of performance. Certainly, this is the simplest solution, if it is available. But SQL*Net's performance characteristics when performing a bulk operation over a network are quite well known; it's really not optimized for bulk operations. And it may not be possible to run SQL*Loader on the remote system.

Whatever the case, it is quite common to use *ftp* or some other similar file transfer utility to copy the "flat file" from the remote system to the local system, staging it locally, so that SQL*Loader can load the data into the Oracle database (see Figure 9.19). The problem here is *latency*. The file transfer has to finish before SQL*Loader starts to be sure that all the records to be transferred are actually loaded. If SQL*Loader "catches up" to the file transfer process and encounters a premature END-OF-FILE, then it will stop loading.

On UNIX systems, there is a mechanism available to eliminate this delay in starting SQL*Loader (see Figure 9.20). UNIX *named pipes* are actually one of the oldest interprocess communication (IPC) mechanisms still in use. Also called FIFOs (for *First In, First Out*), they appear in the UNIX file system much like a regular file. They do not, however, occupy any actual space. They are essentially a memory buffer of fixed size. Although the details vary from one UNIX implementation to another, they essentially operate as a *circular memory buffer*. All writes to a pipe are blocked until a process opens the pipe for reading. Once a pipe is opened for reading, the pipe's memory buffer can be filled. Once the memory buffer fills, any further writes are blocked until the reading process issues read requests. All data written into a FIFO is guaranteed to be read in the same order.

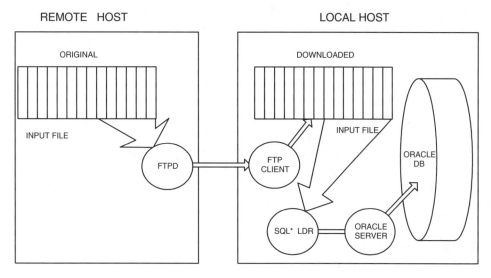

Figure 9.19 Staging a file transfer.

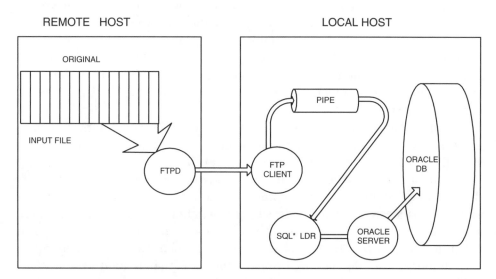

Figure 9.20 SQL*Loader reading from pipes.

Conversely, a process that tries to read from a FIFO or pipe will block until another process writes data into it. Once enough data has been written to satisfy the pending read request, the read will complete. Using this mechanism, the delay while waiting for the file transfer to complete can be eliminated.

First, create the named pipe. Then start the SQL*Loader process, indicating the UNIX named pipe as the input data file. Once the SQL*Loader process is running, it will "hang" immediately as its read request from the pipe is blocked. Then, start the file transfer, directing the file-transfer program to write the remote data into the same UNIX named pipe from which the SQL*Loader process is reading.

Data will be loaded into Oracle as soon as it arrives on the local system. Also, it is not necessary to provide massive amounts of "staging" space for huge file transfers, as the data going through the UNIX named pipe never actually "lands" anywhere but inside Oracle. Therefore, this method might be the only alternative in the event the input data file is too large to fit into a UNIX file or is too big to fit anywhere given the existing disk capacity.

Range Partitioning to *publish* New Data

Historically, using the direct-path mechanism has meant that the table being loaded into is essentially unavailable for query. Although the existing data in the table can still be queried while the direct-path load is occurring, the indexes on the table need to be disabled or dropped while the load is active. Thus, if indexing is important to data access, the table is unavailable.

In Oracle7, this was a limitation that generally meant that using direct path was not possible. If there was no period of *downtime* in which to perform the loads, then using the much slower *conventional-path* mechanisms was an unavoidable evil.

Starting with Oracle8, range partitioning for tables and their associated indexes and the wonderful partition management features of the ALTER TABLE command provide a perfect solution for this.

New data can be loaded into a standalone, nonpartitioned table that has the same logical structure (i.e., column definitions) as the main partitioned table. The data can be loaded in direct path, in parallel, without indexes. Then, when they are needed, the indexes can be created on the standalone table, provided that they match the logical structure (i.e., columns and uniqueness) of LOCAL indexes on the main partitioned table. It is then a good idea to ANALYZE the standalone table and its indexes. If you are using histograms, then analyze those columns as well, as long as those histograms are also used in the main partitioned table.

Finally, when the data in the standalone table is loaded, indexed, and analyzed, it can be *merged* into the main partitioned table as a new partition. The ALTER TABLE . . . EXCHANGE PARTITION command needs to make changes only to the Oracle data dictionary tables. No movement of data, extents, or segments take place during an EXCHANGE operation.

If there are any GLOBAL indexes on the main partitioned table, then these might need to be rebuilt after the new partition is added. If this is necessary, then be sure to remember to ANALYZE INDEX after this is complete!

Thus, during the load cycle, data can be staged in standalone tables that are unavailable to end users. When everything is loaded, indexed, and analyzed, it can then be *published* to end users with a simple DDL operation.

Thus, an important design consideration for frequently loaded tables in the data warehouse is to range partition them according to the frequency of loading. If the tables are loaded daily, then partition them by day.

Range Partitioning to *archive* or *purge* Old Data

Similar to loading and publishing, many tables must have older data purged. This combination of loading new data and purging old data is called a *rolling window*.

Before Oracle8, purging was typically handled with a large DELETE statement. Besides taking a long time to execute, sometimes *prohibitively* long, a mass deletion like this would have a ruinous effect on query performance. This is because of the large *gaps* of empty space opened in both the table and in the index.

If the table was being loaded using conventional-path operations, such as the SQL INSERT command, then those large empty gaps of deleted data in the table would eventually be reused and filled in. Thus, the bad effects of full-table scanning reading empty blocks of table data would eventually resolve themselves.

But if the table was being loaded using direct-path mechanisms, then those large empty gaps of deleted data would *never* be reused. This is because the direct-path mechanism, in order to optimize performance, does not even consider reusing space; it always adds more rows above the currently existing data.

Moreover and even more seriously, the effect on indexes of mass deletions for rolling window purges is disastrous regardless of whether the table is loaded using conventional path or direct path. Oracle B*Tree indexes never shrink. As table rows are deleted, their corresponding index entries are simply marked as empty and reusable, if another row with the same key data is inserted. When purging old data, it is likely that another row with the same data might *never* be inserted. So, the effect of mass deletions on indexes is that they grow more and more inefficient for indexed range-scan operations, and the number of B*Tree levels in the index continues to increase even if the number of table rows stays static.

Essentially, the only remedy for this situation is to rebuild the index. Before Oracle7.3, when the ALTER INDEX REBUILD command was introduced, this meant dropping the existing index and re-creating it with CREATE INDEX.

Although a CREATE INDEX . . . PARALLEL . . . UNRECOVERABLE command has existed since Oracle7.1, this might still take a long time. Even with the ALTER INDEX . . . REBUILD PARALLEL . . . UNRECOVERABLE command introduced in Oracle7.3, it still means that the index (and perhaps the table) is unavailable for a period of time.

All of these considerations tended to add to people's natural reluctance to purge data. Factor in the prevailing conventional wisdom that *disk is cheap*, and the ever-growing data warehouse would begin to enter a cancerous death spiral.

Range partitioning ends all that. If your purging requirements match your loading requirements, then you can accomplish purging without any downtime whatsoever using the simple ALTER TABLE . . . DROP PARTITION command.

If your purging strategy meant some form of archival, then you could facilitate this by simply exchanging the partitions to be purged into separate, standalone tables using the ALTER TABLE . . . EXCHANGE PARTITION command. Once the data is stored separately in a standalone table, it is effectively deleted from the end–users' point of view. You can then export the data to its archive format as you wish and later simply drop the now-useless table.

Tuning the SQL

The tuning of SQL statements is as much an art as a science; at least that is what people would have you believe. Frankly, people who give that impression likely are not sure enough of what they are doing to explain what they are doing. The author Arthur C. Clarke is credited with explaining that "any sufficiently advanced technology is indistinguishable from magic." That beautiful little aphorism can be slightly modified to fit the subject at hand: "Any sufficiently arcane technology can be confused with magic."

In reality, the key is to use the right tools; then tuning SQL statements becomes as easy as determining the lesser or greater of two numbers. Couple that with a spirit of experimentation and some background knowledge of access methods in Oracle, and anyone can become a guru overnight.

The right tools are EXPLAIN PLAN, SQL tracing, and the TKPROF utility. SQL tracing gathers important statistics about a SQL statement while it is running, and TKPROF summarizes those statistics into a formatted report, supplementing the information with EXPLAIN PLAN information as well. These tools are among the oldest in the Oracle product set, having existed with little modification for over a decade. One would think that any tool so venerable would have been well documented. One would be wrong.

Historically, far too many Oracle developers and DBAs have been blissfully ignorant of the power of SQL tracing and TKPROF. Lack of documentation in earlier releases, combined with a lack of coverage in training classes, has stratified the community of would-be Oracle tuners. Those who have stumbled across SQL tracing and TKPROF and have actually learned to use it effectively are the "haves," the keepers of the keys. Those who have not yet discovered these tools remain the "have-nots," doomed to perpetually attend seminars and buy books on how to write SQL (not that buying books is a bad thing!) without ever becoming effective at Oracle tuning.

Documentation for using and interpreting these tools has been sparse and spare. Doubtless, there are those who will find this chapter wanting as well. At the moment, the Oracle *Server Tuning Guide* (for both versions 7.3 and Oracle8) is quite good on this subject, the best yet. Recent publications from Oracle Press and O'Reilly and Associates provide more information on using SQL tracing and TKPROF.

Understanding SQL Tracing

The idea behind SQL tracing is very simple. It started as a debugging tool for development, much as any large-scale system would have a debugging tool for tracing. When SQL tracing is enabled, the background Oracle server process opens an output file stream on the server (see Figure 9.21).

If you were writing a complex program using C or some other third-generation programming language, this is pretty much how you would handle debugging, both during the development phase and later on in production. By default, no such tracing output would be produced, but using one or more methods of signaling, the debugging output can be turned on or off.

In Oracle, there are five ways to enable or disable SQL tracing. But first, we briefly discuss relevant initialization parameters that may need to be set or reviewed.

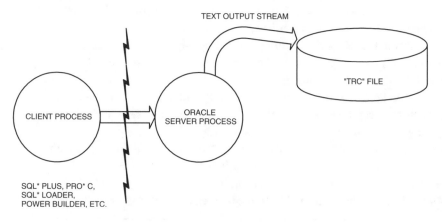

Figure 9.21 SQL tracing output stream on the server.

Relevant Initialization Parameters

The following initialization parameters affect the SQL trace facility:

USER_DUMP_DEST. This refers to a directory on the server where the instance is located that will hold all SQL trace files generated by that database instance. Valid values are dependent on the operating system; check your *Oracle Server Installation and Configuration Guide* for details.

TIMED_STATISTICS. This Boolean parameter defaults to FALSE. If set to TRUE, then the database instance will capture CPU and elapsed time statistics for every operation performed by the instance. Naturally, this adds some processing overhead to everything the database instance does, but it is certainly worthwhile in a development environment and even in some low-intensity production environments.

MAX_DUMP_FILE_SIZE. This is the maximum number of operating system blocks (check the *Oracle Server Installation and Configuration Guide* again) to which an SQL trace file can grow. The default is usually 500. Setting this parameter low helps keep SQL trace files from filling the file system too quickly. Leaving this value too low may cause valuable SQL tracing information to be lost due to file truncation.

ALWAYS SET TIMED_STATISTICS TO TRUE

Many people leave the configuration parameter TIMED_STATISTICS at its default value of FALSE, either because they are unaware of it or because they are trying to reduce processing overhead in an attempt to optimize performance. Setting the parameter to TRUE causes the RDBMS engine to make calls to the operating-system for the current system time frequently, in order to *time-stamp* operations within the database. The reasoning is that this puts additional processing overhead on all operations.

The reality is that the information gathered by having TIMED_STATISTICS enabled would save far more processing cycles than are ever expended. Setting TIMED_STATISTICS to TRUE populates data values in the V$SYSTEM_EVENT, V$SESSION_EVENT, V$WAITSTAT, and V$SESSION_WAIT views, to name a few. Without this timing information in these views, it becomes very difficult to detect any contention in the database efficiently.

Likewise, having TIMED_STATISTICS set to TRUE causes SQL tracing to gather important *elapsed time* and *CPU time* information, which can add valuable insight when reading the *raw* ".trc" trace files or when reading a TKPROF report.

Whatever processing overhead is added by TIMED_STATISTICS is well worth it.

Setting the Current Session
Using ALTER SESSION

The first means of invoking SQL tracing is the most well known, the ALTER SESSION command. As this SQL command implies, it will change a characteristic of the current session for the duration of the session or until it is countermanded. Thus, once a connection to an Oracle instance has been established, any front-end utility such as SQL*Plus, PRO*Precompilers, Oracle Forms, PowerBuilder, Microsoft Access, or Business Objects can issue the following:

```
ALTER SESSION SET SQL_TRACE = TRUE
```

Or:

```
ALTER SESSION SET SQL_TRACE TRUE
```

Although this command can be issued any time during a session, it is best to make this the first SQL statement issued after establishing the connection to an Oracle instance. For example, in PRO*C it would be as follows:

```
/*
 * . . .set up error handling in case any EXEC SQL statements return an
error. . .
 */
WHENEVER SQLERROR DO err_exit();

/*
 * . . .connect to the Oracle instance using the username, password, and
 * possibly the SQL*Net connect-string stored in the host "bind"
 * variable "username_password". . .
 */
EXEC SQL CONNECT USING :username_password;

/*
 * . . .if a UNIX environment variable named "SQL_TRACE" is set to TRUE,
 * then use ALTER SESSION to turn on SQL tracing. . .
 */
if ((p_env = getenv("SQL_TRACE")) != (char *) 0)
{
     if (strcmp(p_env, "TRUE") == 0)
     {
         EXEC SQL ALTER SESSION SET SQL_TRACE TRUE;
     }
}
```

Of course, you are going to need the ALTER SESSION system privilege granted to your Oracle account.

Setting the Current Session Using DBMS_SESSION

Another way to enable SQL tracing is by using the DBMS_SESSION package in PL/SQL. If you are programming in PL/SQL, you can still execute an ALTER SESSION command, but you would have to use the DBMS_SQL package or the new EXECUTE IMMEDIATE command for dynamic SQL, which requires many separate steps. A shorter, more intuitive method might be to use the SET_SQL_TRACE procedure as follows:

```
DBMS_SESSION.SET_SQL_TRACE(true);
```

This is exactly equivalent to the ALTER SESSION command. Of course, using FALSE instead of TRUE, just as in the ALTER SESSION command, will disable SQL trace if it is running. Make sure that your Oracle account (or PUBLIC) has been granted EXECUTE on the package DBMS_SESSION. Now you have two choices in enabling or disabling SQL tracing: using the ALTER SESSION statement or using the PL/SQL packaged procedure DBMS_SESSION.SET_SQL_TRACE.

Setting Another Session Using DBMS_SYSTEM

In addition to setting SQL tracing in your own session, you may want to set it in another session running against Oracle. This is useful for tracing a session that is running from a program that cannot turn SQL trace on by itself. For example, most client/server applications that connect into Oracle databases were not written to enable SQL tracing using either the ALTER SESSION command or the DBMS_SESSION package. Therefore, there might be no way to tune SQL statements being generated from this tool unless the application is rewritten. This, of course, almost never happens!

Never fear! You can log onto Oracle in another session and enable SQL trace from the first session. First you must obtain some unique information about the session to be traced. To get this information, query the V$SESSION view:

```
SELECT username, osuser, machine, process, sid, serial#
  FROM v$session
 WHERE . . .
```

In the WHERE clause of this query, use whatever information is available to you about the session to be traced. If you know the Oracle account to which they have connected, use WHERE USERNAME = '<username>'. If you know what machine or host name from which they are connecting into Oracle, use WHERE MACHINE = '<hostname>'. Or, if worse comes to worst, dump the whole V$SESSION view and try to browse the results.

```
SQL> SELECT username, osuser, machine, process, sid, serial#
```

```
  2    FROM v$session
  3*  WHERE TYPE = 'USER'
SQL> /

USERNAME    OSUSER     MACHINE        PROCESS          SID   SERIAL#
----------- ---------- -------------- ---------------- ----- -------
TED         ted        fester         9845             8     101
SYSTEM                                                 9     43
```

It helps to have a quiet system if you're going to browse the whole thing! Because I know that I'm logged in as SYSTEM, my only other possibility must be user TED.

What you need from V$SESSION are the primary key values of that view, namely SID (a.k.a. session ID) and SERIAL#. These values can then be used in the SET_SQL_TRACE_IN_SESSION procedure in the DBMS_SYSTEM to enable (or disable) SQL tracing in the other session, as follows:

```
SQL> EXECUTE DBMS_SYSTEM.SET_SQL_TRACE_IN_SESSION(8, 101, TRUE);

PL/SQL procedure successfully completed.
```

Again, you will need to have EXECUTE permission for the DBMS_SYSTEM package granted to your Oracle account. Usually, permissions on the DBMS_SYSTEM package are reserved for DBAs only, as there are other powerful procedures available in the package more appropriate for DBAs. You can use the time-honored technique of encapsulating this procedure call inside a custom-built stored procedure and then granting EXECUTE permission on that encapsulating procedure to end-users.

Setting Another Session Using Server Manager

Another method for setting SQL tracing in another session, which is functionally equivalent to using DBMS_SESSION, is using the ORADEBUG facility in SQL*Plus or Server Manager. To do this, enter Server Manager; on UNIX, use the line-mode Server Manager as follows:

```
$ svrmgrl
```

or:

```
$ sqlplus internal
```

On Windows NT with Oracle8*i*, use:

```
C:\> set oracle_sid=oracle-sid-value
C:\> svrmgrl
```

On older versions of Oracle on Windows NT, many Oracle commands include the version number:

```
C:\> set oracle_sid=oracle-sid-value
C:\> svrmgr30
```

Once you've logged on as SYSDBA, you can use the ORADEBUG commands:

```
SVRMGR> oradebug setospid <nnnnn>
Statement processed.
SVRMGR> oradebug event 10046 trace name context forever, level 1
Statement processed.
SVRMGR> oradebug unlimit
Statement processed
```

What these three commands have done is the following:

- "Attached" the current Server Manager session to the process indicated by the operating system PID "nnnnn;" this is the same operating system PID (in decimal format) that we discussed earlier in the chapter.

- Enabled Oracle event 10046 (i.e., SQL tracing) at level "1" (the default level). There are three more levels: 4 (same as level 1 but also dumps the values of *bind variables*), 8 (same as level 1 but also dumps *wait-event* information), and 12 (the combination of levels 1, 4, and 8). All the extra levels of SQL tracing are explained in more detail later in this chapter.

- Disabled the MAX_DUMP_FILE_SIZE initialization parameter so the resulting SQL trace file can grow to an unlimited size if necessary.

It is almost an application of Murphy's Law that the most interesting things that happen while you are tracing a session occur after you have exceeded the MAX_DUMP_FILE_SIZE limit imposed for all SQL trace files generated by the Oracle instance. To prevent this from happening on a very selective basis, enabling SQL tracing from Server Manager gives you the ability to override this limit just for the single session indicated.

WARNING Be aware that the Server Manager ORADEBUG facility is originally intended for debugging. Please do not experiment with it. The purpose of ORADEBUG is to give Oracle Worldwide Support the ability to debug the RDBMS in a wide variety of situations. While it will become obvious that ORADEBUG is capable of a great deal more than setting higher values of SQL Trace, playing with it would be extremely foolish.

Now, we've given you the command to initiate this higher level of SQL tracing, and we've also shown you how to circumvent the safeguards that prevent enormous trace files from being generated. It would irresponsible if we didn't also show you how to turn this enhanced level of SQL tracing off!

Like the default level of SQL tracing, this higher level of tracing stops automatically when the session disconnects from the database. If you want tracing to stop before the end of the session, you can issue the following commands in Server Manager:

```
SVRMGR> connect internal
SVRMGR> oradebug setospid <nnnnn>
Statement processed.
SVRMGR> oradebug event 10046 trace name context off
Statement processed.
```

For long-running batch jobs, it's a good idea to do this when you feel you've gathered enough information. After all, it does no good to fill the filesystem and cause system-wide problems while you're trying to resolve another problem!

Setting SQL_TRACE for the Entire Instance

Last but not least, you can set SQL tracing to TRUE for all the processes in the entire database instance. More often than not, this will generate too many trace files to be examined and therefore is generally overkill. Also, the extra processing overhead incurred by having every single Oracle background process (i.e., PMON, SMON, etc.) as well as every single Oracle server process producing SQL trace output can bring a system to its knees. Also, the number of files can easily run a file system out of space if the system administrators are not prepared. Needless to say, you should be very careful whenever using this option.

This technique, however, has its uses. There can be times when a system is so busy that you may want to "snapshot" it. If you have the freedom to take the database up and down, you can set the initialization parameter SQL_TRACE= TRUE for a short time (i.e., one hour, four hours, eight hours, etc.), then take the database down and set SQL_TRACE back to FALSE. What you will have gathered during the time when SQL_TRACE=TRUE is dozens or hundreds of SQL trace files, which you can examine at your leisure.

Now that we have gathered SQL trace information into a file, what have we really got? What does that information look like? And how can we use it?

What Is Inside a SQL Trace File?

Upon completion of the ALTER SESSION command, the Oracle server process will have created or reopened a file somewhere on the machine where the Oracle instance resides. The directory in which this file resides is determined from the initialization parameter USER_DUMP_DEST, which is set by the Oracle DBA. By default, on UNIX this directory is "$ORACLE_HOME/rdbms/log" and on Windows NT it is "%RDBMSnn%\ TRACE" where the "nn" in "RDBMSnn" is either "73" or "80" depending on your version of Oracle. However, best practices (codified by Oracle's Optimal Flexible Architecture) suggest that it be located somewhere else, not under the "ORACLE_HOME" directory structure. For more on OFA, see Chapter 8.

The name of the file can be constructed if you know a few things about your session. Query the V$SESSION and V$PROCESS views in the data dictionary, and you can find out what the operating system process ID (or PID) is. For example, run the following:

```
SQL> SELECT spid FROM v$process WHERE addr =
  2  (SELECT paddr FROM v$session WHERE audsid = USERENV('SESSIONID'));

SPID
-------
0010A
```

On Windows NT, the column SPID contains a hexadecimal number that must be converted to decimal; on UNIX, the value will already be in decimal representation. Given this value, the name of the SQL trace file can be pasted together as follows:

```
USER_DUMP_DEST || fixed-string || to_char(SPID,'00000') || '.trc'
```

where the following hold:

- *USER_DUMP_DEST* is the directory name specified in the initialization parameter of the same name.

- *fixed-string* is dependent on the operating system. On some UNIX platforms, this string is "ora_" or "$ORACLE_SID_ora_" or "ora_$ORACLE_SID_". On NT, it is simply "ora."

- *to_char (SPID, '00000')* is the operating system PID (in decimal format) zero-padded to five places.

- '*.trc*' is just a file extension.

After running the ALTER SESSION statement, go to the USER_DUMP_DEST directory and look for this file. It is simply a text file, so feel free to view it, but be aware that on some operating systems the file may be locked for use by the process writing to it, or output to it may be buffered and therefore not yet written.

> **TIP** The undocumented initialization parameter _TRACE_FILES_PUBLIC will change the UNIX permissions of the generated trace files so that users other than DBAs may read them. Enabling other developers and users to read trace files is an important step toward empowering them to tune and debug their modules themselves.

What you see when you view the file may not be very helpful for performance tuning, but it ought to give some insight into what is going on "behind the scenes." For example, the following SQL*Plus session was traced using ALTER SESSION:

```
SQL*Plus: Release 8.1.6.0.0 - Beta on Sun Jan 9 18:22:53 2000

Copyright (c) Oracle Corporation 1979, 1994, 2000.  All rights reserved.

Connected to:
Oracle8i JServer Release 8.1.6.0.0 - Production

PL/SQL Release 3.1.6.0.0 - Production

SQL> select spid from v$process where addr =
  2  (select paddr from v$session where audsid = userenv('SESSIONID'));

SPID
-------
13337

SQL> select value from v$parameter where name = 'user_dump_dest';

VALUE
---------------------------------------------------------------
/u01/app/oracle/admin/dev/udump

SQL> alter session set sql_trace true;

Session altered.

SQL> select 'x' from dual;

'
-
x
```

At this point, the resulting trace file at "/u01/app/oracle/admin/dev/udump/
dev_ora_13337.trc" shows the following:

```
Dump file /u01/app/oracle/admin/dev/udump/dev_ora_13337.trc
Sun Jan 09 18:38:58 2000
ORACLE V8.1.6.0.0 - Production vsnsta=1
vsnsql=c vsnxtr=3
Solaris 2.6 SPARC
Oracle8i JServer Release 8.1.6.0.0 - Production
PL/SQL Release 3.1.6.0.0 - Production
Solaris 2.6 SPARC
Instance name: dev

Redo thread mounted by this instance: 1

Oracle process number: 35

pid: 13337

Sun Jan 09 18:38:58 2000
```

```
*** SESSION ID:(9.43) 2000.01.09.18.38.58.687
APPNAME mod='SQL*Plus' mh=3669949024 act='' ah=4029777240
=====================
PARSING IN CURSOR #2 len=33 dep=0 uid=5 oct=42 lid=5 tim=0 hv=1538466435
ad='30ce0c0'
alter session set sql_trace true
END OF STMT
EXEC #2:c=0,e=0,p=0,cr=0,cu=0,mis=1,r=0,dep=0,og=4,tim=0
=====================
PARSING IN CURSOR #2 len=21 dep=0 uid=5 oct=3 lid=5 tim=0 hv=2888538493
ad='30cb850'
select 'x' from dual
END OF STMT
PARSE #2:c=0,e=0,p=0,cr=0,cu=0,mis=1,r=0,dep=0,og=4,tim=0
EXEC #2:c=0,e=0,p=0,cr=0,cu=0,mis=0,r=0,dep=0,og=4,tim=0
FETCH #2:c=0,e=0,p=0,cr=1,cu=2,mis=0,r=1,dep=0,og=4,tim=0
FETCH #2:c=0,e=0,p=0,cr=0,cu=0,mis=0,r=0,dep=0,og=0,tim=0
STAT #0 id=1 cnt=1 pid=0 pos=0 obj=171 op='TABLE ACCESS FULL DUAL '
. . . more . . .
```

At the top of this file we see a banner announcing context: the name of the trace file, the current system date and time, the type and versions of the operating system and the machine it is running on, the Oracle product versions, the Oracle internal process ID and the operating system (Windows NT) process ID, and an acknowledgment that the application (i.e., SQL*Plus) had registered itself using the DBMS_APPLICATION_INFO package.

For each SQL statement, there will be an entry headed "PARSING IN CURSOR #nnn". The cursor number is a numbered entry in the Oracle program global area's (PGA) cursor cache, which is private to each session. The other data in this entry is as follows:

```
len=          the length in bytes (octets) of the SQL statement text
dep=          recursive call depth (0=user SQL, >0=recursive SQL)
uid=          the Oracle user ID (column USER_ID in DBA_USERS)
oct=          the Oracle command type
lid=          the privileged Oracle user ID
tim=          timestamp (hundredths of seconds)
hv=           hash value of SQL statement (column HASH_VALUE in
V$SQLAREA)
ad=           address of SQL statement (column ADDRESS in V$SQLAREA)
SQL           the text of the SQL statement itself
```

The *Oracle command type* is documented in the *Oracle Call Interface User's Guide*.

Also, depending on what kind of SQL statement is being executed there will be entries for the different suboperations of an SQL statement, such as *parse, execute,* and *fetch.* Each of these entries will have the following format:

```
<oper> #nnn        "oper" is either PARSE, EXECUTE, or FETCH
                   "nnn" is the cursor number from the PARSING entry
c=                 CPU time (hundredths of seconds)
e=                 elapsed time (hundredths of seconds)
p=                 number of physical reads
cr=                number of buffers gotten for consistent reads
cu=                number of buffers gotten for current reads
mis=               number of misses in the library cache
r=                 number of rows retrieved
dep=               recursive call depth (0=user SQL, >0=recursive SQL)
og=                Optimizer goal (1=ALL_ROWS,2=FIRST_ROWS,3=RULE,4=CHOOSE)
tim=               timestamp (hundredths of seconds)
```

Additionally, there are entries called STAT with information about the amount of work performed at each level in the SQL access method, also known as the EXPLAIN PLAN:

```
id=                the ID of the step in the EXPLAIN PLAN of the SQL
statement
cnt=               the number of rows visited during this step
pid=               parent ID of this step in the EXPLAIN PLAN
pos=               ordering of all steps with the same ID in EXPLAIN PLAN
obj=               value of column OBJECT_ID in the view DBA_OBJECTS
op=                the actual operation performed at this step
```

Altogether, this information provides a very detailed, if cryptic, look into the inner workings of Oracle.

Familiarity with the format of the SQL trace file is useful for debugging applications. How many times have you wished you could retrieve a log of all the SQL statements executed by a batch program, a form, or a report? As you can see, that is exactly what the "raw" SQL trace file is. It is a sequential record of everything that an Oracle server process does and is therefore a record or a log of everything that comes into the Oracle server process from the front-end program, whether it is a batch program, an OLAP tool, a PowerBuilder form, or an SQR report.

Nobody recommends that you examine a "raw" SQL trace file for SQL tuning purposes. Instead, there is a utility, called TKPROF, that can be used to reformat the "raw" SQL trace information into an actual report, and more.

Formatting a SQL Tuning Report with TKPROF

The TKPROF report format program takes "raw" SQL trace information from an SQL trace file and reformats it into an aggregated report. When used properly, it can sort the SQL statements in the "raw" trace file so the worst SQL statements show up first, making it very easy to identify the problem.

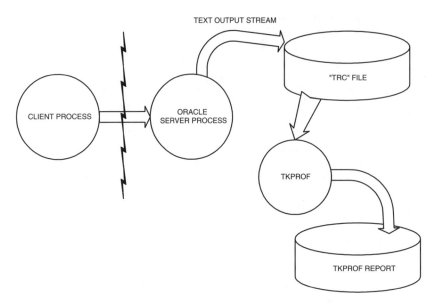

Figure 9.22 The TKPROF utility at work.

The tough part about using TKPROF is that it must be called from the operating system command line, making it rather archaic in terms of user interface! On UNIX, it must be called from the UNIX command line; on Windows NT, it must be called from the Command prompt.

Anyway, the TKPROF utility is quite basic; it takes the "raw" SQL trace file as input and produces a report (see Figure 9.22).

To find out the syntax of TKPROF, just enter the command itself with no parameters on the command line:

```
$ tkprof
Usage: tkprof tracefile outputfile [explain= ] [table= ]
            [print= ] [insert= ] [sys= ] [sort= ]
    table=schema.table    Use 'schema.table' with 'explain=' option.
    explain=user/pswd     Connect to ORACLE and issue EXPLAIN PLAN.
    print=integer         List only the first 'integer' SQL
statements.
    aggregate=yes|no      Default: yes
    insert=filename       Create SQL script of SQL stmts and data.
    sys=no                Do not list SQL statements run as user SYS.
    record=filename       Record non-recursive SQL stmts in trace
file.
    sort=option           Set of the following sort options:
        prscnt        number of times parse was called
        prscpu        cpu time parsing
        prsela        elapsed time parsing
        prsdsk        number of disk reads during parse
```

```
prsqry      number of buffers for consistent read during parse
prscu       number of buffers for current read during parse
prsmis      number of misses in library cache during parse
execnt      number of execute was called
execpu      cpu time spent executing
exeela      elapsed time executing
exedsk      number of disk reads during execute
exeqry      number of buffers for consistent read during
            execute
execu       number of buffers for current read during execute
exerow      number of rows processed during execute
exemis      number of library cache misses during execute
fchcnt      number of times fetch was called
fchcpu      cpu time spent fetching
fchela      elapsed time fetching
fchdsk      number of disk reads during fetch
fchqry      number of buffers for consistent read during fetch
fchcu       number of buffers for current read during fetch
fchrow      number of rows fetched
userid      userid of user that parsed the cursor
```

But what are all these options for? Let's start with the most basic syntax:

```
$ tkprof dev_ora_13337.trc x.tkp
```

In this example here in a Unix environment, TKPROF is reading from the "raw" SQL trace file named *dev_ora_13337.trc* and will write output to another text file named *x.tkp*. In this and all examples, the name given for the output file is completely arbitrary.

This raw SQL trace file was generated by the preceding example, where we pretty much ran a single query, SELECT 'x' FROM DUAL, in SQL*Plus. What resulted in the output file was the following:

```
TKPROF: Release 8.1.6.0.0 - Production on Sun Jan 9 21:59:29 2000
Copyright (c) Oracle Corporation 1979, 1994, 2000.  All rights reserved.
Trace file: dev_ora_13337.trc
Sort options: default

********************************************************************
count    = number of times OCI procedure was executed
cpu      = cpu time in seconds executing
elapsed  = elapsed time in seconds executing
disk     = number of physical reads of buffers from disk
query    = number of buffers gotten for consistent read
current  = number of buffers gotten in current mode (usually for update)
rows     = number of rows processed by the fetch or execute call
********************************************************************

alter session set sql_trace true
```

call	count	cpu	elapsed	disk	query	current	rows
Parse	0	0.00	0.00	0	0	0	0
Execute	1	0.00	0.00	0	0	0	0
Fetch	0	0.00	0.00	0	0	0	0
total	1	0.00	0.00	0	0	0	0

Misses in library cache during parse: 0
Optimizer goal: CHOOSE
Parsing user id: 5
****

```
select 'x' from dual
```

call	count	cpu	elapsed	disk	query	current	rows
Parse	1	0.00	0.00	0	0	0	0
Execute	1	0.00	0.00	0	0	0	0
Fetch	2	0.00	0.00	0	1	0	1
total	4	0.00	0.00	0	1	0	1

Misses in library cache during parse: 0
Optimizer goal: CHOOSE
Parsing user id: 5
****

```
select parameter, value
from v$nls_parameters     where (upper(parameter) in
('NLS_SORT','NLS_CURRENCY',
   'NLS_ISO_CURRENCY',                      'NLS_DATE_LANGUAGE',
   'NLS_NUMERIC_CHARACTERS',
'NLS_LANGUAGE','NLS_TERRITORY'))
```

call	count	cpu	elapsed	disk	query	current	rows
Parse	1	0.00	0.00	0	0	0	0
Execute	1	0.00	0.00	0	0	0	0
Fetch	1	0.00	0.00	0	0	0	7
total	3	0.00	0.00	0	0	0	7

Misses in library cache during parse: 0
Optimizer goal: CHOOSE
Parsing user id: 5

****

```
OVERALL TOTALS FOR ALL NON-RECURSIVE STATEMENTS
```

call	count	cpu	elapsed	disk	query	current	rows
Parse	1	0.00	0.00	0	0	0	0
Execute	2	0.00	0.00	0	0	0	0
Fetch	2	0.00	0.00	0	1	0	8
total	5	0.00	0.00	0	1	0	8

```
Misses in library cache during parse: 0

OVERALL TOTALS FOR ALL RECURSIVE STATEMENTS
```

call	count	cpu	elapsed	disk	query	current	rows
Parse	0	0.00	0.00	0	0	0	0
Execute	0	0.00	0.00	0	0	0	0
Fetch	0	0.00	0.00	0	0	0	0
total	0	0.00	0.00	0	0	0	0

```
Misses in library cache during parse: 0

    2  user  SQL statements in session.
    0  internal SQL statements in session.
    2  SQL statements in session.
*********************************************************************
Trace file: dev_ora_13337.trc
Trace file compatibility: 7.03.02
Sort options: default

    1  session in tracefile.
    3  user  SQL statements in trace file.
    0  internal SQL statements in trace file.
    3  SQL statements in trace file.
    3  unique SQL statements in trace file.
   42  lines in trace file.
```

Although there isn't much going on in this example, its simplicity allows us to examine a few basics. First of all, the header of the report lists information such as the version of TKPROF and when it was run. It shows the name of the input file, the raw SQL trace file, and the sorting options provided. In this example, none were provided.

The bottom of this report header is a standard legend for the statistics displayed in the report:

```
count    = number of times OCI procedure was executed
cpu      = cpu time in seconds executing
```

```
elapsed  = elapsed time in seconds executing
disk     = number of physical reads of buffers from disk
query    = number of buffers gotten for consistent read
current  = number of buffers gotten in current mode (usually for update)
rows     = number of rows processed by the fetch or execute call
```

An OCI procedure refers to the Oracle Call Interface, which is the lowest-level application-programming interface to Oracle. An OCI procedure could be a parse, an execute, or a fetch.

If TIMED_STATISTICS is FALSE, then TKPROF is always going to show 0.00 for both CPU and ELAPSED. While neither of these statistics is necessary as primary evidence in tuning, because they can be affected by other factors on the machine, they still represent valuable secondary information. And, in certain situations such as Oracle Parallel Server, the ELAPSED statistic can provide more information than even *logical reads* because ELAPSED can show the impact of Parallel Server "pinging." Please be sure that the TIMED_STATISTICS parameter is set, either at the instance level or by using ALTER SESSION to set it for the session in question.

The statistics for QUERY and CURRENT together make up the more commonly known statistic of *logical reads*. Logical reads are the number of buffers obtained from the Oracle buffer cache in the SGA. All SELECT, INSERT, UPDATE, and DELETE operations in Oracle operate out of the buffer cache first. If the necessary database blocks cannot be found in that buffer cache then a *physical read* occurs, which is the statistic DISK on this report. The ratio of physical reads to logical reads is typically referred to as the *hit ratio*. More precisely, the hit ratio is calculated as

```
(1 - (physical-reads / logical-reads)) * 100
```

which in terms of the statistics available in TKPROF would become

```
(1 - (DISK / (QUERY + CURRENT))) * 100
```

Following the header is an entry for each of the SQL statements. The first thing printed is the text of the SQL statement itself. Following this are the run-time statistics, which should be vaguely familiar from our examination of the contents of the raw SQL trace files:

call	count	cpu	elapsed	disk	query	current	rows
Parse	1	0.00	0.00	0	0	0	0
Execute	1	0.00	0.00	0	0	0	0
Fetch	2	0.00	0.00	0	1	0	1
total	4	0.00	0.00	0	1	0	1

Except for the *count*, the PARSE information is generally quite insignificant. If you are looking at SQL generated by a form, report, or a batch program, you generally like to see the PARSE operation happen only once for a SQL statement, even if the SQL statement is run several times. If the SQL was generated by an *ad hoc* tool like SQL*Plus, it is generally not so important that the PARSE operation be minimized.

The EXECUTE operation of a SQL statement can mean different things. For an INSERT, UPDATE, DELETE, or SELECT . . . FOR UPDATE command, all the work pertaining to the entire SQL statement occurs during the EXECUTE operation. In the case of a SELECT . . . FOR UPDATE statement, all the rows are fetched and locked during the EXECUTE operation.

The FETCH operation occurs only for SELECT statements other than SELECT . . . FOR UPDATE statements. During SELECT statements, the EXECUTE operation does not retrieve any data. It simply resolves the access methods and leaves "pointers" to the various data structures current inside the cursor. Then, the FETCH operation actually uses those "pointers" to visit the index entries or the rows in the tables, and the data is retrieved. Because a SELECT statement does not have any way of knowing how many rows are eventually going to be fetched, it is common to see an extra FETCH operation occur. This extra FETCH comes up empty, which tells the cursor that no more data can be retrieved.

Last, there is some extra information about the SQL statement:

```
Misses in library cache during parse: 0
Optimizer goal: CHOOSE
Parsing user id: 5
```

From Oracle7 on, there have been two components to a PARSE operation: parsing the SQL statement to obtain the execution plan and storing this information in the Oracle instance's global SQL *shared pool* and parsing the SQL statement for a particular session.

The PARSE statistic mentioned earlier pertains to the number of times this particular session tried to parse the SQL statement. If the application is using Oracle's shared pool correctly, only one of these PARSE operations will actually result in a true PARSE, where the execution plan is determined and an entry for the SQL statement is created in the shared pool. This is known as a *hard parse*. All subsequent PARSE attempts should reuse this entry, making for a very fast, lightweight PARSE operation, also known as a *soft parse*.

If the application is not using the shared pool properly, each PARSE operation issued by the application might result in a hard parse. In a data warehouse environment, this might not be as much of a cause for concern as in OLTP environments, but it can become a problem for frequently executed SQL statements. By far the most common cause of excessive hard parsing is the failure to use *bind variables*. This technique of using a *placeholder* in the text of the SQL statement and then substituting that placeholder with a value stored in a *variable* is strongly encouraged for batch programs, forms, reports, and analysis tools. Oracle *caches* SQL statements in the shared pool based on the text of the SQL statement, and any variations in that text, no matter how slight, cause a new shared pool entry to be created for a SQL statement. If data values are embedded in the text of the SQL statement and these data values are constantly changing, then serious performance degradation could result.

Of course, in a data warehouse environment, there might be a significant amount of *ad hoc* querying. Also, the sheer number of SQL statements might be small enough to make this problem insignificant. Altogether, like many other things, determining the statistic for "misses in library cache during parse" might indicate that a problem requires some knowledge of how frequently the SQL statement is being executed. If the SQL is executed rather infrequently, then "misses in the library cache during parse" may not indicate a problem. If the SQL statement is executed every 30 seconds, 24 hours a day, then perhaps there is a problem that should be examined further.

The Optimizer Goal (an Oracle7 term now completely superceded in Oracle8 by the phrase "Optimizer Mode") is also displayed, along with the USER_ID parsing the SQL statement. Both these factors can have a huge impact on how a SQL statement's execution plan is determined.

For example, remember that there are four Optimizer modes: ALL_ROWS, FIRST_ROWS, CHOOSE, and RULE. The Optimizer mode represents a "bias" on the part of the Oracle Optimizer when it tries to choose an execution method. ALL_ROWS emphasizes throughput, telling the Optimizer to choose a plan that retrieves all the rows the fastest. FIRST_ROWS emphasizes response time, telling the Optimizer to choose a plan that will retrieve the first row the fastest, even at the expense of throughput. RULE is the old rule-based optimizer, which precedes the cost-based optimizer introduced in Oracle7. The rule-based optimizer is very familiar to most SQL programmers, but its rules haven't changed since Oracle version 6, and no new enhancements are being made to it. CHOOSE is the default mode, and it indicates that the Optimizer should choose between using the rule-based and cost-based optimizers, depending on whether there are any statistics on the tables involved in the SQL statement. If even one table has cost-based optimizer statistics, then CHOOSE will choose to use the cost-based optimizer. If none of the tables has ever had the ANALYZE command run to generate statistics, then CHOOSE will choose the rule-based optimizer.

The optimizer mode can be set for the whole database instance using the initialization parameter OPTIMIZER_MODE; valid values are ALL_ROWS, FIRST_ROWS, RULE, and CHOOSE (the default). Alternatively, the Optimizer mode can be set for a single session using the following ALTER SESSION command:

```
ALTER SESSION SET OPTIMIZER_MODE = ALL_ROWS | FIRST_ROWS | RULE |
CHOOSE;
```

Last, the Optimizer mode can be specified for a particular SQL statement using *hints*:

```
SELECT /*+ all_rows */ . . .
UPDATE /*+ first_rows */ . . .
DELETE /*+ rule */ . . .
SELECT /*+ choose */ . . .
```

Unfortunately, the Optimizer mode cannot be set for a particular account, so that each time a user connects his own preferred Optimizer mode would be used. On the other hand, perhaps this is a good thing, as absolute chaos might result if the Optimizer mode is not kept as uniform as possible across all users.

Another factor affecting how a SQL statement execution plan is generated is the schema from which the parse information was derived. The schema for user Joe might present an entirely different set of tables by the same name from those seen by user Mary. User Joe might be looking at the tables belonging to the data warehouse, while user Mary may have made her own copies of those tables, and those much smaller tables are the ones she is querying. This fact should certainly be taken into consideration before trying to use SQL statements generated by Mary against the much larger tables Joe is seeing.

Now that we've had an initial look at some of the information provided by TKPROF, let's use some more of the TKPROF options. Let's use a slightly different example this time, querying the DBA_OBJECTS view in the Oracle data dictionary:

```
SQL> alter session set sql_trace = true;

Session altered.

SQL> describe dba_objects
 Name                            Null?    Type
 -------------------------------------------------------------
 OWNER                                    VARCHAR2(30)
 OBJECT_NAME                              VARCHAR2(128)
 SUBOBJECT_NAME                           VARCHAR2(30)
 OBJECT_ID                                NUMBER
 DATA_OBJECT_ID                           NUMBER
 OBJECT_TYPE                              VARCHAR2(15)
 CREATED                                  DATE
 LAST_DDL_TIME                            DATE
 TIMESTAMP                                VARCHAR2(75)
 STATUS                                   VARCHAR2(7)
 TEMPORARY                                VARCHAR2(1)
 GENERATED                                VARCHAR2(1)

SQL> select owner, object_type, count(*) from dba_objects
  2  group by owner, object_type;
```

OWNER	OBJECT_TYPE	COUNT(*)
DBSNMP	SEQUENCE	1
DBSNMP	SYNONYM	5
DBSNMP	TABLE	8
DEMO	INDEX	10
DEMO	TABLE	10
DEMO	VIEW	1
PUBLIC	SYNONYM	659
SCOTT	INDEX	2
SCOTT	TABLE	4
SYS	CLUSTER	9
SYS	INDEX	116
SYS	LIBRARY	4
SYS	PACKAGE	95
SYS	PACKAGE BODY	92
SYS	PROCEDURE	4
SYS	SEQUENCE	15

```
(. . . 60 lines of output removed . . . )

76 rows selected.

SQL> exit
```

Look in the USER_DUMP_DEST directory for the most recently created file:

```
$ cd /u01/app/oracle/admin/dev/udump
$ ls -lt *.trc
```

The "-t" switch on the Unix *ls* command will sort the output in the order last updated; this will show which is the most recently created trace file. On most systems, unless lots of users are tracing their session, this is sufficient to locate a raw SQL trace file. Now execute TKPROF, but use the EXPLAIN= clause to run EXPLAIN PLAN in the report (see Figure 9.23). When EXPLAIN= is specified, TKPROF actually connects to the database instance as the specified user and runs EXPLAIN PLAN at that time for each SQL statement.

Syntactically, we are using the following:

```
$ tkprof ora00435.trc x.tkp explain=sys/manager

TKPROF: Release 8.1.6.0.0 - Production on Sun Jan 9 23:27:56 2000

Copyright (c) Oracle Corporation 1979, 1994, 2000.  All rights reserved.
```

As you can see, it becomes necessary to write out the password to the SYS account in clear text; using the EXPLAIN= option for TKPROF is a clear security problem. For some reason, there is no way to have TKPROF prompt you for the password, allowing it to be hidden. The user SYS is being used only for this

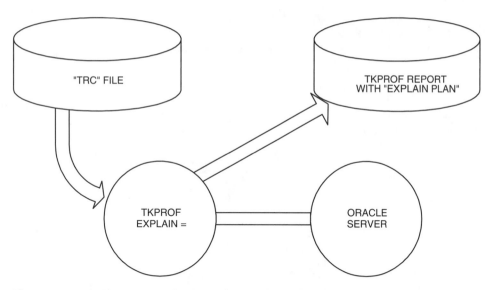

Figure 9.23 TKPROF connecting to perform EXPLAIN PLAN.

example, as SYS privileges are needed to perform EXPLAIN PLAN against data dictionary tables. Normally you should specify the username and password used in the original session.

Looking at the output file *x.tkp*, we see the following:

```
(. . . approximately 14 pages of output removed . . .)


*********************************************************************

select privilege#,nvl(col#,0),max(nvl(option$,0))
from
 objauth$ where obj#=:1 and grantee#=:2 group by privilege#,nvl(col#,0)

call       count    cpu      elapsed   disk    query    current    rows

Parse      1        0.00     0.00      0       0        0          0
Execute    10       0.00     0.00      0       0        0          0
Fetch      10       0.00     0.00      0       20       0          0

total      21       0.00     0.00      0       20       0          0

Misses in library cache during parse: 0
Optimizer goal: CHOOSE
Parsing user id: SYS    (recursive depth: 1)


Rows      Execution Plan
```

```
    0   SELECT STATEMENT    GOAL: CHOOSE
    0    SORT (GROUP BY)
    0     TABLE ACCESS (BY ROWID) OF 'OBJAUTH$'
    0      INDEX (RANGE SCAN) OF 'I_OBJAUTH2' (NON-UNIQUE)
```

****

```
select owner, object_type, count(*) from dba_objects
group by owner, object_type
```

call	count	cpu	elapsed	disk	query	current	rows
Parse	1	0.00	0.00	0	0	0	0
Execute	1	0.00	0.00	0	0	0	0
Fetch	6	0.00	0.00	137	11412	4	76
total	8	0.00	0.00	137	11412	4	76

```
Misses in library cache during parse: 1
Optimizer goal: CHOOSE
Parsing user id: 5   (SYSTEM)
```

Rows	Execution Plan

```
    0   SELECT STATEMENT    GOAL: CHOOSE
 5376    SORT (GROUP BY)
 5376     VIEW OF 'DBA_OBJECTS'
 5376      UNION-ALL
 5375       NESTED LOOPS
   98        TABLE ACCESS (FULL) OF 'USER$'
 5443        TABLE ACCESS (BY ROWID) OF 'OBJ$'
 5543         INDEX (RANGE SCAN) OF 'I_OBJ2' (UNIQUE)
    1       NESTED LOOPS
   98        TABLE ACCESS (FULL) OF 'USER$'
    1        TABLE ACCESS (BY ROWID) OF 'LINK$'
   99         INDEX (RANGE SCAN) OF 'I_LINK1' (NON-UNIQUE)
```

****

OVERALL TOTALS FOR ALL NON-RECURSIVE STATEMENTS

call	count	cpu	elapsed	disk	query	current	rows
Parse	8	0.00	0.00	0	0	0	0
Execute	8	0.00	0.00	0	0	0	0
Fetch	12	0.00	0.00	138	11457	4	86
total	28	0.00	0.00	138	11457	4	86

```
Misses in library cache during parse: 6
Misses in library cache during execute: 1
```

```
OVERALL TOTALS FOR ALL RECURSIVE STATEMENTS
```

call	count	cpu	elapsed	disk	query	current	rows
Parse	18	0.00	0.00	0	0	0	0
Execute	29	0.00	0.00	0	0	0	0
Fetch	57	0.00	0.00	0	132	0	40
total	104	0.00	0.00	0	132	0	40

```
Misses in library cache during parse: 0

    9   user  SQL statements in session.
   18   internal SQL statements in session.
   27   SQL statements in session.
   18   statements EXPLAINed in this session.
********************************************************************
Trace file: ora00435.trc
Trace file compatibility: 7.03.02
Sort options: default

    0   session in tracefile.
    9   user  SQL statements in trace file.
   18   internal SQL statements in trace file.
   27   SQL statements in trace file.
   19   unique SQL statements in trace file.
   18   SQL statements EXPLAINed using schema:
         SYS.prof$plan_table
           Default table was used.
           Table was created.
           Table was dropped.
  392   lines in trace file.
```

Here we had to remove about 14 pages of output to keep this chapter to reasonable size. As you can see, although the SQL*Plus session shows that we executed only three statements (an ALTER SESSION, a DESCRIBE, and the SELECT), the summary at the bottom of this report shows that 9 "user SQL statements" were captured and no less than 18 "internal" or recursive SQL statements were generated and captured.

The reason for this inflation is related to the fact that SQL*Plus itself runs a few SQL statements before the first results are returned. That is, as we ran the first SQL statement ALTER SESSION, SQL*Plus wanted to know what NLS language and conventions we were using, so it checked the view V$NLS_PARAMETERS after the ALTER SESSION was run but before it returned any response from the statement.

Also, the SQL*Plus DESCRIBE command can really best be described as a *macro*, in that SQL*Plus actually expands it into 4 or 5 SQL statements.

Additionally, these 4 or 5 SQL statements generated by SQL*Plus recursively generated about 10 or 12 additional "internal" SQL statements. All in all, 26 SQL statements, both "user" and "internal," result from the ALTER SESSION and the DESCRIBE commands. Finally, the twenty-seventh SQL statement is the query on the DBA_OBJECTS view.

In the output just displayed, note the EXPLAIN PLAN output that has now been added to the run-time statistics. This part of the report comes from two sources: the STAT lines, briefly discussed when we were examining the raw SQL trace output files, and the EXPLAIN PLAN command run during TKPROF. The "rows" information, representing the number of table or index rows visited during the step of the execution plan, comes from the STAT entries from the raw SQL trace file. The rest of the EXPLAIN PLAN output was generated by TKPROF, which created its own PLAN_TABLE, populated it, and dropped it.

> **NOTE** Note that the EXPLAIN PLAN is done at the time of TKPROF reporting and will be based on the available indexes and statistics at that time; this plan may not match the plan that was in effect when the trace file was created.

As illuminating as it is to see all the additional SQL statements resulting from "recursive" or "internal" SQL, there are times when we'd just prefer not to see it, especially in the interests of brevity. So, TKPROF comes with a SYS=NO clause, which filters out all "recursive" SQL statements from the body of the report. Statistics from the recursive SQL are still summarized at the bottom of the report:

```
$ tkprof dev_ora_13337.trc x.tkp explain=sys/manager sys=no
```

Unfortunately, when we read the resulting report, we still have to read through the all the nonrecursive SQL statements generated by SQL*Plus "expanding" the DESCRIBE "macro" before we get to the query on DBA_OBJECTS. What would be most useful would be the ability to sort the SQL statements in the TKPROF report so that the most *interesting* ones "percolated" to the top of the report and the least interesting SQL statements filtered to the bottom of the report. To do this, we would want to use one or more of the 23 different sort options provided by TKPROF:

```
prscnt      number of times parse was called
prscpu      cpu time parsing
prsela      elapsed time parsing
prsdsk      number of disk reads during parse
prsqry      number of buffers for consistent read during parse
prscu       number of buffers for current read during parse
prsmis      number of misses in library cache during parse
execnt      number of execute was called
```

```
execpu     cpu time spent executing
exeela     elapsed time executing
exedsk     number of disk reads during execute
exeqry     number of buffers for consistent read during execute
execu      number of buffers for current read during execute
exerow     number of rows processed during execute
exemis     number of library cache misses during execute
fchcnt     number of times fetch was called
fchcpu     cpu time spent fetching
fchela     elapsed time fetching
fchdsk     number of disk reads during fetch
fchqry     number of buffers for consistent read during fetch
fchcu      number of buffers for current read during fetch
fchrow     number of rows fetched
userid     userid of user that parsed the cursor
exeqry     number of buffers for consistent read during execute
execu      number of buffers for current read during execute
fchqry     number of buffers for consistent read during fetch
fchcu      number of buffers for current read during fetch
```

Which options should we use? If you stop to examine each closely, any one of them has its purpose, but from years of SQL tuning, these are the best recommendations.

Use:

```
SORT=EXEQRY,FCHQRY,EXECU,FCHCU
```

or:

```
SORT=PRSELA,EXEELA,FCHELA
```

The first set of sorting options, EXEQRY, FCHQRY, EXECU, and FCHCU, represent *logical reads*. As you know, logical reads are the reads of block buffers in the Buffer Cache in the Oracle SGA. More than anything else, the accessing and manipulation of block buffers inside the Buffer Cache represent the single best *performance metric* for *work* within the Oracle RDBMS. It is very difficult to find a single numeric metric that represents all of the processing that Oracle does when it executes a SQL statement, but logical reads is the closest to perfect. They are not affected by the size of the Buffer Cache or any other configuration parameter, and they are not affected by other processing occurring on the system as a whole. They represent *work* by the Oracle RDBMS only, and when you are tuning SQL statements, this is what you're trying to tune. Most of time, the most useful metric for sorting the TKPROF report is logical reads.

Sometimes important bits of work occur in the Oracle RDBMS that have nothing to do with block buffers in the Buffer Cache in the Oracle SGA. Examples of this are the following:

- I/O contention
- Delays in I/O processing due to contention within Oracle (i.e., Parallel Server "pinging," latching problems, etc.)
- Other contention problems (i.e., slow parsing, enqueue contention, latch contention)

When you are using Parallel Server or if you suspect that you are having difficulties with your I/O subsystem, continue to sort your TKPROF output by logical reads, but cross-check the results by also sorting by *elapsed time*, which is accomplished by specifying the statistics PRSELA, EXEELA, and FCHELA.

Essentially, sort by logical reads to detect *excessive resource consumption*, but sort by *elapsed time* if you suspect that your problem might be *contention*. If the results from both reports are essentially the same, with only minor differences, if any, then the problem is almost certainly excessive resource consumption, not contention.

Running TKPROF with the SORT= option as well will now give us a TKPROF report with the most expensive SQL statement at the top and the least expensive (and therefore the least important, for our purposes) at the bottom. Let's go further. Standard tuning methodology (whether the subject is Oracle, any other database system, or an operating system) dictates an iterative methodology. Attack the 3 worst, the 5 worst, or the 10 worst problems only; ignore all the others. Fix those first 3, or 5, or 10. Then, after they are fixed, reevaluate again. Again, attack only the worst few problems. Fix them. And reevaluate.

Using this approach, all effort is directed at the worst problems. No effort is expended on small problems or nonproblems. Also, by reducing the scope, focusing on the worst problems becomes easier. It is easier to focus on 5 issues than it is to focus on 50 or 100 issues.

The TKPROF report can support this. The PRINT= clause will limit the TKPROF report output to only the number of SQL statements specified in the PRINT= clause. For example, if you specify PRINT=10, then TKPROF will print report details for only 10 SQL statements, after all the other clauses and options have been processed.

That's about all the limiting you should do. Many people specify the SYS=NO parameter to eliminate *recursive SQL* against the data dictionary from the report. Why would you want to do that? Sometimes it is the recursive SQL that causes the problem. An example of this is a SQL statement that accesses an Oracle SEQUENCE object many times, and the SEQUENCE object is not CACHED. This can be pinpointed easily when SYS=YES (the default), but it would be missed if SYS=NO. So, don't do this.

More options. Let's suppose you just wanted a quick report listing the SQL statements that were not recursive, in the order they were called. The RECORD= clause allows you to specify an output file for such a report.

Now, let's suppose that you did not want TKPROF to aggregate statistics for multiple executions of the exact same SQL statement. This might be the case if different executions of the same query result in vastly different response times not explained by different users parsing the query. In this case, AGGRE-GATE=NO might be useful; the default, of course, is AGGREGATE=YES.

If a large number of people were using TKPROF at the same time, then having each of those TKPROF sessions create, populate, and then drop their own PLAN_TABLES to run EXPLAIN PLAN could get expensive. In this situation you may want to specify a fixed, permanent PLAN_TABLE for TKPROF to use when it does EXPLAIN PLAN; this involves the TABLE=*schema.tablename* clause.

The last option is by far the most intriguing. The INSERT= clause produces, instead of a formatted report, a SQL script that can be run through SQL*Plus or Server Manager to insert all the SQL trace information into a table called TKPROF_TABLE. From this, if you wish, you can generate your own reports, similar to TKPROF. What is so intriguing about this is the possibility of doing advanced analysis on performance statistics. Think about using this feature in conjunction with setting the initialization parameter SQL_TRACE = TRUE to enable SQL trace globally for an entire instance. Once all the raw SQL trace files have been gathered, TKPROF can generate SQL scripts for inserting all the SQL trace information into a table in the database.

Now imagine using an OLAP tool or some other advanced data warehouse analysis tool, not against marketing or campaign data, but against database per-formance data. The possibilities are quite exciting, especially with data mining techniques. You may be able to find something important that can't be gleaned from poring over traditional TKPROF reports.

But the most important thing that TKPROF provides is hard numbers, an empirical set of results against which different hypotheses can be validated or invalidated. TKPROF allows a person doing tuning to unambiguously determine whether one technique works better than another. Is this index more efficient for this query than that one? Test it out. Enable SQL tracing against one version of the query and then against the other. TKPROF the results, and compare.

Would clustered tables be more efficient than regular tables? Test it out; cre-ate the necessary clusters and compare results in TKPROF. Would the optimizer goal of FIRST_ROWS provide better results than CHOOSE? Test it out, using hints or the ALTER SESSION SET OPTIMIZER_MODE command.

Looking for Problems

We've covered four major areas of tuning in Oracle data warehouses:

- Adequately sizing the I/O subsystem
- Pretuning the data warehouse

- Optimizing the load phase
- Tuning SQL statements

Are there more areas to cover? Absolutely! In particular, we need to discuss the techniques necessary to find processes that take an inordinate share of resources. Once we can *screen* for the worst resource hogs, we can then *drill-down* on those intensive processes and fix them. In the previous section on SQL trace and TKPROF we showed how to do this drill-down, this surgical focus on an already identified problem. When you are using SQL tracing and TKPROF, you are not scanning the system looking for problems. When you are using those tools, you have already identified the problem and you are now using very exact tools to fix the problem.

But what do we use to find the problem on a busy system? Finding out who is bringing a busy database to its knees is somewhat similar to trying to find out which cars are emitting the most pollution on a bumper-to-bumper freeway. It's probably not possible to hook up test equipment to every vehicle's tailpipe; personally, we would want to wear a bulletproof vest to do that. You have to have some way of surveying all the vehicles from a distance to determine who is likely emitting the most exhaust first, and then put on the bulletproof vests and try to convince just those drivers to submit to a more invasive, but more definitive, test.

It's the same with databases and data warehouses in particular. In a data warehouse, everyone is using tremendous amounts of resources, just as on the freeway everyone is emitting pollution. The trick is to detect who may be doing too much.

This exercise is usually reactive in nature. Pretuning techniques and SQL tuning can be proactive, in that potentially resource-intensive processes can be examined to determine whether they will consume too many resources. Scanning a system in use for performance problems, however, is strictly reactive.

Here are some tips and techniques for enabling and performing reactive performance tuning.

Reactive Tuning

When a system is running "slow," the reason is either of these:

- One or more contention bottlenecks
- Resource consumption problems due to one or more *resource hogs*

It's either one or the other. The trick is deciding whether it's one or the other. This involves starting at the operating system utilities.

As mentioned earlier, many implementations of UNIX include some form of a "top" command, which displays the top 10 processes in terms of CPU consumption. This is usually a volatile display in that the top 10 processes probably keep shifting around, one sometimes ranking first, then at other times falling out of the top 10 altogether.

If the UNIX platform you are using does not have a "top" command (or anything similar), you can do essentially the same thing using the following:

```
$ uptime
$ ps -eaf | sort -n +3 | tail
```

The first command, *uptime*, provides information about how long the system has been "up" and running, along with a cumulative *load factor*. It is this *load factor*, which is derived from actual statistics from CPU, swap, and I/O consumption, in which we are most interested. On most flavors of UNIX, it is common for this load factor to hover in the low single digits. If the cumulative load factor, which can be explained for your UNIX variant using the "man uptime" command, shows as excessively high, then it is likely that you have a resource consumption problem. The next step is to determine what processes are consuming the greatest amounts of resources. This brings us to the next command.

The second command sequence will first run the UNIX *ps* command, which retrieves UNIX *process status*. The "-eaf" obtains a fairly complete display of information about each process, including the name of the process, the cumulative CPU time, the time when the process started, and the current CPU "clock ticks" consumed. It is this last statistic (CPU "clock ticks") that is most interesting. By passing the output from *ps -eaf* into the UNIX *sort* command, we are instructing *sort* to resort the output by the fourth field, which is the CPU "clock ticks" column. Then, to retrieve 10 processes with the highest number of CPU "clock ticks," we are filtering the output from *sort* using the UNIX *tail* command. Using this homegrown top 10 command, the heaviest consumer of CPU resources will be the last process displayed.

Of course, the "top" command combines all this information into one useful display, but whichever method you use, any process that stays consistently near the top of the list merits attention—especially if it is an Oracle server process. If it is, it may be useful to find out exactly what it is doing. But that would be a *drill-down*; we would no longer be looking for a possible culprit— we would be looking more closely at a single suspect.

The first step is to determine, based on the symptoms, whether the problem is one of excessive resource consumption or contention. Symptoms of the former include CPU resources, memory resources, or I/O resources. Symptoms of the latter involve a conspicuously quiet system, yet still poor performance.

Sometimes, poor performance can be a result of both excessive resource consumption and contention for resources. If this seems to be the case, resolve the excessive consumption problem first, then reevaluate for continued contention. Often, excessive consumption can cause contention, and resolving one resolves the other as well.

Resolving Excessive Resource Consumption

By examining the overall symptoms, you've decided that the primary problem is that the Oracle database instance is consuming too many resources. In other words, the poor performance on the system is caused by an overload of CPU, memory, or I/O resources.

On Oracle systems, excessive resource consumption is nearly always due to inefficient SQL statements. Fixing an inefficient SQL statement could be as simple as adding an appropriate index, or it could be as complex as brain surgery. Attacking any but the largest problem does not make sense. In medical terms this is known as *triage*. This is the basis for a tuning methodology. You want to attend to the worst problems first and leave the less serious problems for later. As in medicine, it is crucial to correctly distinguish between serious problems and ones that are not so serious. Although tuning a database is not nearly as complex as saving lives in an emergency room, both require a methodology.

A Methodology for SQL Tuning

Whether you are tuning an entire database instance or you are trying to tune a specific program module, the methodology includes the following steps:

1. Identify only the 10 to 20 most *offensive* SQL statements.
2. Prioritize them in descending order of *offensiveness*.
3. Select the 2 or 3 top problems.
4. Fix them.
5. Repeat from Step 1.

Tuning is an iterative process. One way to look at it is to visualize the layers of an onion. There might be 12 to 15 layers of an onion, the same way there might be 12 to 15 major performance tuning problems in an Oracle database. The outermost 4 or 5 layers might be some hideously inefficient SQL statements. The next 2 or 3 layers may be a contention problem, such as application locking and deadlocking. The next layers may be some more subtle contention issues, such as redo logging or latches. First, you peel away the biggest layer, the outermost layer. Once that's gone, that exposes the next layer, which is now the biggest layer. You peel that away, and once it's gone, the next layer is now the outermost and biggest. And so on, and so on, until you get to the center and the layers are so small that you don't care anymore.

How do you decide when you are done?

This is important! Tuning is a time-consuming exercise. You must know when to stop.

Keep in mind the *80-20 rule*. This states that the first 80 percent of the problem requires 20 percent of the effort, while the remaining 20 percent of the problem requires the other 80 percent of the effort. If you've fixed 80 percent of the problem, should you bother with trying to fix the remaining 20 percent?

When tuning each statement, stop when you've reduced the statement by 80 percent or so. Leave the remaining 20 percent for another day. Because the tuning methodology is iterative, you'll address the remaining 20 percent only if it prioritizes again as one of the worst two or three statements. If the remaining 20 percent is not *bad enough* to make the triage, then it's not worth working on any further.

Likewise for the number of SQL statements to tune for each iteration of the methodology. As you follow the steps of the methodology and first *identify* the worst SQL statements and then *prioritize* them, you might notice that frequently there is an exponential decrease in severity from item to item.

Let's say we are using *logical reads* as our criterion for identifying and prioritizing SQL statements. We might notice that frequently the *very worst* statement is something like 10 times worse than the next-worst statement. And that next-worst statement is frequently something like 5 times worse than the next-worst statement. And that is frequently 3 times worse than the next one. Finally, when we get down to the fourth or fifth worst SQL statement, they will only be 30 percent worse than the following statement.

So, if you were to graph this, you would notice a steep sine curve as the *seriousness* of the problems quickly drops off beyond the first two or three items. Of course, this may not always be the case, but generally it is.

The *elbow* of that curve is the place to stop tuning. This is the *point of diminishing returns*.

Stop tuning after you fix two or three items anyway, and put the fixes into production, and then repeat the whole process, reevaluating. You might find that what was the fourth or fifth worst items still do not make it to the top two or three because your fixes might have had some unexpected side effects, or something new may pop up altogether. Try to minimize the time spent between iterations; a good frequency is to perform one iteration of the tuning methodology at least once per week. So, how does the tuning methodology work?

Identifying and Prioritizing the Worst SQL Statements

The scope of your tuning is usually either the entire database instance globally or one specific program module or process.

If the scope is just one specific program module or process, then use the SQL trace utility with the TKPROF command to *identify* and *prioritize* the SQL statements in the process. It is vital to use the SORT= parameter of TKPROF to do this. Either:

```
TKPROF trc-file output-file SORT=EXEQRY,FCHQRY,EXECU,FCHCU
```

or:

```
TKPROF trc-file output-file SORT=PRSELA,EXEELA,FCHELA
```

In most cases, sort by *logical reads*, which are the sum of EXEQRY, FCHQRY, EXECU, and FCHCU. If you are using Parallel Server or if you have reason to suspect that there is some form of internal contention affecting performance, then also sort by *elapsed time* for all three phases of SQL execution, which is the sum of PRSELA, EXEELA, and FCHELA.

The TKPROF report will be organized so that the SQL statements are ordered in descending order by the criteria you chose. If you like, you can limit the size of the report by specifying the PRINT=10 option, to limit the report to only the 10 worst. Also, it would be useful to generate an EXPLAIN PLAN for each statement, using the EXPLAIN= option.

If the scope of your tuning effort is the entire database instance, then you'll need to query the Shared SQL Area of the Shared Pool in the Oracle SGA, via the V$SQLAREA view:

```
SELECT      SUBSTR(SQL_TEXT,1,60) SQL_TEXT,
            SUM(BUFFER_GETS) BUFFER_GETS,
            SUM(DISK_READS) DISK_READS,
            SUM(EXECUTIONS) EXECUTIONS,
            COUNT(*) COUNT,
            (SUM(DISK_READS)*100)+SUM(BUFFER_GETS) LOAD_FACTOR
FROM        V$SQLAREA
GROUP BY    SUBSTR(SQL_TEXT,1,60)
HAVING      SUM(DISK_READS) > <minimum-#-of-physical-reads>
AND         SUM(BUFFER_GETS) > <minimum-#-of-logical-reads>
ORDER BY    LOAD_FACTOR DESC;
```

This SQL statement, or something similar, is used by many tuning utilities such as Oracle Enterprise Manager, to identify *offensive* SQL statements.

What the HAVING clause of the query is doing is filtering out all but the most expensive SQL statements in the Shared SQL Area. We don't really care about SQL statements that do not exceed this threshold. Of course, the values for the thresholds *minimum-#-of-physical-reads* and *minimum-#-of-logical-reads* would vary depending on how busy your database is. The threshold values themselves don't really matter; the idea is to get a list of between 2 and 20 SQL statements to look at. For starters, try setting *minimum-#-of-physical-reads* to 100,000 and *minimum-#-of-logical-reads* to 1 million. If you don't get any results, then lower the threshold values until you do. If you get too many results, then raise the threshold values.

The ORDER BY clause is sorting the results by the derived value LOAD_FACTOR in descending order. The LOAD_FACTOR emphasizes the seriousness of the DISK_READS values because physical reads to the I/O subsystem are so much more expensive than logical reads to the Buffer Cache in the Oracle SQL.

This report, or something similar, *identifies* and *prioritizes* the very worst SQL statements executed recently within a database instance. Naturally, if all of the applications on the system are generating shareable SQL statements by using bind variables, then the Shared SQL Area will contain a great deal of valuable information on DISK_READS, BUFFER_GETS, and EXECUTIONS for a very long time. If the *Least-Recently-Used* (LRU) algorithm that manages the Shared SQL Area (which is limited by the total size of the Shared Pool) keeps aging out SQL statements because the application is not generating shareable SQL, then the information in this report might be less definitive.

Depending on the scope of your tuning task, use either one or the other of the two tools to *identify* and *prioritize* the SQL statements to be tuned. If you are tuning an individual program or session, use SQL Trace and TKPROF. If you are tuning an entire database instance, use V$SQLAREA.

Fixing the SQL

So, we've identified the worst SQL statements. The next step in the methodology is to fix them. How do we do this?

The answer is *test cases*.

First, reproduce the problem in a test case using SQL*Plus. Then, if necessary, rewrite the SQL statement to make it more *readable* by you, so that you can understand it easily, **without** changing the behavior of, or the access method of, the statement. This is also called *prettying* the SQL statement, and while this may seem like a waste of time, it is actually an important step in the process of SQL tuning. When you are finished with these steps, you have a *baseline test case*.

Once a baseline test case is established, it is time to try to actually fix the statement. How this is accomplished is based on several factors:

- How much you learned about the SQL statement during *prettying*
- How much you know about the tables and indexes being accessed by the SQL statement
- Your knowledge of SQL access methods
- Your willingness to try any hypothesis, regardless of whether you think it makes sense

First things first. Let's use an example to illustrate . . .

THE IMPORTANCE OF *BIND VARIABLES*

Selecting only the first 60 characters of the SQL_TEXT in the SELECT clause and also using it in the GROUP BY clause are ways of avoiding problems introduced by nonshareable SQL issued by the application. If we did not summarize the results by the first 60 characters of the SQL_TEXT, then bad practices on the part of the application developers could prevent us from identifying bad SQL statements.

The COUNT value returned by the query for each statement should display how many SQL statements made up the values returned for DISK_READS, BUFFER_GETS, and EXECUTIONS. If the value of COUNT is more than 1, then it is possible that, in addition to a SQL tuning problem, the application might be issuing unshareable SQL statements by not using *bind variables*. SQL statement entries in the Shared SQL Area of the Shared Pool are differentiated by their text. Each time a SQL statement is issued, an entry is allocated for it in the Shared SQL Area. Anytime any session uses that SQL statement again, the same SQL statement entry in the Shared SQL Area is reused, saving on parsing costs. SQL statements are differentiated from one another by their text, so if one statement differs from another by only one character in its text, then it is a completely different SQL statement with its own entry in the Shared SQL Area. Using *bind variables* means putting a *placeholder tag* in the text of the SQL statement:

```
SELECT COUNT(*) FROM EMP WHERE DEPTNO = :b1;
```

When the SQL statement is executed, the real data value, such as 1,015, is substituted for the placeholder tag of "b1." This is a SQL statement that will occupy only one entry in the Shared SQL Area, no matter how many times it is executed, no matter how many different values for DEPTNO are supplied, by however many sessions. It is an example of *shareable* SQL. On the other hand, if the SQL statement were issued without a *bind variable*, with the data value of 1,015 embedded right into the text of the SQL statement, it would be parsed like this:

```
SELECT COUNT(*) FROM EMP WHERE DEPTNO = 1015;
```

As each session executes this same SQL statement, it will most likely supply different values for DEPTNO. Written this way, each time the SQL statement is executed with a different value for DEPTNO, it will require its own entry in the Shared SQL Area. As you can imagine, if this statement was executed 5,000 times with 5,000 different values of DEPTNO, the statement would be fully parsed each time, and the same statement would occupy up to 5,000 entries in the Shared SQL Area. Values of more than 1 in the COUNT column returned might indicate that this is happening. Values of more than 50 indicate that this is almost certainly happening. This is a serious *scalability* problem that must be fixed by the application developer. There is nothing that can be done at the database instance level to alleviate this problem.

Let's suppose that, either from the TKPROF report or from the query on V$SQLAREA, we've been handed the following SQL statement, which seems to stink to high heaven, performance-wise:

```
SELECT CUST.ID, CUST.NAME, ORDER.ID, ORDER.SALE_DATE, ORDLINE.NBR,
PART.DESCR, PART.STD_PRICE, ORDLINE.PRICE FROM CUSTOMER CUST, ORDER,
ORDER_LINE_ITEM ORDLINE, PART WHERE 'USA' = CUST.COUNTRY AND
ORDLINE.ORD_ID = ORDER.ID AND CUST.ID = ORDLINE.CUST_ID AND
ORDER.CUST_ID = ORDLINE.CUST_ID AND ORDLINE.ORDER_ID = ORDER.ID + 0 AND
ORDLINE.ORDER_ID = :b1 AND PART.ID = ORDLINE.PART_ID ORDER BY CUST.NAME,
ORDER.SALE_DATE DESC
```

The first step is to *copy* the text of the SQL statement from whichever it was reported into a SQL*Plus script using a text editor. Then, add the following statements around it:

```
whenever oserror exit failure rollback
whenever sqlerror exit failure rollback

variable b1 number
exec :b1 := 1515;

set echo on feedback on timing on autotrace on

spool test1

...paste the SQL statement text here...

exit success rollback
```

The purpose of this SQL*Plus script is to isolate the SQL statement into a reproducible test case. In the event that the SQL statement is an INSERT, UPDATE, or DELETE statement, we don't really want it to change any data. So, the SQL*Plus WHENEVER command, besides exiting SQL*Plus with a failure status, also performs a ROLLBACK before exiting, instead of a COMMIT as SQL*Plus usually does by default. Additionally, even if no errors occur, the SQL*Plus EXIT command at the end of the script still performs a ROLLBACK instead of the default COMMIT. All of this makes it impossible for data to actually be changed in the database, thus making the SQL statement reproducible.

Also, the SQL statement in question has a bind variable, ":b1", in its text. Now, we could edit this in the SQL statement to actually embed the chosen test data value of "1515" into the text of the SQL statement, but this might have the unintentional side effect of changing the execution plan of the statement. We are going to make use of the SQL*Plus VARIABLE command to define a bind variable with a NUMBER datatype. Immediately after, we use the SQL*Plus EXEC macro to execute an anonymous PL/SQL block to initialize the bind variable with the value "1515." Now, the bind variable is ready to be used inside the SQL statement.

Record the results of the test case using the SQL*Plus SPOOL command. This original test case script should probably be named "test1.sql", so the spooled output file should be named similarly, as it is in the example above. As we add new test cases, we're going to want to change the name of the new SQL*Plus scripts and their spooled output files as well.

Running this script through SQL*Plus should also make use of the SQL*Plus AUTOTRACE utility. This utility does three things: It executes the SQL statement normally and displays the output, then it automatically performs an EXPLAIN PLAN and then displays statistics gathered from the V$SESSTAT dynamic performance view, including statistics like "physical reads," "db block gets," and "consistent gets." The former is easy to understand, the latter two sum together to represent "logical reads." So, similar to TKPROF, we can measure the number of *physical reads* and *logical reads* expended during a SQL statement's execution. AUTOTRACE output looks something like the following:

```
SQL*Plus: Release 8.1.5.0.0 - Production on Fri Sep 24 11:24:22 1999

(c) Copyright 1999 Oracle Corporation.  All rights reserved.

Connected to:
Oracle8i Enterprise Edition Release 8.1.5.0.0 - Production
With the Partitioning, Parallel Server, and Java options
PL/SQL Release 8.1.5.0.0 - Production

SQL> set autotrace on
SQL> select count(*) from emp;

  COUNT(*)
----------
     14628
```

This is just a simple example SQL statement to illustrate how AUTOTRACE works. After AUTOTRACE is enabled and the SQL statement is executed, the results are returned as normal.

```
Execution Plan
----------------------------------------------------------
   0      SELECT STATEMENT Optimizer=FIRST_ROWS (Cost=2 Card=1)
   1    0   SORT (AGGREGATE)
   2    1     INDEX (FULL SCAN) OF 'EMP_PK' (UNIQUE) (Cost=28 Card=14353)
```

Next, an EXPLAIN PLAN is run. The Oracle account to which we are connected must have access to the table named PLAN_TABLE for this to work. If such a table does not yet exist for the schema, then you can create one yourself by executing the SQL script named *utlxplan.sql* located in the directory "$ORACLE_HOME/rdbms/admin."

```
Statistics
----------------------------
        0   recursive calls
        0   db block gets
       29   consistent gets
       16   physical reads
        0   redo size
     1087   bytes sent via SQL*Net to client
      673   bytes received via SQL*Net from client
        4   SQL*Net roundtrips to/from client
        1   sorts (memory)
        0   sorts (disk)
        1   rows processed
```

Last, a report of some statistics that changed in the V$SESSTAT view during the execution of the SQL statement is displayed. Notable statistics for tuning purposes are "physical reads," "db block gets," "consistent gets," which together equal "logical reads," and "sorts (memory)" and "sorts (disk)."

Once we have pasted the SQL text into the SQL*Plus script shown here, we can execute the statement to determine if the problem reproduces. If we have an EXPLAIN PLAN of the original statement, we can compare that to the one from the test case. If we have statistics for "physical reads" and "logical reads" consumed per execution from the original statement, we can compare those also to the results from the test case. From this, we should be able to determine whether we have reproduced the problem.

If we have not reproduced the original problem, then it is important that we find out why. Perhaps the underlying conditions in the database have changed since the original problem was detected. Perhaps you are running the test case as a different Oracle account than the original. Perhaps the tables involved had grown significantly and an ANALYZE was performed recently, thereby changing the access methods. Perhaps the problem has even been fixed! In any case, if you are unable to reproduce the original problem exactly, go back and verify that the problem still exists. If you can't verify this, then don't continue on this problem.

If we have reproduced the original problem, then it's time to *prettify* the SQL statement.

This is not merely an aesthetic exercise. It is also not an anal-retentive compulsion to impose one's own sense of order on a lowly SQL statement, although bystanders may feel that this is so.

Reformatting and organizing the text of the SQL statement into some kind of recognizable order means spending time trying to understand it. And it is this intimate understanding of exactly *what* the SQL statement is actually doing that could be crucial to fixing it.

Using the EXPLAIN PLAN output saved in the spooled output file "test1.lst" from the first baseline test case, let's first reorganize the FROM clause so that it matches the order of joins.

The EXPLAIN PLAN looks like this:

```
Execution Plan
```

```
    0       SELECT STATEMENT Optimizer=CHOOSE (Cost=2 Card=1)
    1    0    SORT (ORDER BY)
    2    1     NESTED LOOPS
    3    2      NESTED LOOPS
    4    3       NESTED LOOPS
    5    4        TABLE ACCESS (BY ROWID) OF 'CUSTOMER' (Cost=1)
    6    5         INDEX (RANGE SCAN) OF 'CUSTOMER_FK2' (NON-UNIQUE)
                     (Cost=3731 Card=55)
    7    4        TABLE ACCESS (BY ROWID) OF 'ORDER_LINE_ITEM'
                   (Cost=10)
    8    7         INDEX (RANGE SCAN) OF 'ORDLINE_FK1' (NON-UNIQUE)
                     (Cost=45888 Card=4017)
    9    3       TABLE ACCESS (BY ROWID) OF 'PART' (Cost=1)
   10    9        INDEX (UNIQUE SCAN) OF 'PART_PK' (UNIQUE)
                    (Cost=41333 Card=1458975)
   11    2      TABLE ACCESS (BY ROWID) OF 'ORDER' (Cost=1435)
   12   11       INDEX (RANGE SCAN) OF 'ORDER_FK1' (NON-UNIQUE)
                   (Cost=195889 Card=49363)
```

The way to read an EXPLAIN PLAN report is to follow two rules:

- Whatever is indented the most is executed first.

- When several things are indented to the same depth, then move from the top down.

Therefore, the EXPLAIN PLAN can be read as follows:

1. INDEX (RANGE SCAN) of the index CUSTOMER_FK2.

2. Access the CUSTOMER table from its index CUSTOMER_FK2 by ROWID.

3. NESTED LOOP join from CUSTOMER to ORDER_LINE_ITEM.

4. INDEX (RANGE SCAN) of the index ORDLINE_FK1.

5. Access the ORDER_LINE_ITEM table from its index ORDLINE_FK1 by ROWID.

6. NESTED LOOP join from ORDER_LINE_ITEM to PART.

7. INDEX (UNIQUE SCAN) of the index PART_PK.

8. Access the PART table from its index PART_PK by ROWID.

9. NESTED LOOP join from ORDER_LINE_ITEM to ORDER.

10. INDEX (RANGE SCAN) of the index ORDER_FK1.

11. Access the ORDER table from its index ORDER_FK1 by ROWID.

So, the join order can be listed as follows in the FROM clause:

```
SELECT      CUST.ID,
            CUST.NAME,
            ORDER.ID,
            ORDER.SALE_DATE,
            ORDLINE.NBR,
            PART.DESCR,
            PART.STD_PRICE,
            ORDLINE.PRICE
FROM        CUSTOMER              CUST,
            ORDER_LINE_ITEM ORDLINE,
            PART                  PART,
            ORDER                 ORDER
```

Please note that the contents of the SELECT list are actually quite irrelevant, unless there are a corresponding GROUP BY statement and aggregation functions. In this example, there are not, so in the event that the SELECT list was excessively long it could be trimmed extensively or even pruned down to a single COUNT(*). All that is really needed is enough information to determine whether the query is returning the correct results, and sometimes that can be determined from a simple COUNT(*).

Please note the tabs used in formatting the text of the statement, and note that the fact that each column name and table name are on individual lines. If you don't find this easy to read, then by all means use whatever you are comfortable with. Remember: we are trying to make the SQL statement easy to read, and that may mean different things to different people. This is simply one set of formatting preferences.

Continuing on, we want to prettify the WHERE clause. For our preferences, this involves the following rules:

- Each *predicate* or *logical condition* on its own separate line.

- The *direction* of predicates for table joins is ordered similar to the FROM clause.

- First, *bind predicates* or *join predicates* are listed, followed by *filter predicates*.

- The *direction* of joins within predicates is from *right to left*.

Well, what does this all mean? Let's illustrate first:

```
SELECT          /*+ ordered */
                CUST.ID,
                CUST.NAME,
                ORDER.ID,
                ORDER.SALE_DATE,
                ORDLINE.NBR,
                PART.DESCR,
                PART.STD_PRICE,
                ORDLINE.PRICE
FROM            CUSTOMER              CUST,
                ORDER_LINE_ITEM ORDLINE,
                PART                  PART,
                ORDER                 ORDER
 /* driving table of the query is CUSTOMER,
 * bind-variable into the index on column COUNTRY
 */
WHERE           CUST.COUNTRY        = 'USA'
 /* join from CUSTOMER to ORDER_LINE_ITEM by
 * the index on CUST_ID.  Bind-variable is used
 * as a filtering predicate on column ORDER_ID
 */
AND             ORDLINE.CUST_ID       = CUST.ID
AND             ORDLINE.ORDER_ID              = :b1
 /* join from ORDER_LINE_ITEM to PART by the
 * primary-key index PART_PK
 */
AND             PART.ID             = ORDLINE.PART_ID
 /* join from ORDER_LINE_ITEM by the index on
 * the column CUST_ID
 */
AND             ORDER.CUST_ID       = ORDLINE.CUST_ID
AND             ORDER.ID+0          = ORDLINE.ORDER_ID
ORDER BY        CUST.NAME,
                ORDER.SALE_DATE DESC
```

Please note the comments preceding each predicate in the WHERE clause. They are included to help document how the *rules of prettifying* are applied. Once you settle on some rules for formatting, whether it is these or others, then the comments may not be necessary.

The ORDER BY clause really does not get changed at all, just formatted a little.

Please note the ORDERED hint after the keyword SELECT. The purpose of this is just to ensure that the EXPLAIN PLAN from this *prettified* SQL statement does what we intend; that is, the order of joins should follow the order of the tables specified in the FROM clause. The hint may not be necessary, but as part of the baseline query, it serves as insurance.

Now we have a SQL statement whose EXPLAIN performance exactly matches that of "test1.sql" script, the original baseline. Let's save this SQL statement into another SQL*Plus test case script and change the script's name to "test2.sql." Don't forget to change the SPOOL command in this new script to spool output to "test2.lst." Thus, "test2.sql" is our final baseline test case.

Now, let's fix the danged thing!

Copy the "test2.sql" baseline test case script to another test case script named "test3.sql" and rename the spooled output appropriately. We now have our first hypothesis test case. Unfortunately, it's currently exactly the same as our baseline. What shall we try first?

During the time we spent prettifying the statement, did you notice some strange things? They weren't so noticeable when the SQL statement was just a jumble of words, but once we formatted things, it became more apparent.

Why this particular join order? If you look at the tables, you can readily recognize the tables as belonging to a standard Order Entry schema: customers, orders within customers, order line items within orders, and parts related to order line items. Most people would prefer to see the order of table joins as just described, instead of the somewhat jumbled order currently used.

Why did Oracle choose that order of joins?

Well, Oracle has to start somewhere. When selecting a *driving table* for the query, the Oracle optimizer likes to start from the cheapest, least costly place. Usually, that's a bind variable into an indexed column. Sometimes it's a full table scan of a small table, but in this case, none of the tables is small enough, so it looks at the two predicates with bind values or bind variables:

```
CUST.COUNTRY              = 'USA'
```

or:

```
ORDLINE.ORDER_ID          = :b1
```

From the EXPLAIN PLAN output, it's obvious that there is an index named CUSTOMER_FK2 on the column COUNTRY. That explains why the driving table of the query is CUSTOMER. Also, CUSTOMER is the smallest table of the four, so even if there were no index on COUNTRY, the query might well perform a full table scan on CUSTOMER and still use it as the driving table, unless there was another alternative, such as an index readily available to the other bind value. Is there an index on the column ORDER_ID to use?

Well, querying the USER_IND_COLUMNS view reveals that, yes, there is an index that includes this column, but the columns are CUST_ID, LINE_NBR, and ORDER_ID, in that order. Because the column ORDER_ID is not on the *leading edge* of the index, it is not going to cause the query to use the index by itself. Recall that the column CUST_ID is referenced, in another predicate, and that the index in question, named ORDLINE_FK1, is in fact being used.

Is the ORDER_ID column being used in conjunction with the CUST_ID column, at least? Well, no. You see, the column LINE_NBR is listed in the index after CUST_ID, before ORDER_ID, and the query is not using the LINE_NBR column in the WHERE clause.

Because of this indexing scheme, the column ORDER_ID on the table ORDER_LINE_ITEMS is not being used for indexing.

Let's think. Would it be useful to have an index on the ORDER_LINE_ITEM table starting with the ORDER_ID column? You bet! For one thing, the ORDER table is the direct parent entity of the ORDER_LINE_ITEM table, so an index on the ORDER_ID column should be present anyway to support a FOREIGN KEY constraint. Also, of all the columns on the table, ORDER_ID actually has the greatest number of distinct values, which makes it ideal for Oracle B*Tree indexes. This can be verified by querying the table as follows:

```
SQL> SELECT COUNT(*), COUNT(DISTINCT ORDER_ID),
  2              COUNT(DISTINCT CUST_ID) FROM ORDER_LINE_ITEM;


COUNT(*)    COUNT(DISTINCT O  COUNT(DISTINCT C
----------  ----------------  ----------------
    314628            189222              3341
```

As the results from the query show, the ORDER_ID column is by far the most appropriate column on the table for an index. Now that we've settled that, do we want to create a new index with just ORDER_ID in it? Or do we want to rearrange the existing ORDLINE_FK1 index to put the ORDER_ID on the leading edge?

Well, that answer could go either way, depending on other queries to be performed. For the sake of this example, let's just say that we add a new index on just ORDER_ID, calling it ORDLINE_TESTX1 for now.

With just this new index and no changes to the text of the SQL statement, something cool happens! The elapsed time of the query, which was base-lined at about 3 minutes and 30 seconds, suddenly drops to 40 seconds! The EXPLAIN PLAN changed dramatically (once we removed the ORDERED hint) to the following:

```
Execution Plan
------------------------------
    0       SELECT STATEMENT Optimizer=CHOOSE (Cost=2 Card=1)
    1    0    SORT (ORDER BY)
    2    1      NESTED LOOPS
    3    2        NESTED LOOPS
    4    3          NESTED LOOPS
    5    4            TABLE ACCESS (BY ROWID) OF 'ORDER_LINE_ITEM'
(Cost=13)
    6    5              INDEX (RANGE SCAN) OF 'ORDLINE_TESTX1' (NON-
UNIQUE) (Cost=22 Card=180231)
    7    4            TABLE ACCESS (BY ROWID) OF 'CUSTOMER' (Cost=1)
    8    7              INDEX (UNIQUE SCAN) OF 'CUSTOMER_PK' (UNIQUE)
```

```
(Cost=3 Card=1444)
    9    3          TABLE ACCESS (BY ROWID) OF 'PART' (Cost=1)
   10    9            INDEX (UNIQUE SCAN) OF 'PART_PK' (UNIQUE) (Cost=41
Card=1458975)
   11    2          TABLE ACCESS (BY ROWID) OF 'ORDER' (Cost=1435)
   12   11            INDEX (RANGE SCAN) OF 'ORDER_FK1' (NON-UNIQUE)
(Cost=15889 Card=49363)
```

From 210 seconds to 40 seconds! What a difference! What could have accounted for this difference?

For one thing, notice that one INDEX (RANGE SCAN), on the CUSTOMER table, has now been converted to an INDEX (UNIQUE SCAN). Probing the primary key index for a unique data value is much more efficient than a range scan.

In fact, if you look closely, there is another opportunity available to convert a range scan to a unique scan—the join from ORDER_LINE_ITEM to the ORDER table. Currently, the SQL statement is joining only by the CUST_ID column, but the primary key of the ORDER table is the ID column. For some reason, some joker put the expression "+ 0" next to the reference of the ORDER.ID column, which would "turn off" the index in most versions of Oracle. Removing the "+ 0" expression enables the use of the ORDER_PK index, and suddenly the elapsed time of the query drops yet again, from 40 seconds down to 2.2 seconds!

An important rule of tuning is illustrated here. Most SQL programmers like to write their SQL statements so that the driving table of the query is the smallest table in the set. Generally, the smallest table is the highest-level entity in an *entity-relationship diagram* or ERD. In this example, the highest-level entity is the CUSTOMER table. Then, the conventional wisdom is that you always join from parent-entity to child-entity, recursively. In our example, that would mean a join order of CUSTOMER, ORDER, ORDER_LINE_ITEM, and then back up to from ORDER_LINE_ITEM to the parent PART entity.

However logical that way of thinking seems, it has a real-world cost: It forces you to always perform relatively expensive index range-scans. Joining from parent to child generally involves a range scan because there are usually many children rows for each parent row.

But look at the results from our tuning. From 210 seconds down to 2 seconds! One of the main reasons for this result has to do with the fact that we reversed the order of the joins. Inadvertently, of course. Instead of moving *downward* through the ERD hierarchy, from parent to child, we started at the lowest-level entity of the hierarchy and moved *upward* through the ERD hierarchy. When we did this, our joins went from child to parent. There is an inherent advantage to this because a join in this direction always uses unique indexes! We call this *riding the unique indexes.*

Not only was the new index into the ORDER_LINE_ITEM table extremely efficient, but we had the additional benefit of *riding the unique indexes* on upward through the ERD hierarchy, resulting in a small number of extremely efficient index unique-scans. The result in this example is a query that is 100 times faster! That ain't chicken feed!

Of course, we got lucky. It's not always that we have a bind-variable predicate into such a selective column in the lowest-level entity in the ERD hierarchy. Sometimes you get lucky, and sometimes you make your own luck.

Some tips to remember:

- SQL tuning can be time-consuming. Don't waste time on SQL statements that are not horrible. Use *triage*. Prioritize your tasks so that you attend to only the most important ones.

- Baseline the SQL statement first. Make certain that the problem is reproducible.

- Use the features of SQL*Plus demonstrated here to create test case scripts.

- Use either the SQL*Plus AUTOTRACE feature or SQL Trace and TKPROF. Use both, if necessary.

- Take the time to *really* understand what the query is actually doing. The *prettify* exercise is a good way to do this.

- Understand the *selectivity* or *cardinality* of data in the columns used in the WHERE clause.

- Understand the *entity-relationship diagram* of the tables involved.

- For a *driving table* in the query, start as low as possible in the ERD, and utilize the unique indexes as much as possible to join upward through the hierarchy;

- Don't reject any ideas out of hand. *Test them out!* Even if you don't think they make sense, you may be surprised.

- *Test it out!* Be prepared to ignore every tip listed here—you may find a better idea. Don't reject it. *Test it out!* Don't let anyone talk you out of it based on theory or reasoning. **Test it out!**

And have fun! This isn't life or death—it's just a puzzle.

Resolving Contention for Resources

Suppose the overall symptoms of the performance problem do not indicate excessive resource consumption. In other words, the system does not seem very busy at all, yet performance is not good.

Just as with SQL tuning, the scope of your investigation matters. If you are looking for performance problems due to resource contention in a single session, there are two great ways to begin the investigation. If you are looking for performance problems due to contention in the entire database instance, there is one place to start.

Detecting Contention Globally

Let's start with a global performance problem. The place to start is the V$SYS-TEM_EVENT dynamic performance view, but first let's have a brief discussion of what Oracle's *wait event interface* is.

Introduced with Oracle7, wait events operate very much like a "Gone Fishing" sign on a shopkeeper's door. When the shopkeeper goes fishing, he leaves the sign at his shop while he's gone. When he returns, he takes the sign down.

When an Oracle server process is about to do something for which it will relinquish the CPU, it posts a wait event in the SGA. Then, it goes ahead and makes a system call to the operating-system, goes to sleep to wait for a latch or an enqueue, sets a timer and goes to sleep. Any one of these actions relinquishes the CPU voluntarily. When the server process finally acquires the resource it was waiting for, or when the system call returns, it removes the wait event. Before it continues with its normal processing, it updates some statistics in the SGA: It increments counters, and if the TIMED_STATISTICS configuration parameter is set to TRUE, it records the amount of time spent waiting, incrementing totals.

Four dynamic performance views make up the wait event interface:

V$EVENT_NAME

V$SESSION_WAIT

V$SESSION_EVENT

V$SYSTEM_EVENT

The first view, V$EVENT_NAME, is simply a list of all the wait events for the current version of Oracle, along with a brief description. This view is intended simply as reference. A more complete descriptive list of wait events resides in Appendix A of the *Oracle8i Server* reference manual.

The V$SESSION_WAIT view is a *real-time* display of wait events currently held by sessions in the database instance. If a session currently has a wait event posted, there will be a single row for that session ID (column SID) in V$SESSION_WAIT. The row contains the name of the wait event, up to three qualifying parameter values, and (if TIMED_STATISTICS = TRUE) the total time the session has spent waiting for the event, so far. If a session is busy processing something and is not waiting on anything, then there is no row for that session in this view. As a consequence, V$SESSION_WAIT shows only what is happening right now, in real-time. The information in this view is very transient.

The V$SESSION_EVENT view is a summary of the information posted in V$SESSION_WAIT, cumulative for all of the currently existing sessions in the database. V$SESSION_EVENT summarizes counts and (if TIMED_STATISTICS = TRUE) total time spent waiting by each currently connected session. Each row in this view represents a wait event recorded by a session. When a connected session disconnects, then all its rows in V$SESSION_EVENT are removed.

The V$SYSTEM_EVENT view is a summary of all the information ever posted to V$SESSION_WAIT, cumulatively for the lifetime of a database instance since STARTUP. There is one row in V$SYSTEM_EVENT for each wait event. It summarizes the total number of times each wait event is called and (if TIMED_STATISTICS = TRUE) summarizes the total amount of time spent waiting on the wait event.

If you are trying to find out what kinds of contention are occurring in a database instance globally, it makes sense to start with the V$SYSTEM_EVENT view as follows:

```
SELECT * FROM V$SYSTEM_EVENT ORDER BY TIME_WAITED;
```

This query will display all the information in the view, sorted by the total time that Oracle has spent waiting for the event. This means that the most significant wait events will show at the end of the listing.

Now, one thing to remember: Many wait events are completely normal and are not signs of abnormal contention. Examples of this are timers. Wait events such as *pmon timer* and *smon timer* are just timer events, as their names suggest. The PMON and SMON processes spend most of their "lives" sleeping, waiting to be awakened. This is reflected in the V$SYSTEM_EVENT view, where these wait events are bound to have the highest cumulative totals for TIME_WAITED. Ignore them.

Another "benign" event is *rdbms ipc message*, which represents interprocess communications between the instance's background processes.

The wait event *SQL*Net message from client* should also be ignored, in general. Literally, it represents time spent by Oracle server processes waiting for the client connection to submit a request. A good example is the SQL*Plus program sitting at the "SQL>" prompt. Quite often, this wait event shows with one of the highest values in the TIME_WAITED column. It does not represent a problem in the RDBMS. If anything, it might represent a problem in the client process!

If the wait event is *latch free* and the TIME_WAITED column value is among the highest, then it indicates latch contention. If the wait event *enqueue* is most often waited on, then this might indicate a problem with locking, perhaps row locking in the application.

In the event of latch contention, query the V$LATCH view, which contains cumulative information about the time spent waiting for the latch, cumulatively since the startup of the instance. The V$LATCH view is very much like V$SYSTEM_EVENT in that respect. A good query to use is this one:

```
SELECT * FROM V$LATCH ORDER BY SLEEPS;
```

Latches are extremely low-level synchronization mechanisms used internally by the Oracle RDBMS. They are intended to be accessed extremely quickly and held for extremely brief periods of time. Most of the time, they are either acquired without any waits, or they can be acquired simply by spinning the CPU briefly, a technique called *nonpreemptive waits*. If the latch still cannot be acquired that way, then they must be acquired by relinquishing the CPU and sleeping, a technique also known as *preemptive waits*. If latch processing is congested enough to get this far, then it is useful to know which latches this happens to most often. So, sorting by SLEEPS, by the total count of preemptive waits, is a way of finding out which latch is causing the most trouble.

In the event of contention on *enqueues* (also more popularly known as *locks*), we don't have it so easy. All we have is the view V$LOCK, which is a real-time view showing enqueues currently held or requested by sessions. To query this view, it is perhaps most useful to use the Server Manager script *utllockt.sql*, which is supplied with the Oracle installation in the directory "$ORACLE_HOME/rdbms/admin" on UNIX. This report queries for *blocking sessions* and *waiting sessions* within the database instance, and it reports *who is blocking whom*.

So, when you are trying to detect contention globally within a database instance, utilize the Wait Event Interface, and start with the V$SYSTEM_EVENT view. That will provide a good indicator of where else to continue looking.

Happy hunting!

Detecting Contention in a Single Session

What if the scope of your search is a single job, process, or program module? In that situation, you can utilize some additional, undocumented features of the SQL trace utility. These additional levels of SQL tracing are ignored by TKPROF, so you will need to become familiar with browsing the "raw" SQL trace file.

As we mentioned earlier, one of the methods for enabling SQL tracing in another Oracle session uses the Server Manager's ORADEBUG utility. This is the only way to enable the three extra levels of SQL tracing, which are as follows:

Level 4. Provides all the information with SQL trace's default level (i.e., level 1) and displays the values for any bind variables.

Level 8. Provides all the information with SQL trace's default level (i.e., level 1) and adds information on WAIT events.

Level 12. Provides all the information of levels 0, 4, and 8 combined.

Tracing WAIT Events

From Server Manager, issue the following command:

```
SVRMGR> oradebug setospid NNNNN
Statement processed.
```

```
SVRMGR> oradebug event 10046 trace name context forever, level 8
Statement processed.
SVRMGR> oradebug unlimit
Statement processed.
```

This series of commands will first cause Server Manager to "attach" to the Oracle server process whose operating system process ID (i.e., O.S. PID) is the decimal number represented by *NNNNN*.

Remember: On Windows NT, you have to translate the hexadecimal value you get from the column SPID in the V$PROCESS view. If you acquired the PID from Windows NT Task Manager, then it is already in decimal format.

WAIT EVENTS

Table 9.1 lists some of the basic events most commonly seen.

Table 9.1 Common Oracle Wait Events

WAIT EVENT NAME	DESCRIPTION
SQL*Net message from client	The Oracle server process is waiting for a message to arrive from a client process.
SQL*Net message to client	The Oracle server process is sending a message to a client process.
SQL*Net more data from client	The previous operation was a message from a client process, and this is a continuation.
SQL*Net more data to client	The previous operation was a message to a client process, and this is a continuation.
buffer busy waits	A block is being read into the buffer cache by another session.
client message	The Oracle server process is idle and waiting for an SQL*Net packet.
db file scattered read	The Oracle server process is waiting on a full table scan (i.e., multiblock read).
db file sequential read	The Oracle server process is waiting on an indexed scan (i.e., single-block read).
enqueue	The Oracle server process is waiting on a lock (see V$LOCK).
free buffer waits	DBWR needs to free up some buffers by writing some "dirtied" blocks.

Once Server Manager is attached to the other Oracle server process, you can set the Oracle event number 10046 (i.e., SQL tracing) in that other process. This event will remain set "forever," which means until it is countermanded or until that process terminates. Because level 8 will probably mean more SQL trace output in the trace file, it might be a good idea to remove the size restriction on trace files imposed by the MAX_DUMP_FILE_SIZE parameter. This is not required, but it could keep you from missing something in case there is a lot going on inside the process being traced and the trace file becomes truncated.

Once SQL trace level 8 (or higher) is enabled, you will see lines starting with the phrase "WAIT #" in the SQL trace file. The format of these lines is as follows:

WAIT EVENT NAME	DESCRIPTION
Null event	The Oracle server process is idle.
latch free	The Oracle server process is waiting on a latch (see V$LATCHNAME for P1).
log file sync	The Oracle server process has COMMITed or ROLLBACKed; LGWR has been posted to write the log buffer to the redo logfile.
parallel query dequeue wait	The Oracle server process is waiting on interprocess communication between PQ slaves, which takes place on internal queues.
pmon timer	PMON is idle, waiting to awaken.
rdbms ipc message	DBWR, LGWR, LCKn background processes are idle, waiting to awaken.
rdbms ipc reply	One of the background processes is waiting on a reply from another background process.
smon timer	SMON is idle, waiting to awaken.
write complete waits	The Oracle server process is waiting for DBWR to finish writing a "dirtied" block.

Of course, there are many more events. They are listed online in the V$EVENT_NAME view and in the *Oracle8*i *Server* reference manual, in Appendix A. If you don't have this manual, then you can obtain it from the Internet by registering with the Oracle Technology Network at http://technet.oracle.com/ and accessing the documentation sets in HTML and Adobe Acrobat there. Contact Oracle Worldwide Support for additional explanations, if necessary.

```
WAIT #<cursor>: nam="<event>" ela=N p1=N p2=N p3=N
```

where

cursor	The cursor whose execution is waiting
event	The name of the Oracle event we're waiting for
ela=N	Elapsed time in hundredths of seconds we've been waiting
p1=N	parameter #1 for the event
p2=N	parameter #2 for the event
p3=N	parameter #3 for the event

If you read backward in the trace file, you can find the PARSING IN CURSOR #<cursor> statement that identifies the SQL statement that is waiting. If you read backward from the WAIT event line, you can find the last operation (i.e., PARSE #<cursor>, EXEC #<cursor>, FETCH #<cursor>) that was executed, which would be the operation (or "step") of the SQL statement that the session is waiting on.

The ELA=N shows the amount of time this event was waited on. This is in hundredths of seconds and should not be considered "gospel." Many operations complete far more quickly than 0.01 seconds, so many times this value will be rounded, frequently to 0. The remaining information fields are all dependent on the value of NAM=, which is the name of the event.

These events are also seen in the dynamic data dictionary view V$SESSION_WAIT. Rows in that view exist only for the duration of the wait. Once the process is no longer waiting, the row is removed.

The V$SESSION_WAIT view provides a good snapshot of what all the sessions in the database instance are waiting on at a certain point in time, but it is rather difficult to track what a particular session is waiting on from moment to moment. This level of SQL tracing logs that same information to the trace file, so you can track what an individual session has been waiting on.

Tracing BIND VARIABLE Values

If an Oracle process is doing something unusual or returning unexpected results, it might be useful to see what data values are being passed to each SQL statement that uses bind variables. Of course, it is easy to see what data values are being passed when bind variables are not used, as these values are embedded right in the text of the SQL statement itself. Thus, these data values can be viewed using the default level of SQL tracing.

In order to effectively use the SGA Shared Pool and cache SQL statements, it is usually necessary to use bind variables. To dump the values of bind variables from an Oracle session currently running, use Server Manager or SQL*Plus to enable SQL tracing:

```
SVRMGR> oradebug setospid NNNNN
Statement processed.
SVRMGR> oradebug event 10046 trace name context forever, level 4
Statement processed.
SVRMGR> oradebug unlimit
Statement processed.
```

SQL trace level 4 provides all the information provided by level 0, plus the following entries to display bind variable values:

```
BINDS #<cursor>:
 bind <var>: dty=N mxl=N(N) mal=N scl=N pre=N oacflg=N
  bfp=0xNNNNNN bln=NN avl=NN flg=NN
  value=<value>
```

where

cursor	The cursor to which the bind variable belongs
var	positional number assigned to the variable within the SQL statement (i.e., first variable is "0," second variable is "1," etc.)
dty	data type in internal representation (see OCI Reference Manual)
mxl	maximum length of the bind variable
mal	array length
scl	scale (if numeric)
pre	precision (if numeric)
oacflg	bit-field indicating internal details about variable
bfp	hexadecimal bind address
bln	bind buffer length
avl	actual value length
flg	bit-field indicating internal details about variable
value	actual value of the bind variable

WARNING Be cautious when using the ORADEBUG facility. Be aware that it is intended primarily for use only by Oracle Development and Oracle Support and that the syntax of these commands is subject to change without prior notice. Don't abuse this facility by exploring. You may give Oracle Worldwide Support a good reason to hang up on you.

Summary

This chapter is by no means a complete rundown on tuning Oracle databases or tuning Oracle-based data warehouses. Use the Oracle Server tuning guides; they are quite well written and contain useful advice that it did not make sense to duplicate here. Consider this chapter something of a supplement to that standard piece of Oracle documentation.

Most questions about the behavior of an Oracle process can be answered by examining SQL trace files. If at all possible, ignore the "experts," ignore the pundits as they pontificate, even ignore most of the assertions in this book. Go and find out for yourself. Trace it. Figure it out. Draw your own conclusions based on the empirical evidence.

Parallel Execution in the Oracle Data Warehouse

BRIAN: Look. You've got it all wrong. You don't need to follow me. You don't need to follow anybody! You've got to think for yourselves. You're all individuals!

FOLLOWERS: Yes, we are all individuals!

BRIAN: You're all different.

FOLLOWERS: Yes, we are all different.

VOICE IN THE CROWD OF FOLLOWERS: I'm not!

FOLLOWERS: Shh. Shhhh. Shhh. Shut up!

Monty Python's Life of Brian—*Python (Monty) Pictures, Ltd., 1979*

Parallel operations in Oracle are a direct outgrowth from the trend toward data warehousing. From queries, inserts, updates, and deletes, to index and table creation, to loading, to media recovery, almost every facet of Oracle has gradually been retrofitted with a parallel option.

What Is Oracle Parallel Execution?

In Oracle7, the Parallel Query Option (PQO) was frequently confused with Parallel Server Option (PSO or OPS). Parallel Query Option allowed, for the first time, certain individual SQL statements to be transparently divided into several, concurrently executing operations, providing a dramatic speedup in certain conditions. PQO could be used with single-instance exclusive-mode Oracle, and it does not require PSO. It could also be used in conjunction with PSO to transparently divide certain operations not only among several processes on a single node but across several nodes as well. While PQO and its ability to scale operations within a system are available on just about all the 100-plus platforms Oracle runs on, the availability of the Parallel Server Option is more restricted and is separately licensed.

One additional point of possible confusion: With Oracle8, the Parallel Query Option became a standard feature of the Enterprise Edition of the Oracle8 Server. This has been a long-standing tradition of Oracle: What is originally offered as an unbundled (and separately licensed) additional option is later folded into the base product as standard functionality. This occurred previously when Oracle7 debuted and PL/SQL and row-level locking (together known as the Procedural Option under Oracle version 6) became standard functionality, for instance. Now the same has occurred for the former PQO, and it is now simply referred to as "PX" for *Parallel eXecution*. The older acronyms "PQO" and "PQ," which reflected the emphasis on parallel queries in Oracle7 and Oracle8, are now being replaced in Oracle8*i* by the acronym "PX," which more accurately reflects parallel execution for DML and DDL, as well as queries.

The purpose of this chapter is to explain the history and progression of PX throughout the Oracle RDBMS, how it works, and when it is best to use—as well as when it is best **not** to use—this powerful feature.

PX first became available with Oracle7, version 7.1, and consisted of the following operations:

- Parallel queries (full table scans only)
- Parallel *direct-path* SQL*Loader
- Parallel CREATE INDEX (pCI)
- Parallel instance recovery

Later, with Oracle7, version 7.2, the following parallel operations were added:

- Parallel CREATE TABLE . . . AS SELECT (pCTAS)
- Parallel execution of partitioned UNION-ALL views

Still later, with Oracle7, version 7.3, the following was added:

- Parallel ALTER INDEX . . . REBUILD

And with Oracle8, the following features appeared:

- Parallel queries (indexed scans on non-prefixed partitioned indexes)
- Parallel INSERT on partitioned and nonpartitioned tables

- Parallel UPDATE and DELETE on partitioned tables
- Parallel MOVE PARTITION

Now, with Oracle8*i* the following additional features debut:

- Parallel SPLIT PARTITION for tables and indexes
- Parallel MERGE PARTITION for tables and indexes
- Parallel ALTER TABLE . . . MOVE
- Parallel ALTER INDEX . . . REBUILD
- Parallel ALTER INDEX . . . REBUILD PARTITION
- Parallel ALTER INDEX . . . REBUILD SUBPARTITION
- Parallel ALTER INDEX . . . REBUILD ONLINE
- Parallel ANALYZE (via the DBMS_STATS supplied package only)

Later on in this chapter we discuss each of these operations in detail. First, we will discuss the appropriateness of parallelized operations in general terms.

When Are Parallel Operations Useful?

This issue is neatly summarized by considering the following question: "If it takes a woman nine months to produce a baby, could nine women take one month to do the same?" The answer is *probably not*; the reason the answer isn't *absolutely not* has to do with recent technological advances in cloning and the desire of certain people to appear on late-night talk shows. You just can't tell anymore.

Such speculation (and kidding) aside, it seems certain that parallelism is not the right strategy for speeding up all operations; it may be impossible (due to present technology) or not worth the effort. The same is true with database operations.

TIP Parallelizing any operation adds work to the system. The same amount of actual processing effort is required, plus the work of dividing the task up and then later recombining (or collating) results. While the tasks of dynamically dividing up work and then collating results are relatively minor, remember that PX tries to perform all of the original work in a shorter timeframe, so the system's resources are consumed much more intensely. If the hardware (CPU or disk subsystem) is already running at capacity, then parallelizing will result in diminished throughput on the system.

Think of it this way: *PX is a great way to soak up any excess CPU or disk resources.* If you've got the excess resources and you want to speed up a large operation, then great! Otherwise, be careful.

The main criterion in deciding whether to apply parallelism to a particular operation probably has to do with the duration of the operation. All other issues, such as the number of discretely identifiable steps in the operation, can be altered. But if an operation already completes relatively swiftly, there may be little advantage to trying to speed it up. It is the operations that take a long time that are likely to benefit from the effort involved in parallelizing.

To arbitrarily name a figure, let's say that it generally takes about 10 seconds to break a transaction into several smaller subtransactions. Then, let's say that about 10 percent extra overhead is imposed on these subtransactions during run-time for synchronization. Last, let's say that it takes an additional 10 seconds to collate the results from all these subtransactions to form a single unified result from a single transaction. (These timings aren't representative of real queries, but they make the following example easier to follow. In reality, PX can frequently perform this task in less than a second, but longer times may be required for large queries spread over many instances.)

Now, let's apply these overheads to a small transaction that takes about 2 seconds to complete (see Figure 10.1). Imagine that we are going to try to execute this query using 10 separate, distinct threads of execution. Each of the 10 threads of execution might take one-tenth of 2 seconds, or 0.2 seconds. Tack on the additional 10 percent run-time overhead, and we get 0.22 seconds. Immediately, you can see that the original 2-second transaction would probably take at least 20.22 seconds to complete after parallelization. Certainly, there is no advantage to parallelization here.

On the other hand, consider a query that takes 2 hours to complete (see Figure 10.2). Initiating the parallelized operation may take about 10 seconds, but if the operation is farmed out equally to 10 parallel threads of execution, it seems reasonable to assume that each thread of execution should take approximately one-tenth of 2 hours, or 12 minutes, to complete. Tacking on the extra 10 percent overhead (just because we're conservative) leaves us with an expected execution time of 13.33 minutes. Including another 10 seconds to consolidate

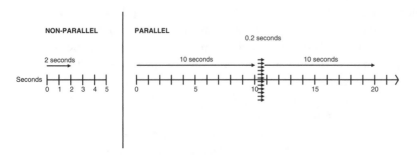

Figure 10.1 Attempting to parallelize brief operations.

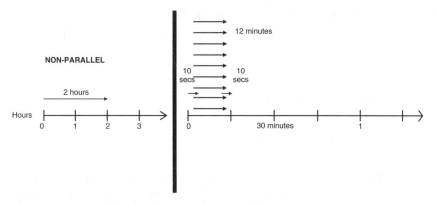

Figure 10.2 Parallelizing long-running operations.

the results of the 10 separate threads of execution and close them down, we could reduce the 2-hour query to less than 14 minutes. Now that's worthwhile.

The majority of "operational" systems can be characterized as online transaction processing, or OLTP. These kinds of systems are designed to process hundreds, thousands, or millions of transactions per hour, each transaction being a relatively short-lived operation. As a result, parallelized operations typically do not benefit OLTP systems except for a few limited exceptions, such as index creation.

In contrast, many of the operations performed in a data warehouse are huge, long-running affairs: a load from a huge "flat file," a massive query against several huge tables loaded with detailed data, summarization of these same huge detailed queries into smaller "summary" tables. Therefore, parallelized operations generally benefit data warehouses and other decision support systems (DSSs) immensely. Almost the entire feature set of the original PX benefits data warehousing and should be exploited.

Basic Parallel Queries

The ability to transparently execute a SELECT statement in parallel was one of the biggest technical triumphs of the Oracle7 product. It first became available with version 7.1 and is the "flagship" feature of the PX.

Most of Oracle's parallelized operations share some common traits. The decision to run in parallel is completely transparent or can be chosen with a simple clause like PARALLEL (DEGREE nn). Behind the scenes, the Oracle server process, which would normally be tasked with performing all the work of the query, is promoted to a management role known as the *query coordinator* (QC). The QC is responsible for the following:

- Dynamically partitioning the work to be done

- Recruiting a *crew* of *parallel query slave* processes to perform the actual work

- Assigning partitions to each of the parallel query "slaves"

- Receiving and collating the results returned by the parallel query slaves to the initiating process

After these tasks are done, the parallel query slave processes used during the operation return to a *pool* of such processes owned by the database instance, and the QC reverts to being just a normal everyday Oracle server process. If the next operation is not parallel, then it will do all the work, as normal. If the next operation is to be in parallel, then the whole process of becoming a QC starts all over again. It's kind of like the old TV game show, *Queen for a Day*.

Consider the following example:

```
SQL> SELECT degree, instances FROM user_tables
  2 WHERE table_name = 'BILLING_DETAIL';

DEGREE       INSTANCES
------       ---------
    1                1

SQL> SET TIMING ON
SQL> SELECT count(*) FROM billing_detail;

    COUNT(*)
-------------
    12384004

Elapsed: 00:58:49.01
```

The first query merely confirms that the table BILLING_DETAIL is currently not set up for parallel queries. The default value of 1 is in effect for both DEGREE and INSTANCES. Please bear in mind that values greater than 1 for INSTANCES are useless unless this is a Parallel Server database with as many active database instances as specified.

The second statement turns on SQL*Plus timing, which will display elapsed time in hours, minutes, and seconds. The third statement is a query that merely counts the number of rows in the BILLING_DETAIL table, and it took just under one hour to complete.

Behind the scenes, the Oracle server process might look as it is shown in Figure 10.3.

Now, let's see what happens when we set a default DEGREE of parallelism on the table. The DEGREE of parallelism is the requested number of concurrent threads of execution to be used on one database instance in order to com-

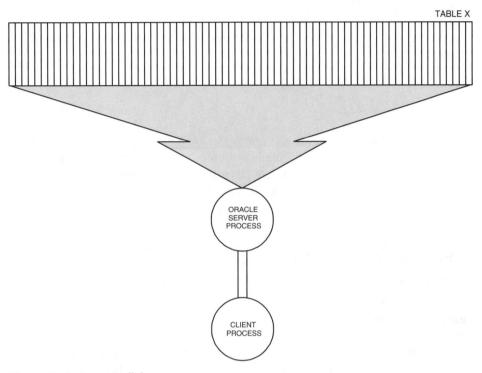

Figure 10.3 Nonparallel query.

plete the query. The other parameter, INSTANCES, indicates the number of database instances to expand the DEGREE over and, as previously mentioned, is usable only in conjunction with Oracle Parallel Server. The resulting number of concurrent threads of execution requested, also known as the *scan factor*, is the product of these two numbers, or DEGREE times INSTANCES. So, if DEGREE = 4 and INSTANCES = 3, then a total of 4 threads of execution will be requested across each of 3 database instances, for a total scan factor of 12.

Let's alter the PARALLEL characteristics of the table and reexecute the same query.

```
SQL> ALTER TABLE billing_detail PARALLEL (DEGREE 8);

Table altered.

SQL> SELECT degree, instances FROM user_tables
  2 WHERE TABLE_NAME = 'BILLING_DETAIL';

DEGREE      INSTANCES
------      ---------
     8              1
```

```
SQL> SET TIMING ON
SQL> SELECT COUNT(*) FROM billing_detail;

COUNT(*)
--------
12384004

Elapsed: 00:08:13.23
```

The row count returned by the query was the same, but the elapsed time dropped from 58 minutes to 8. This is not quite an eightfold improvement, and we'll explore the reasons why shortly. It's not a bad performance improvement, gained with little or no effort on the part of the end user.

Behind the scenes, however, a lot was happening.

Step 1: Dynamic Partitioning

PX uses dynamic partitioning to divide the total work to be performed by a query. Each time a parallel query is executed, this process of partitioning the table to be queried must be done over again, even if the previous operation was the exact same query. It's not as if everything is thrown away, however; partitioned queries executed by each concurrent thread of execution are saved in the SGA's Shared SQL area, just like other queries. So there is some reuse.

The fact that PX provides *internal parallelism* is important because the end user issuing a SELECT statement need not change the SQL statement at all or use a different front-end tool to reap the advantages of parallelism. Many database systems provide functionality similar to that of PX, but they do so *externally*, by forcing the end user to use a different front-end tool or connect to the database differently. PX can be entirely transparent to the end users if they wish.

Dynamic partitioning allows Oracle to adjust, at run-time, to factors such as changing data volume and available CPU resources. *Static partitioning*, available with Oracle8 partitioned tables and solely employed by most other databases vendors, is based primarily on a predetermined partitioning scheme formulated by the system administrator (see Figure 10.4 for a comparison of the two modes). As you might suppose, poor guesses by the system administrator or the DBA will result in queries that perpetually execute poorly. To react to changing data volumes and system resources, static partitioning schemes require, at minimum, that the rules of data partitioning be changed and, at worst, may require a reorganization of the tables involved.

Dynamic partitioning schemes such as Oracle's do incur *front-loaded overhead* because each query must draw on information in the data dictionary to determine how to create partitions. Systems that use dynamic partitioning schemes, like Oracle PX, can experience initial delays while the task at hand is divided equally and each subtask is handed off to parallel query slaves.

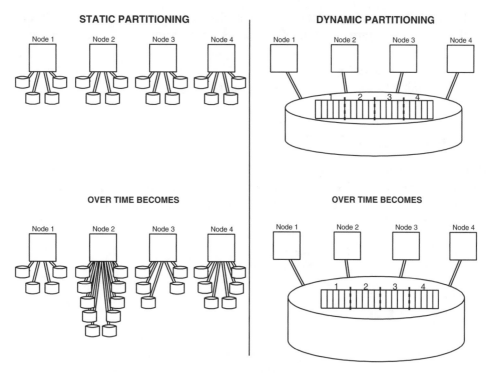

Figure 10.4 Comparison of dynamic and static partitioning.

In Oracle7, PX implemented parallelism for full table scans only. With Oracle8, parallel index scans also become possible on partitioned tables that use partitioned indexes. A parallel query slave process can be assigned to each partition, and each PX slave will scan the index for each partition concurrently. This is similar to the parallel index scan functionality offered by other database vendors.

Nonpartitioned tables in Oracle8 are subject to the same PX limitations as Oracle7, but the addition of parallel index scans on partitioned tables is a powerful feature greatly augmenting Oracle's arsenal of tools for manipulating large bodies of data.

Let's look at how PX dynamically partitions our example query, which is run against a nonpartitioned table, thus requiring a full table scan. The first thing to understand is the *degree of parallelism* (DOP), which indicates the number of threads of execution (i.e., processes on UNIX and VMS, process threads on Windows NT) that will be used to process the SQL statement. The degree of parallelism can be determined from three different levels:

1. At the instance level, using database initialization parameters.

2. At the individual table level, using CREATE/ALTER TABLE commands.

3. At the individual SQL statement level, using hints.

Let's briefly discuss how the value for DEGREE could be derived from initialization parameters in Oracle7, Oracle8, and Oracle8*i*. PX in the Oracle RDBMS has gone through some massive changes during this time, and much has been written over the years. To understand where all the myths and legends may be coming from, let's review some history.

Calculating DEGREE in Oracle7

Strangely enough, the keyword "DEFAULT" is *not* the default value for DEGREE. The default value of DEGREE is 1, meaning no degree of parallelism. Valid values for the DEGREE clause are the keyword "DEFAULT" and numeric values ranging from 1 through 65,535.

```
SQL> SELECT degree FROM user_tables
  2 WHERE table_name = 'BILLING_DETAIL';

DEGREE
------
     1

SQL> ALTER TABLE billing_detail parallel (DEGREE DEFAULT);

Table altered.

SQL> SELECT degree FROM user_tables
  2 WHERE table_name = 'BILLING_DETAIL';

DEGREE
-------
DEFAULT

SQL> ALTER TABLE billing_detail parallel (DEGREE 8);

Table altered.

SQL> SELECT degree FROM user_tables
  2 WHERE table_name = 'BILLING_DETAIL';

DEGREE
------
     8
```

The *degree of parallelism* is calculated based on the following hierarchy, described in the following examples.

If there is a PARALLEL hint in the SQL statement, then that hint will override any other degree of parallelism specified anywhere else.

```
SQL> SELECT degree FROM user_tables
  2 WHERE table_name = 'BILLING_DETAIL';

DEGREE
------
     8

SQL> SELECT /*+ parallel(x, 16) */ COUNT(DISTINCT CUSTOMER_ID)
  2 FROM   BILLING_DETAIL x
  3 WHERE  STATUS = 'ACTIVE';

COUNT(*)
-------
9333817
```

The previous query used a degree of parallelism of 16 threads of execution to count the rows in the table, although the table is defined with DEGREE 8 currently. We don't have any way of showing you this in a two-dimensional printed page, so you'll just have to take our word for it!

If a countermanding hint is not specified for an operation that can be run in parallel, then the Oracle Optimizer uses the DEGREE specified for the table.

In the previous example, with the DEGREE set to 8, the query would use that value for the degree of parallelism. However, if the value for DEGREE was set to DEFAULT, then the degree of parallelism would be calculated based on the settings of some global database configuration parameters, used in the following equation:

```
MIN((size-of-table-in-blocks / PARALLEL_DEFAULT_SCANSIZE),
    PARALLEL_DEFAULT_MAX_SCANS)
```

The size of the table in terms of database blocks (stored in and retrieved from the data dictionary) is first divided by this PARALLEL_DEFAULT_SCAN-SIZE value to get an initial value to use as DEGREE. As you can see, this value is proportional to the size of the table to be queried.

There has got to be a limit on this sort of thing. It doesn't take much imagination to see how this initial calculation could yield a number in the hundreds, thousands, or millions. Most computer systems will balk at supporting millions of parallel query slave processes, one would hope.

To prevent this, the value specified for PARALLEL_DEFAULT_MAX_SCANS was used. If the value resulting from the previous division was smaller than the value of PARALLEL_DEFAULT_MAX_SCANS, then it got used. Otherwise, the value of PARALLEL_DEFAULT_MAX_SCANS was used instead.

Given the following initialization parameter values,

```
PARALLEL_DEFAULT_SCANSIZE = 500
PARALLEL_DEFAULT_MAX_SCANS = 3
PARALLEL_DEFAULT_INSTANCES = 4
```

if a full table scan on a table comprising 1,150 database blocks is to be scanned, then

```
MIN((1150/500), 3)
```

This results in a value of 2 because 1,150/500 = 2 is less than 3. This will result in a value of DEGREE 2 and INSTANCES 4.

If the table is 11,000 database blocks in size, then

```
MIN((11000/500), 3)
```

will result in a value of 3 because11,000/500 is 22, and 3 is less than 22. As a result, a query against this table will result in parallelism of DEGREE 3 and INSTANCES 4.

If you specify a PARALLEL or NOPARALLEL hint for a SQL statement, then that is the degree of parallelism that will be used. Otherwise, if you don't use a hint, then the Oracle Optimizer will examine the DEGREE setting for the table. If this is a numeric value, then that value will be the degree of parallelism. If it is the value default, then the Optimizer will use PARALLEL_DEFAULT_xxx initialization parameters in the ways described previously.

Calculating DEGREE in Oracle8

For the initial release of Oracle8, the rules with respect to the hierarchy of hints, the DEGREE clause with a numeric value, and the DEGREE clause with the value of DEFAULT remained similar. One major difference was the situation with respect to DEGREE DEFAULT, which became much simpler. The PARALLEL_DEFAULT_MAX_SCANS, and the PARALLEL_DEFAULT_SCANSIZE parameters both disappeared. They were replaced by Oracle RDBMS internal calculations that factor the number of CPUs on the node and the number of data files on which the table to be scanned is stored. The CPU information can be verified by examining the configuration parameter CPU_COUNT, and the data file information can be retrieved from the DBA_EXTENTS view.

It is far better to base query parallelism on the resources of the machine (i.e., CPUs and disk drives) to be applied to the table scan rather than simply on the size of the table.

Anyway, moving toward simplicity is a good thing, don't you think? Sorry about that; sometimes Martha Stewart pervades even Oracle database administration. As a matter of fact, if you think about it, don't you think Martha Stewart would make a terrific database administrator?

If you specify a PARALLEL or NOPARALLEL hint for an individual SQL statement, then the Oracle cost-based optimizer will use the specified value as the degree of parallelism. If you did not use a PARALLEL or NOPARALLEL hint, then Oracle will query the data dictionary to find out the value of the DEGREE clause for the table or index. If the value for DEGREE is the keyword DEFAULT, then Oracle8 calculates the default degree of parallelism from the following formula:

```
MIN(CPU_COUNT, #-of-datafiles-segment-located-on)
```

That is, Oracle will use the minimum of either the number of CPUs on the machine (derived from the initialization parameter CPU_COUNT) or the number of data files on which the segment to be scanned is located (derived from the data dictionary table UET$, which underlies the view DBA_EXTENTS).

Calculating DEGREE in Oracle8i

Once again, hints override everything, while explicit numeric values for DEGREE greater than 1 override everything except hints.

If you set DEGREE to DEFAULT, things get quite interesting.

With Oracle8*i*, the move toward simplicity becomes quite overt. Like all simplifications, the underlying mechanisms may seem complicated, but one single initialization parameter should be remembered.

The majority of the PX database parameters from Oracle7 and the initial release of Oracle8 have disappeared, and some new ones appear. The most important is the aptly named PARALLEL_AUTOMATIC_TUNING, which defaults to a value of FALSE. When set to TRUE, this parameter enables *PX automatic tuning*, which changes the default values for several other initialization parameters that establish resource limits for PX (see Table 10.1).

Of course, you can always set any of these parameters explicitly, which (of course) overrides any impact that PARALLEL_AUTOMATIC_TUNING = TRUE has on the parameter's default value. But please don't get bogged down in the details of these parameter settings. Instead, step back and take the long-distance view of these settings.

First of all, Oracle sets some limits high enough so that they do not get in the way. Examples include PROCESSES (and, by extension, SESSIONS, TRANSACTIONS, and other configuration parameters that owe their default values to PROCESSES) and PARALLEL_MAX_SERVERS.

Next, Oracle enables the use of the Large Pool, if it isn't already enabled. Because it was introduced with Oracle8, the Large Pool has been an important adjunct to the Shared Pool. If an Oracle8 database instance is using any one of the features of parallel execution (PX), multithreaded server (MTS), or Recovery Manager (RMAN) and a Large Pool is not created, then each of these features will take memory from the Shared Pool. Now, the Shared Pool is an extremely busy area of shared memory in the Oracle SGA already. The high-velocity demands for memory by PX, MTS, and RMAN place more stress on the synchronization

Table 10.1 New Parameter Defaults when PARALLEL_AUTOMATIC_TUNING = TRUE

PARAMETER NAME	NORMAL DEFAULT VALUE	DEFAULT VALUE IF PX AUTOMATIC TUNING IS ENABLED	COMMENTS
CPU_COUNT	#-of-CPUs	#-of-CPUs	No impact.
PARALLEL_MAX_SERVERS	0	10 * CPU_COUNT	Actually a very wise starting point!
PARALLEL_MIN_SERVERS	0	0	No impact.
PROCESSES	6	**Greatest of:** 1.2 * PARALLEL_MAX_SERVERS **or:** (4 * CPU_COUNT) + 6 + 5 + PARALLEL_MAX_SERVERS	Most DBAs set this parameter explicitly anyway and are aware of its impact on related parameters such as SESSIONS, TRANSACTIONS, etc.
PARALLEL_ADAPTIVE_MULTI_USER	FALSE	TRUE	Important for using PX in a multiuser environment; further detail to follow.
SHARED_POOL_SIZE	16M	16M	No impact.
LARGE_POOL_SIZE	0	600K + PX pool + MTS pool + RMAN pool	Recommended to use Large Pool with PX.
PARALLEL_EXECUTION_MESSAGE_SIZE	2148	4096	No impact.
PARALLEL_MIN_PERCENT	0	0	No impact.
OPTIMIZER_PERCENT_PARALLEL	0	0	No impact.
PARALLEL_BROADCAST_ENABLED	FALSE	FALSE	No impact.
PARALLEL_THREADS_PER_CPU	2	2	No impact.
PARALLEL_SERVER	FALSE	FALSE	*Oracle Parallel Server*, Chapter 11.
PARALLEL_SERVER_INSTAANCES	1	1	*Oracle Parallel Server*, Chapter 11.
PARALLEL_INSTANCE_GROUP	Null string	Null string	*Oracle Parallel Server*, Chapter 11.

mechanisms controlling the Shared Pool, which are likely already heavily contended. Therefore, it is highly recommended, when using one or more of these three features, to specify LARGE_POOL_SIZE. When that happens, each of these three features will cease badgering the Shared Pool for memory resources, and it will instead go after the Large Pool. How large should the Large Pool be? It depends on how many of the three features of PX, MTS, and RMAN you are using, and whether you are using them concurrently. If you are using only PX and RMAN, like most data warehouses, then a good starting point is to allocate at least half the space currently allocated to the Shared Pool. Then, monitor the V$SGASTAT view to determine whether the Large Pool is fully utilized and increase or decrease as you find necessary.

Last, setting PARALLEL_AUTOMATIC_TUNING to TRUE also causes the parameter PARALLEL_ADAPTIVE_MULTI_USER to default to TRUE. This mechanism is the true PX automated tuning utility. It measures other parameters such as CPU_COUNT and PARALLEL_THREADS_PER_CPU, weighs them against the number of data files across which the segment to be scanned is located, and uses the same formula initiated with Oracle8 to arrive at an *initial degree of parallelism*:

```
MIN(CPU_COUNT, #-of-datafiles-segment-located-on)
```

If PARALLEL_ADAPTIVE_MULTI_USER is TRUE, the Oracle cost-based optimizer will then take the additional step to determine exactly how many parallel executions are currently running. If there are none, then the *initial degree of parallelism* calculated previously will become the *effective* value used. If there are already one or more PX operations currently in progress, then the Oracle Optimizer will start to reduce the *initial degree of parallelism* in order to arrive at the *effective* value. An algorithm implementing a *reduction factor* will avoid exceeding the product of CPU_COUNT andPARALLEL_ THREADS_ PER_CPU too quickly.

The purpose of PARALLEL_ADAPTIVE_MULTI_USER is to allow a system using PX to *degrade in performance more gracefully*, rather than simply *hitting a wall*. PX operations that are started when there are fewer other PX operations currently running will receive more resources. PX operations that are started in busier environments will receive fewer resources, right down to the point where the requested PX operation is effectively executed in serial.

Using CREATE/ALTER TABLE to Set DEGREE

As we demonstrated earlier, you can also set the DEGREE clause and the Parallel Server-specific INSTANCES clause to hard-coded numeric values for each table or index, which overrides any of the calculations or functionality described previously. Naturally, the values of DEFAULT and numeric hard-coded values can be mixed. For example:

```
ALTER TABLE x PARALLEL (DEGREE DEFAULT INSTANCES DEFAULT);
ALTER TABLE y PARALLEL (DEGREE 10 INSTANCES 6);
ALTER TABLE z PARALLEL (DEGREE 4 INSTANCES DEFAULT);
```

Table x will use the instance-wide specifications for both DEGREE and INSTANCES. Table y will use only the hard-coded values specified. Table z will use the hard-coded value for DEGREE and the instance-wide default value for INSTANCES. In this way, you can set instance-wide defaults but override those defaults for certain individual tables if you wish.

In Oracle7, setting the parallel DEGREE and INSTANCES clauses was valid only for tables, and it would be used only during *full table scan* operations against those tables.

In Oracle8 and Oracle8*i*, setting the parallel DEGREE and INSTANCES clauses was valid for both tables and indexes. When set for tables, they could be used not only for queries involving *full table scans*, but also for queries involving *indexed scans* on non-prefixed partitioned indexes. Also, when parallel DML was enabled explicitly for the session using:

```
ALTER SESSION ENABLE PARALLEL DML;
```

then the DEGREE and INSTANCES clauses could also be used by parallel INSERT, UPDATE, and DELETE statements.

Individual SQL Statement Level, Using Hints

If you wish to override the instance-wide specifications or the specifications for the particular table you are querying, you can specify SQL *hints* for the degree of parallelism. Hints look very similar to standard SQL *comments* and are specified immediately after the first keyword of the SQL statement. Relevant hints are the following:

```
full(<tbl>)
parallel(<tbl>, <d>, <i>)
```

where

```
tbl   is the name of the table or an alias
d     is either a number or the word "default" to be used for DEGREE
i     is either a number of the word "default" to be used for INSTANCES
```

For example, let's use hints to override the instance-wide defaults to be used for the BILLING_DETAIL table:

```
SQL> SELECT degree, instances FROM user_tables
  2 WHERE table_name = 'BILLING_DETAIL';

DEGREE      INSTANCES
----------  ---------
   DEFAULT    DEFAULT

SQL> SET TIMING ON
SQL> SELECT /*+ FULL(billing_detail) PARALLEL(billing_detail, 8, 4) */
  2        COUNT(*)
  3   FROM billing_detail;

   COUNT(*)
-------------
   12384004

Elapsed: 00:08:13.23
```

Alternatively, a SQL table *alias* can be used in the hint to make the SQL statement a little more concise:

```
SQL> SELECT /*+ FULL(x) PARALLEL(x, 8, 4) */
  2        COUNT(*)
  3   FROM billing_detail x;
```

TIP If a table alias has been specified for a table in the SQL statement, then any hint that references the table MUST use the alias. Specifying the actual name of the aliased table will result in the hint being ignored.

Hints are probably too much of a pain to use regularly, but they are ideal for testing. Using hints, you can try out various values for parallelism in sequence without affecting anyone else.

Step 2: Performing the Partitioning

The product of DEGREE and INSTANCES determines the *effective degree of parallelism*. This number, in addition to being the number of parallel query slave processes that will be requested, is also the divisor used when performing dynamic partitioning (see Figure 10.5).

The Oracle data dictionary contains all necessary information about the number and distribution of database blocks constituting the table to be scanned; the views DBA_EXTENTS or USER_EXTENTS also display this information. The query coordinator (QC) will use the degree of parallelism computed from the requested DEGREE and INSTANCES along with the table size

PARALLEL (DEGREE 4 and INSTANCES 3)

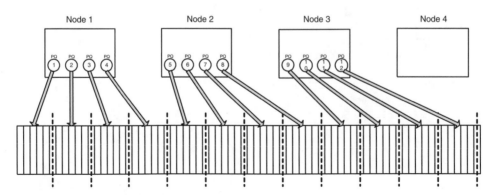

Figure 10.5 Partitioning the table by the DOP.

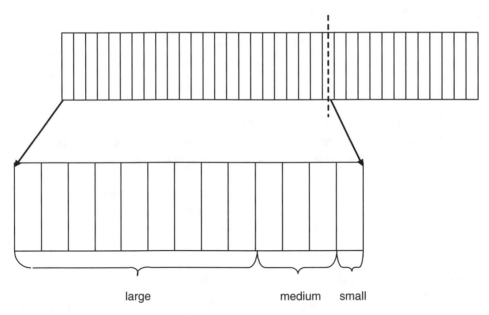

large   medium small

Figure 10.6 Subranges in the initial ROWID ranges.

information in the Oracle data dictionary to divide the table into N roughly equal-sized ranges of ROWIDs, where N is the degree of parallelism.

The QC does not stop with this initial set of ROWID ranges. It then divides each of the initial ROWID ranges into one large, one medium, and one small subrange (see Figure 10.6).

Let's take an example. Starting with DEGREE 4 and INSTANCES 2, we got a degree of parallelism of 8. This resulted in 8 initial ROWID ranges that were fur-

REGARDING THE ORACLE COST-BASED OPTIMIZER

Prior to Oracle7, the Oracle optimizer was rule-based, meaning that a list of prioritized rules was used to determine the access path that each SQL statement would use. The rule-based optimizer (RBO) will be available through the Oracle8 and Oracle8*i* releases, but it is no longer being enhanced. The cost-based optimizer (CBO), which debuted with Oracle7, has been the primary focus for new features.

It is well known that the CBO was almost useless for version 7.0 and that there were significant problems in version 7.1 and 7.2. All in all, even Oracle did not heartily recommend the use of CBO in those releases. The CBO was much improved in version 7.3, but there were still a few well-documented glitches to erode customers' confidence.

In version 8.0, the CBO became "ready for prime-time," provided that cost statistics in the data dictionary are kept up-to-date using the ANALYZE command. Naturally, this caveat is to be expected for a cost-based optimizer, as valid cost data must be available at all times.

Hints, therefore, while remaining a valuable development and testing tool, are generally unnecessary once table default parallelism is defined and statistics are gathered.

The one remaining issue with the CBO in version 8.0 was the fact that the ANALYZE command itself was still not "parallelized," but that has been resolved in Oracle8*i*, not by an enhancement to the ANALYZE command, but by the introduction of the PL/SQL supplied package DBMS_STATS.

Additionally, Oracle8*i* includes new MONITORING functionality that can be enabled for tables using the ALTER TABLE or CREATE TABLE commands. Used in conjunction with the DBMS_STATS package, the MONITORING clause can ensure that tables whose cost-based statistics have become "stale" due to DML activity are re-ANALYZEd when necessary. Consult Chapter 8, "Administering and Monitoring the Oracle Data Warehouse," for more information.

ther subdivided into 3 subranges each. If the table we were querying was 20,000 database blocks in size, then the initial partitioning would have resulted in 8 initial ROWID ranges of about 2,500 blocks apiece. Each of these ranges would then be subdivided into a large, medium, and small subrange, for a total of 24 subranges.

Step 3: Recruiting Parallel Query Slaves

Finally, the partitioning is complete. Given DEGREE 4 and INSTANCES 2, we now have 8 initial ROWID ranges (equal to the degree of parallelism) and a total of 24 subranges. Now, we need to hire a crew to work on those subranges. In our example, we have a degree of parallelism of 8, so the QC is going to try to recruit 8 threads of execution from the database instance.

The term *thread of execution* is used because each thread of execution can consist of either one parallel query slave process, used simply for scanning (reading) data (see Figure 10.7), or two parallel query slave processes that form a producer-consumer relationship. When two processes make up a thread of execution, one parallel query slave process acts as the *producer* by scanning data; the other parallel query slave process acts as the *consumer* by performing some additional processing on the scanned data, such as sorting and aggregating (see Figure 10.8).

Thus, whenever a query includes a sorting or aggregation phase, such as a GROUP BY or ORDER BY clause, or a hash join or sort-merge join, each thread of execution is composed of two parallel query slaves in a producer-consumer relationship. Given a scan factor of 8, this means that the QC will attempt to recruit 16 parallel query slave processes (see Figure 10.9). Whenever the query does not include a sorting or aggregation operation, then the QC will attempt to recruit 1 parallel query slave process per thread of execution. Therefore, given a degree of parallelism of 8, the QC will attempt to recruit 8 parallel query slave processes.

Parallel query slave processes belong to a database instance, as a pool of processes. The number of parallel query slave processes is set using initialization parameters. The first three parameters given in the following list control this pool; the remaining two parameters are used in determining how a parallelized query will run.

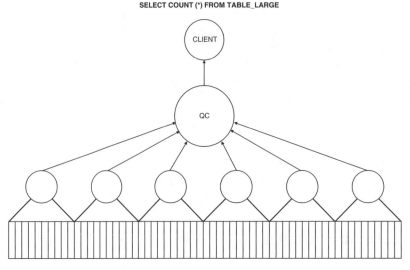

SELECT COUNT (*) FROM TABLE_LARGE

Figure 10.7 Parallel threads of execution consisting of 1 PX slave.

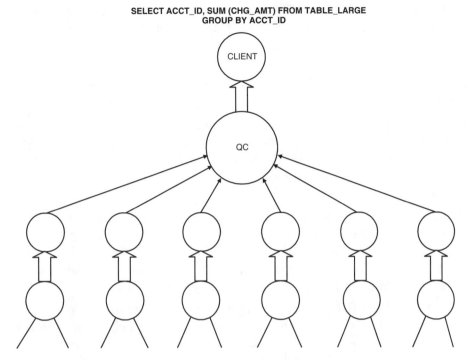

Figure 10.8 Parallel threads of execution consisting of 2 PX slaves.

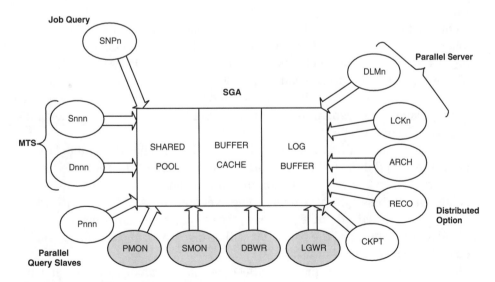

Figure 10.9 Parallel query slave processes.

PARALLEL_MIN_SERVERS. The minimum number of parallel query slave processes for an instance, which are started when the instance starts. As needed, Oracle will increase the number of parallel query slaves up to the maximum specified by PARALLEL_MAX _SERVERS.

PARALLEL_MAX_SERVERS. The maximum number of parallel query slave processes or recovery slave processes for an instance.

PARALLEL_SERVER_IDLE_TIME. The number of minutes that a parallel query slave process remains idle before it is terminated, until the number of processes equals PARALLEL_MIN_SERVERS. This parameter became obsolete in Oracle8*i*, and it has been replaced by a hard-coded value of 5 minutes.

PARALLEL_MIN_PERCENT. The minimum percentage of requested threads in order for a query to be executed. A value of 100 indicates that a query must run with 100 percent of requested DEGREE and INSTANCES or else return an error message. A value of 1 guarantees that a query will at least run nonparallel. A value of 0 disables the use of this parameter.

OPTIMIZER_PERCENT_PARALLEL. Specifies the amount of parallelism that the optimizer uses in its cost functions. A value of 0 (default) means that the optimizer chooses the best nonparallel plan. A value of 100 means that the optimizer uses each object's degree of parallelism in computing the cost of a full table scan operation.

In our example, using DEGREE 4 and INSTANCES 2 representing a degree of parallelism of 8, the QC now has to *recruit* 8 threads of execution, 4 threads on each of 2 database instances. If the QC cannot find 4 (or 8, if necessary) parallel query slaves on 2 different instances, then it checks each instance's PARALLEL_MIN_PERCENT parameter value (set in "init.ora"). If PARALLEL_MIN_PERCENT is 100, then that means that 100 percent of all requested parallel query slave processes should be recruited in order for the query to proceed. If the query cannot proceed, an error message will be returned to the user indicating why the query failed.

If PARALLEL_MIN_PERCENT is 50, it means the DBA has determined that a query can proceed if the QC can recruit only 50 percent of the requested number of parallel query slaves. In our example, this means that at least 4 threads of execution are necessary for the query to be executed. If PARALLEL_MIN_PERCENT is 1 (which is the default), it means the QC can be demoted back to plain old Oracle server process, the partitions will be discarded, and the query will be executed in *serial* instead of using PX.

The DBA determines how many parallel query slaves can be run on each database instance using the initialization parameter PARALLEL_MAX_SERVERS. If PARALLEL_MAX_SERVERS is set to 50, it means that no more than 50 parallel query slave processes can be running at a time on that instance. If there is more than 1 database instance, Parallel Server is being used; then all the instances should have the same value for PARALLEL_MAX_SERVERS.

Once a parallel query slave process has been used and the query it was working on has ended, the DBA can determine how long the process will wait for another QC to recruit it. If the number of minutes specified by the instance's initialization parameter PARALLEL_SERVER_IDLE_TIME is exceeded, then the parallel query slave process will die off.

Many DBAs will recognize that constantly *spawning* parallel query slave processes, which each then *die* after a period of time, only to be *respawned*, can take a performance toll on a system. To make sure that a pool of inactive parallel query slave processes is available, the DBA can set the initialization parameter PARALLEL_MIN_SERVERS to a nonzero integer. When the instance is started, this number of parallel query slave processes will be started automatically. Depending on demand, additional parallel query slave processes can be started, up to the maximum number dictated by PARALLEL_MAX_ SERVERS. If PARALLEL_MAX_SERVERS is greater than PARALLEL_MIN_ SERVERS, then eventually unused parallel query slave processes will die off after PARALLEL_SERVER _IDLE_TIME minutes have passed, down to the minimum value specified by PARALLEL_MIN_SERVERS.

In this way, the costs of spawning these slave processes can be mitigated, if not eliminated. It is common practice to set PARALLEL_MIN_SERVERS and PARALLEL_MAX_SERVERS to the same value. There is nothing inherently wrong in this, as idle processes consume almost no system resources. Also, the slave processes themselves are spared the task of having to constantly check if it is time to die off.

In this way, by setting up a pool of available parallel query slave processes, and by setting a guideline on whether queries requesting PX can proceed if an insufficient number of slave processes are available, the DBA can control the consumption of resources and also control the expected elapsed time of a PX query.

Setting PARALLEL_MIN_PERCENT to 100 enforces a somewhat uniform elapsed time for each PX query, depending on the requested DEGREE and INSTANCES. If a query should run with DEGREE 4 and INSTANCES 2, it will either do so or fail. Thus, fluctuations in query elapsed time will be due purely to overall system load on the cluster.

Setting PARALLEL_MIN_PERCENT to 1, while perhaps making the fullest possible use of PX resources, can also cause severe fluctuations in query elapsed time. The elapsed time for the query to complete will not only be due to overall system resource consumption (i.e., the *busyness* of the system) but also to the number of parallel query slave processes that actually operate on a query at any one time. When a certain query is run at one time when the Parallel Server is relatively idle as a whole, elapsed time on the query can be blindingly fast, as the full number of requested (DEGREE and INSTANCES) parallel query slave processes is actually allocated to work on the query. Should the number of available parallel query slave processes dwindle, fewer and fewer parallel query slave processes may actually process the query. This means that, in addition to query performance being affected by overall system load, it is also affected by a smaller than expected number of parallel query slave processes working on the query. If PARALLEL_MIN_PERCENT is set to 1, then the query may not even utilize PX at all and will execute in serial.

It should be clear that PX does not reduce the total amount of work the system must perform in order to perform a query; as a matter of fact, when you add in the overhead incurred by the PX query coordinator's duties, the overall amount of work required to perform the query is actually greater. However, PX can significantly shorten the elapsed time consumed while performing the query by breaking a large task into many smaller tasks and executing these smaller tasks in parallel.

It should be clear then that PX would work only if there is overcapacity of CPU resources, memory resources, and disk throughput. If your system is nearing capacity on any of these resources, then running a job in parallel may not result in a speedup. But this is where Oracle Parallel Server provides the ability to scale performance. As we've described, if any excess processing capacity exists on any of the machines in your cluster, then PX can utilize it dynamically. If the machine on which the data actually resides has no excess resource capacity, PX can utilize another machine in the cluster that does.

Also, because the partitioning of work occurs dynamically, PX can react to changing volumes of data in database objects at run-time. This avoids the need to continually monitor space consumption by large tables and possibly unload/reload these tables to reorganize the static partitioning structure.

If it becomes clear that there are great inefficiencies in accessing data from a node on which the data does not actually reside, then the DBA can set yet another "init.ora" parameter on all the instances in Parallel Server: _NODE_AFFINITY. If _NODE_AFFINITY is TRUE, then the QC will check the data files in which each of the dynamic partitions resides. If the operating system can provide information about what node the data file resides on, then the QC process will use this information to attempt to acquire parallel query slave processes from the instance on that node. Thus, parallel query slave processes can be assigned to work only on data partitions that are local to the node on which they are running.

Of course, effective use of _NODE_AFFINITY then puts extra responsibility on the DBA to make sure that data for each large table is distributed as evenly as possible across as many nodes as possible. This would prevent PX from using _NODE_AFFINITY to overuse one node to the exclusion of others. But as we described earlier, striping of data (using RAID 0 or by concatenating data files in a tablespace) is a vital consideration when creating the Parallel Server database.

Moreover, the setting of OPTIMIZER_PERCENT_PARALLEL will determine from the start whether the Oracle optimizer chooses between a nonparallel access method, a parallelized full table scan, or parallelized index scan, should such a choice exist. For example, consider a query like this:

```
SQL> SELECT COUNT(*) FROM billing_detail WHERE acct_id > 500000;
```

The column ACCT_ID may have an index on it that can be used by this query. If OPTIMIZER_PERCENT_PARALLEL is left at the default of 0, then the Oracle optimizer will probably choose to use the index. If OPTIMIZER_PERCENT_ PARALLEL is set to 100, then the optimizer may consider the size of the table along with the DEGREE and INSTANCES on the table and may choose to ignore the index and use a parallelized full table scan to perform the query. If the index on ACCT_ID were partitioned (for instance, by transaction date and account ID) then the optimizer could additionally choose to scan each of the index partitions in parallel to find the requested data. (If this index had been partitioned on ACCT_ID ranges then the optimizer could use partition elimination to search only the index partition[s] in which these values could occur.)

Step 4: Assigning Subranges

Once the subranges have been designated, a crew of parallel query slave processes has been recruited, and the query is going to proceed in parallel, then the QC is in charge of keeping the crew busy. Communication between the QC and the various parallel query slave processes is conducted using "PX message queues" in the SGA.

What is the reason for all this subranging? Why wasn't one round of ROWID ranges sufficient?

The key to optimizing a parallelized query is to keep all concurrently executing parallel query slave processes continuously working, each with an equal amount of work. If some kind of guarantee could be made that the initial ROWID ranges would result in equal amounts of work for each parallel query slave process, then it would not be necessary to subrange. Take the pie, cut it into eighths, and keep eight slaves busy.

There is no guarantee, though, that each initial ROWID range will contain the same amount of work. Perhaps some of the extents in the table contain lots of deleted rows. Perhaps an additional filter in the WHERE clause of the query causes most rows found in some of the extents to be skipped over.

Using our simple example, this does not cause much trouble. The rows have to be scanned anyway. But suppose this parallelized table scan is simply the first stage of a complicated join? In this case, each row is not simply something to be scanned and counted, as in our example. Instead, each row could result in joins to other tables. Here, each row represents a discrete and significant *unit of work*. Each row in the driving table might require joins (via indexes, hash joins, or even further full table scans) to several other tables.

Now, with this in mind, the uneven distribution of rows across the initial ROWID ranges becomes quite important. Simply dividing the table by the degree of parallelism would more often than not result in some ROWID ranges being full of work and others having hardly any work at all. As you can see in Figure 10.10, the longest-running parallel query slave determines the overall response time of a parallelized query.

When the parallel query starts executing, the first subranges to be assigned are the large ones (approximately nine-thirteenths of the initial ROWID range). Once there are no more of the large nine-thirteenths subranges, then the next assigned are the medium subranges, which are approximately three-thirteenths of the ROWID range. Once those are all consumed, the last to be assigned for processing are the smallest subranges, which are sized approximately one-thirteenth of the original ROWID range.

In this way, parallel query slave processes that finish their initially allocated subranges faster will be assigned more work. Those processes that are given more work initially will probably not have to process as many partitions (see Figure 10.11).

If you have ever watched a growing litter of puppies eat a meal, then this analogy may help. Consider 8 puppies, with 24 bowls of food put in front of them. Chances are good that they will first each rush to claim the 8 largest bowls. Those who finish their largest bowls first will next rush toward the medium-sized bowls, until all of the medium-sized bowls are finished. At that

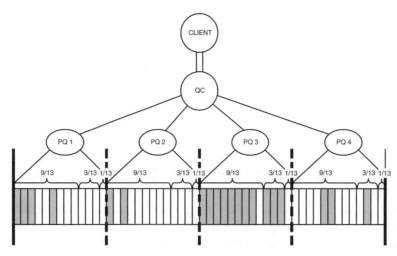

Figure 10.10   Uneven distribution of work in PX partitions.

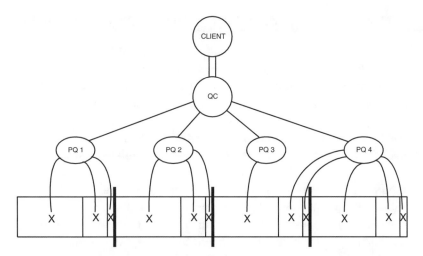

Figure 10.11 Some processes complete more subranges than others.

point, they will turn their attention to the smallest bowls until they, too, are empty. Of course, your experiences with puppies may vary . . .

Step 5: Receiving and Collating the Results

Communication between the QC and the parallel query slaves is accomplished *via PX message queue tables* in the Oracle SGA. Messages from the QC process are sent by placing requests on to the queue. Replies from the parallel query slave processes are sent the same way. See Figure 10.12 for an illustration of interprocess communication in PX.

The arrangement in Figure 10.12, with queue tables, should make something clear: Whenever the parallel query slave processes are returning large amounts of data, the QC can be overwhelmed. Just looking at the diagram should make that clear as well; the QC is a bottleneck.

So, the absolute best kind of query for PX is one that processes a massive amount of data and returns a small number of results. For example,

```
SQL> SELECT COUNT(*) FROM very-large-table;
```

A COUNT(*) operation returns only one row. During a COUNT(*), only one bit of information is being returned to the QC process from the parallel query slave processes. This is quite easily handled.

The absolute worst kind of query for PX is one that queries a massive amount of data and returns a massive amount of data, for example:

```
SQL> SELECT * FROM very-large-table;
```

USING PX CAN BE COUNTER-INTUITIVE FOR SQL PROGRAMMERS

When coding SQL statements with joins to multiple tables, most SQL programmers tend to "drive" the query from the smallest set of data, joining to larger sets of data by indexes. For example, given a query involving tables for CUSTOMERS, ORDERS, and ORDER_LINES, most non-PX queries might have first attempted to query a set of CUSTOMERS rows. From each row in CUSTOMERS, the query would then be expected to join to related ORDERS rows. From there, once the proper ORDERS are identified, the idea is to join to related ORDER_LINES rows.

The use of parallel queries reverses this set of assumptions. Whether partitioned tables with parallel index scans are used, or whether nonpartitioned tables with parallel full table scan are used, the presence of PX means that the "driving table" of the query should be the largest, not the smallest table. Then, the query can perform indexed joins to the next, smaller tables. In the example involving the CUSTOMERS, ORDERS, and ORDER_LINES tables, this would probably be the ORDER_LINES table. Drive the query from the ORDER_LINES table so that PX can be utilized (parallel index scans if it's partitioned, parallel full table scans if nonpartitioned), and join the smaller ORDERS table then to the yet smaller CUSTOMERS table. Note that in this example, we are reaping the additional benefit of utilizing the UNIQUE indexes that support the PRIMARY KEY constraints during the joins, as we are joining in the direction of FOREIGN KEY to PRIMARY KEY. Using the traditional set of assumptions, joining in the direction from PRIMARY KEY to FOREIGN KEY means utilizing the NONUNIQUE indexes that support the FOREIGN KEYs, which generally means less efficient range scans on the index.

This reversal of basic assumptions generally feels counter-intuitive to experienced SQL programmers, and frequently it is the most experienced programmers who have the greatest initial difficulty with PX. Just remember that PX is most effective in scans against large sets of data, not small sets. Give PX room to run, and lose the assumptions based on prior experience once in a while!

Essentially, this query will probably run slower in parallel than it would if run serially. The QC process would be overwhelmed by the volume of data returned by the parallel query slaves.

For data warehouses, the queries that work best are huge queries that summarize, aggregate, filter, or subset the data that is being queried. Huge queries that dump entire tables or otherwise return huge amounts of data will not make effective use of PX.

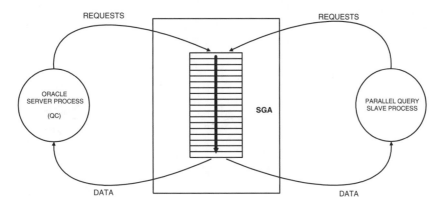

Figure 10.12   Interprocess communication in PX.

Parallel Direct-Path SQL*Loader

SQL*Loader has been available by that name since Oracle6; before that it was known as ODL (Oracle Data Loader). SQL*Loader was designed to read input data files and execute the INSERT commands necessary to load the data into the database. Today, this is still available and is known as SQL*Loader *conventional path* because it uses conventional INSERT statements (see Figure 10.13). To speed up loads or to load huge amounts of data, you could concurrently run several copies of SQL*Loader against the same table (see Figure 10.14).

The direct-path option was added to SQL*Loader with the initial release of Oracle7 (see Figure 10.15). By specifying DIRECT=TRUE on the SQL*Loader command line or in the SQL*Loader control file, the performance of SQL*Loader was dramatically improved by bypassing normal SQL operations and having the SQL*Loader process itself format the data into database blocks and write those blocks into the data files. To accomplish this without interrupting queries against the table, the blocks were added above the *high-water mark* (HWM) of the table. This is done by allocating a new extent for the table but temporarily marking it as TEMPORARY, which means that it is not really associated with the table. When the load finishes, the *block type flags* are changed from TEMPORARY to DATA, and the extent is linked to the table itself.

Another advantage of the direct-path option becomes apparent. During the load, database blocks belonging to the table are not being changed. Instead, the data is being placed into extents marked TEMPORARY. While the load is happening, the data is not available for query, and if the load should fail the TEMPORARY extents are simply removed. This means that it is not necessary to

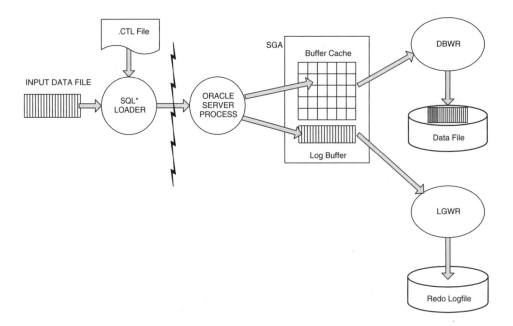

Figure 10.13   SQL*Loader conventional path.

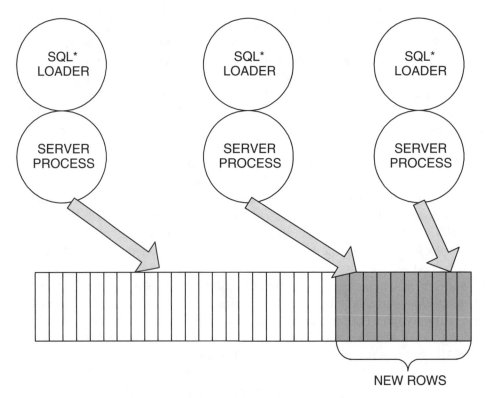

Figure 10.14   Multiple concurrent SQL*Loaders.

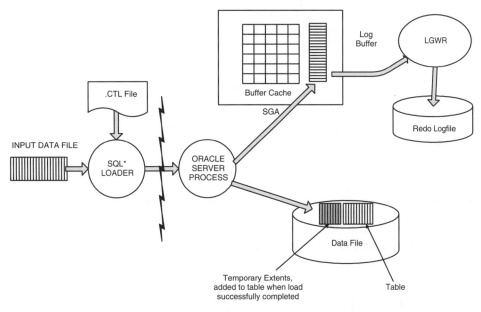

Figure 10.15 SQL*Loader direct path.

record *undo information* in order to perform ROLLBACKs, which means that direct-path SQL*Loader does not affect rollback segments.

Starting with Oracle7, version 7.1, the UNRECOVERABLE option (specified only in the SQL*Loader control file) became available, which meant that redo logging could be disabled for the loaded data. The direct-path option did not allow more than one SQL*Loader process at the same time to load the same table. Thus, for really huge loads, direct path was limited to the speed of a single process, albeit an efficient loading process.

To improve this situation, Oracle7, release 7.1, introduced *parallel* direct-path SQL*Loader. By specifying PARALLEL=TRUE along with DIRECT=TRUE, multiple direct-path SQL*Loader processes could load data into the same table (see Figure 10.16). Each concurrently executing SQL*Loader process allocates its own extent, located above the high-water mark of the table and temporarily marked as a TEMPORARY extent. There is no contention for this extent; each SQL*Loader process owns one absolutely, unlike the extent with concurrently executing conventional path SQL*Loaders. The result is that each direct-path SQL*Loader process can work as fast as it can run. Only table data is loaded, and neither *undo entries* (i.e., rollback segment entries) nor, if specified with the UNRECOVERABLE or NOLOGGING option, *redo entries* (i.e., redo logging) need to be created. No other utility, from Oracle or from other sources, can load data into Oracle as swiftly.

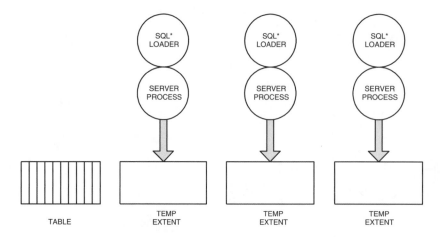

Figure 10.16 Multiple concurrent direct-path SQL*Loaders.

Parallel CREATE INDEX (pCI)

Also available since Oracle7, release 7.1, is the ability to create indexes in parallel. Normally, a single Oracle server process does the job, performing a full table scan on the table in question, sorting the data and then finally creating the index.

Consider the following example:

```
SQL> SET TIMING ON
SQL> CREATE UNIQUE INDEX billing_detail_pk
  2 ON billing_detail (acct_id, bill_date)
  3 TABLESPACE idx_01;

Elapsed: 03:23:56.33
```

This took over three hours to complete. See Figure 10.17 for an illustration of a normal CREATE INDEX.

When the PARALLEL clause is added to the CREATE INDEX command, the Oracle server process becomes a query coordinator (QC). Its first job is to recruit enough parallel query slave processes from the database instance to perform the job. The actual number of parallel query slave processes acquired to create the index is dependent on the value of the initialization parameter PARALLEL_MIN_PERCENT, just as with parallel queries. If PARALLEL_MIN_PERCENT is 100, then the CREATE INDEX will proceed only if 100 percent of the requested number of query slaves can be recruited.

```
SQL> SET TIMING ON
SQL> CREATE UNIQUE INDEX billing_detail_pk
```

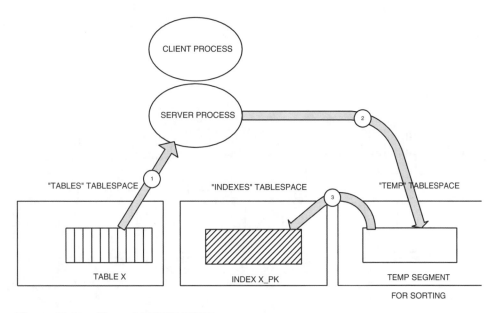

Figure 10.17   Normal CREATE INDEX.

```
  2  ON billing_detail (acct_id, bill_date)
  3  TABLESPACE idx_01
  4  PARALLEL (DEGREE 12);

Elapsed: 00:20:12.05
```

In this case, performing the index creation with 12 concurrent threads of execution on the same instance dropped the elapsed time to create the index from over 3 hours to just about 20 minutes. See Figure 10.18 for an illustration of parallel CREATE INDEX (pCI) on one instance.

If this were a Parallel Server database with four separate database instances accessing the same database, you might be able to run the following:

```
SQL> SET TIMING ON
SQL> CREATE UNIQUE INDEX billing_detail_pk
  2  ON billing_detail (acct_id, bill_date)
  3  TABLESPACE idx_01
  4  PARALLEL (DEGREE 12 INSTANCES 4);

Elapsed: 00:05:38.13
```

In this case, the index creation was performed with 12 concurrent threads of execution on each of 4 separate database instances, for a total of 48 concurrent threads of execution. In this case, the index creation that originally took over 3 hours now takes a little under 6 minutes! See Figure 10.19 for an illustration of parallel CREATE INDEX with Parallel Server.

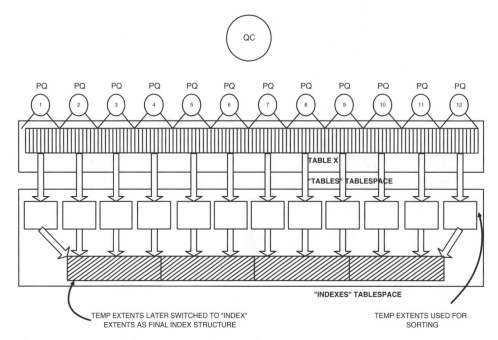

Figure 10.18 Parallel CREATE INDEX on one instance.

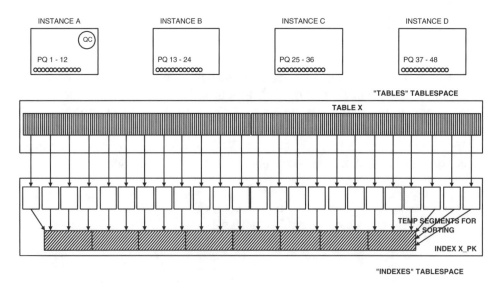

Figure 10.19 Parallel CREATE INDEX with Parallel Server.

Please note that the PARALLEL clause in CREATE INDEX is utilized only at run-time during the index creation itself. The values for the PARALLEL clause do not get stored in the data dictionary for later use by parallel queries, as is the case with the PARALLEL clause used in the CREATE TABLE or ALTER TABLE commands.

The pCI operation utilizes the direct-path mechanism, which means that it generates no undo entries in the rollback segments. Additionally, pCI comes with an UNRECOVERABLE option (NOLOGGING in Oracle8) to eliminate the generation of redo entries for the redo log files. The pCI operation is equally useful in OLTP and data warehouse/DSS environments because no matter what types of transactions are typically executed, everyone needs to create indexes as rapidly as possible.

Parallel Recovery

Available since Oracle7, version 7.1, parallel recovery is completely transparent. During database startup, parallel recovery performs either instance recovery or media recovery in parallel, significantly hastening the *mean time to repair* (MTTR) after an abnormal shutdown of the database or the corruption of a data file.

Instance recovery (see Figure 10.20) occurs after the database has been shut down in an abnormal manner, either due to system failure or a SHUTDOWN ABORT by the DBA. Behind the scenes, when the abnormal shutdown is detected during the STARTUP command, the SMON background process performs a *roll-forward* of all logged operations since the last checkpoint using the information stored in the online redo log files. All these operations are replayed (the roll-forward), and when the last operation is replayed, then any uncommitted transactions are *rolled-back*.

Media recovery must be performed when one of the data files in the database has been corrupted or lost and therefore had to be restored from a backup. The restored data file(s) is then brought *up-to-date* by replaying all changes made to

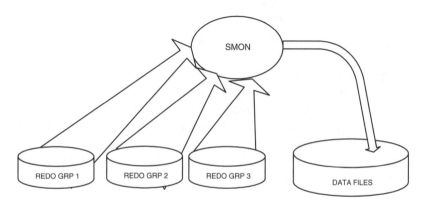

Figure 10.20   Instance recovery.

it from the redo log files. Usually, the changes to be replayed will have to be recovered from *archived redo log files*, so the ability to perform media recovery means the database must be in ARCHIVELOG mode.

As you can imagine, the amount of roll-forward that has to occur during media recovery is dependent on the following:

- The number of data files corrupted and restored from a prior backup
- The amount of time since the backup was taken
- The number of operations recorded since the backup was taken

If 20 data files were somehow corrupted and had to be restored from a backup taken 5 days ago, that means 5 days' worth of operations have to be replayed for those 20 data files. Will this take 5 days to replay? We hope not! Generally, replaying operations recorded in the redo log files takes a fraction of the time required for the original operations because the database is usually not open for general use while instance recovery or media recovery is happening. Also, just the update actions themselves are being applied; in real life, there are frequently dozens or hundreds of queries supporting these INSERTs, UPDATEs, and DELETEs. Last, when these update actions are being reapplied, there is no need to generate undo entries for the rollback segments, nor is there any need to generate redo logging, both of which are usually necessary in real life.

Media recovery can take a long time, and applying parallelism to this process can help significantly. Just like normal recovery, the SMON process reads the redo log files. It is no longer tasked with actually replaying the operations; instead, it has a pool of parallel query slaves available to actually perform the updates to the data files. This is necessary because, obviously, roll-forward operations have to be replayed in exactly the same order they were originally played in real life. Single-threading the read phase of recovery is the best way to accomplish this. (SMON further ensures that two changes to the same block are properly serialized through its handoff algorithm.)

Implementing parallel recovery (illustrated in Figure 10.21) requires nothing more than the setting of an initialization parameter:

```
recovery_parallelism = NN
```

where "NN" is the desired number of *parallel recovery processes* available to the SMON or Server Manager process during recovery. The default value of 0 implies that SMON or Server Manager does all the work. Because no other activity can occur in the database until instance recovery is completed, it makes sense to use the available system resources for this task.

Also, in Server Manager since Oracle7 and in SQL*Plus since Oracle8 version 8.0.5, you can specify a PARALLEL clause with the RECOVER command that can override the setting of the configuration parameter RECOVERY_PARALLELISM.

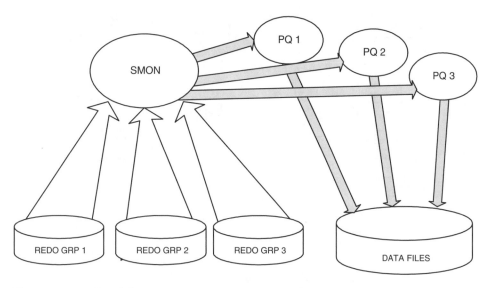

Figure 10.21 Parallel recovery.

If you are performing a RECOVER TABLESPACE or RECOVER DATAFILE command in Parallel Server, you can specify an INSTANCES clauses along with the DEGREE clause.

Parallel recovery is a parallel feature that is equally useful both in OLTP and data warehouse or DSS databases. The types of transactions normally executed on the system are irrelevant; recovery is something that anybody wants to complete as swiftly as possible.

Parallel CREATE TABLE . . . AS SELECT (pCTAS)

Available starting with Oracle7, version 7.2, the parallel CREATE TABLE . . . AS SELECT operation (pCTAS) has turned into one of the most valuable features introduced to benefit data warehousing. Data in data warehouses does not sit still. There are constant reloads and refreshes, and with each load (complete or incremental) there usually comes the need to update summarized data. Whether these summarizations or aggregations take the form of a standalone summary table or whether they exist as part of a *star schema* as a *dimension table*, this operation must be performed frequently and completed swiftly.

Before the advent of the pCTAS operation, data warehouse implementers were faced with having to use a variety of more conventional methods not designed for bulk operations. In some cases, when the base tables in the warehouse were being

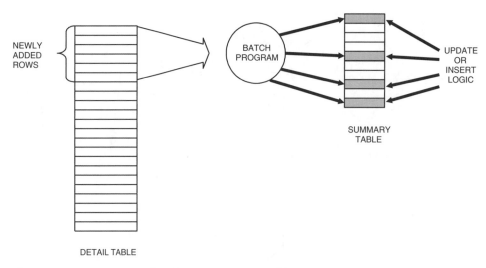

NEWLY
ADDED
ROWS

BATCH
PROGRAM

UPDATE
OR
INSERT
LOGIC

SUMMARY
TABLE

DETAIL TABLE

Figure 10.22 Incremental updates to summary tables.

loaded incrementally, with additional data being appended to existing data, it made sense to update summary tables or dimension tables incrementally as well (see Figure 10.22). This could involve significant programming in PL/SQL triggers or stored procedures or third-generation languages like C or COBOL.

As the very simplest option, an INSERT INTO . . . SELECT statement could do the job (see Figure 10.23), but this operation might have its difficulties, for example, operating too slowly against massive amounts of data. Parallelizing the SELECT portion of this operation could help in certain circumstances (see Figure 10.24), but only if you remember one of the important limitations of parallelized queries: They work best on operations that scan massive amounts of data but return only small amounts of result data.

A number of questions inevitably arise about incremental updates to summary tables and dimension tables. The first involves the fact that *nothing grows forever*. Inevitably, it is necessary to purge. Although this might be easy to do on detail data, it may occasionally become necessary to subtract from related summary tables while the deletions from the detail data are occurring. This is neither an easy nor a swift operation.

The second question grows out of the first one. Because of all the possible complexity involved in custom programming—both the insertion of new data into the summary tables and the purging of old data—how accurate is the summary data after several iterations of both the load operations and the purge operations? And, if it's not accurate, how can it be fixed?

The major problem here is that the incremental approach can be painfully slow even if the programs are written to take advantage of parallelism or multiple concurrent streams of execution. Also, because they were forced to use

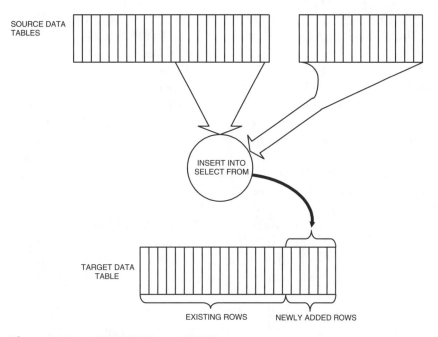

Figure 10.23   INSERT INTO . . . SELECT.

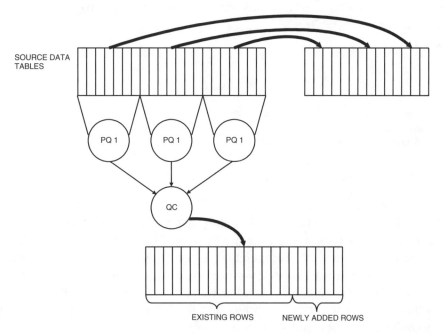

Figure 10.24   INSERT INTO . . . SELECT in parallel in Oracle7.

conventional SQL—with its attendant requirements to generate rollback entries in the rollback segments and redo entries in the redo logs—bulk operations written this way put a great deal of stress on the system.

While the incremental approach may offset this inherent slowness by reducing the amount of work that has to be done (i.e., processing only the changes or *deltas*), the question of *how accurate the summary data is* raises the question of what can be done if it is found to be inaccurate. Reloading the summary tables using processes intended only to perform incremental changes may be unrealistic.

The eventual answer to all these concerns might be to always reload the summary tables. Don't bother with a complicated incremental approach, even if the detail data is substantially unchanged from load to load. Of course, if the detail data is completely reloaded or *refreshed* with each load phase, there is no choice: The summary tables have to be completely re-created. Unless a scheme for saving old copies of the detail data and detecting changes by comparing the old and new copies of detail data is implemented there is no way to detect incremental changes.

The pCTAS operation works somewhat like an INSERT INTO . . . SELECT where the query is parallelized, but with two important differences:

1. The INSERT phase of the operation is parallelized in sync with the SELECT.

2. The INSERT phase uses the direct-path mechanism, similar to SQL*Loader.

A nonparallel CREATE TABLE . . . AS SELECT (see Figure 10.25) has existed since the early versions of Oracle:

```
SQL> CREATE TABLE billing_summary
  2  TABLESPACE summ_data01
  3  STORAGE (INITIAL 4M NEXT 4M PCTINCREASE 0)
  4  AS
  5  SELECT bill_dt, SUM(bill_amt) total_bill_amt
  6  FROM billing_detail
  7  GROUP BY bill_dt;

Table created.
```

In this situation, the new table is created according to the TABLESPACE and STORAGE specifications (which can default if they are not specified). The column names and data type definitions are derived from the elements in the SELECT list of the query (unless specified in the CREATE TABLE's column list). The new table is then populated with the results from the query.

After parallel queries were introduced, it was possible to enhance this command so that half of it was run in parallel, but the INSERT phase of the command was still single-threaded (see Figure 10.26).

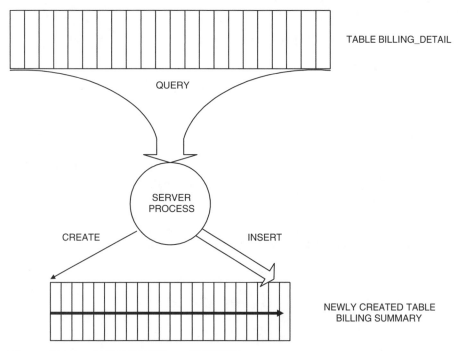

Figure 10.25   CREATE TABLE . . . AS SELECT.

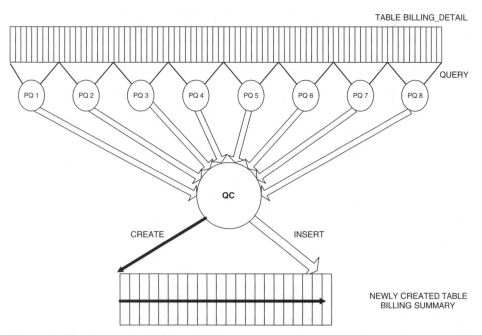

Figure 10.26   CREATE TABLE . . . AS SELECT using parallel query.

```
SQL> CREATE TABLE billing_summary
  2  TABLESPACE summ_data01
  3  STORAGE (INITIAL 4M NEXT 4M PCTINCREASE 0)
  4  AS
  5  SELECT /*+ PARALLEL(billing_detail, 8, 1) */
  6         bill_dt, SUM(bill_amt) total_bill_amt
  7    FROM billing_detail
  8    GROUP BY bill_dt;

Table created.
```

What the pCTAS operation brings to the situation is the full parallelization of both the INSERT and the SELECT phases, so that (with adequate I/O capacity) there are no bottlenecks to impede performance (see Figure 10.27).

```
SQL> CREATE TABLE billing_summary
  2  PARALLEL (DEGREE 8 INSTANCES 1)
  3  TABLESPACE summ_data01
  4  STORAGE (INITIAL 4M NEXT 4M PCTINCREASE 0)
  5  AS
  6      SELECT bill_dt, SUM(bill_amt) total_bill_amt
  7        FROM billing_detail
  8        GROUP BY bill_dt;

Table created.
```

Please note that a *parallel hint* is no longer necessary in the SELECT statement; the PARALLEL clause in the CREATE TABLE statement both functions as a run-time specification for the degree of parallelization during creation and

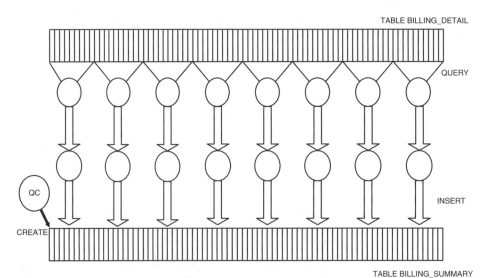

Figure 10.27   Parallel CREATE TABLE . . . AS SELECT.

is stored as the table's DEGREE and INSTANCES values in the data dictionary for future parallelized queries against the new table. If the parallel hint is specified, it will be ignored. If the table being queried from (i.e., in this case, BILLING_DETAIL) has its own DEGREE and INSTANCES values in the data dictionary, they will also be ignored in favor of the CREATE TABLE's PARALLEL clause.

Unlike the INSERT INTO . . . SELECT statement and the older CREATE TABLE . . . AS SELECT operations—whether each used a parallelized SELECT or not—the new pCTAS operation uses the direct-path mechanism originally introduced with SQL*Loader. Therefore, while the table is being created and populated, the pCTAS operation allocates TEMPORARY extents to load into (see Figure 10.28).

The parallel query slave processes themselves are not performing INSERT statements using the conventional SQL mechanism that operates through the SGA buffer cache and the LGWR and DBWR processes. Rather, they are bypassing the SGA buffer cache and log buffer, formatting the database blocks directly, and writing directly to the data files (see Figure 10.29).

Therefore, not only has the pCTAS operation removed bottlenecks from its architecture, but it also uses a mechanism ideally suited for bulk data loading. This mechanism, by loading into TEMPORARY extents, eliminates the need for undo information to be generated in rollback segments. Additionally, like other Oracle operations that employ the direct-path mechanism, an UNRECOVERABLE or NOLOGGING clause is available also to eliminate much of the redo

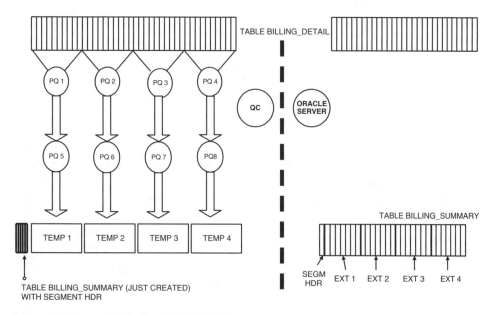

Figure 10.28   pCTAS using TEMPORARY extents.

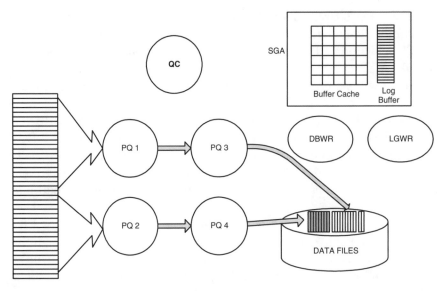

Figure 10.29 pCTAS using direct-path mechanism.

information logged to the redo log files by the LGWR process for future recoverability.

```
SQL> CREATE TABLE billing_summary
  2 PARALLEL (DEGREE 8)
  3 UNRECOVERABLE
  4 TABLESPACE summ_data01
  5 STORAGE (INITIAL 4M NEXT 4M PCTINCREASE 0)
  6 AS
  7     SELECT bill_dt, SUM(bill_amt) total_bill_amt
  8       FROM billing_detail
  9      GROUP BY bill_dt;

Table created.
```

So now we have an operation that allows summary tables and dimension tables to be re-created quickly and efficiently. In data warehouses, this opens all kinds of possibilities for data cleansing, data transformation, and data mart creation.

In any kind of database—OLTP, data warehouse, or otherwise—the pCTAS operation is also useful for performing mass UPDATEs or mass DELETEs. For example, if the following DELETE statement will be deleting a large portion of the following large table, it could literally take days to perform:

```
SQL> SET TIMING ON
SQL> DELETE
  2 FROM BILLING_DETAIL
  3 WHERE BILL_DT < '01-JAN-96';

1803773 rows deleted.

Elapsed: 22:44:55.03

SQL> COMMIT;

Commit complete.
```

Instead, the following pCTAS operation could perform this operation in a fraction of the time:

```
SQL> SET TIMING ON
SQL> CREATE TABLE new_billing_detail
  2 PARALLEL (DEGREE 8 INSTANCES 4)
  3 TABLESPACE bill_data01
  4 STORAGE (INITIAL 4M NEXT 4M PCTINCREASE 0)
  5 AS
  6     SELECT *
  7       FROM billing_detail
  8       WHERE bill_dt >= '01-JAN-96';

Table created.

Elapsed: 00:50:03.43

SQL> RENAME BILLING_DETAIL TO OLD_BILLING_DETAIL;

Table renamed.

Elapsed: 00:00:01.01

SQL> RENAME NEW_BILLING_DETAIL TO BILLING_DETAIL;

Table renamed.

Elapsed: 00:00:02.03
```

The exact same result is obtained in less than an hour as opposed to almost 23 hours. The downside is that the new table does not have any indexes (yet), table GRANTs have been lost, and any views or procedures referencing BILLING_DETAIL will have to be recompiled.

A similar operation can be performed for mass UPDATEs.

Extent Trimming in Oracle

In Oracle, the operations for parallel direct-path SQL*Loader, parallel CREATE INDEX, and parallel CREATE TABLE . . . AS SELECT all have something in common: They all use a parallel implementation of the direct-path mechanism. This is a good thing. The direct-path mechanism is well optimized for writing massive amounts of data into the database, and that is—after all—the primary goal of each of these operations. See Figure 10.30 for an illustration of direct-path operations.

But, in achieving the goal of throwing data into the Oracle database by the truckload, one of the basic assumptions of Oracle space management was in danger of being violated, and the remedy was one that irritated many DBAs. When the direct-path mechanism is in use, it does not share the space in which it is working with other processes. The space in which it is loading is "private," temporarily marked as a TEMPORARY segment, accessed and modified only by the single process doing the work.

All other "conventional" SQL operations (see Figure 10.31) work through the SGA buffer cache, performing all modifications on database blocks located in the shared memory buffer cache. Conventional SQL operations (i.e., INSERT, UPDATE, DELETE, and CREATE) do not write to the data files; rather, the

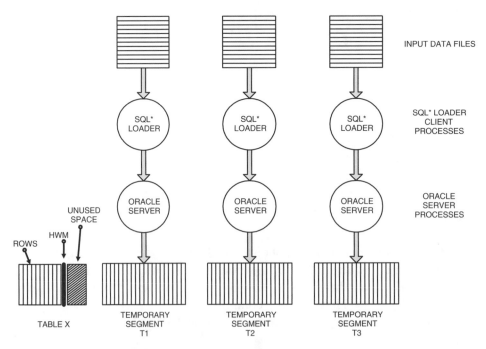

Figure 10.30 Direct-path operations.

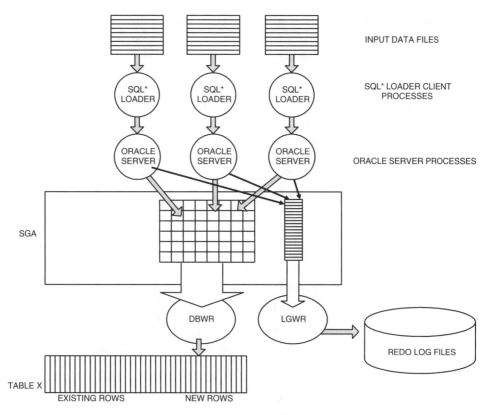

INPUT DATA FILES

SQL* LOADER CLIENT PROCESSES

ORACLE SERVER PROCESSES

SGA

Figure 10.31 Conventional SQL operations.

memory-resident images of the database blocks in the buffer cache are modified, and those modifications are later written to the data files by the DBWR process.

So far, so good. Direct-path operations running in parallel, however, have a special problem. In this case, there are multiple independently executing operations, none of which are sharing anything with each other. They are all (by definition) operating on the same task on the same object, but they are working independently.

This in itself is not a problem, except for a basic rule about Oracle space management. Each segment (table, cluster, or index) extent has all used space contiguously allocated, and all unused space is also contiguous. In other words, think of a table or index as being a sequential array of information, allocated by extents. Naturally, because the space for the segment is allocated in extents and space is used row by row, this means that unused space will exist at the "end" of the allocated space. The imaginary line drawn at the last row in a table (or entry in an index) is called the high-water mark (HWM), and space beyond that line is referred to as being *beyond (or above) the high-water mark* (see Figure 10.32).

So, up until Oracle8 and the advent of partitioned objects, one of the basic rules of Oracle space management indicated that, for each segment, one and only one extent could house a high-water mark, and only that extent could have unused space above that high-water mark.

Now, rewind to the discussion about direct-path operations. What you have is umpteen processes, each operating independently of one another. Each of N processes is going to load a certain number of rows into however many extents are required, and when they each finish you can bet that each of those N processes is going to find that it has not completely filled the last extent it was working on. See Figure 10.33 for an illustration of parallel direct-path operations, each leaving a high-water mark.

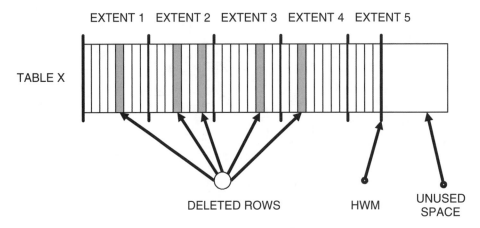

Figure 10.32 The high-water mark and unused space.

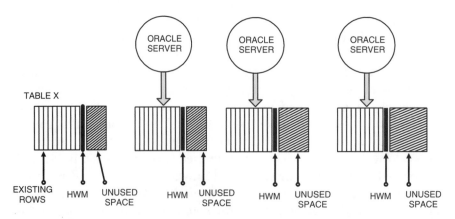

Figure 10.33 Parallel direct-path operations each leaving a HWM.

Although the direct-path operations are ongoing, each process is working on its own TEMPORARY segments. But, when all the parallel operations are finished, the QC will change the BLOCK_TYPE flag in the headers of each of those segments, flipping them from TEMPORARY to DATA (for tables) or TEMPORARY to INDEX (for indexes). At this point, the QC is also supposed to merge these formerly TEMPORARY segments into the base table or index being loaded.

But, to do so while each of the TEMPORARY segments had unused space above the high-water mark would violate the rule stated earlier. The very last thing each parallel query slave process has to do after finishing direct-path operations is "trim" its last extent to eliminate any unused space above the high-water mark from the TEMPORARY segment (see Figure 10.34).

Then, and only then, can all the TEMPORARY extents be merged into the base object. Why might this be a problem? A basic and well-known goal of experienced Oracle DBAs is to eliminate fragmentation by utilizing uniform-sized extents in various tablespaces. Tablespace fragmentation (see Figure 10.35) is the often-discussed problem wherein the space inside a tablespace is "chopped up" into many differently sized extents. This in itself is not a problem, but eventually after tables and indexes get dropped and re-created, the

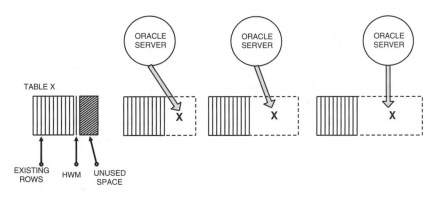

Figure 10.34 Extent trimming.

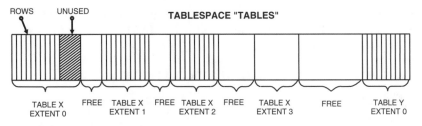

Figure 10.35 Tablespace fragmentation.

resulting odd-sized extents of free space can make it impossible to create or extend anything in that tablespace. This topic was discussed in depth in the "Monitoring Tablespace Fragmentation" section of Chapter 8. Recall the analogy of laying floor tiles of different sizes.

In this way, there can be huge amounts of free space available in a tablespace, but it's all chopped up into small enough extents that it becomes practically unusable. In response to this, a number of products from a number of vendors have sprung up to *reorganize* tablespaces. What they do is export all the table and index definitions in a given tablespace, drop and re-create the tablespace, and then reimport all the tables and indexes. Typically, the INITIAL storage parameter of all these tables and indexes has been reset so that all data in the tables and indexes resides in a single extent. After this export/import is finished, all the free space in the tablespace formerly scattered in many unusable small chunks of space is now coalesced into one large usable chunk.

The problem with these reorganization utilities is that when they coalesce a table or index into a single large extent, they only address the symptoms instead of fixing the problem. After all, these utilities would get used only once per tablespace if they actually solved the problem, wouldn't they?

There is a myth about Oracle space management that states "a segment should have only one extent" for optimal performance. It implies that multiple extents, especially hundreds of extents, are somehow bad for performance. This is almost always complete balderdash. There is no performance advantage to having data compressed into a single extent versus having it spread out over hundreds of extents, all other factors being equal. The habit of *compressing extents* for a segment into a single extent simply perpetuates the segment fragmentation problem, which suits the vendors of reorg tools just fine.

The permanent solution to tablespace fragmentation is to use uniformly sized extents, for all segments (table, clusters, and indexes) within a tablespace. If every extent in a tablespace is 1 MB (to pick a number) in size, then tablespace fragmentation cannot exist.

Some may argue that objects aren't always sized at 1 MB or whatever number is chosen. True, that's why Oracle allows multiple extents. Those steeped in the one-extent-only myth just mentioned may argue that multiple extents hurt performance. False, so there's nothing to worry about (unless the extents are very, very small in relation to DB_FILE_MULTIBLOCK_READ_COUNT). The only thing to worry about when letting segments extend is not to exceed MAXEXTENTS. Prior to release 7.3, the maximum value of MAXEXTENTS for a segment is tied to the database block size.

DB_BLOCK_SIZE	MAXIMUM MAXEXTENTS
1 KB or 1,024 bytes	57
2 KB or 2,048 bytes	121

4 KB or 4,096 bytes	249
8 KB or 8,192 bytes	505
16 KB or 16,384 bytes	1,017

The most common DB_BLOCK_SIZE for data warehouse databases is usually 8 or 16 KB. Realizing this, experienced Oracle DBAs try to keep the number of different extents to a minimum—ideally only one size, but possibly two, three, four, or five. As a result, these DBAs never have to worry about segment fragmentation, and they never need to buy one of those reorganization utilities.

Into the midst of this idyllic world come valuable operations like parallel direct-path SQL*Loader, parallel CREATE INDEX, and parallel CREATE TABLE . . . AS SELECT, which make it almost impossible to keep *uniform-sized extents* in a tablespace. Very annoying! The problem does not get fixed until Oracle8, when extent trimming is no longer necessary and does not occur for these operations. For Oracle7, the problem is not addressed until version 7.3.3, when event 10,901 can be set to disable extent trimming. Call Oracle Worldwide Support for information on setting this event if you are using version 7.3.3 or above.

Or better yet, upgrade to Oracle8 or Oracle8*i*. As with so many other things, extent trimming is simply not a problem in Oracle8. There is no need for event 10,901, and there is no wasted space. Any unused space left over after the direct-path operation completes is then put onto the free lists, so it may eventually be used.

Parallel Indexed Queries on Partitioned Tables

In Oracle7, only queries based on *full table scans* could be executed in parallel. In Oracle8 and Oracle8*i*, indexed range-scans can also be executed in parallel.

Let's assume the following query:

```
SQL> SELECT COUNT(*) FROM BILLING_DETAIL WHERE STATE = 'RI';
```

Assume that BILLING_DETAIL is a partitioned table, range-partitioned on the column TXN_DATE. Further, assume that the column STATE has a local partitioned index. In order for this index to be local, it must include the partition-key column TXN_DATE, so the index is created on the columns STATE and TXN_DATE, in that order.

Because the partition-key is not the *leading edge* of the index, this means that the index is a *nonprefixed local partitioned index*. Finally, let's assume that the DEGREE clause on the index has been set to the numeric value of 8.

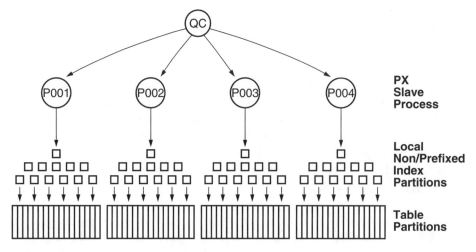

Figure 10.36 Parallel index range-scans.

The Oracle cost-based optimizer parses the query and decides to use the index on STATE. Realizing that the index is partitioned and it has a degree of parallelism of 8, it spawns a parallel query that performs index range-scans against each of the partitions where STATE = 'RI'. If the partitions are for a single day apiece, and there is 3 years worth of data in BILLING_DETAIL, then it is possible that almost all of the almost 1,100 partitions in this index contain entries where STATE = 'RI'. Naturally, each index range-scan is likely to be relatively quick, but 1,100 individual index range-scans can take a long time. With 8 concurrently executing parallel query slaves, the process can take up to 8 times less elapsed time (see Figure 10.36).

Parallel DML

In Oracle7, only a SELECT statement could be executed using parallel execution.

In Oracle8 and Oracle8i, this changes if you explicitly enable parallel data manipulation language (DML) statements using the following:

```
SQL> ALTER SESSION ENABLE PARALLEL DML;
```

Data manipulation language (DML) is another fancy way of grouping INSERT, UPDATE, and DELETE statements together. Parallel DML means parallel INSERT, parallel UPDATE, and parallel DELETE statements.

There are actually two different variations on parallel INSERT statements, so the total number of choices is really four, not three.

Parallel INSERT APPEND

For nonpartitioned tables, only the parallel INSERT APPEND option is available of all the four choices. The keyword APPEND is another name for the *direct-path* mechanism, which is used in SQL*Loader and parallel CREATE TABLE . . . AS SELECT. This means that a parallel INSERT INTO . . . SELECT operation works much like the pCTAS operation, described earlier (see Figure 10.37).

The only difference is the actual CREATE operation, which happens serially anyway. The real parallel execution, the INSERT and SELECT operations, work similarly in both operations.

```
SQL> ALTER SESSION ENABLE PARALLEL DML;

Session altered.

SQL> INSERT /*+ append nologging parallel(X, 8) */ INTO BILLING_DETAIL X
  2 SELECT /*+ parallel(y, 8) */ . . .
  3 FROM TEMP_BILLING_DETAIL Y
  4 WHERE . . . ;

10628998 rows inserted.

SQL> COMMIT;
```

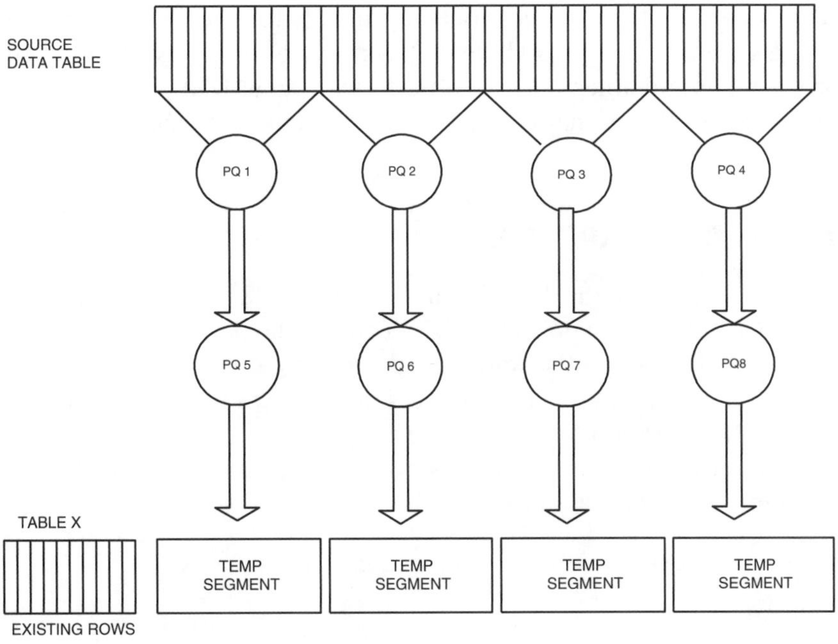

Figure 10.37   Parallel INSERT APPEND on a nonpartitioned table.

Although APPEND is the default mode for an INSERT . . . SELECT statement in a session where PARALLEL DML is enabled, it doesn't hurt to explicitly specify it in a SQL statement hint.

Also, when using the direct-path mechanism, further performance gains can be achieved by using the NOLOGGING (formerly UNRECOVERABLE in Oracle7) mechanism, which disables about 97 percent of all redo logging (except for modifications to the data dictionary). The NOLOGGING hint can be used, as it is here, or it can be turned into a table attribute using the CREATE TABLE or ALTER TABLE commands. As always, be absolutely certain that you fully understand all of the recovery implications of using the NOLOGGING mechanism; you can end up in a world of hurt by using it when it is not appropriate. You might end up with an unrecoverable table full of data if you don't perform a backup soon after completing a NOLOGGING operation.

The PARALLEL hint is also used, although the DEGREE of 8 might also be stored as a table attribute using the CREATE TABLE or ALTER TABLE commands.

Note that the SELECT statement also has a PARALLEL hint. Be certain that the degrees of parallelism for both the source table (table TEMP_BILLING_DETAIL with the table alias Y in this example) and the destination table (table BILLING_DETAIL with the table alias X) is the same. If they are different, you will get parallel execution for each operation, but it may not be the degree of parallelism you expect. Either verify (by querying the DBA_TABLES view) that the DEGREE clauses are the same in the data dictionary, or use explicit SQL statement hints (as shown here) to be certain.

While SQL statement hints are generally useful only for testing, with parallel DML they are generally a very good idea. They provide readily available documentation of the programmer's intent to perform parallel DML, and their use limits the number of things that can go wrong, preventing consistent parallel execution.

Parallel INSERT NOAPPEND

For partitioned tables, both the APPEND and the NOAPPEND mechanisms are available but only if there are no GLOBAL indexes on the partitioned table.

Using the APPEND option (also known as the direct-path mechanism), a parallel INSERT statement requires that triggers and constraints be disabled for the duration of the operation (see Figure 10.38).

Like other direct-path operations, existing indexes are automatically disabled and rebuilt by the operation.

```
SQL> ALTER TABLE partitioned-table DISABLE CONSTRAINT . . . ;

Table altered.

SQL> ALTER TRIGGER trigger-name DISABLE;
```

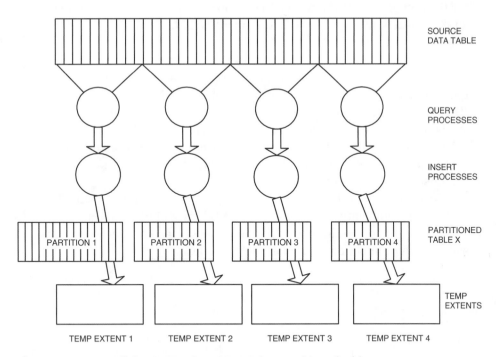

Figure 10.38 Parallel INSERT using APPEND into partitioned tables.

```
Trigger altered.

SQL> ALTER SESSION ENABLE PARALLEL DML;

Session altered.

SQL> INSERT /*+ append nologging parallel(X, 8) */ INTO BILLING_DETAIL X
  2 SELECT /*+ parallel(y, 8) */ . . .
  3 FROM TEMP_BILLING_DETAIL Y. . .
  4 WHERE . . . ;

10628998 rows inserted.

SQL> COMMIT;
```

Immediately after each parallel DML statement, a COMMIT or ROLLBACK must be issued; any other SQL statement will fail until the transaction is ended. The reason for this is that all parallel DML statements are very similar to *distributed transactions* performed over a database link. Each of the parallel threads of execution is operating independently, each with its own individual transaction within Oracle. At some point, a *two-phase commit* is necessary to first synchronize and then commit or cancel (rollback) the transaction. So, after the completion of the parallel DML operation and the completion of the overall transaction, no other SQL statements can be issued because the data changes are in an *in-doubt* status.

At any rate, if the table being inserted into (in this example, BILLING_DETAIL) is partitioned, you have the choice of performing the INSERT with the direct-path APPEND option or the conventional SQL NOAPPEND option.

The main reason for using the slower, conventional SQL NOAPPEND option is availability of the table partitions being inserted into. The APPEND option disables indexes for the duration of the INSERT, and triggers and constraints must also be disabled or dropped. Thus, for all intents and purposes, the table partitions involved are not available.

This can be avoided by not using the direct-path APPEND option. Instead, specifying the conventional SQL NOAPPEND hint will cause the parallel DML operation to use conventional INSERT statements, and then there is no need to disable anything and indexes remain fully usable.

```
SQL> ALTER SESSION ENABLE PARALLEL DML;

Session altered.

SQL> INSERT /*+ noappend parallel(X, 8) */ INTO BILLING_DETAIL X
  2 SELECT /*+ parallel(y, 8) */ . . .
  3 FROM TEMP_BILLING_DETAIL Y. . .
  4 WHERE . . . ;

10628998 rows inserted.

SQL> COMMIT;
```

Please note that the NOLOGGING mechanism works only with direct-path operations, so specifying the NOLOGGING hint here will be ignored. Likewise, if NOLOGGING is specified on the table and its associated indexes, full redo logging will occur anyway.

Besides ignoring the NOLOGGING hint or table attribute, like all conventional SQL operations, INSERT NOAPPEND also generates *undo information* to be logged in the rollback segments, in the event that the transaction is cancelled. Because direct-path mechanisms are inserting data into TEMPORARY segments, rolling back the transaction is easily performed by dropping the TEMPORARY segment. Not so with conventional SQL statements; each changed database block must have its *before image* stored in a rollback segment. So, the cost of a conventional INSERT statement is that the rollback segments are used as well as the redo logs. A direct-path INSERT statement never uses the rollback segments, and it can even do without the redo logs.

This accounts for much of the performance difference between a conventional INSERT statement and a direct-path INSERT statement.

Like many dilemmas in computing, choosing between APPEND and NOAPPEND is a clear trade-off between *speed* and *flexibility*.

Parallel UPDATE and DELETE

Parallel UPDATE and DELETE statements are never direct-path; they always use conventional SQL statements, and therefore they use both the rollback segments as well as the redo logs, regardless of the setting of NOLOGGING.

Additionally, parallel UPDATE and DELETE statements will become "parallel" only if executed against partitioned tables; they are not available for non-partitioned tables (see Figure 10.39).

```
SQL> ALTER SESSION ENABLE PARALLEL DML;

Session altered.

SQL> UPDATE /*+ parallel(X, 8) */ BILLING_DETAIL X
  2 SET STATUS = 'ACTIVE'
  3 WHERE . . . ;

107288 rows updated.

SQL> COMMIT;
```

As with parallel INSERT statements, parallel UPDATE and DELETE statements must be committed or rolled back immediately after they complete, so

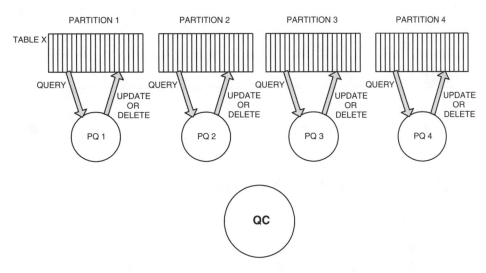

Figure 10.39 Parallel UPDATE or DELETE on partitioned tables.

that a *two-phase commit* mechanism can correctly complete the multiple independent parallel processes.

There is one thing to consider with parallel UPDATE and DELETE statements. If you are going to be updating or deleting a very large proportion of the rows in a table, it just might be much faster to re-create the table using parallel CREATE TABLE . . . AS SELECT or parallel INSERT APPEND. Instead of updating 50 percent of the rows within a very large table, it might be faster to use the direct-path mechanism (with NOLOGGING, perhaps) to simply pull the data from the original table, make the data modifications in the SELECT portion of the statement, and INSERT the rows into a new table. Then, the old table can be renamed to move it out of the way and the new table can be renamed to replace the old.

Similarly, instead of deleting 30 to 40 percent of the rows in a very large table, consider simply re-creating the table, selecting the rows that you would like to *keep*.

The elapsed time of a direct-path, NOLOGGING parallel INSERT APPEND or parallel CTAS could be a fraction of the time of even a parallel UPDATE or DELETE command.

It is difficult to devise a *rule of thumb* for knowing when to do this. Sometimes it simply isn't possible to substitute for the UPDATE or DELETE statements. Obviously both the parallel INSERT APPEND and parallel CTAS options require that the table be unavailable for a period of time; perhaps that is simply not possible. Also, both direct-path options imply a lot of extra steps not mentioned here, such as dropping and re-creating indexes, constraints, permissions, and triggers, followed by recompilations of invalidated database views and PL/SQL program modules.

It is good to have options, though, and it is good to know the trade-offs for each option.

Parallel DDL

Besides the previously mentioned parallel CREATE TABLE . . . AS SELECT, parallel CREATE INDEX, Oracle8 and Oracle8*i* debuted some additional useful parallel operations.

Parallel ALTER INDEX . . . REBUILD

This operation actually became available with Oracle7, version 7.3. Essentially, this operation can replace the old steps of dropping and re-creating an index. Besides being able to be executed in PARALLEL using the direct-path mechanism, it also accepts the UNRECOVERABLE clause, which becomes the

NOLOGGING clause in Oracle8. This means that redo logging is almost completely eliminated. Unlike a NOLOGGING operation on tables, there is very little reason for performing redo logging on index creation. After all, if you lose the index for some reason, just rebuild it!

The other reason that this operation is so fast is that, unlike a CREATE INDEX, it does not construct the index by reading the table data. Instead, it scans the existing index's leaf blocks. This means that it scans much less data because the number of index leaf blocks is generally much less than the number of database blocks in a table. Furthermore, scanning the existing index's leaf blocks means that the data is already sorted, so the ALTER INDEX REBUILD command skips the sorting phase that CREATE INDEX is required to do.

It runs in PARALLEL, it runs NOLOGGING, it doesn't sort, and it scans less data.

Parallel MOVE PARTITION

One of the reasons people hesitate to convert an existing nonpartitioned table to a partitioned table is because they are unsure about how, in which tablespace, to locate the partitions.

While it is useful to make sound up-front decisions, you can still act with the full assurance that you can correct any mistakes rather easily using the ALTER TABLE . . . MOVE PARTITION statement, executed in parallel and with NO LOGGING. Performed without parallel execution, this statement is done using conventional SQL. When the PARALLEL clause is specified, it uses the direct-path mechanisms, which also allow the use of NOLOGGING. Thus, if you need to move a partition to another tablespace quickly, you can do so.

Let's say that a huge deletion of rows occurred to a partition. Or, perhaps a huge UPDATE occurred that resulted in excessive row migration. You would now like to *reorganize* this partition, either to reclaim space freed up by deletions or to reinsert migrated (chained) rows. The ALTER TABLE . . . MOVE PARTITION PARALLEL command does this quickly.

Parallel SPLIT PARTITION

If one partition is growing too large and you would like to split it into two partitions, this can also be done in PARALLEL and with NOLOGGING. This operation reads from the original partition and creates two new ones. The original partition is removed only when the operation is completed.

Parallel MERGE PARTITION

Available with Oracle8*i*, this is the only table partition operation that was missing from the initial Oracle8 release. This is the converse of the SPLIT PARTITION operation. It reads from two partitions whose partition-key data range are adjacent to one another, and it creates a new partition. When the operation is complete, the two original partitions are dropped.

Parallel ALTER TABLE . . . MOVE

New with Oracle8*i*, this operation simplifies the process of moving a table from one tablespace to another or *reorganizing* a fragmented table to reclaim deleted space or migrated/chained rows. This operation is very similar to the previously mentioned ALTER TABLE . . . MOVE PARTITION.

This operation uses the direct-path mechanism when executed in PARALLEL, and it can also utilize the NOLOGGING clause.

Parallel ALTER TABLE . . . MOVE ONLINE

Also new with Oracle8*i*, this operation is available only for *index-organized tables* (IOTs) in the current releases of Oracle8*i*. This operation allows a table to be moved or rebuilt while still *fully accessible* for all SELECT, INSERT, UPDATE, and DELETE statements.

Parallel ALTER INDEX . . . REBUILD PARTITION

This is very similar to the previously mentioned ALTER INDEX . . . REBUILD operation, except that this runs against individual partitions.

Parallel ALTER INDEX . . . REBUILD SUBPARTITION

This is very similar to the previously mentioned ALTER INDEX . . . REBUILD and ALTER INDEX . . . REBUILD PARTITION operations, except that this runs against individual subpartitions in a composite partitioned Oracle8*i* index.

Parallel ALTER INDEX . . . REBUILD ONLINE

Possibly the only drawback to the ALTER INDEX . . . REBUILD command is that it must lock the index that is being rebuilt, restricting DML against the associated table. This presents an availability issue.

New with Oracle8*i* is the ability to perform this operation against indexes with *no loss of availability* to the index or to the associated table.

There is more to the availability equation than simply preventing database outages. This is another important direction for Oracle; making objects available during maintenance.

Parallel Statistics Gathering

Ever since the introduction of the cost-based optimizer (CBO) in Oracle7, release 7.0, almost 10 years ago, analyzing statistics that could be used by the CBO has been plagued by the fact that the ANALYZE command could not be performed in parallel.

Now, with Oracle8*i*, it still can't!

But the PL/SQL supplied package DBMS_STATS has three packaged procedures that perform the same function as the ANALYZE command, and they include the ability to specify a degree of parallelism.

The three procedures are GATHER_DATABASE_STATISTICS, GATHER_SCHEMA_STATISTICS, and GATHER_TABLE_STATISTICS. Finally it is possible to gather statistics from a single command while behind the scenes it performs parallel execution. Check the Oracle8*i* *Server Supplied Packages Reference* manual for more detail on these procedures.

Summary

Parallel operations in Oracle are a direct reaction to the rise of data warehousing. Bit by bit, since Oracle7, version 7.1, in 1994, more and more operations in Oracle can be transparently decomposed and run in parallel. With Oracle8 and its partitioned tables and indexes, this trend has leaped forward impressively.

Additionally, Oracle has "spun on a dime" and branched off into a completely unexpected direction with *direct-path* operations. Until Oracle7, version 7.1, the obvious primary focus of the Oracle RDBMS was toward supporting large numbers of concurrent OLTP operations. Since version 7.1, that evolution has continued, but there has been dramatic movement toward adding nonshared direct-path operations, optimized for speed and volume, that bypass the all-important buffer cache. This is a shift toward supporting a relatively small number of very large concurrent DSS operations.

With Oracle8, there is now a single RDBMS that can be optimized for both major kinds of databases: OLTP and data warehouse. This is no one-trick pony, like Red Brick or Sybase. This is a technological tour de force, and it continues to improve.

Warehousing with Oracle Parallel Server

MRS. MOORE (*in labor*)**: What's that for?**

OBSTETRICIAN: That's the machine that goes 'ping'. [*PING!*] You see? That means your baby is still alive!

DOCTOR SPENSER: And that's the most expensive machine in the whole hospital!

OBSTETRICIAN: Yes, it cost over three quarters of a million pounds!

DOCTOR SPENSER: Aren't you lucky?!

Monty Python's Meaning of Life—*Python (Monty) Pictures, Ltd., 1983*

There are occasions when the demands of the application exceed the capacity of a single machine. There are also situations when the demands for nonstop availability exceed the probable reliability of a single machine and its subsystems. To address these situations, Oracle Parallel Server is available for clustered and massively parallel processing (MPP) systems.

CLUSTERED AND MPP SYSTEMS

Refer to Chapter 2, "Hardware Architectures for Oracle Data Warehousing," in this book for a detailed discussion of clustered, MPP, NUMA, and other multinode computer architectures.

What Is Oracle Parallel Server?

The Parallel Server option of the Oracle RDBMS allows a single database to be accessed and maintained by more than one instance. The usual arrangement for most Oracle installations involves a database with a single instance, whereas the files of an Oracle *database* are accessed and maintained by the processes of only one *instance* of Oracle. When the Parallel Server option is purchased and installed, more than one instance can be used to access and maintain a single database. See Figure 11.1 for an illustration of an exclusive database versus a parallel database.

In the vast majority of Parallel Server implementations, each instance resides on a separate node in a cluster. Each node, with its Oracle instance, has complete, equal, and full read/write access to all the files or volumes that make up the Oracle database. This is the concept of *shared* disk (see Figure 11.2). Oracle is the only major database vendor with this requirement on clustered systems; all other vendors implement what is known as a *shared nothing* parallel database architecture (see Figure 11.3). With shared nothing implementations, each database instance on each node of the cluster has exclusive access to the portion of the database residing on that node. Examples of shared nothing par-

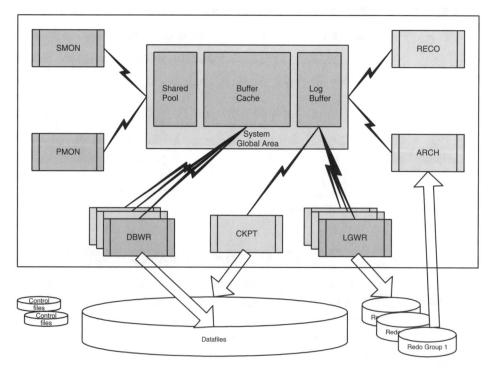

Figure 11.1 Exclusive database versus parallel database.

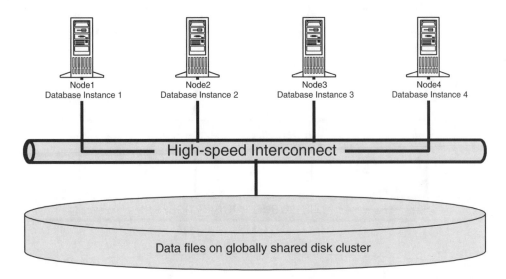

Figure 11.2   Shared disk parallel database architecture.

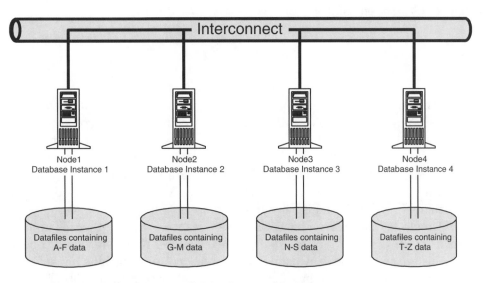

Figure 11.3   Shared nothing parallel database architecture.

allel database architectures include IBM DB2/PE, Informix XPS, and Teradata. As we just mentioned, Oracle has the only shared disk parallel database architecture.

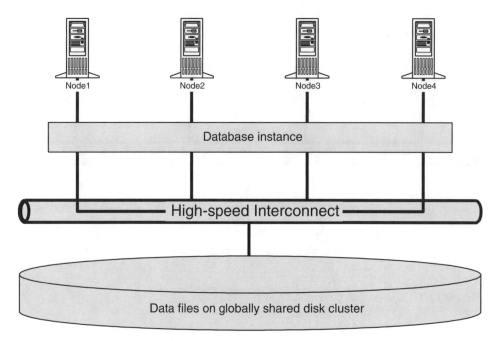

Figure 11.4 Shared everything parallel database architecture.

There is another parallel database architecture that is possible for clustered or massively parallel processing (MPP) machine architectures: *shared everything* (see Figure 11.4). So far, there has yet to be a commercial implementation of a shared everything architecture. It could be argued that exclusive, non-Parallel Server Oracle on NUMA architectures presents this architecture, but NUMA platforms are only now becoming available, and there is nothing to indicate that the availability of NUMA systems can survive component failures.

In Oracle Parallel Server, each database instance is a *peer*; there is no concept of a *master* instance or of *subordinate* instances. Therefore, should one or more instances become unavailable for any reason (i.e., a machine "crash"), the remaining instance or instances can keep the database fully operational, provided that full access to all the files and volumes that comprise the physical database continues (see Figure 11.5).

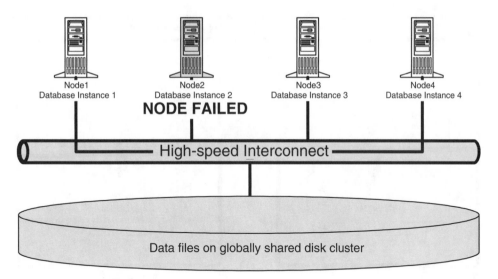

Figure 11.5 Availability in Parallel Server.

Parallel Server versus Distributed Databases

The concept of Parallel Server should also not be confused with the concept of a distributed database. A distributed database is a logical concept, consisting of two or more separate physical databases, each operating completely independently of one another. Each can be backed up and recovered separately; each can be started up or shut down independently. Distributed Oracle databases are linked together using Oracle "database links," which allows transparent server-to-server communication. Distributed Oracle databases are discussed in more depth in the next chapter. A distributed homogeneous database is illustrated in Figure 11.6.

In heterogeneous environments involving Oracle and other database vendors, *gateway* products may be used to represent the foreign data stores as part of the Oracle database, and vice versa (see Figure 11.7). Alternatively, access to each of the heterogeneous data stores can be presented to end users by middleware using X-Open's XA distributed transaction control protocol, which is used by transaction processing monitors such as BEA's Tuxedo, IBM Transarc's Encina, IBM's CICS, and NCR's Top End (see Figure 11.8).

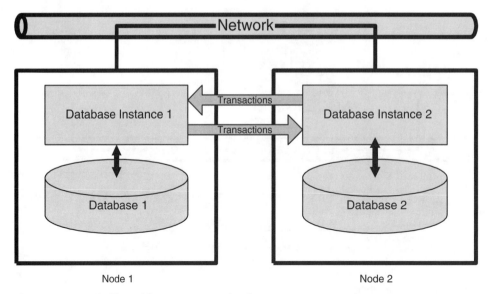

Figure 11.6 Distributed homogeneous databases.

Last, distributed and/or heterogeneous databases can be linked together by the front-end applications; many development environments provide transparent connectivity to various data stores simultaneously (see Figure 11.9). Of course, a network of distributed databases could also include Parallel Server databases. In fact, it is not uncommon to see one or more so-called data marts, implemented as either single-instance exclusive Oracle databases or multiple-instance, multiple-node Parallel Server databases, extracting data from a centralized data warehouse, which also might be a single- or multiple-instance database (see Figure 11.10).

Again, What Is Parallel Server?

Bear with us while we employ a simple analogy to illustrate the following:

- The difference between an Oracle database and an instance
- How reads and writes are performed by an Oracle instance
- How Oracle with the Parallel Server option is different from single-instance Oracle
- How reads and writes are performed by many Oracle Parallel Server instances

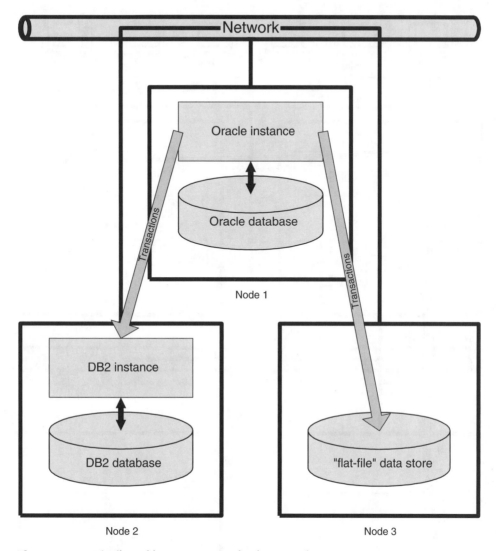

Figure 11.7 Distributed heterogeneous databases and gateways.

Some of these issues were also covered in Chapter 3, "Oracle Server Software Architecture and Features," but they bear revisiting.

File Cabinets and File Clerks

The distinction between a database and an instance can be illustrated with a simple example involving file cabinets and file clerks. File cabinets, where

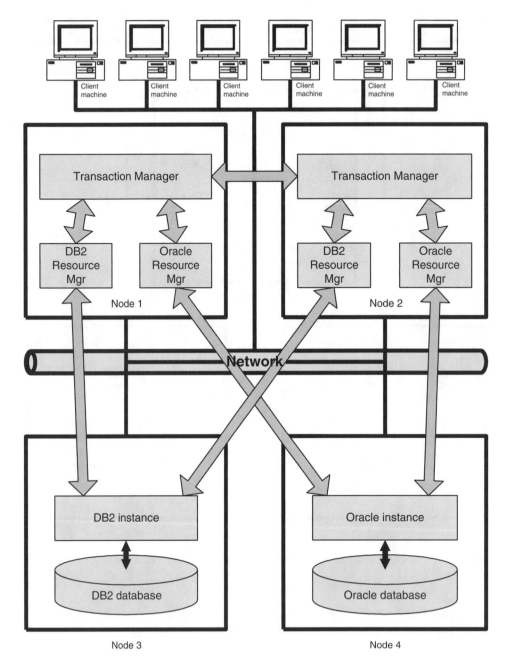

Figure 11.8 Distributed environment using XA.

paper files are stored, are just racks, drawers, and cabinets where information, in the form of file folders, is stored. Someone or something has to organize these file cabinets and store data there in an orderly fashion; otherwise, data

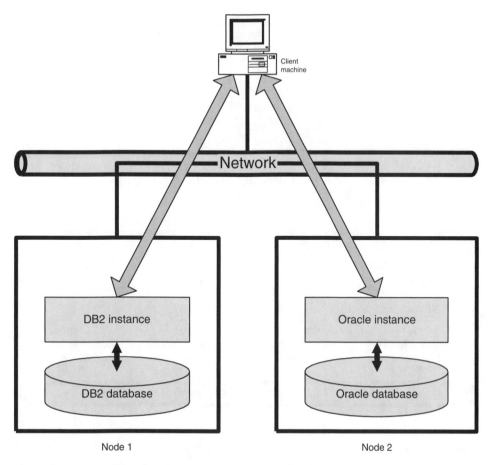

Figure 11.9   Distributed environment joined by application.

would be stored there in a jumble, with no hope of being able to retrieve it again. That someone or something is the file clerk.

In this analogy, the role of the Oracle database itself is played by the file cabinets, which are just places to store data. On a computer, operating system files or disk volumes are used. The role of the Oracle database instance is played by the file clerks, who decide where and how data will be stored to facilitate retrieval. A database is inert storage, while an instance is active processes and data structures. In an office, the file cabinets are inert storage bins, while file clerks are the people who access those file cabinets.

Now let's build on this analogy a little and make it more closely fit the reality of what an Oracle database is and how Oracle works. (Please bear with us on this; if it gets too corny, then just skip ahead to the next section.)

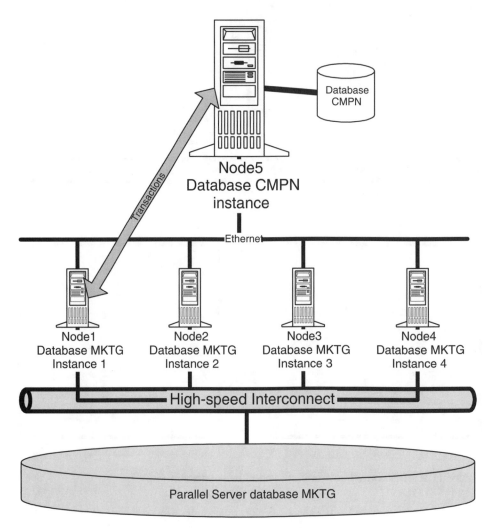

Figure 11.10 Distributed environment including Parallel Server.

Because they hold valuable data the file cabinets themselves reside in a room set apart from the rest of the office. Anybody accessing these file cabinets has to walk to this other room, which takes a little bit of time. Because of the amount of time it takes to walk from their office to the room where the file cabinets are kept, the file clerks keep the most frequently accessed files with them, on their desks in their office. This tends to save many trips back and forth to the file cabinets.

This part of the analogy illustrates the expense of accessing disk drives. The desks in the file clerks' office represent the Oracle SGA, which contains caches of information stored in shared memory. The file cabinets themselves, because they represent Oracle data files on disk drives, are depicted as being a certain distance away from the file clerks and their desks.

Now, some rigid rules define how file clerks and their coworkers work together. It has been decided that, when anybody wants to access data, either to just read it or to update it, he should first check to see if the appropriate file or folder is already present on the file clerks' desks. If so, then the information should be read or updated right there. Once again, this scheme cuts down on the number of trips back and forth to the file cabinets.

If the information to be read or updated is not present on the file clerks' desks, then the coworkers themselves, not the file clerks, must trek out to the file cabinets and retrieve the information. They are not allowed to update the data (if that is their intention) at the file cabinets, but rather they must make photocopies of the files and then bring the copies with them back to the file clerks' desks. Then and only then are they allowed to read or update the data contained in the files.

This makes sense because if the small group of file clerks was tasked with performing every single request to retrieve data from the file cabinets, the clerks would quickly become overloaded. Rather than keep people idle while a clerk retrieves information from the file cabinets, they go and do it themselves. This arrangement is much more *scalable*. The file clerks themselves, however, are responsible for making sure that *changed* file folders get back to the file cabinets.

The basic rules in the fictitious office in this analogy are rather simple, as they are in real life in an Oracle database. Any Oracle server process (i.e., a coworker) must first check in the buffer cache (the file clerks' desks) to see if the information to be accessed or manipulated is already there. If it is not, it makes the trek to the database (file cabinets) to bring a copy back to the buffer cache (file clerks' desks), where the data can then be used.

Once an Oracle server process (a coworker) has used a file folder, it can just leave the folder in the buffer cache (file clerks' desks). If the data gets updated, the background processes of the database instance (file clerks) are responsible for putting the changed data back into the database (file cabinets).

There is an additional responsibility not previously mentioned: Because only so many file folders can fit on the file clerks' desks, the file clerks are also responsible for removing little used files to make room for more heavily used ones. This is, of course, analogous to the least recently used (LRU) buffer cache recycling scheme employed by Oracle, which allows a fixed-size buffer cache to efficiently accommodate a database of unlimited size, for all intents and purposes.

Extending the Analogy to Include Parallel Server

Take a deep breath because we're not quite through with this analogy yet.

Adding Parallel Server option to the picture simply extends this analogy. Now there are two or more separate sets of file clerks, all of whom are operating on the same file cabinets. Each set of file clerks, however, is located in a different building (i.e., different computers), but they all have equal access to the same set of file cabinets.

Each instance (set of file clerks) caches data locally in its buffer cache (on the file clerks' desks). Oracle server processes (coworkers) in each computer (building) work with their local database instance (set of file clerks). When a server process (a coworker) wants to access or update data, it must first do so in the local instance's buffer cache (on the local set of file clerks' desks).

Now, perhaps you can see a problem. As long as the server processes (i.e., workers) are only reading the data, they can both do so at the same time and not cause a problem. But if both server processes (coworkers) wish to simultaneously update the same bit of information from the same file folder, then there could be a problem. Both instances could cache the information and make their updates in their respective caches. Subsequent reads and updates of this same information would then be different, as each instance has its own (now different) copy of what was read from the database. Eventually, each instance will write different information back to the same location in the disk drives, corrupting the database. If there are going to be multiple caches, they have to be kept *coherent*.

What has to happen to prevent this is a form of locking called *parallel cache management* (PCM). PCM is necessary only when two or more instances are trying to update the same parts of a database. If update activity (which includes INSERTs, UPDATEs, and DELETEs) is not occurring, if the environment is *read-only*, then there is no need for PCM. Oracle performs parallel cache management by assigning individual PCM locks to cover one or more database blocks in the database (see Figure 11.11).

The tables used to map from *database blocks* to *PCM locks* are in the Oracle SGA. Before any process can update the database block in the buffer cache, it must first acquire the related PCM lock in *exclusive* mode. By definition, before an exclusive lock can be acquired, any other instance holding an exclusive lock has to release it. Before it can do that, the other instance has to write all changes it has made to the database block back to the database. This is known as a *ping*.

Additionally, any instances that had acquired the PCM lock in *shared mode* must also release the lock, so the copies of the database blocks resident in the cache cannot be used again. To read those database blocks again, a shared lock on the related PCM lock must once again be acquired. Figure 11.12 shows one instance trying to change a cached block.

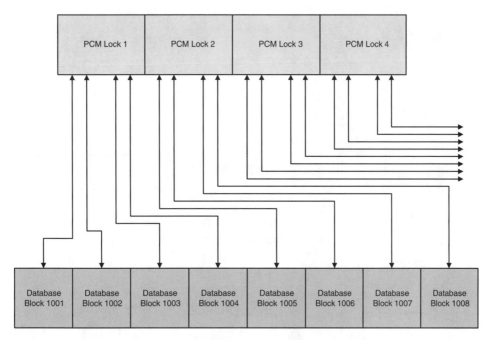

Figure 11.11 PCM locks covering one or more database blocks.

When the process performing the change finally acquires the exclusive lock, it makes the change. It is not immediately required to write the changed buffer to the database unless someone else requests another shared or exclusive lock. So, multiple changes to the same block can occur until another lock request comes across. At that time, the block can be written down to the database, and if the requested lock mode is shared, the exclusive lock will then be converted to shared as well.

In the terms of our analogy, these locks are *sign-up sheets* that each coworker must sign before he takes a file folder back to his reading room. That way, if each bit of information is "signed out" when it is read up to the local buffer cache, then any later coworkers, perhaps from different buildings, know whether they can safely change the data or whether they must first inform all other departments about the change. If everyone is just going to read the file folder, then they simply indicate this on the sign-up sheet. Reading is no problem; many people are allowed to read at the same time, as long as you tell everyone else that you're reading.

Think about what happens when a change occurs. There are numerous copies of the file folder in different departments. If someone makes a change to his copy, then this change must be immediately propagated to the other copies in the different departments, so that everyone sees the same data.

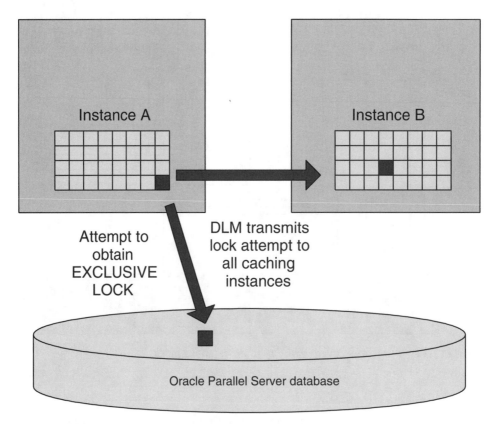

Figure 11.12   One instance tries to change a cached block.

How can this propagation occur? Continuing with our analogy, it's possible that whoever is going to make the change gets on an intercom and announces the change to the whole company. A less obnoxious alternative might be to set up a telephone system from each of the clerk's desks; anybody about to make a change has to first notify all the other departments. This is *messaging*, and Oracle does this. A message, similar to a short telephone call, is sent to all instances holding locks, telling them someone is going to change that database block. Each instance must surrender its shared lock in order for the updating instance to obtain the necessary exclusive PCM lock covering the block to be changed.

The data changes themselves are not transmitted in the message. In Oracle, the data changes are made to the database block and are then written to the database. Any instances wishing to see those changes must read the block from the database back into their buffer caches. See Figure 11.13 for an illustration of messages and database writes.

Completing the analogy (finally!), the different departments (i.e., machines in a cluster), each with its own sets of file clerks (database instance) and its

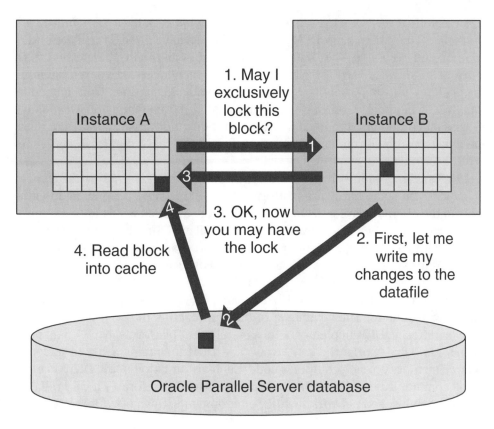

Figure 11.13 Messages and database writes.

local supply of information on top of the clerks' desks (buffer cache) copy file folders (database blocks) from the file cabinets (database). To copy the file folders, the workers in the company (Oracle server processes) have to check out the file folders on a sign-up sheet, telling everyone that they've got the folder. Then they can carry a copy of it back to the file clerks' desks and read it.

If anyone in any of the departments wishes to change the contents of a file folder at his file clerk's desk, he first has to check the sign-up sheet and call all the other departments on the list, telling them that the file folder is going to be changed. Once they've been notified, the copies of the file folders in the other departments are discarded, and their entry on the sign-up sheet is deleted. When the sign-up sheet for the file folder is finally clear, the change is made, right at the file clerk's desk.

Is there any need to put that changed file folder back into the file cabinet? Not until some other department wants to read it or write it. Once again, this write-down is known as a *ping*.

In real-life terms, Oracle Parallel Server uses what is called a *distributed lock manager* (DLM) to manage PCM locks. PCM locks have three basic states: *null*, *shared*, and *exclusive*. The DLM maintains a list of all the PCM locks and their current states. It is part of a class of program peculiar to networked environments known as a *distributed service*. It is available anytime, from any computer. If it is updated on one computer, it must be instantaneously updated across all computers. If one computer is shut down or crashes, the DLM must be able to continue running on all other nodes in spite of that (also known as *fault tolerance*).

For Oracle version 6.2 and Oracle7, the DLM was external to the Oracle instances. On some hardware platforms, the DLM is *kernelized* as an integral part of the operating system. On other platforms, the DLM is just another application running under the operating system, similar to the Oracle RDBMS itself. Check with your hardware vendor or Oracle Corporation to determine whether the DLM for your platform is provided by the hardware vendor (i.e., kernelized DLM) or by Oracle (i.e., nonkernel DLM).

With Oracle8 release 8.0, the DLM became an integrated part of the Oracle database instances. The advantage of this approach is that you don't have to rely on differing DLM implementations on different platforms. Now, on all platforms, the DLM works the same way. The DLM maintains a list of locks in shared memory on each computer node. Each instantiation of the DLM on each node communicates with each other over a network, preferably a very reliable and very high-speed network. In MPP environments, this network is known as the *interconnect*.

The DLM has a very simple job. The application (in this case, the local instance of the Oracle RDBMS) requests locks in different modes: null, shared, and exclusive. The DLM grants those requests according to a series of rules. The main trick is to tell everyone the same thing at the same time.

In our earlier analogy, these mysterious sign-up sheets seem to be everywhere at once. This is the magic of the DLM: to be everywhere at once, to be reliable, and to be fault tolerant. As you may have guessed, all this messaging and pinging replace what, in "normal" exclusive-mode Oracle, used to be simple accesses of buffered database blocks in shared memory. What was once a very fast, efficient, and scalable operation—caching—is now a liability. Writing to a cached database block now involves an expensive operation that includes writes to the database known as *pinging*. This effect is referred to as the *paradox of pinging* (see Figure 11.14).

Pinging is, therefore, to be avoided if possible. Is the way to avoid pinging to simply avoid using local buffer caches? Figure 11.14 would suggest so. But, no, this would be an erroneous conclusion. Rather than avoiding buffer caching, one should try to avoid *cross-instance writes*, the situation that spawns the necessity for pinging. If the I/O from each database instance can be *segregated*

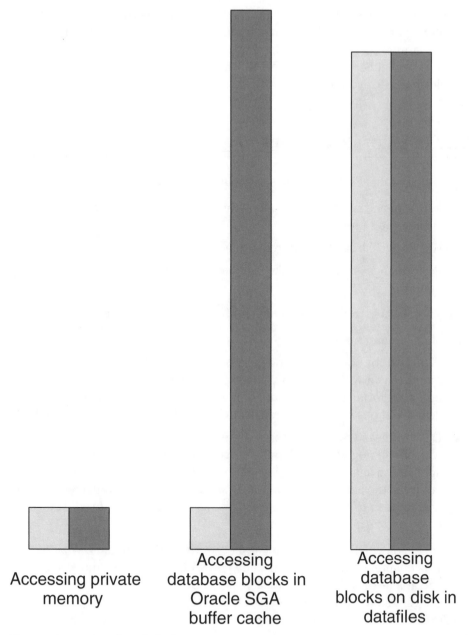

Figure 11.14   Paradox of pinging.

effectively among the database instances, then cross-instance writes wouldn't happen, and therefore pinging could be eliminated or minimized. This too is discussed later in the chapter.

We've now discussed the basics of how the Oracle RDBMS and the Oracle Parallel Server option work. This discussion outlines some of the complexities of using Parallel Server option and, we hope, helps form a framework for understanding Parallel Server to help decide whether the Parallel Server option is a suitable choice for your data warehouse.

Why Use Parallel Server?

In general, Parallel Server provides the following benefits:

- Performance and capacity scaleup through additional instances operating against the same database
- Higher availability through redundancy
- Performance speedup when used in conjunction with Parallel Query option

In general, these advantages could be offset by the following costs:

- Much greater system management complexity.
- The need for some applications to be built (or rebuilt) specifically to be "parallel-aware;" if not, the expected performance benefits can readily turn into a performance degradation; query-intensive applications typical in a data warehouse do not generally suffer from this potential disadvantage.
- Lack of disaster-recovery tools. Using current clustered and MPP hardware technology, Oracle Parallel Server is not yet capable of protecting an application against the massive failures within a data center or a massive failure of the entire data center itself. In other words, Parallel Server does not address *disaster-recovery* issues, as Oracle's *standby database* or *data replication* products do.

The decision whether to use the Parallel Server option should be made carefully. This chapter is intended to provide you with most of the knowledge necessary to make that decision. We will not, however, cover all details of all concepts related to Parallel Server. We highly recommended that you read the Oracle8*i Parallel Server Concepts and Administration Guide*.

Benefit: Performance and Capacity Scaleup

It's simple. You've estimated how much disk storage and how many concurrent users the data warehouse is going to need, and the hardware vendor is skeptical that one machine could handle that load. Or worse, you've proved this empirically, finding out after the fact that your machine is not able to handle the load. But perhaps 2, 10, or 100 machines can handle the load. Perhaps more machines can provide the necessary storage capacity. Parallel Server allows one database to be spread over 2 or more machines in a clustered environment.

There are several alternatives for dividing the load across several machines. In the case of two-tier (i.e., client/server) or multitier applications, the load can be distributed vertically by tier. For example, starting with the initial client/server application on one machine, the "client" tier can be moved onto one or more separate machines. Thus, the "horsepower" required to drive the client-side programs can be separated from the Oracle instance and the server processes. This is a common remedy for older versions of the Oracle Applications, such as Oracle General Ledger or Oracle Inventory, which were primarily two-tier (dumb terminal or client/server GUI) applications.

Another option is to distribute the load horizontally. If 2,000 online users are too much for one machine, buy another machine and put 1,000 online users on each. If you choose this route, there are again two choices. The existing database can be divided up into 2 (or more) separate databases. If each of the resulting databases needs to access or manipulate data in the other database, then segregation can be made syntactically transparent to the application by using database links and synonyms. See Figure 11.15 for an illustration of distributed databases.

Creating two databases linked together is relatively easy if there is some natural segregation (as in Figure 11.15). For example, perhaps application A is primarily financial data while application B is primarily marketing data. But if there is no clear separation point, it might work best to leave the database whole and distribute this single database across several machines, as shown in Figure 11.16.

How can the load be distributed evenly between each instance? Oracle's Net8 product is capable of distributing connections that use a Net8 *connect-string* among multiple instances of a Parallel Server database. This involves describing each connection to each instance in separate "DESCRIPTION=" specifications, then grouping them together within the same *connect-string* using the "DESCRIPTION_LIST=" syntax. The default behavior for this Net8 configuration is to randomly distribute the connections between all of the DESCRIPTIONs within the DESCRIPTION_LIST.

Another strategy is to use an external load balancer such as a Cisco Load Directory (CLD) device from Cisco Systems, Inc.

Benefit: Higher Availability

Higher availability in traditional mainframe systems was usually the result of higher reliability of components. Mean time between failures (MTBF) in mainframe components was generally quite high, meaning that component failure

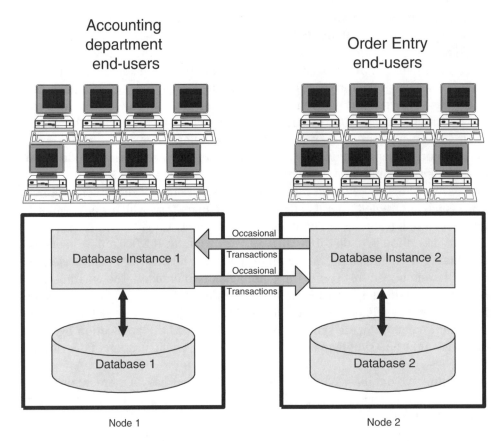

Figure 11.15 Distributed databases.

occurred infrequently enough to enable close to 100 percent system uptime. The problem here is that such component reliability is expensive.

Open systems such as UNIX rely on component redundancy, not component reliability, to enable close to 100 percent system uptime. Components produced on a commodity basis have lower MTBF individually, but their lower price allows redundancy. Moving beyond component redundancy, Oracle Parallel Server enables the use of clustered systems to provide *system redundancy*. Each individual database instance in Parallel Server can continue to operate as long as all parts of the database are still available. So, if one machine should fail or be shut down, the remaining database instances can continue operating unimpaired (see Figure 11.17).

How can disk drives survive machine failure? For the most part, disk drives used in clustered systems do not physically reside in the same cabinet as the CPU. Rather, storage arrays residing on their own power supplies can be connected to more than one CPU. Should one CPU or node in the cluster fail, the

Data
Warehouse
end-users

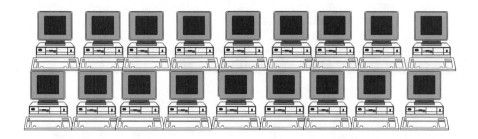

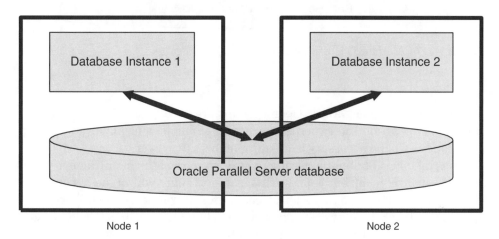

| Database Instance 1 | Database Instance 2 |

Oracle Parallel Server database

Node 1   Node 2

Figure 11.16   Parallel server.

partner node detects this and orders the storage array to fail over or transfer control of the array to itself (see Figure 11.18).

In addition to having all parts of the database available to each database instance on each node, each disk drive is usually connected to two or more nodes. Most of the technology to implement this redundancy has been developed only in the past decade. At the moment, most of this complexity is exposed to developers and administrators, making redundant open system environments exceedingly difficult to manage. The evolution, however, continues. Within a few more years, administering redundant systems will be almost as simple to manage as individual systems. In fact, the redundancy may be quite transparent, blurring the lines of separation between mainframes and large open systems. The

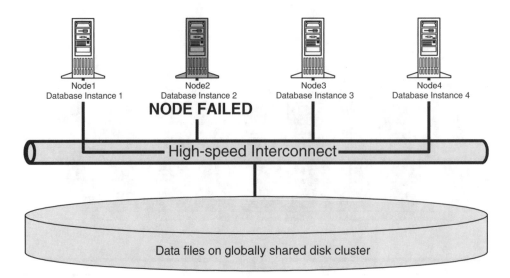

Figure 11.17 Machine failure in parallel server.

mainframe is not going away. Open systems are rapidly acquiring mainframe-quality features, and the expertise necessary to implement mainframe-quality applications will be necessary in greater numbers than ever.

It has taken UNIX about a decade to scaleup to rival the mainframe in terms of performance, availability, and manageability. Many will argue successfully that it is not there yet in the last two categories. It will be interesting to watch how long it takes Windows NT-based systems to match this feat. UNIX still has a long way to go and NT even further, but both have a lot of momentum.

Benefit: Performance Speedup

As we mentioned in the previous chapter on parallel operations, on most UNIX platforms (IBM RS/6000 SP and Pyramid RM1000, for example) Parallel Execution (PX), in conjunction with Parallel Server, can transparently scale a query or DML statement across nodes. Instead of the query being executed by a single process or multiple processes on the same machine, it can actually be scaled across multiple database instances (see Figure 11.19).

This is actually quite an awe-inspiring feat, and the performance increases can be stunning. The IBM RS/6000 SP machine from IBM has a wonderful graphical 3-D performance statistic monitor named, appropriately, "3dmon." If a particular table is striped properly across all disk drives on all nodes, it is possible to execute a simple query, such as:

```
SQL> SELECT COUNT(*) FROM <really-big-table>;
```

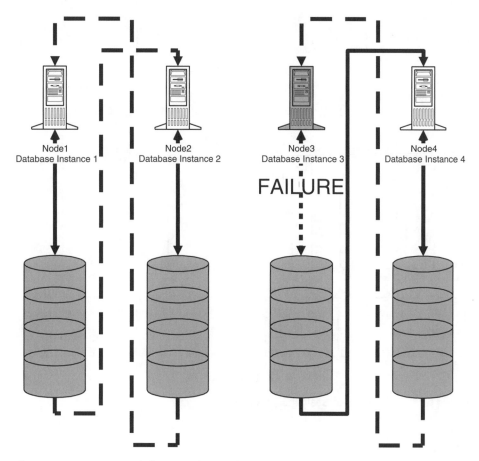

Figure 11.18 Storage failover in clustered systems.

and watch "3dmon" display all the little three-dimensional colored columns representing the disk drives on all the nodes in the cluster just stand right up and start pumping. Querying a 20 GB table could take a single machine that is otherwise idle 20 minutes; spreading the table across 20 machines and having all 20 participate in the query can result in the query finishing in well under a minute.

Cost: Greater Management Complexity

Consider the maturing status of the components in clustered and massively parallel systems. Features and performance are clearly top priority, while manageability may be considered far down on the list of priorities. Initial manageability weaknesses are shown in the tools supplied by the hardware vendor as well as in other systems management packages from third-party suppliers.

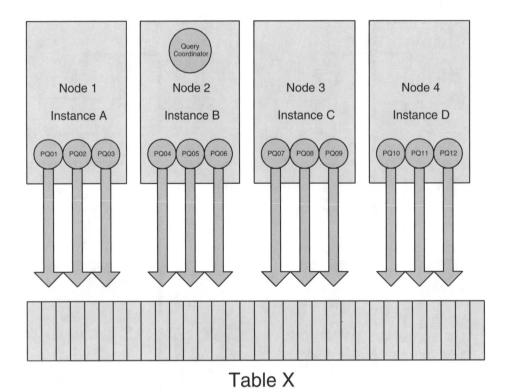

Table X

Figure 11.19 Parallel query scaling across instances.

Illustrating this, Oracle Parallel Server did not have any database- or system-management utilities prior to Oracle7, version 7.2. Starting with version 7.2 (circa 1995), a short-lived utility named "dbtool" was introduced to facilitate startup and shutdown. With Oracle7, version 7.3 (circa 1996), "dbtool" disappeared and another utility named "opsctl" appeared, which also performed startup and shutdown only. Additionally, Oracle Enterprise Manager was introduced in 1996, and it was instrumented to manage many additional Parallel Server operations. Currently, startup and shutdown operations can be scripted for batch execution using the "opsctl" utility and most other operations can be performed using the GUI-based Oracle Enterprise Manager.

This illustration is not an indictment of Oracle's administration tools—the same points can be made about the evolving nature of all management tools for these newer, somewhat exotic, clustered environments. The point is that you must not assume that the same level of monitoring and control that you have over your existing systems will be readily available on the "bleeding edge." Be prepared to develop additional shell scripts to bridge the gap until the system administration tools mature.

If your organization is seasoned, has good policies and procedures, and thrives on making new gizmos work, then clustered systems and Parallel Server should work out just fine. Mainframe-trained users invariably liken UNIX systems to tinker toy sets that are used to build Ferraris: All the pieces are there for you to use, but you have to fit them together yourself. If your organization likes doing this, then this is good news. If the organization is not technically confident, seems overwhelmed, has limited success adapting to change, or doesn't welcome a possible tinker toy Ferrari, then perhaps the project should scale back somewhat.

Another proof of the added complexity of a clustered or MPP environment is the fact that there are numerous training classes by the vendors on installing, administering, and tuning clustered environments. In some cases, the hardware vendor (anticipating increased call volume to its technical support lines) will insist that the customer's System Administrators take this training and be "certified" as capable of supporting clustered configurations. Check your hardware vendor's Web site for education offerings specific to clusters and MPP systems.

This is good advice for Oracle database administrators as well. Oracle Education has a Web site at http://education.oracle.com/, and there is at least one three-day course on "Oracle8i: Parallel Server Implementation," which should be mandatory for anybody considering Parallel Server.

Each of these training courses costs at least $2,000 per person for the course alone. If you are not fortunate enough to be located near a training center, then you'd need to tack on the cost of boarding, feeding, and airfare.

If you do not already have cluster experience among your UNIX system administrators, either you'll need the training or you'll need to hire contractors with this experience, or both. Same for Oracle database administrators: Either get the training, hire expensive contractors with prior experience, or do both.

Attempting to learn this stuff on your own is also an option, but it will undoubtedly be the most expensive option of all, in the final analysis.

Either way, these are required costs that vendors are not anxious to discuss during the sales cycle, to nobody's great surprise. And these costs are simply indicators of the complexities involved in installing, configuring, and maintaining these systems. Do not underestimate this; there is no such thing (yet!) as a clustered system or an Oracle Parallel Server database that is "ready to go" or "shrink-wrapped."

Cost: Not Transparent to Some Applications

To avoid pinging, some applications may require segregation of query and data manipulation, dividing activity in the database in such a way that each database instance does not frequently try to access database blocks outside of its designated segment of tables or tablespaces. Obviously, most applications are not written this way. Therefore, most applications not originally designed for Parallel Server will not perform well if rehosted without change to a Parallel Server environment. In fact, if no effort is made to tune for Parallel Server, it is quite likely that an application will run much slower in Parallel Server than when it was running on a single machine! So, applications must be written in such a way that they perform well on Parallel Server, and the cost of making those changes might very well be prohibitive.

HEY! WE'LL JUST USE ONE INSTANCE FOR REAL WORK AND ONE INSTANCE FOR REPORTING!

As Oracle consultants, we frequently hear from customers who are aware of the fact that applications not built explicitly for Parallel Server will suffer serious performance problems. They, however, want to make use of clustered or MPP systems for the availability benefits. They propose a two-node configuration with Parallel Server, each node with one instance accessing the same database. On one node, the "primary," they intend to place their existing application, unaltered. In the event of node failure, then the second instance on the second "backup" node can act as a "hot standby," continuing normal operations of all but transactions that had been "in-flight."

So far, so good. It is difficult, though, to allow the second backup node to remain "unused" under normal circumstances. Thus, the proposal includes the scheme to use the second node with its second database instance as a "reporting" server. While all the "real work" is performed on the primary node, the backup node (while it is still a "backup") will be used for read-only "reporting."

An attractive thought, but even read-only activities cause pinging when requesting blocks that have been updated in another instance. As a result, the performance of "real work" on the primary node will be severely affected by contention with the read-only query activity on the backup node.

In brief, this scheme won't work; the backup instance must remain completely quiescent to avoid contention with the primary. To put it another way, for this primary/backup use of Parallel Server to work as intended, the backup node will have to be a "room warmer" until the primary fails.

One possibility: The backup node can be used to perform backups. Backup activities are generally image copies of the underlying data files to the Oracle database, and they do not cause pinging (although Oracle8's Recovery Manager does have modes that do block reads and would induce pinging).

The other alternative: Retrofit the application to accommodate Parallel Server.

Luckily, data warehouse applications do not suffer from many of these issues. For the most part, data warehouses are read-only during most of their available hours, and read-only is not a problem. During the load phase, when inserts, updates, and deletes are occurring, it may be easier to segregate activities from load programs than it would be to segregate the activities of, say, online forms. Because of the need to enforce segregation, it might be more properly said that the cost of making changes to accommodate segregation may be prohibitive for OLTP applications. For DSS applications, the batched nature of the loads may make the task much easier to control.

There are a few ways to group database objects to make segregation easier. There are two primary ways to group tables, clusters, and indexes for Parallel Server segregation: read-only objects and read/write objects. Because pinging is a problem only when objects are being written, significant improvements are possible just by separating read-only objects into separate tablespaces from read/write objects. Isolating the objects being written may make a large task a little smaller.

In a data warehouse, the vast majority of objects are *supposed to be* read-only. The catch is load cycles, when even read-only objects must occasionally be written to, so some objects may switch between read-only and read/write modes depending on whether they are in a load cycle. Because read-only segments cause no PCM difficulties, they should be grouped into tablespaces according to whether the following is true:

- They contain data (i.e., tables and clusters) or are indexes.

- They are on the same load or purge schedule (i.e., they are updated similarly at the same time).

- They have similar size and growth characteristics.

Data segments such as tables and clusters should be separated from indexes. Primarily, this is because tables and their associated indexes have different I/O characteristics: Indexes are always accessed with single-block, random I/Os, and tables could be accessed with either single-block random I/Os or with multiblock, sequential I/Os. These characteristics have direct impact on how PCM locks will be allocated. Also, tables and indexes typically have different size and growth characteristics; typically, indexes are smaller than the tables they are associated with and grow more slowly. Last, indexes don't necessarily have to be backed up, as they are *derived supporting* data structures and do not actually contain data. This brings up the whole debate over how to recover from a media failure: *restore from backup* or *rebuild*. With the size of data warehouses and the somewhat less stringent *mean-time-to-repair* recovery requirements associated with decision support databases as a whole, it may be much more attractive to rebuild indexes and their tablespaces rather than back them up.

If tables are on different load schedules from each other, they should be placed into different tablespaces. This allows maximum flexibility in using the ALTER TABLESPACE . . . READ ONLY command in Oracle to reduce PCM contention by setting entire tablespaces into READ ONLY mode, thus absolutely preventing writes.

As far as size and growth characteristics are concerned, placing similar-sized segments in the same tablespace allows you to use a single extent size for that entire tablespace. This issue was discussed back in Chapter 8, "Administering and Monitoring the Oracle Data Warehouse." If all extents for all segments in a tablespace are the same size, then there is no problem with *freespace fragmentation,* which can cause "bubbles" of unusable space to form, which can subsequently lead to false "out of space" conditions or simply wasted space. Many software vendors make a pretty fair living for themselves by selling "database reorganization" products to facilitate unloading and reloading tablespaces. The typical reason for wanting to do this in Oracle is generally freespace fragmentation. What the vendors of these reorg tools fail to mention is that freespace fragmentation is *completely unnecessary* if segments are assigned to tablespaces so that uniform-sized extents can be used. For example, consider a tablespace containing segments that range in size between 10 MB and 500 MB. Setting the tablespace's DEFAULT STORAGE to INITIAL 4M NEXT 4M PCTINCREASE 0 MAXEXTENTS 400 and then removing STORAGE clauses for all segments created in that tablespace will result in nothing but 4 MB extents in that tablespace. Some segments will use only 3 or 4 such extents, and other segments may use 100 or even up to 400 such extents, but there would be absolutely no fragmentation issues. The Oracle8 parameter, MINIMUM EXTENT, may be applied to a tablespace to ensure that all extents are multiples of this size.

If tables are to be read/write at all times, then further break down the types of update that will occur: INSERTs or UPDATEs. DELETEs should be considered a given, as all data must eventually be purged, but the manner in which purges occur is not necessarily in online transaction. They can be done via periodic batch transactions, or they can be grouped under the category of UPDATEs for the purposes of further discussion. Also, in a data warehouse environment, deletions can frequently be performed using the TRUNCATE command or by simply DROPing the table altogether. For now, let's just consider DELETEs as being the same as UPDATEs.

If tables are primarily INSERTed into but rarely UPDATEd, then access to them can be segregated in at least two ways: either by data routing or randomly using FREELIST GROUPS. If tables are INSERTed into and UPDATEd or DELETEd from frequently, then the best method for segregating access involves data routing only.

Load Segregation Using Data Routing

Data routing means that data will be manipulated according to the value of a key column or group of columns (see Figure 11.20). With Parallel Server, it means that each instance will be assigned to work on data according to the value of this key. This simplified example might involve customer information, keyed by CUST_NAME. Data is routed to Parallel Server instances according to the initial letter in the CUST_NAME. If there are four instances accessing the Parallel Server database, then each instance will be responsible for INSERTs, UPDATEs, and DELETEs to any customer information where the CUST_NAME starts with a letter from the preassigned range.

Data routing can be performed explicitly by the application software, or it can be performed by a Transaction Processing Monitor (TPM), the middle tier in a three-tier application architecture.

The data routing (sometimes called *application partitioning*) and table partitioning schemes must be coordinated. This helps to ensure that the set of transactions routed to one Parallel Server instance will access a different subset of

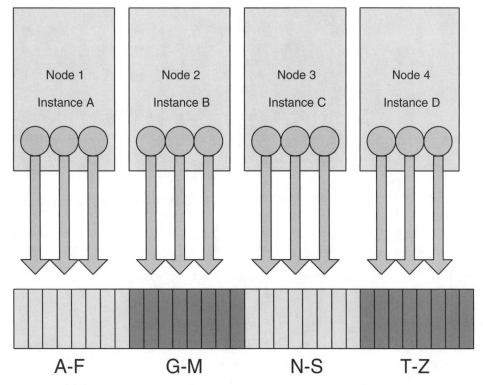

Figure 11.20   Data routing.

MULTICOLUMN PARTITIONING KEYS

Oracle8 partitioned tables with partition keys based on multiple columns can be tricky. The data values supplied are compared against the partition range bounds in the order in which the partition key has been defined. The first column (from the left) in the row's partition key that is not equal to a partition's corresponding boundary value will determine which partition will hold the data row.

This behavior can be confusing. As an example, if you specify REGION and TRANS_DATE as the partitioning key, rows with different values in the REGION column may end up in the same partition. In the following example, the COMMENTS column tells where the row will be inserted:

```
CREATE TABLE multikey
                (region              VARCHAR2(4),
                 tx_date             DATE,
                 comments            VARCHAR2(20))
             PARALLEL (DEGREE 4)
             PARTITION BY RANGE (region, tx_date)
             (PARTITION P1 VALUES LESS THAN
                          ('EAST',to_date('19970101',
                          'YYYYMMDD'))),
              PARTITION P2 VALUES LESS THAN
                          ('EAST',to_date('19980101',
                          'YYYYMMDD'))),
              PARTITION P3 VALUES LESS THAN
                          ('EAST',to_date('19990101',
                          'YYYYMMDD'))),
              PARTITION P4 VALUES LESS THAN
                          ('WEST',to_date('19970101',
                          'YYYYMMDD'))),
              PARTITION P5 VALUES LESS THAN
                          ('WEST',to_date('19980101',
                          'YYYYMMDD'))),
              PARTITION P6 VALUES LESS THAN
                          ('WEST',to_date('19990101',
                          'YYYYMMDD'))) );

         insert into multikey values ('CENT','15-oct-98',
         'partition 1');
         insert into multikey values ('EAST','15-oct-96',
         'partition 1');
```

database blocks in the data files than those transactions routed to each other instance. Data segregation may be aided in an implementation through the use of *partitioned tables* and *local partitioned indexes*. As long as the data routing is segregated using the same ranges as the data partitioning, then the Parallel

```
              insert into multikey values ('EAST','15-oct-97',
              'partition 2');
              insert into multikey values ('EAST','15-oct-98',
              'partition 3');
              insert into multikey values ('EAST','15-oct-99',
              'partition 4!');
              insert into multikey values ('EAST', null,
              'partition 4!');
              insert into multikey values ('WEST','15-oct-96',
              'partition 4');
              insert into multikey values ('WEST','15-oct-97',
              'partition 5');
              insert into multikey values ('WEST','15-oct-98',
              'partition 6');
              insert into multikey values ('WEST','01-jan-99',
              'rejected');
              insert into multikey values ('WEST', null,
              'rejected');
              insert into multikey values (null,  '15-oct-98',
              'rejected');
      commit;
```

Several rows end up rejected or in partitions other than where you might intuitively expect them! A user who queried specifically from partition P_4 thinking that this partition includes just the 1996 transactions from the WEST region might be surprised to also receive two EAST region transactions!

A null value in the partition key column of an inserted row is sorted above all other values and will therefore sort into the highest partition that satisfies the boundary criteria of any columns defined earlier in the partition key. Therefore, there should be a partition bounded by MAXVALUE in any column that may contain nulls, or the row containing the null value will be rejected or inserted into the next higher partition based on previous columns. (Inserts 6, 11, and 12 in the example demonstrate this behavior.) Better still, try to avoid partitioning on columns that allow null values.

Using a date column to define partition boundaries (single column or multicolumn) can also be confusing. Although it isn't well documented, you must specify the boundary value with a to_date function that includes century along with the year, month, and day in the date format. The example just presented demonstrates this. Failing to specify the century (YYYY) as part of the date format will result in an error.

Server will be able to efficiently distribute the work load without inducing excessive pinging. Segregating database instance activity to different partitions guarantees that multiple instances will never contend for the same database blocks.

Unfortunately, for the data warehouse designer, the most common data partitioning plan is based on date ranges. This approach facilitates warehouse administration through simplified purges and read-only tablespaces. Partitioning by date does not, however, generally lend itself to data routing or application partitioning because most activity occurs only within the most recent time partition. On the other hand, application partitioning by, say, region would nicely balance workload across OPS instances, but it would hinder the easy administration of the database.

Luckily, Oracle8*i*'s composite partitioning (using both range and hash partitioning) can help. Range partitioning by a date column can still be employed to aid administration of the data, by permitting the loading of data by partition. Within each range partition, composite hash partitioning can be used to segregate data by another column (say, customer ID or region) that matches how your database instances segregate access the data. By always accessing data by specific customer ID or region, you can be sure that the hashing algorithm in Oracle8*i* composite partitioning will not cause your accesses to physically coincide with accesses by another database instance.

The key to data routing, however, is to have some mechanism outside of Oracle route transactions to specific connections to database instances based on certain data values. This implies some form of middleware, or it implies some form of restriction in the client layer of the application.

Randomly Segregating Load

Freelist groups are a mechanism used by Oracle during INSERTs. When a row is to be inserted into a table, a database block in which to place the row has to be identified. A freelist identifies database blocks that have sufficient room to allow a new row to be inserted. A segment can have multiple freelists; this can be specified during table creation only. Multiple freelists reduce contention when many different processes are rapidly inserting rows into the same table (see Figure 11.21). They do this by keeping separate lists of available database blocks.

Freelist groups are separate groupings of one or more freelists. When FREELISTS GROUPS is set to a value greater than 1, a separate database block is added to the segment header for each freelist group. Having each group in a separate database block allows Parallel Server to avoid pinging when accessing and manipulating freelists. Therefore, in a Parallel Server environment, the value of FREELIST GROUPS is usually set to the number of instances, allocating different groups of FREELISTs for each instance. When an insert into that table occurs, it will attempt to find a block on a FREELIST belonging to a FREELIST GROUP belonging, in turn, to the instance performing the insert. If

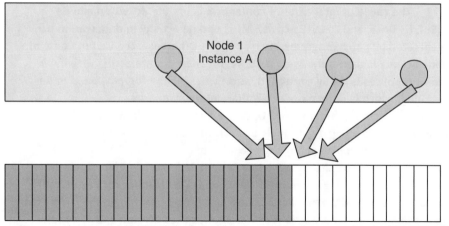

Four concurrent INSERTs into the front block on a single FREELIST

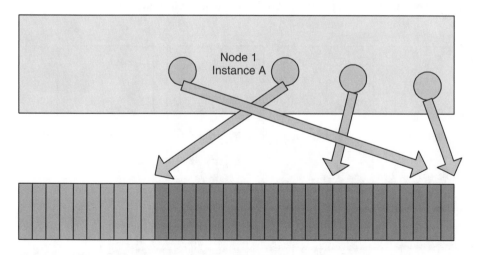

1st INSERT into first block of FREELIST 3, 2nd INSERT into front block of FREELIST 1, 3rd INSERT into front block of FREELIST 2, 4th INSERT into front block of FREELIST 3

Figure 11.21   Multiple FREELISTs reducing contention.

none of the FREELISTs belonging to an instance has any space for additional rows to be inserted, then a new extent will need to allocated, and either the entire new extent or just a portion of it will be allocated to this session's FREELIST in this instance's FREELIST GROUP. See Figure 11.22 for an illustration of multiple FREELIST GROUPs reducing contention.

NOTE The cause of interinstance contention is update activity, meaning INSERT, UPDATE, and DELETE activity. Most update activity in data warehouses is generated by batch programs, such as loads. Otherwise, the vast majority of online activity is read-only. As a result, segregation of data access activity in data warehouses is easily controlled, as only the batch programs need to be controlled, which is done more easily than interactive users.

OLTP systems are a different story. Update activity comes from online as well as batch modules, making it extremely difficult to segregate effectively.

The best way of implementing segregated applications is by the use of data routing. The most controllable way to implement data routing is by using a three-tier architecture involving a transaction processing (TP) monitor such as BEA's Tuxedo. The front-end tier handles business and presentation logic, the middle tier handles the routing of transactions to various instances according to a key value embedded in the data, and the back-end tier is the Oracle Parallel Server database.

When considering Oracle Parallel Server, start off with the assumption that a data warehouse application can be two-tier (client-server), while an OLTP application should be expected to be three-tier (client-monitor-server).

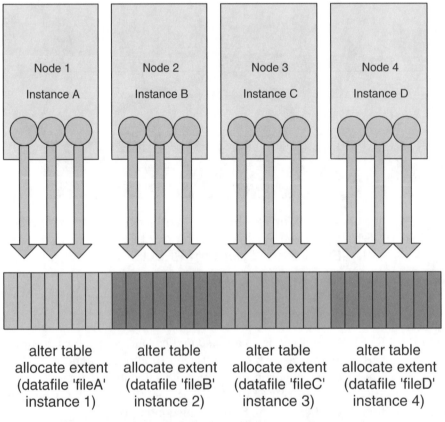

Figure 11.22 Multiple FREELIST GROUPs reducing contention.

More on PCM Locks

There are two kinds of PCM locks: *hash* locks, which are statically allocated, and *DBA releasable* locks, which are allocated and deallocated dynamically on demand. Hash locks are assigned to database blocks within data files and tablespaces using the GC_FILES_TO_LOCKS "init.ora" parameter at instance startup. DBA releasable locks are assigned to specific database blocks that are about to be updated and are released when the updated transaction is ended.

The "init.ora" parameter GC_DB_LOCKS controls the total number of hash locks to be used by all database instances and the DLM; the parameter GC_RELEASABLE_LOCKS does the same for DBA releasable locks. How these pools of locks are assigned is specified by the parameter GC_FILES_TO_LOCKS.

PCM locks cover only database blocks occupied by tables, indexes, and data structures such as segment headers, rollback segments, and temporary tablespaces. Non-PCM locks are *enqueues*, which must now be acquired *globally* across multiple database instances. Therefore, the parameters GC_DB_LOCKS, GC_RELEASABLE_LOCKS, and GC_FILES_TO_LOCKS should not cover tablespaces containing rollback segments and tablespaces designated for temporary segments only or explicitly marked as TEMPORARY tablespaces.

The GC_FILES_TO_LOCKS parameter is specified with a rather complicated syntax:

```
GC_FILES_TO_LOCKS="{ file-list=#locks[!blocks][EACH]} [:] . . . "
```

where

file-list is the FILE_ID of each data file to be covered. FILE_ID values can be translated from file names using the following query:

```
SELECT FILE_ID, FILE_NAME FROM DBA_DATA_FILES;
```

The FILE_IDs should be specified as follows:

```
FILE_ID{ -FILE_ID} [,FILE_ID{ -FILE_ID} ]
```

For example, "1" would indicate FILE_ID = 1 by itself; "1,2,3,4,5" indicates files with FILE_IDs 1 through 5. This last can also be specified using "1-5," indicating all FILE_IDs in the range from 1 through 5, inclusive. Individual FILE_IDs as well as ranges of FILE_IDs can be specified in comma-separated lists, such as "1-5,10-20,23,30-40."

#locks is the number of PCM locks to cover the data files specified by the *file-list*. For example, "1-5=100:10-20= 200:23=300:30-40=400" indicates that files 1 through 5 are to be covered by 100 PCM locks, files 10 through 20 are to be covered by 200 PCM locks, file 23 is to be covered by 300 PCM locks, and files 30 through 40 are to be covered by 400 PCM locks.

Unless the "R" qualifier is used, these locks will be *static* or *hashed* PCM locks. If the "R" qualifier (see text that follows) is used, then these locks will be *fine-grain* or *releasable* PCM locks. These locks, also known as *dynamic* or *fine-grain* or *DBA* (Data Base Address) locks, are not permanently assigned to specific database blocks for the duration of the database instance, as static or hashed PCM locks are. Instead, these locks are assigned to individual database blocks as needed, drawn from the fixed-size pool of locks specified by the GC_RELEASABLE_LOCKS parameter.

The two locking schemes, *static* and *releasable*, can be used together at the same time in the same database. Each data file can use only one or the other locking scheme; they cannot be mixed at that level. Therefore, some tablespaces or data files can use static PCM locks while other tablespaces or data files can use releasable PCM locks.

!blocks is the blocking factor for the database blocks to be covered. It is a nonzero positive integer value. If !blocks is not specified, it defaults to a value of 1. Syntactically, it is specified like this: ",1-5=100!20:10-20=200!20:23=300!30:30-40=400!20", which indicates that all the files specified (i.e., 1-5, 10-20, 23, and 30-40) will have a blocking factor of 20, except for file 23, which was specified with a blocking factor of 30. The significance of the blocking factor, as well as guidelines for setting it, will be discussed in more detail shortly.

R, if specified, indicates that this entry uses *releasable* or *fine-grain* or *dynamic* PCM locks, not the default *static* or *hashed* PCM locks. If you are using Oracle7, please be aware that releasable PCM locks were not generally available until version 7.3.3.

EACH, if specified, means the #*locks* and !*blocks* values will apply to each of the files in the *file-list*, instead of cumulatively to all.

To determine how each of these values is derived, let's approach them separately. The value of #locks is dependent on the amount of expected update activity in the data file and the size of the data file. Data files from tablespaces with high levels of update activity should get more PCM hash locks; data files from tablespaces that are marked READ ONLY only need 1 PCM hash lock.

The value of !BLOCKS is dependent on what kind of activity will be performed in the tablespace. If it will be primarily random index scans, smaller values of !BLOCKS are suggested. If it will be primarily full table scans with multiblock reads (as specified by DB_FILE_MULTIBLOCK_READ_COUNT), then the value of !BLOCKS should be two to four times the value of DB_FILE_MULTIBLOCK_READ_COUNT.

HOW ARE THE TWO LOCKING SCHEMES TO BE USED?

How are the two locking schemes intended to be used? What are the advantages and disadvantages of each?

Static locks inherently require less processing. As a database block is requested, its physical address on disk is converted using a hash algorithm into a lock number. This is a very simple and very fast operation. The database instance does not need to maintain a mapping of blocks to locks, as each block's address simply hashes to a lock number. Also, each of these locks can cover more than one database block, so this scheme is useful for covering large numbers of database blocks with small numbers of locks. Because each lock occupies several hundred bytes in the shared memory allocated by the distributed lock manager, this is an important consideration. If PCM locking required a lock for each database block, then databases would either quickly run out of shared memory as the numbers of locks increased or databases would have to limit their size. Naturally, this is an unacceptable requirement with most data warehouses.

Releasable locks reside in a fixed-size pool associated with the database instance, whose size is specified by the parameter GC_RELEASABLE_LOCKS. When a database block is about to be accessed by any Parallel Server database instance, a releasable PCM lock is allocated from the pool. This lock is associated with one and only one database block. This scheme requires more processing for maintenance of the pool of locks, but it also allows a relatively small pool of locks to cover a large number of database blocks provided the simultaneous number of database blocks being accessed does not exceed the size of the pool of locks.

Static locks are more efficient for covering large numbers of database blocks that are being read by more than one Parallel Server database instances. But because the setting of a single static PCM lock to *exclusive* mode can cause a large number of database blocks to be locked, this scheme can be very problematic when updating occurs. Contention between database instances for exclusive locks on the same database blocks is known as *true pinging*. When pinging results from database instances contending for exclusive locks on different database blocks that are covered by the same PCM lock, it is known as *false pinging*. True pinging cannot necessarily be avoided; if two or more instances need to update rows in the same database block, then contention cannot be avoided. But false pinging is unnecessary and can be reduced by allocating larger numbers of static PCM locks to the data file. This will not eliminate false pinging, but it will make it less likely.

Because releasable PCM locks are each assigned to one and only one database block, false pinging is not a possibility at all. Thus, in tablespaces that will be updated heavily and often, releasable PCM locks are a favorable choice. In tablespaces that are predominately read-only or read-mostly, static PCM locks are suitable.

Administering Parallel Server

There are a few requirements for implementing Parallel Server that are different from normal "exclusive"-mode Oracle:

- Install and link Parallel Server option (PSO) into the Oracle RDBMS kernel (required)

- Create separate threads of redo log files for each Parallel Server database instance (required)

- Optimize each redo log file thread for its associated Parallel Server database instance

- Create separate rollback segments and tablespaces to hold them for each Parallel Server database instance

- Optimize temporary tablespaces for the clustered environment

- Optimize the loading of data

Installing and Linking in the Parallel Server Option (Required)

The Parallel Server option is additional code that must be installed with and linked into the Oracle RDBMS. It is not a separate product, and only a few key sections in the Oracle RDBMS software are made different by linking the Parallel Server option.

All instances of Parallel Server must be running the same Oracle RDBMS software. This means that Oracle Parallel Server must run on a homogeneous cluster of nodes. A Parallel Server database cannot run partly on one platform and partly on another; for example, a four-node cluster cannot consist of a Sun server, an HP server, a Pyramid server, and a Compaq OpenVMS server. Generally, the hardware manufacturer stipulates that all nodes in a cluster must be running the same operating system (i.e., UNIX, OpenVMS, MVS) and the same version of the operating system. This is a requirement just to get the clustered systems up and running.

The same is true for Oracle. Separate Parallel Server instances for the same database must be running the same platform (i.e., platform and platform version) as well as the same version of Oracle. Oracle RDBMS version numbers have five separate digits: *version, major release, minor release, port-specific release*, and *patch level*. For example, Oracle RDBMS 7.3.2.3.1 can be read as follows:

- *Version* 7
- *Major release* 3
- *Minor release* 2
- *Port-specific release* 3
- *Patch level* 1

Oracle Parallel Server instances should be running the same platform of software—always. Instances are also required to be running the same version and major release of the software components. However, even though Oracle says it's OK if the minor release, port-specific release, and patch level are different among different instances on the same database, it is not recommended.

The reason? Oracle Development does not test all possible combinations of Parallel Server releases for all the platforms it supports. If a primary reason for choosing to use Parallel Server was to improve database availability, why would you jeopardize availability unnecessarily by simply not keeping versions of software synchronized?

Separate Threads of Redo Log Files (Required)

Each database instance in Parallel Server must have its own separate set of redo log files. These sets of redo log files are also known as *threads*.

Redo logs are essentially a sequential record of every action performed in the database. In one sense, they are a second copy of the Oracle database. The database itself is consistent in time; it presents a consistent image of all its composite data to a single point in time: right now. Archived redo log files, along with the online, active redo log files, present a different picture of the exact same database. The redo log files present a record, collected over time, of all the changes that have been made to the database by a database instance.

Because Parallel Server can consist of more than one instance, and because each instance has its own record of changes applied to the database, or *redo thread*, Parallel Server databases must consist of multiple, separate threads of redo. This is actually quite easy to implement. The creation of a Parallel Server database starts off exactly like the creation of a "normal," single-instance database: with the CREATE DATABASE command. The CREATE DATABASE command creates the data structures listed in Table 11.1.

Table 11.1 Components of CREATE DATABASE Command

DATA STRUCTURE	FILENAMES SPECIFIED IN	SIZE DETERMINED BY
Control files	"init.ora" configuration file	The following clauses in the CREATE DATABASE command: MAXDATAFILES, MAXLOGFILES, MAXLOGMEMBERS, MAXLOGHISTORY, MAXINSTANCES, etc.
SYSTEM tablespace	DATAFILE clause in CREATE DATABASE command	SIZE qualifier to DATAFILE clause
Redo log file thread #1	LOGFILE clause in CREATE DATABASE command	SIZE qualifier in LOGFILE clause

Following a successful CREATE DATABASE command, additional redo log file threads can be added using the ALTER DATABASE ADD LOGFILE THREAD command. The number of groups in the thread, the number of members in each group, the size of each member, and the file names of the members are specified in this command insofar as they were specified for the redo log file thread 1 in the CREATE DATABASE command. After a new log file thread is created, it must be enabled using the ALTER DATABASE ENABLE LOGFILE THREAD command.

How are redo log file threads assigned to the instances?

In the "init.ora" configuration file, there is a THREAD parameter that defaults to a value of 1 when not specified. This is useful when not using the Parallel Server option; because CREATE DATABASE implicitly creates redo log file thread 1 and because the THREAD parameter defaults to 1, a DBA not using Parallel Server option can ignore the whole issue quite safely.

After the database has been created (with redo thread 1) and threads of redo have been added for the other instances, the additional instances can be started as long as the THREAD parameter is set appropriately in each instance's "init.ora" configuration file. For the instance using redo thread 2, the parameter THREAD should be set to 2. For the instance using redo log thread 3, the parameter THREAD should be set to 3.

Please note that it is not strictly necessary to have the redo threads numbered sequentially starting with 1; it's merely a convention. Although the CREATE DATABASE command does not allow you to change redo thread 1 to another number initially, there is nothing to stop you from dropping redo thread 1 and assigning the instance that formerly used it to a different thread.

How can a user detect which instance and redo log file thread he is currently connected to from inside Oracle? Query the V$PARAMETER view for the row where the NAME column has the value "thread." The column VALUE on that row will contain the redo log file thread number. Additionally, if you wish to know the value of ORACLE_SID for the instance to which you are connected, execute the following query:

```
SELECT REPLACE(instance, chr(0), '') instance
  FROM V$Thread
 WHERE thread# =
           (SELECT TO_NUMBER(value)
              FROM v$parameter
             WHERE name = 'thread');
```

Please note the REPLACE() function around the INSTANCE column. In some circumstances, the INSTANCE column contains NULL characters [i.e., CHR(0)]. The use of the REPLACE() function here eliminates those unprintable, undisplayed characters. Hey, don't laugh! It's trivia like this that allows otherwise ignorant people to consult at a rate of $350 per hour!

Optimizing Parallel Server for Data Warehouses

Some of the characteristics of Parallel Server call for the consideration of additional issues when optimally configuring the database. These issues may not be present for non-Parallel Server environments.

Initialization Parameters

Oracle Parallel Server has changed dramatically with each version and major release. Many initialization parameters have become obsolete, while a couple new ones have been introduced for Oracle8*i*. If a parameter is not listed below, then it is obsolete; a great many parameters have become obsolete.

The following are some suggestions for setting Parallel Server-specific configuration parameter values. For more information, see the Oracle8*i Parallel Server Concepts and Administration Guide.*

PARALLEL_SERVER

Defaults to FALSE. Set it to TRUE to enable Parallel Server.

When it is set to TRUE, then the STARTUP command in Server Manager and SQL*Plus defaults to STARTUP SHARED. When set to FALSE, the STARTUP command defaults to STARTUP EXCLUSIVE. Of course, you can still explicitly specify STARTUP EXCLUSIVE when PARALLEL_SERVER = TRUE, if you wish.

GC_RELEASABLE_LOCKS

This is the default method of PCM locking in Oracle8*i* Parallel Server. The default value is equal to DB_BLOCK_BUFFERS, which is generally sufficient for any database. This means that there is one PCM lock for each buffer in the database instance's Buffer Cache. If DB_BLOCK_BUFFERS is the same across all the database instances in a Parallel Server database, there should be no reason to override this default.

It sets the maximum total number of fine-grain releasable locks for data files with zero PCM locks specified in GC_FILES_TO_LOCKS.

GC_ROLLBACK_LOCKS

The GC_ROLLBACK_LOCKS parameter string consists of one or more entries, separated by a colon (":") character. Each entry has the format of:

```
rbs-list = #locks [ EACH ]
```

The rbs-list is either a single integer, a comma-separated list of integers, an integer range, or a combination of all these. Each integer is a rollback segment number, as shown in the view DBA_ROLLBACK_SEGS by the column SEGMENT_ID.

The #locks value is the number of PCM locks to devote to the list of rollback segments. If rbs-list has more than one item in the list, then the keyword EACH is required as PCM locks cannot be shared across rollback segments.

For example, the GC_ROLLBACK_LOCKS string might look like:

```
gc_rollback_locks="1=100:2-10=50EACH:11-20,30,33-36=30EACH"
```

which means that rollback segment 1 (i.e., the SYSTEM rollback segment) has 100 PCM locks, while rollback segments 2 through 10 each have 50 PCM locks. For rollback segments 11 through 20, 30, and 33 through 36, each is allocated 30 PCM locks.

GC_FILES_TO_LOCKS

GC_FILES_TO_LOCKS is used to hard-code the mapping of either static hashed or dynamic releasable PCM locks to data files and also sets blocking factor. It is required when specifying static hashed PCM locks (as they cannot be specified any other way!), but it is optional when using dynamic releasable PCM locks. This is because dynamic releasable PCM locks are not associated with data files by default. Setting GC_RELEASABLE_LOCKS and leaving GC_FILES_TO_LOCKS blank is a valid configuration, implying that any releasable PCM lock can be used in association with any data file. When GC_FILES_TO_LOCKS is used to specifically associate releasable PCM locks to a data file, only those locks will be used in that data file (or data files) and they won't be used anywhere else.

GC_FILES_TO_LOCKS is generally used only to specify static hashed PCM locks. A good rule of thumb for determining how many static hashed locks to assign to a data file is to start with the idea of a *density*, namely, the density of database blocks per PCM lock. For want of a better rule, it's probably a good idea to start with a density of 100:1—that is, 100 database blocks to 1 PCM hash lock. Once this is determined, it is not difficult to start calculating how many locks will be required for each data file. The following query can help:

```
SELECT file_id, blocks, ROUND(blocks/<density>,0) LOCKS
  FROM dba_data_files
 WHERE tablespace_name <> 'TEMP'
   AND tablespace_name NOT LIKE 'RBS%'
 ORDER BY file_id;
```

Remember, the TEMP tablespace used for sorting is not explicitly covered by PCM locks (either hash or releasable), and the other GC_ parameters cover rollback segments, so tablespaces containing nothing but rollback segments should be excluded from the calculations as well. The output from this query may look something like the following:

FILE_ID	BLOCKS	LOCKS
1	25600	256
2	4096	41
4	1024	10
5	1024	10
6	2048	20
7	1024	10
8	1024	10
9	4096	41
10	4096	41

The GC_FILES_TO_LOCKS string that results from this output might look something like this:

```
GC_FILES_TO_LOCKS="1=256:2,9,10=41EACH:4-5,7-8=10EACH:6=0"
```

What this translates to is this: File 1 has 256 hash locks; files 2, 9, and 10 each have 41 hash locks; files 4, 5, 7, and 8 each have 10 hash locks; and file 6 has 0 hash locks, meaning that it will be covered by dynamic releasable locks (if GC_RELEASABLE_LOCKS has not been set to zero).

Of course, if some tablespaces are likely to receive heavier amounts of write activity, then perhaps it would be a good idea to lower the ratio from 100:1. If the total number of locks resulting from this calculation using the 100:1 ratio is too high, or if some tablespace is going to receive very low write activity, then feel free to raise the ratio from 100:1 to 1,000:1 or higher. Of course, if you are going to set the tablespace in question to READ ONLY, then a single PCM hash lock can be used to cover all the data files belonging to the tablespace.

What is not addressed in this example is the blocking factor, which would probably differ depending on whether the tablespace contains tables that are frequently fully scanned or indexes that are randomly accessed. In the former case, you would want to use a higher blocking factor of about twice the value of the configuration parameter DB_FILE_MULTIBLOCK_READ_COUNT. For randomly accessed objects, you would want to use the default blocking factor of 1. See the section explaining PCM locks and GC_FILES_TO_LOCKS syntax earlier in this chapter.

FREEZE_DB_FOR_FAST_RECOVERY

Setting this to TRUE speeds instance recovery by freezing I/O from all Oracle processes. If it is set to FALSE, then other database instances continue processing as normal, which can delay the completion of instance recovery due to contention.

This parameter defaults to FALSE if all data files are using static hashed PCM locks. Else, if any data files are using dynamic releasable PCM locks, it defaults to TRUE.

LM_RESS

This parameter specifies the total number of locking resources that the DLM can handle. It should be the same on all instances of the database; it has a minimum value of 256 and defaults to 6,000.

Setting this parameter can be quite a challenge. The *Oracle8i Parallel Server Concepts and Administration Guide* does present a formula for calculating the correct value for LM_RESS, based on the anticipated number of PCM and non-PCM locks.

If there is a formula to follow, then why doesn't Oracle just encode it into the RDBMS? It's a mystery! It certainly would make things a lot easier.

Regardless, the formula specifies that the parameter LM_RESS, which represents "resources" to be held by the Integrated Distributed Lock Manager (IDLM), is made up of the sum of the number of PCM locks and non-PCM locks.

PCM resources we've discussed; they are specific to Parallel Server, and they are synchronization data structures (OK, they're *locks* then!) assigned to tables, clusters, indexes, and rollback segments for *parallel cache management*. Thus, the sum of resources implied by the parameters GC_RELEASABLE_LOCKS, GC_ROLLBACK_LOCKS, and GC_FILES_TO_LOCKS takes care of this half of the formula. Just add them up, and then Oracle recommends multiplying them by two. Why *two*? Because each database instance has to keep track of at least two states for each resource: local and remote. So, the first half of the formula to calculate a good starting value for LM_RESS is:

```
2 * (GC_RELEASABLE_LOCKS + sum(GC_ROLLBACK_LOCKS) +
sum(GC_FILES_TO_LOCKS))
```

What then are *non-PCM resources*? They are all of the high-level synchronization structures (yup, another fancy name for *locks*) that Oracle uses that are *not* particular to Parallel Server. The best example is *enqueues*. To add up all of the non-PCM resources, add together all of the following standard Oracle initialization parameters for each database instance:

```
(3 * PROCESSES) + (10 * SESSIONS) + DML_LOCKS + TRANSACTIONS +
ENQUEUE_RESOURCES + (2 * DB_FILES) + 221
```

We're not done yet. If you plan to make use of Parallel Execution (PX), which typically means parallel queries or parallel DML, but can also mean such things as parallel CREATE INDEX, then you'll need to add these factors to the formula as well:

```
7 + (#-instances * PARALLEL_MAX_SERVERS) + #-instances +
PARALLEL_MAX_SERVERS
```

The first formula, for adding up PCM resources, makes perfect sense. Simply summarize the PCM resources specified to date. The second half of the formula, for adding up non-PCM resources, seems suspiciously like a witch's incantation. It is documented in Chapter 16 of the *Oracle8i Parallel Server Concepts and Administration* manual. We've taken some algebraic liberties to simplify the formula somewhat, but feel free to use the version that is documented; they are equivalent.

Be aware that the resulting number for LM_RESS from these formulas is likely to be extremely high. They are very pessimistic values, which represent the *maximum possible size* for the IDLM in the shared memory of the Oracle SGA. It is possible that you will not need the numbers to be this high in actual usage.

To determine this, use the value specified by the formula to set LM_RESS for your initial application testing. Monitor the dynamic performance view V$RESOURCE_LIMIT, where there will be an entry showing the current utilization, the maximum utilization since the database instance was started (i.e., a *high-water mark*), and the initial allocation (i.e., the "init.ora" setting) of the parameter. If, after some representative workload has been run for some time, you find that the high-water mark for LM_RESS does not come close to the "init.ora" setting, then you can consider reducing LM_RESS.

LM_LOCKS

This parameter specifies the number of locks that the DLM can handle, and it should be the same on all instances of the database. It has a minimum value of 512, defaults to 12,000, and can be set according to the formula "LM_RESS +

(LM_RESS * (nbr-nodes – 1)) / nbr-nodes". In shorthand, LM_LOCKS should usually be set to a little less than (2 * LM_RESS).

Once you calculate LM_RESS, it's easy to derive LM_LOCKS.

As with LM_RESS, this formula is simply a good (and pessimistic) starting point. Monitor the view V$RESOURCE_LIMIT to see if you might have opportunities to reduce (or the need to increase) this parameter.

LM_PROCS

This parameter specifies the number of processes that the DLM can handle, and it should be the same on all instances of the database. It should be set using the formula "(PROCESSES * nbr-nodes)," where PROCESSES is the Oracle configuration parameter PROCESSES and "nbr-nodes" is the number of instances for the database.

As with LM_RESS and LM_LOCKS, monitor the V$RESOURCE_LIMITS view during normal system usage to determine whether you might need to increase or decrease LM_PROCS the next time the database instance is restarted.

THREAD

This parameter identifies which thread of redo that the database instance will use. If not set specifically, then it defaults to the order in which database instances were started. In situations such as MPP environments, where the choice of redo threads has severe performance impact, it should be required to set this parameter and never change it. This is a good practice anyway to reduce some of the mystery that can result from Parallel Server.

INSTANCE_NUMBER

This number is used to uniquely identify a specific database instance for use with FREELIST GROUPS. It is also the number used by the ALTER . . . ALLOCATE EXTENT (INSTANCE . . .) command to "assign" a segment's extent to a specific instance's freelist group. Even though it is not necessary to set this parameter if freelist groups are not in use, it would be wise (but not required) to set this to the same value as THREAD to reduce confusion.

INSTANCE_NAME

This parameter is used primarily to uniquely distinguish database instances for Net8 service registration. In prior versions, the ORACLE_SID environment variable was often named uniquely to accomplish this purpose, but there are many situations where one would prefer that the ORACLE_SID value be the same for all instances in a Parallel Server database.

INSTANCE_NAME is used by Net8 to distinguish between the instances belonging to the database implied by the parameter SERVICE_NAME. If the ORACLE_SID environment variable values for each instance are different, then it is a good idea to set INSTANCE_NAME to correspond to those values. If the ORACLE_SID values are the same across all instances, then (while it is possible to set INSTANCE_NAME to any arbitrary value) it is advisable to set this parameter string to the concatenated values of ORACLE_SID environment variable and the THREAD parameter.

INSTANCE_GROUPS

This parameter is a string that lists a series *groupnames*. Each *groupname* in the list represents a grouping of Parallel Server instances. The purpose of this grouping is to control parallel execution (PX) operations across instances. This parameter lists all of the groups to which this database instance belongs. The naming of the groups is completely arbitrary.

For example, you might have an eight-node cluster, with each node running an instance of a Parallel Server database. For PX operations, you'd like four of the nodes to be separated from the other four, so that all PX operations initiated within one group are not propagated across all eight nodes.

By default, when this parameter is not set, all instances in the cluster belong to a single DEFAULT instance group.

This parameter can be set only at database instance startup in the "init.ora" file; it cannot be modified after startup by ALTER SESSION or ALTER SYSTEM.

PARALLEL_INSTANCE_GROUP

This parameter designates the INSTANCE_GROUP to which this database instance currently belongs. The list of available values is any of the *groupnames* listed from any of the active database instances. If the groupname specified in this parameter is not part of the list, then parallel execution will be disabled, and operations will execute serially. The current database instance does not have to be part of the specified instance group; that is, you can set this parameter to a groupname that is not in the list specified for this instance by the parameter INSTANCE_GROUPS.

This parameter can be set in the "init.ora" file, and it can be changed using ALTER SESSION and ALTER SYSTEM.

DML_LOCKS

This parameter controls whether "table locks" will be acquired for processes that are performing row locking, during DML operations such as INSERT, UPDATE, and DELETE. These "table locks" (i.e., "TM" locks from V$LOCK) ensure that DDL (i.e., CREATE, ALTER, DROP) commands are not performed while a process is changing data in the table. If the data warehouse application will not (foreseeably) be issuing DDL commands, then the acquisition of "table locks" during DML (i.e., INSERT, UPDATE, DELETE) can be disabled, thereby optimizing performance. Because these are data dictionary locks, this can help Parallel Server performance in particular, since the data dictionary (i.e., SYSTEM tablespace) is shared among all database instances, and is sometimes a source of unavoidable contention. Eliminating DDL during run-time, by setting DML_LOCKS = 0, can eliminate a major source of contention in Parallel Server. Of course, this comes at a cost to flexibility during run-time, as DDL commands will not be permitted, but this can be a win for controlled change-management anyway.

By default, this parameter defaults to (4 * TRANSACTIONS). In turn, TRANSACTIONS defaults to (1.1 * SESSIONS), which itself defaults to (1.1 * PROCESSES). Most commonly, database administrators set only PROCESSES, and they allow the related parameters SESSIONS, TRANSACTION, DML_LOCKS, and ENQUEUE_RESOURCES to default automatically. Doing so is a very sound policy, as the defaults are quite sufficient for most implementations.

In a Parallel Server environment, eliminating "TM" table locks can be an effective way to reduce global enqueue acquisition. Setting DML_LOCKS to 0 to accomplish this can be a somewhat draconian solution, due to the restrictions on DDL commands. A more controlled alternative is to use the ALTER TABLE ... ENABLE|DISABLE TABLE LOCKS command, which will eliminate the need for "TM" table locks for an individual table. This command will have the same effect of restricting most DDL commands (such as CREATE INDEX) on the table, but at least the effect would not be global, as happens when DML_LOCKS is set to 0.

This parameter and its usage as described here are valid for Oracle 7.3, Oracle8, and Oracle8*i*.

DB_BLOCK_SIZE

Larger database block size can affect Parallel Server at least two ways. One negative effect is that larger database blocks can result in greater contention as each block contains more rows of data. But if steps have already been taken to segregate data access in the application to optimize Parallel Server, this should not be an issue at all. A positive impact is that larger database blocks can reduce the number of PCM locks necessary to manage a database of a given size. If a database is about 100 GB, then it will contain about 13.1 million Oracle database blocks, if each is 8 KB. This means that any PCM locking scheme may have to cover up to around 10 million blocks. If the same 100 GB database was created with DB_BLOCK_SIZE = 16384 (16 KB), then, of course, the number of blocks would be roughly half. Halving the number of blocks to cover might

ENHANCEMENTS WITH ORACLE8/ RELEASE 2 (A.K.A. V8.1.6)

Oracle Parallel Server has been optimized for a two-node, high-availability configuration. In this special high-availability mode, one node is designated to be the *primary* database instance, while the other node is designated as a *secondary* or *failover* database instance. This secondary instance can be used to perform some limited DBA tasks, report generation, and other read-only or nonbuffered-write database activities. The trick is to ensure that the secondary instance does not acquire any PCM locks in exclusive mode or acquire exclusive access to any enqueues (a.k.a. session locks).

If the primary instance fails, then the secondary becomes the primary. In version 8.1.6, this configuration is optimized to provide better throughput by efficiently managing the locks on only the primary node, resulting in less processing overhead and much better response times. Thus, some of the issues just discussed in the section concerning DML_LOCKS parameter now become moot. Because enqueues no longer incur additional overhead by involving the distributed lock manager, it is now possible to rehost an application to this simple two-node, high-availability configuration without incurring the pervasive additional overhead of globally mastered enqueues.

halve the number PCM locks to cover them, in the event that system memory is short in supply.

Although 2,048 bytes or 2 KB is the default Oracle database block size, standard recommendations by Oracle Consulting's System Performance Group state that the standard configuration today should be at least 8,192 bytes or 8 KB. Optionally, data warehouse databases using DB_BLOCK_SIZE = 16,384 (16 KB) or higher can optimize read-intensive I/O. Database block size is changeable only at database creation; once you choose, you are stuck with your choice.

Detecting Contention Specific to Parallel Server

How can you determine whether Parallel Server is having problems with pinging ?

Oracle provides a series of dynamic performance ("V$") views and dynamic database instance statistics to help determine whether additional contention is being introduced by parallel cache management.

The *Oracle8 Parallel Server Concepts and Administration Guide* contains a more complete source of information on all these topics. There is little purpose served in duplicating the excellent treatment of this topic by the standard documentation set, but we discuss some information that may be supplemental.

Dynamic Performance (V$) Views

The following sections briefly describe the monitoring points with which all DBAs administering Parallel Server databases should be familiar.

catparr.sql script

The dynamic performance views for Parallel Server are created by the *catparr.sql* script, which is run under Server Manager while you are connected as SYS or CONNECT INTERNAL. This script is normally run during an installation of the Parallel Server software.

The *catparr.sql* script itself provides some interesting documentation of the dynamic performance views, in addition to what can be found in the standard documentation. Take the time to read through this script.

VBH, VCACHE, and V$CACHE_LOCK

These views are essentially synonyms for each other. They all depict the real-time, current contents of the Buffer Cache in the Oracle SGA. They all show the current state of the buffer, as well as the address and name of the PCM locks currently covering the database block. This information can be used to cross-reference to the V$LOCK_ELEMENT view. Querying these views can also be used to get an idea of the composition of the Buffer Cache, in terms of what types of objects are being cached, what tablespaces and data files they are located in, and, in fact, what the names of the objects are.

V$PING

The V$PING view, as the name implies, displays information about pings, or I/O activity resulting purely from parallel cache management. Table 11.2 briefly describes the columns shown in the view and the meaning of their values.

The columns FORCED_READS and FORCED_WRITES provide a good picture of the amount of wasteful I/O occurring due to parallel cache management only. The column XNC is provided for backward compatibility to previous versions of Oracle Parallel Server, and it is useful for a quick summary of the most destructive type of contention: *exclusive-to-null* conversions.

By querying this view, you can detect exactly which objects (or their partitions) within which tablespaces or data files are suffering the most from *pinging*:

```
SELECT    F.TABLESPACE_NAME,
          F.FILE_NAME,
          U.USERNAME || '.' ||
                P.NAME || decode(P.PARTITION_NAME,
                                 null, null,
                                 ':' || P.PARTITION_NAME) NAME,
          DECODE(P.CLASS,
```

Table 11.2   Columns in V$PING

COLUMN NAME	DESCRIPTION	
FILE#	the file number of data file (see column FILE_ID in DBA_DATA_FILES)	
BLOCK#	the database block in the data file (see column BLOCK_ID in DBA_EXTENTS)	
CLASS#	*Value Description*	*GC Parameter*
0	SYSTEM rollback segment	N/A
1	data block	gc_files_to_locks
2	temporary segment block	N/A
3	rollback segment block in offlined TS	gc_save_rollback_locks
4	segment header block	gc_segments
5	rollback segment header in offlined TS	gc_save_rollback_locks
6	freelist group header block	gc_freelist_groups
7 + (N*2)	rollback segment header block	gc_rollback_segments
8 + (N*2)	rollback segment data block	gc_rollback_locks
	(Note: "N" is the rollback segment number from V$ROLLNAME.USN)	
STATUS	*Value Description*	
FREE	not in use	
XCUR	held exclusive by this instance	
SCUR	held shared by this instance	
CR	only valid for consistent read	
READ	is being read from disk	
MREC	in media recovery mode	
IREC	in instance (crash) recovery mode	
XNC	number of times block has converted from exclusive (X) to null (N) for this database instance	
FORCED_READS	number of times block had to be reread from disk because another instance had forced it out of cache by requesting a PCM exclusive lock	

continued

Table 11.2 Continued

COLUMN NAME	DESCRIPTION
FORCED_WRITES	number of times block was written by DBWR because another instance had requested a shared or exclusive PCM lock
NAME	name of the segment
PARTITION_NAME	name of the partition within the partitioned segment
KIND	type of segment
OWNER#	owner of the segment (see column USER_ID in DBA_USERS)
LOCK_ELEMENT_ ADDR	foreign key to V$LOCK_ELEMENT view, which contains one row for each static (hashed) lock specified by GC_DB_LOCKS
LOCK_ELEMENT_ NAME	the name of the lock element

```
                    0, 'SYSTEM RBS',
                    1, 'DATA',
                    2, 'TEMPORARY',
                    3, 'RBS DATA OFFLINE',
                    4, 'SEG HDR',
                    5, 'RBS SEG HDR OFFLINE',
                    6, 'FREELIST HDR',
                    DECODE(MOD(P.CLASS, 2),
                           0, 'RBS DATA',
                           'RBS HDR')) LOCK_CLASS,
                    P.STATUS LOCK_STATUS,
                    SUM(P.FORCED_READS) FORCED_READS,
                    SUM(P.FORCED_WRITES) FORCED_WRITES
FROM       V$PING          P,
           DBA_DATA_FILES   F,
           DBA_USERS        U
WHERE      F.FILE_ID = P.FILE#
AND        U.USER_ID = P.OWNER#
GROUP BY F.TABLESPACE_NAME,
           F.FILE_NAME,
           U.USERNAME || '.' ||
                  P.NAME || decode(P.PARTITION_NAME,
                                   null, null,
                                   ':' || P.PARTITION_NAME),
           DECODE(P.CLASS,
                  0, 'SYSTEM RBS',
                  1, 'DATA',
                  2, 'TEMPORARY',
```

```
             3, 'RBS DATA OFFLINE',
             4, 'SEG HDR',
             5, 'RBS SEG HDR OFFLINE',
             6, 'FREELIST HDR',
             DECODE(MOD(P.CLASS, 2),
                     0, 'RBS DATA',
                     'RBS HDR')),
     P.STATUS;
```

One way to reduce pinging is to increase the value of the parameter associated with the block class (see CLASS# column in Table 11.2). If this value is already judged to be high enough, then it may be wise to consider other ways of reducing interinstance contention, such as implementing FREELIST GROUPS (if the pinging is due to INSERT activity) or data-routing (if the pinging is due to UPDATE or DELETE activity).

V$FALSE_PING

If *static* or *hashed* PCM locks are being used in the data file in question, then remember that there are two categories of pinging that can occur: *true* and *false*. *True pinging* results from contention between two (or more) database instances for the same exact database block. *False pinging* results from a database block buffer being pinged because it is covered by the same hashed PCM lock as a database block buffer that is actually being locked. To determine whether this is so, query the view V$FALSE_PING, which has all the same columns as V$PING. In V$FALSE_PING, the view is making an *educated guess* at whether blocks are being pinged due to the fact that they belong to the same hashed lock and the fact that they have been converted more than 10 times.

If V$FALSE_PING shows large numbers of rows, then consider either increasing the hashed PCM locks on the affected data files or changing the locking scheme from hashed PCM locks to *fine-grain* or *releasable* PCM locks, which never cause false pinging.

V$CLASS_PING

This view summarizes information in V$PING by the *class* of database blocks. Block classes are numeric and are documented for the V$PING view.

V$LOCK_ACTIVITY

Another useful view is V$LOCK_ACTIVITY, which summarizes the types of PCM activities performed on the system. Columns for this view are shown in Table 11.3.

Healthy PCM lock activity includes any number of actions like "Lock buffers for read" and "Lock buffers for write." Contention between database instances is indicated when all the other actions achieve high numbers, relative to the "Lock buffers for . . ." actions.

Table 11.3 Columns in V$LOCK_ACTIVITY

COLUMN NAME	DESCRIPTION
FROM_VAL	PCM lock conversions from: NULL (unused), S (shared), X (exclusive), SSX (shared exclusive)
TO_VAL	PCM lock conversions to: NULL, S, X, SSX
ACTION_VAL	description of the FROM/TO action
COUNTER	total number of conversions

V$RESOURCE_LIMIT

This view is not specific to Parallel Server, but it allows you to monitor whether you have allocated sufficient resources during configuration. It shows the current utilization of resources, but the really useful feature is that it remembers the maximum utilization of these resources, much like a high-water mark. This way, you can raise parameters based on facts, not supposition.

It is especially useful for monitoring the use of resources allocated by the initialization parameters ENQUEUE_RESOURCES, PROCESSES, SESSIONS, TRANSACTIONS, DML_LOCKS, LM_RESS, LM_LOCKS, and LM_PROCS.

V$DLM_LOCKS and V$DLM_ALL_LOCKS

This is a real-time view listing all the locks (PCM as well as non-PCM) currently held. It is essentially a superset of the standard V$LOCK view. It is capable of showing which Oracle processes on which instances are waiting for locks, as well as which processes are currently holding locks.

V$DLM_RESS

This view is a dump of all resources currently active in the IDLM. It is used primarily for debugging.

V$DLM_CONVERT_LOCAL

This is a cumulative view, containing the number and average conversion times of PCM lock conversions performed by this instance on behalf of other database instances.

It is important to set the TIMED_STATISTICS initialization parameter to TRUE, so that timing information is collected in this view. Without this information, this view would be of very little interest.

V$DLM_CONVERT_REMOTE

This is another cumulative view, containing the number and average conversion times (in 1/100ths of a second) of PCM lock conversions performed for this instance by other database instances.

Again, please set the initialization TIMED_STATISTICS to TRUE in order to collect timing information, without which this view would be useless.

V$DLM_MISC

This view is an extension of the V$SYSSTAT view, specifically depicting miscellaneous IDLM statistics.

Global Dynamic Performance Views

All of the dynamic performance ("V$") views display information for an individual database instance. With Oracle8, *global* dynamic performance ("GV$") views are available, which display information on *all* running instances of the Parallel Server database. The GV$ views have all the columns of the V$ views, with the addition of a column INST_ID, which is an integer corresponding to the INSTANCE_NUMBER configuration parameter value. All of V$ views have corresponding GV$ views, except for V$ROLLNAME.

Parallel Server-Specific Statistics

The following statistics can be queried from V$SYSSTAT for cumulative statistics since the database instance was started or from V$SESSTAT for cumulative statistics for a particular Oracle session.

global lock gets

The actual statistics are "global lock gets (non async)," "global lock gets (async)," and "global lock get time." These are the total requests made to upgrade PCM locks to either shared or exclusive mode, starting from null mode.

global lock converts

The actual statistics are "global lock converts (non async)," "global lock converts (async)," and "global lock convert time." These are the total requests made to either upgrade PCM locks from shared to exclusive mode or downgrade PCM locks from exclusive mode to shared mode.

global lock releases

The actual statistics are "global lock releases (non async)," "global lock releases (async)," and "global lock release time." These are the total requests made to release PCM from shared or exclusive mode to null mode.

releasable freelist waits

This is the number of times the database instance exhausts the pool of releasable PCM locks specified by the configuration parameter GC_RELEASABLE_ LOCKS. Naturally, this value should be kept as close to zero as possible. This may include increasing the GC_RELEASABLE_LOCKS value or reducing usage of releasable PCM locks.

remote instance undo requests

This is the number of times this instance tried to read the "before image" stored in a rollback segment belonging to another database instance, for the purpose of satisfying a "consistent read."

remote instance undo writes

The number of times this instance had to write down "dirtied" (or changed) rollback segment blocks so that another instance could read the "before image" information, for the purpose of satisfying a "consistent read."

DBWR cross instance writes

This is the number of "dirtied" (i.e., changed) database block buffers written to disk to allow another instance to acquire a shared or exclusive PCM lock on the block.

physical writes

This is the total number of "dirtied" (i.e., changed) database block buffers written to disk by the DBWR process(es).

The ratio of "(DBWR cross instance writes/physical writes)" indicates how many of the writes performed by DBWR were due to pinging. When this ratio approaches 1.0, then use the V$PING and V$FALSE_PING views to locate the sources of cross-instance contention and to mitigate the pinging problem.

Once again, the standard Oracle8 documentation set has an excellent section on tuning Parallel Server in the *Oracle8 Parallel Server Concepts and Administration* guide; read it thoroughly and utilize it.

Reducing Enqueue Processing by Disabling "Table Locks"

This topic was discussed briefly in the section on the initialization parameter DML_LOCKS, but it bears further discussion.

Whenever the Oracle RDBMS starts a transaction, due to an INSERT, UPDATE, DELETE, or SELECT FOR UPDATE statement, a "TX" or *transaction* enqueue is acquired. This TX lock represents the actual transaction, and it is released with the transaction ends, due to an explicit COMMIT or ROLLBACK or due to the termination of the session.

Alternatively, another enqueue, known as a "TM" or "DML enqueue," is also acquired against the database objects being acted on. The purpose of this enqueue is, quite simply, to prevent the object from being dropped or otherwise modified while the transaction is in progress.

As a result, if you query the V$LOCK table, you'll notice that sessions acquire TX and TM enqueues, seemingly in tandem. This is indeed the case.

TM enqueues, however, are optional. They can actually be eliminated by disabling most of the DDL commands available in Oracle. *What's this? Disabling most of the data definition language commands? Am I understanding this correctly? How the heck are we supposed to get anything done without DDL commands?*

In answer to those questions, consider this: When you examine the life-cycle of a database application, there comes a time when, after the initial design and development phases, the tables and indexes themselves are modified quite infrequently. In fact, if your environment is well controlled, there is only occasional need for DDL commands at all. Not all systems reach this level of maturity, but it can be done.

Why? What is the purpose?

By eliminating the need for TM enqueues, you eliminate roughly half of the enqueue processing for each transaction initiated on your database. This can be extremely useful in Parallel Server environments because enqueues are *global resources*. This means that, before they can be acquired by a session on a database instance, the RDBMS must first check the global resource's status in the Distributed Lock Manager. Before the DLM can provide the enqueue's status, it might have to message all of the remote database instances. So, the operation of acquiring a lock using an enqueue, which is a rather simple activity in a single-instance environment, now becomes quite complex and potentially slow. Thus, anything we can do to reduce the number of times we have to process enqueues, the faster transactions are initiated.

Let's use an example. Let's say you were running a PL/SQL stored procedure that did the following:

- Opened a cursor loop that queried a table. While inside the cursor loop, we performed the following actions for each row retrieved:
    - Insert a row into one table
    - Update another row in another table
    - Possibly delete several rows from yet another table
    - Commit
- Repeat the above steps until the cursor reaches the last row

Each time the cursor loop is iterated, a transaction is implicitly begun with the first INSERT statement. At that time, a TX and a TM enqueue must be acquired by the session. For the UPDATE statement, another TM enqueue must be acquired. The DELETE, which seems to be optional, might also mean the acquisition of another TM enqueue. Upon COMMIT, the enqueues are released, at the bottom of the loop. Then, the whole process repeats when the cursor loop iterates again.

So, if each iteration of the loop acquires, then releases 1 TX and 3 TM enqueues, and the loop iterates 10,000 times, then we have about 80,000 enqueue operations to process. That's 4 enqueue-acquisition operations plus 4 enqueue-release operations per iteration, times 10,000 iterations.

In a single-instance environment, enqueue processing is relatively unnoticed. But in a Parallel Server environment, even when only one of the database instances is open, enqueue processing is more expensive as the DLM becomes part of the game.

Eliminating TM enqueues, in this example, would dramatically reduce the number of enqueue operations, to only 1 enqueue-acquisition plus 1 enqueue-release operation per iteration, times 10,000 iterations, for a total of 20,000 enqueue operations. Your mileage may vary, but that can result in very noticeable performance improvements for certain types of batch processes. For the example given, which is terminating transactions within each loop iteration, you could see improvements of 20 to 50 percent in total processing time.

If the COMMIT statement were moved out of the cursor loop and instead executed only once after the looping completed, there would not be as many enqueue-acquisition and enqueue-release operations. In fact, there would only be 8: 1 TX and 3 TM enqueue-acquisitions during the first iteration of the cursor loop, and 1 TX and 3 TM enqueue-releases at the commit. No TM or TX enqueues would be processed during the 9,999 subsequent iterations of the cursor loop. In this scenario, disabling TM enqueues would result in a reduction of only 6 enqueue operations (i.e., from 8 to 2). In the previous scenario, with the COMMIT occurring inside the cursor loop, disabling TM enqueues would result in a reduction of 60,000 enqueue operations (i.e., from 80,000 to 20,000); you would certainly notice that!

There are two ways to disable TM enqueues: globally for the all tables in the database or selectively for certain tables. Disabling them globally can be accomplished by setting the initialization parameter DML_LOCKS to a value of zero. This parameter can be changed only at database instance startup, so altering it back to a nonzero value involves "bouncing" the database instance.

The ALTER TABLE . . . ENABLE / DISABLE TABLE LOCK command allows a database administrator to selectively enable and disable TM enqueues for individual tables. In order for this command to work, of course, there can be no active transactions against the table, but at least it does not require "bouncing" the database instances.

The key is to analyze your application, especially where INSERTs, UPDATEs, and DELETEs are occurring, and determine whether they are implemented as large numbers of short transactions or as relatively small numbers of large, long-running transactions. For a variety of reasons, the former are usually preferable, but when it comes to minimizing enqueue processing, smaller numbers of larger, longer-running transactions work best. The ability to reduce or eliminate one-half of the transactional enqueues can prove invaluable in a Parallel Server environment.

Reducing Enqueue Processing with Locally Managed Tablespaces

The new feature of *locally managed tablespaces* in Oracle8*i* may not seem very important if you are not familiar with the problems they resolve.

With the introduction of this feature as the EXTENT MANAGEMENT LOCAL clause to the CREATE TABLESPACE command, the "old" method of space management (and still the default) is EXTENT MANAGEMENT DICTIONARY. What this means is that all information about extents used by tables, indexes, sort segments, rollback segments, and the like are stored in the *data dictionary*, which is located in the SYSTEM tablespace. Specifically, the table holding *used extent* information is named UET$, and the table holding *free extent* information is named FET$.

Allocating extents to segments means inserting rows into UET$ and removing them from FET$. Dropping or truncating segments means removing rows from UET$ and inserting them into FET$. Whenever these operations were happening, a single ST enqueue must be acquired by the session.

The existence of this single ST ("space transaction") enqueue means two crucial things: Every space-management operation is essentially single-threaded, and this single ST enqueue must be shared by every session on every database instance. In databases with high volumes of transactions, there might be a great deal of space-management occurring. One of the advantages of Parallel Server is trying to bring more processors and processes to bear on a problem, but if space-management is occurring frequently and is single-threaded to boot, then we have a grave scalability problem.

Moreover, beyond this single-threading issue, Parallel Servers have additional challenges. First of all, as *global resources*, enqueues require more processing in Parallel Server than in typical non-Parallel Server databases because the Distributed Lock Manager must be consulted before enqueues can be acquired and after they are released. It is possible that the DLM will have to send and receive messages to and from remote database instances in the cluster, to determine the true global state of the enqueue. This means that enqueue processing in Parallel Server environments requires significantly more processing time. So, we've introduced a concurrency challenge by throwing more CPUs and more processes by moving the database to multiple clustered nodes. Then, we introduced more concurrency challenges by single-threading certain operations, and we've added to those challenges by making those single-threaded operations much, much slower. *But wait! There's more.*

Once we've acquired the ST enqueue and we start inserting and removing rows from those two tables in the SYSTEM tablespace, we now have a *pinging* problem! After all, this *is* Parallel Server, and after all we do have processes from different database instances trying to modify the same database blocks in the same tables.

So, space-management operations in Parallel Server introduce massive new opportunities for poor performance, caused by factors that were simply not noticeable in non-Parallel Server databases.

In one fell swoop, *locally managed tablespaces* provide a solution to all of these problems. Because the extent information is no longer stored in centrally located data dictionary tables, but are rather stored in decentralized, local *bitmap* structures in the header blocks of each data file, the *single-threading* and the ST enqueue are both eliminated at once.

Furthermore, the pinging problem on the centrally located data dictionary tables is also reduced. It can even be eliminated, depending on how well the application developers and the database administrators have *segregated* activity from different database instances from each other.

In summary, Oracle8*i* presents the opportunity to utilize locally managed tablespaces in every tablespace, including SYSTEM. Take advantage of this, and use this feature.

When using locally managed tablespaces, be aware of the administration procedures in the DBMS_SPACE_ADMIN package. These procedures are used for detecting errors in the bitmap data structures containing extent information. In particular, the procedure TABLESPACE_VERIFY should be used regularly. It compares the extent information in each bitmap structure with the extent information in the header blocks of all segments in the locally managed tablespace. Another procedure, SEGMENT_VERIFY, does the same thing for a single segment.

Other procedures in the DBMS_SPACE_ADMIN package either dump bitmap structure information for analysis or can be used to repair them. If either TABLESPACE_VERIFY or SEGMENT_VERIFY detect problems, be sure to consult with Oracle Support before utilizing the repair procedures.

A last procedure in DBMS_SPACE_ADMIN is interesting: TABLESPACE_MIGRATE_FROM_LOCAL will convert a locally managed tablespace back to dictionary-managed. This is provided in the event you wish to downgrade from Oracle8*i* to a previous Oracle8 release. Not a very confidence-inspiring thought, but interesting to note, regardless.

Optimizing Redo Log Files in Parallel Server (Optional, but Highly Recommended)

One important thing to remember about redo log files in general, Parallel Server option or not: the redo log files are likely among the busiest objects in the Oracle database in terms of I/O. They are continuously receiving large sequential writes from the Oracle LGWR background process. If the database is in ARCHIVELOG mode, they are frequently receiving large sequential reads from the Oracle ARCH background process.

As a result, the redo log files should be situated on the most optimal disk devices for large sequential writes and reads. What represents an "optimal disk device?" At the most basic level, it simply means a "fast" device. Redo log files are typically not accessed concurrently by more than one process at a time; LGWR is the only process that writes to redo log files when they are active; the ARCH process is typically the only process that reads from them. Of course, it is possible to start more than one ARCH process manually, but each ARCH will read from only one redo log file apiece.

Because the level of concurrency of redo log files is very low, good performance gains can be achieved by utilizing RAID 0 nonredundant data striping with a fine-grain stripe width to parallelize the write- and read-requests across several devices at once. The fine-grain stripe width, which indicates that the stripe size is relatively small (i.e., 4,096, 8,192, or 16,384 bytes), implies that each LGWR write-request or ARCH read-request will make I/O requests of several different devices at once, achieving a degree of parallelism.

While RAID 0 data striping cannot improve on the inherent data transfer rates of the devices included in the RAID "parity group," the parallelism achieved by writing to and reading from multiple devices does improve overall data transfer throughput.

Please note the term *nonredundant* in the name "RAID 0 nonredundant data striping." By itself, RAID 0 striping is a classic example of how a feature with clear *performance* advantages can have serious negative *availability* consequences. In this case, the fact that data is striped across multiple devices without any redundancy considerations means that the data is *more susceptible* to device failure than if data striping is not employed. Luckily, the solution is quite simple: RAID 1 mirroring (or *shadowing*) or RAID 5 block-interleaved distributed-parity mirroring can be employed to provide the necessary redundancy to guard against device failure. Check with your hardware vendor or system administrator for the most advantageous option.

Whatever option is chosen, be sure to optimize I/O to the redo log files. In general terms, the use of the combination of RAID 0 striping plus RAID 1 mirroring (also known as RAID 0+1 or RAID 01 or RAID 10) is the best option for the high I/O rates that Oracle redo log files generate.

On many clustered systems where Parallel Server option is used, there is another factor to be considered when creating the redo log files: locality of storage. Some clustered environments (i.e., Compaq VMS Clusters) used a *star-coupler* arrangement to provide each node with access to the cluster's disk drives. Other clustered environments (i.e., IBM RS/6000 HACMP) provide *direct connections* from each node to each disk drive. Therefore, each drive might have *multitailed* connections to two or more (up to eight) different nodes. With both of these arrangements, each storage device is equally accessible to all the nodes, and there is no disk drive that may be considered *local* to a particular node.

With some environments (i.e., IBM RS/6000 SP), though, disk drives are actually connected to particular nodes, and the ability to provide access to all disk drives from all nodes in the cluster is provided via *virtual shared devices*, which operate over a high-speed network interconnect. Therefore, while each node can access all disk drives, some disk drives (because they are local and do not have to be accessed over the interconnect) are more advantageous to use than others.

If the clustered environment you are using falls into the category of clustered systems with *local* and *nonlocal* disk drives, be sure to situate the redo log files for each instance on disk drives local to that node. With the combination of local disk resources and fine-grain RAID 0 striping, you can be certain that the Oracle background processes that write to (i.e., LGWR) and read from (i.e., ARCH) the redo log files will do so most optimally. When using RAID 1 mirroring/shadowing or RAID 5 interleaving in conjunction with the striping, you can be more comfortable that these all-important data structures are not subject to device failure.

One last note: Which is better? Mirroring provided by the hardware or operating system (i.e., RAID) or mirroring provided by the Oracle RDBMS (i.e., multiple members for each redo log file group)? In general, there is nothing wrong with trying to use both methods at once. Naturally, this can be considered wasteful in terms of space utilization: twice the level of redundancy or essentially four copies of data! As with all redundancy schemes, the duplication is wasteful if the data structures being protected are unimportant. Oracle's redo log files, however, are crucial to the Oracle RDBMS's ability both to run and to recover from any kind of failure. Because redo log files generally consume a fairly small percentage of the total warehouse database size, extra redundancy may not be that costly to implement. But because Parallel Server needs a separate complete set (or thread) of redo log files for each instance, it stands to reason that the more instances you use, the more space the redo log files will consume in total. If you are mirroring log files at the hardware/operating-system level and again at the Oracle RDBMS level, using both methods of mirroring together may become prohibitively expensive.

If this is the situation, there is one extra failure scenario that mirroring at the Oracle RDBMS level (i.e., multiple members per redo log file group) can cover and that mirroring at the hardware/operating-system level (i.e., RAID 1 or RAID 5) cannot handle: corruption of write requests issued by Oracle. Because the Oracle RDBMS method of mirroring can handle one more small scenario than the other option (even if the probability of this failure scenario is infinitesimally rare), we would tend to choose to create multiple members for redo log file groups rather than use RAID 1 or RAID 5 for redo log files.

Optimizing Rollback Segments in Parallel Server (Optional, but Highly Recommended)

There are two kinds of rollback segments in Oracle: public and private. The concept of public rollback segments was originally designed specifically for use in Oracle Parallel Server environments, but they are rarely (if ever) used even here, and it is advisable to avoid them. Rollback segments (both public and private) are claimed by a database instance and used exclusively by that instance until the instance is shut down. The difference between the two kinds of rollback segments lies in how they are claimed by an instance.

Private rollback segments are the default (and preferred) type. They can be claimed by an instance by specifying a list of rollback segment names in the ROLLBACK_SEGMENTS parameter in the instance's "init.ora" configuration file so they are claimed (and onlined) by the instance on startup. Or they can be claimed by an instance after instance startup using the ALTER ROLLBACK SEGMENT . . . ONLINE command.

Public rollback segments were designed to be used as a pool of rollback segments, which are intended to be claimed by any instance that needs extra rollback space on demand. The idea sounds attractive but is actually faulty in practice. The reason public rollback segments are a bad idea is twofold. The first reason concerns the fact that, after the redo log files, the rollback segments can be considered the second-busiest data structures in the typical Oracle database in terms of I/O. Of course, this depends on the type and nature of the application being run on the database; some applications may access other data structures more heavily, of course. Also, I/O to and from the rollback segments can usually be reduced by increasing the size of the buffer cache in the SGA; this is not an option for redo log files. Regardless of the type of application, the rollback segments can usually be counted on to provide very high levels of I/O. This can be true even in primarily read-only environments like data warehouses.

Because of this, it is advantageous to separate rollback segments into their own tablespaces, separate from all tables, indexes, clusters, and especially temporary (sorting) segments. This prevents the expansion of these other types of segments from interfering with the growth of the rollback segments. Conversely, this also prevents the dynamic expansion of rollback segments from interfering with the growth of these other types of segments.

Temporary (sorting) segments and rollback segments are particularly incompatible because they both have the same nasty habit of growing very rapidly in a short amount of time. Detecting a conflict between temporary segments and rollback segments can be made more difficult by the fact that temporary segments tend to disappear when they're no longer in use. If an operation requiring a sort fails because the associated temporary segment was unable to grow any further due to a clash with an active, growing rollback segment, the temporary segment disappears after the operation finishes. Additionally, via the use of the OPTIMAL storage clause, rollback segments themselves can shrink back to an optimal size. Because of the ability of both of these kinds of segments to "cover their tracks" (as it were) following a clash (one disappears completely, the other can shrink so that it doesn't appear to be a problem), detecting the cause of a space shortage in a tablespace where temporary segments and rollback segments can coexist can be like chasing the will-o'-the-wisp.

It is also advantageous to try to situate the rollback segment tablespaces on the most optimal devices for I/O, if possible. The reasons here are the same as those cited for redo log files. You should situate data structures that you know are likely to generate the most I/O on devices capable of providing the fastest I/O. If the concept of local disk drives is relevant on your clustered system, then the devices capable of providing the fastest I/O differ from instance to instance. By explicitly naming rollback segments for each instance, they can be isolated into different tablespaces and therefore made local.

The second reason public rollback segments are a bad idea involves the way Parallel Server handles contention between instances. Although it is possible for two or more instances to update data in the same tablespace or segment or extent, it is easiest to guarantee that there will be no interinstance contention if the contents of tablespaces can be *dedicated* to a specific instance. Because rollback segments are effectively dedicated to the instance that brings them online, this makes it possible to guarantee that an entire tablespace, if it contains only private rollback segments for a particular instance, handles reads and writes only from that particular instance. The same guaranteed dedication to an instance cannot be made for tables, indexes, or clusters.

For all these reasons, the best practice is to create separate tablespaces for rollback segments only, one tablespace per instance, in a Parallel Server database. Each tablespace should be created on disk devices optimized for the node on which each particular instance resides. Each tablespace should contain private rollback segments for that one—and only one—instance. Upon startup, each instance should bring its own private rollback segments online using the ROLLBACK_SEGMENTS parameter in the instance's "init.ora" configuration file.

Optimizing Sorting in Parallel Server

With Oracle RDBMS version 7.3, the TEMPORARY clause became available with the CREATE TABLESPACE and ALTER TABLESPACE commands. By default, tablespaces can contain both "permanent" segments (i.e., tables/clusters, indexes, rollback segments) and temporary segments. When an entire tablespace is created as TEMPORARY, or if it already exists and contains nothing and is altered to TEMPORARY, then it is optimized for use only by the temporary segments used during sorting.

Before version 7.3, and in PERMANENT tablespaces from 7.3 on, temporary segments are allocated on demand and are removed as the final task of the SQL statement that created them. All this allocation and deallocation can strain the Oracle RDBMS and its data dictionary. When a tablespace is marked TEMPORARY, then the extents belonging to temporary segments are not deallocated once they are created. The extents remain allocated but available for use by subsequent SQL statements. The fact that extent deallocation and reallocation no longer occurs can remove quite a bit of contention from each Oracle instance, as well as the database's data dictionary, which is global to all the instances. If multiple instances no longer have to update the global data dictionary when a lot of sorting is happening, then the performance of each instance as well as the overall performance of all instances is improved.

Also, marking a tablespace TEMPORARY further emphasizes the nature of I/O performed on that tablespace. Because tables, clusters, indexes, and rollback segments can no longer be created in the tablespace, the data files that make up the tablespace can be optimized for the kind of I/O generated by sorting operations. If a lot of sorting is performed by the SQL statements used by the data warehouse application, then you may want to consider placing these tablespaces on optimal I/O devices as well.

Temporary tablespaces, however, can safely be shared by all the instances of a Parallel Server database, so you may need only one such tablespace. But that one tablespace may have to be huge, and here's why: Data warehouse applications on Oracle typically require *very large* amounts of sorting space. The kinds of SQL statements issued against data warehouses are generally large queries that perform summarizations, aggregations, or filtering against massive amounts of data. Sometimes these massive queries might also involve joining several tables, which may require additional sorting.

Add to this the probable involvement of the Parallel Query Option (PQO), which transparently takes a single SQL query running on one Oracle server process and divides the work to be performed so that many concurrently executing parallel query slave processes can perform the work in parallel. If the original query was large enough, then instead of a single long-running query process generating huge temporary segments for sorting, you may have dozens of parallel query slaves, each generating large temporary segments for sorting. Where only one process was consuming space at a relatively slow pace, you may now have dozens of processes, each clamoring for more sorting space at the same time. If you have a handful of such queries running at the same time, each using PQO, then Oracle can gulp down sort space at a dizzying rate and just as quickly release it when the queries finish.

Quite frequently, the temporary tablespace in an Oracle data warehouse is the single largest tablespace in the database. In fact, in a data warehouse that makes heavy use of both Parallel Query Option and Parallel Server Option, the temporary tablespace can represent anywhere from 10 to 25 percent of the total size of the Oracle database. To illustrate this, in an Oracle data warehouse database that measures 750 gigabytes in total, it is not unreasonable to have a temporary tablespace sized at 100 to 125 gigabytes. The size of the temporary tablespace is dependent partially on the amount of "raw" data in the database (i.e., tables and clusters, not including indexes) and partially on the number of concurrently executing query processes requiring sort space.

Another issue that arises when optimizing temporary tablespaces and sorting in general is to set the SORT_DIRECT_WRITES parameter in each instance's "init.ora" configuration file to TRUE (default is FALSE). Enabling this parameter causes each query process to write directly to the temporary segments, bypassing the buffer cache in the SGA. As a result, there is less contention in each instance's SGA, each query server process performs the I/O to the temporary tablespace's data files (instead of the DBWR background process), and the overall code path in performing sorting is made significantly shorter.

All in all, the redo log files, the rollback segments, and the temporary tablespace may put huge demands on the I/O subsystem underneath an Oracle data warehouse, whether Parallel Server is in use or not. If Parallel Server is in use, then the redo log files and rollback segments should be isolated from data files accessed by other database instances and optimized for the instances and nodes with which they are associated. Because it can be shared by all the instances in the Parallel Server database, the temporary tablespace should probably be striped or concatenated across all the nodes in the cluster to ensure that no single node (or group of nodes) bears the brunt of the I/O associated with sorting.

Concatenating, as the word is used here, is similar to data striping, but at a less sophisticated level. RAID 0 striping causes the data to be striped in small discrete chunks (i.e., 4 KB, 16 KB, 64 KB, etc.). Concatenation merely means dividing the tablespace evenly into a certain number of separate files and then placing each one of those files on a separate node or device.

An example of tablespace concatenation is shown in the following CREATE TABLESPACE command:

```
CREATE TABLESPACE TEMP DATAFILE    '/dev/dsk/node1/temp01.dbf' SIZE
1024M,
    '/dev/dsk/node2/temp02.dbf' SIZE 1024M,
    '/dev/dsk/node3/temp03.dbf' SIZE 1024M,
    '/dev/dsk/node4/temp04.dbf' SIZE 1024M,
        TEMPORARY;
```

In this example, a temporary tablespace named TEMP is created with an initial size of 4 gigabytes (i.e., 4,096 MB). The data file named *temp01.dbf* is created on *node1*, the data file named *temp02.dbf* is created on *node2*, and so on. This tablespace is concatenated across four nodes, each chunk (or stripe width) being 1 gigabyte.

Of course, each data file itself might be RAID 0 striped across several disk devices. For example, the data file named *temp01.dbf* may actually reside on 16 disk drives on *node1*. The size of each chunk (or stripe width) on each disk drive might be 16 KB. Whether each data file is itself striped at the hardware or operating system level is, of course, completely transparent to Oracle.

Some clustered systems, such as the IBM RS/6000 SP, provide the ability to perform RAID 0 striping not only across disk drives within a node but also across nodes. On the SP platform, these are referred to as *hashed shared devices* or HSDs. In this case, the 4 data files in the example just shown may themselves be RAID 0 striped in relatively small widths (i.e., 16 KB) across all 4 nodes, as well as being RAID 0 striped across all 16 disk drives on each node. In this situation, the only reason for using 4 data files to create the tablespace is due to a possible 2 gigabyte file size limitation on AIX, not because of a desire to spread I/O across all 4 nodes. If the AIX operating system (as well as Oracle for AIX) fully supported file sizes larger than 2 gigabytes (which will be true with AIX 4.2 and above), then the tablespace TEMP in the preceding example could have been created with a single HSD and still provided all the benefits of RAID 0 striping across all nodes and all disk drives.

Optimizing Data Loading in Parallel Server

Strategies for populating the data warehouse were discussed in detail in Chapter 6, "Populating the Oracle Data Warehouse," but there are two basic methods for loading data into Oracle:

1. Using "conventional" SQL.
2. Using direct path.

The first approach includes any mechanism involving SQL: conventional-path SQL*Loader, custom-written programs using Precompilers or OCI, or third-party vendor solutions using Precompilers or OCI. The other approach has only one alternative: direct-path SQL*Loader. Oracle does not provide an API for using the direct path mechanism, so SQL*Loader is the only utility available for loading data that uses it.

The best approach to loading with Parallel Server is the same regardless of which mechanism is being used: The fastest approach is to use as many instances as possible. Segregating the loads so that there is no contention between instances varies based on the mechanism.

Direct Path Loading

The SQL*Loader utility can be used with the direct-path mechanism in parallel, that is, with several concurrent programs running at the same time. SQL*Loader does not transparently "parallelize" the way parallel queries do. Rather, parallel direct path SQL*Loader just means that you can have two or more SQL*Loader processes running in this fashion at the same time. For example:

```
$ sqlldr control=x.ctl data=x1.dat direct=true parallel=true . . .
$ sqlldr control=x.ctl data=x2.dat direct=true parallel=true . . .
$ sqlldr control=x.ctl data=x3.dat direct=true parallel=true . . .
```

What will happen here is that the SQL*Loader processes will each create its own "private" TEMPORARY segments to load into, each essentially *appending* data onto the table in question.

The problem here is that we have provided Oracle no guidance about where to physically locate these extents, so in Oracle7 it guesses. It may guess well and locate the extents in data files that are "local" to the node on which the SQL*Loader processes are running, or it may guess poorly and locate these extents in data files that are not "local." This is illustrated in Figures 11.23 and 11.24.

Naturally, you can see that locality can be important for performance; having to send data across a network, even a high-speed network, is certainly much slower than sending the data to locally connected disk drives. You can also see that, all other things being equal, it would be even more advantageous to locate each of these three SQL*Loader processes on separate database instances. But which of the scenarios illustrated in Figures 11.25, 11.26, and 11.27 is more efficient?

Obviously, it's Figure 11.27. Little or no networking is involved; each process is simply shoveling data from the input flat files and loading the local data files in the tablespace. Oracle7 chooses where the extents will go if you don't.

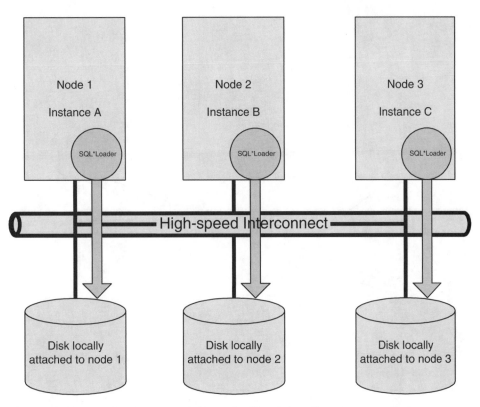

Figure 11.23 Loading into extents located on local data files.

Frankly, you shouldn't allow it to do so if you are concerned about optimizing performance. So, using the FILE= clause you can explicitly specify where the extents will be located, ensuring locality of work.

```
$ sqlldr control=x.ctl data=x1.dat direct=true parallel=true file='x1.dbf'
$ sqlldr control=x.ctl data=x2.dat direct=true parallel=true file='x2.dbf'
$ sqlldr control=x.ctl data=x3.dat direct=true parallel=true file='x3.dbf'
```

The FILE= clause can also be specified inside the SQL*Loader control file; in some cases, this is the only option—for example, when data from the input file is being loaded into two or more different tables or when data from the input file is being loaded into two or more different partitions in a partitioned table. Check with the *Oracle Server Utilities Guide* or Chapter 6 in this book.

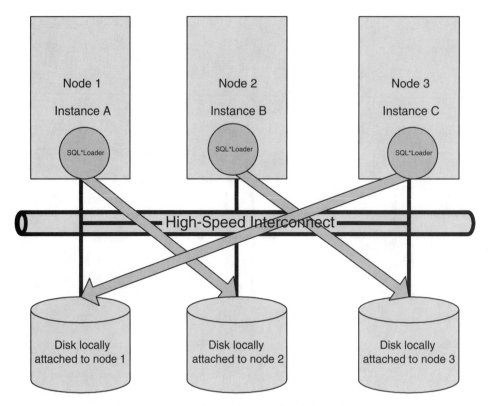

Figure 11.24   Loading into extents located on nonlocal data files.

Conventional SQL Loading

For some reason, many people are under the impression that any program written in C, COBOL, or Fortran simply must be faster than SQL*Loader. Even if the task at hand is simple insertion, they still feel that writing a program in a third-generation language (3GL) such as C simply must be faster than the SQL*Loader conventional path.

Not true. To help explain this, just think of SQL*Loader as a C program that has already been written. All you have to do is write a control file that describes what the input data looks like. Right away, this is a performance increase; creating a 3GL program takes a lot of time to write and test, and writing a control file is a heck of a lot faster and easier.

SQL*Loader can handle a surprising number of complex file formats and situations, such as loading from one input file into several tables or partitioned tables or merging multiple input records into a single input record. But there are a few basic ones that it cannot handle—for example, if data from each input

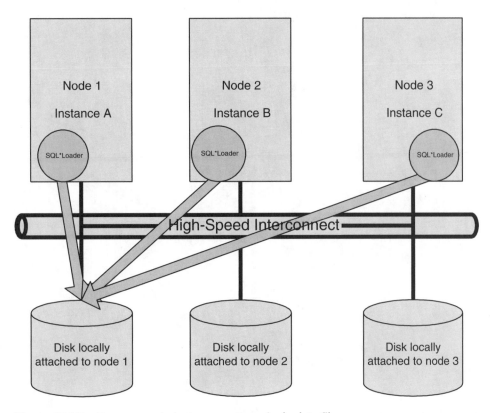

Figure 11.25   From separate instances onto a single data file.

record must go to more than one table or if data from two or more input files must be merged, to be loaded into one or more tables. Also, SQL*Loader is capable only of inserting data; it cannot perform an update of a duplicate record.

Whichever conventional SQL mechanism is used, the performance challenges in a Parallel Server environment are similar to those faced with the direct-path mechanism: reducing contention between instances. For SQL INSERT statements, the mechanism is *freelist groups*. As described earlier, freelist groups are a way of associating contiguous blocks with a specific database instance.

If freelist groups are specified for a table or an index, then groups of database blocks will be allocated to an instance using the values specified in the GC_FILES_TO_LOCKS parameter. For example, if GC_FILES_TO_LOCKS includes a specification of "!50", meaning 50 contiguous database blocks for PCM locks covering the relevant data file, then blocks will be automatically allocated to the freelist group for the current instance in increments of 50 blocks at a time.

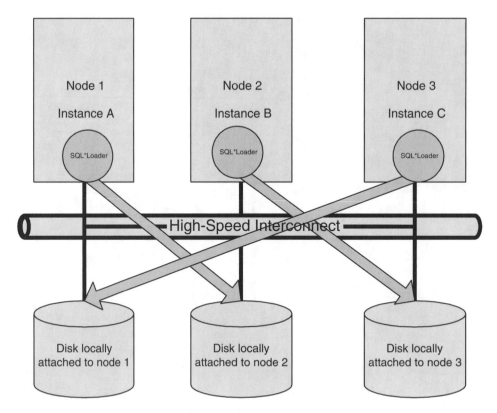

Figure 11.26 From separate instances onto different data files.

Preallocation of extents is a far more reliable method for ensuring that insertions occurring from database instances end up in the most efficient location for each database instance. Preallocating extents to freelist groups allows you to "map" extents to specific data files with complete certainty, and they therefore serve the dual goals of reducing contention between database instances and "localizing" disk traffic.

```
SQL> CREATE TABLE X
  2  (. . .)
  3  STORAGE (INITIAL 1 NEXT 8M PCTINCREASE 0
  4  FREELISTS 4
  5  FREELIST GROUPS 3);

Table created.

SQL> ALTER TABLE X ALLOCATE EXTENT
```

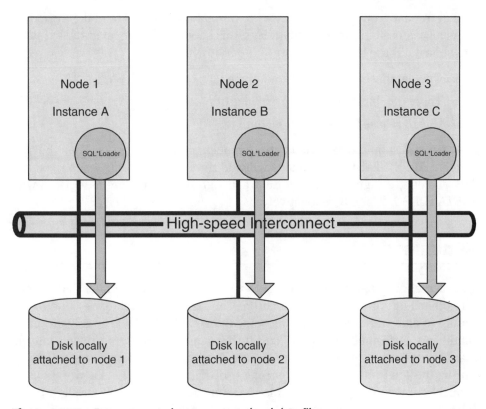

Figure 11.27 From separate instances onto local data files.

```
     2          (DATAFILE '/dev/rv_node1_02_X.dbf' INSTANCE 1);

Table altered.

SQL> ALTER TABLE X ALLOCATE EXTENT
     2          (DATAFILE '/dev/rv_node2_03_X.dbf' INSTANCE 2);

Table altered.

SQL> ALTER TABLE X ALLOCATE EXTENT
     2          (DATAFILE '/dev/rv_node3_04_X.dbf' INSTANCE 3);

Table altered.
```

Here, table X is initially created with a minimally sized initial extent; note that only one byte was requested. This initial extent will not belong to any particular freelist group, so the best way to mitigate this fact is to make the extent as small as possible. On most platforms, this should result in an initial extent of only one database block, as a part of the following:

- One database block for segment header
- Three database blocks for freelist groups
- One database block for initial extent

The result should total five database blocks on table creation. Then the subsequent ALTER TABLE commands will add three more extents, each sized at 8 MB, and each assigned to one of the freelist groups, which are associated with INSTANCES 1, 2, and 3, respectively.

Summary

Data warehouse applications are better suited to Oracle Parallel Server than any other kind of database application. The risks are much lower due to the nature of data warehouses. Troublesome data manipulation is largely programmatic and performed in "batch," and if this can segregated to prevent interinstance contention, Parallel Server can demonstrate impressive scalability during the load phase. The real strength of Parallel Server data warehouses, though, comes during queries. This is when the full power of Oracle's parallelized operations, described in Chapter 10, "Parallel Execution in the Oracle Data Warehouse," can fully exploit the hardware architecture.

CHAPTER

12

Distributing the Oracle Data Warehouse

All right, you knuckleheads! Spread 'em out!

Moe Howard, **The Three Stooges—***1930s, '40s, and '50s film shorts*

Data warehouses are without any doubt the largest relational databases being developed today. Data warehouses tend to push the limits of database storage capabilities and performance. Oracle8 has greatly increased the physical limits on the size of a database and has provided new capabilities for managing larger databases. Physically storing and administering data warehouses with multiple terabytes of data are now feasible. At the same time developments in both hardware and Oracle Parallel Server have greatly increased the capability of data warehouses to handle hundreds or even thousands of simultaneously connected users.

With such capabilities available to the warehouse development team, one has to wonder why any organization would ever need to consider any architecture more complex than a single large database. There are several reasons for considering a distributed database architecture. Chief among these is *increased availability*; secondary is *cost*. Modern (exotic) MPP hardware makes it *possible* to develop and administer a multiterabyte warehouse. But the added complexity of these architectures has made them, to date, much less reliable than expected, reducing availability instead of increasing it. Also the economics of this architecture may make it unfeasible, which begs another approach entirely.

It may be far less expensive to maintain the large central data warehouse using conventional SMP or newer NUMA computer technology. The storage costs of disk and controllers is not reduced in this configuration, but processor costs can be reduced by literally millions of dollars. What is given up by making this hardware change, of course, is the capability to support hundreds of simultaneous parallel queries. Many of the queries that need to be processed in the warehouse, however, are using relatively small summary tables for which parallel operation across dozens of CPUs is not required. It is possible, in some cases, to move some of the data and some of the users to separate servers and databases and thereby reduce total costs.

Another reason to consider a distributed database is to provide "local" access to a data mart that contains a subset of the data stored within the total warehouse. By keeping a copy of the data most likely to be needed by a particular department or workgroup on a server nearby, we can reduce the need for our entire user base to access the centralized warehouse, which reduces our need for massive computing resources. Because the department's data mart is physically close to its users we can reduce telecommunications cost and network delays for widely dispersed global corporations. Using data marts in this way may increase the total warehousing costs for an organization but will provide increased availability and performance in return.

Reasons to Consider a Distributed Data Warehouse

Each feature of Oracle addresses some problems extremely well, but it may not address other issues as effectively. It is vital to understand the strengths and weaknesses of a feature before deciding whether to use it. The following sections contrast replication against clustering solutions.

Increased Availability

The old adage about keeping all one's eggs in a single basket says just about everything here. While clustered and MPP architectures promise fault tolerance against *component* failure, they do not provide any protection against *data center* failure. As of this writing, no commercially available clustered hardware can be geographically dispersed.

Additionally, clustered and MPP architectures are relatively *tightly coupled* in comparison to multiple distributed databases on standalone servers linked together by a network. A failure to one component is relatively more likely to affect other components than a distributed architecture, where the only linkage between components is likely to be a local area or wide area network.

Cost

Cost provides one criterion by which distributed data warehouses are justified. Let's consider a hypothetical MPP hardware architecture that costs $10 million for 16 interconnected SMP nodes and 1.2 terabytes of shared disk storage. We anticipate that we will need the processing capability of those 16 nodes to handle the query load of several hundred users. To support the loading, indexing, summarizing, and other administrative tasks of our terabyte warehouse, we determine that we will need the processing power of 4 of those nodes. The cost of those 4 MPP nodes (and the same amount of disk) might be $3 million. We might be able to satisfy the query processing needs of our large user community by purchasing four large SMP machines at $1 million each. Figures 12.1 and 12.2 provide an idea of these two configurations and the potential savings.

The databases on each of these four query databases can be much smaller because they will not store the very large volumes of detail data. If each of these machines is assigned to a different group of users, we may well find that we can further limit the local storage on each to even a subset of the various summaries that we produce. Thus, with a distributed configuration, we might provide the same or better level of query performance at a cost savings of $2 million dollars.

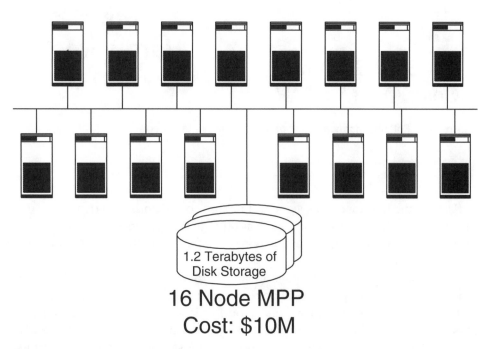

Figure 12.1 Potential hardware cost of an MPP data warehouse.

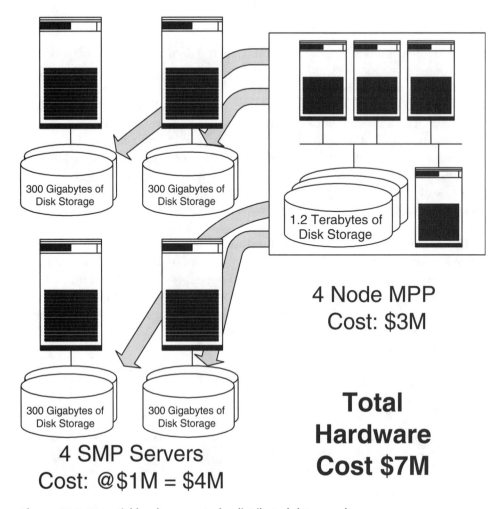

300 Gigabytes of
Disk Storage

300 Gigabytes of
Disk Storage

1.2 Terabytes of
Disk Storage

300 Gigabytes of
Disk Storage

300 Gigabytes of
Disk Storage

4 Node MPP
Cost: $3M

4 SMP Servers
Cost: @$1M = $4M

**Total
Hardware
Cost $7M**

Figure 12.2 Potential hardware cost of a distributed data warehouse.

Further, the four machines serve as backups to each other so that, in case of one machine's failure, users can reach another of the servers to have their query processed. So, in addition to saving money, we may actually be able to increase net system availability.

For global corporations, another advantage to this distributed architecture is that the four secondary servers in our example may be placed in different parts of the world. This can improve query performance by keeping the database closer to a selected group of users. It can greatly decrease the total telecommunications costs of the warehouse because most queries can be performed "locally." This leaves periodic data load file transfers and occasional drill-down queries (which need to access detailed data) as the only warehouse demand on the global network connections. This advantage also extends to simplified administration. Because each machine is potentially supporting a group of users spanning only a few time zones instead of the entire world, it is easier to schedule loads and cold backups in times when the users don't need access. A database supporting only query users in the United States and Canada may be easily taken offline every Sunday evening; if the database supports worldwide users, there never is a "Sunday evening" window—for users in Europe it is now Monday morning and for those in Asia it is already Monday evening!

This alternative architecture with a smaller central complex augmented with four large SMP servers does, however, come at some additional operational costs. After the data has been loaded onto our central server and then summarized and indexed, we have another generation of data loading to perform. We must create several extracts of the summarized (and perhaps some of the detailed) data and then transport, load, and index our four additional databases. This process is greatly simplified, however, because the hard work of organizing and integrating the data was performed during the load of the central server. Extracting data from an architected warehouse to build these smaller warehouses (often called "data marts") requires minimal additional analysis to decide which subset of the total warehouse should be copied closer to each user group.

Also, because of the redundant nature of this distributed architecture, we may well be able to forego making backups of the four secondary warehouse databases. Should one of these machines suffer a disk failure, we may find that reloading the data into the affected tablespaces from either the MPP central database or one of the other secondary servers is faster than performing database recovery.

If we decide that we should do backups on the distributed servers' databases, we will find our task streamlined by the fact that we are doing very simplified processing on each of these servers. We can take full advantage of read-only tablespaces so that much of our recovery requires only file restoration from backup.

Our backup and recovery of the distributed data marts is made simpler by another feature of this design. Most of our loads and index builds can be done with the UNRECOVERABLE (Oracle7) or NOLOGGING (Oracle8 and Oracle8i) options and therefore will generate minimal redo. Not having to perform large summarizations or other processing will minimize the redo generation on these satellite systems. This means we may avoid the usual complexities while still running the database in ARCHIVELOG mode—we are likely to have fewer archived log files to manage and may be able to retain them on disk until the next system backup.

> **NOTE** NOARCHIVELOG mode is an option for Oracle databases, but only in a rare set of circumstances, and almost always for databases that are considered expendable. It is strongly recommended in almost all circumstances to operate the database in ARCHIVELOG mode. Whenever you are operating an Oracle database in NOARCHIVELOG mode, you can easily recover any read-only tablespaces in the event of media failure. The SYSTEM tablespace and the tablespace holding rollback segments cannot be made read-only. These tablespaces must be given additional protection from failure through some form of disk mirroring. When running NOARCHIVELOG, you cannot perform hot backups, so warehouse downtime for cold backups after each load must be scheduled. When loads are performed weekly or monthly and the warehouse is not being accessed globally, this backup window is usually easy to schedule. If a disk failure does occur to a database operated in NOARCHIVELOG mode, the administrator must either restore the entire database from the last cold backup or re-create the database and reload all of its data. In essence, NOARCHIVELOG mode is desirable only when simplicity is preferable to recoverability and availability. Whenever this is not true, use ARCHIVELOG mode.

Given these potential advantages of a distributed data warehouse, let's consider Oracle's distributed database features and then examine several alternative distributed architectures.

Distributed Database Terminology

Before examining the specific Oracle features that support distributed data warehousing, it is appropriate to introduce some terminology used to describe database operations in both local and distributed configurations.

We use the term *query* to describe a retrieval of data that does not attempt to modify any database data. In the Oracle SQL language, queries are performed using the SELECT command. A *transaction*, on the other hand, may involve multiple SQL statements and makes some modifications to data through some combination of data manipulation language (DML) verbs, namely INSERT, UPDATE, and DELETE. Each of these commands locks the specific rows being modified, so that no other transaction is able to make additional changes until the first transaction completes. (There are other SQL statements that can lock data for the purpose of making changes—SELECT . . . FOR UPDATE and LOCK TABLE request locks without actually changing any data. This type of *intention locking* allows the transaction to ensure that the data needed will be available and not locked by another transaction.)

A *transaction* is terminated by the SQL COMMIT statement. COMMIT (or COMMIT WORK to meet ANSI SQL standard syntax) makes all the modifications permanent and releases all the locks held by the transaction. Alternatively, the transaction can be ended with the ROLLBACK (or ROLLBACK WORK for ANSI compliance), which restores all the data modifications to the state in which they existed before the start of the transaction. ROLLBACK reverses the effects of the transaction and releases all its locks. A new transaction is started by the first DML statement after the initial user connection to the database or the last COMMIT or ROLLBACK that ended a previous transaction.

A *local query* is a SELECT statement that is executed entirely within the database where the user is connected. In Oracle's two-task implementation this type of query follows the client/server model. The user process passes the query to an Oracle server process that will perform the work and then return results to the user process. The user process may reside on the same server as the database instance or it may submit the query over Net8 from another computer, typically a desktop PC or an Internet application server. Only a single database is required to satisfy the local query.

A *local transaction* is a transaction that locks and/or modifies data only within the single database to which the user is connected. Again, only a single database is required to complete the entire transaction. There are several query and transaction processing models, however, in which more than the single connected database is required. These include remote and distributed queries and transactions. A special case of prepackaging distributed transactions, known as replication, is also available as part of the Oracle environment.

Remote Query

The most basic distributed database operation is the *remote query*. A remote query requires data from only one database, but not the database to which the user is connected. The database to which the user is connected determines that the entire query can be shipped to a remote database for processing.

Figure 12.3 illustrates a query submitted by the client while connected to the database instance LOCL on Database Server number 1. LOCL recognizes that the query requires only data that is located in the database instance RMOT on Database Server number 2. LOCL reissues the query directly to RMOT using its own client/server connection. The query is executed entirely on RMOT, and then the final results are passed back to LOCL, which merely passes them along to the client user.

Distributed Query

A distributed query is a SELECT statement that requires data from more than one database. The data from one database must be combined (either through a join or a set operation such as UNION ALL) with data residing on another

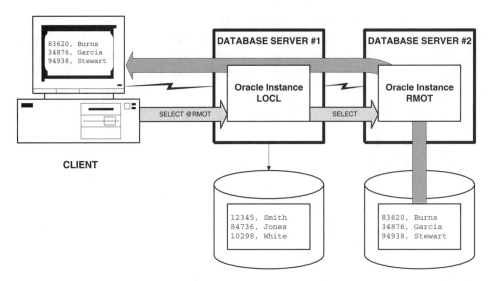

Figure 12.3 A remote query.

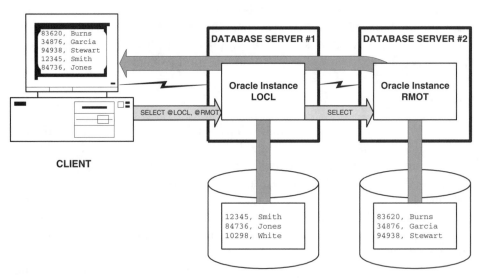

Figure 12.4 A distributed query.

database. Figure 12.4 demonstrates a distributed query being submitted to LOCL. The query requires data from both LOCL and RMOT, so the LOCL instance examines the statistics about both tables (and their indexes) to determine the optimal plan for combining the data. In some cases, the amount of data from LOCL is much smaller than the amount of data needed from RMOT. In such a case, LOCL will reformulate the query and ship it, along with the LOCL data, to RMOT for processing. In other situations, RMOT data will be much smaller than LOCL data, and LOCL will generate a query to RMOT to bring back the needed data for processing in LOCL. Wherever the data is combined, it will be passed back through LOCL to the requesting user. The DRIVING_SITE hint is available to give the SQL programmer control over this decision making. The hint takes as a parameter a *table name* or *table alias*. The optimizer will consider the database on which the indicated table is physically located to be the *driving site* of the distributed query.

Remote Transaction

A remote transaction involves locking or changing one or more rows in a single database other than the one to which the user is connected. As long as each subsequent DML statement continues to refer to the same remote database, the local instance continues to simply pass the DML statements along to that remote instance for processing. When the transaction-ending COMMIT is issued by the client, the local instance verifies that all INSERT, UPDATE, and DELETE and other locking statements were directed to the same instance. If so, the COMMIT statement is passed along to the remote database instance for normal single-phase completion.

An example of a remote transaction is provided in Figure 12.5. One row is updated in the RMOT database instance. The UPDATE statement is passed along to that database. When this single statement is committed, only the RMOT instance will have any changes to make permanent. No special two-phased commit protocol will be required.

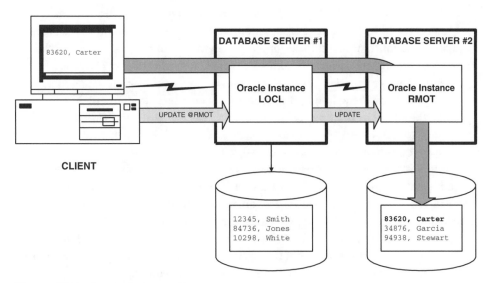

Figure 12.5   A remote transaction.

Distributed Transaction

A distributed transaction involves data manipulation in more than one database that must be treated as a single unit of work. The changes in the two (or more) databases have to be coordinated and either made permanent (committed) or reversed (rolled back) identically at each site.

Ensuring that all the sites either commit or roll back together requires special processing at the end of the distributed transaction. This special processing is known as a two-phased commit. The local database instance where the client is connected will coordinate the two-phased commit processing. In the first phase, all sites (except the coordinator) are put into a *prepared* state. From this state each site is guaranteed to be able to either roll back or commit the transaction. In Oracle terms this means that all the transaction's changes, including the prepare request, are written out to the online redo log. Once all sites have responded (to the coordinator) that they are prepared, then the second phase, *commit*, is initiated.

A simple distributed transaction, with one data change in LOCL and another single row modified in RMOT, is illustrated in Figure 12.6. The LOCL instance that receives each request from the connected client determines which statements it can process, and which must be passed along to another instance. As soon as a DML statement is encountered that must be handled by a second instance, the transaction is marked as distributed and two-phased commit processing will be required when the transaction ends.

LOCKING DURING TWO-PHASED COMMIT

All but one site in the distributed transaction will require special locks to be taken on the blocks that have been modified in the transaction. These locks are called in-doubt transaction locks, and are generally held only for a short period between the two phases of the commit process. These locks are, however, potentially very expensive because they prevent any user from updating or even reading any data in the in-doubt blocks. This is necessary and acceptable during the normally brief period of committing because the local Oracle instance cannot accurately rebuild a consistent view of the block until it receives the commit or rollback message in the second phase.

This can cause concurrency problems when distributed transactions need to modify data in the same blocks as other transactions or queries. Another concurrency problem is introduced when, in rare circumstances, a failure of the network, a server, or a database instance prevents completion of the second phase of the commit after a site has entered the prepared state. In such a situation the expensive, in-doubt transaction locks will be maintained until the failure is corrected and the commit processing can be completed.

Replication

Replication is a facility for propagating changes made in one database to another. When a row is inserted, updated, or deleted in one database, a corresponding insert, update, or delete is automatically performed in the other. Replication may be either synchronous or asynchronous. Synchronous replication occurs as part of the initial transaction—if the change can't be propagated immediately then the transaction fails. The advantage in performing synchronous replication is that both databases are kept perfectly synchronized. The drawback, however, is that a failure of any server or network component prevents the transaction from completing.

In asynchronous replication, changes are propagated after the initial transaction by a separate independent transaction. Asynchronous replication is more resilient to outages of either the network or the remote database and server. Performance of the original transaction is also less impacted by asynchronous replication than by immediately performing the remote work with synchronous replication. Figure 12.7 shows a simple transaction inserting a single row into the database associated with instance LOCL. Replication has been defined on the particular LOCL table that received the insert. Oracle's replication facility

To minimize the impact (and perhaps the probability) of such situations, Oracle7, Oracle8, and Oracle8*i* allow the administrator to set the initialization parameter COMMIT_POINT_ STRENGTH in each instance. Whichever participating database instance has the highest value of COMMIT_POINT_STRENGTH, it will become the commit point site of the transaction and will not have to enter the prepared state. The commit point should be directed to the database in which in-doubt transactions would have the greatest impact. In many cases, this will be the busiest database; in others it might be the one supporting the most critical application. A database instance on an unreliable server, however, would not be a good choice because failures of the commit point site can leave in-doubt blocks of other databases unavailable.

Oracle also provides a means for the administrators of the distributed database to manually force the local portion of a distributed transaction to complete the commit (or rollback) when an outage causes a severe contention problem. Care must be taken, though, to ensure that any manually forced transaction is handled consistently with the action taken by the commit point site. Committing part of a distributed transaction at one site and rolling back at another will cause an inconsistency (also known as corruption!) in the distributed database.

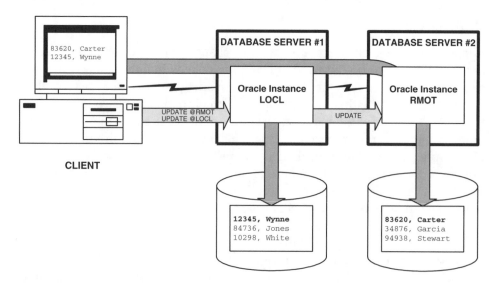

Figure 12.6 A distributed transaction.

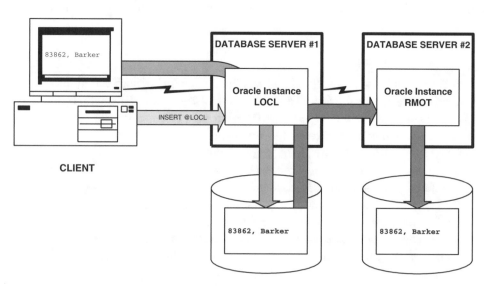

Figure 12.7 A replicated transaction.

will automatically copy the row as part of a separate transaction into the database opened by the RMOT instance. The second, asynchronous replication transaction (shown in the darkest shading) operates independently of the first under a schedule defined during the setup of replication. Should the network connection to RMOT be unavailable for some reason, the row will be replicated when the connection is restored.

Oracle Distributed Database Technology

The Oracle RDBMS has included distributed database features since version 5. The same basic "SQL*Star" architecture that provided distributed query capability over a dozen years ago has been preserved with several major enhancements. Chief among these has been the introduction of distributed transactions in Oracle7. Building on this capability, Oracle's replication facilities allow changes made in one database to be automatically propagated to a corresponding table within another database. Finally, constant improvements in the Oracle optimizer have greatly improved the performance characteristics of distributed queries. The Oracle8*i* cost-based optimizer is able to use statistics on both local and remote database objects to determine an efficient plan for distributed queries. Although such queries are never as quick as the equivalent query performed entirely within a single database, they are far more efficient than in earlier releases, which were not able to determine the relative volumes of data and available indexes in each database.

Beyond changes in the optimizer several other Oracle features provide location transparency—the ability for the administrator to hide distributed complexities from the end user.

Database Links

A *database link* is Oracle's means of establishing a connection from one database to another. Just as user connections are made over Net8 to allow client application code to communicate with an Oracle database using SQL and PL/SQL, one database can become a client requesting services from another database. The connection between databases is defined through an underlying network protocol, such as TCP/IP, and a layer of Net8, Oracle's communication software. Net8 does not replace the network communication protocol but rides on top of it.

To avoid having to specify physical connection information as part of SQL queries, Oracle provides a means for predefining connection data. This predefined connection is called a database link. The syntax to create a database link is as follows:

```
CREATE [ PUBLIC ] DATABASE LINK rmot
    CONNECT TO username IDENTIFIED BY password
    USING 'connect_string';
```

In this example "*rmot*" is the name given to the database link. It is a good idea to name the database link the same as the GLOBAL_NAME of the remote database, to ensure compliance with Oracle's global naming standards. The GLOBAL_NAME can be retrieved from a view named GLOBAL_NAME, and it can be changed (if necessary) using the ALTER DATABASE RENAME GLOBAL NAME command. The name of the database link will be used as part of each remote query or DML statement. This avoids having to specify the other details again in the query or transaction. To query data from the PROJECTS table in the database pointed to by this link, the user would add the database link name to the table name in his SELECT statement:

```
SELECT *
  FROM projects@rmot;
```

The keyword "PUBLIC" can be used by the DBA to define a link that can then be used by any user of the database. General users may be allowed to create their own private database links without the "PUBLIC" keyword.

The "CONNECT TO . . . IDENTIFIED BY . . . " clause allows a remote operation to be conducted through a connection to a specific schema and password within that remote database. The administrator might use this feature to direct all remote queries to a particular schema that has read-only access to all of the warehouse tables in a database. If this clause is not included in the definition of the database link then connections will be made using the same username and password that were used to make the initial local connection. This is common practice when each user has been provided with an account in each database that they are allowed to access. This would allow the administrators of each database to control what data is visible to each individual user or group of users. It does, however, require the user to change his or her password in every database each time one is changed.

The final clause, "USING *'connect_string'*" is where the detailed database connection is defined. Usually, the connect string is the name of a service already defined to SQL*Net (or Net8). This definition is made by an administrator, not a general user, as an entry in either a TNSNAMES.ORA file or within an Oracle Name Server.

When an Oracle Name Server has been configured, a third type of database link can be used—a *global* database link. This is the simplest type of link for the administrator to create and maintain since only a single, centralized definition needs to be made. There is no need for the administrator of each database (or any user) to issue a CREATE DATABASE LINK command. For a large distributed database environment this can be a great time-saver. Using global database links still requires each database administrator to carefully control the privileges provided to users who can now reach any database in the network. Whether they should have access to the data in every database is not as straightforward as providing the connection path!

> **TIP** Net8 (the upgraded and renamed SQL*Net product shipped with Oracle8) also allows for resolving connection strings through host naming (such as Domain Name Services, or DNS) or through external naming (such as the NetWare Directory Service). These features are defined in the *Net8 Administrator's Guide*.

Synonyms

Synonyms provide another level of location transparency to the distributed Oracle environment. A synonym may be created to define an alternative name for some database object, either local or remote. The SQL SELECT statement used in the database link example earlier had to include the "@RMOT" designation appended to the PROJECTS table name. The user would be required to remember that the PROJECTS table was physically stored in the database pointed to by the RMOT link.

To avoid this burden on the user, the administrator might predefine a public synonym that would incorporate both the table name and the location definition:

```
CREATE PUBLIC SYNONYM projects
   FOR projects@rmot;
```

(Note that the synonym name does not have to be the same as the name of the object to which it refers.) Now any user who needs to reference this remote PROJECTS table can simply use the synonym in the SQL statements:

```
SELECT *
  FROM projects;
```

Without the "PUBLIC" keyword, an individual user may create a private synonym that can be used to simplify his own personal accesses but will be unknown to other users.

Views

Views are created by the administrator (or by a user) for a variety of reasons. In some cases, the view will be used to predefine complex join or selection logic. In other situations the view might be used to provide a level of security or convenience by limiting the amount of data visible to user.

Views can also serve the same purpose as a synonym when the goal is to make a remote object appear to the user as if it were a local object:

```
CREATE VIEW projects
    AS SELECT *
  FROM PROJECTS@RMOT;
```

This view would provide the same function as the synonym definition in the previous example. The view processing requires some additional overhead not needed by the synonym. Therefore, the view approach would be used only if some requirement other than transparency were to be met. An example would be when an optimizer hint or WHERE clause restrictions were needed to control the access to the remote data. Another example would be where the local administrator wishes to impose a level of security on the access. An explicit grant of privileges is required before a user can access the view; no privileges are associated with public synonyms, so the only security would be enforced at the remote site where the object physically resides.

Views are a very handy way of controlling access to remote databases. The local database administrator can create a specific user for accessing remote databases. That user account would own a set of views accessing the remote tables. Whenever another user needs access to remote data, the DBA can grant privileges on these views. This can do away with private database links and the issues that prevent the changing of their passwords that can hinder proper security practices.

UNION ALL Views

UNION ALL views are a special case of using a view to simplify the accessing of multiple remote objects as if they were one. We may wish to allow our users to easily select from identically defined tables containing different data rows located in multiple databases. By defining a UNION ALL view that includes the data rows from each of these tables, the user query can appear to select from just a single local object:

```
CREATE VIEW all_projects AS
    SELECT *
      FROM projects
  UNION ALL
    SELECT *
      FROM projects@canada
  UNION ALL
    SELECT *
      FROM projects@europe
  UNION ALL
```

```
SELECT *
  FROM projects@asia;
```

This view will present all PROJECTS data from these four databases to the user who enters a simple query such as the following:

```
SELECT project_name, start_date
  FROM projects;
```

Of course, there are performance considerations with retrieving data from multiple remote databases. As we discuss later in this chapter there are trade-offs in deciding to distribute the data.

Gateways or "Heterogenous Services"

Oracle8*i* introduces the concept of *heterogeneous services*, where access to foreign datastores (such as file-based systems like VSAM) or other database management systems (such as DB2 or Informix) are made accessible as Oracle tables or through Oracle stored procedures. *Heterogeneous services* is the overall name for this capability, and *Oracle Open Gateways* is the name for the services provided by Oracle Corporation using this application programming interface (API).

Oracle provides these *gateway* products to provide a different type of transparency. Gateways allow data maintained by another RDBMS or file management system to appear exactly like another Oracle database. The Oracle Open Gateway serves as a black box that translates the Oracle dialect of SQL into the appropriate dialect for the RDBMS. In situations where any dialect of SQL is inappropriate (i.e., VSAM or APPC), heterogeneous services can be used to encapsulate procedural-language functions into PL/SQL.

Some of the Oracle Open Gateway products allow read-only queries while others allow for additional DML commands. The difference involves whether the foreign data store or database is capable of distributed transactions, involving two-phase commit, or not. Most file management systems do not offer this, while most other DBMS products do. Additionally, Oracle provides procedural gateway capabilities that allow a programmer to write procedures in the language of a non-Oracle application and then invoke those procedures via an Oracle PL/SQL procedure.

Figure 12.8 illustrates an Oracle Open Gateway that transparently allows Oracle queries to be directed to a DB2 database. The Gateway modifies the SQL as necessary to meet the requirements of the DB2 RDBMS. Although this example shows a remote query, the Gateway may also be incorporated into a distributed query or transaction.

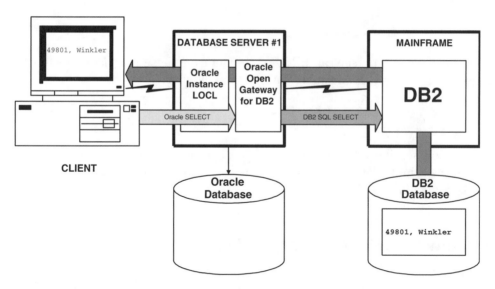

Figure 12.8 An Oracle Open Gateway.

Location transparency of the homogeneous RDBMS connection through a gateway is provided through the same synonym or view facilities as remote or distributed Oracle. Overview documentation of the Oracle8 Open Gateways is provided in the Oracle8*i* *Server Distributed Database Systems* manual, with more detailed documentation provided in separate manuals for each of the specific gateway products.

Oracle Replication Facilities

Basic replication facilities were first introduced in Oracle7, release 7.0, which allowed the creation of read-only snapshots. Additional capabilities for advanced (symmetric) replication were incorporated with release 7.1. Releases since then have incorporated many small enhancements to these facilities, especially related to increased performance and throughput in Oracle8*i*. In Oracle8*i*, *snapshots* have been generally renamed as *materialized views*, as their role has expanded into *summary management* in addition to their traditional role in *data replication*. Chapter 7, "Post-Load Processing in the Data Warehouse," deals extensively with the use of *materialized views* in the area of summary management; this chapter deals with *materialized views* or *snapshots* in their original role in data replication. Please note that, mainly for brevity, we continue to use the older term *snapshot* throughout this chapter, as does the standard Oracle documentation. After all, the phrase *materialized view* is quite a mouthful!

Basic Replication

Basic replication consists of the ability to create read-only snapshots. A snapshot is an automatically maintained copy of remote data. In the simplest form, the snapshot is a complete copy of a remote table. Whenever a row in the base table is added, modified, or deleted, Oracle performs a corresponding INSERT, UPDATE, or DELETE statement in the snapshot. These secondary changes are not made as part of the original transaction but are propagated as part of an asynchronous refresh process controlled by Oracle. The snapshot definition includes a declaration of how and when the refresh should take place.

Oracle can refresh a snapshot (or a group of snapshots) automatically under a regular schedule such as every 15 minutes or at 1:00 A.M. each day. The snapshot owner or DBA may also choose to manually refresh a snapshot group. The refresh can be a COMPLETE refresh in which the copy is truncated and then all rows are retrieved to repopulate the snapshot. Any snapshot can be refreshed in this manner.

An alternative for doing FAST refreshes, in which only changed rows need to be copied, is available only for so-called simple snapshots. A simple snapshot is one whose defining query is based on a single table without joins, set operations, or GROUP BY functions such as SUM() or COUNT(). It may include some or all of the columns in the base table, and may include all the rows or restrict the copy to a subset of the base table rows. Snapshots that do include joins of data from multiple tables or are defined using summary functions are considered complex snapshots and cannot be FAST refreshed.

The query that defines the simple snapshot could not, prior to Oracle8, include a subquery. This new feature greatly extends the capability of Oracle8 replication to precisely define the appropriate rows to be included in a simple snapshot. Consider, for instance, a snapshot site that is designed to keep only information about West area consultants and their timecards. No column in the CONSULTANT table or the ACTIVITY table provides the area. This information is maintained in the ORGANIZATIONS table, based on the consultant's ORG_ID. In Oracle7 it would be necessary to either denormalize both the CONSULTANT and ACTIVITY tables at the master site, to include this additional data or to use a complex snapshot based on a view that joins these tables to ORGANIZATIONS.

In Oracle8, it is possible to code the query using a subquery to help filter the necessary rows using filters defined in a parent table. In the following example, three snapshot logs are created on the tables in the master database. Two snapshots with subqueries are then defined in a remote west area data mart.

```
CREATE SNAPSHOT LOG ON organizations WITH PRIMARY KEY (area);
CREATE SNAPSHOT LOG ON consultants WITH PRIMARY KEY;
CREATE SNAPSHOT LOG ON activity WITH PRIMARY KEY;
```

```
CREATE SNAPSHOT west_area_consultants
        REFRESH FAST WITH PRIMARY KEY
        AS
        SELECT * FROM consultants@dw_master c
         WHERE EXISTS
                (SELECT o.org_id
                   FROM organizations@dw_master o
                 WHERE c.org_id = o.org_id
                   AND o.area = 'West');

CREATE SNAPSHOT west_area_activity
        REFRESH FAST WITH PRIMARY KEY
        AS
        SELECT * FROM activity@dw_master a
         WHERE EXISTS
                (SELECT c.employee_id
                   FROM consultants@dw_master c
                 WHERE EXISTS
                        (SELECT o.org_id
                           FROM organizations@dw_master o
                         WHERE c.org_id = o.org_id
                           AND o.area = 'West')
                 AND a.employee_id = c.employee_id);
```

There are many restrictions on the use of subqueries in defining simple snapshots. These are documented in the *Oracle8i Server Replication* manual.

Basic snapshots allow for only query access at the remote site. All changes to the data must be made at the base site on which the snapshots are defined. This limitation is not generally a problem with data warehouse replication but sometimes is inappropriate for certain OLTP requirements. Allowing for data modifications in multiple distributed databases requires more advanced replication facilities.

Advanced Replication

Oracle7, release 7.1, provided new replication facilities that have been carried forward into each subsequent release. *Advanced Replication,* or symmetric replication as it was originally titled, allows for updateable simple snapshots so that DML activity at any of the snapshot sites can be replicated back to the master database site. Multiple master sites can also be defined in which each site serves an equal partner in owning the replicated objects.

Oracle Advanced Replication further allows the combination of these facilities so that snapshots, both read-only and updateable, can be defined based on any of the masters in a multimaster configuration. Because data changes can occur to the same data at multiple sites, Advanced Replication introduces the possibility of conflicts. A conflict might occur when two users, at different sites, each make a change to copies of the same data row. One might delete the row while the other updates a column. Advanced Replication provides conflict detection features to identify such a conflict. The person implementing replication then has to define an appropriate conflict resolution strategy.

TIP Snapshot replication in Oracle7 is maintained based on the ROWID of each row in the master site. This capability is maintained in Oracle8, but an improved method based on the primary key values of the table data has been added. Primary key snapshots require the master table to have a primary key constraint. To facilitate migration, an Oracle8 master can support both primary key and ROWID snapshots. Unless data needs to be replicated between an Oracle7 and an Oracle8 or Oracle8*i* database, it is recommended that the newer primary key method be used in pure Oracle8 replication environments.

Such configurations with multiple masters and many snapshots can become very complex to administer. The Oracle8 Replication Manager is used to help the administrator control the distributed environment and maintain the replication catalogs maintained at each participating site.

One final capability of replication that may have merit within a distributed data warehouse environment is to automatically maintain two identical copies of the warehouse for performance and throughput by supporting twice as many users. Using replication in this way has another advantage, in that it also provides a backup site for continued availability in case of a server crash or other outage that would prevent access to a single warehouse database. This should not be considered a complete disaster recovery solution, but it can increase warehouse availability. It is probably not possible to replicate all detail data in this manner, but keeping copies of all summary tables may be feasible.

NOTE Using replication to maintain a backup site contrasts to the Oracle standby database feature (introduced in release 7.3) that maintains a complete remote copy of a database by constantly applying redo log files from the primary database to the backup database, which is kept in recovery mode. The replicated site can be accessed and queried by users whereas the standby database allows only very restricted access unless the primary database is lost.

Because of the nature of data warehouse processing, there are limited opportunities or requirements to utilize Advanced Replication to propagate changes within the warehouse environment. Because most activity is read-only, basic replication of some tables between databases is generally sufficient.

The other problem with both basic and advanced replication features in the data warehouse environment is based on data volume limitations. The commonly accepted rule of thumb for Oracle7 replication has been to expect propagation of no more than 20 or so rows per second in any single replication group. Major rewriting of replication code in Oracle8 and Oracle8*i* provides for significantly higher throughput, but extremely high propagation rates of many hundreds of rows per second should not be depended on without adequate testing.

Another facility, however, exists within the Oracle Advanced Replication facility, which is designed to handle certain large volume operations within the distributed warehouse. Procedural replication allows for a remote procedure call (RPC) to a PL/SQL stored procedure on a different database. If your warehouse has a monthly purge procedure that is expected to delete a very large number of rows, row-based replication would require a very large number of individual rows to be deleted in each data mart. Network performance of this operation would likely be unsatisfactory. By avoiding the normal replication of row deletes and then defining a packaged procedure to issue the same delete statement at each site, the warehouse can propagate a single call to each data mart. Procedural replication will ensure that the procedure is completed at each site. Consider using procedural replication whenever a single large set operation can be defined that will perform the needed maintenance at each site based on a general WHERE clause condition rather than individual primary key (or ROWID) values. Note, however, that Advanced Replication's normal row-level conflict detection is disabled for these RPCs, so care must be taken to ensure correct handling of any possible conflicts.

One final replication feature, which is new to Oracle8, is the ability to propagate changes from one database to another in parallel. Parallel propagation uses the same query slaves mechanism as Oracle Parallel Execution (as described in Chapter 10, "Parallel Execution in the Oracle Data Warehouse"). Unfortunately, this feature is incorporated into the Advanced Replication facility and does not support refreshes of individual simple snapshots.

Tablespace Replication with Oracle8i TTS

With the introduction of the new Oracle8*i* feature of *transportable tablespaces*, a new wrinkle in the replication of masses of data becomes feasible.

Instead of replicating large volumes of data, row by row or transaction by transaction, data can now be copied from one Oracle8*i* database to another Oracle8*i* database by copying the entire data files making up the tablespace.

For data warehouses, this can be especially useful, presenting new options in extracting data from source operational databases or in moving data from data warehouses to data marts.

When copying a tablespace from one database to another, both databases must be versions of Oracle8*i* or later. Additionally, both databases must be based on the same hardware platform and both must be based on the same version of the operating system.

The technique of transportable tablespaces has been discussed previously in the chapters on designing, loading, and transforming data. The specific checklist for copying a tablespace from one database to another follows:

1. Verify that the tablespace(s) in the *transport set* to be copied do not violate any of the restrictions imposed by your current version of Oracle. The procedure TRANSPORT_SET_CHECK in the package DBMS_TTS populates the data dictionary view TRANSPORT_SET_VIOLATIONS.

2. Resolve all violations shown in the view, then repeat Step 1 until no more violations are detected.

3. Set all of the tablespaces in the transport set to READ ONLY using the ALTER TABLESPACE command.

4. Export the data dictionary contents pertaining to the tablespace(s) in the transport set using the command documented in the *Oracle8i Server Utilities* manual:

```
EXP TRANSPORT_TABLESPACE=Y TABLESPACES=ts-list...
```

5. Using operating system file-copy commands, copy the data files in the transport set to the locations allocated for them in the destination database.

6. Import the data dictionary contents pertaining to the transport set using the command documented in the *Oracle8i Server Utilities* manual:

```
IMP TRANSPORT_TABLESPACE=Y TABLESPACES=ts-list DATAFILES=file-list...
```

7. Reset the tablespace(s) in the transport set back to READ WRITE in either the source or the destination databases, as desired.

As you can see, replicating data in this manner is not at all *transparent* in the manner that transactional replication is. While the data magically appears and can be published in the destination database, it must (temporarily) be put into READ ONLY on the source database. Also, the process of resolving the issues detected by the DBMS_TTS packaged procedures might cause temporary invalidation or other temporary losses of service.

But for situations where large volumes of data need to be copied from one database to another, and some temporary downtime is permitted, there is no faster method.

If neither the Oracle Advanced Replication product nor the ability to copy tablespaces meets your needs, then you may need to consider designing and building your own replication mechanisms.

"Roll Your Own" Replication with Triggers

Before symmetric (or advanced) replication was introduced in release 7.1, we had occasional application requirements to keep two updateable copies of data in different databases. Database triggers can be used to perform synchronous replication as part of the transaction that changes data. The row-level trigger is written to immediately propagate the equivalent row modification to the remote database. Synchronous replication has the disadvantages of decreased availability and performance. Availability is reduced; a failure of either server, database, or their network connection prevents the transaction from completing. Performance is diminished because of the additional work required to perform distributed transactions and the requisite two-phased commit.

Database triggers can also be used to develop your own primary key-style asynchronous replication. The database trigger is written to insert a row into a separately defined "to-do list" table every time a row is inserted, updated, or deleted in the base table. This "to-do list" tracks the primary key and type of action performed. A user-written process is scheduled to periodically read from the to-do list, perform the required action in the remote database, and then delete the row from the to-do list. The entire transaction is then committed using the two-phased commit protocol. This approach is very similar to the Oracle8 design. The only reasons to consider building your own asynchronous replication facility in this manner would be to implement primary key replication in Oracle7. Because this is all custom code that has to be developed, tested, and maintained, there would have to be an extremely strong reason for going this route!

Optimizing PL/SQL Performance across Database Links

If the decision is made to write custom code to perform transactional replication, there are some newer features of PL/SQL in Oracle8*i* that should be considered, in order to optimize performance. Using these new features in conjunction with some little-used features of Oracle7 can lead to dramatic performance gains in replication that is fully transactional. That is, bulk masses of data can be swiftly replicated with full COMMIT and ROLLBACK functionality.

The older feature of Oracle7 that comes in handy is the ability to pass large amounts of data across database links by passing PL/SQL tables into stored procedures. Most programmers regard parameters in PL/SQL as single-value, scalar data types. But, PL/SQL tables can also be defined and passed across the database link in far smaller numbers of network operations. In some environments where the network is a particularly slow LAN or WAN, this can lead to unbelievable efficiencies.

The first issue is to use PL/SQL packages (instead of standalone stored procedures) while programming. PL/SQL packages provide an important element in defining the necessary data types to accomplish this task. It is not necessary to use packages on both the *local* and *remote* databases, but it is necessary that a package be defined on the *remote* database.

Next, on the *remote* database, define PL/SQL table *types* for all of the PL/SQL parameters that will be passed from the *local* packaged procedure to the *remote* packaged procedure, as follows:

```
create table test_table
(
    col1   number        not null
);

create or replace package test_remote_pkg
is
    type NumTab is table of number;
    procedure one_at_a_time(in_nbr in number);
    procedure use_the_array(a_nbr in NumTab,
                            n_cnt in number);
end test_remote_pkg;
/
show errors

create or replace package body test_remote_pkg
is
    procedure one_at_a_time(in_nbr in number)
    as
    begin
        insert into test_table
        values(in_nbr);
    end one_at_a_time;
    --
    procedure use_the_array(a_nbr in NumTab,
                            n_cnt in number)
    as
    begin
        forall I in 1..n_cnt loop
            insert into test_table
            values(a_nbr(i));
    end use_the_array;
end test_remote_pkg;
/
show errors
```

Please note how the USE_THE_ARRAY procedure uses the new FORALL syntax, which does a *bulk bind* of the encapsulated INSERT statement. By performing N_CNT number of distinct INSERT operations, the FORALL syntax binds all of the data values at once and performs a single mass INSERT operation.

Now, on the *local* database, you can create a package like the following:

```
create or replace package test_local_pkg
is
    procedure one_at_a_time;
    procedure use_the_array;
end test_local_pkg;
/
show errors

create or replace package body test_local_pkg
is
    procedure one_at_a_time
    as
        i          binary_integer := 1;
    begin
        for i in 1..1000 loop
            test_remote_pkg.one_at_a_time@Remote(i);
        end loop;
    end one_at_a_time;
    —
    procedure use_the_array
    as
        arr        test_remote_pkg.NumTab@Remote;
        i          binary_integer := 1;
    begin
        for i in 1..1000 loop
            arr(i)  := i;
        end loop;
        test_remote_pkg.use_the_array@Remote(arr, i);
    end use_the_array;
end test_local_pkg;
/
show errors
```

Please note how the PL/SQL table in the *local* package was declared. It references the type declared within the remote package. This is very important; this whole scheme of passing PL/SQL tables as parameters fails without that small detail!

Also, this is a very simplified test case; it generates its own data and there is no error handling. The new bulk bind operations in PL/SQL will allow you to roll back either individual failed operations or the entire bulk bind operation; it depends only on how you code the error handling. In this case, with no explicit error handling coded, using the defaults, the entire bulk bind operation would fail and need to be rolled back.

Testing this simple code example over a slow network can be mind-boggling. To fully appreciate the differences, query the view V$SESSION_EVENT after each test, and notice that the difference in the TOTAL_WAITS and TIME_WAITED columns will be dramatic, especially with the reduction in the "SQL*Net message to db link" and "SQL*Net message from db link" wait events.

For the test case previously coded, the procedure ONE_AT_A_TIME will generate a thousand of each of the "SQL*Net message . . ." wait events. By contrast, the USE_THE_ARRAY procedure will generate only one of each wait event, along with a small number of additional "SQL*Net more data to db link." These additional wait events indicate the need for Net8 *continuation packets* because the entire PL/SQL table probably would not fit into a single network packet.

Even the "SQL*Net more data to db link" messages can be reduced by increasing the size of the *session data unit* or SDU in the Net8 TNS description. Consult the *Net8 Administrator's Guide* for more information on setting the SDU. Please note, however, that modifying the SDU will generate only very slight performance improvements beyond that already achieved by the use of PL/SQL table parameters and PL/SQL bulk bind operations, and modifying the SDU might possibly cause other performance problems. Test changing the SDU carefully and completely, to monitor its complete impact.

Alternative Distributed Architectures

The distributed database features of Oracle8*i* can be used in a variety of ways within an Oracle data warehouse environment. The remainder of this chapter looks at these distributed warehouse design alternatives.

Oracle8*i* provides multiple alternatives for developing a data warehouse in configurations other than a single database. Some of these alternatives are, however, more reasonable than others. We discuss each of them in the following sections.

Data Marts

It is a tempting euphemism for warehouse developers (and warehouse product vendors) to justify laziness or sloppiness by invoking the mantra of "distributed" and "data mart." The term *data mart* is, unfortunately, misused in many cases where what is actually being created is a series of disjointed data warehouses. Figure 12.9 portrays this dangerous situation.

Each of what might (incorrectly) be called data marts in Figure 12.9 is really an independent data warehouse. As such, there is no coordination in the identification of source systems or in the extract, reformatting, and summarization processing. Each of the warehouses has some data that overlaps the data in the others, but none of them is consistent with the others. Developing independent data warehouses in this uncoordinated manner should be avoided. The end result will frustrate users who obtain conflicting answers and will undermine any possible success of the data warehousing effort.

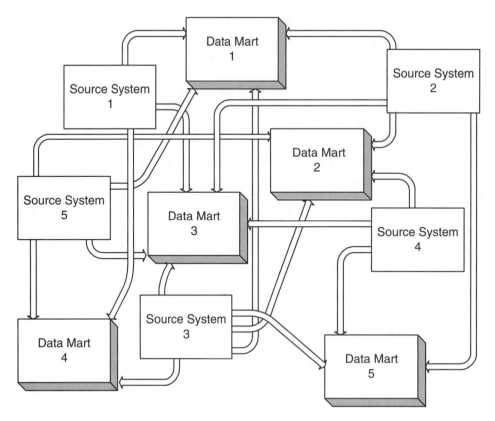

Figure 12.9 Improper data mart design.

A data mart is not just a small, independent data warehouse—avoid the temptation to build small data warehouses without an overall integrated design! Remember the analogy of a warehouse that distributes products to various retail outlets. This is the model to follow in creating your data mart strategy.

A proper data mart design, as illustrated in Figure 12.10, shows data from various sources being integrated into a centralized warehouse. The integrated data then flows from the data warehouse to the various data marts. This approach provides the true benefits of local data marts without forfeiting control. The proper data mart approach takes as much work as building the single centralized data warehouse (even a bit more). Any attempt to circumvent that necessary work by throwing together a handful of quick and dirty mini-warehouses will inevitably lead to the chaos of Figure 12.9.

The data marts shown in Figure 12.10 can be maintained by using the Oracle RDBMS or alternatively by using an Express Server. Using the Oracle Express Server as the manager of a data mart is covered in the next chapter.

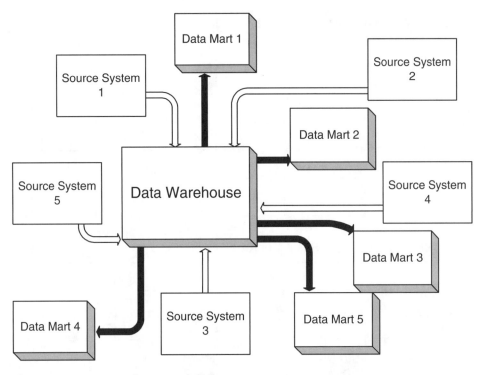

Figure 12.10 Proper data mart design.

Distributed Data Warehouse

A single data warehouse need not be housed entirely within a single Oracle database. A single logical database design may be physically distributed. This physical distribution of a single logical model requires careful analysis in order to avoid a chaotic mess like that shown in Figure 12.9. It is not acceptable to simply create separate data warehouses for different departments as a means of avoiding the tough analysis and design necessary to create the unified data model. The data warehouse can, theoretically, be distributed in three ways: We can separate objects from subject areas, or we can partition specific objects, either horizontally or vertically. Only the first two of these three options are likely to be used in data warehousing with current technology.

Distributing Warehouse Subject Areas

When there is a clear line of demarcation between certain subject areas and when we can be sure that very few (or no) queries will want to access tables from more than one subject area, then the two subject area's tables can be placed in separate

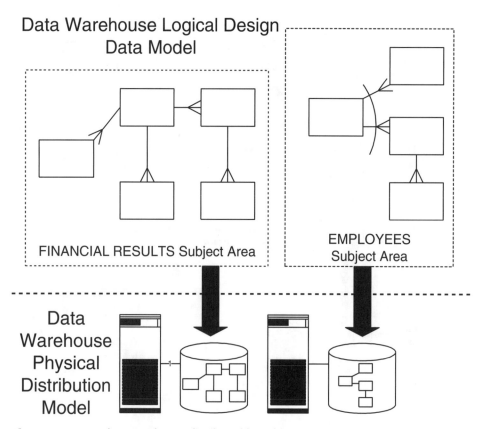

Figure 12.11   A data warehouse distributed by subject area.

databases. Figure 12.11 illustrates the separation of two subject areas in the data model that have no anticipated intersection.

Extreme care must be exercised to ensure that data that is likely to be needed together is stored in the same physical database. Although Oracle is able to distribute a query to more than one database, a performance penalty is incurred whenever joins (or subqueries) are forced to operate over the network. This performance penalty has been greatly reduced with the improvements in the Oracle cost-based optimizer introduced in each successive release of Oracle7, Oracle8, and now, Oracle8*i*.

Distributing the warehouse as a first deployment strategy leads to a risk of slipping into the easy (read "lazy") approach of "wishing" that two areas be completely separable when more careful analysis or experience would indicate that they are not. While the warehouse is small, there are probably no hardware limitations that force the issue of distribution. This type of distribution may be a better direction after the organization has gone through several iterations of data warehouse rollout. Consider migrating to this approach as the warehouse grows and requires either a major hardware upgrade or a second server. Delaying the distribution action while doing the initial analysis and logical design will help enforce the necessary discipline for a successful design.

This approach of distributing the data warehouse later in its life is facilitated by the recommendation made in Chapter 4, "Designing the Oracle Data Warehouse," to place each subject area into its own schema during physical design. If you have initially separated the subject areas in this way, you will have an easier time physically separating them to multiple databases later.

By using roles to control user access to the various subject areas (as recommended in Chapter 8, "Administering and Monitoring the Oracle Data Warehouse") it will be easy to verify whether users accessing one subject area are or are not also accessing the other. In the example of Figure 12.11 we expect that financial analysts should have roles that permit them to query various subject areas of a financial nature. The analysts in the human relations group are probably working only with roles that allow them to see data relating to the EMPLOYEES subject area. If we discover a group of users who have requested both roles, then they need to be questioned to determine how they see the data—are they using the tables of the different subject areas completely separately, or have they found some unexpected connection in the data?

Distributing Dimensions for a Single Logical View

One common problem encountered when distributing a data warehouse is the issue of dimensions—dimension table definitions in particular. With multiple databases, especially when they are not replicated, it is easy to have different dimension tables on each database.

This can be disastrous for user friendliness, especially if the end users are accessing the databases using *relational online analytical processing*, or ROLAP, utilities. Many of these utilities require the use of dimension tables in the underlying database in order to generate SQL queries. Many of the generated SQL queries will take the form of a *star query*, with one or more dimensions being joined to a fact table.

If the dimension tables are not defined to a common format across all of the distributed databases, then it would be necessary for end users using OLAP utilities to define a new set of definitions for each database. This can be quite an onerous task, and nobody is thankful for having to repeat it, especially if the differences are minor. This is especially true for ROLAP utilities, which generate SQL statements against the data warehouse or data mart databases directly.

Thus, it is highly recommended to define a single set of dimension tables to be used across all decision support systems, then make use of Oracle replication

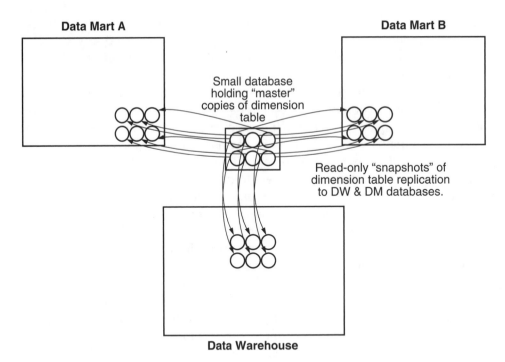

Figure 12.12 Replicating dimension tables.

(i.e., *materialized views*, also known as *snapshots*) to distribute this single logical view across many physical databases, as illustrated in Figure 12.12.

Besides saving time and effort and avoiding confusion on the part of end users, replicating a single logical set of dimension tables also enforces unity among distributed decision support databases. As discussed in the chapter on data warehouse design, there can be two primary ways to implement a data warehouse:

- Build an enterprise-wide data warehouse first and then distribute subject-area specific data marts afterward, an approach that guarantees architectural coherency but can impose deadly design and implementation delays

- Build one or more subject-area specific data marts first, then coalesce them into an enterprise-wide data warehouse afterward, an approach that can optimize rapid *return on investment* (ROI) but jeopardize a coherent architecture by fragmenting decision support data

If the latter approach is chosen, then the task of later coalescing the multiple data marts into a larger, coherent data warehouse can be made easier by using a single logical set of dimensions replicated across the databases.

Horizontal Partitioning of Data Warehouse Objects

Partitioning refers to the dividing of a single object into multiple objects. Horizontally partitioned tables have the same logical design of columns, but rows are placed into one of the partitions based on some specific criteria. The new partitioned tables (and indexes) in Oracle8 are horizontally partitioned. Each partition has an identical table layout but contains a different subset of the total table's rows. Oracle8 allows the different partitions of a partitioned object to be placed in different tablespaces of a database. In some future release of Oracle there may be an enhancement of the distributed capabilities to include distributed support for partitions, but in the current release the partitions must remain in the same physical database.

True horizontal partitioning, such as the partitioning of Oracle8, ensures that the rows entered into a partitioned table are unique and no duplicates can "sneak" into different partitions. (In the case of vertical partitions, the DBMS would ensure that a matching row piece would occur in every partition. A single INSERT or DELETE statement would operate on all vertical partitions at the same time.) Of course, in the data warehouse we frequently relax the normal OLTP constraint requirements, and we may also choose to distribute parts of a logical table without insisting that the database enforce all the strict rules of a distributed database.

If the warehouse designer has a valid reason to do so he may manually "partition" by creating separate tables (with the same column layout) in separate databases. Oracle7 and Oracle8 will treat these as completely separate objects, and any rules for which rows are placed into which table will be entirely the responsibility of the programmers building the extract and load processes. Duplicated rows in different partitions will not be automatically prevented by an Oracle primary key constraint. An example of partitioning by division in our case study warehouse is illustrated in Figure 12.13. In this case there is a "clone" of each table in each database. Some dimension tables, such as FISCAL_PERIOD and FUNCTION_CODE are likely to contain the same data in each database. Others, such as ORGANIZATION, PROJECT, and CONSULTANT, along with the ACTIVITY fact tables, can be expected to contain only the rows that pertain to the specific division being stored.

A decision to separate our European Division warehouse data from our Asia-Pacific Division and North American Division data is not one to be entered into lightly. The ability of each division to work with its own data may be enhanced by having the data physically closer to its divisional headquarters and by having a smaller collection of data to process. For a company with totally autonomous operations this might be an overwhelming advantage. By taking this approach, though, we have surrendered an easy way to do comparisons of operations

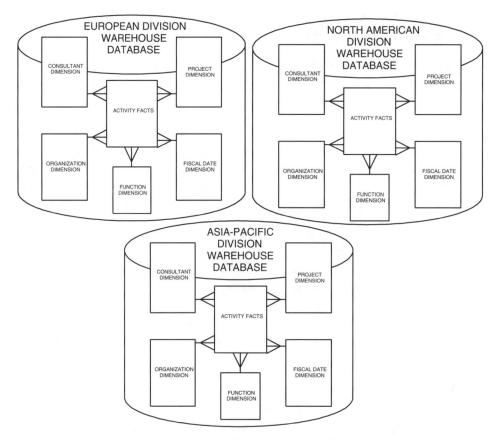

Figure 12.13 A horizontally partitioned data warehouse table.

across the divisions. This might be an important type of query for an operations analyst in worldwide headquarters to perform.

Oracle can allow a single query to access the data in the three physical databases, but there will be a severe performance penalty if large amounts of data from one database need to be retrieved to another database to complete the query. A SELECT . . . GROUP BY, for instance, on any dimension other than organization will have to retrieve data from two remote databases and then sort it in the database instance where the user is connected.

Vertical Partitioning of Data Warehouse Objects

Less common than separating entire subject areas or horizontal partitioning of logical tables is the possibility of partitioning a table vertically. Vertical partitioning refers to the division of a logical table based on one subset of columns being stored in one physical table and other columns being stored in a separate table.

NOTE Vertical partitioning is not directly supported by either Oracle7 or Oracle8, although a foreign key constraint and two identically defined primary keys can provide most of the required support for vertical partitioning within a single database. Database triggers are needed to automatically support any partitioning across distributed databases. The performance impacts of this approach make it infeasible for most warehouse tables.

Vertical Partitioning in OLTP Systems

Vertical partitioning is sometimes used to improve the performance and storage efficiency within an OLTP application when a large amount of data potentially needs to be stored for a particular entity, but only a small portion of the total attributes are commonly needed for online update.

Figure 12.14 shows a table that has been partitioned vertically in order to separate a LONG column from the rest of the table's data. By separating the infrequently used LONG data from the other columns that are used regularly, the designer provides for more rows of data to be stored in each block of the primary table, and thus reduces the possibility of chaining rows across multiple blocks. The LONG data is stored in a table that has different storage parameters defined and in which possible chaining may be isolated and better controlled.

While each consultant's resume might well be "normalized" into the same logical table as the rest of the data about consultants, it isn't required in the operational timecard system. The resume data is used infrequently to aid in staffing projects but is not used by the various online TEAM system's screens or by the billing system. The designer chose to vertically partition the CONSULTANTS table so the resume data wouldn't slow down OLTP access to the other data.

The designer might have chosen to further separate the resume data by storing it in a completely separate database. If the two tables are not stored in the same database, then it is impossible to define the foreign key constraint, as shown in Figure 12.14. Maintaining this referential integrity rule across multiple databases would require creating database triggers. Most OLTP systems designers would attempt to avoid enforcing referential integrity across multiple databases for both performance and availability issues.

Vertical Partitioning in the Data Warehouse

Vertical partitioning data in the data warehouse environment is even less common than in OLTP systems. The primary objective in the warehouse is not to perform online access and updates. Making data accessible in a useful and convenient format is more critical. Because vertical partitioning is not widely used

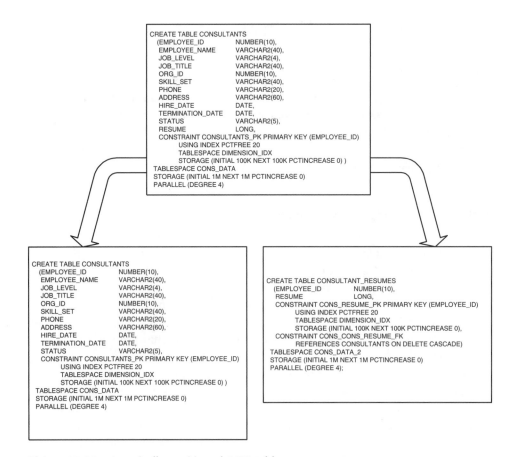

```
CREATE TABLE CONSULTANTS
     (EMPLOYEE_ID           NUMBER(10),
     EMPLOYEE_NAME          VARCHAR2(40),
     JOB_LEVEL              VARCHAR2(4),
     JOB_TITLE              VARCHAR2(40),
     ORG_ID                 NUMBER(10),
     SKILL_SET              VARCHAR2(40),
     PHONE                  VARCHAR2(20),
     ADDRESS                VARCHAR2(60),
     HIRE_DATE              DATE,
     TERMINATION_DATE       DATE,
     STATUS                 VARCHAR2(5),
     RESUME                 LONG,
     CONSTRAINT CONSULTANTS_PK PRIMARY KEY (EMPLOYEE_ID)
          USING INDEX PCTFREE 20
          TABLESPACE DIMENSION_IDX
          STORAGE (INITIAL 100K NEXT 100K PCTINCREASE 0) )
TABLESPACE CONS_DATA
STORAGE (INITIAL 1M NEXT 1M PCTINCREASE 0)
PARALLEL (DEGREE 4)
```

```
CREATE TABLE CONSULTANTS
     (EMPLOYEE_ID           NUMBER(10),
     EMPLOYEE_NAME          VARCHAR2(40),
     JOB_LEVEL              VARCHAR2(4),
     JOB_TITLE              VARCHAR2(40),
     ORG_ID                 NUMBER(10),
     SKILL_SET              VARCHAR2(40),
     PHONE                  VARCHAR2(20),
     ADDRESS                VARCHAR2(60),
     HIRE_DATE              DATE,
     TERMINATION_DATE       DATE,
     STATUS                 VARCHAR2(5),
     CONSTRAINT CONSULTANTS_PK PRIMARY KEY (EMPLOYEE_ID)
          USING INDEX PCTFREE 20
          TABLESPACE DIMENSION_IDX
          STORAGE (INITIAL 100K NEXT 100K PCTINCREASE 0) )
TABLESPACE CONS_DATA
STORAGE (INITIAL 1M NEXT 1M PCTINCREASE 0)
PARALLEL (DEGREE 4)
```

```
CREATE TABLE CONSULTANT_RESUMES
     (EMPLOYEE_ID           NUMBER(10),
     RESUME                 LONG,
     CONSTRAINT CONS_RESUME_PK PRIMARY KEY (EMPLOYEE_ID)
          USING INDEX PCTFREE 20
          TABLESPACE DIMENSION_IDX
          STORAGE (INITIAL 100K NEXT 100K PCTINCREASE 0),
     CONSTRAINT CONS_CONS_RESUME_FK
          REFERENCES CONSULTANTS ON DELETE CASCADE)
TABLESPACE CONS_DATA_2
STORAGE (INITIAL 1M NEXT 1M PCTINCREASE 0)
PARALLEL (DEGREE 4);
```

Figure 12.14 A vertically partitioned OLTP table.

in data warehousing, we will have to stretch a somewhat artificial example to demonstrate the concept. We will close this section with an example of partitioning across data marts that has more practical value.

Warehouse design sometimes leads to a denormalized structure in which a time series of data is stored within a single row. An example might be a summarization of consultants' monthly utilization that includes a separate column for each month. Storing the data in this manner may enhance certain types of analysis. Figure 12.15 illustrates such a denormalization, which includes three years' utilization data for each consultant. In this example, we would create a monthly summarization job that would update each row to populate the utilization column for the most recent month and calculate the appropriate quarterly and annual utilization columns.

The simple denormalization adopted in Figure 12.15 leads us to make another design decision, however. Once we decide to store multiple months'

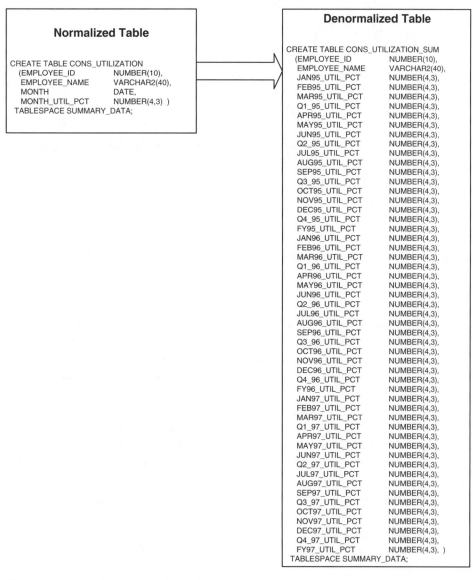

Figure 12.15 A denormalized warehouse table.

values in the utilization table, we have to determine how many months of data should be included. If we were expected to retain summarization data for 5 years we would require 60 monthly columns, 20 quarterly columns, and 5 annual columns. Ten years would therefore require a total of 165 columns.

We have to consider how, with this design, we'll handle the rolling window of the data to be kept. We can't easily drop the initial 17 columns (12 months, 4

Partitioned Denormalized Table #1	Partitioned Denormalized Table #2	Partitioned Denormalized Table #3
CREATE TABLE CONS_UTILIZATION_95_SUM (EMPLOYEE_ID NUMBER(10), EMPLOYEE_NAME VARCHAR2(40), JAN_UTIL_PCT NUMBER(4,3), FEB_UTIL_PCT NUMBER(4,3), MAR_UTIL_PCT NUMBER(4,3), Q1_UTIL_PCT NUMBER(4,3), APR_UTIL_PCT NUMBER(4,3), MAY_UTIL_PCT NUMBER(4,3), JUN_UTIL_PCT NUMBER(4,3), Q2_UTIL_PCT NUMBER(4,3), JUL_UTIL_PCT NUMBER(4,3), AUG_UTIL_PCT NUMBER(4,3), SEP_UTIL_PCT NUMBER(4,3), Q3_UTIL_PCT NUMBER(4,3), OCT_UTIL_PCT NUMBER(4,3), NOV_UTIL_PCT NUMBER(4,3), DEC_UTIL_PCT NUMBER(4,3), Q4_UTIL_PCT NUMBER(4,3), FY_UTIL_PCT NUMBER(4,3)) TABLESPACE SUMMARY_DATA;	CREATE TABLE CONS_UTILIZATION_96_SUM (EMPLOYEE_ID NUMBER(10), EMPLOYEE_NAME VARCHAR2(40), JAN_UTIL_PCT NUMBER(4,3), FEB_UTIL_PCT NUMBER(4,3), MAR_UTIL_PCT NUMBER(4,3), Q1_UTIL_PCT NUMBER(4,3), APR_UTIL_PCT NUMBER(4,3), MAY_UTIL_PCT NUMBER(4,3), JUN_UTIL_PCT NUMBER(4,3), Q2_UTIL_PCT NUMBER(4,3), JUL_UTIL_PCT NUMBER(4,3), AUG_UTIL_PCT NUMBER(4,3), SEP_UTIL_PCT NUMBER(4,3), Q3_UTIL_PCT NUMBER(4,3), OCT_UTIL_PCT NUMBER(4,3), NOV_UTIL_PCT NUMBER(4,3), DEC_UTIL_PCT NUMBER(4,3), Q4_UTIL_PCT NUMBER(4,3), FY_UTIL_PCT NUMBER(4,3)) TABLESPACE SUMMARY_DATA;	CREATE TABLE CONS_UTILIZATION_97_SUM (EMPLOYEE_ID NUMBER(10), EMPLOYEE_NAME VARCHAR2(40), JAN_UTIL_PCT NUMBER(4,3), FEB_UTIL_PCT NUMBER(4,3), MAR_UTIL_PCT NUMBER(4,3), Q1_UTIL_PCT NUMBER(4,3), APR_UTIL_PCT NUMBER(4,3), MAY_UTIL_PCT NUMBER(4,3), JUN_UTIL_PCT NUMBER(4,3), Q2_UTIL_PCT NUMBER(4,3), JUL_UTIL_PCT NUMBER(4,3), AUG_UTIL_PCT NUMBER(4,3), SEP_UTIL_PCT NUMBER(4,3), Q3_UTIL_PCT NUMBER(4,3), OCT_UTIL_PCT NUMBER(4,3), NOV_UTIL_PCT NUMBER(4,3), DEC_UTIL_PCT NUMBER(4,3), Q4_UTIL_PCT NUMBER(4,3), FY_UTIL_PCT NUMBER(4,3)) TABLESPACE SUMMARY_DATA;

Figure 12.16 Vertically partitioning the denormalized warehouse table.

quarters, 1 annual). Reusing the same columns within the long list of columns for the new year could easily lead to confusion. A further complication arises when we consider that we have consultants joining and leaving our practice each month. Storing 60 months' history for a consultant who started last month (or who left 3 years ago) is a bit wasteful.

Figure 12.16 takes the denormalized table of Figure 12.15 and partitions the data into separate tables to hold the monthly data from each year. (Note that because of the chosen denormalization to store time-series data, this vertical partitioning scheme actually looks a lot like horizontal partitioning based on year.) With this approach, retention or deletion of particular years' data is simplified, and we waste at most 11 months' storage for a consultant who doesn't remain with us for a full 5 years.

If these partitioned tables were used in different ways or by different users, they could be moved to different warehouse databases. An entire database could be created to house data older than 1996. Assuming that this old data was not needed often, we might choose to house this data on a low-powered server, saving our high-powered server resources for more critical queries on more current data.

This example illustrates the concept of vertical partitioning without demonstrating much practical benefit. As a slightly more practical example, consider a warehouse table that maintains data about customers. Some of the columns store data about our customers' sales history. Perhaps other columns are used to contain information about the history of warranty claims and technical support calls made by each customer account.

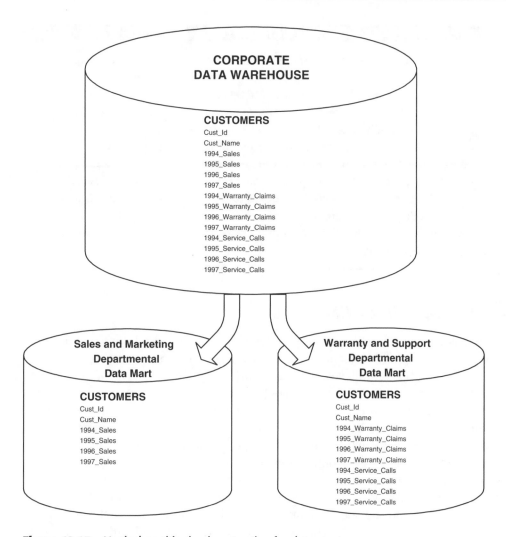

Figure 12.17 Vertical partitioning in extracting for data marts.

If we have decided to create multiple departmental data marts with subsets of the warehouse data, we may find it helpful to vertically subset the table when extracting it to the data marts. Figure 12.17 shows this situation. The data mart in the sales department may include a different subset of data than the data mart created for our warranty and support department. Each user community has quick, local access to the customer information that is of primary interest to the users. Because the data marts are all fed from an integrated warehouse the risk of inconsistent data is greatly reduced. Note that this flavor of vertical partitioning as part of an extract can be implemented using Oracle replication. A different snapshot query would be used to perform each extract.

OTHER ADVANCED REPLICATION FACILITIES

Materialized views, known as *snapshots,* allow changes made to the master database to be automatically copied to one or more databases where they can be seen (but not modified). In addition to this basic read-only replication facility, Oracle7, Oracle8, and Oracle8*i* also provide for more advanced replication capabilities, in which changes can be made in more than one site and replicated to others. These advanced replication facilities are not addressed in this book, because they are not appropriate in the recommended model of a centralized data warehouse that may feed multiple distributed data marts. If the warehouse designer chooses to directly update data marts and then feed changes from them to either other data marts or a centralized warehouse, then further investigation of the advanced replication capabilities would be warranted.

Replicated Data Warehouse

Just as we can choose to distribute pieces of the data warehouse into multiple databases, we may also choose to replicate or copy some warehouse components to multiple databases. For data mart designs that follow the recommendations given earlier for structuring each data mart as an extract from a centralized data warehouse, replication is a valuable and useful tool. Entire summary tables may be replicated from the warehouse to a data mart. Alternatively, the designers may choose to incorporate horizontal or vertical partitioning into the replication scheme, and copy just a subset of table data into each distinct data mart.

Oracle's replication facilities allow for easy declaration of objects that need to be copied and the schedule under which they should be synchronized. For replicating summary tables (or subsets, as shown in Figure 12.18) from the centralized data warehouse to data marts, the designer may choose to use the snapshot feature of Oracle7 or Oracle8, which is now known as *materialized views* in Oracle8*i*. Please see Chapter 7 for a more complete discussion of *materialized views* for the purpose of maintaining *summary tables*. This approach would involve creating read-only snapshots at each data mart for each table that is to be copied, in total or in part, from the data warehouse.

NOTE *Materialized views* (also known as *snapshots*) are a major part of Oracle8's replication features and are documented in the Oracle8*i Server Replication* manual. The Replication Manager tool is provided to aid the administrator in managing the replication environment. Unfortunately, this tool is not yet described in these manuals. Review the text files that are supplied with Replication Manager for documentation.

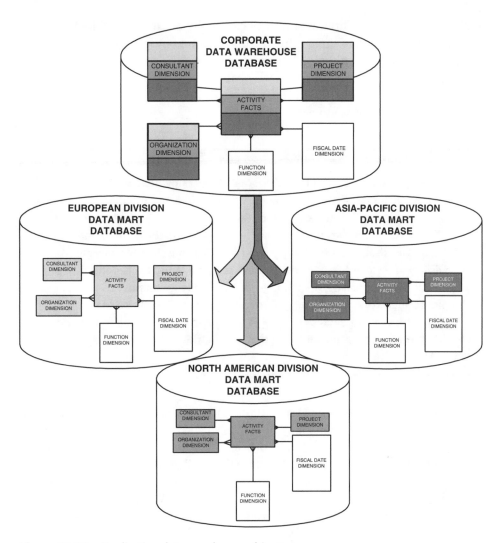

Figure 12.18 Replicating data warehouse objects.

The snapshot creation process involves defining a query that will be used to refresh the snapshot. The refresh may be performed automatically by the replication facility based on a time schedule defined at the time the snapshot is created. Alternatively, the refresh process may be executed manually by the administrator. In the data mart and data warehouse environment there may be good reasons to choose to ignore the automatic refresh capability. The administrator will want to ensure that the data mart snapshots are not performed until after the warehouse summary tables have been completely updated, or rebuilt and then validated. Because the automatic refresh capability is based on a time schedule and our regular warehouse loads and summarization processes may have varying execution times (or may occasionally not even complete), we will want to prevent the data mart refresh from starting before the warehouse processing is done. We would also like to avoid scheduling our data mart refresh based on a "worst case" schedule—we probably don't want to regularly waste hours or even days updating our data marts only to allow for occasional processing delays in the warehouse.

SNAPSHOT GROUPS

It is possible to maintain and refresh snapshots as individual objects. It is recommended, however, that they be included in snapshot groups and refreshed as a group. For the data mart, this is particularly important to ensure that all related data in various summary tables gets updated simultaneously. If individual snapshots are individually refreshed, it is possible for one query to get a different answer than a second query issued against a different level of summarization. Refreshing snapshot groups with a large number of tables containing large volumes of changed rows will require the entire snapshot refresh process to be handled as a single large transaction. The administrator should be prepared for this and assign an appropriately large rollback segment to this transaction.

A better alternative to using Oracle replication's normal automatic time-based refresh of data mart snapshots may be to trigger the refreshes based on completion of the final step in the warehouse processing. A manual refresh is invoked by calling the DBMS_MVIEW.REFRESH or DBMS_SNAPSHOT.REFRESH procedure. This causes all the snapshots in a refresh group to be refreshed together, maintaining consistency across the various snapshots. Where possible, all snapshots related to a particular subject area should be included in a single refresh group.

PACKAGES DBMS_MVIEW AND DBMS_SNAPSHOT

The package DBMS_MVIEW is implemented merely as a public synonym to the DBMS_SNAPSHOT package, reflecting the fact that the terms *materialized view* and *snapshot* are simply synonyms for one another.

Snapshot refreshes are based on a pull model—the snapshot site must initiate the query against the master, so this command has to be issued from the data mart where the snapshot is created. Remember, normal Oracle snapshot replication will initiate this pull based on the passage of time. To trigger it based on an event in the warehouse, we have two choices. We can have the data mart poll the warehouse—issue regular queries against the warehouse metadata store to determine whether a particular job has ended. These queries might be issued every 15 minutes starting at the time we expect to be ready, and continuing until we find the successful completion record in our job status metadata table. This approach requires somewhat sophisticated scripting, either with shell script and cron (assuming the data mart is running on a UNIX platform) or with PL/SQL and the DBMS_JOB utilities inside the Oracle database.

DBMS_JOB

DBMS_JOB is one of several utilities built into the Oracle database kernel. It provides a job scheduler function similar to the UNIX cron utility. Oracle snapshots use this facility to automatically invoke refresh jobs at scheduled times. When snapshots were initially introduced in Oracle7, the job queue was created to manage the refresh processes, but not documented for other customer use. Because of its usefulness in various situations other than just refreshing snapshots, the facility was documented and made available for customer use in Oracle7, version 7.2. This utility is documented in *the Oracle8i Supplied Packages* reference manual as well as the *Oracle8i Server Administrator's Guide*.

There's a disadvantage, however, to placing all of these scripts at each remote data mart server. In general, we want to maintain as simple an environment as possible at each data mart. We'd like to perform the majority of our administration from the centralized warehouse. This is partly because of an assumption that the data marts may be located in sites without a regular Oracle administrator. The simpler each site's programming and administration can be made, the more likely it is that the mart will remain functional and available. Another motivation for centralizing our control of the data mart refresh cycles is to provide a simple capability for adding data marts. If our administrator can monitor, administer, and tune all refreshes from one site, then the additional burden of adding another site is minimal. If, on the other hand, he needs to specifically connect to each remote data mart database to verify its status and possibly perform some administration tasks, then each new site will add significant workload for each routine task.

In keeping with this desire for distributed data with centralized control, we have a second way to approach triggering the remote "pulls" of data from the warehouse. Oracle's distributed capabilities provide for execution of remote procedure calls. These RPCs are developed in PL/SQL and allow for execution of a stored procedure on a remote database. In this case, when the centralized warehouse completes the load, summarization, and validation cycle, a remote procedure call is issued to each satellite data mart to invoke the refresh. The centralized job would call the DBMS_MVIEW.REFRESH procedure on each remote database. In this model, all of the scheduling and triggering scripts can be maintained on the centralized warehouse server. (If a customized replication facility were used instead of the standard snapshot facility, then the centralized job would call DBMS_JOB.SUBMIT to request execution of a custom procedure.)

Unfortunately, neither of these two approaches is as simple as using the default snapshot timing mechanism. If, as expected, the central warehouse has occasional processing delays that affect the time when data is ready to be replicated, then it is important to assume manual control of the replication timing.

Summary

There are several potential motivations for creating a distributed database architecture for an organization's data warehouse. Among these are decreased cost, increased availability, and increased performance. Oracle provides several distributed database facilities that allow the warehouse designer to implement a distributed warehouse solution. Among these are database links, synonyms, and views that enable remote and distributed queries. Oracle gateway products allow non-Oracle data to be queried and in some cases updated as if it were managed by Oracle. Oracle's *materialized view* or *snapshot* facility allows for automatic copying of selected data from one database to another. This greatly simplifies the development of data marts as satellites of the central warehouse, and facilitates the important task of presenting a single logical set of dimension tables replicated across many decision-support databases.

These Oracle features allow the designer to adopt any of several styles of distributed warehouse architecture. One of these options is the data mart, in which a subset of the centralized warehouse is copied to a smaller, local database for user access. Another option is a truly distributed data warehouse in which certain subject areas are physically housed in one database, while others are maintained in a separate database. Variations allow for the partitioning of certain objects or for replication of objects (or even subsets of the data in those objects) to more than one database in the distributed warehouse.

Analytical Processing in the Oracle Data Warehouse

BEDEVERE: Quiet! Quiet! There are ways of telling whether she is a witch.

CROWD: Tell us! Tell us!

BEDEVERE: Tell me. What do you do with witches?

CROWD: Burn! Burn them up! Burn!

BEDEVERE: And what do you burn apart from witches?

VILLAGER #1: More witches!

VILLAGER #2: Wood!

BEDEVERE: Exactly! So, why do witches burn?

VILLAGER #3 (*after a long pause, hesitantly*): Be . . . cause they're . . . made of . . . wood?

BEDEVERE: Good! Good! So, how do we tell whether she is made of wood?

VILLAGER #1: Build a bridge out of her.

BEDEVERE: Ah, but can you not also make bridges out of stone?

CROWD: Oh, yeah. He's right. Hmm . . .

Monty Python and the Holy Grail—*Python (Monty) Pictures, Ltd., 1974*

Overview and Agenda

To this point, the main discussion of this book has been to build the data warehouse. But once we have it built, what are some of the things that we can do with this all this *data*, to turn it into *information*?

The most obvious reporting tool is the SQL language itself. Using any of a number of reporting utilities, traditional, ANSI-standard SQL statements can fulfill most of the reporting needs of the enterprise.

Pure ANSI-standard SQL commands, however, have never been sufficient for building real-world, complex applications, whether they are data warehouses or operational systems such as billing or order entry systems. Vendors such as IBM and Oracle have always led the way in implementing new features and extensions to the SQL language. The ANSI standards always lagged behind, providing a *baseline* of ground-floor functionality to which database vendors must adhere. It is the extensions to the SQL language, such as *parallel execution* (discussed in Chapter 10, "Parallel Execution in the Oracle Data Warehouse"), *partitioned tables and indexes* (discussed throughout the book), and the analytical functions (discussed later in this chapter) that really make large, complex database systems possible. If the ability to perform pure ANSI-standard SQL commands were the only criteria, then everybody would use a freeware or shareware package such as *MySQL*.

In this chapter we discuss some options for advanced reporting and analytical processing. To do this, we concentrate on three areas:

- Analytical functions in Oracle SQL
- Browsing and ad hoc reporting
- Online analytical processing (OLAP)

In addition to the standard analytical functions that have been present in the Oracle RDBMS for years (such as SUM, AVG, VARIANCE, STDDEV, etc.), a number of newer and more useful functions have been added in Oracle8*i*. In the first release of Oracle8*i* (versions 8.1.5 and below), the ROLLUP and CUBE extensions to the GROUP BY clause were introduced, allowing subtotals to be generated as part of a single SELECT statement. In the second release of Oracle8*i* (versions 8.1.6 and higher), a whole new family of advanced analytical functions has been introduced, aimed primarily at statistical processing packages such as SAS. We talk about these functions in the first part of this chapter.

In the middle part of this chapter, we focus primarily on a class of tools that is well exemplified by the Oracle *Discoverer* product. Using a remarkably intuitive graphical interface, the Discoverer product enables easy browsing in a spreadsheet-style format, along with the ability to easily publish crafted reports to an intranet or to the Internet. Discoverer also integrates easily with spreadsheets such as Microsoft Excel, giving users who are most comfortable with spreadsheets a familiar interface. The Discoverer product is aimed at the middle-of-the-road of reporting and analytical needs, combining advanced features such as *drill-down* and *summarization* with everyday reporting.

The last (and by far the largest) part of this chapter focuses on the subject of the advanced techniques of *online analytical processing* or OLAP. OLAP products generally address the types of reporting and querying for which the SQL language is simply not well suited, either in terms of getting the job done or in terms of returning results quickly enough to enable *train-of-thought* analysis. OLAP products generally extract information from the data warehouse into a compact, fully indexed data repository sometimes referred to as a *cube*. Every data element in this cube is indexed in multiple ways, greatly speeding access to this information from multiple perspectives. We focus on the Oracle Express online analytical processing product during our discussion.

Analytical Functions in Oracle SQL

In Oracle8*i*, Oracle's variant of the SQL language has been enhanced in several directions. The end result is that more can be done in the database server than ever before, reducing, even possibly eliminating, the need for low-end query tools and laborious programmatic post-processing of data fetched from queries.

For example, prior to Oracle8*i*, retrieving both query details as well as subtotals and grand totals required a reporting utility outside of the server. A SQL statement could retrieve the detailed results, and then the reporting tool, such as SQL*Plus, would total the results separately. Or a PL/SQL stored procedure would fetch the data from a cursor, and the developer would have to laboriously perform the totaling using PL/SQL variables and cursor loop control techniques.

Other, more advanced reporting requirements, such as statistical analysis and linear regression, required large-scale statistical packages such as SAS, layered above Oracle. While there is no inherent problem with this, this method implicitly requires the extraction of potentially massive amounts of data out of Oracle, to be transported and stored in the statistical package's repository. The new statistical analysis functions of Oracle8*i* (release 2) can now perform the same processing as a statistical processing package while eliminating the need to extract, transport, and import the data. At least, the volume of data can be reduced.

ROLLUP Extension to GROUP BY

The ROLLUP function creates subtotals in increasing order of aggregation, all the way to a grand total if all expressions in the GROUP BY clause are being rolled up.

The function is best illustrated by example:

```
SELECT        time, region, dept, SUM(amt) amt
FROM          sales
GROUP BY      time, region, dept;


TIME    REGION    DEPT          AMT
----    -------   -----------   ----------
1998    EAST      VIDEOSALES     75,000.00
1998    EAST      VIDEORENTAL     6,500.00
1998    CENTRAL   VIDEOSALES    111,233.50


3 rows returned.
```

Now, adding the ROLLUP extension to the GROUP BY function causes additional summarization by each of the dimensions:

```
SELECT        time, region, dept, SUM(amt) amt
FROM          sales
GROUP BY      ROLLUP(time, region, dept);


TIME    REGION    DEPT          AMT
----    -------   -----------   ----------
1998    EAST      VIDEOSALES     75,000.00
1998    EAST      VIDEORENTAL     6,500.00
1998    EAST                     81,500.00
1998    CENTRAL   VIDEOSALES    111,233.50
1998    CENTRAL                 111,233.50
1998                            192,733.50
                                192,733.50


7 rows returned.
```

The first two rows are identical to the original unmodified query. But the third row returned is a subtotal of DEPT; please note the NULL value in place of the DEPT column. There really are no NULL values in this column; this is just an artifact of the ROLLUP function. The next row is another detail row, identical to the original query, while the fifth row is another subtotal by DEPT. Now that all three detail rows have been returned, and because the subtotals by DEPT are complete, the final rows are higher totals. The sixth row is a subtotal by REGION as well as department, and the last row is a total by TIME, REGION, and DEPT, which also makes it a grand total.

Has Oracle ever been capable of this kind of combined detailed and summarized data? Of course, if you utilize the UNION clause to paste together multiple queries in go, as follows:

```
SELECT      time, region, dept, SUM(amt) amt
FROM        sales
GROUP BY    time, region, dept
UNION
SELECT      time, region, '', SUM(amt) amt
FROM        sales
GROUP BY    time, region, ''
UNION
SELECT      time, '', '', SUM(amt) amt
FROM        sales
GROUP BY    time, '', ''
UNION
SELECT      '', '', '', SUM(amt) amt
FROM        sales
GROUP BY    '', '', '';
```

This query is the exact functional equivalent to the query using ROLLUP. But notice how verbose and difficult to read this query appears. More importantly, notice how many times the table is scanned. The ROLLUP function, while more concise and easier to read, is also vastly more efficient in that only one pass is made through the table. For extremely large sets of data, this is the difference between feasible and infeasible.

It is not necessary to specify all of the columns (also known as a *full rollup*); *partial rollups* are also possible:

```
SELECT      time, region, dept, SUM(amt) amt
FROM        sales
GROUP BY    time, ROLLUP(region, dept);
```

TIME	REGION	DEPT	AMT
1998	EAST	VIDEOSALES	75,000.00
1998	EAST	VIDEORENTAL	6,500.00
1998	EAST		81,500.00
1998	CENTRAL	VIDEOSALES	111,233.50
1998	CENTRAL		111,233.50
1998			192,733.50

6 rows returned.

In this case, no grand total, or total by all dimensions, is produced. Also, notice that, if N columns are specified inside the ROLLUP function, N + 1 subtotal types are produced.

CUBE Extension to GROUP BY

The CUBE function is closely related to ROLLUP. Where ROLLUP summarizes at increasing levels of aggregation, in a straight line from right to left, CUBE summarizes all possible types of aggregation.

Just like ROLLUP, CUBE is best illustrated with an example. Starting with the same example used above, CUBE totals across every possible combination of dimensions:

```
SELECT      time, region, dept, SUM(amt) amt
FROM        sales
GROUP BY    CUBE(time, region, dept);

TIME    REGION     DEPT          AMT
----    -------    -----------   ----------
1998    EAST       VIDEOSALES     75,000.00
1998    EAST       VIDEORENTAL     6,500.00
1998    EAST                      81,500.00
1998    CENTRAL    VIDEOSALES    111,233.50
1998    CENTRAL                  111,233.50
1998                             192,733.50
1998               VIDEOSALES    186,223.00
1998               VIDEORENTAL     6,500.00
                   VIDEOSALES    186,223.00
                   VIDEORENTAL     6,500.00
                                 192,733.50

11 rows returned.
```

Just as before, there are only three original detailed rows. But, where the ROLLUP function will produce N + 1 subtotal types the CUBE function will produce all possible combinations, or 2**N subtotal types.

Like the ROLLUP function, the CUBE function can either be a *full cube*, incorporating all of the expressions in the GROUP BY clause, or a *partial cube*, incorporating only a subset.

GROUPING Function

One characteristic of the ROLLUP and CUBE functions might already be obvious to you savvy developers. Namely, how do you distinguish between dimensions that have valid NULL values and the NULL values returned as artifacts of the ROLLUP and CUBE functions?

The GROUPING function can provide an indicator to distinguish between actual NULL values and summarization artifacts, returning a value of 0 for the former case and a value of 1 when a subtotal is detected:

```
SELECT          time, region, dept, SUM(amt) amt,
                GROUPING(time) t,
                GROUPING(region) r,
                GROUPING(dept) d
FROM            sales
GROUP BY        CUBE(time, region, dept);
```

TIME	REGION	DEPT	AMT	T	R	D
1998	EAST	VIDEOSALES	75,000.00	0	0	0
1998	EAST	VIDEORENTAL	6,500.00	0	0	0
1998	EAST		81,500.00	0	0	1
1998	CENTRAL	VIDEOSALES	111,233.50	0	0	0
1998	CENTRAL		111,233.50	0	0	1
1998			192,733.50	0	1	1
1998		VIDEOSALES	186,223.00	0	1	0
1998		VIDEORENTAL	6,500.00	0	1	0
		VIDEOSALES	186,223.00	1	1	0
		VIDEORENTAL	6,500.00	1	1	0
			192,733.50	1	1	1

```
11 rows returned.
```

Please note the 1s and 0s to the right of the actual data. The 0s correspond to actual data while the 1s correspond to subtotaled columns.

The GROUPING function can also be used for *filtering* returned rows, using the HAVING clause normally used to filter rows returned by the GROUP BY clause. For example, suppose you didn't even want any detail data rows and, in fact, are interested only in the subtotals by REGION:

```
SELECT          time, region, dept, SUM(amt) amt,
                GROUPING(time) t,
                GROUPING(region) r,
                GROUPING(dept) d
FROM            sales
GROUP BY        CUBE(time, region, dept)
HAVING          GROUPING(time) = 0
   AND          GROUPING(region) = 1
   AND          GROUPING(dept) = 0;
```

TIME	REGION	DEPT	AMT	T	R	D
1998		VIDEOSALES	186,223.00	0	1	0
1998		VIDEORENTAL	6,500.00	0	1	0

```
2 rows returned.
```

Simple in concept and efficient in implementation, the ROLLUP and CUBE functions can simplify a great deal of processing currently laboriously implemented in 3GL or 4GL code.

> **TIP**   All functions usable in the GROUP BY clause can be used in conjunction with ROLLUP and CUBE. These functions include SUM, COUNT, MIN, MAX, VARIANCE, and STDDEV.

Analytical Functions

The ANSI SQL standard, as well as Oracle's superset of it, has never been strong at advanced business analysis processing. Geometric functions and simple statistical function have been available since the early versions of Oracle all the way up through the initial release of Oracle8*i*:

ABS	COSH	SIN
ACOS	EXP	SINH
ATAN	LOG	SQRT
ATAN2	LN	TAN
COS	POWER	TANH

Beginning with Oracle8*i* Release 2 (version 8.1.6 and above), the Oracle SQL language now boasts an impressive suite of functions for ranking, moving averages, lead/lag, and more advanced statistical calculations, including linear regression.

Let's deal with the simplest functions first. Giving Oracle new capabilities in calculating geometric coordinates for charting results for graphical display, *linear regression* functions calculate *least-squares regression* on pairs of numbers representing coordinates. The list of new regression functions includes the following:

REGR_COUNT	REGR_SLOPE	REGR_SXX
REGR_AVGX	REGR_INTERCEPT	REGR_SYY
REGR_AVGY	REGR_R2	REGR_SXY

Each of these functions has more traditional syntax, namely:

```
Function ( nbr1, nbr2 )
```

Now, on to the more complex, remaining new functions, which can be divided into the following five categories, listed in Table 13.1.

Each is made possible by an additional third stage of SQL statement processing. Previously, all SQL statements consisted only of one-stage or two-stage processing.

Table 13.1   Categories of Analytic Functions

RANKING	WINDOWING	REPORTING	LAG/LEAD	STATISTICS
RANK	*Aggregate(expr)* OVER . . . [(PARTITION . . .] (ORDER BY . . .)	*Aggregate (Aggregate(expr))* OVER . . .	LAG . . . OVER . . .	VAR_POP and VAR_SAMP
DENSE_RANK		RATIO_TO_ REPORT(*expr*) OVER . . .	LEAD . . . OVER . . .	STDDEV_POP and STDDEV_SAMP
CUME_DIST				COVAR_POP and COVAR_SAMP
PERCENT_ RANK				CORR
NTILE				
ROW_NUMBER				

Simple, one-stage SQL operations in Oracle include basic queries and joins. Two-stage processing would accompany clauses such as ORDER BY and GROUP BY clauses that take results from the first stage of processing and either sort or aggregate the output.

The new analysis functions in Oracle take advantage of a third stage of processing that can occur after the second stage of aggregation or sorting. Within this new stage of processing Oracle is able to group the data temporarily into *windows* or *partitions* of data. Using this method, the SQL statement is able to apply analytical functionality to each row, sometimes referring *backward* or *forward* to values within other rows within the partition.

To permit control by the SQL programmer over this new stage of processing, all of the remaining analytic functions share syntax new to the Oracle SQL language. The *partitioning* capability is specified by the clause PARTITION BY. It would be nice if Oracle had chosen another word from the incredible array of words available in the English language, to relieve the burden on that already overloaded keyword PARTITION, but it appears that we'll have to live with this. The reserved word PARTITION is thus doomed to mean multiple things in the Oracle universe, and those of us working with all of those different meanings are thus doomed to a future of forever specifying the difference.

Please note that this form of partitioning is (as mentioned earlier) a postprocessing step that occurs after rows have been retrieved and aggregated, but before they have been sorted for final display. The purpose is merely to break this resulting intermediate data into *windows* of data against which the analytic functions will be applied.

Each of the functions also performs a separate sorting step that has nothing to do with the order in which the rows are returned. Instead, this sorting step merely affects the order in which the analytic function is applied, internally within the *partition* or *window*.

Each of the analytic functions has syntax similar to the following:

```
Function ( expression ) OVER
[ PARTITION BY ( expression ) ]
ORDER BY ( expression )
```

The *function* names themselves were listed earlier. Each of the *expressions* is a value expression using columns, aggregate functions, or a list of those items. The PARTITION clause is optional, while they all require some form of an ORDER BY clause. If PARTITION is not specified, then by default the entire result set from the query represents one large partition.

To illustrate the new stage of SQL processing and how it is used, let's use the simplest of the new functions to provide an example.

RANK and DENSE_RANK are two slight variations on one another. Both rank the value of their initial *expression* in either ascending (the default) or descending order, but DENSE_RANK does not leave gaps in rank numbers following a tie. To illustrate:

```
SQL> SELECT C1,
  2         RANK() OVER (ORDER BY C1) RANK,
  3         DENSE_RANK() OVER (ORDER BY C1) D_RANK
  4  FROM   T;

C1       RANK   D_RANK
------   ----   ------
  2722   5      4
  1871   6      5
  3303   3      3
    38   7      6
  3303   3      3
 10015   2      2
 27888   1      1

7 rows returned.
```

With the RANK function, please note that there are two data values tied for third and that the next lowest value was ranked fifth, not fourth. If there had been three values (not two) tied for third, they all would have been ranked third together, but the next lowest value would have been ranked sixth.

With the DENSE_RANK function, see that the same exact situation yields a slightly different result. Here, two values once again are in a tie for a ranking of third, but the next-lowest value is ranked fourth. If three values (or more) had also been tied for third, the next-lowest value would still have been ranked fourth. There are no gaps in the sequence, and consequently the highest ranking value returned by DENSE_RANK is also equivalent to the number of distinct values returned (i.e., output from the expression COUNT(DISTINCT *)).

Suppose that we wanted to see what happens with the PARTITION BY clause?

```
SQL> SELECT C2,
  2         C1,
  3         RANK() OVER (PARTITION BY C2 ORDER BY C1) RANK,
  4         DENSE_RANK() OVER (PARTITION BY ORDER BY C1) D_RANK
  5   FROM  T;

C2  C1      RANK    D_RANK
--  -----   ----    ------
XX  2722    2       2
XX  1871    3       3
YY  3303    3       3
YY    38    4       4
XX  3303    1       1
YY  10015   2       2
YY  27888   1       1

7 rows returned.
```

In this situation there were no ties, so both RANK and DENSE_RANK returned the same results. But we're not focusing on that anymore. Instead, please notice that within the result-partition of rows where C2 equals XX, rows are ranked by the value of C1. Same is true for those rows where C2 equals YY. With everything jumbled up as they are, perhaps adding an ORDER BY clause on the entire query might make it easier to see:

```
SQL> SELECT C2,
  2         C1,
  3         RANK() OVER (PARTITION BY C2 ORDER BY C1) RANK,
  4         DENSE_RANK() OVER (PARTITION BY ORDER BY C1) D_RANK
  5   FROM  T
  6   ORDER BY C2, RANK;

C2  C1      RANK    D_RANK
--  -----   ----    ------
XX  3303    1       1
XX  2722    2       2
XX  1871    3       3
YY  27888   1       1
YY  10015   2       2
```

```
YY    3303   3      3
YY      38   4      4

7 rows returned.
```

Chapter 17 of the *Oracle8i Release 2 (8.1.6) Data Warehousing Guide*, which is entitled *SQL for Analysis*, provides an excellent, complete description of each of these analytical functions, along with examples and suggestions for even more creative uses. This manual is part of the standard Oracle documentation set, which is shipped via CD-ROM with each Oracle license and is also available for free via the Internet at `http://technet.oracle.com/`.

Browsing and Ad Hoc Reporting

Enhanced SQL functions are fine if you are going to write your own reports. You can use SQL*Plus (or any other simple command-line utility). You can use a 3GL language such as C++ or Java (using the Precompilers like PRO*C or SQLJ, ODBC, or JDBC). You can use a reporting utility such as Oracle Reports or PowerBuilder. But each of these methods requires intimate knowledge by a programmer of both the reporting utility (or language) itself and the vagaries of Oracle SQL. Any one of these solutions is not optimal if you are trying to *eliminate the middle-person* and empower end users to perform their own queries.

Over the years, quite a few products have purported to empower *ad hoc* queries and simple analysis by end users. In the late 1980s and early 1990s, many of these products called themselves *executive information systems*, which implied that they could be used by nontechnical, high-level managers and business analysts.

Ironically, one of the most effective querying and analysis tools has turned out to be the lowly spreadsheet. Over the years, probably more high-level managers and executives who were comfortable with Microsoft Excel and Lotus 1-2-3 would simply import data sets into various spreadsheets and perform their analysis that way. As a data warehouse or data mart designer, you may find that sometimes the most effective requirements gathering can be simplified by just asking end users for the spreadsheets that they like to use for reporting.

Following on this observation, many query browsing tools have implemented interfaces similar to those of spreadsheets, along with tight integration with spreadsheets. An end user could perform analysis in the database utility and then import the results to a spreadsheet for report formatting, or he could extract data from the database using the database utility and import the raw data to the spreadsheet for analysis and report formatting.

One utility that has proven to be an excellent implementation of a midlevel query utility, acknowledging the role that spreadsheets play with end users, is the Oracle Discoverer product. It is a grave injustice to characterize Discoverer as simply a browsing utility and spreadsheet; it also has significant analysis capabilities. Thus, we would like to focus on the Discoverer product as an ideal middle-level solution, somewhere between *roll-your-own* and full-fledged *online analytical processing* (OLAP).

Oracle Discoverer

This is a product that has been around for quite a long time. Its genesis is actually in several Oracle products, namely gateways to various spreadsheets and other data browsing tools written for dumb terminals. Over the years, the product coalesced as *Discoverer* with an MS-Windows GUI front-end and then migrated to the Web. The current implementation, known as *Discoverer 3i*, is fully integrated with the Oracle8*i* database server and has Web-based components to allow access to reports and the ability to analyze those reports over the Web.

Administration Edition and the End-User Layer

The *administrator edition* of Oracle Discoverer is intended primarily to set up the *metadata repository* in the database that is utilized by end users. This metadata repository is the *end-user layer* (EUL) and can reside in an Oracle database anywhere on the network. The *administration edition* software is (generally) the only modules with *read-write access* to the EUL; all other editions (*user* and *viewer*) have *read-only* access to the EUL.

Upon installation, the Discoverer administrator software is capable of performing *discovery* of the Oracle RDBMS data dictionary, to initially populate the EUL with metadata about the tables to be reported on. It is well worth the effort for a data modeler or other administrator to enhance this metadata information with labels, names, and comments that would help make end users' understanding of the data model easier.

At the present time, the *administration edition* is available only on Windows 95/98/NT. This then requires a client-side installation on an administrator's PC.

User Edition and Viewer Edition

The *user edition* of Oracle Discoverer includes the *ad hoc* query and *browsing* capabilities that will be used by most end users. It is available on UNIX (via

X-Windows/Motif), MS-Windows, and Web browsers. It includes the ability to create reports and store them for reuse, as well as run reports. It is intended for business analysts and developers who are not administrators, as well as end users who fall into the classification of *power users*.

The *viewer edition* is available from Web browsers only, and it provides the ability to run reports and perform analysis on those reports built by the *user edition*.

Both the *user edition* and the *viewer edition* use the EUL metadata repository created and maintained by the *administration edition*.

Reporting and Browsing Using Discoverer

The simplicity of creating reports in the *user edition* of Discoverer relies heavily on the amount of work spent by data modelers in creating referential-integrity constraints in the database and on the amount of work spent by administrators in supplementing the *end-user layer* with easily understandable information. With well-documented metadata in the EUL, creating reports with the *user edition* becomes quite fast and simple.

These reports can then be saved either to the current workstation or within the database. If the reports are saved to disk on the current workstation, then access to the saved reports depends on access to those files by other workstations. If the reports are saved to a local drive that can be shared by other workstations, then they can be used by many other users using the *user edition* of Discoverer only. If the reports are saved to a network drive, then the same is true. But saving reports to disk in this manner may not make the reports available from the Web-based *viewer edition*.

The *viewer edition* can run only reports that have been saved back to the database. Saving reports to the database is also a guaranteed way of making sure that reports are available across all platforms, such as UNIX, Windows, and the Web.

Close integration with Excel also allows reports to be saved as .xls spreadsheets and .csv flat files, as well as .pdf Acrobat documents and .html files, which can be posted directly on most Web sites.

Analysis Using Discoverer

Once a report has been run using either the *viewer* or the *user editions*, then the report results can be further manipulated using filters, conditions, and other restrictions. Moreover, if the report contains summary information, then summarized results can be *drilled down* to the detailed level, using standard point-and-click hyperlinks. Thus, reports can be built to show high-level summary results first, with access to lower-level summary information as well as the bottom-level detailed information.

Online Analytical Processing

Finally, for advanced analysis above and beyond what the SQL language itself is capable of performing in terms of functionality and performance, a class of products is available that uses your data warehouse or data mart as a data source. These utilities then build extremely specialized and highly indexed internal repositories of data that enable more advanced analysis functions with better performance. This is known as *online analytical processing*, or OLAP.

What is OLAP and why is it so different from relational technology? This chapter sheds some light on these questions and gives some idea of how to go about implementing an OLAP system. Online Analytical Processing (OLAP) utilizes software that adds value to the huge volume of data most organizations collect through their transaction processing. Most of this data remains unused in large data stores until it is purged or archived and forgotten.

The Origins of OLAP

The term *OLAP* was coined by Dr. E. F. Codd to describe a technology that could bridge the gap between personal computing and enterprise data management. The relational model falls short of providing the analytical capabilities required by management, analysts, and executives. Dr. Codd recognized the need for an additional multidimensional model that would allow faster and more capable analysis of the growing relational databases. A multidimensional model would allow the data to be represented in ways that more closely fit the way managers and analysts understand their businesses. Marketing and salespeople tend to think of their sales in terms of products, markets, and time, and financial managers tend to view their data by line, organization, and time.

The multidimensional model allows users to change their "reports" by simply reorienting their dimensions. Frequently, the reports requested within an organization are merely different orientations of the same data, perhaps viewed at different levels of summarization across various keys. It should be possible to change the selection of data and the view interactively, without rerunning complex queries or creating many separate reports. It should not require large amounts of time to rewrite the report just for simple changes in layout. With an OLAP engine, the calculations and design work are done once, resulting in a multidimensional database that, by its very nature, can deliver reports and analysis with flexibility and power that standard relational technology cannot match. Figure 13.1 illustrates multiple views of the same data as required by various managers.

The multidimensional model is inherently better at representing different views of the business by comparing different facets of the business environment

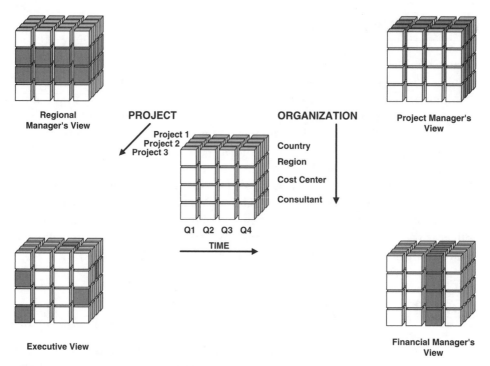

Figure 13.1 Multiple views of the data.

at different levels of detail. Some of the terms used in OLAP are *slicing*, *dicing*, *rotating*, and *drill-down*. The true power of a multidimensional structure is in its ability to quickly and easily manipulate or rotate the view to do a comparison along different criteria. The other "abilities" are more technology-specific. Express is particularly good at slicing and dicing and has powerful analytical functionality built into the engine.

What does "slicing and dicing" mean? To easily visualize an example it is best to limit ourselves to a three-dimensional cube. For example, you may have a cube of hours worked. The cube may be dimensioned by project, organization, and time. Let's assume the organization dimension has several summary levels, like region, cost center, and consultant at the lowest level of detail. *Slicing* means limiting the view of the data to a selection of consultant, region, or cost center. It would take a "slice" of data from the cube as shown for the three managers' views in Figure 13.1. You could have a slice for a particular cost center or a slice for a particular quarter or one for a particular project.

Dicing, just as in cooking, is slicing in multiple directions—making the selection along more than one dimension. Using persistent selections, you essentially keep the slice of data already selected and refine the selection by adding or removing more of the data cube. This could be the number of hours or revenue for a particular cost center during a specific time period. It could represent region and quarter for specific projects. When you add the other features of an analytical engine to the picture it gets interesting because you can select via interrelationships of the data, perform exception analysis, and calculate rankings by a wide variety of criteria.

Rotating data is changing the axes along which you orient your data. If we review cost centers by placing organization down the page, we might analyze our data across time or across projects. In a case where we have multiple hierarchies in a project, like industry or service line, we can compare cost centers across those, too. Another rotation would be to set cost centers as page values, with each page displaying time for one cost center across the page and projects on the vertical axis.

Drilling is being able to open up a subset of data that corresponds with a particular value of a dimension. A good example in our sample data schema would be drilling down within an organization. By starting at region, perhaps "EAST," "CENTRAL," and "WEST," the analyst might click on WEST to examine the next lower level of detail, the cost centers in Seattle, San Francisco, and Los Angeles.

Other typical operations in the analysis of the data would involve top/bottom or exception analysis. *Top/bottom* analysis selects the top and/or bottom ranges based on certain other criteria. For example, we could look at the top 5 cost centers based on margin. Within a cost center, we could select the top 10 *and* bottom 10 projects based on the ratio of expenses to revenue. Exception reporting involves selecting data based on exceptions—all the data that does not meet some specification. For instance, one could request the cost centers where margin is less than 10 percent.

Why bother with an OLAP component to a data warehouse? Keep in mind that different types of systems (OLTP, warehouse, and OLAP) all serve specific purposes and are optimized accordingly. The complex analytical queries of an OLAP engine might bring a relational system to its knees. The Express engine, on the other hand, is not capable of handling many simultaneous online transactions.

Table 13.2 shows a popular way of comparing the different types of systems and their typical characteristics. There are other characteristics not mentioned, but this gives a pretty good comparison. Obviously, there are many similarities between the relational warehouse and OLAP characteristics. If some users have a need for strong analytical capabilities then an OLAP component to the warehouse may be desirable.

Two striking differences between relational and OLAP processing are the OLAP capabilities for performing different types of time-series analyses and complex calculations such us multiple linear regressions, forecasting, or other built-in financial or statistical functions. Anyone who has written SQL for time-series reporting should appreciate multidimensional OLAP on first sight. The general user can change the selections and selected periods with ease, interactively. This interactive use is a keystone of decision support systems (DSS)

Table 13.2 Types of Systems and Their Characteristics

	OPERATIONAL	RELATIONAL WAREHOUSE	OLAP
Activity	Updating	Reporting	Analysis
Queries	Periodic	Ad hoc and periodic	Ad hoc
Transaction size	Small	Small to large	Large/complex
Transaction volume	Large	Medium	Small
Age of data	Current	Current and historical	Current, historical, and future
Data sources	Internal/keyed	Internal and external	Internal and external
Predictability of usage	Predictable	Unpredictable	Unpredictable
User interaction	Low	Medium to high	High

because the investigative nature of analysis requires the reformulation of queries to further narrow down areas of interest. There is no need to reexecute queries just to see the new selections or format.

The Express Data Model

In discussing the Express data model, it is important to understand the different components and how they fit together. On the client side we often speak of *cubes* that represent the data elements, even when they represent data with five, six, or more dimensions as opposed to only three. Data with more than three dimensions is still represented as an essentially three-dimensional view, with the extra dimensions grouped on either the x-, y-, or z-axis. A dimension may also be hierarchical, allowing us to drill down, but this is not required. In the engine itself a dimension is a specific type of database object. What is called a dimension in the application is really a composite structure of dimensions and other database objects, such as relations, variables, and value sets that support the functionality of the application's front-end.

Dimensions

Dimensions are the keys to the data. It is through the dimension values that you select the data that is to be analyzed. They are also the means of indexing into the data. For example, in the time dimension we may have the months JAN97, FEB97, and MAR97 as values, while a geography dimension may have specific cities or sales offices. Dimensions correspond to the key values in a relational table. Just as the key values define the data, the dimensions define the measures in a multidimensional database, so that if our variable is dimensioned by time, there exists a "bucket" for each and every value of time. Unlike a relational database, when analyzing or reporting Express data you do not generate a result set of data. Instead, you manipulate the data available to the Express analytical engine by setting the *status* of the dimensions. The dimension status is a selected subset of the dimension's values. One way to describe this is that all values not included in the current status are invisible. You cannot see other data, and Express calculations, reports, and other commands won't have to deal with it. From a relational perspective, think of status as a dynamically created view that limits the underlying table's view, which is visible.

Hierarchies

Dimensions are usually used in the form of *embedded total hierarchies*. These special hierarchies are made up of a dimension whose values include all the different levels within a hierarchy. This means that the summary levels are in the same database object (dimension) as their children. It is through this structure that the most effective drill-down is made possible. The embedded total dimension is actually a complex object made up of several components. It usually will have the dimension itself, a relation to itself that represents the parent-child relationship, and also related dimensions for hierarchies and levels. In its simplest form, the embedded total hierarchy in Express is similar to a self-join in a relational database.

Hierarchies are made up of different levels of detail, each value having a parent relation and a level relation, indicating the parent value and level for at least one of the hierarchies. Because Express is multidimensional relations can also be multidimensional. This allows for multiple hierarchies. For example, if the project dimension has two hierarchies, one for industry and one for service line, the relation would contain a parent value for each of the two hierarchies. The hierarchy dimension is one that allows the main dimension to have alternative or multiple hierarchies. In the following Express example, P1.HIERDIM is the hierarchy dimension, while P1.LEVELDIM is the level dimension, and the P1.PARENT and P1.LEVELREL are the parent and level relations, respectively:

```
DEFINE PROJECT DIMENSION TEXT

DEFINE P1.PARENT RELATION PROJECT <PROJECT P1.HIERDIM>
LD Parent-child relation for PROJECT
```

```
DEFINE P1.LEVELDIM DIMENSION TEXT
LD List of hierarchy levels for PROJECT

DEFINE P1.LEVELREL VALUESET P1.LEVELDIM <P1.HIERDIM>
LD Levels used by each PROJECT hierarchy

DEFINE P1.LEVELREL RELATION P1.LEVELDIM <PROJECT P1.HIERDIM>
LD Level of each PROJECT in each PROJECT hierarchy
```

Within the Express environment, we refer to the relationships between the dimension members using the family tree metaphor. Terms like parents, siblings, children, ancestors, and descendants are all used here. Dimensions are grouped together by level. Month, quarter, and year would be typical levels for the time dimension.

Parent. The dimension value that represents the next higher level of aggregation within each hierarchy.

Sibling. Other dimension values at the same level of detail.

Children. Those dimension values that have the dimension value as parent.

Ancestors. The dimension values above each value (the parents, the parents' parents, etc.).

Descendants. The corresponding lower-level values (the children, the children's children, etc.).

Attributes

Sometimes we would like to select, sort, or categorize data without calculating all the totals for each category. In such cases, it is wise to use attributes. *Attributes* are really just relations to the dimensions. Attributes are similar to lookups or joined tables in relational databases. For instance, if we may want to select projects by type, but we are not interested in totals by type, we would use type as an attribute. We accomplish this by defining another dimension called type and then defining a relation between the two. Indeed, you could also create an aggregate or other calculation using this relationship.

Measures

Express includes two basic types of measures: variables and formulas. *Variables* are predefined "buckets" in which calculated or loaded data is stored, either permanently or temporarily, during a session. *Formulas* calculate or retrieve their values as they are accessed.

NOTE Some other OLAP tools support only single cubes and are limited by requiring all data to have the same dimensionality. This is a serious limitation when trying to model the complexity of the real world.

Express allows multiple cubes, which may or may not share common dimensions. Having multiple cubes is an important feature because it allows different data to have different dimensions. Calculations can be performed even where all dimensions are not shared. Take our example where we have measures of HOURS, EXPENSES, and REVENUE. Measures share dimension values where the dimensions are common. If HOURS and EXPENSES are both dimensioned by PROJECT, then they are both dimensioned by the *same* PROJECT dimension. If the variables do not share dimensionality then the natural dimension set of the result is the union of the input variables' dimensions. The following example demonstrates a result that has the full set of the variables' dimensions:

```
DEFINE HOUR_RATE VARIABLE  DECIMAL <TIME ORGANIZATION CONSULTANT MONTH>
DEFINE HOURS_BILLED VARIABLE DECIMAL <TIME ORGANIZATION PROJECT
LIMIT TIME TO AUG97 TO DEC97
LIMIT PROJECT TO FIRST 2

REPORT HOURS_BILLED*HOUR_RATE

PROJECT: 334535
              --------HOURS_BILLED*HOUR_RATE--------
              -------------TIME-------------
ORGANIZATION     AUG97      SEP97      OCT97      NOV97      DEC97
------------   --------   --------   --------   --------   --------
BOB            2,061.93   2,044.37   1,560.21   3,102.57   3,928.67
JIM            2,496.12   5,447.33   5,462.96   3,168.02   2,451.28
MARY           6,393.59   4,952.59   5,527.89   5,349.60   4,026.10
CINTHIA        2,263.69   1,752.84   1,900.22   1,683.16   1,874.65
JOANNE         1,665.23   1,453.19   2,980.58   1,574.94   2,585.95
ELROY          1,734.90   2,912.60   3,616.01   2,063.45   2,649.98

PROJECT: 124858
              --------HOURS_BILLED*HOUR_RATE--------
              -------------TIME-------------
ORGANIZATION     AUG97      SEP97      OCT97      NOV97      DEC97
------------   --------   --------   --------   --------   --------
BOB            2,324.71   4,087.13   3,906.41   4,314.90   2,148.17
JIM            2,025.50   3,055.48   4,149.35   4,445.50   2,363.84
MARY           5,762.75   6,763.80   6,481.53   7,761.13   8,158.61
CINTHIA        2,230.26   2,325.09   3,729.94   1,794.86   1,992.37
JOANNE         1,195.04   1,533.00   3,320.61   2,215.31   1,532.00
ELROY          2,982.99   2,832.65   2,010.95   1,339.40   2,101.53
```

Variables

Variables are the Express structure used to represent stored data. They are usually quantitative; however, other types are supported. Most of the labeling for the data is indeed just text variables, defined by the dimension they describe. Sometimes there might also be a language dimension to provide for multiple-language versions. For the purposes of the application, variables are collected under a dimension that allows the user to rotate and use the selector tool to add and remove different measures to and from the view.

Formulas

Formulas are measures that are evaluated on the fly when accessed. Essentially, each is a stored procedure, like an Express program, which has dimensions (similar to a variable) and can be accessed precisely like a variable. When a formula is accessed, Express loops over its dimensions to perform the specified calculations. The Express engine is extremely efficient at calculating formulas. In many cases formulas may be used quite efficiently instead of storing derived variables.

In its most simple form, a formula is just a calculation based on existing values in the Express database. For example, if we have the variables HOURS and REVENUE, dimensioned by PROJECT, ORGANIZATION, and TIME, we could divide REVENUE by HOURS to obtain REVENUE_RATE. To perform this calculation, Express would have to open two separate data areas and then perform the calculation. Depending on how it would be used, this could be a pretty large transaction. We could make a smaller, simpler calculation by predefining a RATE variable that was just dimensioned by CONSULTANT and TIME. Figure 13.2 shows another simple example of calculating SALES as the product of UNITS multiplied by PRICE.

More complex formulas can use Express functions or logical operators or call stored procedures. For instance, the data may reside in a relational database and be queried and summarized for display. Oracle Sales Analyzer, Analyzer, and Express Objects allow users to create what are called *custom aggregates*. The user creates these by selecting a set of dimension values for which a total is then calculated. This custom aggregate gives the flexibility of reporting or analyzing totals on an ad hoc basis, even where the values haven't been precalculated.

Programs and Models

Express includes a powerful language for developing stored procedures. These procedures are the basis for applications developed in Express. Various front-end options exist, but the Express 4GL does the data manipulation work. Pro-

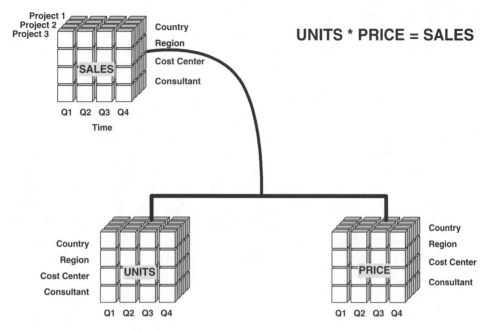

Figure 13.2 Formula arithmetic.

grams and models are compiled objects within the Express environment. Programs are independent and free-standing while models are defined to perform calculations over dimensions. Models are heavily used in financial applications such as Oracle Financial Analyzer.

The History of Oracle Express

Express was originally written in the early 1970s by MIT graduate students Jay Wurths and Rick Karrash while they were doing marketing analysis programming for three MIT professors, John Little (ex-dean of MIT's Sloan School of Business, now professor emeritus), Glen Urban (current dean of Sloan), and Len Lodish (currently at the University of Philadelphia's Wharton School). The software was first used to model market data for several large consumer products companies, to which John Little was consulting. This early work resulted in the founding of a company, Management Decision Systems (MDS), which did consulting in consumer market research.

Express started out as a mainframe system available only under the IBM VM/CMS operating system. It was later ported to Prime systems. In the beginning, Express was made available via a time-sharing service. It was made available for customer installation in the early 1980s.

Information Resources, Inc. (IRI) purchased MDS in 1985, primarily to acquire the Express technology. It wanted to use Express for analysis of scanner data and therefore had a strict marketing focus. Shortly thereafter, Express was converted to the C language, resulting in a two-tier product architecture comprised of PcExpress as a PC-based client and MDB as a back-end server component. Some features for advanced statistical analysis (factor, cluster, or discriminant analysis) that were present in the early product are no longer included. IRI later expanded from its strict marketing focus and developed FMS, the Financial Management System.

Oracle acquired the Express software from IRI in July 1995. This acquisition included the set of products based on Express technology. About two-thirds of the IRI field staff and the development teams in Waltham, Massachusetts, also joined Oracle in the acquisition. PcExpress and MDB were renamed Oracle Personal Express and Oracle Express Server, respectively. The other IRI application products then evolved into Oracle Sales Analyzer, Oracle Financial Analyzer, Oracle Analyzer, and Oracle Express Objects. (Note that the Financial Analyzer database names are still prefixed with "FMS.")

NOTE Since the acquisition, Oracle has greatly improved the integration of Express to relational (SQL) databases using RAA/RAM (Relational Access Administrator/Relational Access Manager) and added new composite dimensions to transparently handle sparse data. Continued product development is underway under Oracle Corporation's ownership.

The fundamental data model is still very similar to that of the original product. It has undergone very few changes over the years. Express has always been both multidimensional and relational. Yes, relational. When Dr. Codd composed the 12 rules for relational database management, Express met more rules than many accepted "relational" databases at the time. Just because Express meets many of the rules documented for relational databases does not mean it has been designed to be used as a transactional database. The arena where Express performs best is where it should be—in analytical processing. Incidentally, Dr. Codd documented the rules for OLAP tools in 1992, 20 years after Express was first made available!

The Technology of Oracle Express

The following section introduces a few elements of the Express technology. Express is a robust product, and this book does not allow a complete discussion of the technology. We will explore a few areas that can have an impact on the performance of an Express database implementation. Perhaps this discussion can help you understand enough about how Express works to avoid problems. You can read about other issues in the Express product documentation.

Data Storage and Access

Express manipulates the data as multidimensional arrays with indexes on each dimension object. It does this by storing each variable, both on disk and in memory, in pages whose layout is mapped to the dimensional array. This means that each and every cell in the database is indexed, allowing very rapid retrieval of data from the database. As long as the dimension values are already defined, the keys are not stored with the variables so as not to require more segments, which makes data storage very compact on pages. This is important for performance considerations.

This is quite different from typical relational storage where the key values are stored along with the data values, and related rows might be spread across multiple pages. (The nearest Oracle RDBMS structure is an index cluster.) Figure 13.3 illustrates the storage of all values for HOURS together and all values of EXPENSES together, organized by their dimensions. Retrieving a large number of data values across time, for instance, will be much faster than scanning through a correspondingly large table to collect key values for every data item retrieved. This reduces I/O significantly and also allows matrix arithmetic and complex functions to be performed very efficiently.

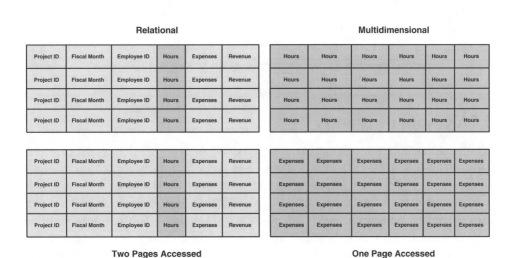

Figure 13.3 Data access.

Offset Addressing

Offset addressing is another facet of the way Express organizes measure data on whole pages. Offset addressing helps retrieve data that has a high degree of locality. For instance, when you are viewing January data and next want to look at February's, it is not necessary for the engine to seek the next "chunk" of data; it knows to look "4 bytes to the right" to find the value corresponding to that dimension's next value. This is especially important to time-series analysis, where you may be performing calculations involving many data "buckets" that are literally stored next to each other.

Persistent Selections

Much analysis is performed on specific slices or views of data. For example, a particular cost center may show a higher result on some measure than other cost centers. It is normal to make comparisons during analysis, frequently across some other dimension. It may be interesting to take the results from the current month and expand the time dimension to the past half-year. This second selection doesn't affect the status of the first selection. It is persistent. In this way, the user can add or take away dimension values very quickly, not by generating new results tables, but just by reshaping the current view.

Inversions

An inversion is an internal structure that holds information about relationships between dimensions. It is essentially the set of related values that correspond to a particular dimension value. Table 13.3 lists an example based on the demo database.

The inversions allow very fast lookups and limit operations on related dimensions. The level relations in the hierarchies we discussed earlier are an excellent example.

XCA Communications

The Express Communications Architecture (XCA) is a high-performance, peer-to-peer architecture that allows databases to communicate with each other across different platforms in a way that is transparent to the user. This topological independence can be important in maximizing performance when working in distributed architectures. It is important to evaluate the communications requirements and methods for transferring/loading data when designing the Express architecture. The various architectures supported by Express are discussed in the next section.

Table 13.3 Relations and Inversions

RELATION	INVERSION			
1	ATLANTA	EAST	EAST	1, 2, 7, 8
2	BOSTON	EAST	CENTRAL	3, 4
3	CHICAGO	CENTRAL	WEST	5, 6, 9
4	DALLAS	CENTRAL		
5	DENVER	WEST		
6	LOS ANGELES	WEST		
7	NEW YORK	EAST		
8	PHILADELPHIA	EAST		
9	SAN FRANCISCO	WEST		

The retrieve command is useful for exchanging data between host and client sessions where the information is for a specific purpose and expected to be used infrequently. It provides seamless integration of the remote and local data. It allows the user to get any data so long as the dimension of the data exists in both sessions. The formula would check against the local memory cache to see if the value had been retrieved and, if not, would call a program to query the details and return them.

The *EIF* (Express Interchange Format) *pipeline* is best for transferring larger amounts of data between Express sessions. It uses data compression to make the transfer more efficient. This transfers data via an EXPORT directly from one session into the objects of another. Arguments can be used to transfer only data, only definitions, or both. Dimension values can be appended or replaced. This technique is also useful in updating slices of data.

An *EIF file* is especially effective for cases where communications may be undependable or where the client must be able to work with the data while disconnected from the primary database. A manager may wish to perform analysis using a laptop while flying to a meeting. An EIF file is created using the XCA compression algorithm to compress and store the data in a platform-independent binary file. The platform independence of this file also makes it an excellent method for distributing data in cases where no network connection is available. (An EIF file is conceptually similar to the dump file used by Oracle EXP and IMP utilities.) As with the EIF pipeline, the import command can be used to transfer just definitions, only data where dimension values are present, or even to replace all objects.

Application Architectures

When implementing an Express OLAP solution, there are several different options for the overall application architecture that can be implemented. There are many factors that play a role in determining how the application should be structured. These factors can be grouped as follows:

Data distribution architecture. How the data is distributed to or accessed by users. The architecture options include thin client, thick client, Web access, or a combination of several different approaches depending on the needs of the user community.

Load and storage strategy. The overall style of solution, whether purely multidimensional, relational access (ROLAP), or a hybrid, with summary-level data stored in the OLAP tool but detail maintained by a relational database.

Physical database design. The structure of the database objects themselves and how the data will be organized.

We explore the first two groupings next. The third, database design, is covered throughout the rest of this chapter.

Data Distribution Architectures

Express applications can be set up to allow access or distribution of data following three basic configurations. The primary drivers for determining how information will be distributed are whether the user needs a local copy of data for disconnected use, the maintenance costs of installed software, and the performance issues surrounding both loads of distributed "slices" and system response. The three alternatives are as follows:

- Client/server with thick client or thin client, or via a browser using Web Agent
- LAN installation with shared databases on a LAN
- PC installation

Figure 13.4 presents a graphical view of these three architectures.

The three variations on the client/server model are discussed in the following three sections. They are shown in Figure 13.5.

Thick Client-Server

Thick client typically consists of the client application (running under Microsoft Windows), a local version of the database engine (Personal Express), and the Express server located on a host system. The local database on the PC client

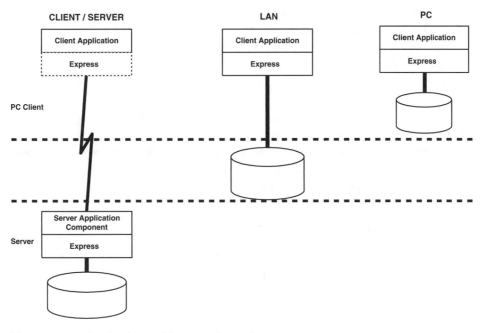

Figure 13.4   Application architecture alternatives.

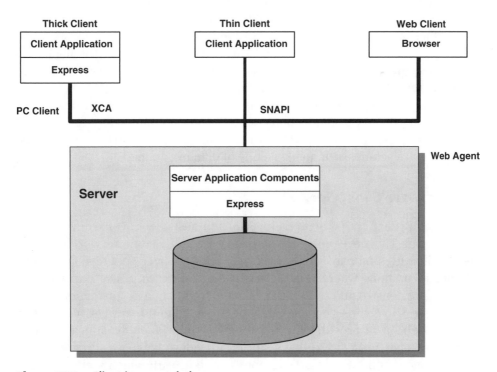

Figure 13.5   Client/server variations.

communicates with the host using XCA to retrieve and load data from Express Server. This means that when the server has new data, the client can refresh the local database with the new version of server data. This is particularly useful when Personal Express is used on a laptop and usually presents a slice of data. The data can be refreshed, then used as needed, while you are disconnected from the server. The thick client is limited by disk space and network performance, so care must be taken in determining the slices of data that will be distributed to the clients. A complete copy of a large database may not be appropriate. The PC is the most common client component in a typical Express implementation. This will probably change as more Web applications are made available and network computers appear on more desktops.

Thin Client-Server

A somewhat "thinner" alternative to the thick client on which data is permanently stored involves the use of a local cache database. The GUI application communicates with the local cache database via SNAPI (Structured N-dimensional Application Program Interface), and the cache uses XCA to retrieve data from the host as needed. The data is stored in the cache (memory) for the duration of the session, minimizing the repetitive retrieval of data.

One advantage the cache has over a true thin client without cache is that the cache database eliminates the need to retrieve data from the server more than once per session. Once the data has been retrieved, it resides in the cache, so that further analysis using that data can use the Express engine to manipulate it. There is, however, a negative impact on performance because the IF clauses check to see if the buffer is filled. This can be significant in cases where the cache database has a large number of dimension combinations to check.

Starting with Express Server version 5.03, a true thin client is available. In this scenario, the client application uses SNAPI to communicate directly with the Express Server component. Only the Windows application itself is installed on the client machine, with no local copy of data maintained.

Web Browser Client/Server

Web-enabling the Express Server allows the thinnest client of all—any standard Web browser. This development is also in line with Oracle's Network Computing Architecture and may represent a significantly lower cost for maintaining all implementations where remote sessions are necessary. The Express Web products are constructed as four-tier CGI and four-tier Java applications.

Web access to Express can currently be provided in three ways. In all cases, Express Web Agent provides the environment to produce dynamically generated Web pages through Express's stored procedure language. Provided with the Web Agent is the Express Developer's Toolkit, with which you can create

Express programs that generate dynamic HTML pages that, in turn, contain views of Express data. These programs also support special formatting such as tables, frames, and other capabilities defined by the HTML 2.0 standard.

The Express Web Publisher is used in conjunction with either Express Objects or Express Analyzer. With it, Web "sites" can be created and managed and tables and graphs published. Within Web Publisher you can create and publish *WebSites* that are units of storage for *WebBriefings*. WebBriefings are, in turn, groups or subsets of *WebPages* that contain tables, graphs, and other HTML content. The published WebPages are supplied within briefings and include the controls for selecting pages, rotating, and exporting data.

Sales Analyzer version 1.6 is also Web-enabled, and through its administrative features it allows users to publish their own reports to libraries. The public libraries are then accessed from the Web via the Sales Analyzer Web Server. The Web pages generated by Sales Analyzer are like the Web Publisher pages and provide the same tool set for later rotating and selecting from a Web browser.

LAN Installation

In a LAN installation the application code, shared databases, and even the user's databases would exist on the shared disk of a server on the local area network. The temporary data files used for paging should always be on the client side. It is important to note that the software is run completely in the memory space of the client PC using the client CPU. This can cause a significant amount of network traffic as data is transferred between the database and the client. The chief advantage of this architecture is that it provides the analytical independence of a PC installation, but simplifies the software and database maintenance through centralization. The release of Express Server on Windows NT has made the more efficient client/server model available to smaller systems. Increasing acceptance of NT Server has virtually eliminated new LAN installations of Express.

PC Installation

A single user installation of Personal Express can be performed on a personal computer. With the processing power of modern PCs, this is a viable solution for many analysts. A local installation on a notebook computer allows Express capabilities to become completely portable for small to moderate-size databases.

Load and Storage Strategy

While there are many ways to strategize storing data, the first alternative stores data within an Express multidimensional database. This approach will most surely deliver the best performance in data retrieval and presentation.

Multidimensional OLAP

Such activities as drilling down, rotation, and analytical calculations have the best response in a purely multidimensional setup. Frequently, though, there is a great deal of corresponding relational data that needs to be processed to load the multidimensional database. Achieving speed-of-thought multidimensional database performance requires that staging, loading, and aggregating of data be performed in batch. This process can take quite a bit of time depending, of course, on the structures being updated. Figure 13.6 illustrates Express retrieving data from its own database.

This approach is especially suited for systems where the data is updated on a periodic basis, typically monthly or even quarterly. The time required for the loading and aggregating makes this less suitable for situations requiring frequent updates. There is also some inflexibility in making changes to the multidimensional front-end, as it is heavily dependent on the database structure. Making significant structural changes involving large amounts of data will require correspondingly long times associated with reloading and aggregating along the new structures. Even changes in hierarchies involving no "structural" changes can have a significant impact on the build process.

Relational OLAP

The ROLAP alternative uses the relational database to store the data, which is then mapped into a multidimensional cache where the structures are more

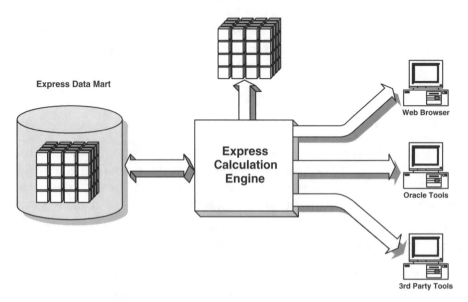

Figure 13.6   Multidimensional OLAP.

tuned for display and analytical purposes. On the relational side, the data would be stored in either a star (or snowflake) schema. Ideally, the Express metadata layer would then be maintained as relational tables so that a variety of end-user applications could be used, depending on the individual needs of the user or group. The data is queried into the Express database as needed and kept there for the session. This marriage of the Express engine to a relational warehouse database is shown in Figure 13.7.

The drawback with any pure ROLAP solution is that every time the system is started it must start from scratch and reload the cache. Heavily indexed databases with summary tables can mitigate degradation in response time. This, however, comes at the cost of introducing more overhead during updates of the relational database. Performance of this architecture depends greatly on the relational server platform. If this is the desired solution, be sure to invest in adequate hardware. Each loading of the Express cache can represent a significant query load on the warehouse server.

Hybrid

The hybrid approach uses the power of the multidimensional structures and storage for performance in analytical processing while allowing "reach-through" to the relational system for more detailed data supporting the summary data the

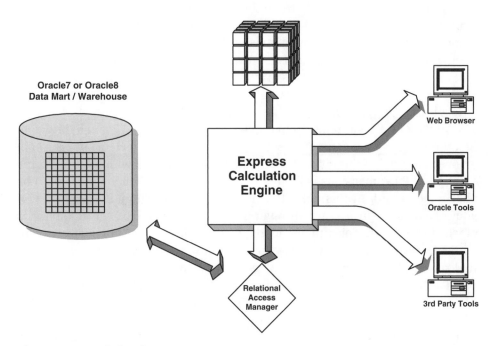

Figure 13.7   Relational OLAP.

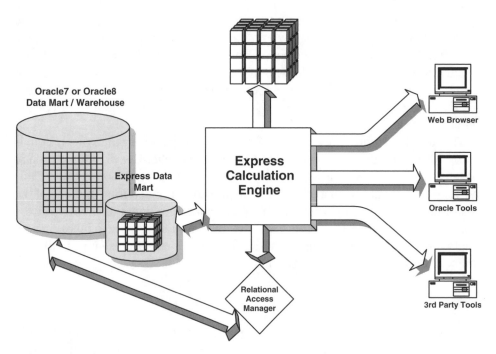

Figure 13.8 Hybrid OLAP.

user is analyzing (see Figure 13.8). In this model, some of the data is preloaded and aggregated in the Express database, while the rest of the data is left in a relational database. This is accomplished by defining a local cache with a reach-through to a ROLAP database. Then, with the Express database attached with write access, the upper levels of summary data are loaded into the Express database.

Relational Access Administrator (RAA) and Relational Access Manager (RAM) are special tools to assist in the development of ROLAP and hybrid configurations. These tools are discussed in the section on Oracle Express Applications at the end of this chapter. For a database generated with RAA/RAM, the status of all the dimensions is limited to those values for which data should be loaded and stored. At this point the "normal" fetch program is run, just as it would have been in a reach-through situation, except that the database is attached read/write. This process loads the data into the buffer usually used to hold data during the session. Once it is loaded, we can update Express, saving the loaded values in the cache database. Now when the data is accessed, the formula that evaluates whether the buffer is already populated will determine that it is and avoid the additional cost of reaching through.

Using the hybrid approach also allows an extra degree of "tuning" for performance by adjusting how much data is stored in the multidimensional side and how much remains in the relational. Use of the two environments can also be optimized by splitting the different reporting needs by the applicability of the different technologies—some reports are better provided in the purely relational world. Don't assume that Express must be used to satisfy all needs. This awareness may save loading a lot of detail into Express for very little additional benefit.

Implementing an OLAP Solution

This section deals with some of the issues related to implementing an OLAP application. Most conventions for application development and implementation can be adapted to apply to OLAP. It is not within the scope of this chapter to discuss project methodology or coding, naming, documentation, and project administration issues, except where those issues are specific to OLAP or to Oracle Express. That said, this section delves into basic project phases in order to group certain issues together. Be aware, however, that many activities are intertwined, and the related issues are not unique to a particular project phase.

Requirements Definition

If the OLAP implementation is part of a larger data warehouse project, much of the requirements definition has more than likely been done. Even so, at minimum a review of the business requirements, data sources, and extraction and loading plans as well as the resultant entity relationship models is necessary from the point of view of the OLAP implementation process. In OLAP implementations it is good to keep in mind that it will be the analysts and business managers who will determine the success of the project. While the reporting and analysis needs for a given group of users will change to keep pace with evolving the business environment, the underlying data needed to support the information requirements will generally remain fairly stable. To support a wide array of decision support needs, the data model must be very flexible.

Business Requirements

To fully understand what the objectives and informational needs of the business users are, it is useful to review current and proposed report layouts as well as any proposed organizational changes and any external factors expected to alter how the business will be run. It is critical that the business issues are fully understood and represented in the business model and that all calculations and models currently in use are fully documented. An organization chart of the users should be created as well as documentation of the business entities and how they relate to each other. At this point, a high-level data model should be created containing the main entities and data elements needed to support the business views.

Data Sources

The analysis of the data sources should compare the data requirements coming out of the business requirements analysis with the existing data sources. If the data sources do not exist within the existing schema, other sources may need to be found or else the business views need to be adjusted to balance the availability of data with the users' expectations. If an Express OLAP solution is being added to an existing relational data warehouse, much of this work will already be complete.

Data quality should also be addressed because data of poor quality can have a severe impact on the success of an OLAP project. The source data's granularity needs to be documented and correlated between the different source systems because comparison of data will require a set of common keys. This may mean that for some external sources you will be able to load data only at a very high summary level. Often, information from associations or governmental agencies is based either on some geographic code like country or by some industry-unique identifier.

This can pose a difficult problem. You may wish to combine your internal sales figures with data from the OECD, the United Nations Statistical Office, or the Direct Marketing Association. Users may demand state-level summaries but want to look at their data by DMA code. This, of course, would seem simple for many DMA codes because in areas like the northeastern United States the codes may be like supercountries. This is not true in other areas where population density may be much lower. Here we find DMA codes that overlap state boundaries! It should also be noted that DMA codes don't exist internationally. This is just one example. Reports should be evaluated carefully to identify data that is "grouped" by some of these codes. As often as not, even if it makes sense to the users, careful investigation will reveal that it is in error because of mismatches in groupings. Some of these reports can easily be produced via SQL, where a subtotal will be generated by each of these groups. If you add up the subtotals, you may find double counting, missing data, or some of both.

Star and Snowflake Schemas

The star schema is the simplest relational schema that supports the multidimensional model effectively. To what extent summary tables are created (and how extensively they are indexed) is determined by factors such as the available Express load window, the frequency and volume of updates, and the type(s) of access to the relational warehouse. The star (or snowflake) simplifies loading in that all the dimension maintenance can be done on smaller lookup tables instead of the fact tables, which usually represent the largest component of the relational data.

Extraction and Loading

There is a good chance that source data for a standalone OLAP database will be coming from several places. Ideally, however, data reconciliation and integration is all done through the relational data warehouse. If the data is coming directly from source transaction systems, it should first be extracted to intermediate tables in a relational database or flat files. This can be accomplished using extraction tools or just as reports/extracts from the systems in question.

The most efficient method for reading data into an Express database is by using the FILEREAD command. This advantage may be outweighed by other factors, such as maintenance of the source data in a warehouse or data cleansing issues.

Cleansing the Data

If the data is not coming from a verified data warehouse and an extraction tool with data scrubbing capabilities is not being used, then the data will need to be verified and corrected. Care must be taken to ensure that all the necessary parent values exist so that rollups can be successful. Express (starting with version 6) has a utility called HIERCHECK for checking hierarchies for circularity. To deal with circular references prior to version 6, refer to the ROLLUP command in the *Language Reference Manual* for sample code to write your own verification programs.

Distribution and Access Control

Requirements for access and distribution of data should be determined based on the need of the various users or user groups. Generally, it makes the most sense to allow export of slices to those who need a local copy of data to update during the analytical cycle or to those who need to view the data while disconnected from the network. This is especially true with Financial Analyzer because of its budgeting capability.

Distributing data may make sense if the user base is skilled with regard to computers or if the users' workstations are powerful. This can be a way of distributing the processing load. Generally, this is not an issue because the server is likely to have enough capacity to outperform even the fastest PCs. Creating and distributing EIF files or exporting via the pipeline would also require host CPU and disk resources, so the distribution of data may not greatly reduce the total load on the server.

Another consideration regarding access and distribution is, naturally, security. Allowing users to take slices of data may complicate the management of data security. This is a general issue related to how people use laptops and personal workstations. As such it is beyond the scope of this chapter.

Analysis

With the requirements fully understood and with clearly identified sources, it is possible to put together some size estimates and some predictive metrics regarding performance. During the analysis phase, we will want to take those requirements and determine the best of the many alternative methods for structuring the database. This will be done by assessing the characteristics of the data, determining the appropriate dimensions and granularity of the data, and determining how dense or sparse the data may be. Finally, we need to establish the impact of the available time window, the frequency of loads, and any processor and disk constraints.

Dimensionality

An important issue is the dimensionality. When should an entity be considered in a separate dimension? When is it just a level within a hierarchy? In typical hierarchies, the relationships are always one too many. Should you try to make separate dimensions out of them they are likely to be extremely sparse. If, for example, you would make state and city separate dimensions and then view the data in table form, it would normally be fairly sparse. Denver would probably only have data for Colorado, leaving the remaining rows and columns empty. This obvious example illustrates the potential use of a hierarchy. It might not be so obvious, however, if the data is billing information for a telephone company and CITY is the origination city and STATE the destination state. In this revised example, the CITY and STATE fields are not hierarchically related. Making separate dimensions of them would result in a cube that would probably be very dense. So the entity relationship diagram can't be simply mapped directly to a physical model in OLAP. Care needs to be taken to understand how the elements relate to each other.

Likely candidates for dimensions are naturally TIME, because a particular month is always in a specific quarter, year, and so on. Others are PRODUCT, ORGANIZATION, and GEOGRAPHY hierarchies. For example, Denver is always in Colorado, which, in turn, is always in the United States.

Another common question is how many dimensions can a cube have. Theoretically, Express can support objects with up to 32 dimensions. This is really not necessary. Try to imagine a table on your screen with the columns across the screen representing TIME, and with GEOGRAPHY as the vertical axis, and then the unique combination of 30 keys defining each page definition. Now think about drilling down or making a specific selection. This would mean that to truly use the tool, you would need to drill and select through all 32 dimensions as keys. The relational equivalent would be equally complex. Imagine having to specify 32 key columns in each SELECT statement. That wouldn't be user friendly by anyone's definition. A far better solution is to utilize the Express multiple cube facility. Then smaller cubes could be defined to support different types of analysis. In our case study database project time accounting, we probably wouldn't want to include the Strategic Service Line, Industry, or Project dimensions in a simple report of consultant utilization. A smaller cube of the data that had dimensions of Consultant, Organization, and Time would be sufficient for this analysis.

Granularity

The level of detail stored in the Express database will have an impact on loading and maintenance performance as well as responsiveness. Less detail will allow enhanced performance but will limit the users' ability to drill down. Balancing these objectives is an important function of analysis.

Sparsity of Data

Generally, we refer to data as being 80 percent sparse when only 20 percent of the variable's cells—unique combinations of the dimensions—for that variable contain data. Where data is sparse, dimensions should be set up as either *composite* or *conjoint*. If the database is large or if the data is sparse for certain subsets of dimensions, there may be other methods for managing the sparse data and improving performance. Some other techniques (discussed later in this chapter) are subsetted dimensionality, record relational structures, indirect references, and capstone databases. Most of these techniques partition the data into smaller pieces and then join the pieces together through the use of formulas. This corresponds to the definition of a relational view that predefines a join of multiple tables.

Precision of Data

The required precision of data should be evaluated carefully. Both variables and dimensions should be defined with the least precise definition possible. Is rounding error going to be a problem for the type of analysis to be performed? Whether to maintain SALES data with whole dollar values or with dollars and cents will be determined by whether you're selling cars for thousands of dollars or canned foods for less than a dollar.

Reducing precision will make the dimensions smaller, so they'll take less storage and be more efficiently accessed. Specifying a decimal variable instead of a short integer will double the amount of storage for that variable. Need we say more? It is, however, important to provide sufficient precision to meet the analytical needs of the business.

Order of Dimensionality

In determining the order of dimensions for the variables, certain things must be taken into consideration. Data loading and typical view layouts are factors that influence the order. In the example data, we assume that time should be used as an "across" dimension in many views—this is fairly typical. Time is expected to be one of the "most variable" variables. If we take a look at our case study data, we see that we have thousands of consultants and projects and even hundreds of organizations. It is typical that a consultant will work on one project and perform one function for several months. Therefore, time is the dimension that varies fastest—it changes every period, even when other aspects of a consulting assignment remain the same.

To optimize our application for performance we want to represent time as the fastest-varying dimension. This would make it the "across" dimension in the default layout of a table. The second fastest is the down dimension, and third, fourth, and so on become pages. Because the order of dimensions will also dictate how the data is physically stored, this decision will make this setup the fastest for retrieval as well.

Some systems will have frequent loads or updates and will need to have the dimensions ordered accordingly. If you are loading data daily, you may want time to be the slowest-varying dimension. This would allow the data for a single data to be loaded together onto a single page (or small set of pages).

DEFINING SPARSE DIMENSIONS

In Express version 6 the definition for hours would include the sparse keyword to designate which dimensions are sparse:

```
DEFINE HOURS VARIABLE INTEGER <TIME SPARSE <CONSULTANT PROJECT
FUNCTION>>
```

In releases prior to version 6 you would more than likely use a conjoint dimension to manage the sparsity:

```
DEFINE MAIN.CJT DIMENSION <CONSULTANT PROJECT FUNCTION>
DEFINE HOURS.CJT VARIABLE INTEGER <TIME MAIN.CJT>
```

Design and Build

The design of a multidimensional database is conceptually quite different from that of an OLTP relational database. Of course, some characteristics are common to both types of systems. The largest difference is in the approach to design. It is important to remember that the primary reason for the development OLAP databases is for decision support. For a decision-support system (DSS) to be successful, it must accurately represent the business model, not an effective transaction processing model.

Many of these multidimensional relationships will be similar to joins that could be done at run-time in an RDBMS. Within the multidimensional database, they must be defined carefully to fit within the business model. Although this requires more work at design time, a properly designed multidimensional database can offer a great deal of versatility and flexibility at run-time because of its very nature.

One of the more difficult transitions for experienced relational database designers to make is to work in more than two dimensions simultaneously. One typical mistake is to develop the design of the multidimensional database based on reports from either a legacy or current relational system. While this input is an important part of the information needed for analysis and design, it is not an end. The physical schema should be optimized for interactive performance and for maximum flexibility in regard to reporting layouts.

Do the planning up front—it will save countless headaches later.

Constructing a small prototype of the multidimensional database is always a very good idea. Don't forget that multidimensional databases are new to many people. The users may do a thorough job of describing their current reporting and analysis needs, but if they haven't worked in a multidimensional database before, they won't be able to conceptualize what they want in the appropriate terms. After working in a prototype for a short while, they will be much more prepared to give appropriate feedback.

One of the first steps in the actual design of the multidimensional database is to determine which data elements should be included. Next it will be necessary to determine the source of the data, or how it will be entered. The atomic level "facts" need to be identified first. Then the corresponding hierarchies are determined for each dimension. Finally, the key values for each dimension must be verified. These elements and the necessary dimensional objects will form the basis for the database design.

Design Trade-Offs

Just as in relational database design, the primary activity during the design of an OLAP environment is evaluating the trade-offs between multiple objectives and alternative solutions. Most trade-offs revolve around how much work to do ahead of time, during, and directly after the load process and how much to do on the fly. Some of the trade-offs to consider are the following:

- Load time versus retrieval time
- Load time versus required granularity
- Precalculation of aggregates versus calculated-on-demand
- Loaded aggregates versus rolling up in Express
- Loading of detail versus reach-through-on-demand
- Loading all desired data versus disk limitations
- Object definition versus cell limitations

Calculated Variables

Whether to precalculate and store variables often depends on how the calculation affects performance and the load window. Calculating on the fly saves storage space but may adversely affect the performance. Some calculations are simple or require a small subset of data, perhaps by utilizing offset addressing.

When presenting cumulative sums, one could use the *cumsum( ) function.* This would require calculating over the entire time series—and would probably take much too long for on-the-fly calculations. If the cumulative sum is precalculated and stored, however, you could use a formula to present the monthly values by calculating the difference between the current and previous month. This calculation would be very fast, because Express just needs to look a few bytes to the left and return the difference.

If your database size is not an issue and your load window is adequate, precalculating and storing both of these variables may be the best alternative. Where processing speed is the primary concern, lean toward calculating and storing a variable. When database size or load processing are critical, consider calculating on the fly.

Entity Relationship Diagram

An entity relationship diagram (ERD) of the data and various entities is a typical method for determining what needs to be in the database and what objects will be defined. Using standard modeling techniques will help the database designer to better communicate the data feeds and source requirements necessary to support the multidimensional database. The ERD is ideal for understanding the various elements and their interrelationships and dependencies. The data model will be somewhat different from an OLTP database design, but the ERD can be the link between different technologies. This will be particularly important if Express is being used to reach through to an underlying relational database.

Mapping to Multidimensional Structures

Entities and relationships map to dimensions, levels, and attributes, while facts generally map to variables and formulas. One of the core concepts in OLAP terminology is the *data cube*. A data cube is the multidimensional object, referred to as a *financial data item* in Financial Analyzer or as a *measure* in other Express front-end tools. These structures are indeed multidimensional arrays; a three-dimensional object would be conceptually similar to a Rubik's cube. These normally dimensioned structures are fine for densely populated data sets, but in many cases the data is not at all dense. To compare the different alternatives for the physical structure of our database, we will start with our example database consisting of ORGANIZATIONS, PROJECTS, and TIME. This example is simple and easy to follow.

To create our sample database, suppose our dimensions are defined as follows:

```
DEFINE PROJECT DIMENSION TEXT
DEFINE ORGANIZATION DIMENSION TEXT
DEFINE TIME DIMENSION TEXT
```

and we define our data in a simple cube by placing it within the three dimensions:

```
DEFINE HOURS VARIABLE INTEGER <TIME, ORGANIZATION, PROJECT>
```

Furthermore, suppose our dimensions had 10 values each, 10 PROJECTS, 10 ORGANIZATIONS, and 10 MONTHS. Our cube could then store up to 1,000 values of HOURS. If only 250 of these distinct combinations contained values, the cube would be 1,000/250 or 25 percent dense. (This is the same as 75 percent sparse.) The cube may not, however, be uniformly dense. For instance, it is possible that each actual PROJECT and ORGANIZATION combination might have corresponding values for every value of TIME. This would mean that TIME is dense relative to PROJECT and ORGANIZATION. PROJECT and ORGANIZATION, however, would be sparse relative to each other.

Normal Multidimensional Structures

Where data is dense across its defining keys, normal dimensional structures can be used. For instance, as we demonstrated earlier:

```
DEFINE HOURS VARIABLE INTEGER <TIME, ORGANIZATION, PROJECT>
```

Using standard dimensional and hierarchy structures simplifies both the build process and aggregation and facilitates using various tools and functions. The standard structures keep all of the hierarchical information in a simple set of relations that are then used for both aggregating the data as well as drilling down from a front-end tool. Alternative structures, in which the applications can become more complicated, are discussed in the following sections. The direct, simple structures allow all the analytical power to rotate, slice, dice, and drill down via the dimensions. If it is possible to keep the application simple, do it!

Conjoint Dimensions

In Express versions prior to 6.0, the *conjoint dimension* was one of the primary methods for controlling sparse data. A conjoint dimension is a dimension whose values point to values of its base dimensions and represent an intersection. This allowed the variables to be stored very densely. The downside to conjoint dimensions was the extra work required to set up hierarchies. Additionally, conjoint dimensions can get very large. The indexing algorithm for conjoint dimensions should be hashed. (If it is initially defined as *nohash* the indexing algorithm can be reset to either *hash* or *btree*.) Were our example to have sparse data, we would first need to define the conjoint dimension:

```
DEFINE ORGPROJ DIMENSION <ORGANIZATION, PROJECT>
```

The data would then be stored using the conjoint dimension rather than the original two dimensions:

```
DEFINE HOURS_CJT VARIABLE INTEGER <TIME, ORGPROJ>
```

Reporting on this structure wouldn't be very convenient or flexible. That HOURS_CJT is dimensioned by ORGPROG means that the combination of ORGANIZATION and PROJECT must always be on the same axis. This limits the ability to rotate the output. In the following example we limit the time to only four months:

```
LIMIT TIME TO LAST 4
REPORT DOWN ORGPROJ HOURS_CJT

                          ----------HOURS_CJT----------
     -----ORGPROJ----------------TIME----------------------------------
ORGANIZATION   PROJECT    SEP97      OCT97      NOV97      DEC97
------------   -------    -----      -----      -----      -----
BOB            334535     60         57         55         80
BOB            124858     63         63         73         69
JIM            334535     55         61         52         63
```

JIM	124858	75	59	79	79
MARY	334535	67	63	68	72
MARY	124858	58	64	56	69
BOB	394893	73	64	78	75
BOB	342382	56	65	70	79
MARY	394893	75	76	67	74
MARY	342382	73	78	70	61
JOANNE	124858	59	62	62	53
JOANNE	394893	79	77	69	53
JOANNE	342382	65	59	51	53

The hours variable could be represented via a formula instead, so that the full dimensional power could be used to allow pivoting, rotating, and the like:

```
DEFINE HOURS_F FORMULA INTEGER <TIME, ORGANIZATION, PROJECT>
EQ HOURS_CJT

REPORT HOURS_F

PROJECT: 334535
                  ---------HOURS_F---------
                  ---------TIME---------
ORGANIZATION          SEP97     OCT97     NOV97     DEC97
------------          -----     -----     -----     -----
BOB                   60        57        55        80
JIM                   55        61        52        63
MARY                  67        63        68        72
JOANNE                NA        NA        NA        NA


PROJECT: 124858
                  ---------HOURS_F---------
                  ---------TIME---------
ORGANIZATION          SEP97     OCT97     NOV97     DEC97
------------          -----     -----     -----     -----
BOB                   63        63        73        69
JIM                   75        59        79        79
MARY                  58        64        56        69
JOANNE                59        62        62        53


PROJECT: 394893
                  ---------HOURS_F---------
                  ---------TIME---------
ORGANIZATION          SEP97     OCT97     NOV97     DEC97
------------          -----     -----     -----     -----
BOB                   73        64        78        75
JIM                   NA        NA        NA        NA
MARY                  75        76        67        74
JOANNE                79        77        69        53
```

```
PROJECT: 342382

                    ---------HOURS_F---------
                    ----------TIME----------
ORGANIZATION            SEP97        OCT97        NOV97        DEC97
------------            -----        -----        -----        -----
BOB                      56           65           70           79
JIM                      NA           NA           NA           NA
MARY                     73           78           70           61
JOANNE                   65           59           51           53
```

As you can see, having the dimensions separated provides multidimensional functionality to the data. Even though creating a viewable structure is easy, it is more complex to build the structures for performing rollups of data and to maintain the multiple levels and hierarchical information.

In order to perform a rollup of the data, store the aggregates, and provide drill-down, you need to make parent structures for the conjoint. (Now comes the fun part!) For each of the base dimensions of the conjoint, a parent conjoint value must be added. First, we will need to define a parent relation for each of the base dimensions:

```
DEFINE ORGPROJ_ORG RELATION ORGPROJ <ORGPROJ O1.HIERDIM>
```

Notice that this relation is also dimensioned by the hierarchy dimension (its name shows that we assume the administrator tool is being used), so that the conjoint rollup can support multiple hierarchies. Otherwise, a separate relation is needed for each hierarchy.

The following is a simple method for using the parent relation to build the parent structures; Sales Analyzer does this in a much more sophisticated way.

```
vrb lvlcount int
lvlcount=0
lvlcount=obj(dimmax 'O1.leveldim')
while lvlcount gt 0
do
  maintain ORGPROJ merge    -
  < O1.PARENT(ORGANIZATION -
  key(ORGPROJ PROJECT))>    -
  relate ORGPROJ_ORG

lvlcount=lvlcount-1
doend
```

After building the parent structures, the ROLLUP command can be issued as it normally would:

```
ROLLUP HOURS_CJT OVER ORGPROJ USING ORGPROJ_ORG
```

A later section of this chapter, "Aggregation/Rollup," provides general rules on performing rollups.

Composite Dimensions

Starting with Express version 6.0, another means of dealing with sparsity is provided. As measures/variables are defined, combinations of their dimensions can be designated as being sparse. This allows Express to manage their storage more efficiently. Express version 6.0 handles this transparently. No extra structures need to be created or maintained as required with conjoint dimensions. Express maintains the *composite dimension* automatically.

The conjoint example above, if re-created using a composite dimension, would be:

```
DEFINE HOURS VARIABLE DECIMAL <TIME SPARSE <ORGANIZATION PROJECT>>
```

At this point the data is as usable as in the normal dimensional model. There is no need to create any extra structures just for viewing the data or aggregation.

```
PROJECT: 334535
                 ---------HOURS_F---------
                 ---------TIME---------
ORGANIZATION      SEP97       OCT97       NOV97       DEC97
------------      -----       -----       -----       -----
BOB               58.29       55.52       54.22       74.81
JIM               60.55       61.03       69.36       65.64
MARY              53.95       58.83       51.38       60.75
CINTHIA           70.66       57.45       74.29       73.96
JOANNE            64.19       61.03       64.80       68.72
ELROY             56.86       61.52       55.04       65.85

(Note: Full report output not shown.)
```

Subsetted Dimensionality

Creating subsets of large objects is one of the more common ways to improve performance when sparse data is not equally distributed but occurs in large "chunks." This places the data into separate cubes in which the data is dense. In some cases, it may even make sense to separate the data into individual databases. Using indirect references, you can join them seamlessly. This can make the complexity invisible to the user.

Record Relational

Record relational structures can be useful as an alternative to building very large conjoint structures. A record relational structure makes use of the Express capability for storing data in a relational manner based on a record ID. This feature would be used only when you have a very large number of transaction details that need to be loaded into an Express database. One situation where this might be handy is where data must be counted using a dimension at the detail level. Calculating this type of measure requires the detailed base elements to be available.

Consider the need to maintain a count of the number of different projects that a consultant worked on during a specified period of time. The data could be calculated at the detail level, but you will have to recalculate higher levels based on the lowest level. Simple aggregation would be wrong. As an example, Bob worked on three projects during January and his work on two of those projects extended into February, along with work on a new project. If the two months' data were simply aggregated, it would appear that Bob worked on six projects even though he actually worked on only four. To calculate the proper count for higher levels in the TIME hierarchy, the details must be preserved and used. To allow such a large number of records we could use the record relational structure.

In this scenario, a dimension would be created to act as a record identifier, and then the "columns" would be relations to the base dimensions. Accessing data dimensioned by the "record dimension" requires using qualified data references within formulas.

The primary drawback to this method is one of data integrity. It is conceivable that duplicate rows of data could quite easily be loaded into such a structure unless custom integrity checking code is written. One alternative is to use meaningful *record ID* codes. If the record ID were to be a concatenation of the "base dimension" values, then it would be relatively simple to check for duplications. The fact remains that it would be a customization.

As an example, we can take our example data and define a record ID dimension, some relations, and an hours variable that will act as "columns":

```
DEFINE RECDIM DIMENSION INTEGER
DEFINE REC_PROJ RELATION PROJECT <RECDIM>
DEFINE REC_ORG RELATION ORGANIZATION <RECDIM>
DEFINE REC_TIME RELATION TIME <RECDIM>
DEFINE REC_HOURS VARIABLE DECIMAL <RECDIM>
```

We can then define a formula to retrieve some data from the record relational structure:

```
DEFINE REC_HOURS.F FORMULA DECIMAL <TIME PROJECT ORGANIZATION>
EQ TOTAL(REC_HOURS REC_TIME REC_PROJ REC_ORG)
```

We may also use the REPORT command to view the record relational data:

```
REPORT REC_TIME REC_PROJ REC_ORG REC_HOURS
```

RECDIM	REC_TIME	REC_PROJ	REC_ORG	REC_HOURS
1	JAN95	334535	BOSTON	321.50
2	FEB95	334535	BOSTON	325.50
3	MAR95	334535	BOSTON	430.50
4	APR95	334535	BOSTON	576.00
5	MAY95	334535	BOSTON	811.50
6	JUN95	334535	BOSTON	890.00

A REPORT (or the graphical user interface, or GUI) can use the formula to provide us with a multidimensional view of the data. We could test this using our example data, rotating it a few different ways:

```
REPORT REC_HOURS.F

ORGANIZATION: BOSTON
                 -----------REC_HOURS.F-----------
                 -------------TIME-------------
PROJECT            JAN95      FEB95     MAR95     APR95     MAY95
-------            -----      ------    --------  --------  --------
334535            321.50     325.50    430.50    576.00    811.50
124858            660.00     761.00    917.50  1,256.00  1,267.00
133555            524.00     568.50    588.50    693.50    902.50
394893            532.00     589.00    628.00    678.50    688.50
342382            914.00     868.50  1,002.00  1,075.50  1,201.50
```

Or we might set ORGANIZATION across and set TIME down the y-axis. PROJECT then becomes the page dimension.

```
REPORT DOWN TIME ACROSS ORGANIZATION: REC_HOURS.F

PROJECT: 334535
                -----------REC_HOURS.F-------------
                -----------ORGANIZATION-----------
TIME      BOSTON    ATLANTA   CHICAGO   DALLAS    DENVER    SEATTLE
-----     ------    -------   -------   -------   ------    --------
JAN95     321.50    406.50    291.00    477.50    365.00    435.50
FEB95     325.50    442.50    290.00    501.50    336.50    412.00
MAR95     430.50    512.50    395.50    671.00    453.00    515.50
APR95     576.00    784.50    488.00    873.00    574.50    770.50
MAY95     811.50    936.50    666.00  1,154.00    795.50  1,043.50
```

Or, with ORGANIZATION defaulting as the page, we might report TIME down (and PROJECT across):

```
REPORT DOWN TIME REC_HOURS.F

ORGANIZATION: BOSTON
                    -----------REC_HOURS.F-----------
                    -----------PROJECT------------
TIME              334535   124858       133555     394893   342382
-----             ------   --------     ------     ------   --------
JAN95             321.50     660.00     524.00     532.00     914.00
FEB95             325.50     761.00     568.50     589.00     868.50
MAR95             430.50     917.50     588.50     628.00   1,002.00
APR95             576.00   1,256.00     693.50     678.50   1,075.50
MAY95             811.50   1,267.00     902.50     688.50   1,201.50
```

Indirect References and Capstone Databases

One of the most common approaches to insulating the users from complex structures is the use of indirect references. Data can be partitioned into smaller components either in the same database or in separate databases. Indirect references can also be used to view and manipulate data stored in the record relational structures described in the last section. The downside of this approach is in the additional complexity of the application for administration and modification. The users are insulated from this complexity, however, because they are able to see just the formulas that reference the otherwise awkward schema. These formulas are normally dimensioned and look like other multidimensional data.

Reconciling the physical and logical data models is achieved by creating a dimension that is a superset of the dimension values. This superset dimension serves as a view in an Oracle relational database that combines data joined from multiple tables. This approach insulates the users from the additional variables and dimensions (and possibly different databases) chosen by the designers.

In our example, this might allow the data to be physically separated regionally (e.g., Americas and Europe). This should be a pretty clean breakdown because most projects will be staffed by consultants from the same region as the organization owning the project. For each summary value at the top levels of the superset dimension, the formula would check whether there was a value and, if so, retrieve it from the subdatabase/cube. This is similar to the way a cache database is set up or to the use of the SQL reach-through feature.

A *capstone* is a shell database that is the only database the users directly access. Just like indirect references within a single database, they contain the supersets of dimension values and access the subordinate data slices residing in separate databases via formulas. One way of conceptualizing a capstone implementation is to see it as a partitioned database. The databases can be par-

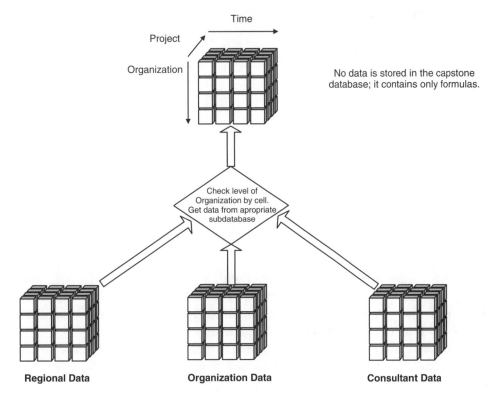

Time

Project

Organization

No data is stored in the capstone database; it contains only formulas.

Check level of Organization by cell. Get data from apropriate subdatabase

Regional Data

Organization Data

Consultant Data

Data is retrieved from sub-databases where the actual values are stored.

Figure 13.9 Capstone database.

titioned vertically or horizontally. Figure 13.9 demonstrates a capstone database that retrieves its actual data from three other databases.

There are performance trade-offs in the use of capstone databases. There may be some loading advantages from spreading the load process over several file systems. There will be some extra overhead, however, from evaluating the formula to determine the proper location from which to retrieve data.

Using our PROJECT example, we could have a vertical partition by separating the different levels of the ORGANIZATION hierarchy into different databases. Given the following hierarchy within the ORGANIZATION dimension:

⌐ Totorg

   ⌐ Division

      ⌐ Region

         ⌐ Cost Center

            ⌐ Consultant

then our formula for accessing the different "cubes" would be as follows:

```
DEFINE HOURS_F DECIMAL FORMULA <PROJECT ORGANIZATION TIME>
eq if  O1.LEVELREL eq 'TOTORG then
if isvalue(T.PROJECT PROJECT) and
               isvalue(T.ORGANIZATION ORGANIZATION) and
               isvalue(T.TIME TIME)
    then T.HOURS_F
else if O1.LEVELREL eq 'DIVISION' then
if isvalue(D.PROJECT PROJECT) and
   isvalue(D.ORGANIZATION ORGANIZATION) and
   isvalue(D.TIME TIME)
           then D.HOURS_F
else if O1.LEVELREL eq 'REGION' then
if isvalue(R.PROJECT PROJECT) and
   isvalue(R.ORGANIZATION ORGANIZATION) and
   isvalue(R.TIME TIME)
           then R._HOURS_F
else . . .
```

In this example, each of the objects within each "partition" database will need a prefix where the objects would otherwise have identical names. This is similar to the owner qualification required in the Oracle relational database when referencing objects from multiple schemas.

You will also need an AUTOGO program to attach all the subdatabases when starting the system. An AUTOGO program would be run automatically upon attaching the capstone.

```
DEFINE AUTOGO PROGRAM
PROGRAM

DTB ATTACH TOTORG.DB
DTB ATTACH REGION.DG
DTB ATTACH COSTCNTR.DB
DTB ATTACH CONSULT.DB

END
```

Data Loading and Integration with External Systems

Source data typically comes from many different places. It would not be at all strange to get financial data from the corporate general ledger system, production statistics/costs from text files, and perhaps sales and marketing data from another relational system such as a data warehouse, perhaps organized in a star schema. Express can efficiently load from diverse sources into one database.

**THE SOURCE FOR EACH DATA MART SHOULD BE
AN INTEGRATED DATA WAREHOUSE**

To maintain a consistent data snapshot across the enterprise, it is important to control the integration of data from these multiple sources. The majority of readers of this book are likely to be incorporating Express and OLAP into an environment with a relational data warehouse. As we recommended in Chapter 12, "Distributing the Oracle Data Warehouse," a centralized warehouse should be used to bring data together from many sources before it is distributed to various data marts (whether Oracle relational or Express multidimensional). Individually sourcing multiple data warehouses or data marts is virtually guaranteed to eventually result in multiple users receiving different answers to what looks like the same question.

Loading Data

Express provides alternative methods for loading data from extracted files or directly from a relational database.

Text Files

The FILEREAD command represents the most efficient (fastest) way for Express to load data. Express processes records very quickly using this method, and still allows quite a bit of processing during the load. Using the Express administrator tool to map text files will generate code that simplifies the use of FILEREAD. This generated code can then be further modified as needed to maintain conjoint dimensions.

FILEVIEW is used to individually read each record from the data file and process it. The FILENEXT command is then used to explicitly read and process the next input record. This is effective where more extensive processing would be necessary during the build/load of data. FILEVIEW and FILENEXT are used infrequently because FILEREAD usually has enough flexibility to deal with most load situations.

SQL/ODBC

The SQL capabilities in Express enable it to communicate with an ODBC-compliant (Open Data Base Connectivity–compliant) relational database. Express Server can also access Oracle8 directly via OCI. This connection allows for both data retrieval and modification; however, it is less common to update the relational database from Express. Express uses embedded SQL for accessing the relational database. There are four primary uses for SQL connectivity in Express, as described in the following sections.

Loading Express Using SQL

Express can use SQL to capture data from a relational database for storage in its multidimensional database. This is similar to loading from text files in that it is usually a batch loading process that happens to pull data from a relational source. Loading using SQL involves the creation of a data loading procedure that connects to the SQL database, declares and opens a cursor, and then fetches data from the cursor into Express dimensions and variables. Here are the significant parts of a load programs:

```
SQL.DBMS='ORACLE'
SQL CONNECT 'scott/tiger@projectdb'
SQL DECLARE c1 CURSOR FOR -
SELECT -
     month, -
     project_number, -
     delivery_org_id, -
     SUM(hours) -
     FROM PA_olap.activity -
     GROUP BY -
     month, -
     project_number, -
     delivery_org_id

SQL OPEN c1
_i = 0
WHILE SQLCODE EQ 0
  DO
_i = _i + 1
    SQL FETCH c1 INTO -
            :APPEND period     -
            :APPEND project    -
            :APPEND organization    -
            :hours_SQL_LOAD
DOEND
SQL CLOSE c1
SQL ROLLBACK
```

Drilling through to Relational Data (Details)

In the ROLAP and HYBRID architectures, Express retrieves data from a relational database for temporary use. Express checks a local data cache location to see if it is populated. If it isn't, then Express will fill the cache location by generating a SQL SELECT statement to retrieve the specific data requested.

Here is a formula, as generated by the Administrator tool, for retrieving HOURS data when the local cache value is NULL:

```
DEFINE HOURS_SQL FORMULA DECIMAL <TIME ORGANIZATION PROJECT>
EQ IF bookdemo_CACHE0 EQ XP_NULL THEN NA -
ELSE NAFILL(bookdemo_CACHE0, XP_SQLGen('hours_SQL',-
        CONVERT(time, TEXT) -
        CONVERT(organization, TEXT) -
        CONVERT(project, TEXT) ))
```

Updating SQL Databases

SQL DML statements can be used within the Express embedded SQL model. Because most OLAP applications are limited to reporting and analysis, this type of direct updating or inserting data via SQL is very unusual. This feature might conceivably be used to store the results of some ROLAP analysis back into a relational table. Here is a somewhat contrived example:

```
SQL PREPARE h1 FROM PA_OLAP.activity, -
   SET hours=:hours -
   WHERE :organization = TO_CHAR(delivery_org_id)-
   AND :project = TO_CHAR(project_number) -
   AND :time = TO_CHAR(month)


FOR organization
   DO
   _i = _i + 1
      SQL EXECUTE h1
      IF SQLCODE NE 0
      THEN BREAK
   DOEND
```

Dynamic Generation of SQL Code/Selections

This is really a variation of the first three categories for using SQL. The Express stored procedure language can generate SQL queries based on currently selected dimension values. These dynamically generated queries could, in turn, be passed to another tool or could direct SQL output to another window rather than filling a data cube. This technique can be used, for instance, to provide detailed reports to substantiate on-screen views.

Aggregation/Rollup

Several steps should be taken to ensure good rollup performance. As long as the database design is sound, most steps are related to data storage or paging behavior. The most significant performance effects are related to how much data is to be aggregated.

When Express performs a rollup of data it loops implicitly though the dimensions of the data variable being aggregated. The status of the variable's dimensions determine how much of the data is used as input for the calculations. The rollup will populate the higher levels based on the current status of dimension values.

Storage

Before rolling up a variable, it should be changed to *INPLACE* storage. This can significantly cut down on paging because Express doesn't need to copy data back and forth into memory just to change the values and save it back to disk. Changing the storage to INPLACE just before rolling up the data means that the rolled-up data is written directly to the address on disk. To do this safely, you must ensure that no one else will have access to the database while the rollup is in progress, because the database will be in a state of change.

If other users must be attached (with read-only access), set the storage to PERMANENT—users then will see the last saved version of data when they load from disk. This will, of course, have an impact on the ROLLUP performance. Setting the storage of a variable to either INPLACE or PERMANENT is done with the CHGDFN command:

```
CHGDFN HOURS_CJT INPLACE
CHGDFN HOURS_CJT PERMANENT
```

Always use the UPDATE command to ensure that all data is written to the database. If you exit before updating the database, the data may be inconsistent because some of it may have been written to the database. To resolve the inconsistencies, just execute the ROLLUP again to ensure that it is complete, then UPDATE.

Segment Size

Express stores data in segments of disk space allocated for each variable. The segments are divided into pages of 4 KB each. You shouldn't have to change the size of the segment in Express Server 6.01 because the default segment size is probably adequate.

In earlier versions of Express, however, it may be useful to calculate and then set the appropriate segment width needed for the variables. If all the dimension values are loaded first, Express will allocate enough segment space to keep the data for each respective variable all in one segment. If the dimension values will be loaded intermixed with the data, there may be a significant growth in the number of segments. Express will always add segments as each new dimension values is added, except for the last (slowest-varying) dimension. If a composite dimension is defined anywhere but in the last position, segment growth could be extreme—instead of a single segment, this can result in hundreds of thousands of segments.

To avoid creating a multitude of new segments each time a new dimension value is added, use the CHGDFN SEGWIDTH command to allocate enough space for all the values. Calculate the product of a variable's dimension lengths, and set the segment width to that value. In the case of conjoint or composite dimensions, calculate or estimate the total number of unique combinations of the conjoint/composite dimension and set the segment width equal to that. While use of this command will ensure the best performance of all variables, it is most critical to use the command on any variable where conjoint or composite dimensions are not in the slowest-varying (last) position.

Limit Status

Limit the status of the dimensions to those children without descendants by using the COMPLEMENT keyword. Note that this example does not show a rollup over a conjoint dimension. It also does not detach the database to free up memory between ROLLUPs—normally this would be done.

First, set the status for all dimensions of HOURS to the lowest level of detail. Then increase the status of each dimension before rolling up over its values. In this fashion, the rollup loops only over the dimension values for which values have been calculated. The values in status are the "input" for the rollup so each level becomes the input for the next level. The ROLLUP command will still process all the levels in the hierarchy, but based on the parents of the "input" that is in status. Rolling up over data that will be replaced either because it is null or just old data is only a waste of CPU and developer time. Once the first level of rollup is complete, then that level can be used to populate the next level.

Figure 13.10 illustrates the rollup of the HOURS variable as performed in the following example code:

```
LIMIT ORGANIZATION COMPLEMENT O1.PARENT
LIMIT PROJECT COMPLEMENT P1.PARENT
LIMIT TIME COMPLEMENT T1.PARENT

LIMIT TIME TO ALL
ROLLUP HOURS OVER TIME USING T1.PARENT
UPDATE
LIMIT PROJECT TO ALL
ROLLUP HOURS OVER PROJECT USING P1.PARENT
UPDATE
LIMIT ORGANIZATION TO ALL
ROLLUP HOURS OVER ORGNIZATION USING O1.PARENT
UPDATE
```

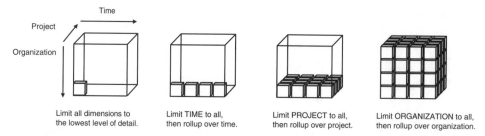

Figure 13.10 The rollup of the HOURS variable.

Rolling Up Selectively

Normally, data will be added incrementally. Corrections and regular monthly updates are two examples of this. If only a smaller subset of data is changing, why roll up all the data? To selectively roll up the data correctly, you must limit the dimensions in the hierarchy to the following:

1. The initial value(s) that changed.
2. The changed value's siblings.
3. All ancestors of the changed value.
4. All siblings of the ancestors.

If we take a look at our ORGANIZATION hierarchy once again, we see that at the lowest level we might have "Cost Center." Just imagine that cost center "DENVER" has just been updated. Figure 13.11 shows this situation.

Here is the code that is needed to selectively roll up the changed HOURS for DENVER:

```
LIMIT organization TO 'DENVER'
LIMIT organization ADD ANCESTORS USING O1.PARENT
LIMIT organization ADD CHILDREN USING O1.PARENT
ROLLUP HOURS OVER organization USING O1.PARENT
```

Check for Circularities

It is critical that hierarchies not include circular references that would suggest a value was its own ancestor. To check for such anomalies in Express version 6.0 and above, you can run HIERCHECK either as a function or a program. As a function it returns a YES if the hierarchy is OK. When run as a program, it generates an error if the hierarchy contains loops.

The syntax for the HIERCHECK program is as follows:

```
Call HIERCHECK(relation)
```

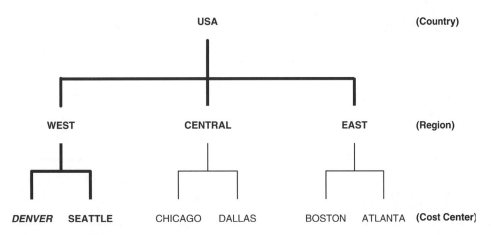

Figure 13.11 Rolling up because one variable value has changed.

where relation is the name of the parent relation being checked. NOSTATUS can also be supplied as a second argument to tell the program to ignore the present status of the dimension.

You can also access several system variables to check the results of the program. The variable HIERCHK.LOOPFND will contain a YES if a loop was found, and NA if HIERCHECK terminated abnormally. If no loop is found, the HIERCHECK.LOOPEND will contain a NO. HIERCHK.LOOPVALS shows the dimension values where problems were found. This helps to identify where to begin correcting the data. HIERCHK.XTRADIMS provides the names of the hierarchy in which a loop was found in situations where the dimension has multiple hierarchies.

For versions of Express before 6.0, refer to the ROLLUP command in the *Express Language Reference Guide* for some example code to check for circularity.

TIP If the amount of data being rolled up is larger than available memory, you can control the amount of thrashing and significantly decrease the amount of time the rollup takes by rolling up subsets of data. Set the status of the variable's dimensions, then loop through the subsets explicitly in the rollup program.

Clustering of Dimension Values

The best performance will result if the physical order of the dimension values are clustered according to their level, as opposed to interspersed with the child values. At a minimum, cluster at least the lowest-level values because they

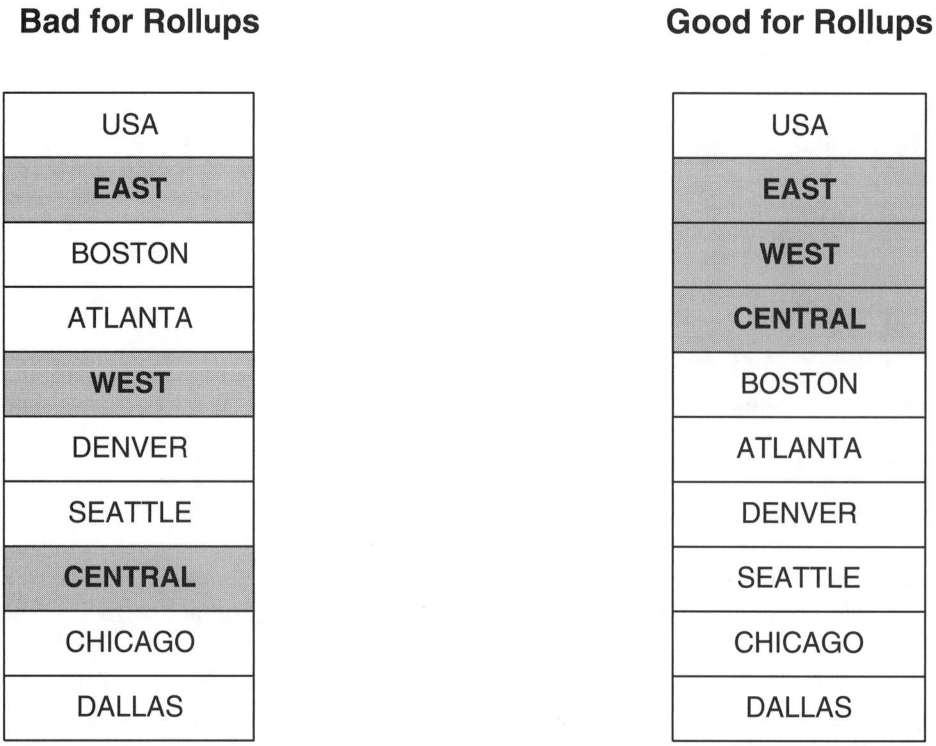

Bad for Rollups   **Good for Rollups**

Bad for Rollups
USA
EAST
BOSTON
ATLANTA
WEST
DENVER
SEATTLE
CENTRAL
CHICAGO
DALLAS

Good for Rollups
USA
EAST
WEST
CENTRAL
BOSTON
ATLANTA
DENVER
SEATTLE
CHICAGO
DALLAS

Figure 13.12   Clustering of the organizational hierarchy dimensions.

account for the largest number of values. Also try to keep the children of the same parents adjacent to each other. This is best done by sorting the input files prior to loading the database. Otherwise, the values can be moved via the MAINTAIN MOVE command, then exporting and importing the EIF file into a new database. Figure 13.12 shows the effect of clustering dimension values.

Performance Issues and Tuning

In general, Express is self-tuning, and you are limited to adjusting memory allocation, job priority, disk allocation, and I/O settings. More critical to performance are changes in applications and data structures. There are several Express utilities for gathering information relating to performance. There are also operating system-specific utilities (commands) that can be useful. In many cases, upgrading hardware is the quickest and most cost-effective way to boost performance.

Always be sure that all objects related to or dimensioned by the dimensions you are maintaining are loaded into memory before the maintenance is performed. This will help prevent deferred maintenance, which is costly. For instance, if we are loading values or updating the ORGANIZATION dimension, we would do the following:

```
LIMIT NAME TO OBJ(ISBY 'ORGANIZATION')
LOAD &CHARLIST(NAME)
```

Then perform the required maintenance:

```
MAINTAIN ORGANIZATION ADD 'PHILADELPHIA'
UPDATE
```

Gathering Information to Help Tune

There are utilities and commands both within Express and at the operating system level that can give valuable information to help identify slow-performing programs, I/O problems, and the like.

Express

The following list is a sample of the most common utilities and commands used to help tune an Express application and database. More detail on each of these is provided in the Express reference manuals. Not all these commands or their options are available on every operating system.

SYSINFO(CPUSECS) shows the number of CPU seconds accumulated since the start of the current session. The use of SYSINFO is platform-dependent. The CPUSECS option is available on most Express Server platforms (NT is different). Check the reference manuals for other choices, depending on your operating system.

DATABASE command can reveal information about the attached databases. Observing paging activity in a database can help you check the impact of stored procedures.

DATABASE(PAGEREADS 'databasename') shows the number of pages read from this database during the current session.

DATABASE(PAGEWRITES 'databasename') shows the number of pages written to this database during the current session.

DATABASE(PAGES 'databasename') displays the total number of pages in this database.

DATABASE(FREEPAGES 'databasename') provides the total number of pages available for reuse.

DATABASE(PAGESIZE 'databasename') shows the number of bytes in the per page used by Express. (**DBPAGESIZE** provides the same information in versions prior to 6.0.)

OBJ (object) command provides information specific to a particular database object.

OBJ(NUMSEGS ['object-name']) displays the number of storage segments associated with the object.

OBJ(DISKSIZE ['object-name']) shows the number of disk pages used to store the object.

OBJ(INORDER ['object-name']) indicates whether the object's logical order matches the physical order.

OBJ(NAPAGES ['object-name']) provides the number of logical pages that are not physically stored because they are entirely filled with null values.

OBJ(NUMDELS ['object-name']) displays the number of deleted cells for a dimensioned object.

OBJ(NUMCELLS ['object-name']) shows the number of logical cells, both active and deleted, for a dimensioned object.

OBJ(NUMVALS ['object-name']) shows the number of active cells for a dimensioned object.

OBJ(VALSIZE ['object-name']) indicates the number of pages used to store the object's values.

OBJ(DISKSIZE ['object-name']) displays the total number of pages used to store an object.

The following OBJ commands are related to RANSPACE (Random Access Pagespace). Even if you have been careful in capacity planning and sized the variables and dimensions, there can still be memory shortages. This is due to the shared memory pool that many objects use. The objects usually sized and planned for have their own pagespace allocated and therefore have that memory space independently managed. Objects that share the common pagespace are text variables, program object definitions, key value tables, and inversions.

OBJ(RSSIZE ['object-name']) returns the amount of text in RANSPACE.

OBJ(IRSSIZE ['object-name']) displays information about the size of inversions.

OBJ(KVSIZE ['object-name']) shows the space used by key values.

In addition to the DATABASE and OBJ commands, several other Express utilities provide important information for monitoring and tuning performance.

PRGTRACE = YES|NO sets an option to force the redirection of all non-stripped code to the current output device. (*Stripped* code includes just the run-time application without source code.)

TRACE prgname modifies the control list of programs and models that will be traced by the Express debugger.

TRACKPRG command tracks the performance cost of all programs executed while it is turned on.

MONITOR displays the amount of time spent on each line of executed code to help isolate poorly performing code.

DBREPORT is included in the DBREPORT.DB database that comes with Express. When run, it produces three reports: the "Dimension Space Report," the "Detailed Space Report," and the "Summary Space Report."

REORGANIZE is used to remove deleted values from dimensions and variables, remove segments from variables, and change the physical order of dimensions. The main results of this are usually that Express can access data faster. It also puts freed space into contiguous areas so that data can be written without expanding the database file size. Note: This will not make the database file smaller. On the contrary, it may actually make it larger. The file, though, may not grow as fast after a reorganization. *Always make a backup before reorganizing!*

RANSHOW is a monitoring tool to show the total RANSPACE used in the database. It is mostly used by Express developers, but it can give you a quick view of the RANSPACE utilization.

DBCACHE can help performance when the application reads and writes to consecutive database pages. This option is not available in version 6. Instead, see the Windows NT section later in this chapter.

UNIX

The following tools can be useful in isolating issues with regard to CPU usage, disk utilization, memory usage and I/O requests:

```
iostat
vmstat
sar
ps
top
```

Space limitations prevent us from giving a detailed explanation of each of these UNIX utilities. If you are not already familiar with them, then the tuning effort should be coordinated with the UNIX systems administrator, who will be experienced in using these commands. Check the system vendor's command reference or use the UNIX *man* (manual) command for description and usage information. For example, to obtain the reference manual page on the vmstat command, enter the following:

```
man vmstat
```

Windows NT

On Microsoft Windows NT, the Express Server is integrated with the Performance Manager. To enable this functionality, the Performance Manager module must be installed. In the Performance Monitor, Express Server provides the following counters:

- %Processing Time
- %CommittedBytesInUse
- PageFaults/Second
- FileReadOperations/Second
- FileWriteOperations/Second

Of these, the most commonly used are probably *%Processing Time* and *Page-Faults/Second.*

Express NT Server Configuration Manager Settings

Express for Windows NT changes the way we work with configuration settings. The Express Configuration Manager, along with closer integration with the NT Performance Monitor, allows us to tune the way Express interacts with the operating system more easily than before. The three main areas we can affect are the Express cache, paging activity, and the I/O thread.

Express Cache

Adjusting the size of the Express cache can help the performance if there is operating system paging, Express paging, or both. Increase the Express cache to decrease Express paging when the operating system is not paging. Decrease the cache if there is operating system paging. The size of the Express cache is determined by the value of the *PageBufferCount* parameter in the Express Configuration Manager. By default Express uses 75 percent of the total number of pages available. To calculate the actual value divide the total system memory by 4,096 to determine the total number of pages. Express will use 75 percent of that total.

Paging

Two parameters that control how Express recycles pages are *FreePageLow-Count* and *FreePageHighCount*. *FreePageLowCount* determines at what page count Express starts to discard pages, and *FreePageHighCount* defines the number of pages that need to be available before Express stops discarding them. If, while executing a rollup, there are spikes in the process time counter in the NT Performance Monitor, increasing both of these may be the solution. If the system provides more than 128 MB of physical memory then both of these should be set higher. The defaults are 100 and 250, respectively.

I/O Thread

You can adjust the parameters *ModifiedPageWriterSleep* and *ModifiedPage-Count* to improve the performance of updating the database and of data loading procedures on multiprocessor computers. These determine how long the I/O thread waits to check for modified pages to write and how many modified pages to keep in modified state. The default for *ModifiedPageWriterSleep* is 30 seconds on a multiprocessor machine and 0 (zero, disabled) on a uniprocessor. The default setting for *ModifiedPageCount* is 200. Some performance improvements may be gained by experimenting with different values here if there are multiple processors.

Front-End Alternatives

There are several alternative interfaces by which a user may interact with an Express database. In selecting a front-end alternative, care must be taken to evaluate the administrative needs as well as the interface. The Express applications offer substantial functionality in maintenance, distribution, and standardization. When developing and defining the requirements, review the available Express applications to see how closely they fit the business's needs. It may even be worthwhile to revisit some of the requirements for cost justification of custom development as opposed to a more standard approach through the prepackaged applications.

Should a custom-developed solution be necessary, review the different tools available and choose wisely. Much can be said for Express Objects' tight integration with the Express engine. Consider building multidimensional data-aware objects using other programming environments.

The Oracle Express Applications

Sales Analyzer and Financial Analyzer are *packaged* applications that meet most of the needs of a large number of users. Both include many robust administrative and loading functions that would otherwise need to be custom developed. Sales Analyzer, as well as custom solutions developed with Express Objects, can make use of the Relational Access Manager. Financial Analyzer is tightly integrated with the Oracle General Ledger application through the G/L (General Ledger) Link. Cleansing and loading data can represent a sizable portion of the project time line and budget—it may make sense to evaluate these products as components in an overall solution, even if they don't provide the complete solution for your data warehouse project.

Oracle Sales Analyzer

Originally used as a consumer goods marketing and sales analysis tool, Sales Analyzer has grown to be a versatile tool that can be used in a wide variety of ways. Sales Analyzer is expected to be a component in Oracle's Data Mart Suite for Sales and Marketing. It is the OLAP component of Oracle's Applications Data Warehouse. Sales Analyzer is also designed to work with Oracle's Relational Access Manager (which evolved from Sales Analyzer's SQL Bridge component). See the section on Relational Access Manager later in this chapter to gain a better idea of how this alternative works.

There is a utility to allow the Sales Analyzer to obtain its data from text files instead of RAA/RAM. Preparing for the Data Loader requires building sets of files for establishing dimensions, levels, hierarchies, variables, and measures. See the Data Loader Guide for details on the file structures and exact instructions for running the loads.

Oracle Financial Analyzer

Oracle Financial Analyzer was developed to support the specific needs of financial analysts. It can support multiple levels of administration and distribution.

There are essentially four types of workstations in a Financial Analyzer implementation: Super DBA, Sub-DBAs, Analyst, and Budgeting workstations. The users of Budgeting workstations can enter data via worksheets, submitting the budget data to their administrator. The subadministrators then review, combine, and submit the data from their users and so on.

The Super DBA sits at the top of the pyramid and controls the distributions of data, structures, and reports. The Super DBA also sets up the access privileges, user definitions, and other administrative functionality. The Super DBA is also responsible for launching the load processes to pull data from Oracle General Ledger, from other systems, or from text files. Through use of the G/L Link, the Super DBA can also submit budget data back to the Oracle General Ledger.

Oracle Financial Analyzer/General Ledger Integration

The General Ledger (G/L) Integration has made the Financial Analyzer application extremely popular for performing financial functions. The G/L Link has two basic components:

On the General Ledger side there is an interface for mapping the G/L segments to dimensions and providing the administrator with functionality to set up and run the extracts. These screens are accessed through the Application Manager.

Generally, the Express Server side of Oracle Financial Analyzer needs to use the concurrent manager to find the extracts. If Express Server cannot be installed on the same machine as the concurrent manager, you will need to ftp the files to a location accessible to Express Server. You must then update the *rg_dss_requests* table in General Ledger so that it will be able to find the extracts. This must be done each time the extracts are run. The Super DBA can then load the data into the shared database and run Solves, distributions, and so on.

The budgeting capability has been extended to include uploads to the Oracle General Ledger by the OFA Super DBA. There are also hooks to enable drilling down into more detailed data; however, this is not standard functionality in the current release.

Relational Access Manager/Administrator

The Relational Access Administrator (RAA) and Relational Access Manager (RAM) are the client and server components (respectively), which allow the management of metadata conforming to standard as Discoverer and the Oracle Applications Data Warehouse. The metadata is stored as *projects*. Each project contains the necessary data for establishing connections and building the necessary Express structures for performing SQL reach through via mapped dimensions and facts.

The Relational Access Administrator is a graphical user interface tool for creating and managing projects that control the mapping of data in a relational star (or snowflake) schema to the dimensions and variables within an Express database. RAA uses ODBC to connect to the relational data warehouse. RAA provides two choices for building a project: The user may utilize the Project Wizard or manually define the multidimensional data model and then map the relational structures to it.

The Relational Access Manager then performs a build. This creates an Express database that is defined by the metadata layer of the relational warehouse. RAM uses a direct connection to the Oracle database (through OCI) to load data whenever it is requested through either Sales Analyzer, Express Objects, Express Analyzer, or an Express Web Agent access tool.

The Express engine handles the multidimensional representation and generates the necessary SQL code to fetch the data.

It is also possible to use a RAA/RAM database in a hybrid configuration. As discussed in the "Data Distribution Architectures" section earlier in this chapter, a hybrid configuration stores summary data within the Express multidimensional database while allowing reach-through through the relational database to obtain detail data for drill-down processing. To implement a hybrid architecture, the Express database needs to be attached read/write while the procedures for fetching data from the star schema are executed. Which data is fetched and stored depends on the status of the dimensions when the data is retrieved. During normal access, Express checks the buffer to see whether the data has been retrieved. By preloading and updating the database the buffer can already be populated for certain values, improving performance. Upon drilling down to nonstored data, an empty cache is encountered, and the data is automatically retrieved from the relational database.

Oracle Express Objects and Express Analyzer

Express Objects is an object-oriented application development environment. It can be used to create Briefing Books or to create applications for Express Analyzer. A *Briefing Book* is an application that allows the user to create page objects and populate them with data-aware tables and graphs. Users can also modify Briefing Books created by Express Objects. Express Objects is the most effective way to build custom applications for Express multidimensional databases.

The Express Analyzer tool provides a subset of the tools available in Express Objects. Express Analyzer users can only run the application built in Express Objects; it cannot alter it. The standard applications (such as Financial Analyzer) are more complete packages that can be executed by the Express Analyzer software but not modified.

Other Development Tools

The Express Structured N-dimensional Application Program Interface (SNAPI) allows custom development of applications using a variety of tools, including C++, PowerBuilder, and Visual Basic. It is not within the scope of this chapter to provide details on the use of these tools.

Express and the Web

Beginning with version 6, Express is Web-enabled, that is, it is capable of generating dynamic Web pages. This is done through the Express Web Agent, which is a Web listener interface. It allows Express Server to respond to requests from the Web Request Broker in one of two ways. It can be configured either as a Common Gateway Interface (CGI) or as an Oracle Web Request Broker Cartridge. The Cartridge configuration is more efficient and can support many more users. Other components of the Web Agent include Web modules and the Web Agent Developers Toolkit.

Express Web Agent Developers Toolkit

The Express Web Agent includes the tools necessary to build custom Web applications developed in the Express stored procedure language. This is a module of the Express Server (version 6.0+) that allows Express to produce HTML output in response to requests received from the Web Request Broker.

The Express Web Publisher

The Express Web Publisher is a component of the Oracle Express Objects development tool set that allows you to publish Web sites. Web sites are the containers for Briefing Books. With the Web Publisher, a user with no knowledge of HTML can publish tables and graphs on a Web site. The resulting pages are complete, with a rotation tool, an export tool, and a saved selection tool. Web Publisher utilizes either the Express Analyzer or Express Objects environments to develop the tables and graphs. The tool can also be started on its own and has features to create and manage Web sites and to create new Briefing Books.

Sales Analyzer Web Server

Publishing reports and graphs to the Web is as simple as copying the reports to a common library. The created Web pages are extremely similar to Web Publisher pages. They have folders like Briefing Books in Web Publisher, the rotation tools, a graph/table, an export-to-Excel button, and a saved selection button. One advantage of Sales Analyzer's Web capabilities is that the user doesn't need to do anything different from normal distribution policy. The objects are simply copied from the personal library into a public library, just as they would be for other users of the client tool. Once made public, they can be viewed using a standard Web browser.

Summary

The Oracle Express products provide an OLAP component for the Oracle data warehouse. The features of Express extend the usefulness of the data warehouse by providing additional analysis capability not available in standard relational query tools. Express includes its own multidimensional database facilities. It has also been integrated with the Oracle8 relational databases to allow the Express user to transparently access data stored relationally.

In this chapter we introduced several concepts of multidimensional databases and OLAP. We described elements of the Express technology as well as several alternative architectures for implementing Express. The chapter discussed topics related to analyzing, designing, building, loading, and tuning an Express database as well as several Express tools and alternative interfaces.

Index

NOTE: Page numbers in **bold-face** indicate the primary discussion of that term.

A

Absence, of natural keys, 185
ACCEPT command, 229–230
Accessing data
  in data warehouses, 19–20
  in implementing OLAP, 831–832
  with Oracle Express, 819
  during warehouse refresh processing, 152–153
Account information, 230–231
  security of, 230
Account locking, 460
Accuracy of data
  in query rewrites, 437–439
  for space requirements, 473–474
  after updates, 652–654
Active DML transactions, rollback segments and, 482
ACTIVITY_TS tablespace, case study with, 253, 257–258
Actuaries, data warehousing for, 10
ADD DATAFILE parameter, of ALTER TABLESPACE command, 250
ADD TEMPFILE clause, with ALTER TABLESPACE command, 251
Ad hoc querying, 12, 13, 536, 537

disabling, 472
and documenting outbound data, 471–472
rollup summarization and, 407–409
SQL tracing and, 580
system availability and, 453
usage tracking and, 549
Ad hoc reporting functions, **806–808**
Administration
  basic principles of, 449–450
  business requirements of, 450–452
  of data warehouse configuration, 463–508, 508–514
  of data warehouses, **447–514**
  need for, 447–449
  of Oracle Parallel Server, 700–701, 714–717
  roles in, 454–456
  security in, 456–462
  system requirements of, 452–454
Administration edition, of Discoverer, 807
Administration tools, 450
Advanced queuing (AQ), 343–344, **375–376**
Advanced Replication Option, 142, 770–772
Aggregate computability, in query rewrites, 434
Aggregate data, 406–407, **407–410**
  dimensions and, 435–436

in logical schema design, 170, 171–172
with Oracle Express, 849–854
parallel query slaves and, 634
updating, 651–652
AI. *See* Artificial intelligence (AI).
Aliases
  information concerning, 154
  of objects, 129–130
  problems with, 156
ALL_COL_COMMENTS, viewing comments with, 157–158
ALLOCATE parameter, with ALTER TABLE command, 257
ALL_ROWS mode, for Oracle Optimizer in SQL tracing, 580–581
ALL_TAB_COMMENTS, viewing comments with, 157–158
ALL_TABLES view, 125
ALTER commands, 479
ALTER DATABASE command, 251
  for locally managed temporary tablespaces, 251
ALTER DATABASE ENABLE LOGFILE THREAD command, 716
ALTER DATABASE RENAME GLOBAL NAME command, 764
ALTER FREELISTS command, 513
ALTER INDEX command, 108

N